THE B

D1280540

F. W. DEAKIN, Warden of St. Antony's College, Oxford, was born in London in 1913 and graduated in Modern History from Oxford. He has taught Modern History in Oxford and served as literary assistant to Sir Winston Churchill on his historical publications and his War Memoirs. During World War II he served in Yugoslavia as head of the first British Military Mission to Tito, in North Africa, and in Italy before he transferred to H.M. Foreign Service and became First Secretary to the British Embassy in Belgrade. He holds the Distinguished Service Order (British), Legion D'Honneur (French), Medal for Valour (Russian), and Bundes Verdienstkreuz (West Germany).

940.535
D34

THE BRUTAL FRIENDSHIP

Mussolini, Hitler and the Fall of Italian Fascism

By F. W. DEAKIN

PART I, REVISED BY THE AUTHOR

ANCHOR BOOKS
DOUBLEDAY & COMPANY, INC.
GARDEN CITY, NEW YORK

THIS BOOK IS DEDICATED TO MY WIFE

The Brutal Friendship: Mussolini, Hitler and the Fall of Italian Fascism was originally published by Harper & Row, in 1962. The Anchor Books edition is Part I of the original volume, has been revised by the author, and is published by arrangement with Harper & Row, Publishers.

Anchor Books edition: 1966

Library of Congress Catalog Card Number 66–17409
Copyright © 1962, 1966 by F. W. Deakin
All Rights Reserved
Printed in the United States of America

CONTENTS

145919

BOOK III

BOOK IV

PREFACE TO THE NEW EDITION (1966)

The present volume is a revised version of the first half of the original edition of *The Brutal Friendship: Mussolini, Hitler, and the Fall of Italian Fascism,* and bears the same title. It is a self-contained study of the events leading up to the destruction of the Fascist régime from within at the historic meeting of the Grand Council on the night of July 24, 1943, and the dismissal of the Duce by King Victor Emmanuel III on the following afternoon.

A second volume, composed of the latter section of the original edition, is being published separately under the title *The Six Hundred Days of Mussolini.* It contains an analysis, complete in itself, of the establishment by the Germans of the rump neo-Fascist Republic of Salò in the North of Italy, under the nominal authority of Mussolini, after his liberation from internment by Badoglio and the signing by the latter of the Italian Armistice with the Allies in September 1943. This study ends with the death of the Duce at the hands of Italian partisans in April 1945, which grimly completed the cycle of over twenty years' Fascist rule in Italy.

In the two present volumes, certain documents and appendices have been omitted, translations corrected, and most footnotes deleted. The chapters dealing with the interlude of the Badoglio government in the original version have been replaced by a new Epilogue at the end of the first volume, and by an Introduction to the second.

The new edition also embodies comments and corrections which have reached the author since the first publication of this book. A contemporary historian has one particular advantage over his colleagues working in more sheltered fields of history: his work, which is both provisional and provoking, is exposed not only to reviewers, but to survivors. This present record of the fall of Italian Fascism and the fate of the Axis alliance has been subjected to this rewarding treatment.

Apart from these modifications, the present two-volume edition, which is at the same time two self-contained works, is identical with the text of the original version.

PREFACE

This is a book by an Englishman, in part based on German documents, on the fall of the Fascist government in Italy. It has grown in labour out of a short study of the events leading up to the meeting of the Grand Council on July 24, 1943, which seemed to give a deceptively tidy illustration of the technique of the coup d'état in contemporary history. Further and lengthy investigation destroyed the neatness of the original interpretation, and, as material accumulated, it became clear to me that I should attempt to marshal and select the massive, and at the same time fragmentary, unpublished evidence, which might throw new and detailed light on the collapse of Italian Fascism under the impact of military disaster. The study of contemporary history is fraught with the temptation of uttering premature personal judgments, and with the snare of the uncritical assembly of excessive material. In spite of the uneven wealth of written sources, much has been destroyed by chance of war, and perhaps more buried by the death of leading witnesses or withheld by the living. In spite of such hazards, which are the lot of the historian, it seems that the prime and humble duty of the student of contemporary history is to establish the elementary record before it is dissipated.

In the case of this work, the author has deliberately attempted to unfold, with a minimum of apocalyptic commentary, the account of the disintegration of the régime in Italy from the moment when military events from the autumn of 1942 onwards reacted savagely and progressively on the internal structure of Italian Fascism, and he trusts that the reader will be patient with such a direct and first-hand presentation of the evidence, most of which is original, and much is tempered by numerous discussions with surviving witnesses.

The weighing of oral evidence in such an enterprise is risky and imprecise, and perhaps its only justification is that from time to time vital fragments are snatched from oblivion. One word on this subject belongs to Dr Johnson. 'Nothing but experience could evince the frequence of false information, or enable any man to conceive that so many groundless reports should be propagated . . . Some men relate what they think, as what they know; some men of confused memories and habitual inaccuracy, ascribe to one man what belongs to another; and some talk on, without thought or care. A few men are sufficient to broach falsehoods, which are afterwards innocently diffused by successive relators.'

This portentous warning should not however deter the contemporary historian from seeking confirmation or denial of matters arising from the plethora of documents with which he is confronted. His work at best is the provisional creation of a pioneer.

'My attachment to the person of the Duce has not changed . . . but I regret not having listened to reason, which imposed on me a brutal friendship in regard to Italy.'

ADOLF HITLER, APRIL 1945

ACKNOWLEDGMENTS

In the writing of this book I am indebted to friends and colleagues in England, the United States, and Italy and my formal expression of thanks would be inadequate. Any views expressed, however, or errors committed, are mine.

In the early stages of the work, I have a special debt to the Hon. Margaret Lambert who led me with a sure and experienced hand into the jungle of the German diplomatic records, and encouraged me to undertake a detailed study of the subject; to Professor Howard M. Smyth, now of the Historical Division of the State Department, who put at my disposal, with a rare generosity, the drafts of his invaluable forthcoming official American history of the war in Italy; and to their Excellencies Dr Manlio Brosio and Count Vittorio Zoppi, successively the envoys of the Republic of Italy at the Court of St James for persuading me that my task was not, as a foreigner, a total impertinence, and for the courtesy of introducing me to certain leading Italian witnesses.

I am grateful to my colleagues at St Antony's College, Oxford, for their patience over an excessively long period, and in particular to Sir John Wheeler-Bennett, Mr James Joll, and Mr David Footman, for their helpful criticism.

I have also profitably inflicted the draft manuscript on friends in the University, and my warm thanks are due to Professor Sir Isaiah Berlin, Professor A. J. Ayer, Professor Sir Ronald Syme; the Master of St Catherine's, Mr A. L. C. Bullock; and the Warden of Rhodes House, Mr E. T. Williams. I have an equal debt to the Earl of Birkenhead, Count Julian Dobrski, and the Hon. Anthony Samuel.

It is a special pleasure to pay tribute to the late Professor Federico Chabod for his serene and perceptive advice; to Professor Mario Toscano, the Director of the Italian Foreign Office Archives, for his courteous assistance; to my Oxford friend, Professor Count Alessandro Passerin D'Entrèves; to Professor Franco Venturi; and to Dr Leo Valiani.

I was fortunate to have the benefit of talks with the German Ambassador to the Republic of Salò, Dr Rudolf von Rahn, who patiently submitted to interrogation, and to correspond with the former Japanese Ambassador to Italy, Dr Hidaka, who was good enough to answer importunate questions. I would also wish to thank Count Dino Grandi for the courtesy of discussing with me the central theme of this work, and for permission to publish certain correspondence.

Finally this book would never have been completed without the sturdy and uncomplaining labours beyond the call of duty of my secretary, Mrs Patricia Kirkpatrick, of Miss Mary Worthington, and their colleagues on the staff of St Antony's College, and to them I would like to express my specially warm thanks. My task has been lightened by the helpful efficiency of Miss Margaret Carlyle and Miss Jill Myford in handling documentary material.

'A régime never falls for internal reasons, moral questions, economic stresses. Party struggles do not hazard the existence of a system. A régime, of whatever kind, collapses only under the weight of defeat.'

MUSSOLINI, THE HISTORY OF A YEAR

BOOK I

CHAPTER ONE

'The Fourth Punic War'

THE AUTUMN of 1942 marked for Italy the crisis of the Second World War. By that time all the assumptions upon which she had entered the conflict just over two years previously had been destroyed. The war aims of Italian Fascism had been outlined by the Duce in private at a meeting of the Grand Council on February 4, 1939. His speech was drafted to guide this supreme consultative body in Italian foreign policy 'for a short or for a long, even very long, term'; it summarized the aspirations of his government and was a quintessence of its foreign aims since the take-over of political power in October 1922.

'The premise from which I argue is the following: States are more or less independent according to their maritime position . . . Italy is bordered by an inland sea which communicates with the ocean through the Suez Canal—an artificial means of communication which is easily blocked even by accident—and by the Straits of Gibraltar, dominated by the government of Great Britain. Italy has in fact no free access to the oceans. She is really a prisoner in the Mediterranean, and the more populous and powerful she becomes, the more will she suffer from her imprisonment. The bars of this prison are Corsica, Tunisia, Malta, and Cyprus. Its sentinels are Gibraltar and Suez.'

From this situation Mussolini drew the following deductions. The task of Italian policy 'which has not and never can have as objectives continental European territory, except Albania, is in the first place to break the prison bars'. Once this was done, Italy could have only one watchword: 'The March to the Ocean. Which Ocean? The Indian Ocean linking across the Sudan and Libya to Abyssinia; or the Atlantic Ocean across French North Africa? In the first, as in the second, hypothesis we find ourselves face to face with Anglo-French opposition. To brave the solution of such a problem without having secured our backs on the Continent would be absurd. The policy of the Rome-Berlin Axis therefore answers the historical necessity of a fundamental order. The same applies to our conduct in the Spanish Civil War.'[1]

The conception of an Italo-German alliance, apart from its ideological significance, was therefore, from the Italian point of view, to cover and secure by treaty with the greatest European land power the continental position of Italy, and free her to pursue her 'vital interests' in the Mediterranean and in Africa. As Mussolini expressed it three years later in a speech to senior Party officials, 'The question of our land frontiers was settled by the war of 1915–18. We are faced today with the problem of the maritime frontiers, and this conflict has for us a very special character, that of the Fourth Punic War.'[2] The weakness of any alliance between Germany and Italy must be, as he realized at the Munich Conference in September 1938, that Italy might be dragged into a major war, the timing of which would be decided by Germany in her own political and strategic interests, before her ally was in a condition to fight. The Czech crisis was a warning.

As Mussolini analysed the position to the Grand Council, 'Are we today, February 1939, in ideal conditions to engage on a war? No State is ever in ideal conditions to make war, when by this you mean to imply the mathematical assurance of victory . . . But there is no doubt that our preparations will be better in a few years' time, and more exactly when we have renewed all our artillery (during 1941–2), when we have in service eight battleships and perhaps double the existing number of submarines, when the empire is completely pacified, self-sufficient, and can provide us with a native army, when we have realized at least fifty per cent of our autarchic plans and when we have held at the end of 1942 the Exhibition, which should reinforce our reserves.' This last plan of marking the twentieth anniversary of the March on Rome by a celebration of the achievements of Fascist rule was thus established, with a neat symbolism, as the most appropriate and convenient date for an Italian entry into a war.

The progress of events in Europe moved harshly in the fol-

Superior numbers refer to Notes beginning on page 511.

lowing months, and with little relation to Italy's position or interests. The signing of the Axis Pact in the following May brought little change.* This treaty was the personal creation of Hitler and Mussolini, and the alliance between the two countries rested essentially on the relationship between the two men. Hitler's admiration of his Italian colleague was of long standing. As he told his entourage on one occasion, the Duce had overcome Bolshevism 'not by military force but by superior intellect, and we have to thank him for showing for the first time, by his decisive defeat of the inner power of Bolshevism, that even in this twentieth century it is possible to recall a people to a sense of purely national pride'.[3] The Duce had been therefore the precursor of the original crusade. The master of the technique of modern mass dictatorship, he had also inspired a new conception of rule, and Hitler regarded himself as his pupil. 'When I read the history of Fascism I feel as if I am reading the history of our movement.' In Germany 'things had developed spontaneously and subsequently acquired a speed comparable with that of developments in Italy. The Duce himself has told me that at the moment when he undertook the struggle against Bolshevism, he didn't know exactly where he was going . . . What crowns these parallel destinies is that today we are fighting side by side against the same Powers and against the same personages. At the same period, the Duce and I were both working in the building-trade. This explains that there is also a bond between us on the purely human level. I have a deep friendship for this extraordinary man.'[4]

The historical and temperamental differences between the two peoples could not conceal, in Hitler's mind, the identity of outlook of the two dictators. But such a conception was cerebral and spurious, and onlookers observed during the summit meetings between the two men a lack of real understanding and comprehension. There was no familiar intercourse between them, and their successive encounters created an increasingly distorted image of their relationship.† The

* For a brilliant and exhaustive account of these negotiations see Mario Toscano *"Le Origini Diplomatiche del Patto D'Acciaio"* (Second edition, 1956).

† In 1926 or 1927 the Italian Embassy in Berlin received a request from a certain Mr Adolf Hitler for a signed photograph of the Duce, which was forwarded to Rome. The Embassy were instructed to transmit a polite refusal. See Donosti, *Mussolini e l'Europa*, p. 80.

only reality of the personal bond between them lay in their mutual and lonely isolation at the summit of supreme power. There was an artificiality also about the political and ideological bond which they had forged between their two countries, and this arbitrary and fragile structure could ill stand the reality of war. Hitler perhaps more than Mussolini was aware of its personal nature. As he told his generals as early as August 1939, 'There will never be in the future a man who possesses more authority than I do. My very existence is also a great factor of value. But I can be put out of the way at any time either by a criminal or a lunatic. The second personal factor is the Duce. His existence also is decisive. If anything happened to him, the loyalty of Italy to the alliance would be no longer secure.'[5]

Mussolini was more realistic than Hitler as to the limitations of the Pact. He never completely lost sight of the fact that the power interests of Italy were both distinct from those of Germany and in some instances conflicting. From the military point of view, the treaty laid down prior consultation between the allies in event of one or the other being engaged in armed conflict, which was regarded as inevitable. The occupation of Czechoslovakia in March 1939 by Nazi Germany as a forward base for any eventual assault in the East, was countered on the Italian side by the occupation of Albania a few days later, in order to mark Italy's separate, if limited, interests in Europe which were not confined, as Mussolini had stated to the Grand Council in February, to Albanian territory, but which included the 'unfinished business' of the First World War in the Adriatic and at the expense of Yugoslavia. Control of his inland sea was essential to Italy's conception of her position as a Mediterranean power, and the Peace Treaties of 1919 had left Italy unsatisfied in this direction.

But her ultimate success in achieving her objectives might be achieved by the diplomatic ability of Mussolini in restraining Hitler from pursuing immediate German interests which might endanger the peace of Europe. He had acquired at Munich in the previous year a view of his position as an arbitrator, and in terms of prestige and ideology he was quick to grasp one aspect of this crisis. In a private address to a gathering of Italian Prefects at the end of 1938 he had shouted: 'The word Munich means that for the first time since 1861 Italy has played an extremely prominent and decisive role in an event of world importance (loud applause) . . . What happened in Munich was simply colossal, and I use the word advisedly as it is one of ours. What happened at Munich spelt the end of Bolshevism in Europe, the end of all Russian political influence on our continent. Prague was the principal headquarters of democracy and of Bolshevism. Prague housed the archives of the Third International. With the conquest of Prague we had already practically captured Barcelona.'[6] The connection between Munich and the events of the Spanish Civil War was that it gave Mussolini the pretext to withdraw the Italian contingent from Spain and to liquidate this commitment prior to the gathering storm in central Europe. But whatever the 'moral' victory, there remained the brutal inadequacies of Italian armament and industry. After the signature of the Axis Pact, Mussolini sent one of his generals, Ugo Cavallero, the future Chief of the General Staff, to Germany with a personal note to Hitler dated May 30, 1939, outlining Italy's position in the event of a European war, and repeating, in some passages word for word, his speech to the Grand Council in the previous February. Mussolini recognized that war was inevitable, but added: 'The two European powers of the Axis need a period of peace lasting not less than three years. It is from 1943 onwards that a war effort will have the greatest prospects of victory . . . Fascist Italy, although convinced that it is inevitable, has no desire to anticipate a European war . . . Italy can mobilize proportionately more men than Germany. But with its abundance of manpower there is a corresponding modesty of materials.'[7]

The Axis Pact did not lead to corresponding Staff talks, or to any serious consideration of building up Italy's war potential from German sources. Hitler had no intention of preparing for a long conflict, and at no time did he show any interest in Italian military co-operation in the event of a major war. Her role at best would be to neutralize by the threat of intervention British and French forces in the Mediterranean and North Africa, if Germany were to be involved in hostilities with the Western Powers as a result of German action in the East.

The steps leading to the Nazi-Soviet Pact were taken by the German leaders without any reference to Rome or any consideration of Italian interests. The German attack on Poland in September 1939 equally was not a subject of prior consultation as laid down in the Axis Pact between the two partners. The German conception of a Blitzkrieg in Europe presented certain dangers for Fascist Italy, and overwhelming German power on the Continent, and possible German expansion, in the event of the total defeat of Britain and France, in their imperial possessions in Africa, would be at the expense of the long-term aims of Italian policy.

Until the spring of 1940, however, Mussolini reluctantly maintained a neutral position. On September 17 the King had telegraphed to him, 'I would like to hope that, when Poland has been liquidated, you will be able to negotiate diplomatically, and if, in spite of the sinking of their merchant shipping, the British want to treat, one can perhaps reach a good solution'.[8] But Mussolini's basic assumptions underwent successive changes as events developed. On March 31, 1940, in a memorandum sent to the King, Mussolini referred to the inevitability of Italian entry into the conflict, but in 'a war parallel to that of Germany to obtain our objectives, which can be summed up in this phrase: liberty on the seas; a window on the ocean'.[9] Hitler had also discussed such an action at a meeting on the Brenner earlier that month, and it was established that the timing of such a decision concerned Italy alone. His conception of Italy's role was somewhat contemptuous. At the moment of an Anglo-French collapse Italy should be allowed a modest pound of flesh, acquired by a nominal show of force.

The original Italian time-table for entering the conflict in 1942 was rendered meaningless by the march of the German armies. Their successes in Norway, then in the Low Countries and France in the late spring and early summer of 1940 revolutionized the whole position. At a meeting of the Italian military leaders in the Duce's room at the Palazzo Venezia on May 29 the die was cast. The decision to go to war had already been outlined in the Duce's memorandum to the King on March 31. 'That left the date, the most important problem to settle in connection with the tempo of a war. This date had originally been fixed for the spring of 1941. After the easy conquest of Norway and the domination of Denmark, I had already brought this date forward to early September 1940. Now, after the conquest of Holland, the fall of Belgium, the invasion of France and the resultant general situation, I have brought the date still further forward, and consider that any day from June 5 next is suitable for entering the war. The present situation rules out any further delay, as otherwise we run the risk of greater dangers than would have resulted from a premature intervention. Moreover, in my opinion, the situation is—so far as the so-called allies are concerned—decisive. If we delayed two weeks or a month, we should not improve the situation, while we might give Germany the impression of arriving after the *fait accompli* when the risk is slight; besides the fact that it is not in our moral code to strike a man when he is down. Finally, all this could be important when peace is signed.'[10]

Mussolini's decision to enter the war on June 5 was accepted by Hitler without enthusiasm. There was no co-ordinated military planning to meet such an event. A nominal and ineffectual Italian assault on the French advance positions in the Western Alps was to have the intended effect of giving Italy a place in the armistice negotiations with France. Even before this attack was launched, the French armies had collapsed.

On June 17 Marshal Pétain from Bordeaux sought an armistice in Berlin, and Hitler called at once for a meeting with the Duce, who was taken by surprise, without a pondered solution and without a token victory. When the Italo-German conference opened at Munich on June 18 the real subject of debate was the cutting down of any eventual Italian claims against France in order to permit Germany to seek a working compromise with the new Vichy government. The German attitude was conditioned by the fear that a French government-in-exile might be set up in North Africa, and the hope that England might be persuaded to consider a compromise peace. Although Hitler seems to have agreed in his first private talk at Munich with Mussolini that Italian claims would be respected, there was little conviction in his tone.

It was not only a question of territorial claims, but also of the fate of the French Fleet which, as both belligerent parties realized, held the balance of not only the Mediterranean but also the war at sea throughout the world. As Hitler expressed it, 'the best thing that we can hope for is that the French will sink it. The worst is that the fleet should go over to the British'. This would enable the latter to protect their convoys, and garrison and supply their bases 'from Egypt to Portugal, keeping alive or creating a series of theatres of operations, thus leading to a long war and the impossibility of hitting the enemy decisively. I far prefer a compact and concentrated enemy as France was, which I can grasp and beat, to enemies who may be weak, but who are scattered here and there.' It would be impolitic therefore to ask the French to hand over their fleet to the Axis powers, but it should be concentrated 'in a position where it could neither move nor fire', either in French or neutral (preferably Spanish) ports. 'On the whole, there was agreement with the Fuehrer's point of view.' Italian territorial demands were to be shelved 'until peace negotiations are started'.[11] The evidence as to how this fatal step was taken is contained in an unpublished letter of June 22, from Mussolini to Hitler: 'With the aim of making it easier for the French to accept the armistice conditions, I have not included in the clauses the occupation of (French) territory on the left bank of the Rhône, of Corsica, Tunisia, or Djibouti, which we agreed on at Munich. I confined myself to the minimum—i.e. to demanding a demilitarized zone of 50 kms. I think this minimum is indispensable for avoiding incidents. For all the rest, I adopted the clauses of the German armistice.'[12]

These decisions set the future frame of 'the French problem' in Axis policy, and had been taken on the assumption of a rapid military victory over Great Britain or of an early negotiated settlement with her. But if Italy were to pursue in earnest hostilities against the British in the Mediterranean, such concessions from France were essential to the conduct of this campaign. The Italian General Staff pointed this out in a memorandum drafted for the Munich conference, and Mussolini agreed to press them. Why did he change his mind? The significance of this meeting with Hitler was that the latter was able to persuade the Duce of the imminent collapse of Great Britain and that, given this assumption, the importance of the immediate neutralization of France in the Mediterranean, of her fleet and her North African possessions, was vital to the successful and quick conclusion to the war.

The notes taken at the conference by the Vice-Chief of the Italian Army Staff, General Roatta, read: 'The Duce sent for me and told me the following: "The Fuehrer, who is not anxious to see the appearance of American intervention and to pass a second winter at war, has given the clear impression that he wishes to conclude in the shortest space of time peace with England. He only referred vaguely to offensive action against her, and in completely hypothetical terms." '[13] When Ciano presented the Italian claims to Ribbentrop, the latter said: 'One must be moderate and not have eyes bigger than one's stomach . . . but Ciano has formed the conviction that Germany is in the state of mind of a poker player who, far beyond his hopes, finds himself in front of a pile of chips. Would it not be better to close the game?'[14]

Mussolini's decision to enter the war had been a calculated risk. A token campaign on the Western Alpine frontier would bring him to the conference table with the French, and make it possible to settle, at least in part, the historic claims to Nice, Corsica, and Tunis. An operation on the Libyan border against the British in Egypt would entitle the Italians to take their seat at the armistice with the British which, it was calculated, would rapidly follow Operation 'Sea-Lion' and the invasion of the British Isles. In August Marshal Badoglio, the Chief of the Italian General Staff, was still hoping 'for a quick end to the war through the activities of the German Air Force and a landing in Great Britain. There is only sufficient food in Italian East Africa until the spring. An offensive against Egypt can only achieve *tactical* success.'[15]

Mussolini had received over many months due warning of the state of the Italian armed forces and of the economy of the country in the event of war. No decrees or reorganization could change the brutal reality of this position. The Italian army was neither a highly equipped and trained élite striking force, nor a Napoleonic conscript army. Italy was totally deficient in anti-aircraft defence. In 1940 she possessed two searchlights and some 230 anti-aircraft batteries for the defence of the mother country. There were only 42,000 vehicles for the whole metropolitan army in July 1940; she possessed no modern artillery or tanks. Much out of date equipment and war material at the disposal of the Italian armed forces had been lost in Ethiopia and in Spain. These stocks had not been replenished, and she had not the industrial machinery to maintain an effective Air Force whose plans and training were far behind that of the Western Powers. The Navy, though better equipped, possessed no battle experience and was dependent for oil supplies on forces beyond her control. The closing of Suez and Gibraltar at the outbreak of war with Britain meant that Italy would henceforward be totally dependent on Germany for the transport of raw materials to Italian industry. According to reports from the Italian Commission of War Production, which reached Mussolini at the end of 1939, Italian industry could begin to meet in full the needs of the three armed services by 1944, and in order to enter the war with sufficient stocks to maintain hostilities for one year only the date would be 1949. By February 1940

General Favagrossa, head of the Commission, was able to report that the former date could be brought forward to 1943.[16]

This was the background of Mussolini's gamble. In any event, however short the period of the war might be, Italy would be dependent during the ensuing months in transport, communications and supplies of raw materials on her German ally. Nevertheless, the Duce was determined to fight his own 'parallel war', to achieve the aims which he had outlined to the Grand Council in the previous year and at the same time, somewhat unrealistically, to seek liberation from economic dependence on Germany and to bolster up the Italian system of economic autarchy. The incorrigible slowness of the British to surrender, and the limited tasks and resources allotted to Graziani in Libya, thereby excluding any decisive results in the African theatre, led Mussolini, prompted by Ciano, to snatch at quick profits in another region where Italian interests were traditionally involved, and before the Germans could further extend their control. Mussolini was not only determined to pursue his own war without German military aid, but also if necessary at the expense of certain German interests.

The Fascist mission to complete the unachieved war aims of 1915–18 was specially linked with the whole Balkan area. Even if Italy had not come into the war on the side of Germany in 1940 against the British and French, she would probably have sought compensation at the expense of Yugoslavia in a separate and distinct expedition. As Graziani put it at his post-war trial, referring to the time when he had been Chief of the Italian Army Staff which was planning for such an enterprise in April 1940, 'they wanted to make a little war for the mines as they had done in Albania, and not a large-scale war alongside the Germans which they hoped to avoid'.[17]

Italy's interest in Yugoslavia was both historic in terms of Dalmatia and the Adriatic coast and economic in regard to the valuable copper and bauxite. The attack on Yugoslavia was stood down temporarily until after the fall of France, when 37 Italian divisions were again put on the alert for this purpose. If Mussolini's time-table were accurate, and the French armistice were followed by negotiations with the British, and Italian aims in Egypt and East Africa were fulfilled, the acquisition of parts of Yugoslav territory and her economic resources would round off Italian claims in the Mediterranean, and complete the cycle of Italy's 'parallel war'. But as so often in the past the Duce, perhaps discouraged by the frigid German attitude to the Yugoslav adventure, cancelled the operation and orders were given to demobilize 600,000 men. The war, it seemed, was practically over, and the Italians could be resigned to collecting their pieces of silver from the French and the British.

As the first winter of the war drew on, however, there were no signs of a British collapse, and Ciano, in particular, thought to snatch a further lightning compensation for the Italian Mediterranean empire in the form of a sudden attack on Greece, in spite of the recent disorganization and demobilization of a large part of the Italian army which had just begun. It could be argued that in military terms the Greek expedition was linked with the stalemate on the Libya-Egypt border and by tempting the British into Greece a far more important decision might follow in the direction of Egypt and Suez. But the Greek campaign, and the failure of the Italians to defeat the Greek armies extended German intervention in the Balkans—an area which the Italians hoped to keep for themselves, and brought a stage nearer the Italo-German combined military operations which Mussolini hoped so much to avoid. The Axis occupation of Greece, bringing with it a wave of Italian profiteers and dubious businessmen to exploit the resources of the country in the interests of Italian economy, as had happened the previous year in Albania, also increased the Italian military commitment overseas to garrison and contain the Greek peninsula.

A separate Italian adventure against Yugoslavia, in light of the Greek experience, was now out of the question. By joint diplomatic pressure Yugoslavia might be forced into the Axis camp, thus completing control of the whole of the European fortress. Yugoslavia represented the last remaining neutral power in Europe outside the Iberian peninsula and Switzerland. The failure of these diplomatic moves, and the Yugoslav rising in March 1941, caught both the Italians and the Germans by surprise. The planning of the Russian campaign was now far advanced, although as usual unknown to the Italians and Hitler was about to embark on his major gamble. The sharp Yugoslav campaign, which followed in April, led to the destruction of the State of Yugoslavia, the partition of the country to include the setting up of the independent satellite state of Croatia, German military government in Serbia, and Italian military occupation of Montenegro and the annexation of Dalmatia. This situation was to produce one of the main frictions between the Axis allies in the conduct of the war, and to feature at intervals henceforward at every summit conference between the two dictators. In fragile fashion the Italians had achieved their territorial aims in the Adriatic, but the physical presence of the Germans in these regions brought with it the revival of the historical ghosts of the Habsburgs and their claims on former Austrian territory in the Balkans, and in particular in Slovenia and Croatia. The copper-mines in Serbia and the bauxite deposits in Herzegovina became of central concern to the German aircraft industry. An inevitable clash with Italian economic interests followed.

The German attack on Russia brought a further revolution in the position in the Balkans. The Germans were now actively allied to Roumania, and the supplies of wheat, and oil from Ploesti and the other Roumanian oilfields vital to the Axis war effort, could reach Germany and Italy only along the main railways running through Yugoslavia and Hungary. These communications were now of major importance to both Axis Powers, and in addition represented the supply route to the Piraeus and thence to the Italian and German garrisons in Greece and to Rommel in North Africa. They were the main life-line of the Axis.

The German attack on Russia changed the face of the war, and precluded any major German military effort in the Mediterranean theatre as an alternative operation to the assault on the British Isles itself which had now been indefinitely postponed. Italy alone was incapable of reaching a decision against the British Mediterranean positions. Spain could not be brought into the war except at the expense of the French, and Hitler's Montoire policy towards the Pétain government precluded any such sacrifice. The Italian possessions in East Africa, cut off from all supplies and contact with the mother country, fell piecemeal into British hands. After the wholesale surrender of the Italian armies in Ethiopia, and with the see-saw campaigns in North Africa, the Italians were unable to achieve a temporary decision, let alone a victory.

Although the main German attention was now directed towards an Eastern Blitzkrieg, the German High Command realized that limited military reinforcements to Africa might just tip the balance. In any event it would be but a secondary episode. As General Ambrosio, the future Chief of the General Staff, wrote later, 'The politico-military conduct of the present war is characterized on the German side by a completely continental strategy and a total incomprehension of the decisive importance of the Mediterranean theatre. In fact, apart from the episode of the air assault on England and the battle of the Atlantic—to which can probably in the main be attributed a secondary role in favour of the battle for Northern Europe—the whole German effort has always and only been directed against the continental Powers.' But Mussolini's initial obstinacy in fighting his own 'parallel war' led to the rejection on more than one occasion of German armoured reinforcements for the Libyan Front. The German appreciation of the military value of the Italian army was such that appeals for more tanks and material alone were never met. As Ambrosio wrote: 'From 1940 onwards armoured equipment was requested for the Italian troops in Italian North Africa to put them in a condition to undertake a rapid offensive against the British forces in Egypt. The requests for material were not conceded, in spite of the fact that during the whole of the second half of 1940 and the first quarter of 1941 the German army was not engaged in any operations of war. A few hundred tanks at that time would have probably been enough to occupy the zone of Suez.'[18]

Mussolini had been dazzled by the mirage of a cheap triumph in 1940. His justification for entering into the war, apart from reasons of prestige and a sense of inferiority in regard to the might of Nazi Germany, was to secure sufficient gains for Italy to counter-balance total German supremacy in Europe. But such calculations, which had been quickly disproved by the military events following the French armistice, were swept away by the German attack on Russia, and Mussolini rapidly conceived of a new set of false premises. The Italian 'parallel war' which had been begun to seek limited aims in the Mediterranean, the Balkans and Africa, was now incongruously merged in a German crusade against a Bolshevik East. Mussolini's pose as the leading prototype of the anti-Bolshevist leader was now put to a rude and brutal test. Just as he had felt compelled to enter the war in June 1940 to gain some territorial advantage in face of a German victory in the West, so now in 1941 he could hardly stand aside from this fateful extension of the conflict.

The Libyan campaign was conceived of as a token operation which would strengthen Italy's position at the conference table. Mussolini telegraphed to Graziani in North Africa in October 1940, 'We must bring home to the peace conference our military conquests; it is not worth the trouble of having sixteen months' time in which to prepare and equip fifteen divisions just in order to bring home Sidi El Barani.'[19] In similar fashion he forced on a reluctant Hitler, in the winter of 1941, the Italian Expeditionary Corps on the Russian front to take part in the victorious march to the East as a claim on the economic resources of the Soviet Union at yet another triumphant peace, and told the Italian Commander, General Messe, 'We cannot count less than Slovakia and the other minor states. I must be at the side of Hitler in Russia as he was at mine in the war against Greece, and is henceforward in Africa. The destiny of Italy is intimately bound up with that of Germany.'[20]

In 1940 his calculations were destroyed by the continued resistance of Great Britain, and those of 1941 were shattered by that of the Soviet Union. The myth of the invincibility of the German army on which both dictators had staked their régimes lay derelict. They could only hope, by desperate and co-ordinated efforts, to achieve sufficient initiative on the Eastern Front and in the Mediterranean, to create a stalemate which would form the basis for a compromise peace. Such was the reality of the situation facing the Axis powers in 1942. Hitler and Mussolini, who had never discussed at their sporadic meetings a joint overall politico-military strategy, were reluctant to face such a logic. The Duce drew the conclusion that Italy was at war primarily with England backed by the United States, and that he could not conduct such an effort without German aid in terms of troops, air force, armaments, and supplies in the Mediterranean theatre. Hitler was driven fatally to seek at whatever the cost a victorious solution of his crusade in the East.

His gamble with Operation 'Barbarossa' included a complementary plan to strike, after the rapid defeat of the Soviet armies, through the Caucasus and to form a massive concentration on the highlands of Anatolia—with or without Turkish consent—whence to strike a decisive blow at the British Empire in the Middle East through Iraq, and onwards to a Napoleonic rendezvous with the Italians and Rommel's Afrika Korps at Alexandria and Suez. He outlined this strategic task in his Directive of June 30, 1941. 'Prosecution is envisaged of the fight against the British position in the Mediterranean and the Near East by a concentrated attack from

Libya through Egypt, from Bulgaria through Turkey, and also, under certain circumstances, from Transcaucasia through Iran.'[21] With the failure to reach a decision on the Russian Front by the winter of 1941, any operational planning, other than that for the Russian Front itself, was abandoned. The Germans and Italians were faced at the beginning of 1942 with the bankruptcy of the whole conception of a Blitzkrieg against either the West or the East and with the added, and indeed decisive, burden of the entry of the United States into the war, counterbalanced inscrutably by the declaration of war by Japan on the Axis side. It was not only the myth of the Blitzkrieg but also of the Italian 'parallel war' which had vanished by the end of 1941.

Speaking at the Italian Council of Ministers in December 1941, Mussolini made this reluctant admission: 'The war will last long—three to four years. The situation of the Eastern Front will gradually be stabilized. Germany will occupy those territories which she regards as essential. Russia will be liquidated as an opponent. To win the war, Great Britain must be defeated; either by invasion or the capture of her world bases. The key is the Suez Canal; the attack must come not only from one side, but "also from the East".'

The entry of the United States into the war produced a threat of massive Anglo-American intervention in the Western Mediterranean and on the Atlantic coast of French West Africa, and with it the increased possibility of the ultimate defection of Vichy and the fading chance of Spanish intervention on the Axis side. An early decision in the North African theatre was now not only imperative for Italy, but also for the Germans, and, for the first time since the outbreak of hostilities, the German High Command was forced to pay increased attention to the Mediterranean war. Mussolini for his part was forced to withdraw his opposition to direct German military aid. The German Air Force had, since October 1940, been operating from Sicily against Alexandria, and after a temporary transfer to Greece for the Crete operation in the summer of 1941, Field-Marshal Kesselring, with a German Air Fleet based on Sicily, set up a permanent command at Frascati outside Rome. In February 1941 the German Expeditionary Corps in Africa under General Rommel was sent to stiffen the Italian positions in Libya and Tripolitania, with a view to achieving a military decision in the direction of

Egypt before an Anglo-American threat in the Western Mediterranean might materialize.

The fortunes of the see-saw fighting in the North African desert were linked with the ability to maintain air superiority over the battlefield, and a preponderance of supplies in fuel, munitions, and men at the front. Secure in their bases at Gibraltar, Malta and Alexandria, the British were able to control the skies, and decimate Axis shipping on the sea routes between Italy and North Africa to a sufficient degree to emasculate any serious offensive which might be mounted in the direction of Egypt. The Italian Supreme Command decided therefore to concentrate on Malta, and began planning in earnest early in 1942 for what was christened 'Operation Hercules' to carry out an air-sea combined operation against the island to open on June 10.[22] If this could be timed to coincide with a thrust southwards from the Caucasus in the direction of Egypt, the balance of power in the Mediterranean might be decisively altered in favour of the Axis.

The Germans showed at first little enthusiasm for 'Operation Hercules'. The losses in the Crete operation of 1941 were not forgotten, and, although there were now two German Air Corps in the Mediterranean theatre, one in Sicily and Southern Italy, and another in Greece and on Crete and Rhodes, there was no clear Axis superiority in the air. It was not until April 21, 1942, that the German General Staff agreed in principle to the plan.[23] At Berchtesgaden, however, on April 30, the German and Italian leaders met in a military conference, which followed the political discussions at Salzburg on the previous day. The main issue under discussion between the representatives of the Axis General Staffs was the relation between the planned operation against Malta and the opening of the offensive along the North African coast in the direction of the Nile Delta. The thesis of Marshal Cavallero, who had succeeded Badoglio as Chief of the Italian General Staff after the Italian fiasco in Greece in December 1940, was that Malta must be taken before marching on Tobruk, which guarded the eastward land route to Egypt. The German military leaders insisted however that, unless Tobruk were first occupied and the Axis forces reached at least the Egyptian border, the British would take the initiative in the desert with the decisive support of the Royal Air Force based on Malta. Cavallero was forced as usual to accept the German plan. Rommel was to move against Tobruk and up to the frontier of Egypt, starting at the end of May and in a campaign of two weeks. The Malta operation would then begin. Cavallero recorded the debate in his diary: 'As to Malta, the Fuehrer is of the opinion that it must be taken from the British. I point out the difficulties in regard to means and preparations to such an end. The Fuehrer envisages an operation based on the use of troops landed from gliders, who will pave the way for parachutists . . . One must go into action in Libya at the end of May, and on Malta in the middle of June. As an item of curiosity, I show the Fuehrer Napoleon's plan of 1798 for the conquest of the island.'[24]

German air activity in the ensuing weeks of May over the Central Mediterranean enabled the Axis to build up sufficient supplies in North Africa for Rommel to move eastwards from his Libyan bases.[25] He launched his offensive on May 26, by which time the convoy battle in the Central Mediterranean was being lost by the Axis, and the British position in Malta strengthened by reinforcements at heavy sacrifice. On June 21 the Duce wrote to Hitler: 'At the centre of our strategic plan is the problem of Malta . . . August is the last period of the year for carrying out the operation; after that we would have to wait until the summer of 1943, with consequences of which you are fully aware. Besides solving the problem of Mediterranean traffic, the operation against Malta would allow us to dispose freely once more of our air forces, which today are tied to the Mediterranean sector, and will remain so as long as the enemy has Malta. The freeing of the air forces together with the other advantages of taking Malta would mean that our freedom of manoeuvre would be restored—a factor of prime importance for victory.'[26]

The rapid advance of Rommel, however, threw out of gear the strategy of a simultaneous action against Malta and towards Egypt. On June 21 Tobruk fell to the Axis forces. On the following day Cavallero obtained Mussolini's agreement to issue orders limiting the Axis advance to the Egypt frontier line, and withdrawing a proportion of the air forces for the pending Malta operation. On June 23 Rommel, on receiving Mussolini's directions, told the senior Italian liaison officer attached to his staff that he intended to continue his advance into Egypt, and press on to the Persian Gulf. On the same day Rintelen in Rome informed Cavallero that he had instructions to this effect from the German General Staff. As Kesselring wrote later: 'Rommel at this time had an almost hypnotic influence on Hitler, which made the latter incapable of an objective judgment on the military situation.'[27]

The fatal confirmation that Hitler had personally ordered the abandonment of the Malta operation came on June 23 in his letter to Mussolini.[28] 'Destiny has offered us a chance which will never be repeated in the same theatre of war. The main military objective must be, in my opinion, to exploit it as totally and rapidly as possible. So far I have always had every defeated enemy followed as far and as completely as our forces allowed. The British Eighth Army is practically destroyed. In Tobruk, whose port installations are almost intact, you possess an auxiliary base, Duce, which is all the more important since the British themselves have built a railway from there almost as far as Egypt. If the remnants of this British Army are not now followed by every soldier to his last breath, the same thing will happen which deprived the British of success when, within a very short distance of Tripoli, they suddenly stopped in order to send troops to Greece in March 1941. Only this capital error on the part of the British Command made it possible for our efforts to be crowned with the reconquest of Cyrenaica.

'If our forces do not now advance into the heart of Egypt as far as is humanly possible, we shall see first of all an influx of American long-range bombers which will be able to reach Italy easily. Moreover this will be followed by a concentration of all British and American forces, wherever they can be assembled. The situation will very shortly turn against us. But if we pursue the enemy mercilessly they will be undone. This time, under certain conditions, Egypt could be wrested from England. The consequences of such a stroke would be of world-wide importance. Our offensive for which we are opening the road by conquering Sebastopol, will contribute to the fall of the whole Eastern structure of the British Empire. Therefore, Duce, if in this historic hour, which will not be repeated, I can give you a piece of advice straight from my eager heart, it would be: "Order operations to be continued until the British forces are completely annihilated, as far as your Command, and Marshal Rommel, think that they can do it militarily with their forces."

'The goddess of fortune passes only once close to warriors in battle. Anyone who does not grasp her at that moment can very often never touch her again.'

The gamble was irresistible, and the prize a revolution in the balance of the whole war. Reserves were strained recklessly to the limit. The warnings both of Cavallero, and of Kesselring went unheeded. If Rommel outran his supplies, the disaster would be irretrievable, with the British falling back on their bases at Alexandria and Suez, and the Axis forces stretching their lines of supply and air cover to breaking point.

On June 26, at a conference at his headquarters, Rommel gave his analysis of the tactical situation. The objective of the advance was the position of El Alamein. 'If today the army succeeds in breaking the enemy position, we shall be at Cairo or Alexandria on June 30.'

The Duce crossed to Africa for the final parade, accoutred with the Sword of Islam, while Hitler launched his armies for the long-awaited thrust on the Southern Russian Front. Plans for the administration of an occupied Egypt were already being discussed through diplomatic channels. An Italian civil administrator was nominated, and Hitler agreed that Egypt 'would belong to the Italian zone of influence'. But disappointment was swift, and the doubters were proved to have been justified in their caution. Rommel, now a Field Marshal and military commander designate of Egypt, came to a halt at the Alamein positions.

On his return from the African front, Mussolini wrote to Hitler to explain the reasons for the 'hold up' at El Alamein. They 'could be summed up in one word: the physical exhaustion of the troops, particularly of the Italian infantry'. In an enclosure to his letter dated July 22, Mussolini amplified his views. 'The battle which began on May 26 and which can be called the battle of Tobruk, ended in the first days of July in front of the line of Bir el Alamein. The results of the battle were impressive for a whole enemy army was destroyed, but the objectives hoped for—Cairo and Alexandria—were not attained because, after chasing the enemy for over five hundred kilometres, the Axis troops arrived exhausted. One (Allied) air group and the appearance of a small number of fresh forces sufficed to stop an advancing army which had no reserves to throw into the line . . . The battle of Tobruk is over: the battle of tomorrow will be the battle of the Delta. The time needed to prepare for this new battle must be counted in weeks, but not a single moment must be lost in this competition of speed between the enemy and ourselves.'[29]

In order to carry out Mussolini's instructions on his return from Africa to reinforce the Alamein front and strengthen the Axis hold on the advanced bases and ports in Libya, the Italian reserves of men and shipping intended for the Malta operation were diverted to Rommel. 'Operation Hercules' was abandoned, and with it any hope of regaining the initiative by the Axis in the Mediterranean.

On August 4 Hitler replied sympathetically to Mussolini's comments on the position at El Alamein. 'However long it takes to consolidate our position, I have, like you, given orders to throw into North Africa everything of value in the way of support, reinforcements and replacements . . . It will be difficult and complicated for us to do this. The formation and maintenance of such a strong group of air transport for Africa at the moment of our big offensive in the Caucasus means slowing up the advance of our armoured divisions out there. In the eastern bend of the Don particularly our movements will automatically slow down, because in a vast unroaded zone the necessary fuel supplies can in bad weather often only be brought up by air. There are in addition certain precautionary measures which I am compelled to adopt or keep up in the West.'[30]

The advance of Rommel to the Egyptian border coincided with the launching of the main German offensive on the Russian Front. In order to drive southwards to the oilfields of the Caucasus, it was essential as a first step to establish the German armies in a central strategic position at Stalingrad on the Volga and thus to cover the left flank of the German armies and hold a strong front protecting the southern advance against an eventual Russian counter-offensive. Just as Rommel over-extended his lines of communication and supply in a race for Egypt in June, so the Germans pressed deep into the Caucasus in August, diverting forces needed for the capture of the keypoint of Stalingrad.

Once irretrievably committed on the Southern Russian front, Hitler turned to his Italian ally for reinforcements. Since the dispatch of the first Italian units to Russia in July 1941 as a symbolic counter-aid to the German expeditionary force of Rommel in North Africa, the Germans had been sceptical of the value of an Italian contribution to the war on the Eastern Front. The failure to reach a military decision against Russia by the winter modified this reluctance on the part of Hitler. Ciano had pressed, on Mussolini's instructions, during his visit to Berlin in November 1941, for sending Alpine divisions, and Hitler admitted that especially after the passage into the Caucasus, the intervention of Italian forces would be most useful. The moment had now arrived.

In his letter of August 4 to Mussolini, Hitler wrote: 'I would now like to suggest, Duce, that you allow the three Alpine divisions to be employed alongside our mountain and light divisions on the Caucasus front. This is the more important because the forcing of the Caucasus will bring us into territories which do not belong to the German sphere of interests, and where, therefore, on psychological grounds it would be better if we were accompanied by Italian detachments—if possible by the Alpine Corps, which is the most suitable for this purpose . . . For the rest, I fervently hope that in a few weeks Russia will have lost her most important source of petrol supplies, while in consequence our own disastrous lack of these supplies will be definitely eliminated.'

Mussolini had already been preparing since the previous winter to send the Italian Eighth Army to Russia in spite of gloomy warnings from General Messe, commanding the original Italian force on the Eastern front. Late in July came a formal German request to send Alpine reinforcements to the Caucasus. The proposed move of Italian Alpine troops from the Italo-French frontier to Russia reveals the basic weakness of the Axis military position in the Mediterranean. The failure of a quick gamble to occupy Egypt and gain supremacy in the Eastern Mediterranean exposed the lack of balance of Italy's front in the West. If the Italian Eighth Army went to Russia, the French frontier would be uncovered, and at a moment when there might be an Allied landing in North Africa—an obvious riposte to Rommel's eastward advance—or a coup d'état in France which would create a situation long overdue, in which the unoccupied zone must be taken over by the Axis and the one remaining northern shore of the Mediterranean finally sealed against enemy invasion.

As autumn approached, the military scene on the Axis side was thus dominated by two failures: Russia and Egypt, and a threat: an Allied attack in the Western Mediterranean on North Africa.

The Germans could not afford another indecisive winter in the East. But the personal commitment of Hitler to the Russian war was obsessive and limitless. Everything depended on the early fall of Stalingrad, to which action on other fronts must be subordinated. Just as control of the Ukraine was vital to the Axis in terms of food supplies, so the possession of the Caucasian oilfields was indispensable for the further decisive conduct of the war against the Anglo-Americans. A sinister aspect of the Egyptian gamble had been the exhaustion of stocks. As Keitel had telegraphed to Cavallero on June 27: 'The handing over of 160,000 tons of fuel oil to the Italian Navy has effectively exhausted the last remaining (German) reserves.'[31] After the Italian capture of Mersa Matruh two days later, Cavallero noted in his diary: 'There is no more fuel for the destroyers at Tripoli . . . The oil tanks are empty and two cruisers as well.'[32]

In pressing the Italian Ambassador in Berlin, Alfieri, for three Alpine divisions for the Caucasus, 'a region which interests Italy more than Germany', Hitler was merely underlining this stark reality.[33] The Caucasian mirage was to dominate Hitler's military thinking through the year. As he told the Italian Fascist Party Secretary, Vidussoni, during the latter's visit to his headquarters, his plan was: 'to push forward from West to East into the South Caucasus in order to reach the oil regions of the British. Once this was accomplished, the British would be prevented further from operating in the Mediterranean.'[34]

With the failure of Rommel to reach Suez, the initiative in the North African theatre passed to the Allies. It was too late in the year to mount the Malta operation, nor indeed would the supply position or the state of Axis air power, after the Egyptian effort, permit it. The Italian parachutists destined for Malta were now fighting as infantry in Egypt. The Italian Command was strangled and tied by the Egyptian front on which, as Cavallero plaintively noted, 'depends the fate of the Middle East'.[35]

It was inconceivable that the Western Allies should not act in such a situation. Both Hitler and Mussolini were, however, convinced that they would not have to face a Second Front in Europe in 1942.

In a memorandum headed 'Considerations on the military situation', addressed to Cavallero on July 19, Mussolini had expressed his view of Allied strategic intentions. There would be a mounting air offensive against German cities, and on land a front would not be opened 'in Norway nor in any of the countries bordering the Atlantic, nor even in the African territories on the shores of the same ocean (Morocco). The Second Front will take place in the Middle East, that is, in Egypt, Palestine, Syria, Iraq, in countries in which men and equipment can land without fighting in lands which constitute the great crossroads of the British Empire.'[36] As the Fuehrer wrote to Mussolini at the beginning of August, 'I think this Second Front is quite mad. However, since in democracies it is the majority and therefore human folly which makes the decisions, we must reckon with the possibility that madmen will take control and will try to open a Second Front . . . I have nevertheless decided to leave a large number of first-class divisions in the West and even to take more over there so as to have compact armies always at hand for counter-attacks. . . . If the English and Americans really make this mad attempt, they will get unpleasant technical surprises, which from 1942 onwards will make them lose all desire to repeat this experiment on the European continent.

'Unfortunately, for the moment I am not able to leave General Headquarters even for a few days. But as soon as joint operations on the Eastern Front are under way, I hope to make you my promised visit. I am convinced that by then the picture will have become much clearer and will have changed in our favour.'[37]

The summer of 1942 proved to be the watershed of the war, or rather of the two 'parallel wars' fought by the Germans and Italians in the East and in the Mediterranean. It witnessed the end of the last hopes of a Blitzkrieg. On August 17 the American Strategic Air Force began operating against Germany on a massive scale and three weeks earlier, on July 24, after bitter and obstinate staff talks on the highest level, the Allied leaders had decided to launch the planning of a major operation against French North Africa, under the code name of 'Torch', as the first stage of a grand design to liquidate the war in the Mediterranean and a prelude to opening a Second Front in Europe in 1943. Only a drastic revision of a grand strategy together with careful joint planning and a survey of existing military commitments could re-establish the military initiative of the Axis. Both dictators were victims of their own strategic obsessions.

Although Hitler was correct in his view that no landing would take place in the West in 1942, and Mussolini in his in regard to the opening of the Allied air offensive against Germany, neither grasped the intentions of the Allies in the Mediterranean, and their failure to do so changed the course of the war.

* * *

Apart from the basic strategic errors of the Axis leadership, the absence of a co-ordinated machinery of military and political consultation was fatal to the conduct of the war. There were no secret military clauses in the Axis Pact, and no formal machinery of consultation on a General Staff level set up after the entry into the war in June 1940. The experts on both sides in practice only met as part of the delegations to summit conferences between the two leaders called hastily and irregularly in moments of crisis.

On the German side neither Keitel nor Jodl visited Italy before the collapse of the Fascist régime in July 1943. Goering, as head of the Air Force and a self-appointed specialist on Italian affairs, was the main channel of intermittent high-level contact. When the Germans were forced to pay urgent and anxious attention to the supply problems of the African Front at the turn of the year 1942, Admiral Doenitz was sent twice on a special mission to Rome. Apart from these sporadic and infrequent visits, the channel of communication ran through the Military Attachés in the two Embassies in Berlin and Rome and the German commanders in Italy to their respective ministries and chiefs in Berlin. The German Military Attaché in Rome, General Enno von Rintelen, was the main and most reliable and perceptive source of information on Italian affairs. He had been in this post since 1936, and was by far the best observer of the Italian scene. His reports and dispatches form the most accurate picture of events as seen from Rome during these years.

Field Marshal Kesselring had been transferred from the Eastern Front to command the German Air Force based on Sicily in November 1941, and was the senior German officer in the Mediterranean theatre. His meetings with Mussolini were held on a more or less regular basis, and in times of crisis almost daily. His headquarters at Frascati just outside Rome was in theory an expeditionary force under Italian command, and nominally directly under the Duce himself, but any real decision in regard to the African war was made in correspondence between Mussolini and Hitler, or by direct orders issued by the latter to the Commander of the German Afrika Korps.

On the Italian side the conduct of the war was the personal province of Mussolini. His meetings with his Chief of the General Staff, Cavallero, and the heads of the Armed Services, although held regularly, bore little resemblance to the equivalent machinery on the Allied side. Marshal Cavallero had succeeded Badoglio in December 1940 after the Greek fiasco. He was both efficient and unpopular in carrying out his functions.

After the First World War he had abandoned his military career to work for the Pirelli rubber company. In 1925 Mussolini appointed him Under-Secretary of War, but three years later he returned to business life as a director of the giant Ansaldo shipbuilding yards, and there were certain scandals relating to contracts for building cruisers which were hushed up at the time by the veteran Costanzo Ciano, but which were widely known in Italian military circles. Cavallero was, nevertheless, a man of outstanding gifts of organization and a brilliant administrator.

These characteristics led him inevitably to admire the efficiency of the German war production and military structure, and on his return to active service on the Italian General Staff he became identified at an early stage with the pro-Axis party in Italy. After the outbreak of war, Cavallero headed the liaison office of the Italian High Command with the German military missions in the country. His appointment as Chief of the General Staff in December 1940 was regarded in Berlin as an encouraging sign of future improvement in the Italian conduct of the war and of closer co-operation between the two allies. Cavallero, with his own experience of industry, also made his influence felt in the chaotic sector of Italian war production. His future position would in fact depend largely on relations with the Germans. As Rintelen reported later to Berlin, 'Within the bounds of possibility he (Cavallero) is fulfilling all German wishes.'[38]

From the Italian side, however, as Chief of the General Staff, he was at the mercy of Mussolini's changing attitudes, and the intrigues of the clans within the Italian service ministries. Unless the war in the Mediterranean could be won in the ensuing months, Cavallero would be sacrificed. He was the symbol of the idea of an Italian Blitzkrieg in the Mediterranean, and time was running out. By the beginning of 1942 his position had reached the point of weakening. Rintelen reported on February 13 that this was now endangered.

'Cavallero has carried through, in a fashion hitherto unknown in the Italian Armed Forces, a strong military leadership, and in particular he has forced the Navy—in spite of opposition from them—to take action in supplying Libya. He has used his influence with the various military and civilian officials to increase war production. He is working in a close and trustworthy manner with the German military agencies, which is regarded in some circles as going too far.' The Duce was beginning, however, to lose confidence in him, and his career would henceforth increasingly depend on German protection.[39]

Diplomatic relations between the two Powers were also seldom conducted in traditional style. The German Embassy in Rome and the Italian Embassy in Berlin would normally have been regarded as fulfilling such a function. But as the war progressed an unofficial network of contacts grew up between individual Ministers in both countries, Party politicians and specialists, which bedevilled the work of both diplomatic missions to such an extent as to sabotage any efficient conduct of business. The Italian Ambassador in Berlin, Dino Alfieri, was in particular exposed to this climate. He had been nominated to his post as the successor to Count Attolico, who had fought with all his skill and experience to preserve Italian neutrality after September 1939. Alfieri should have been, in theory, a central pivot of contact in the wartime affairs of the two countries. A lawyer from Milan, he had made his career in the Fascist Party along conventional lines, firstly in the Ministry of Corporations at intervals between 1929 and 1936, and then as the first Minister of Popular Culture dealing with press and propaganda from June 1936 until his appointment to Berlin in May 1940. He came to his post with no training in diplomacy, but was viewed by the Nazi leaders as an adequate representative of Italian Fascism. He had established good relations with Goebbels during his period at the Ministry, and Hitler had special regard for him as Alfieri had, at the time of the Austrian crisis in 1934, warmly supported German policy.

Baron Hans Georg von Mackensen, the German Ambassador in Rome, came from a different school. He had succeeded Ulrich von Hassell as Ambassador in Rome in April 1938, and his predecessor, like Attolico in Berlin, had striven both to avoid the outbreak of hostilities in Europe and to avert the fatal commitments which led to the Axis Pact. Hassell was later to perish as one of the civilian leaders in the July Plot in 1944. Mackensen was an old-world diplomat, son of the Field Marshal of the First World War, and his innate correctness of approach to the problems of diplomacy made it difficult for him to interpret with any subtlety or skill the irresponsible and often contradictory mechanism of Roman politics.

The real decisions relating to the conduct of the war by the Axis did not pass, however, through such channels. They were made at irregular summit conferences between the two dictators, and initiated and implemented by unofficial visitors at all levels from both sides; from Berlin, in particular by Goering or Ribbentrop and occasionally Himmler, and from Rome by Ciano and on occasion special economic or military missions.

The two Embassies in Berlin and Rome operated therefore in an atmosphere of resentment and confusion, plagued by sporadic personal visits of political and military figures of varying importance reflecting a criss-cross of private intrigues and conflicting organs of power, bedevilling and impeding the routine business of the official representatives. In addition, each political organ and Party boss in both countries established his own unofficial agents.

The lengthening of the conflict had also revealed the artificiality of the Axis alliance. The longer the war lasted the greater the aversion towards Germany in political circles in Italy. In Italian eyes the justification of the Axis Pact and the linking of the destiny of Fascist Italy to that of Germany could only be the achievement of quick results, of historic Italian aims in the Mediterranean, the Adriatic, and Africa, as the appendix of a German victory in Western Europe. Such a programme failed even before it could be implemented. By the autumn of 1942 the temporary optimism which had marked Italy's declaration of war two years earlier had evaporated, and a sense of fear and frustration pervaded the Italian scene. Historically Italy had always sought freedom of action; to ally with one great power or another. The basic principle of her foreign policy had always been freedom of choice. What alternative now lay ahead if only Germany were left in Europe as a great power? And if Germany were defeated, what would be the fate not only of the Fascist régime, but of Italy herself? There was also a strong feeling that Germany did not sincerely regard Italy as an equal partner, and that the war was being conducted without any regard for Italy's susceptibilities or interests. In spite of protestations to the contrary, Germany had penetrated economically into the one Italian sphere of influence in Europe, namely the Balkans. Italy was now totally dependent on Germany both militarily and economically for the continuance of her war effort, and there was no frank discussion or even propaganda as to the future construction of a New Europe in event of victory, nor of Italy's place in such a world.

Disillusionment in Italy in regard to the German ally in its turn stimulated criticism of the régime itself, calling in question the prestige and personal authority of the Duce.

CHAPTER TWO

Twenty Years After

On July 21, 1942 the Duce returned from his African expedition, leaving behind him a tactical and strategic stalemate. As he wrote in a memorandum the next day, 'We must rake up everything that can be taken without danger from Libya and send for everything else from Italy.'[1] But he knew intuitively that a final chance had been missed to redress the balance of military power in favour of the Axis in Africa. His sense of an irretrievable loss of initiative in the conduct of the war in the Mediterranean extended to a profound weariness in the management of affairs at home. For the first time in his career, the burden of responsibility became unbearable and was outwardly manifested in a breakdown in health.

At the end of July, Mussolini left Rome for the Adriatic resort of Riccione, and spent the remainder of the summer there, partly with his mistress Clara Petacci, whose existence and the activities of whose family were at last precipitating a political scandal on the fringes of government circles. The physical crisis in the Duce's health intensified during the ensuing months, coming to a head in October. Apart from three brief visits to Rome, he was either at Riccione or his retreat in the Romagna at La Rocca delle Caminate, between the end of July and the middle of October. Such absences of the Head of the Government from the seat of authority inevitably disturbed the routine of administration, and the confusion was the greater because of the peculiar climate of Mussolini's personal rule.

Throughout the twenty years of the régime, the traditional organs of rule had atrophied or been abolished, and a strange and unique amalgam of unco-ordinated bodies and conventions had taken their place, all stemming from the immanent authority of one man. The formal structure of Fascist power lay in the national machinery of a totalitarian party. Its roots as a revolutionary movement had been in origin regional. The organization of the March on Rome, and the capture of the State machine in October 1922 had been the work of the provincial organizations. Both the strength and the weakness of the Party in its early history was its loose and decentralized structure. The authority of the original Milan Fascio, for example, was never imposed on groups outside that city. As Mussolini wrote in July 1919, 'The Fasci are not, do not wish to be, and cannot become a Party. Fascism has neither statutes nor rules.'[2] It was not until November 1921 that a Party statute and a national directorate were set up and a Director-General appointed to curb the activities of the regional Action Squads. Indeed, underlying and permeating the whole history of Italian Fascism were two opposed conceptions of party organization within the ranks of the leaders of the first generation: the Jacobins of Italian Fascism, represented by Roberto Farinacci, who believed in a highly organized revolutionary machine to safeguard the permanent revolution: and the believers, such as Giuseppe Bottai, in an opposition within the Party which should be a decentralized system of discussion clubs with voluntary membership and freedom of speech. The issue between these two opposing views of the nature of Party government was settled early in the history of the movement. With the parliamentary crisis after the murder of the Socialist leader Matteotti in 1924, and the vertiginous decline in popularity of the Fascist Party throughout Italy, the extreme elements of the Action Squads now incorporated in the Party Militia, and with Farinacci as their spokesman, won the day—and decisively. It was he who, as Party Secretary after the crisis of January 1925, broke the original Fascist Party machine which had carried through the political revolution three years earlier. He also set the frame for the future development of the whole movement, and the effects of his draconian actions were never basically reversed. By massive purges of the membership, he broke the strength of the provincial bosses and their organizations, and the political fiefs of the city states of Northern Italy, which had been the strength of the early Fascist movement, lost their independence. The elements of a centralized Party machinery in Rome were now set up. It is therefore primarily due to Farinacci that the Italian Fascist Party assumed a rigid frame. His successors followed his example. The Party machine became increasingly organized on lines of military discipline, and it was the Party Secretary himself who now controlled all local appointments at all levels of the Party hierarchy, with power to dismiss any nominee. The general result of such a procedure was to replace the provincial 'tyrants' by local clans, whose existence and enjoyment of office depended on the favours of a central secretariat in Rome.

In the inter-war years the functions of the Party Secretary extended into the machinery of government. Already in 1932 he had exclusive control of Party affairs, and the selection of the central Party directorate lay in his hands. He himself was always a personal nominee of the Duce. The Party Directorate itself was a body meeting weekly, consisting of three Vice-Secretaries, the Administrative Secretary, and eight nominated members, acting as a sort of Party Cabinet. Below this body lay a National Council, consisting of the 92 provincial secretaries, the members of the Directorate, certain honorary nominees, and a number of national inspectors. The essential function of this body was to impress upon the provinces the unity of the Party through directives issued at the meetings held usually once or twice a year, and often presided over by the Duce himself. In 1938 the Party statute was again revised, and the Secretary now became both Secretary of State in the Council of Ministers, secretary of the Grand Council, leader of the youth organizations, and of para-Party organizations. In addition he had in practice a certain control over the activities of the Fascist syndicates and was at times even commander of the Party Militia. With the outbreak of war in 1940 the activities of the Party, under the direct control of the Secretary, extended into such fields as the mobilization of shop-workers in agriculture, and setting up committees—as at the time of the Ethiopian war—to attempt to regulate and control prices.

The Party machine had its own liaison office with the Militia and its own political police organization. Through the provincial secretaries a machinery characteristic of Italian Fascism developed alongside that of the Prefects and of the traditional civil administration, and through the Party national headquarters from time to time it would send out requests for secret information on local reactions to Party politics, just as in the same way the Prefects would report to the Ministry of the Interior.

Throughout the twenty years of Fascist rule there was a

continuous debate on the concept of Party membership, and thus on the relationship of the Party to the population as a whole. The three early tests of membership had been: participation in the March on Rome, membership of the Party during the Matteotti crisis, or later training in the Party youth organizations and special schools. The original apparatus was manned by the pre-1922 generation, and as late as 1934 two-thirds of the provincial organizations were still controlled by members of the old guard of the Action Squads. In 1923 recruitment was halted and a temporary stop put to the election of new members. The lists were open again after the murder of Matteotti the following year. In 1932 regulations were enforced whereby civil servants, school and university teachers, and officers in the Army were obliged to take out Party cards, thus widening the circle of membership; but it was seldom that any member of this generation reached any responsible office within the Party itself. In 1938, in an endeavour to meet the basic problem of the second generation of Fascists, Party membership was thrown open to the graduates of the now massive youth organizations under Party control. In 1940 the lists were opened to all members of the armed forces, with the result that the total figures reached over three and a half million, in addition to the now highly developed youth cadres of nearly eight million.

From the time of the take-over of power in October 1922 until the outbreak of war in 1940, the organs of Fascist control had been gradually extended and perfected, invading the jurisdiction and prerogatives of the traditional State machinery. Throughout the whole system of government ran a basic dualism of authority and activity, ranging from the undefined relations between Mussolini as Prime Minister, appointed with all legal propriety in 1922, and the King as constitutional monarch, through the ill-defined and parallel existence of the Party and the Civil Service, the Militia and the Army, to the provincial Party secretaries and the Prefects.

Finally, as a cornerstone of a supreme collective authority within the régime developed the functions of the Grand Council of Fascism. This unique body was to play a decisive part in the history of the movement. It was set up originally early in 1923 as a sort of central committee of the Party, and indeed as 'shadow Cabinet'. In 1932 it was transformed from a Party institution into the highest governing authority of the Fascist State, by-passing the traditional Council of Ministers or Government, and co-ordinating and integrating all the activities of the régime. As Farinacci put it, 'The State and the Party have, in the Grand Council . . . the unifying centre through which the antithesis between Party and government is rendered no longer possible.'[3] There was even a touch of Platonic ritual in the conception of a nocturnal council to make the Laws of the State. The Party Secretary acted, among his other functions, as secretary of the Grand Council, and, in the absence of the Duce, as its Chairman. The Grand Council, among its many functions, regulated the succession to the Party leadership, and just before the war—to the controlled fury of the Sovereign—that of the Crown itself. The membership of the Grand Council consisted of some twenty individuals who represented the élite of Fascism. There were the life members, and these were the survivors of the Quadrumvirs, the leaders of the columns in the March on Rome; then the holders of key offices, such as the Cabinet Ministers, the President of the Special Tribunal, the Party Secretary and vice-Secretary, selected members of the Party Militia, and the President of the Institute of Fascist Culture. Finally, certain special members were appointed for three years; four Ministers and Party Secretaries, and 'eminent men' of the revolution. The Grand Council provided the audience for the historic decisions of the Fascist government, and it was at a meeting on December 8, 1939, that the principle of Italian non-belligerency in the war was enunciated. But no minutes were ever kept or any vote taken. The body had not been summoned since that date.

The machinery of the Fascist Party, together with its armed embodiment in the Militia and with the Grand Council of Fascism as its apex, governed Italy through its own special organs and by extensive and persistent penetration of the three traditional pillars of administration and authority —the Army, the Police, and the Civil Service.

The Legislature had survived the shock of the March on Rome, and with the revised electoral procedure of a single list, continued even after the Matteotti crisis and the secession from Parliament of the 'Aventini'—the opposition deputies in 1924—as a rump assembly. But the fiction of such an elective body was eliminated in December 1938, and replaced by a nominated Chamber, the deputies being National Councillors of the Fascist Party and appointed as such partly by the Party machine and partly from the various professional Corporations of employers, technicians, the professions, and the workers. To these were added *ex officio* the high officials of the Party, the holders of ministerial office, and the Undersecretaries of State. In violation of the constitutional statute of the Kingdom of Italy, this legislative body was sanctioned by a law passed by the expiring Chamber of Deputies and ratified by the Senate and the King. Indeed, the continued existence of the Senate and undefined privileges of the Crown were the sole remaining fragments of the edifice of the Albertine Statute of 1848. It was primarily against these two surviving historical enclaves that the Fascist revolution stopped short of a totalitarian frame.

The entry of Italy into the war in 1940 produced first hidden and then revealed pressures, which brought to light the essential flaws in the whole structure of Fascism. By 1942, when the conflict approached its military crisis, the internal weakness of the régime became manifest. Apart from the inconveniences of the highly personal rule and style of government of the Duce himself, the rigid and conformist structure of a mammoth Party machine became progressively exposed. As in the field of State administration, so in the higher levels of the Party, Mussolini's inevitable solution was a series of 'changes of the guard', exhausting the cadres and depressing their morale. After twenty years of government, and according to paper planning, a new and enthusiastic generation trained in the youth organizations, the Militia, and the Party schools, should be awaiting in the wings, in fervent Fascist enthusiasm, their summons onto the stage. Their absence was only too painfully apparent, and the exigencies of the war effort, quite apart from the peculiar mentality of the Duce himself, made any drastic reform of the Party machine out of the question. It was this problem of the second generation, or as it was called 'the second wave', which was the recurrent and central theme in Party discussions in the late 1930's and again during the first two years of the war. With the failure of the long-expected élite cadres of Fascist youth to appear, the only temporizing recourse in each crisis within the Party would be a search for the ghosts of the old discarded leaders of the Action Squads of the 1920's, whose enthusiasm could not be recaptured and whose very existence was difficult to trace. The fluctuating history of the Fascist Party in the later months of its life revolves round this antithesis and the unreal choice between the survivors of the revolutionary generation and the 'second wave'.

In December 1941 Mussolini appointed as Party Secretary a young man called Vidussoni. He was 28 years old, and had not yet finished his Law studies. He came from the model provincial Fascist world of Trieste. As a Militia officer he had been wounded in the fighting during the Civil War in Spain and decorated with the military Gold Medal. As Ciano put it, 'One cannot say more about him.' He was not intelligent, but equally not disloyal, and he was to act as a kind of cheerful and eager aide-de-camp to Mussolini. As the latter expressed it in his speech to the Party Directorate on January 3, 1942, the nomination of Vidussoni was 'a symbol of youth and heroic commitments. One has now reached a point where the generation which made the Fascist revolution has become old, feeble, or ill, and is on the decline, while the new generation is on the move . . . The tasks of the Party are in the first place of a moral nature, and lie in a purely political sphere, and these tasks, from the point of view of the State, are above all a police function. The more successful the work of the Party in the moral sphere, the less work for the police.'

The Duce drew attention to the essential importance of the millions of members of the Fascist youth organizations, where 'the loss of 400,000 Party members is unimportant in itself'. In accordance with customary rhetoric, mention of the faithful was followed by that of the enemy within, in this case the too familiar caricature and butt—the Italian middle classes—together with the external scarecrow, international capitalism. Regarding the first, 'We will bring these fat sheep into the pen and shear them'; as to the second, 'On January 3, 1925, we were faced with the internal opposition of the Aventine. Today we have to deal with a much more powerful Aventine, which stretches from Moscow to Washington and is created by capitalism. The inner relationship between Bolshevism and capitalism has not surprised me.'

The maintenance of the Italian war effort was dependent not only on massive German aid, but also on the resistance of the Home Front. 'New military disasters could only be borne if the whole nation were prepared to face up to them.'[4] Effective political control was in turn bound up with the morale and prestige of the Party, and in the last resort of the Militia. At the same time the whole structure of Italian government was characterized by an ill-defined dyarchy ranging from the relations and balance of authority between the King and Mussolini, to the respective functions of the Party regional machine headed by the Federal secretaries and the civil administration represented by the Prefects nominated by the Crown; the competing roles of the Militia and the royal military police in keeping public order, and the position of the Army in relation to both bodies. Within the confusion of these rival organs of control and unresolved dualisms, Mussolini had imposed his own supreme authority, and in a sense his unique position, as he conceived it, depended on its continuance.

By 1942 Benito Mussolini embodied the following attributes of power. As Duce of Fascism he controlled in the last resort all manifestations of the Party, changing its Secretary at will; packing the National Directorate, and presiding over the supreme organ and symbol of Fascist power, the inner conclave of the leadership, the Grand Council, whose theoretical functions had no counterpart in the traditional structure of the Italian State, regulating not only the life of the Party and its armed embodiment in the Militia, but even charged with deciding the succession to the Duce, and to the Throne itself.

In keeping with conventional usage, however, the Duce of Fascism was also Prime Minister of a government, appointed with due form by the King in October 1922. In virtue of such an office, Mussolini was received in audience twice a week, and the Monarch was duly informed of the progress of public affairs, keeping his own counsel and stretching to the limit the fiction that he was dealing with a constitutional Prime Minister. Throughout twenty years the main rôle of King Victor Emmanuel had been to keep up appearances, and when the inevitable crisis of the régime came, it was Mussolini who proved to be the self-deluded victim of the fictitious relationship between the two men.

It was, however, not only as President of the Council, or Prime Minister, that Mussolini held supreme executive authority. On the outbreak of war he assumed the office of Minister of War and the Commandership in Chief of the Armed Forces, a position constitutionally held by the Monarch. The service Ministries were thus directly subordinate to him, and the ultimate responsibility for the conduct of the war lay exclusively in his hands.

In dealing with routine affairs, civilian and military, Mussolini had evolved over the years his own peculiar and highly personal style. He was methodical in planning his day and his time-table rarely varied, but he was capricious in employing any machinery of consultation, and destructive of any ordered dispatch of business. As Bottai put it, 'Investiture to office by rotation and changes of the guard were his highly personal method. Names were chosen by chance, often from the parliamentary directory, and often even mistakes of name were made.' Italy was governed by clans of functionaries and not by a ruling class. 'If three Ministers agree on a subject, it is a conspiracy . . . the balcony of the Palazzo Venezia has completely substituted the Council of Ministers and even the Grand Council itself.'[5]

The Council of Ministers was a disjointed body of subordinates, summoned on paper to meet at 10.30 on the last Saturday morning of every month at the Viminale, but the date was never fixed in practice and meetings were often postponed at the last moment. In principle an agenda of draft legislation was prepared for discussion between the Ministers. In practice the intermittent occasions on which the Council of Ministers was summoned were employed by Mussolini to clarify in confidence his thoughts aloud, and usually a second meeting had to be summoned to deal with the routine business.

One such session is refreshingly described by Giuseppe Gorla, who was Minister of Public Works from October 1940 to February 1943.[6] 'Suddenly the door of the President's study opened, and Mussolini appeared. Everyone was silent, and saluted in Roman fashion . . . In front of each Minister was placed a sheet containing the agenda, which is very long. It contains a list of draft legislation to be introduced for the approval of the Ministers. Mussolini having sorted out the documents in front of him begins to speak, but does not follow the agenda, and announces that he has confidential statements to make to the Council alone.' Gorla, seeing that the secretary of the office of the President was keeping no record, began to take notes. 'Mussolini notices almost at once and asks me what I am doing. I tell him. I stop for a moment. "Do not do so. You can see that even the secretary of the Council is keeping no record, on my orders. Because I want to talk freely and I can only do so in this body which alone can keep a secret. Not even in the Grand Council can I speak openly, as the walls seem to have ears . . . Yes, in eighteen years, nothing has been repeated outside this room. Perhaps because the ministers share the responsibility. So no records."' Gorla continued however to take notes under the table, and at subsequent meetings.

The Council of Ministers was thus a private sounding-board rather than a consultative body. The effective conduct of business radiated from the Duce's private office, the Sala del Mappamondo in Palazzo Venezia, in individual audiences and myriad telephone calls. On a normal morning when in Rome, Mussolini would usually receive the head of the political police (the OVRA), the Foreign Minister, the Minister of Popular Culture who controlled the Press, the Secretary of the Party, the head of the Ministry of the Interior, and the Chief of the Armed Forces. In addition a mass of reports and memoranda would filter on to his desk through the private secretariat, police and spy reports from the competing and rival agencies of the Interior, the Chief of Police, the special offices of the Party and–separate again–of the Militia and of the Military Intelligence; reports of the Prefects from the provinces, the telegrams of the Foreign Office, and the war bulletins and memoranda from the Chief of the General Staff. These documents would be scrutinized without minuted comment, and returned with a bare majestic 'M' in blue pencil. Decisions would usually be taken verbally or by telephone.

The reading of the Italian and foreign press occupied a central position in this activity, and the daily directives to the Ministry of Popular Culture were the essence and revelation of the personal direction of the Duce. A study of these directives would give a detailed picture at any given moment of the shifts and trends of Italian policy. A change in headlines or pagination in the totally-controlled Press would indicate imminent and future developments and recent decisions. This was Mussolini's real world, and the measure of his genius lay essentially in the manipulation of the masses by the written and spoken word. But his increasing isolation in recent years from the public arena had led to a certain loss of contact with the Italian people. His last public appearance of national importance had been on the balcony of Palazzo Venezia to announce the declaration of war in June 1940. The explanation of the 'mission' of the Fascist government came to depend increasingly on the written directives to the Press, but the brutal reality of military defeat and stalemate, of Allied bombing and short rations deprived words of their meaning, and under such an impact Fascism began at last to exhaust its vocabulary. In a sense Mussolini governed Italy as if he were running a personal newspaper single-handed, setting the type, writing the leaders, interviewing everybody, chasing the reporters, paying the informers, sacking staff incessantly, defining the policy to be adopted and the causes to be defended, and basically ignoring the supreme responsibility of political power as extraneous to the business.

The twentieth anniversary of the March on Rome fell on October 28, 1942. It had been hoped to celebrate the occasion with due pomp and to demonstrate to the Italian people the fruits of twenty years of the Party and the Régime. There had indeed been plans initiated in 1938 for a world exhibition, and even for a moment a tidy and artistic notion of the Duce to enter the conflict at such a moment. But under existing circumstances the ceremonies were by his orders to be muted. The historical significance of the occasion was unhappily dwarfed by the harsh realities of war and the first perceptible signs of the disintegration of the very structure of the régime, whose creation was to be the solemn subject of celebration.

Mussolini had intended to make a speech to a mass gathering of the Party leaders on October 29, but orders were given to cancel everything. Ciano noted in his diary: 'Three current interpretations: that the doctors have forbidden the strain of a long speech; that Mussolini does not wish to say anything until the Libyan offensive is decided; that he intends to make big changes in the Party and, as would be logical, he wants to speak to the new leaders.'[7]

The only public ceremony held to celebrate the March on Rome was the inauguration of the Museum of the Revolution. It was the first time that Mussolini had appeared in public since his illness. It was a cool and hollow occasion, but with a harsh significance. It was an implicit and unexpressed indictment of the Party, whose triumphant accession to power twenty years earlier was the formal subject of commemoration. As Ciano wrote, 'The organization of the ceremony was far from coming up to par, lacking even the least sense of comradeship among its members. The fact is that the present secretariat of the Party is made up of obscure men, to whom we are in turn unknown . . . On this very day of the recurrence of the Fascist celebration, the inefficiency of the Party is felt more strongly than ever.'[8]

The real celebrations of the historical triumph of Italian Fascism in 1922 were marked by the British in Libya and the Royal Air Force over the towns of Northern Italy.

CHAPTER THREE

The Problem of the Succession

'From October 1942 onwards I had a constant and growing presentiment of the crisis which was to overwhelm me. My illness greatly influenced this.'* The rumour in informed circles in Rome that expert medical diagnosis showed that the Duce had no more than four or five months to live produced consternation. On September 26 Ciano received a letter from his wife, who had just arrived at the Rocca delle Caminate, and which 'disturbs me a great deal . . . Under the circumstances, for the Duce to be ill would be really disastrous.'[1] Bottai saw Mussolini on the evening of October 7 on his return to Rome: 'His face grey and ashen, the cheeks sunken, his look troubled and tired, his mouth expressing a sense of bitterness, and thus revealing clearly the illness which, according to rumour, has attacked him again. But the man does not seem to be so much ill as dejected and saddened, no longer fighting triumphantly against age . . . He has in himself killed the man that he was. All bonds of confidence are broken. Even to ask after his health makes him suspicious.'[2]

The physical incapacity of the Duce created a vacuum at the summit of power and a crisis of leadership which coincided with a weakening of national confidence in the régime, both in its handling of internal affairs and in view of the mounting tide of military defeat. For the first time since 1924 there were spreading doubts as to the continued viability of the personal rule of the Duce, and agitated speculation as to the political succession in the event of his disappearance or demise.

The machinery of Fascism provided in theory for such a

* *Pontine Notes.* Written during the internment of Mussolini at Ponza after July 26, 1943. See p. 547 of the original edition.

situation. It was one of the functions of the Grand Council to maintain a list of deputy leaders, the senior of whom would receive formal and automatic nomination. Such a convention had been under cursory review in the months following the first grave crisis of Fascism in 1924. It was in no way geared to the political realities of the régime, but was conceived in a moment of fleeting danger. The only personality designated was Count Costanzo Ciano, who had been intimately concerned with the inner councils of the movement at the time of the March on Rome and was one of the leading figures of the early Party. He had been nominated the first President of the Fascist Chamber on its inauguration, but died shortly afterwards in the summer of 1939. He had been an honorific figure, trusted by Mussolini, and unhampered by a following in the Party machine. His very designation as the official successor to the Duce signified his lack of political significance. The Grand Council met after his death, in December 1939, but to discuss the realities of Italian policy in regard to the outbreak of war in Europe. The theoretical issue of the succession was not raised, and the Council itself ceased to meet.

The trusted intimacy of Count Costanzo Ciano with the Duce was perhaps more significant in forwarding the career of his son, Galeazzo.[3] After brilliant high school and law studies in Rome, the young man sought to make his mark in the journalistic and literary clans of the capital which passed for the intellectual circles of the régime. The young Ciano was soon at ease in this café society of political leader-writers, critics, and writers, and marked by his contact with this climate of licensed comment on the régime. Coming from a prosperous Leghorn family with widespread shipping interests he typified that upper middle class which had viewed with benevolence the rise to power of Fascism, but which did not seek advancement through the channels of the Party. His ambitions, unfulfilled as a playwright, soon changed direction. He sat for the regular Foreign Service examination in 1925, and passed among the first successful candidates. He was first posted to Brazil and then to China. In 1929 Ciano returned to Rome on his appointment as secretary at the Vatican Legation. It was at this time, through his sister, that he met Edda Mussolini, and his marriage to the Duce's daughter the following year was to launch him into the centre of the government.

His career henceforth was the personal creation of the

Duce. In August 1933 he was appointed head of the Press Office in the Foreign Ministry and a year later Undersecretary in the newly created Ministry of Press and Propaganda. In 1935 he was appointed Minister. In this capacity he was the intimate spokesman of Mussolini in a characteristic field of Fascist activity, and the channel of interpretation, through the organs of a controlled Press, of the manifestations of the régime. The young unsuccessful playwright had become the intimate interpreter of the veteran journalist. Mussolini gave his affection easily, but his confidence rarely. Since the death of his brother Arnaldo he had accepted no collaborator. His son-in-law seemed destined to fill the void.

In June 1936, at the age of 33, Ciano became Foreign Minister, a post hitherto held by his father-in-law.

The influence and prestige of Ciano in Italian politics was both subtle and fragile. He was in the last resort immutably dependent on his father-in-law, and possessed no constant personal following of his own, although at any given moment he commanded a series of fleeting loyalties. In general the upper ranks of the Fascist Party were hostile to him. He did not belong to the generation of the March on Rome, and was thus alien to the core of Party bosses, and on the whole he was indifferent to the vagaries of internal Party intrigue. His meteoric rise had not been through the channels of the Party, but by family accident, and inevitably multifarious jealousies concentrated around him. However, his position as Foreign Minister brought with it closer access than any other public figure to the Duce, on whom every decision depended not only in foreign affairs but throughout the whole machinery of government. It was this that gave Ciano a special and unique importance, but at the same time any action by him was totally circumscribed by the will and indeed the whims of Mussolini.

Ciano's support was constantly enlisted from every quarter, and his agile, imaginative mind was perpetually active in creating shifting alliances of mutual and usually temporary convenience within the political and social world of Rome. At the beginning of 1942, for example, he was in close and constant touch with Buffarini, who controlled the working of the all-important Ministry of the Interior. Colonel Dollmann, Himmler's representative in Rome, reported that Ciano was in a leading position, before the Greek campaign, 'not in popularity but in influence'. He was followed hand in glove by Buffarini. Both men had succeeded in winning over the Duce's private secretaries 'which means in Italian politics the suppression of every disagreeable report'.[4] Ciano was, as Acquarone put it, 'a man badly viewed and attacked by all'[5] and his essential weakness was his basic isolation. He seemed cast by nature for the eventual role of scapegoat, and although the basic decisions of policy, which had led to the entry of Italy into the war, had been the personal responsibility of Mussolini, in the popular mind Ciano was intimately identified with them. The mounting crisis of the conduct of the war in the autumn of 1942 represented a potential threat to his personal position, and the illness of the Duce affected him even more immediately and acutely. It might also, however, create an opportunity.

One of the characteristics of Mussolini's political technique of rule was to regard his collaborators of the moment as both immediately expendable and always available. He was not concerned with creating a loyal team, but maintaining a reservoir of clients, totally dependent on him for the favours and fruits of office, awaiting their turn or return and thus circumscribed in their loyalties to each other, and reluctant to establish more than an effusive camaraderie among themselves, or to push a momentary cabal beyond private consultations.

Nor would Mussolini allow even the outline of a rival personality to appear in his vicinity. As Italo Balbo once remarked: 'As soon as he sees too much light shining on us, he turns off the switch.' This deliberate fragmentation of the Fascist governing class ultimately brought about its self-destruction. Each leading figure was contained in his activities by a direct relationship to the Duce, to which every other position or office which he might hold was secondary, even in the Fascist movement itself.

Dino Grandi was perhaps both the most outstanding product and victim of this 'system'. His early career was like that of his generation in the Fascist movement. A gallant officer in an Alpine regiment in the First World War, a law student who completed his studies, an early member of the local Fascist organization and a leader of the action squads in Emilia. The pattern of his local position follows that of his contemporaries: control of the squads in the region and then of the Party machine in Bologna; a journalist on the local paper *Il Resto del Carlino*, an activity essential to the influence and prestige of a successful politician; and then a member of the Party Directorate by 1921.

By the time of the March on Rome, Grandi in Bologna, like Balbo in Ferrara, could answer for his regional clan, and was in a position to exercise a certain influence on the direction of the movement. In this early period, when Mussolini's authority was not absolute over his followers, Grandi clashed with him openly both over the former's attempt to make a pact with the Socialists, and again in opposing the leader's short-lived anti-monarchical campaign. Although designated as a member of the 'General Staff', set up to organize the March on Rome, Grandi, who had already opposed the idea of insurrection on the grounds that the battle could be won without effort by legal means, stayed in Rome to take a leading part in the intricate negotiations with Antonio Salandra, the interventionist Prime Minister of the First World War, and other Liberal politicians, in order to bring about a coalition ministry with the Fascists, a plan approved by the Crown and rejected by Mussolini. Grandi claims that this action on his part 'excluded him from any political activity for nearly two years'. He was, however, summoned to Rome in March 1923, and his official career begins with his appointment as Undersecretary at the Ministry of the Interior. Two years later, he transferred to the same post in the Foreign Office to become Foreign Minister in 1929.

Grandi was now imprisoned in the 'system'. 'What should I have been if I had not met you? At the very most, an obscure provincial lawyer.' A series of such letters from Grandi was published by Mussolini in his thrashing booklet first issued in August 1944 as a supplement to the Milan paper *Il Corriere della Sera.* There is no reason to doubt their authenticity, and they illustrate the style of 'double-talk' which became increasingly and inevitably a familiar part of every dialogue between the Duce and his collaborators, containing an element of genuine effusion within a general convention of language, which was not intended wholly to deceive the recipient.

During the years in which Grandi controlled the Foreign Ministry, and after 1932 when he was sent as Ambassador to Great Britain, he was influenced by the necessity, in the interests of Italy, of avoiding a clash with the Western Powers and he devoted much energy, charm, and persistence, particularly when in London, to improving relations between the Italian and British governments. Grandi was recalled in the early summer of 1939 and nominated, without his prior knowledge, Minister of Justice, and in December he was appointed President of the new Fascist Chamber, on the death of the first holder of this office, Ciano's father. The former post brought Grandi into the Council of Ministers; the latter provided an as yet unexplored political sounding-board, and made him an *ex-officio* member of the Grand Council.

In the desperate controversy in Italian political circles over the attitude to be taken by Italy after the outbreak of war in Europe, Grandi openly favoured Mussolini's immediate and reluctant declaration of non-belligerency. In March 1940, when Mussolini began talking openly of entering the war on the side of Germany, Ciano noted, 'Against the adventure are Grandi and Bottai.'[6] In the following month, on April 21, 1940, Grandi expressed his views in a wide-ranging personal letter to Mussolini. It was a forceful plea that Italy should remain neutral in existing circumstances. 'It is never "late" to enter a war. Italy has not the means equal to those of any of the protagonists in the present European drama, but could, under certain conditions, become "the decisive weight" . . . These conditions depend on what Russia does or does not do, the third great absentee power. Depending on the future attitude of Russia the future position of Italy can be judiciously considered . . . Until such a time, let us remain as we are, neutral, non-belligerent, abstainers. The formulae are irrelevant provided that Italy keeps out. In the meantime let us prepare and arm ourselves in a serious manner.'

With the news, however, of the vertiginous collapse of the Western Front in May, no single leading figure in Italy was exempt from the ensuing wave of euphoria. Grandi made an anti-Allied speech in the Chamber, which he seems promptly to have regretted. Ciano maliciously recorded that Grandi only received three telegrams of congratulation: two from well-known Fascist figureheads, 'and one from an inmate of a lunatic asylum in Catania, who offered to put the speech into verse for one hundred lire'.[7] But as the general optimism as to a war of weeks evaporated and after the fiasco of the 'parallel' war in Greece in the winter of 1940, the muted chorus of critical comment recovered its voice.

In the months leading up to Italy's entry into the war, Mussolini had noticeably and exceptionally made use of the formal machinery of government. The Council of Ministers met frequently, major policy decisions regarding non-belligerency were discussed in the Chamber, and recorded solemnly in the Grand Council at the beginning of December 1939. There was, however, no consultation on the declaration of war. This step was the supreme personal act of the Duce himself, and as abruptly as he had previously taken soundings, henceforward—apart from irregular meetings of the Council of Ministers where he was accustomed to think aloud and unreported—the administrative and executive organs of the State, apart from working technical committees, ceased to function. Such was his conception of government that, in moments of panic or in an atmosphere of pessimism, he regarded each body as merely a potential forum of criticism and discontent, however passing and impotent.

The Greek fiasco had generated just such a climate. As Grandi put it 'Parliament virtually vanished'.[8] It was so in a literal sense, as most of the Ministers, and National Councillors of the Party, were mobilized and sent to the Albanian-Greek front as a puckish means of dissipating incipient plotting. This move of Mussolini's was greeted with anxious astonishment. Some people, such as Bottai, went so far as to speak of 'a real coup d'état by the Duce in order to get rid of Fascism and place his reliance on other political currents'.[9] Bottai, who was at the time Minister of Education, received without warning a telephone call from Mussolini telling him that he was mobilized. The Duce was said to be in excellent humour. 'I will show the country how one governs with only senior civil servants.' Bottai commented, 'We are the object of a new dictatorial experiment.' The same fate befell Grandi later in the month, and he too found himself on the Greek front. Ironically, it was here that the discontented caballed. As Grandi wrote later, with a certain telescoped and grandiloquent exaggeration, 'I made contact with my friends, and jotted down, there in the trenches of Greece, the plan of the resolution which later marked the end of Mussolini.'[10]

There have been numerous references in contemporary memoirs and documents to Grandi's 'circle' or 'Grandi and his friends', implying the existence of a shadowy but coherent political group. Such a concept is at the same time too precise and misleading. But with two men of his own political generation Grandi enjoyed a particular intimacy and an interchange of ideas, which became increasingly marked after his return from Greece and which intensified in the late autumn of 1942. They were Giuseppe Bottai, and Luigi Federzoni, both in distinct ways leading personalities in the formative years of Fascism and drawn together subsequently by a similar approach to the problems created by Fascist rule. They both held a series of high offices, and were, in the prevailing climate of the régime, both beneficiaries and critics. Grandi was the diplomatic expert; Bottai the theoretician of 'constitutional' Fascism; and Federzoni the elder statesman, and potentially, as in October 1922, a respected link with the Crown.

Bottai, like Grandi, had been a young officer at the front and had fought in those commando units—the *Arditi*—which supplied so many recruits to D'Annunzio's adventure at Fiume, and to the early action squads of Fascism. In 1919 he had taken part in the founding of the Rome Fascio, and led its detachment in the March on Rome. Unlike many of his companions he had literary pretensions beyond the immediate field of local journalism, and possessed serious intellectual qualities. 'Even if I have always recognized the origins of Fascism as being neither theoretical nor logical . . . I have never believed that intelligence was absent from those origins.' Through the pages of his review 'Critica Fascista', founded in Rome after 1922, he made obstinate and not entirely forlorn attempts to enunciate a 'moderate' programme for a triumphant Fascism, of fundamental reform by legal revolution, achieved and modified by constant self-criticism and revision within the élite of the Party. 'I pleaded for an opposition on interior lines.' Bottai was arguing for formal acceptance by the Party leadership of such an approach, but the weakness of his case was that the essential problem created by the occupation of the State machine by Fascism—namely the demarcation of the frontiers between illegality and legitimacy in the exercise of power—could never be faced owing to the limits, both in terms of brute strength and moral ascendancy in the country as a whole, of the very Fascist movement itself. He glimpsed this at one early moment. 'In a certain sense one can say that it is not that Fascism is in a state of crisis, but that Fascism is a synthesis of the crisis of Italian life as a whole, a crisis of formation, of growth, and of a definition of values.'[11] Between the ultra-revolutionary conception of Farinacci and the 'slow but sure revolution' by legal process of Bottai, developed the personal dictatorship of Mussolini. The historic dilemma of Fascism was that it did not possess the vital force or the united will to achieve a total political and social revolution, nor the coherence and discipline to be compressed into the role of a governing political party in a traditional constitutional frame, however modified by reform.

In 1936 Bottai became Minister of Education and occupied himself with the formation of a second generation, more comprehending than his contemporaries in his conceptions of the structure of the Fascist régime. He still held this office in the autumn of 1942.

Luigi Federzoni represented in the history of the Fascist movement the later arrival of an older political grouping, the Nationalist Party, which he had founded in 1910 with Enrico Corradini, and which formed the advance guard of the interventionist campaign in 1914–15. In the years immediately following the armistice, Federzoni and his party were rivals of and hostile to the early manifestations of Fascism, and the temporary allies of D'Annunzio. The Nationalist and pro-monarchist 'Blue Shirts' were also a particular source of disquiet to Mussolini in the regions of Italy south of Rome, where the Fascist hold was weak. The personal relations between Federzoni and Grandi dated from the intricate negotiations in the capital preceding the March on Rome, and the latter played a role in the subsequent absorption of the Nationalist group into the ranks of Fascism. Federzoni formally joined the Party in 1923, but with mental reserves, which survived his appointments as Minister of the Colonies, of the Interior, and President of the Senate. Like Bottai, he possessed marked intellectual gifts. In 1942 he was President of the Italian Academy, and as such was also a member of the Grand Council.

This private grouping of Grandi and his friends, however, did not constitute a distinct political force. As Bottai put it, 'We are consumed with inactivity. We are only isolated individuals: we do not form a governing class, nor even a government team.'[12] It was nevertheless among these 'isolated individuals' that a programme and a platform were conceived which, in July 1943, as Grandi wrote, 'marked the end of Mussolini'. The essence of Grandi's solution was the ultimate intervention of the Crown, the revival of the constitutional organs of government, the setting up of a 'moderate' Fascist administration, the resumption by the King, as head of the Nation, of the supreme command of the Armed Forces, and a probing search for contacts with the Western Allies with a view to a separate peace. Its implementation depended exclusively on the action of the King, and in the absence of any sign from him no move could be made. It was a time for analysis and definition rather than action.

The continued existence of the institution of the Monarchy under Fascism was a tacit reminder that the Fascist revolution had its limits set, and that in the event of any disputed succession to the Duce the ultimate decision could only lie with the King. As Hitler on one occasion told his advisers: 'In Rome I saw what Fascism is like. It could not prevail over the Court circle . . . The Fascists and the Quirinal crowd are all jumbled together . . . How does he judge Italy's chances in the event of a waning of the Fascist revolution, or of the Royal House? . . . For either the Royal House supersedes the Fascist Revolution—how would he judge the prospects of his people in that case? . . . Or how does he judge them if the Royal House alone should take over power? It is hard to say. In Klessheim he made a remark while we were having dinner together. He suddenly said, "My Fuehrer, I don't know; I have no successor in the Fascist revolution. A chief of state can be found to succeed me, but no one who will continue the Fascist revolution." That is certainly a tragedy.'

The decline or disappearance of Mussolini must inevitably lead to a reactivation of the prerogatives of the Crown. Much turned on the personality of the Monarch. As he told General Puntoni, the head of his military household, 'In 1922 I had to call on "these people" to govern, as all the others, some in one way and some in another, had abandoned me. For forty-eight hours I had to give orders direct to the Police Commissioners of Rome and the Corps Commander to prevent Italians killing each other.'[13] Twenty years of Fascist rule had progressively shorn the royal prerogative, but in spite of the tacit complicity of the Monarchy with the régime, the prestige of the Crown survived. The ultimate sanction of Italian politics, as in 1922, still lay in the constitutional intervention of the King. He was a close taciturn man, both obstinate and diffident, secretive and distrustful, keeping absolutely his own counsel. His attitude to public affairs was conditioned by his rigid and formalistic conception of his duties as a constitutional monarch. Even if Fascist rule had circumscribed and diminished the royal authority, the outward forms remained intact.

It was also of salient importance that, although Mussolini had assumed nominal command of the Armed Forces in June 1940—the latest violation of the royal prerogative—the oath of loyalty of every officer was to the King, and in a major political crisis the Army would not only be the decisive factor, but would also as in October 1922, obey and await the orders of the Crown. Just as at the time of the March on Rome the Army accepted the new régime following the example of the Monarchy, there was every reason to believe that, in changed circumstances, the military power might become the loyalist instrument for the overthrow of Fascism. According to Hitler, 'The work of the Duce is mainly hampered by the fact that his power is limited by the Crown. One cannot lead a nation when the army, for example, has sworn fealty to another who is not the effective head of the state. Just as a man cannot run a commercial firm if others hold a majority of the shares and thus have the power to cancel all his decisions.'[14]

But in spite of the mounting internal weaknesses of the Fascist system, the growing loss of contact of the Party with the masses, and the declining authority of the Duce, only two events, together or separately, could lead to the collapse of the régime: the disappearance of Mussolini or total defeat in war. The military situation, though grave, was not hopeless so long as the African front could be held and the invasion of the Italian mainland averted. But the crisis of the Duce's health must inevitably endanger the existence of his rule, and excite speculation and anxiety in every quarter. 'Must hold one's tongue. Spies on the Staff . . . Political situation not clear. Duce ill.' This entry appears in the diary of General Ambrosio, Chief of the Italian Army Staff, on October 17, 1942. The course of the war and the internal state of the country gave further cause for alarm. Intensive Allied bombardment of Italian cities, the problems of evacuation of damaged areas and of rationing, added to the war-weariness of the population a sharp pervasive criticism of the régime.

The King was aware that any move which he might make would be decisive not only for the country but also for the future of the Monarchy. He was conscious of his exclusive and unique role which could be played only once, and its manner and timing would depend on him alone. He also knew that, with the exception of a few Party extremists, every circle and clan in Italian public life looked in the last resort for such action as the supreme catalyst. General Puntoni recorded, 'They all hope for an intervention of the Crown and think it necessary for the Sovereign to be in close union with the Army, which, in the event of a crisis, can alone save the situation.'[15]

The King, as was his nature, proceeded with secretive caution. Early in October he had retired to San Rossore, one of the Royal estates near Pisa. Since the declaration of war in 1940 he had avoided appearing in public or receiving in audience more often than his routine duties as monarch required. His main confidant and link with the world of public affairs was the Duca Acquarone, who since 1939 had held the post of Minister of the Royal Household. The King, slow to give his confidence, was impressed by Acquarone's grasp of business and his handling of the Royal finances and estates. The Minister was a wealthy Genoese aristocrat and former cavalry officer, loyal, discreet, ambitious, and active. Victor Emmanuel came to rely on him more and more as a source of political information and as an intermediary behind the political scene. By the winter of 1942 not only was this special role of Acquarone assured, but the Monarchy might well require the widest possible personal contacts in the event of an internal crisis transcending the Fascist régime.

On October 10 the King was considering a visit to Rome. Acquarone telephoned to fix an audience with the Duce, but was told that the latter intended to meet Hitler in Russia. Two days later it appeared that Mussolini was suffering again from the internal malady which had followed his recent North African trip, and had postponed his journey. There were rumours of cancer. The King, however, appears to have been less concerned about the gravity of the Duce's condition than other observers. As he said to Puntoni, 'Mussolini's womenfolk complain that he is a bizarre invalid and does not want to look after himself. I would advise him to take care and remember that he is sixty years old.'[16]

On October 27 the King came to Rome, and received Mussolini the same morning. He learnt 'nothing particular' from his Prime Minister, but 'spoke to him clearly about the internal position'. It is not without significance that the main informant of the Court for some time had been General Hazon, one of the senior officers of the military police, the very body responsible for the maintenance of public order and incidentally by tradition and sentiment deeply royalist. In the event of any disturbance, their role would be of prime importance. Any weakening of control would be the precursor of a national crisis, and to this threat the King, with his clear memories of the events following the end of the First World

War, turned his attention. In his methodical way, he addressed himself to one problem at a time.

The internal malaise of 1942 indeed presented certain features in common with the grave tensions in Italian affairs in 1917; the same picture of military disaster as at Caporetto, and of war-weariness and political strains on the Home Front. As this latter situation had been the political school of King Victor Emmanuel his judgment of the former must be to some extent inevitably influenced by a particular historical pattern. The recurrence of the same stresses might lead to the revival of the role of the Crown in Italian affairs, but under conditions totally modified by twenty years of Fascism. The destruction of all organizational forms of a parliamentary opposition after 1924 had also removed the means of appointing an alternative government by constitutional process. The open removal of the Duce would now be a revolutionary act, and this the King intended to avoid at all costs. He was by temperament and training opposed to radical solutions, and in particular because the chances of a successful counter-coup by the Fascist Party aided by the Germans were difficult to estimate or at least analyse with any certainty.

But the danger of the disintegration of the Fascist State as the direct result of the death, by natural causes or violence, of Mussolini, or through a military collapse followed by enemy invasion, or both, had in the autumn of 1942 become real and menacing. The candidates for the succession, in the absence of any system of political parties, might be found among the 'moderates' of the older generation of the Fascist movement itself, men like Grandi, Bottai, and Federzoni, who had always regarded themselves in part as a self-elected opposition within the system, or from the exiguous band of survivors of the political and military élite of pre-Fascist Italy. It was unlikely that any of these elements, even in an emergency, could form into an administration by themselves, but they were in a sense possible candidates to the succession; and each had his own particular solution and in every case this depended in the final resort on the action of the Monarchy.

Any new government, formed from whatever elements, and in the shadow of military defeat, would need the prestige of a senior military figure in order to ensure the political support of the Army and to create some psychological basis of support and confidence among the masses, the extent of whose allegiance to the cult of the Duce was another undefined element in the situation. One aspect of the case, therefore, was the appearance in the wings of the Marshals of the First World War, and the abrupt prospect of a vacancy at the summit of political power, for which they might be competitors. The least retired and most obvious candidates were Badoglio and Caviglia, linked in an ironic and mutual hatred in the historical controversy over the responsibility for the Caporetto disaster in 1917, the Italian Gallipoli of the First World War. Their subsequent careers too had sharply diverged.

It was Caviglia who had suppressed D'Annunzio's rebellion at Fiume in 1920, after Badoglio had displayed his natural wariness. Caviglia had regarded the successful march of Fascism with a consistent and distant sarcasm, and both D'Annunzio and Mussolini were in his eyes 'the charlatans of power'. He commanded a certain following among the older generation of survivors in the Senate, the only enclave of murmured and licensed discontent under Fascism, but he remained aloof, independent, and untouchable. A police report suggested that in the first politico-military crisis of the war—in October 1940—Caviglia was 'prepared to assume the liquidation of the régime'.[17] There is no reliable evidence to elucidate or confirm this, but it does appear that in the succeeding months he was received by the King on more than one occasion.

Badoglio, on the other hand, although by legendary account he had in October 1922, as Farinacci put it, 'boasted that in five minutes of machine-gun fire he would clear away all the Black Shirts',[18] had become a major beneficiary of the régime, ennobled and enriched by Mussolini, the victorious commander in Ethiopia, Duca di Addis Ababa, and Chief of the General Staff at the outbreak of war. His direct responsibilities, however, made him closer than Caviglia to leading Army circles, and his position in regard to the war, though he retained his functions, was unequivocably opposed to Italy's entry. With the Greek disaster in the winter of 1940, his abrupt dismissal modified the impression of his Fascist past. He had thus closer and more recent links than Caviglia with the upper ranks of the Army, and a special advantage in the virulent personal hatred of Farinacci and thereby of those extremist Fascist elements compromised with and bound to the German ally.

On the eve of the war there is a fleeting but unconfirmed indication that the King had proposed to both Caviglia and Badoglio that action should be taken by them against Mussolini. They both evaded the hint, and as the police report added, 'These Marshals have no contacts between themselves.'

In any event, both rivals were by the autumn of 1942 active and expectant observers of the political scene.

The Germans in their turn were alerted. Against the opposition of his rival Ribbentrop, Himmler announced that he would visit Rome in early October. It appears to have been a private move inspired by Ciano, as a plaintive telegram from Alfieri, the Italian Ambassador in Berlin, shows: 'The rumours which have been circulating in recent weeks in Germany, and I imagine also in Italy, over Himmler are certainly known there. This morning I learnt from a reliable German source that Himmler will be visiting Rome at the invitation of Minister Ciano on the 10th or 11th of this month. It would have been very interesting for me, if at the same time as this news had been given by you to the German Embassy, I had received a confidential indication, and in fact for several reasons which I will pass on to you another time.'[19]

It was natural that Himmler should wish to sniff the political air in view of the increasing reports of the decline in Mussolini's health, and to investigate the intricate balance of forces behind the scenes which might follow a disappearance of the Duce from public life. Ciano's motives in encouraging such a visit are less clear. Perhaps he was anxious to quieten Himmler's suspicions as to the fragility of the Italian political scene, and as to the attitude of the Italian royal house—and in particular the Prince of Piedmont—with whom Ciano seems to have been increasingly in contact as a possible ally in the event of a hiatus of power.

On October 11 Ciano, by an unusual protocol, went to the station to meet the head of the German SS. In a later conversation, he found that 'what counts is the extremely reserved tone of his conversation . . . He wanted to find out a good deal about Italy. In particular he wanted to know about the Monarchy and the Vatican . . . I praised the loyalty of the first and the discretion of the second.'[20]

In a subsequent report to the Fuehrer, Himmler described his formal reception by Mussolini, who seems to have made a special effort for the occasion. The memorandum has the mark of a prissy schoolmaster. 'The Duce gave me a very cordial reception. He was in civilian clothes and looking particularly well, extremely fresh and in the best of humour . . . (He) gave me, in the course of conversation, an outline of the Italian political situation. He described the mood of the population as not enthusiastic, but as resolute. The Italian people was well aware of what was at stake in the war. He, the Duce, and the Party had the people well in hand, and there were no grounds for misgivings of any kind. The only question that was serious, though neither dangerous nor catastrophic, was the food position . . . Italy had, in general, a good many problems to face; and one of these problems was of course the fact that, as he phrased it, "there are three of us in Rome: myself, the King, and the Pope." In spite of this things were better than was generally thought. The Pope was not going to make things too difficult for him, and he was, after all, an Italian at heart. He added that the lower ranks of the Italian clergy were moreover very patriotic, though some of the higher clergy dabbled in politics. Referring to the Royal Family, the Duce said that "the King was of course very old, but he remained loyal, and had indeed been loyal to him from the very first days of his Premiership. The Crown Prince was a Fascist and had completely subordinated himself to him, the Duce; he was equally loyal." I replied that this struck me not merely as gratifying, but also as good policy on the Crown Prince's part, since the House of Savoy owed its throne in the last resort to the Duce, whose intervention had alone rescued Italy from Bolshevism and upheld the monarchy. I said that it was to be hoped that the House of Savoy would be duly grateful and never forget this fact. The Duce, however, rejoined that one should never expect gratitude from princes, for they were not as other men: princes were the last International.'

But the real purpose of Himmler's visit becomes clear from the rest of his report. He spent three days in Rome touring the city, sometimes in mufti, and accompanied on different occasions by Buffarini, who controlled the Ministry of the Interior, Senise, the Chief of Police, and Ricci, the Minister of Corporations—and, in the background, his own representative in Rome, Colonel Dollmann. These were his main sources of information. Buffarini at the Interior had long been such a source and a key through the intermediary of Dollman. Senise was a professional expert on police affairs, and, although his loyalties may have lain elsewhere, his duties required that he should brief the distinguished visitor. Ricci, apart from being in charge of the important Party stronghold, the Ministry of Corporations, had close links with the Militia, which would be the essential element in an internal crisis.

During this visit, which was primarily to gain a first hand impression of the Italian political scene, there was clearly speculation in private conclave of the possible course of events if the Duce should disappear from the stage, and the establishing of confidential contacts with reliable Italian Fascists to act in such an event. It is significant that just after Himmler's departure Dollmann should report in the following terms: 'May I begin these lines by emphasizing the deep and enduring impression which the Rome visit of the Reichsfuehrer SS has left behind everywhere here. I can best summarize this fact in the statement made repeatedly to me by Excellency Ricci. "The best offensive of this autumn in the Axis camp is called Heinrich Himmler in Rome." Again Ricci recently stressed how vitally necessary this contact was for the friends of the Axis in Rome, whose positions are undermined from so many sides.'[21]

The reserve nucleus of an eventual Fascist counter-coup, among the leaders of which can be identified Buffarini and Ricci, can for the first time be discerned, and indeed their later role after the events of the following July provides such a confirmation.

Apart from rallying internal support to maintain a pro-German régime in power in event of a sudden collapse, Himmler was anxious to study the immediate situation of Mussolini. 'I am convinced that so long as the Duce is alive, Italy will hold firmly and steadfastly to the Axis, and will fight the war to the finish.' But if an untoward event occurred, the only rallying point of opposition to Italian Fascism could, in German eyes, come from the circle of the Royal House. This had always been the basic interpretation of Italian affairs both by Hitler and his entourage. Himmler's particular interest was therefore focused on this aspect of the Roman world. He was but half convinced by the Duce's assurances. 'The good relations maintained with the Royal Family and with Crown Prince Umberto were stressed with quite striking unanimity by most Italian ministers and dignitaries. However, I heard *through links confidentially established with Italian circles* that despite this external emphasis the Italian police are busily compiling a dossier on the Crown Prince, as in fact he is still not quite trusted.' Rumours continued to cluster round the Prince of Piedmont as a possible successor to the régime, and as the leader of such a movement, but as a result of his visit to Rome Himmler would now be better informed, and able to observe more closely the labyrinthine moves of Italian affairs.

CHAPTER FOUR

'Torch'

On October 17 the German Embassy in Rome sent a report on the views of Italian political and military circles on the Mediterranean war. 'A considerable intensification of military activity' must be expected. The Italian Foreign Office had already at the beginning of the year felt that, in the event of an Axis failure in Egypt in the summer, they must reckon with an American landing either at Dakar or at a Moroccan port. Since the Italians had been halted at El Alamein, 'these anxieties have increased. Although the Italian General Staff are quietly awaiting the British offensive, there are other disturbing factors: an English air superiority of three to one; and Axis shipping losses and supply difficulties in North Africa. An English flanking attack at El Alamein is expected, coupled with the certainty of American operations against Dakar. I learn reliably,' the German Ambassador wrote, 'that the Italian High Command has decided to make at once the necessary preparations to occupy Tunis, if military developments require.'[1]

From the Italian strategic point of view, the Western Front ran from the French Alpine frontier through the islands of Corsica and Sardinia and Sicily to the Tripolitanian and Tunisian borders. As the Duce put it in a survey of the war to his service advisers at a meeting on October 1 at Palazzo Venezia: 'This front could become active at any moment, in all probability in relation to the attitude of France, which seems ambiguous. That is so much the case that our Allies have already agreed on ways and means of occupying the whole country should the government be forced to go over to the enemy. If this should happen, it is for us to occupy Southern France and Corsica; such a task, if one considers the experience of the Germans in France, and ours in the Balkans, will not be easy. The assault on the cities will be particularly difficult, and we will have to attack Toulon and Marseilles . . . We must also take into account that, if we proceed to the total occupation of France, the French government may go to settle in Algiers and become the ally of the Anglo-Saxons, thus opening to them those landing areas which today it asserts that it wishes to defend. French Equatorial Africa is also threatened. For this reason, I have decided to send one division into Tripolitania to be followed by two others . . . We should try to have sufficient forces in Tripolitania to extend our occupation up to the western frontier of Tunisia before enemy forces could land in strength.

'Above all it seems to be the Allied intention to launch an offensive against Libya simultaneously from Egypt and from West Africa. It is certain that Churchill and Roosevelt regard the North African theatre as Front Number One. Their plan is to destroy Italy as the weaker Axis partner.'[2] But several months must elapse before such an enemy operation could be mounted. The Italian High Command reckoned on, first an attack by the British at El Alamein, followed by a simultaneous assault from both sides on Libya. The Duce however was optimistic. 'He still has not written off a decisive thrust against Egypt. If the Americans set foot first in Morocco, he will march into Tunis and occupy Tunisia, irrespective of whether Vichy reacts.' Preparations against this must be made on the Alpine frontier. No Italian initiative as such would be taken in this region, not even in the direction of Nice. 'Under present circumstances, Italy will take no action against France. The emphasis of the war has moved to the Mediterranean. The need is to strengthen the Axis positions there and to step up the U-boat war in the Atlantic.'[3]

On October 19 Goering had arrived in Rome to review with the Duce the war situation on both the Eastern and Mediterranean fronts. As head of the German Air Force, he had a major interest in the Italian contribution to the war, both because of the stationing of the German Second Air Fleet under Marshal Kesselring in Italy, and its role in supporting the North African campaign, and also because on the successful resistance of Italy depended the air defence of Germany herself. It was also Goering, rather than his other colleagues, who came to Rome as the personal envoy of the Fuehrer in times of particular stress, and as the interpreter of the latter's immediate preoccupations.

Hitler and Mussolini had met on the Russian Front in the autumn of 1941. There was still a year later no sign of a German breakthrough to the oilfields of the Caucasus, and the mirage of a Middle Eastern meeting linking up the two war fronts of Russia and the Mediterranean was still beyond the horizon. A critical battle was now imminent on the Don, and the German advance into the Donetz basin was barred at Stalingrad. Until this major deadlock was broken, Hitler could hardly turn his attention to the other problems of the war, which Goering was now sent to discuss in Rome. He arrived in the Italian capital on October 19 on the heels of Himmler, but business was delayed by an attack of dysentery which as Ciano noted 'did not permit him to leave his throne even for ten minutes'. His meeting with Mussolini took place on October 23, and lasted for two hours, with the assistance of the inevitable interpreter Schmidt.[4]

Goering's first duty was to describe the situation on the Eastern Front. The Russians must be driven out of the Caucasus, and the Stalingrad battle should be over in the next eight days. As Goering said subsequently at breakfast in the German Embassy, he had been deliberately optimistic as the Duce had a pessimistic impression from Rommel of the African Front—a view which was supported by the British assault at El Alamein on the day of this conversation at the Palazzo Venezia.

The regrettable pause at Stalingrad had nevertheless increased the danger of the British and Americans being 'forced' by the Russians to open a Second Front in the West. Goering stressed that there were crack German divisions on the West Wall in France and that it was also unlikely that the enemy would land in Spain or Portugal. 'The main anxiety arises in the Mediterranean, in an eventual attack on French Africa, Libya, Sardinia or Crete. He (Goering) did not reckon on a landing in Italy. Crete and the Peloponnese, as well as the endlessly long Mediterranean coast of Africa were threatened, but the question of a landing in the Adriatic or in Croatia did not arise.'

The Axis armies in Africa could again become operative only if adequately supplied. 'If a major landing in the Mediterranean does not happen in another area (than Libya) and if supplies via Greece and Crete can be assured, which has proved useful in contrast to earlier experience in supplying

Tobruk, the Axis need not fear anything from the direction of Egypt.'

Mussolini's main preoccupation was inevitably with the situation in North Africa, where the decisive military engagement was already in progress. He summarized the results of the Axis failure in the Mediterranean since 1940, and he was talking under the shadow of a fatal and decisive reckoning—the omission to occupy Tunis, to take Malta, and to protect the supply lines to the battle front in Libya. 'The Duce continued that he wanted to discuss one internal and two military problems. The latter were the question of oil supplies and Malta. To protect the convoys the fleet escorts required certain quantities of oil, and to safeguard the supply routes Malta must be neutralized . . . Then the routes from Italy to Tripoli and from Greece to Tobruk could be safeguarded. The Duce was preparing to send three further divisions to Africa. One division had already been moved by air to meet a threat from the Sahara to the south. The other two, whose presence in Africa raised again a supply problem, he would station on the Tunisian frontier and would occupy Tunis at once in the event of an Anglo-American landing in French Africa. For if they occupied Tunis there arose the possibility of an English landing in Italy, even if it were not successful. The French population was adopting a waiting attitude . . . In event of an Anglo-American attack France would only put up a token defence as in Syria and Madagascar, to save its honour. One should not forget that the Axis had released much war material to the French and that all Frenchmen hated the two Axis allies. They hated the Germans with respect, and the Italians with contempt.

'In this connection the Reichsmarshal expressed his regret that Tunis was not in the hands of the Axis, to which the Duce answered that naturally if this had been the case the question of supply would be absolutely assured.' Goering then asked 'why at the time of the armistice negotiations with France the occupation of Tunis had not been demanded. After some hesitation the Duce replied that he must admit that this had been a failure by omission. Italy had been too modest.'

The conversation ended with Goering expressing the hope of the Fuehrer that he could meet the Duce next month, as he must in any case be in Munich on November 8.

While the two men were in conclave in Palazzo Venezia, the British Eighth Army opened its long-planned and awaited assault on Rommel's positions at El Alamein. During the night of November 2, after a decisive Allied breakthrough, he ordered a general retreat, in spite of orders and counter-orders from above. As Rintelen wrote later in his memoirs, 'It is not possible to interfere in tactical decisions from East Prussia, or even from Rome, in a battle in Egypt.'[5] The 'battle for the Delta' was over, and the remnants of the Axis army in North Africa were disengaging at speed from the British assault.

On November 5, the Italian Supreme Command received precise intelligence of a large Allied convoy in readiness to leave Gibraltar. Cavallero, at a meeting of the Italian Chiefs of Staff, commented on the news. 'One does not know whether this will be to supply Malta or whether it has an operational purpose: a landing at Casablanca or Oran. Our surface naval forces cannot take action owing to lack of fuel.'[6] At 8.30 that evening, the Italian Naval Chief of Staff reported to Cavallero that the convoy had left Gibraltar half an hour earlier. 'One did not yet know in which direction.' The Duce summoned his service advisers on the following morning. It was agreed that if the Allies landed in French North Africa, the Italians must occupy Corsica immediately, and be prepared to move into the unoccupied zone of Southern France. At a meeting that evening Rintelen was present. The Duce had a presentiment of disaster and talked at length of the sacrifices in men and material which had been made in Libya.[7] The 'omission' of Tunis at the time of the Franco-Italian armistice might now cost the Italians their North African territories. As Mussolini told Rintelen: 'We must settle the French question. Otherwise the further conduct of the war will be difficult. I shall speak to the Fuehrer at the end of November.'[8]

The Germans were also considering the reports of the moves of the Allied armada. Jodl had already telephoned to Rintelen to instruct him to emphasize to Mussolini that Hitler was personally convinced that the Allied intention was to land in Rommel's rear at Tripoli or Benghazi.[9] This was confirmed in a telephone conversation between Goering and Kesselring, which had been intercepted on the same day, November 6, by the Italian Intelligence:

Goering: In my view, they will attempt a landing in Corsica or Sardinia, at Derna or Tripoli.

Kesselring: It is more likely to be in a North African port.

Goering: Yes, but not in a French one.[10]

Hasty orders were issued to concentrate all air and naval forces in an attack on the convoy. But the main German U-boat packs were operating in the Atlantic in anticipation of an Allied operation against West Africa, and, thanks to this strategic error, the 'Torch' convoys passed unscathed in their appointed direction.

In the small hours of November 8, reports from the Italian Intelligence in Algiers confirmed landings throughout French North Africa. At 5.30 a.m., Ribbentrop woke Ciano from his sleep to tell him the first news on the telephone. In the next crucial hours it was vital to the Italians and to the Germans to form an accurate assessment of French reactions to the Allied landings, and to reach with speed an agreed line of action in regard to France.

During the course of the morning of November 8, the Duce formed his own preliminary view of the situation, and at noon summoned Rintelen who sent at once the following personal message from Mussolini to Hitler.

'If the French government is seriously prepared to fight with us together against the English and Americans, I am ready to agree. It seems to me requisite that France should not only break off diplomatic relations with America, but also declare war both on England and the United States, as would be obvious in the case of an attack on her own territory. In order to defend aggression against the North African theatre, agreement to a landing of ground troops in Tunisia is absolutely necessary. If these conditions are not met, and there is no question of a common struggle as an ally, I think it is essential to occupy immediately the rest of France and Corsica. At all costs Corsica must not fall into enemy hands, for a threat from Corsica would be fatal to Italy. Of these two possibilities, I prefer collaboration with the French.'[11]

The immediate balance of power in the Mediterranean lay, as in 1940, with the French battle fleet. The first reports led Cavallero to note in his diary on November 8: 'The French fleet is ready to put out from Toulon in an hour. I do not dare to hope, but if this collaboration comes off, we have won the war. I am a convinced partisan of collaboration with the French, although I have no friendly feelings towards them . . . But today we must seek for this collaboration by every means.'[12]

* * *

During the day, Hitler confirmed his agreement with the Duce's appreciation of the French attitude, and Rintelen had a further meeting with the latter that evening. 'The Duce summoned me again on November 8 at 7 p.m., together with Marshal Cavallero. After I had reported that the Fuehrer agreed with the Duce's analysis (as outlined in the above message), the latter made the following points: "In this morning's talk I omitted to draw attention to one point, namely, supposing that the Vichy government accepts an agreement with the Axis powers and then the population rebels against the government? In this case, too, nothing remains but to occupy the rest of France and Corsica.

'"If the French government raises the question of what to expect after the war, my view is that we should not discuss it. Territorial issues do not play the same role as at the beginning of the war, we are now fighting for our existence. It is a matter of winning and postponing all territorial questions until later. When we have won, there will be sufficient points of compensation for the French. Whatever decisions are made, I am determined to defend Libya to the last man."'

That night, Ribbentrop again telephoned to Ciano to say that it was essential that either the Duce or Ciano should come at once to Munich for talks with Hitler, and that Laval would also be summoned. 'It is time to consider our line of conduct towards France,' wrote Ciano in his diary on November 9. He does not seem to have been present at the various meetings held by Mussolini the previous day, and there is no evidence to show that he was directly aware of the Duce's views as expressed to Rintelen and Cavallero. Ciano now told the Duce of his conversation with Ribbentrop. 'I wake the Duce. He is not very anxious to leave, especially since he is not yet feeling at all well. I shall go, and on the instructions: if France is ready to collaborate loyally, she will receive all possible aid from us; if, on the other hand, she plays hot and cold, we are going to adopt preventive measures: the occupation of the Free Zone and a landing in Corsica.'[13]

The picture of events, as seen in Munich and Rome, and in French metropolitan and African territory, was changing hourly. There was no further news of the French fleet, except that the French Admiralty, on November 9, had asked the Italian Armistice delegation for collaboration with the Axis forces in Sardinia, and a French Naval Mission had arrived in Rome for talks. It was not clear how far Pétain and

Laval were in active agreement with such a move, or whether the French naval authorities were seeking their own revenge for the sinkings by the British at Oran in 1940. The Germans had already made certain preliminary demands at Vichy. Even before the landings in North Africa they had asked for permission to send German aircraft across the Unoccupied Zone for reconnaissance in the Western Mediterranean. At 3 a.m. on November 8, they offered the support of the Axis air force based on Sicily and Sardinia. The French Cabinet met at 11 a.m. that morning. Laval was opposed to military collaboration with the Germans, but careful not to give a categorical refusal.

At 2 p.m. the German request for bases in Tunisia, so long delayed, was handed in by the Control Commission at Wiesbaden. An hour later a message from Hitler to the French government asked whether they were prepared to fight on Germany's side against the Anglo-Saxons. Otto Abetz, the German representative at Vichy, specified that all that was required was military collaboration in Africa. Early that evening, Laval received the invitation to meet Hitler and Ciano at Munich. Just before midnight the German General Staff insisted on immediate agreement for the use of the Tunisian airfields and requested a reply within an hour. Consent was by now a grudging formality.

On the morning of November 9, Ciano arrived at the station at Munich to find Ribbentrop awaiting him 'tired out, thin and courteous. Laval, who is making a long journey by car, will arrive during the night.'[14] Ciano's first conversation with Hitler took place that evening.[15] The latter immediately launched into a ranging monologue, minimizing the present dangers, and sketching an apologia for his past attitude towards France. 'Generally from the point of view of the military expert, the American landing in North Africa was not so dangerous as that of the English in Norway (in 1940) . . . At that time the landing took place in an area where both the military and the civil population were firmly on the English side. The present situation in North Africa was different: the country was half-heartedly co-operating with the Americans and nevertheless offering some resistance. If in addition the enemy were decided on a Second Front such as the present one in North Africa, the military dispositions to be adopted by Germany and Italy would be easier. It would no longer be necessary to maintain a large number of troops along a gigantic front which could be attacked at any point—no one knew where. Fifty-two armoured and infantry divisions were concentrated in France. The moment it transpired that danger no longer threatened, they could disperse all the troop concentrations there.'

The situation had been much worse in the winter of 1940–1. The threat to Germany from the East was only a few hundred miles from the frontier of the Reich. No one then knew from what quarter the attack from the East would come: through Roumania, the Balkans, or with the help of Yugoslavia. At the same time the British were in Crete and in Greece and had almost reached the Syrte in North Africa. Hitler stressed that he had not changed his attitude towards France. 'The French loved neither Germany nor Italy. Some admitted this with brutal openness, others were rather more reserved, and a third category sought slyly to hide it.'

In regard to French affairs, he had always tried to get the best out of each situation. 'Whether, in the present situation, much or little was to be obtained from the French it was not yet possible to judge.' In agreement with the Italian General Staff, Germany had demanded from the French the evacuation of their air bases in Tunis, and had sent in two wings of Stukas. It was unlikely that a direct attack from the sea by the Allies would follow in view of the proximity of the Axis air bases in Sicily. The Americans would attempt to advance on Tunis from the land side. It was therefore important that the Axis should be installed in Tunis beforehand.

If the Allied landing was in effect a Second Front, the military situation of the Axis in Africa would be held and improved. 'This would be especially true if the French really defended themselves against the Americans. In Western Morocco and Southern Algeria this seemed to be the case, whereas in the city of Algiers itself there was treachery, and Darlan and Juin appeared to have been arrested. Here it was certainly a case of a plot. Even Marshal Pétain was to have been lured to Africa, and would in fact have been there if the Germans had not declared his journey inopportune.'

The decisive point was that the advance of German infantry and armoured divisions up to the French demarcation line would have been completed by midnight, so that, if the French should collapse, these troops could march in at dawn the following morning. Hitler had asked the Duce also to make arrangements to move into Southern France, and to occupy Corsica whose importance for the air protection of Italy was immense. If this were not done with lightning speed and the Americans were to establish themselves there, this would be a catastrophe for Italy. 'One could not predict what would come out of the conversations with Laval. Whether he would bring an offer of alliance, or request deliveries of weapons or demand further release of war prisoners, one could not foresee. Hitler thought it right that an Italian representative should be present at these talks, since quick decisions would probably have to be taken to which the Italian Foreign Minister, in case of doubt, could seek the Duce's agreement by telephone.'

Ciano then summarized Mussolini's first reactions to the Allied landings in Africa. 'If the French asked for help, and fought with a minimum of loyalty, the Duce would be ready to accord them such assistance.' If they were 'ambiguous', rapid decisions must be made. Above all, Corsica must be occupied at once.

As Ciano explained, 'either co-operation or occupation—that was the Duce's standpoint—and he was now waiting to know what measures the Fuehrer intended to take. The Duce would also be ready at any time of the day or night to telephone the Fuehrer if the latter wished to speak to him direct.' Ribbentrop then referred to rumours that Weygand was to take over control in French Africa. Hitler was strongly distrustful of the latter, and added, 'Laval must take a clear stand tomorrow. The French knew anyway that Germany was decided to go to the limit. They could certainly not be unaware of the troop movements. In the course of the last six weeks alone a further eighteen divisions had been sent to France.' Ciano noted in his diary: 'Hitler has not built up any illusions about the French desire to fight. . . . He will listen to Laval. But whatever he says will not modify his already definite point of view: the total occupation of France, a landing in Corsica, a bridgehead in Tunisia. Hitler is neither nervous nor restless, but he does not underrate American initiative, and he wants to meet it with all the resources at his disposal. Goering does not hesitate to declare that the occupation of North Africa represents the first point scored by the Allies since the beginning of the war.'[16]

Laval was travelling by car from Vichy to Munich because of the hurry, but had been stopped on the way by fog, and could not reach the Bavarian capital until about four in the morning. Joint conversations with him were postponed therefore until about noon on the following day. Ciano met Hitler again briefly the next morning. News had come in that, during the night of November 9/10, both German and Italian air units had arrived in Tunisia. The French reception of the Italians had been 'cool, almost hostile'. The Germans had also been very coldly received. On the basis of the latest reports of the fighting in North Africa, Ciano pressed hard for the occupation of Corsica by the Italians, and the Fuehrer warmly concurred. It was decided to telephone to the Duce the Fuehrer's agreement.[17]

While Ciano was telephoning to Rome, and Laval, who in the meantime had arrived at the Fuehrerbau, the official building used by Hitler on public occasions when in Munich, was on the line to Vichy on the latest developments in North Africa, Hitler was briefed on the partly contradictory reports on the attitude of the French in Africa, particularly events in Algiers and the arrest of Darlan and Juin. Abruptly the meeting with Laval was postponed until the afternoon. There had been a sudden and dramatic change in the position in North Africa. Darlan had opened negotiations with the Americans. Early in the afternoon Pétain had disavowed him over the radio, and assumed command of the French armed forces.

This news reached Laval only in Munich. He had already had a brief preliminary talk with Ribbentrop and rejected the formal offer of an alliance. Early in the afternoon Abetz, the German political representative with the Vichy government, who had come with Laval, showed him the German monitoring of Darlan's cease-fire order, and the Frenchman telephoned to Rochat, the head of the Vichy Foreign Ministry. The Germans were recording the conversation. 'I shall be received presently by Hitler: therefore do nothing for the moment. Everything will be broken off and I shall resign, if you negotiate with the Americans without my having got back and been able to talk to you. I want to know what is the Marshal's decision.' A second telephone call from Vichy informed Laval that Pétain had given formal orders to defend Africa.[18] Such was the latest position when Laval, who had been already waiting over two hours in the Fuehrerbau, was shown into the main salon. It was in this room that Daladier and Chamberlain had been received by Hitler in September 1938. Ciano observed the entry. 'Laval, with his white tie and middle class French peasant attire, is very much out of place in the great salon among so many uniforms. He tries to speak in a familiar tone about his journey, and his long sleep in the car, but his words are unheeded. Hitler treats him with frigid courtesy.'[19]

Hitler began curtly. 'A situation had arisen that he had always feared . . . There were two courses open to France: either to lean definitely and clearly on the Axis or to lose her entire colonial empire. At Montoire he had explained to Marshal Pétain that someone had to pay for this war, France or Britain, anyway not Germany, who had not wanted the war, had not begun it, and deeply regretted its outbreak.' Hitler nevertheless still wanted to work with France, and to help to maintain the French colonial empire. 'It was clear that France alone could not effectively oppose the Americans and British in North Africa, but would need strong Axis support. Fundamentally it was desirable that the whole European stake in Africa should be guaranteed and defended in common. The question therefore arose as to whether France was prepared to accept such support. The Fuehrer asked Laval to tell him how he judged the situation in Africa and whether France were ready to accept Axis aid.'

Laval began his exposition. His presence at the head of the French government since the previous April meant in itself a policy of understanding and reconciliation between Germany and France. But this could not be promoted by routine political contact, and he had repeatedly sought a personal meeting. He thanked Hitler for agreeing to such a talk, 'and only regretted that, owing to its late realization, it was being held under the shadow of unfavourable events'. It was not only in the interest of France but also of the whole of Europe if France were allowed to arm herself more effectively for her defence. The situation in Africa was serious. According to report, Darlan had ordered the cessation of hostilities. Under these circumstances it was as well that no conversations had taken place in Munich that morning, so that Laval could press Vichy the whole time on the telephone, and finally induce Marshal Pétain himself to take over command of the three armed forces, to disavow Darlan's order, and to strengthen anew his own (Pétain's) instructions whereby resistance should be offered to the Allies. It was not yet clear what had happened with Darlan . . . It was unlikely that, being a prisoner, he had any further freedom of decision. Nevertheless Laval was surprised that Darlan should have given the order to cease hostilities. Since his arrest Darlan had so far sent only one telegram in which he intimated that he would negotiate through the Americans for the handing over of the administration in Algiers. A reply was sent that he should undertake nothing. This cable crossed with a further telegram from Darlan saying that he had already ordered all units to cease fighting. Whereupon, persuaded by Laval on the telephone, the Marshal himself, after a talk with the War, Navy and Air Ministers, had taken over command of the Armed Forces, and in this way had firm control of the three services together. Laval stressed the need 'for very great and urgent counter-measures' against the danger in North Africa. Hitler interposed at once a demand that 'the harbours of Tunis and Bizerta must be placed at the disposal of the Axis as a prerequisite to building up a counter-offensive.' Had this happened earlier, there would never have been a landing in West Morocco.

Laval then spoke of the meeting at Montoire, 'which represented a generous gesture of the victor to the vanquished, which was certainly unique in history. He must say quite sincerely that France would not have so behaved if she had beaten Germany.' Hitler went on: 'The fate of France lay in her own hands . . . If she pursued the wavering path which she had so far followed, she would lose all her colonial territory.'

There could be no doubt that Germany would vanquish England. It was true that Germany had to make 'an excursion to the East', but this was also in France's interest. Because of this, the reckoning with England was at the most postponed. The East would certainly be liquidated. This would have happened earlier if France had shown herself to be more understanding. And then Germany would have devoted her attention to England.

Laval then turned to the question of political collaboration in Europe. 'Whereas earlier wars had been waged from village to village, and later from country to country, now a whole continent ought to be organized for peace. This would of course not be possible if each country insisted on putting forward claims to satisfy its natural greed. Such a way meant rejecting the possibility of organizing Europe on a solid enduring foundation.' He 'spoke of these things with great passion as a man whose heart lay not only in his own country but also in Europe. As such he did not want certain egoisms (*sic*) to hinder the erection of the structure for which the peoples of Europe longed.' He had taken a great personal risk in coming out publicly in favour of a German victory, and had done so because he wanted to save his country from Communism. But in order to further his intention he needed the help of the victors 'in creating a suitable atmosphere'.

At this first conference since Montoire between the victors and vanquished some political concessions must be made to the French if Laval was to be able to maintain his own line of support for collaboration in general terms with Germany and Italy. 'He felt it his duty to try to obtain more favourable conditions of support from Germany, which would also be in the interests of Europe.'

Hitler's attitude was categorical. 'If Germany lost the war, Bolshevism would overrun Europe: no Atlantic Charter could be erected against the wild eastern storm of the Soviet savages. There had been a time when France too had seen the situation in this light. There was much talk then in French circles representing the view that France should devote herself to her colonial empire and that Germany should be given a free hand in the East. Among others, Monsieur Flandin, who hitherto had been an opponent of Germany, shared this view. In recognizing the extent of the threatening danger from the East, every nationally-minded Frenchman must wish fanatically for the victory of Germany . . .' Laval retorted: 'Nevertheless it was not entirely easy to convince the French of this obvious truth. The country had existed a very long time in happy peaceful conditions and had been poisoned by the doctrines of the Popular Front.'

The Frenchman's persuasive advocacy reached its peroration. The Fuehrer must help 'in creating the moral conditions in France in favour of collaboration with Germany. The present state of German-French relations was pictured by many Frenchmen as a one way street.' Laval asked for a gesture by Germany to lighten his task, and for more frequent personal contacts. Hitler's only answer was that 'he hoped that it would be realized in France that the Anglo-Saxons were aiming at world supremacy.'

Laval now took his leave and expressed again, 'with obvious emotion, the wish to do all in his power to collaborate and also the hope that in future Germany and France would between them find a relationship of friendly co-operation'.[20] He had never in his career played so hard for time, nor from such a position of weakness. His dialogue with Hitler, brilliant in form, neither altered nor modified a single decision, in particular the total occupation of France. As Ciano wrote, 'Not a word was said to Laval about the impending action.

The orders to occupy France were being given while he was smoking his cigarette and conversing with various people in the next room. Ribbentrop told me that Laval would only be informed next morning at eight o'clock that, because of information received during the night Hitler had been obliged to proceed to the total occupation of the whole country.'[21] That evening Ciano returned to Rome.

The Allied landing in North Africa had forced on the Axis powers, in unplanned and barely co-ordinated haste, the decisions originally taken at the conference in Munich in June 1940. As in the past, the Germans acted first and on their own. Marshal von Rundstedt, commanding the German armies in occupied France, transmitted a letter to Marshal Pétain on the morning of November 11—there was a fortuitous irony in the date—announcing the crossing of the demarcation line by his forces. On the same day, German armoured units were landed at Tunis and Bizerta. German and Italian air units were already in occupation of the Tunisian airfields.

The Italian war machine was less highly geared to such lightning action. The decision to occupy Corsica was made on November 10, and orders given to move that night. The expedition was delayed by rain and heavy seas, and ultimately put to sea, in part literally in sailing cutters, the following afternoon. The Italian Fourth Army on the French frontier was 'a little behindhand',[22] and eventually began to move the same evening. An Italian convoy was due to arrive in Tunisian ports on November 12. As Cavallero noted in his diary: 'The Duce says if we do not gain time, the game is lost. It is not enough to occupy France, we must not lose Libya.'[23] But Rommel was withdrawing so fast that Cavallero, on a lightning trip to Africa, was unable to locate his headquarters three days later. 'Now Mussolini thinks,' wrote Ciano in his diary on his return from Munich, 'that we shall have God to thank if we can succeed in stopping at the old Agedabia line. I see a few people, and gather the impression that the events of the last few days have been a sad blow for the country which, for the first time, is asking many questions without finding answers.'[24]

CHAPTER FIVE

The Axis and North Africa

THE MENACING presence of the Anglo-American forces in North-West Africa created a military revolution in the Mediterranean, shattered the structure of German relations with France as defined at Montoire, and drove both Axis powers to occupy positions and undertake commitments regardless of the political consequences at Vichy. Having resisted Italian claims on Nice, Corsica, and Tunis in 1940, Hitler was now obliged from military necessity to press for their fulfilment by the French. Even so, there was a note of meanness.

Following the Munich Conference on November 9/11, 1942, Ribbentrop asked the German Ambassador in Rome to summarize the present Italian attitude to eventual claims against France, insinuating that perhaps Germany had no ultimate obligations in this respect towards her ally. Mackensen minuted the conversation: 'There was no evidence to show that the Duce had in any way changed in regard to Italian claims on Djibouti, Tunis, Corsica and Nice, but there were certain signs that, at least seen from outside at a given moment they would be upheld in their entirety . . . In addition I wanted to point out that the Fuehrer had repeatedly and also in his letters to the Duce, plainly stated that he would support Italian claims against France as presented by the Duce. As I saw it, there could be no question of giving the Italians to understand even by a hint that on our side there was any desire for a reduction of these claims. With these four demands the Duce had brought his people into the war and had firmly relied on the Fuehrer's word. The whole Italian population had still lively memories of the gulf between the promises of the Allies in May 1915 and that which was in reality conceded to them in November 1918, so that their trust in their present Ally would be shattered even by a hint. The German Foreign Minister agreed with my presentation completely and answered that for him it was beyond any discussion and that we had to abide unswervingly by the Fuehrer's assurances.'[1]

The immediate issues, vital to the future conduct of the war in the Mediterranean, were the exploitation in time of the Tunis bridgehead and the fate of the French fleet. Rintelen reported an optimistic conversation with Mussolini: 'The Duce summoned me at 8.30 p.m. on November 13 and instructed me to convey the following to the Fuehrer:—"Now that five days have passed since the American landing in North Africa, I do not view unfavourably the development of the situation in the interval. It is particularly good that we have taken possession of Tunis and Bizerta. The occupation of Tunis is of decisive importance for the further conduct of hostilities in the Mediterranean and therefore our first and most urgent task is to build up the Tunis bridgehead . . . I regard it as an excellent measure to have obtained the word of honour of the French fleet at Toulon." '[2]

On the immediate credit side, also, the French merchant fleet was to be handed over to the Axis. This acquisition might prove decisive in the battle of the African convoys. It was agreed at once that the bulk of the ships would be transferred to the Italians. But since the events of November 8/9, the attitude of the French Navy to the course of the war in the Mediterranean had been menacingly obscure. The Axis powers were now faced with a situation not unlike that of the British at the time of the 1940 armistice, and the grim solution was similar.

On the evening of November 26 Kesselring delivered to the Duce an urgent letter from Hitler. It was an announcement, without previous consultation, of the entry of German troops into Toulon. 'The information from the Italian Consul in Toulon about the incidents in the French fleet, which was passed on to me on your instructions, confirms numerous reports from other sources and, together with the treachery of North Africa, gives now incontestable proof of the disloyal attitude of all the French Armed Forces, including the Fleet. After the appeal which Darlan broadcast over the wireless, we must particularly expect political sedition in the Toulon fleet. Not only will the latter not oppose an enemy attack, but from now on there is great danger that it will suddenly leave port and join the enemy. The same can be said for the

French Army and Air Force. As an uncertain factor they constitute a threat to our rear for which I think I can no longer be responsible. I have therefore decided to disarm the French Army and Air Force as far as is necessary, and to occupy Toulon suddenly so as to make sure of the French fleet. German submarines are already off the French naval base with instructions to attack immediately every French warship which may attempt to escape.

'Duce, Marshal Kesselring will give you the details of my orders. Likewise I have asked General Field Marshal von Rundstedt to inform the Italian Fourth Army promptly and seek its support. And now, Duce, I would like to ask you, in support of these—in my opinion—absolutely necessary measures, to issue general orders to your Armed Forces authorizing them to co-operate with Field Marshal von Rundstedt. Since the success of this plan, which may well be of decisive importance for the war, depends on complete secrecy, I would ask you, Duce, to inform as few people as possible and above all not to give telephoned or more precise orders, but, as I have done with my Armed Forces, only to direct your Army to collaborate.' Instructions had also been given to distribute the French merchant fleet, 'so as to take into account in the fullest possible way the heavy Italian losses'. The Germans only needed relatively few ships for North African, Cretan and Black Sea convoys. 'As for the French Navy, I fear that it will not come to us intact, but if this does happen, Italy is the only lawful possessor.' The Germans required only temporarily light escort vessels for convoys which would be returned after the war. 'I hope, Duce, that the motives which I have given for my action seem reasonable to you.'[3]

The Axis was confronted in the following hours with the total sabotage by the French of their Mediterranean fleet in Toulon, and the dragging commitment of a military occupation of Southern France, thus tying down divisions needed in Russia and North Africa. Such was the final result of Montoire. The concept of a strong collaborationist French Government neutralizing the Western Mediterranean had disappeared. The German army in the West was now forced to garrison the Unoccupied Zone of France with inevitable adverse political repercussions at Vichy. The stationing of the Italian Fourth Army on the Southern coast of France came at a moment when the battle of North Africa was reaching a decisive stage, and such an extension of Italian military commitments represented a dangerous stretching of her resources.

* * *

The Allied invasion of French North Africa also brought into sharp relief the issue of Spain's continued neutrality in the war, and forced equally on both belligerent parties a reappraisal of their own policies towards the Spanish government. The Allies, at the moment of the 'Torch' landings, had given formal assurances to respect Spanish territory, both European and African. On the other hand, the Axis might well have an interest in reviving the strategy of Hendaye, when in October 1940, at the meeting between Hitler and Franco, the former had pressed for Spanish co-operation in a German advance across Spain against Gibraltar. The Spanish demands had been excessive, and the guarantees of military co-operation unsatisfactory. Mussolini's attempt to appeal to Franco's sense of obligation for the decisive support given by Italy during the Civil War in Spain met with little success when the two men met at Bordighera early in 1941, and this failure on the part of the Axis to inveigle Spain into the war deprived them of any means to liquidate the British base at Gibraltar, or establish themselves in Spanish Morocco, and thus control the Western entry into the Mediterranean. As the Italian minutes of the meeting in April 1942 with Hitler at Salzburg read: 'Regret for not having carried out the operation of Gibraltar for which everything was ready, including a mountain in the Jura which looked like Gibraltar, and round which innumerable exercises had been carried out.'[4] Just as Hitler had met the nemesis of his French policy in the fracas of the North African landings, so Ciano was driven to face, under the same impact, the bankruptcy of the whole assumption underlying that Italian intervention in the Spanish Civil War, of which he had been the instigator.

The reactions of Franco to the new revolution in the balance of forces in the Mediterranean were carefully and ably reviewed by the German Ambassador in Madrid, in a telegram to Berlin on November 16. His initial assumption was that Stohrer, in spite of Party and Army talk in Spain about burning boats and intervening on the Axis side, Franco and his government were determined to avoid war. 'Spanish fears of being drawn unwillingly into the war are not only based on the threatening new power position of the Anglo-Saxons, but also in the recognition that Germany could have an interest in threatening the enemy flank in North Africa and in blocking the Straits of Gibraltar by an advance through Spain . . . Did we intend to attack through Spain?'

The Spaniards saw in a further success of Allied plans a grave threat to Italy, whose powers of resistance 'one does not estimate very highly here since the experience in the Spanish Civil War. The Government and public opinion reject entry into the war either on the side of the Anglo-Saxons or the Axis. Spain would attempt to resist attack on the Spanish motherland. She would fight the Anglo-Americans with weapons in her hand. In the event of a German invasion, orders for military resistance would be given, but it is not likely to come to this. In any case we must reckon with an active opposition from Red elements, which would receive supplies from the enemy. A German invasion would mean total war for Spain . . . An early breakdown of the food situation would be inevitable; in view of the strong Red elements present in Spain one must reckon with severe sabotage. Spain has made no preparations for a war . . . There is also no spiritual mobilization.

The main need was military aid, both to strengthen Spain, and to discourage the Allies from regarding her as 'a glacis for their offensive against Europe'. If things developed better for the Allies in Africa, an increase in armaments to Spain would help her to resist pressure. This was the best means to prevent her sliding on to the other side. In any case, conversations should be held. 'We must not today allow the Spaniards to give themselves up.'[5]

Four days later, the German Ambassador had an interview with Franco. As Stohrer reported, 'Towards the end of the conversation of November 20, Franco asked me quite abruptly how we viewed the attitude of Italy. It seemed to him that Italy's powers of resistance were not very great . . . I answered of course reassuringly that we were firmly convinced that Italy possessed every requisite power of resistance, and that there was no demoralization, nor was it to be expected. But as there is no doubt that, by asking this question, Franco wanted to give a hint, and as naturally an unfavourable appreciation of Italy's will to resist must influence Franco's judgment of the whole situation, I thought that I should report the above.'

The German government, although dubious of the advantages of Spanish belligerency, demanded a guarantee from Franco that, if he was supplied with war material, he would at least fight if attacked by the Allies. Hitler was not prepared to be rushed. At a meeting on December 3, he decided after a lengthy exposition that 'it would be best for our conduct of the war if Spain remains neutral. An invasion of Spain under present conditions, both military and economic, would place exceptional demands on us.' Hitler would equip Spain with modern weapons only if she would fight with them. 'If she only wants to preserve her neutrality, let her seek equipment in America. We do not intend to attack Spain, hence we are indifferent as to where Spain obtains weapons to preserve her neutrality.'[6]

Mussolini had already reached the same conclusion independently, but as always tentatively. 'Spain will move increasingly in the direction of complete neutrality. Nothing much has been lost, as the entry of Spain into the war would require a very strong support in weapons and other things.'[7] And again on December 9 he told Ciano that 'he does not intend to move a finger to accelerate Spain's intervention in the war, because it could be more of a hindrance than a help'.[8]

The Allied landings in North Africa had created a new war front on the Tunisian border. The other lay, separate and unco-ordinated, along a rapidly disintegrating line in Libya as a consequence of the British victory at Alamein. If the shrinking Axis bridgehead in Africa were to be held—and the politico-military consequences of its loss would be incalculable—major strategic decisions at the highest level must be taken. A conference between Hitler and Mussolini on Africa might have led to a revision of Axis strategy, but the former was nailed in isolation in East Prussia with his maps of the Eastern Front, and the Duce confined by ulcers in Rome.

Rommel was by now sceptical of any stand being made, even in Tunisia. He had no hope of parrying a British outflanking drive. Only one-third of his fighting power was left and all reserve stocks and supply dumps had been lost. On November 11, having failed to persuade Cavallero or Kesselring to come to Africa, he had sent one of his officers to the Fuehrer's headquarters in the hopes of getting a precise directive. The officer 'met with little understanding. The Fuehrer had instructed him to inform me that I should leave Tunis out of my calculations and simply act on the assumption that the bridgehead would be held.'[9] In writing to Mussolini on November 20, in answer to requests for aircraft and artillery to defend Tripolitania on the Agheila line, Hitler assured him that guns would be sent 'as and when each gun is produced' and 'everything possible' would be done to strengthen the air force. But the immediate German interest was concentrated in Tunis. 'The aim of operations in Tunisia should in my opinion be that of advancing towards the west in order to break up the North African-Mediterranean positions of the Franco-Anglo-American troops.'[10] This was small comfort to Rommel. He had received orders from the Duce to hold on at all costs. His own conviction was that the only purpose of a delayed withdrawal would be to evacuate the remnants of an élite corps for action in Europe. 'In the long run neither Libya nor Tunisia could be held, for the African war was being decided by the battle of the Atlantic.'[11]

An Italo-German staff conference on November 24 revealed that the Afrika Korps now consisted of only one weak German division. It also showed a profound divergence of view between Rommel and Kesselring, the latter being obsessed with the consequences of Allied air bases being set up in Tunisia, and the creation of an air triangle Malta-Algiers-Tripoli which would control communications in the Central Mediterranean. In final exasperation, Rommel decided abruptly to fly in person to Hitler's headquarters to ask for a strategic decision and request as a long-term policy the evacuation of North Africa. The Fuehrer received him on the evening of November 28 in a thunderous mood. Rommel was barely able to state his case, and was lectured on the political necessity of holding a major bridgehead in Africa. Hitler was at last and belatedly convinced that the continued participation of Italy in the war depended on such action. The effect of Rommel's visit was at least to force the Fuehrer to make some decision. As a personal meeting with Mussolini was for the moment impracticable, Goering was sent to Rome, together with Rommel, and full powers to negotiate with the Italians.[12] As Ciano put it, 'Goering comes to Rome without advance notice. From what was said by members of the General Staff, the visit was prompted by the fact that Rommel left Libya secretly to see the Fuehrer. We protested, and the assistant German Military Attaché has been told that if an Italian General had behaved in this way he would have been brought before a court martial. Now Goering comes to settle the trouble, but this discord is not a matter of form . . . We shall see what decisions emerge from the conference that is to be held today at Palazzo Venezia.'[13]

It was a grumpy journey in Goering's special train. Rommel suspected Goering of wishing to supplant him, and of creating a private army and air force under his own command in Africa. The two men quarrelled all the way to Rome, which they reached on November 30, preceded by a telegram from Hitler to Mussolini complaining blandly of Italian delays in supplying Rommel's forces.[14] On arrival Goering, Kesselring and Rommel first attended a meeting at the Italian Supreme Command Headquarters to review the military position, particularly in regard to supplies for the African front.

Goering's speech on this occasion was a blustering lecture. 'We no longer have in Africa one battlefield divided into two separate sectors, but one united zone. The enemy is, as is known, superior there in numbers, material, and principally in tonnage. Our submarines will from now on act with particular energy against these new enemy supply routes. For us the central problem is that of supplies. For the first time we are not far away from our battlefield—a mere "panther's leap". Hence we can ship rapidly men and material to Tunisia . . . Both for Tunisia and for Rommel one thing is certain and that is: if the supplies continue to be sent at the present rhythm we cannot hold either Tunisia or Tripolitania. Air transport is out of the question . . . The normal route is thus by sea. There is the question of mines, and in a meeting held by the Fuehrer there was a long discussion about these mines. We have the example of the British, which is the most eloquent of all. The English minefield which runs from Scapa Flow to the Thames has made it impossible for German U-boats to approach the English coast . . . We must without fail produce a similar one between Sicily and Tunis. This is the view of the Fuehrer and he will make available the necessary material.[15]

At a further conference with the Duce, Goering emphasized that the Germans were sending three armoured divisions to Africa, the Adolf Hitler, the Hermann Goering, and the Deutschland, 'three names which mean much to German honour'. This news seems to have heartened Mussolini, whom Ciano found 'optimistic both as regards the war and the internal situation',* and it was in this mood that the Duce supported Rommel when the latter was openly attacked by Goering at the meeting for leaving the Italians in the lurch at Alamein. 'Before I could make a worthy reply to this mon-

* Ciano, *op cit* December 1, 1942, p. 530. It is noticeable that Ciano was not present at the meeting. There is no record available of the talk, though Ciano mentions 'the Duce sent me a report of his conversation with Goering'.

strous statement,' Rommel recorded, 'Mussolini said, "That's news to me; your retreat was a masterpiece, Marshal Rommel."'[16]

Ciano had watched Goering's visit to Italy with distant asperity. D'Ajeta, the head of Ciano's private office, reported to him a private talk with the German Minister in Rome, Prince Bismarck, who was quoted as saying: 'The Germans themselves are convinced that there is nothing more to be done in Africa, and that all Goering's promises are destined to remain in the kingdom of the clouds. But it is a matter of saving Rommel's reputation . . . Goering's principal task therefore is to create confusion and prove that the fault lies with our defective organization of shipping . . .' Bismarck added that the military experts of the German Embassy were amazed at the number of stupidities which the Reichsmarshal could accumulate. 'Can it be that Goering is really thinking of appointing himself the Reichsprotektor of Italy?'[17] It is not inconceivable that Goering may have considered such a project in the event of a sudden disappearance of the Duce from the scene, through illness or a political coup. The defence of the Italian mainland would then become a German responsibility and form the outer bastions covering the fortress of Europe and possibly more effectively organized by direct military government, backed by the divisions now being sent to Italy which, together with the Air Force, were closely connected with Goering. A similar thought had occurred to Rommel on the train journey to Rome. 'Goering also possessed inordinate ambition and had no scruples about the means he used to advance it. Thus he thought that there were easy laurels to be earned on the African Front, and was angling to manoeuvre the Air Force into control of it. Units of his Praetorian Guard, the Armoured division "Hermann Goering", were already on their way to Tunis.'[18]

In any event, Goering now appeared as the leading exponent, on the German side, of bolstering up the Mediterranean theatre. He presided over meetings of Italian civilians and technical experts, creating confusion, obstruction and resentment.[19] Rommel noted: 'Particularly interesting was Goering's political attitude towards the Italians in relation to the difficult situation in Africa. Although we had always been forbidden to say a word to the Italians about the shortcomings of their Army and State, or to demand improvements, Goering now began to talk to Cavallero about really fundamental questions, such as the poor Italian armament, their sea strategy and similar thorny subjects. The only result, of course, was that he put their backs up without having any hope of getting anything put right . . . Many Italians felt very deeply that the Axis was a sham, and consequently believed that in final victory we would have scant regard for their interests. It was generally felt that, if Tripolitania were lost, Mussolini would be threatened by a political crisis in Italy. His position may well have been further weakened by Goering's sudden heavy-handed behaviour. A great many Italians had had enough of the war, and were considering how best they could get out of it.'[20]

CHAPTER SIX

'The Beresina Wind'

'The Fuehrer wanted to bring the battle for Stalingrad to a conclusion. This would probably happen in the next eight days, as already eight-tenths of the city was in German hands . . . Then the fighting on the Volga in this region would be closed.'[1] These remarks by Goering during his talk with Mussolini in Rome on October 23 masked the real situation on the Eastern Front.

Hitler was counting to reach a final decision within the year 1942 in the Russian war, which tied down over 200 German and satellite divisions and 70 per cent of the total German armed forces. He had set himself a two-fold and simultaneous task: firstly a thrust south-eastwards to the Caucasus which would bring into German hands the granaries of the Kuban, the industrial regions of the Donetz Basin, and the oilfields of the Caucasus; secondly, having achieved this conquest, a final flanking assault on the main concentration of the Russian armies in Central Russia ending with the occupation of Moscow—an operation which had failed in the blitzkrieg of the previous winter. By the middle of August the southern advance had already been carried out according to plan, and the concentration of oilfields at Maikop was already in German hands. But the communications of their armies were now stretched to the limits, and the mountainous terrain of the southern Caucasus lay ahead of them, and beyond that the Grozny oilfields and the ultimate objective, Baku. The limit of the southern advance was reached during the first days of November.

The first stages of the second part of the German plan consisted of a major thrust conducted by forty German divisions to break through from the Southern Don to the Volga, and towards the industrial keypoint of Stalingrad lying on that river, the possession of which would cut off Central Russia from the Caucasus. From here the northern offensive along the right bank of the Volga would be pursued against the main Russian armies protecting the approaches to Moscow. The attack against Stalingrad was launched and the outskirts of the city were reached on September 3. In the early planning of the German campaign Stalingrad had not been a major target, except in the sense that the city lay on the main axis of the ultimate gigantic German flanking manoeuvre against Moscow. The fatal diversion to the Caucasus resulted in neither the Central, Northern, nor the Southern offensives being successful. The Russians were able to withdraw their forces on the central sector behind the Don, and create a Stalingrad front. During September and October the issue of the Russian war, and indeed that of one of the major fronts of the world conflict, was fought out in and around the city.

From the beginning of September the German air forces were flying up to 2,500 sorties a day over the battle area. The climax of the campaign was sudden and dramatic. During these weeks of grim fighting, the Russians had massed sufficient forces east of the Volga to launch an encircling offensive against the German armies in front of embattled Stalingrad. On November 19 the Russians attacked the German forces north of the city, and on the following day assaulted the positions to the South. Within five days, 22 German divisions were encircled and another 14 destroyed. By the end of the month the German 6th Army under General Paulus was totally surrounded, and the whole operational plan of the Germans for 1942 lay shattered. Meanwhile the Caucasus offensive had come to a standstill, and the German Commander, von Manstein, was ordered to divert forces in a combined move to liberate the Stalingrad pocket. On December 12 this abortive thrust from the south was launched, together with a similar operation due eastwards from positions on the Don. On December 16 the Russians struck southwards from their positions east of Stalingrad against Manstein's divisions, and he was driven rapidly southwards. By the second half of December another 22 German satellite divisions had been broken to pieces.

The catastrophic course of the war on the Eastern Front had coincided with the destruction of the Axis position in North Africa at El Alamein. The mirage of a rendezvous at Suez had been brutally dispersed, and the initiative lost on the two land fronts of the war.

On the evening of November 6, after the Alamein battle, Mussolini had told Rintelen, 'I would like to convey to you personally my impression that we must make a separate peace with Russia as soon as possible.'[2] Only in such a manner could the deadlock of the war be broken on the Axis side, and the only person who could raise such an issue personally with Hitler was the Duce himself. Unless such a drastic summit decision were made, there would be a total strategic disaster.

On December 4 Goering came again to Rome, and in private conversation with Mussolini, at which no interpreter was present, the latter pursued this delicate and vital theme. 'The Duce believed that, one way or another, the henceforth pointless chapter of the war against Russia should be closed. If it should prove possible to arrive at a second Brest-Litovsk* —and this one could do by giving Russia territorial compensation in Central Asia—care must be taken to set up a defensive line which will destroy all enemy initiatives and with the minimum commitment of Axis forces. Goering says this would be Hitler's ideal.'

The attitude of Goering on this occasion is unresolved. No German leader could openly express scepticism at the victorious outcome of the Russian campaign. This would amount to treason. The only hope, however meagre, of persuading Hitler even to consider a compromise peace with the Russians, must lie in the subtle pattern of relations between the Fuehrer and the Duce. Hence the intense, wary, and at times alarmed, speculation in certain German circles during the autumn and winter of 1942, and again in the spring of 1943, as to the very political existence and future of Mussolini. The historic role of the Duce might be to persuade Hitler to come to such a decision, and there are signs, even though as yet, in the present state of the evidence, faint, that Mussolini was cast in just such a political part, not only by his own entourage, but also in certain German quarters.

There is a posthumous account by Ribbentrop, which is understandably not corroborated in any formal minutes of diplomatic talks during these weeks, but coincides in time with the first indication of the Duce's own intention to ap-

* The Treaty of Brest-Litovsk was signed between the Central Powers and Russia on March 3, 1918.

proach Hitler on the subject. 'When the Anglo-American landing in North Africa took place in November 1942, I happened to be in Berlin. The very first reports showed the remarkable tonnage employed—four million was mentioned. Clearly, an operation of such vast dimensions was very serious, and we had apparently been very wrong in our estimates of enemy tonnage. Indeed, Hitler later admitted as much. Since fortunes in the African theatre had always swayed backwards and forwards, I now feared the worst concerning the Axis position in the Mediterranean.

'After contacting the Fuehrer I invited Count Ciano to come to Munich immediately for a conference; the Duce could not be spared to leave Italy. I flew to Bamberg, where I boarded the Fuehrer's special train, which arrived there from the East. I briefly reported as follows: the Anglo-American landing was serious, for it showed that our estimates of enemy tonnage, and therefore of the prospects of our U-boat war, had been radically wrong. Unless we could expel the British and Americans from Africa, which seemed very doubtful in view of our transport experiences in the Mediterranean, Africa and the Axis army there were lost, the Mediterranean would be open to the enemy, and Italy, already weak, would be confronted with the gravest difficulties. In this situation the Fuehrer needed a decisive reduction of his war commitments, and I asked for authority to make contact with Stalin through Madame Kollontay, the Soviet Ambassadress in Stockholm. I suggested that, if need be, most of the conquered territories in the East would have to be given up. To this the Fuehrer reacted most strongly. He flushed, jumped to his feet and told me with indescribable violence that all he wanted to discuss was Africa—nothing else. His manner forbade me to repeat my proposal.'[3] It does however appear that on December 14 an agent of Ribbentrop's, Edgar Clauss, first contacted Madame Kollontay.

On December 15, on the eve of the forthcoming talks with the Germans, Mussolini aired his views to Bottai on a possible settlement with Russia, which to him was now the cardinal issue of the war. Mussolini seemed 'worn out, unshaven, his face livid and shrunken. I referred to the . . . fixation of German thoughts on the Russian front, which they now call the Soviet sphinx. He reacted at once, reminding me that he had already attempted on one occasion to draw the attention of Hitler and "that dilettante Foreign Minister of his" to the "decisive" Mediterranean front. But in vain. It would have been better if we had dealt with the Russians. Having swallowed the Non-Aggression Pact, it was better to reach an alliance. And he alluded to the expediency, even today, of making peace with the Russians.'[4]

But one brutal set of facts was seldom reviewed. The basic raw materials of the Italian war economy, steel, iron, and oil must also come from German-controlled territories. Here again the vital sources of supplies lay in occupied Russia, and on the imminent possession of the Donetz Basin and the Caucasus, in spite of any wishful thinking in Rome of a separate peace with the Russians, depended the future successful maintenance of the Axis war effort. Negotiations had just taken place on December 14 in Berlin between German and Italian technicians on the failure of the Germans to maintain their steel deliveries essential to keep even a minimum level of production by the Italian war industry. The Italian representative, General Favagrossa, the Undersecretary at the Ministry of War Production, was received by Ribbentrop, and treated to a survey of the war. The weight of the German forces lay in the East: 1,000,000 men as against less than 50,000 in Africa. But there would be no early Russian collapse. It had taken two and a half years in the First World War. In regard to oil, there was an unfortunate dependence on Roumania, but the Caucasus fields were in sight. 'Next year the oil problem will be solved.'

The military crisis on the Russian front, and the revolution in the position of the Axis in the Mediterranean, now forced Hitler to call a summit meeting with his Italian ally. The two leaders had not met since the previous April at Salzburg. On December 6, the German Ambassador in Rome, Mackensen, officially extended the long-postponed invitation to the Duce to come to Germany. Laval was to be summoned for the second part of the meeting. According to Ciano, Mussolini was prepared to go 'but without enthusiasm'. He said that he would want his meals alone 'because he does not want a lot of ravenous Germans to notice that he is compelled to live on rice and milk only'.[5]

The Germans had suggested that the meeting should be held at Klessheim where the Axis leaders had last met in April 1942, but late on December 15 Mackensen called on Ciano to say Hitler 'cannot leave the High Command, nor can he postpone the meeting'. He therefore asked that, as the journey would be long for the Duce, Ciano should come, together with Cavallero, to East Prussia. The Duce agreed that Ciano should go 'and this time provided with exact instructions'. The Germans had given no precise indication as to an agenda. Mackensen had merely told Ciano that 'the conversations would be important and last a few days'. Bismarck however told D'Ajeta, the head of Ciano's private office, that Hitler had tried to avoid the meeting with the Duce, because he did not want to enter into general political discussions. 'It seems,' wrote Ciano, 'that we shall speak only of France, and that Laval will be present.'

On December 16 Ciano received his instructions for the conference, 'Mussolini is especially anxious that Hitler should know, as he had already spoken of it to Goering, that he considers it extremely advisable to come to an agreement with Russia, or at least to fix upon a defensive line which could be held by small forces. 1943 will be the year of the Anglo-Saxon effort. Mussolini considers that the Axis must have the greatest number of divisions possible to defend itself in Africa, the Balkans, and perhaps in the West.'[6]

It appears that Ciano placed 'elsewhere' a copy of his instructions, and although this document has not yet come to light, a page of notes clearly made from them, possibly on the journey to East Prussia, is among his papers. The main entries read: 'Policy—1943. Effort of the Anglo-Americans—North Africa and also West Africa. If we do not want two fronts—Brest-Litovsk is necessary, if possible; if not, at least a systemization of the Eastern Front—withdrawal of strongest Axis units. War with Russia has no point. See if one can use intervention by Japan.

'1943. Italy will make military effort and in January call up 1907 and 1923 age-groups; in March, 1924; and after the harvest, 1925. 1,000,000—weapons and equipment. Without a stable air superiority which makes provisioning possible, the position in North Africa will become uncertain and in the end untenable.'[7]

While Mussolini was brooding on the consequences of the war in the East, Hitler was obsessed with the impossibility of retreat from the clash of armies at Stalingrad and was cut off from all reality save the impulse to endure all the implications of his anti-Bolshevist crusade. Living in the physical isolation of a secret headquarters on the East Prussian front, where it was dark early in the afternoon, he had retreated mentally from every other preoccupation with the war save the imperative need to avoid military disaster in the East.

Neither the Germans nor the Italians seem to have been able to face up to the problems of joint planning and command. The occupation of the Tunis bridgehead had at once created such an issue. Should there be a unified command in Africa for both the Eastern and Western fronts, Libya and Tunisia, and if so, under whom? At a military conference at Hitler's headquarters on December 1, Jodl touched on the matter and the ensuing dialogue lights up the German reaction to their Italian allies. 'May I add something on the question of leadership in Africa? Of course that is a question of organization. This is a very touchy point with the Italians: before long they will say, "of course we must have full command in this theatre of war". Up to now they have not raised the question.' Hitler retorted, 'At the moment we are handling the show, and if we do start another offensive you can be sure that there will be no Italians in it.' Jodl added that 'this was also the reason why they never spoke of the fact that we are quietly in command' in the African theatre. 'How can they?' Hitler answered. 'With seven divisions we are running the war alone anyway. They are not running it.'[8]

On December 12, at a further meeting with his military advisers Hitler, talking of the misfortunes of Rommel in North Africa, referred to 'the tragic distractions with the Italians, the eternal uncertainty. We are expecting that too; I didn't sleep last night; that's the feeling of uncertainty. If I had a German front, it would still be possible that something might happen, but I would have the feeling that it would be made up again. At least a whole army would not fall apart in a day . . . We won't succeed with the Italians anywhere. Therefore, if anybody breaks through there, there will be a catastrophe.'[9]

It was to study this 'uncertainty' that the present conference had been summoned, although the formal reason was the new situation in France. 'The Germans want to study thoroughly our will to resist.'*

The Italian delegation led by Ciano and Cavallero, and accompanied by Mackensen, left Rome by train on the evening of December 16. They were joined in Berlin by the Italian

* Simoni, *Berlino Ambasciata D'Italia*, p. 296. Simoni is the pseudonym of the Italian Minister at the time in Berlin, Baron Michele Lanza, who accompanied Alfieri to the conference.

Ambassador, Alfieri, and by Lanza, his senior Embassy official. The journey has been described by the latter.

'Thursday, December 17. Travelling since last night. Sumptuous train. Ciano, Mackensen, Cavallero; each has a special carriage. Then there is a "radio" car, full of the most ingenious contraptions, which at the critical moment never work; then a carriage for the General Staff which is so cold, dark, and abandoned that no one dare put their feet inside. The train seems to be dragging with difficulty a dead weight behind it. The food is refined, the service perfect, and there are fresh flowers at each meal. At each stop in the railway stations in Germany, radio contact is made in a few minutes with Rome. But Rome has nothing to say, and our Minister (Ciano) does not believe that he has any succulent meditations to expound. His table talk, brilliant and amusing, is disconcertingly vacuous and extremely monotonous. The Germans seem to be his favourite target and he enjoys himself by talking of them in the worst possible way. Mackensen must be used to hearing every kind of insult, for he keeps quiet with dignity at the all too open asides against his country. One never sees Cavallero. Ciano, whenever he refers to him, calls him "that bum with short legs". Bum here, bum there; imbecile Germany here, cretinous Germans there; "that delinquent Ribbentrop"; "that criminal Hitler" and so on. Slowly, to the rhythm of these phrases, the train carries us, without bumping or deviating, towards the goal.'

The following day, the train reached a siding beyond Rastenburg, where Ribbentrop and Keitel were awaiting their Italian colleagues. The formal conference was preceded by a brief private talk between Hitler and Ciano. The former expressed anxiety at the Duce's state of health on which so much depended. Ciano explained that 'the Duce, as the result of his stomach trouble, has lived for a long time almost exclusively on milk, but he is now able to take some nourishment again and it is hoped that he will be fully recovered in two or three months. The Fuehrer answered that he had followed the course of the Duce's illness with special sympathy as he himself had suffered for a time from a stomach complaint which had indeed been of nervous origin and caused by overwork.'

At noon the two men were joined by Ribbentrop, Keitel, Jodl and Cavallero. The Fuehrer opened the meeting by saying that it had not been possible to work out a formal agenda. 'He would probably be called away many times during the talks in order to make military decisions . . . It would therefore be a matter of a business discussion without formalities or a conventional frame.'

Hitler began by reviewing in detail the reasons which had led him to begin the Russian campaign; 'a struggle for the existence not only of the totalitarian régime but of our very countries'. The greatest danger which now threatened them was that of Bolshevism. If the Axis were to suffer defeat from Bolshevism, all Europe would be infected by it, because the Democracies, who had not had the strength to bring it to a halt in Russia itself in 1920, would not now be capable of hindering its westward march.

Speaking of the military position, Hitler postulated the existence of four fronts: the Eastern, the South-Eastern, the North African, and the Far Eastern.

The Eastern Front, 'which represents the protective front of Europe. Its purpose is to destroy the Bolshevik colossus and to assure ourselves living space from which Europe can draw not only the necessary foodstuffs, but also the indispensable raw materials for the prosecution of the war, such as coal, petroleum, and iron . . . Russia is now making a desperate effort to wrest from us the advantages already gained. . . . Countermeasures have already been taken, and we are sure that the situation will be controlled and corrected.'[10]

The South-Eastern Front. Hitler did not know how many Anglo-American divisions were marching on Tripoli, but they might be in a position simultaneously to bring forces to Syria and prepare to attempt a landing in the Balkans. 'It is obvious that, as long as we have bases in the Dodecanese, Rhodes, the Peloponnese, Crete, Greece, and Dalmatia, all efforts to make a landing will fail, on the condition that together with the bases we also control the rear.

'The following measures are basic in order to avoid the threat of a Balkan front: the strengthening and securing of communication between the Dodecanese, Crete, Rhodes, the Peloponnese; the building of a striking force; contacts with Hungary and Bulgaria, to work out eventual action with them; taking all measures to ensure order in the Balkan hinterland as well as supplies to our forward bases. It cannot yet be said whether the Anglo-Saxons will launch such an enterprise, but we must take steps to meet the worst eventuality.'

The North African Front. German policy towards France was based on the experiment of Montoire. 'Then began the so-called collaboration which was regarded by the Germans simply as a business proposition. Germany has gained certain advantages but it must be recognized that in reality she has paid a higher price than France, and even more so as the French have only partly carried out their obligations. Hitler has never believed in the sincerity of France and now believes therein even less. It is clear that Pétain himself has conducted a policy only based on gaining time, on thus obtaining advantages for his country, and on sowing discord between Germany and Italy. On this all Frenchmen including Laval are united, and Hitler never again wants to receive Laval alone. This mistrust of France has had the effect that Hitler has never forgotten that, while he has been placing his troops on the Atlantic coast in a defensive role against England, he has in his rear a France which is at the same time an unknown quantity and a threat. When it came to the events in North Africa, it was clear that there must be no ultimatum, in order above all to avoid the Fleet going to Algiers and taking up a position against us. In any event it is better to know that the Fleet is sunk in Toulon rather than intact in Algiers. He is by no means convinced that the Generals and Admirals betrayed Pétain. There is evidence that the Marshal himself was aware beforehand, was essentially in agreement, and had in mind a trip to Algiers himself. The German government refused permission for such a journey although he had stated that he would not go to Tunisia in order not to "annoy" the Italians.'

Hitler emphasized the importance of the whole of French territory and particularly of Corsica, Tunisia and Bizerta. 'Tunis was strategically of great importance to the Axis. It was no coincidence that the first Punic War had been fought for Tunis, and the domination of ancient Rome in the Mediterranean was only completed by the conquest of Tunis. And now the Axis was here faced with a series of decisive tasks. First in importance was the transport question. If this could not be solved, Tunis could not be held. If it could, then Germany could and would send her best divisions to Tunis and drive the British and Americans from these regions. If it proved possible to bring to Tunis supplies, oil, and men, Algeria would be lost to the Anglo-Saxons and the Axis would be soon outside Melilla, which might well bring about a change in the attitude of Spain. If the transport problem could not be solved, it would be a waste of each man and each item of equipment brought to Tunis. One could not answer for sending further troops there. If the operation succeeded, the efforts and commitments of the Anglo-Saxons would be in vain and they would have to supply their positions in the Eastern Mediterranean by the long route via the Cape, where they were again threatened by U-boats. It was clear that on both sides the problem of transport was basic. To solve the Axis problem of supplies to Africa there must in any event be a widespread sacrifice on the part of the civilian population[11] . . . The Italian Navy must be impelled beyond the bounds of the possible to assure communications with Tunis and Bizerta. The solution of this problem was of the greatest importance for the conduct of the war itself, and one must not shrink from the possibility of losing ships, for either the war was won and the ships could easily be replaced, or the war was lost and then one need have no illusions about the fate of the fleet, even if it had been carefully spared during the conflict.'[12]

In conclusion Hitler said that 'he was determined to give of his best, because he regarded the North African question as decisive for the war, and wanted to stand by Italy out of warm friendship towards the Duce. The enemy was seeking advantages each for himself, while Germany and Italy had no conflicting interests and existed in completely separate living spaces.'

At five o'clock that evening, December 18, the meeting reassembled. Ciano, speaking from his instructions, placed squarely before the conference the main proposal of Mussolini.

'The Duce took the view that the British and Americans would in 1943 carry out large-scale operations in North Africa, in South-East Europe, and in Western Europe. Under these circumstances he wondered whether it was not possible to avoid the war on two fronts by making a political settlement with Russia. An ideal solution seemed to him to be a new "Brest-Litovsk Treaty", although he was also aware that it would be exceptionally hard to reach such an agreement with Russia. If it did turn out to be too difficult to arrive at that sort of arrangement, he would be of the opinion that they should take up a position on the Russian Front which would allow the Axis to transfer greater numbers of troops as soon as possible from East to West. Ciano emphasized that these considerations were mere hypotheses which had not assumed any concrete shape. The Duce believed that one could possibly use Japan to explore the chances of a political solution with Russia. By these means Russian dynamism must be steered in another direction—towards Central Asia.'

Ciano recorded in his subsequent memorandum for the Duce: 'When I spoke of the possibility of a separate peace with Russia, Hitler expressed his own negative point of view in the following words. Germany had already in the past posed the problem of coming to an understanding with Russia, and precisely in the winter of 1940–41 every attempt was made to push the Russians into Central Asia. This was particularly discussed at the time of Molotov's visit to Berlin. But the Russians did not follow this course. Instead they brought up their historic claims on Finland and the Dardanelles, against Roumania, and in the direction of Bulgaria. If Germany had given way at that time, the Russians would first have attacked Finland, and then after they had taken over the Roumanian oil, the Axis would have been placed in an untenable position.

'The Russia of Stalin still follows the path chosen by Peter the Great for the expansion of his people to the North and South-West. Russia has in no way shown herself prepared to follow the course proposed to her towards India and the Persian Gulf because she regards these aims as secondary. If she were first assured of hegemony over Europe, the rest would follow of its own accord.

'The break between Germany and Russia arose out of the increasing danger which this latter threat presented. When Hitler knew for certain that nine hundred airfields, an enormous quantity of war material and numerous troops were concentrated on the frontier, he had to take defensive measures. Can yet another attempt now be made to reach a settlement of the struggle with Russia? The Fuehrer asked himself this question some months ago, when the rumour was spreading that Japan had sounded the Fuehrer in this sense. But, as we had assumed, we learnt that these rumours had been artificially spread by the Russians themselves to bring pressure on their allies to give more support in armaments, and to obtain the opening of the Second Front.

'What would the position be today if we somehow came to an agreement? It is certain that the Russians would devote six months to a complete overhaul of their equipment and strength in order to fall on our rear again. The Brest-Litovsk line is out of the question. These are regions which represent indispensable reserves of foodstuffs and raw materials for

Germany and Russia alike. Thus any line drawn which might satisfy the requirements of one people would sacrifice the needs of the other.

'Even if we came to an understanding with Russia, we would not be able to move larger forces to Africa, because the only reason for the crisis which has arisen in Africa is to be found in our transport difficulties and not at all from lack of material and troops.' Also in regard to air strength an understanding with Russia would bring no noticeable gain. 'No air force could be moved effectively to another front in under six months . . . but in any case, the removal of these forces from Russia would be disquieting as their deployment in the event of a treacherous Russian attack would need many months.' There was only one great advantage, the reduction of losses in manpower; but the risk was too great. In short, Hitler saw no advantage in ending the war in the East. Finland would then probably sever with the Axis and join the enemy. The forces required for the security of Norway and France need not be taken away from the Russian front. Four divisions were already prepared for Africa and could be sent as soon as transport was assured. These divisions would, together with the Italo-German forces already available in Tunisia and Libya, amount to a total of four hundred thousand men, whose maintenance produced transport problems of enormous size, and this number certainly could not be increased.

Ciano broke into the conversation by saying that 'he had taken down the interesting observations of the Fuehrer exactly and would make an exhaustive report to the Duce. The latter had incidentally made no proposal, but only wanted to know the Fuehrer's opinion on certain matters.'

On her side Italy would do everything possible to make a major military effort in 1943. Between January and the summer one million men would be under arms. There would be the problem of equipping them, and Cavallero must talk about this separately to Keitel. As to the situation in North Africa, Mussolini thought it essential to protect the supply routes through the establishment of a permanent air superiority. Without such superiority, the transport position would become increasingly precarious and finally untenable.

Ciano then turned to the French situation. 'The Duce had from the beginning had the gravest mistrust of, and a very modest and limited confidence in, the Laval government,' which certainly represented the real France to a far less degree than the Darlan administration now set up by the Allies in Algiers.

Laval was due to arrive at the conference on the following day. Hitler told Ciano that, 'after Laval has been heard' decisions would be taken about France. He agreed with Mussolini's view. 'The French are eighty per cent *attentistes,* five per cent collaborationists in more or less good faith, and the rest follow Darlan and de Gaulle. All are united in the thought of freeing themselves from the Germans. One must make an exception only for those few who, like Laval, have completely compromised themselves, and know that on the day the Germans leave France they will be shot. The greatest reservations are also made as to the loyalty of Pétain.' But in any case it was proper to support a French government since it at least could neutralize the action carried out by Darlan in North Africa. 'The majority of Frenchmen are not without spirit or enthusiasm. Darlan calls on them to fight; Pétain invites them to avoid battle. Many Frenchmen prefer to live with Pétain rather than die with Darlan . . . Germany is only ready to give way on a few formal questions without giving the Laval government any real element of strength.'

Hitler warmed to his own defence of his French policy. 'Pétain ought to be kept peacefully going as a kind of ghost, inflated from time to time by Laval when he appears to be sinking too low.'[13] Hitler did not know what kind of requests Laval wished to bring forward. In any case he would only talk to him in Ciano's presence. Laval would probably want a sort of final peace treaty, but of this there could be no question while Darlan and de Gaulle were sitting in North Africa. 'As to internal concessions Laval will probably put forward requests for a new army. This must be discussed with Field Marshal Keitel. Fundamentally France should not be allowed to have much more than a kind of fire brigade.'

Hitler now invoked his special bogey—the menace of partisan warfare in the Balkans. 'He stressed again the utmost importance of the pacification of these regions in face of an eventual British front in the Balkans. Every measure must be taken to prevent the outbreak of fire in our rear in case an Anglo-Saxon landing takes place. For otherwise all the heroic courage of the Axis troops in Crete and the Peloponnese (in 1941) would have been in vain; for apart from the above-mentioned railway line, no other route was available. If this was lost the Balkans were finished for the Axis. The recent blowing up of a bridge had shown how disagreeable for supplies such a disruption of traffic could be* . . . The enemy must therefore be prevented from continuing with their partisan war against Axis communications, otherwise a catastrophic situation would arise. The partisans, with Mihailović at their head, were working closely with England, whence they received material from submarines at night on the Dalmatian coast, and also information and gold from parachutists . . .'[14] Owing to weather conditions in the Balkans, no troops could be sent there to undertake bigger operations before March. The Axis would therefore be helpless in the event of an Allied landing.

The conference was punctuated throughout its proceedings by the disintegration of the whole German front in the East. The line of the river Don from the north of Stalingrad, stretching to the German armies on the sector facing Voronezh, was held by Roumanian and Italian armies. It was here during these December days that the Russians launched a massive thrust, scattering in particular the Italian 2nd Armoured Corps which formed the main body of the Italian force in Russia, and rupturing the whole line.

On the evening of December 18 Ciano returned to his carriage on the official train, and noted in his diary: 'The atmosphere is heavy. Perhaps one should add to the bad news the sadness of this damp forest and the boredom of collective existence in the huts of the High Command. There is no touch of colour, no lively note . . . a smell of kitchen, uniforms and boots . . . Since my arrival no one has hidden from me and my collaborators the uneasiness caused by the news of collapse on the German front in Russia. They seek openly to make us responsible. Hewel,† who lives in Hitler's immediate circle, had the following conversation with Pansa.‡

Pansa: "Had our army many losses?"
Hewel: "No losses at all; they are running."

* The Gorgopotamos bridge by a British-led party of Greek partisans, on the main railway line to Piraeus—the supply route to North Africa.

† The political adviser attached by the German Foreign Office to Hitler's headquarters.

‡ The Vice-Chief of Protocol at the Italian Foreign Office.

Panza: "Like you did in front of Moscow last year?"
Hewel: "Exactly."'[15]

The Fuehrer went so far as to insist that the Duce should be asked 'personally to telegraph to the Italian troops in Russia not to yield an inch of territory'. Throughout the day Hitler hammered on this theme. That evening Ciano cabled to Mussolini that the situation appeared grave, and there was little possibility of persuading Germany to come to terms with Russia.[16]

Laval had now arrived at German headquarters. That evening the Frenchman was received by Hitler in the presence of Ciano and the other Axis leaders. Ciano recorded that the ensuing talks 'were without the slightest political interest. They took place first round a tea-table and then at a dinner table. Thus the French Premier, whose journey took him eighty hours, had only three hours with the Fuehrer, during which, when it came to the point, he was able to speak for twenty minutes. The Fuehrer repeated his view about France and avoided every precise demand on the part of Laval. The latter had a long list of questions written on a piece of paper. But he only got out the first one: the request to be able to dissolve the other parties and to found a united party. When this was refused, he did not find the courage to produce the others. Basically he confined himself to seeking a proof of confidence from the German side, as he is aware that this is the only positive element on which he can base his tenure of office, which he recognizes as very difficult. In one of his own phrases, "It is very hard for him to govern a France in which he only hears shouted: Laval to the scaffold."'

Hitler confirmed his general confidence of a personal kind in Laval, 'and a complete mistrust of all his colleagues. It could not be otherwise since during the short conference in Munich Laval had personally stood guarantee for men such as Noguès and Darlan, who in the course of a few hours had shown their true faces.'[17]

'Nevertheless,' wrote Ciano in his diary, 'how the Germans respond to the charm of the French, even of this Frenchman! Except for Hitler, all the others were crowding round him trying to talk to him or to get close to him; it looked like the entrance of an erstwhile great lord into a circle of new-rich parvenus.'[18]

* * *

The final meeting of the conference took place on the morning of December 20. Hitler announced that he could not come to Italy, 'but Count Ciano had seen for himself how much the Fuehrer was committed to his tasks at Headquarters'. He then commented on the talks of the last days. 'There was complete agreement between Germany and Italy in their judgment of the so-called French government and on the methods to be employed in France. The aim was to maintain at least the fiction of a French government and to leave Pétain as Head of the State, because this made operations in North Africa easier.' The problem of the French fleet had been settled one way or the other at Toulon. 'As to the problem of the East, the Fuehrer referred to it as a purely military matter. The question of a settlement of the Eastern problem by an agreement with Russia was not ripe for discussion.'

Turning to the war in North Africa, Hitler repeated the historical importance of the area for Italy. 'The possession of North Africa was also essential to Italy on grounds of military geography. Thus North Africa was vitally necessary to the Axis for the successful conduct of the war. One might well say that the Axis could withdraw to the fortress of Europe. But in the long run one could not put up with such a self-contraction, but must, through the possession of North Africa, compel the enemy to commit his forces and above all his shipping, which was his very lifeline . . . For this reason alone the transport problem of supplying North Africa must not go unsolved. It was decisive for the war, and every conceivable effort must be made. Moreover, when peace was concluded, Italy would find herself in a more favourable position to claim territories in North Africa if she already held them. Events after 1918 could only strengthen this view.'

Ciano returned to Rome on December 22. 'I find considerable panic over the news from the Russian front, especially since the Duce, in speaking to people of a possible peace with Russia, has kindled many hopes . . . In my verbal comments I do not conceal any unfavourable impressions.'[19]

The Goerlitz visit had sharply affected Ciano's spirit and he had come back with a sense of frustration and failure. The 'Beresina Wind',* fatal to Napoleon, was blowing across Europe from the steppes of Asia, and the barometer was falling at a remorseless speed.

* A phrase of Grandi's.

APPENDIX A

Goering-Duce Conversation in Rome
(December 6, 1942)

On December 6 Goering called on the Duce, and the two men reviewed the war situation alone. At Mussolini's request neither Schmidt nor Dollmann was present. It seems that the Duce himself drafted a brief note the following day which summarized the talk, and this hitherto unpublished document exists among those of Ciano's papers later captured by the Germans.

During the talk between the Duce and Marshal Goering the following subjects were discussed:

'1. Russia: The Duce believes that, one way or another, the chapter of the war against Russia, which has no more purpose, must be closed. If it should prove possible to arrive at a second Brest-Litovsk (and this one could do by giving Russia territorial compensation in Central Asia), it must be so provided that a defensive line is reached that destroys any enemy initiative and with a minimum of commitments of the Axis forces. Goering says that this would be Hitler's ideal.'

'2. All resources must be directed to the West and the Mediterranean, as it is clear that enemy number one is still England and the industrial effort of the United States is such that she will produce an air superiority on the Anglo-Saxon side. Goering says that the Axis can count on a joint monthly production of 5,000 machines.

'3. *Croatia:* The Duce considers the situation very precarious, and foresees the need for a joint command, that will group and exploit all available Italian, German and Croat forces. Goering agrees that Pavelić is still the man the Axis must use.

'4. *Spain:* The Duce suggests that arms should be delivered gradually to Spain (Goering says that Germany is doing this), but she should not be pressed to intervene prematurely as this would be more of a burden than an advantage.

'5. *Turkey:* From the latest reports it seems that Turkey fears Russia, but also is anxious about the Anglo-Saxons who have extended their occupation of Iran and the Middle East.

'In order to bring about a decisive change in Turkish policy it is necessary: (a) to drive down from the Caucasus;

(b) to strengthen the Bulgarian army, which will never be used against Russia but can represent a threat to Turkey.'

APPENDIX B

The Concept of a separate Peace in 1942 between Russia and the Axis, with Japan as Mediator

IN the Goerlitz talks on December 18–20, 1942, Hitler revealed for the first time publicly at a conference, and in answer to the Italian view that a separate peace with Russia must be explored, that the Japanese had approached the German government earlier in the year with a similar proposal. Hitler's words were: 'Some time ago the question was raised by Japan as to whether it was not possible to reach agreement with the Russians on a workable basis.'

Ever since the Japanese had entered the war they considered the German campaign in Russia solely in relation to whether or not it contributed to the ultimate victory of the Tripartite powers against England and the United States. If the German plan of a lightning and decisive campaign on the Eastern Front succeeded, there would be no cause for Tokyo to comment; and the Far Eastern War was parallel to that in Europe in the sense that the Italians strove to regard the Mediterranean theatre and their war activities as separate from the German conduct of the war in the East, North and West of Europe. But the failure of the German offensive in Russia in the winter of 1941–2 caused the Japanese leaders to reflect with some concern on the whole course of the war.

Soundings as to the possibilities of a contact between the Germans and the Russians seem to have begun early in 1942, and continued through the summer and autumn. The available evidence is fragmentary.

The first cautious hint appears to have been made by the Japanese Navy, whose clear concern was to interest their European partners in concentrating their war effort against the British and Americans in the Atlantic and Mediterranean. On March 14, 1942, the German Ambassador in Tokyo had sent the following telegram to Berlin: 'Naval attaché has informed the Japanese Admiralty that "Germany from her point of view does not see the possibility of making a peace with Russia, which would establish those conditions essential to cover Germany's rear in her further pursuance of the war against the Anglo-Saxons and would safeguard her in the East. In any event it is felt in Berlin that Russia will suffer further blows this year which will force the Russians to seek peace. The representative of the Japanese Admiralty was receptive to these explanations."

'Naval attaché informed his Japanese colleagues that no information existed in Berlin to show that the Soviet government intended to treat with Germany. But as the communications from the Japanese Navy suggest a change in the attitude of the Soviet government in regard to the continuation of the war with Germany, Berlin would be interested to know what caused the Japanese Navy to hold this view, and in particular did the Soviets, directly or indirectly, take the initiative in bringing to the knowledge of the Japanese their wish to make peace now with Germany?

'German Naval Attaché stressed that Germany would never undertake any such initiative, and received the answer that naturally Japan would never take such action unless requested to do so by Germany.

'The Japanese official concerned pointed out that "the desire" of the Japanese Navy that Germany should postpone her differences with Soviet Russia, and reach an agreement with the Russians, stemmed from the wish that Germany could then turn all her efforts to destroying British forces in the Middle East, and the British position in the Eastern Mediterranean, and in this way and as quickly as possible implement a direct collaboration between the Axis powers and Japan.'

The failure of Rommel's attack in Egypt in the summer of 1942, and of the hopes of an early German break-through in the Caucasus, prompted the Japanese to put out further feelers, in particular through their Ambassador in Russia. The Italians seem to have been aware of these moves. On July 30, Mussolini told the King 'that it seems confirmed that Japan is working to conclude a separate peace between Germany and Russia'.

On August 31 Ribbentrop expressed his irritation at these 'rumours' in a conversation with General Oshima, the Japanese Ambassador in Germany.

'The rumour in the world of a separate peace between Germany and Russia has not died down. Unfortunately we have to state that once again it was also Japanese sources which nourished this rumour. It gives strong support to

Stalin's propaganda, and he uses it to spur the English to greater efforts. If Japan is using the rumour as cover, to lull the Russians into false security before attacking them, then Ribbentrop has nothing against it. But if not, would Oshima tell his government that "rumour of a separate peace merely helps our enemy". A separate peace was impossible for Germany "for Stalin could not accept the conditions which we would put to him, and which–thanks to our military position –we feel strong enough to make". Also there was, Oshima added, a group in Tokyo, who thought for example that a separate peace between Germany and Russia would be politically useful.'

In September the German Embassy in Tokyo reported that the plan to mediate a peace between Germany and Russia 'has not come to the fore again since the feeler put out earlier this year'. On December 11, Oshima was able to tell Ribbentrop that, 'The theme of a separate peace between Germany and Russia had been very strongly (*sic*) handled at the conference of Japanese Ambassadors in Europe in Berlin, as very many rumours were in circulation. He did not believe himself that Stalin could make peace because of the conditions which Germany would have to make, but in the event of Stalin–having been militarily thoroughly beaten–being finally ready to do so because of the fear of internal revolt, his Japanese government asked to be speedily informed . . . This would be very important to Tokyo as the Army under Yamashida, the conqueror of Singapore, stood on the permanent alert in Manchuria.'

CHAPTER SEVEN

The Winter Crisis

THE CRISIS on the Home Front in the winter months of 1942, which opened with the illness of the Duce, was also closely bound up with the deterioration of the position of Italy in the military theatres overseas, and the contracting menace of war closing in on the mother country. The collapse of the Axis front at Alamein brought home to the Italian public the threat of invasion of the islands and mainland of Italy itself. The failure of Hitler's gamble in the East, demonstrated by the opening of the great Russian offensive on the Stalingrad front on November 19, marked the end of a grand illusion of a short and victorious war conducted out of sight and almost of mind.

The King returned to Rome from San Rossore on November 13. He had prepared a note for the Duce. 'Serious steps must be taken for the defence of Italy by concentrating the maximum forces on metropolitan territory . . . Everything must be done to obtain the repatriation of our units in Russia . . . starting with the Alpine divisions.' The next day the Duce had an audience of the King, and promised to study this question with care.[1]

In mid-November the seeming recovery in health of the Duce relaxed the political climate. On November 16 the King said, 'I have the impression that Mussolini has entirely recovered, and has a reasonably clear head. His judgment on certain men appeared to me to be clear and precise.'[2] Victor Emmanuel was by instinct opposed to violent change, and his natural preference lay in supporting his Prime Minister in striving to redress the balance of the military situation, and using his royal authority, which Mussolini had always accepted as a political factor, to such an end. As the anonymous Italian informer of the German Embassy reported, 'The state of feeling in the Royal Family is "preoccupied", though the King is co-operating with the Duce in unaltered fashion in the hope of final victory.'

But, in event of a stalemate on the war fronts, the King was aware of the possible contribution which he alone could make in seeking a negotiated peace with the Allies, both by exploiting the international connections of royalty, and by stressing his role, uncompromised by the present and untouched by the responsibilities of Fascism. In this sphere he would take no separate initiative. The threat to the internal stability of the country, however, which had stemmed from the temporary incapacity of the Duce, implied at least an examination by the Crown of the eventual possibilities of a breakdown of the machinery of administration, and the study of preliminary counter-measures.

On November 26, for example, the Undersecretary of War, General Scuero, cautiously warned the King's aide-de-camp, General Puntoni. He 'spoke of the perils of the internal situation. I get the impression that the Undersecretary seeks to learn from me what the Sovereign thinks. He assured me of his devotion to the King, and expressed his conviction that the Army is closely bound to the Crown. Scuero is urgently worried that the Grenadier Division should be recalled to Rome, and I calm him by saying that it is on the way at the King's express desire.' The King's personal intervention in the early stages of the winter crisis was thus limited to securing the stationing of one élite army division in Rome, and, in the same line of thought, pressing Mussolini to withdraw the Italian Expeditionary Force from Russia, especially the Alpine units.

There is evidence, however, that with or without express instructions from the King, Acquarone had moved further in the direction of precautionary measures. The role of the Police, particularly the Public Security, in event of an internal threat, would be as vital as that of the Army. The Director-General of Security, Carmine Senise, was peculiarly fitted for such special duties. He had begun his career in the Ministry of the Interior, and at the time of the March on Rome was head of its Press Office, and in the confidence of the Minister in Facta's government, Taddei, who was foremost in resisting the Fascist assault. Senise had thus acquired invaluable experience in the technique of the coup d'état, which proved to be a decisive element in the historical reversal of these events twenty years later.

During the 1930's he had served under a brilliant technician in the person of Arturo Bocchini, who controlled as Chief of Police the security of the régime until his death in November 1940. Cynical, corrupt, observant, and ruthless, the latter built up the Police as an independent arm of the State, extending its powers with the creation of the OVRA as a special branch to protect the person of the Duce against assassination, and in suppressing anti-Fascist agitation and organization inside and outside the country. His supreme achievement was to block any attempt by the Fascist party to penetrate or control the Italian police. It was characteristic of Mussolini that he should both accept and encourage such a situation, and also permit within the Ministry of the Interior, of which he retained the nominal control as Minister, a standing rivalry between the Undersecretary and the Chief of Police.

Since 1933 the former office had been held by Guido Buffarini Guidi, a Tuscan lawyer, elusive, subtle, effusive, obsessed by the political game.[3] It was he, already in the years immediately preceding the war, who held in his hand the private links between the Italian and German security organs, and he had established close contacts, in particular with Himmler. Unlike Bocchini, he sought to play a political role and was in a perpetual search for allies, of whom one was Ciano. He also intrigued in Party circles, and there was much pressure on him from this quarter to appoint a Party nominee to the Police on Bocchini's death in 1940. Senise, however, had paid careful attention to his relations with his Undersecretary even to the extent of enlisting the backing of Himmler's representative in Rome, Dollmann,[4] and it was Buffarini who secured Mussolini's consent to Senise's appointment as Bocchini's successor. Senise's powers of deception exceeded even those of his volatile chief. Ciano, in his flippant and self-revealing way, described the new Chief of Police after the first lengthy meeting between the two men: 'He is a Neapolitan, a queer mixture of intelligence and ignorance; he follows his natural instincts and is a blackmailer; fundamentally he is easy-going, a chatterbox, superficial, and a gesticulator. It is enough to think that such a man is Chief of Police in the twentieth year of Fascism to be convinced that, in this country, *plus ça change, plus c'est la même chose*. He might better have been a Minister under the Bourbons . . . I shall see him more often because it is amusing.'[5]

It was characteristic of Ciano that he should be unaware of and incurious as to Senise's real abilities and attitude. Not only was the new Chief of Police a brilliant administrator and organizer, a planner with a gift of detailed preparation, but he was untouched by any myth of the régime, and was by temperament a pre-1922 Monarchist, by inclination devoid of any fundamental allegiances.

According to his own account, Senise seems to have considered at an early stage after his appointment in 1940 the precautions to be taken in event of a crisis of the régime. The police was kept independent of the Party; the force was increased by twelve thousand men; in October 1942 the Questore of Rome, the official controlling order and security in the capital, was replaced by the former head of the Milan OVRA, a nominee of Senise's; close relations were established with the Military Police Headquarters, particularly with General Hazon, its vice-commander; help was forthcoming from the Minister of Finance, Thaon di Revel, and General Scuero at the War Office provided equipment for the Police units.[6] Senise claims that he had established close relations with the latter since the summer of 1942 in order to study counter-measures in event of 'a Fascist coup'. Cavallero was also aware of these moves, and sent Senise a message offering arms to the Police. 'Evidently the reason for reviving the plans to maintain public order, on which Scuero and myself had agreed, had not escaped him, and he indicated that he shared our view.'[7]

It appears that by November 1942 therefore some elementary liaison plans between the Police and the Army had been discussed, and that the routine directives to both bodies in event of a crisis of public order had been subject to revision. The only source of reaction on the part of the régime in an emergency lay in the heads of the command of the Party Militia. In theory this protecting force of the régime should be able to act in twenty-four hours.

Senise seems to have probed the intentions of the Militia Commander, General Galbiati, in such an event, and sought to establish the semblance of a combined security plan. Galbiati made it clear that he would make separate arrangements. Like other public figures he was aware of the feverish and disjointed speculation in all circles during these weeks as to the succession of the Duce. The testing enquiries of the Undersecretary of War and the Chief of Police on the dusty standing instructions for the maintenance of public order drawn up by the Ministry of the Interior years before, and even linking with measures designed originally to combat the predecessors of the Militia, the Action Squads of the days before the March on Rome, could not but arouse his suspicions. Incipient and precautionary plotting in the Ministries of War and the Interior was a minor alarm signal.

Early in December, Galbiati addressed the Militia Commanders in the presence of Buffarini and Vidussoni. According to Scuero's alarmed report to Puntoni, 'special groups of the members of the former Action Squads have been formed to keep internal order, and the Militia Command has insisted with Senise to have control of the radio-telegraph stations.'[8]

It was typical of the climate of the régime that the Militia should maintain its own political office, and that one of its main functions should be to report to Mussolini on the activities of the Police, particularly in the light of its permanent vendetta with the Public Security authorities. These reports reveal the depth of these feuds. Since January 1941 secret instructions had been issued by the Director of Public Security to the local Chiefs of Police to keep an eye on their opposite numbers, the Federal Secretaries, and particularly to report any matters of a scandalous nature. There was 'in effect a real system of espionage'. Party activities were everywhere obstructed. Senise's contacts with anti-Fascist groups in the Ministries, and in particular the War Office, were reinforced. Scuero, the Undersecretary of War, had a complete plan of action in the event of a 'disturbance of public order which might follow the imminent collapse of the régime, which is regarded as certain, or on the death of the Duce. In such an event all the Party bosses will be immediately arrested, and the combined forces of the Police and the Army used to suffocate any attempts at Fascist insurrection. The Chief of Police, master of the situation, has offered to the King the possibilities of setting up a constitutional government . . . Everything that happens at Militia Headquarters is under surveillance and particularly anything which might be organized for the defence and maintenance of the régime.'[9]

By November 1942 Senise appeared to share the widespread view of the imminent disintegration of the Fascist structure. He was by now in touch with the Minister of the Royal

Household, Duca Acquarone, and the latter's confidential secretary and stenographer was one of Senise's agents. On the other hand, his relations with Buffarini at the Ministry of the Interior had declined and he had been unable to maintain regular and direct contact with the Duce and the private secretariat at Palazzo Venezia.

Although the activities in the shadows of the Court could in no way be defined as a Palace conspiracy, it is clear from fragments of evidence that the lineaments of a cabal can be traced, involving, with the active knowledge of Acquarone, leading individuals in the Police, the Army and the Military Police, and indeed, as in the case of Thaon di Revel, in the government ministries, with the object of enabling the Crown to intervene in the event of a political breakdown. But any advance in this direction must depend on the personal decision of the King alone, and in spite of the apparent seriousness of the situation at the end of 1942, there is no sign that the King had as yet any intention of making such a move. As Puntoni explained to Scuero, 'Only in a desperate case will the Crown be able to intervene. At the moment it is as well that His Majesty should be above everything in order to be one day the arbiter of events.'[10]

The origins of Badoglio's search for a 'personal solution' during these weeks is still obscured by lack of convincing evidence. According to his own account, the first appeal to him came from the Princess of Piedmont in the summer of 1942. He 'advised her to report to her father-in-law and husband what she had told him, as he could not ever take by surprise and overthrow the government without a suitable organization, nor would he lend himself to it without orders from the King'.[11]

His notorious prudence is sarcastically depicted by Caviglia. Badoglio told a private gathering at the beginning of 1941, 'I am like the flag that is presented when the regiment is on parade. At that moment I take command and one moves off. You prepare everything, acting like a kind of secret society, and think of me as the leader.' The others present told him, 'No one can organize something on the lines which you propose. One must take an organization which exists, and that is the army. You could take that in hand and we will prepare the country.' Badoglio, as Caviglia commented, 'did not want to take any initial responsibility, he wanted everything fixed and then he would put himself at the head'.[12]

Caviglia had as yet not ventured to make any soundings and was content to observe. Mysteriously, in November, his country house was searched by the Italian police, and almost at the same moment the German War Office asked Rintelen in Rome for his curriculum vitae.[13]

Both Marshals were the subject of discreet German interest. The recent example of Darlan in North Africa could be infectious, and had perhaps been noted in comparable quarters in Rome.

'My anxiety is for the present internal situation. From my last conversation with you, I formed the impression that you were not well informed, and I do not know for what reason . . . Honest Italians are suffering a momentary lack of confidence . . . There are traitors who would willingly see our armies defeated in order to strike at Fascism.'[14]

Farinacci wrote to the Duce on November 19 in these terms. To him the present climate of alarm and discontent in these winter months stemmed logically from the mistaken direction taken over the years by the Fascist movement under Mussolini's leadership. The violent and polemical interventions of Farinacci were a familiar feature of the régime, and his career was symbolic of the defeat of the early extremism of the regional Action Squads. He was the only genuine National Socialist of the Revolution, whose conception of the future of Fascism was totalitarian. He was also one of the few who were really present at the foundation of the Milan Fascio on March 23, 1919. He started life as a station master near Cremona, had struggled to educate himself. He created in his area his own action squads, and Cremona, a Socialist stronghold, was literally taken by assault, and organized as a 'model' fief. He became the natural spokesman of the renegade Left extremist elements of militant Fascism, republican, proletarian, national-socialist, preaching the abolition not only of parliamentary government but of the State, pressing for an all-embracing, all-powerful, Party machine led by an incorruptible dedicated élite, the guardian of a permanent revolution.

The inevitable clash with Mussolini had come soon after the accession of Fascism to power, and it was savage and final. The March on Rome, in Mussolini's view, marked for the moment the historic limits of Fascist illegality, and after his arrival in office it became increasingly clear to his followers that he intended to govern with a minimum violation of existing practice, accepting the continued existence of the Monarchy, and—subject to good behaviour—the presence of a parliamentary opposition. Such an attitude, on the part of the Leader, must arouse the puzzled hostility of the extreme elements among the inchoate mass of the provincial Party organizations, and it was Farinacci who crystallized this reaction into a formidable pressure group, aided by the armed formations of the Party now legalized as the Militia, with the official task of preparing the Revolution and with the deliberate purpose of forcing Mussolini back into the path of totalitarian dictatorship.

The murder of the Socialist deputy Matteotti in 1924, after two years of Mussolini's personal experiment in compromise, gave Farinacci his chance. The Leader was driven back into the arms of the faithful by the nation-wide reaction to this political assassination. Mussolini's speech of January 3, 1925, under the impact of this unexpected disaster, marked the historic beginning of Fascist rule. Farinacci became Secretary of the Party. This was his only opportunity, and it never recurred. In one year, during the temporary weakening of Mussolini's personal position and prestige following the Matteotti crisis, Farinacci conducted a large-scale purge of the whole machine, striving to give shape to his own apocalyptic vision. In reality Farinacci, with uncontrolled violence, aimed at a detailed and planned attempt to create a party machine in his own image, which was intended to be the decisive and dominating factor in the political scene. His activities had, however, the effect of breaking the spirit and enthusiasm and indeed the idealism which had been an intrinsic element of the early movement. All that he had built was an imperfect clientele.

By 1926 Mussolini had recovered his nerve and prestige as the Duce of Fascism. Farinacci was removed, and was never to hold active office again outside nominal membership of the Grand Council. He was now relegated to Cremona and through his local paper *Regime Fascista,* conceiving of himself as the conscience of the Party, he became an impotent Cassandra, dangerous and violent in his pursuit of personal feuds, a dissolving and demoralizing influence, bombarding Mussolini with advice in bitter frustration and recrimination at his expulsion into the wilderness. In January 1932, for example, he referred in such a letter to the fact that the Duce 'publicly deplores my existence as a member of the Grand Council, as a Deputy, journalist and lawyer'.[15]

Throughout his correspondence in the succeeding years, he evolved the elements of a personal political programme. His relations with Mussolini were soured for ever, but coloured by a reluctant and disapproving admiration for the figure of the Duce, and the obstinate hope that circumstances would force the Leader again to expel the traitors from within the gate and to march at the head of the revolution. In the same letter of January 1932 to Mussolini, he wrote 'I am and always will be a faithful soldier of the cause, and if dark times for our country came tomorrow, you would find me at my battle station, my enthusiasm unchanged, and my loyalty intact.'

The political future of Farinacci lay, if at all, only 'in dark times' and he remained remorselessly and almost hopefully the prophet of disaster—in Spain, in Ethiopia, and after the outbreak of war in 1940. The deficiencies of the Italian war effort and the tragi-comedy of the Greek Campaign in October 1940 brought new life to his polemical outbursts. With the pent-up violence of his temperament Farinacci now pursued his longstanding vendetta with the real culprits in his eyes, the Army leaders. His organ of attack, his paper *Regime Fascista,* launched this campaign in November 1940 in an article directed against the incompetence of the General Staff and particularly of Badoglio. As he also wrote to Mussolini at the time: 'If our Revolution has marched into every sector, it has been absent in one and that the most delicate and important—the Army. The old Italy is still at the head of the army with an obstinately anti-Fascist mentality or better still, to describe Badoglio more exactly, with the mentality of a Gamelin.'[16]

The winter crisis of the war in 1942 and the anxieties on the Home Front, together with the Duce's illness, offered Farinacci the promise of a wider field of action. On the problem of the succession, he had written on the same theme nearly ten years before, at Mussolini's request. The latter himself had said that there could not be a second Duce. But there must be strong safe men to carry on the work; where were they? 'The supreme duty is to prepare the governing cadres' though the best members of the régime had been discredited and set aside by the political police (the OVRA). One day Mussolini would realize the harm done by this body to his work of material and spiritual reconstruction. 'What is the State? Faith in Mussolini.'[17]

In the winter of 1942 the country and the régime were in mortal danger. But Farinacci must seek also his personal solution. The axiom of his programme was that Fascism could only survive in close and loyal alliance with National Socialist Germany, and by a heightened and purified joint war effort. It was, however, an implicit peril in the situation at hand that the personal structure of Mussolini's rule might disintegrate before a counter-action could be organized. Quite apart from the possibility of his death, there was always the obsessive theme, in Farinacci's mind, of an all-pervading treachery in the air, of the Royal House, the Army leaders, and within the Party itself. He was by now convinced that even if the Duce survived it was too late to save Fascism except by drastic measures, perhaps even including the sacrifice of Mussolini himself.

Although he had no close allies, Farinacci still could perhaps count on well placed supporters in the Party hierarchy, most of them former political clients. His first step, therefore, was to renew these connections with a view to a 'revival' of the Party on the pattern of 1925. His veteran enemies, the police, were close behind. 'Excellency Farinacci continues his activities aimed at increasing the number of proselytes to carry out his programme of removing the Duce at an opportune moment. He has a house in Rome where his henchmen, having worked on picked Party bosses, invite them to lunch.' His political influence was concentrated in Lombardy. Apart from his personal fief of Cremona, he was assured of support in Milan, Bergamo and Brescia. He had come to terms with the former Party Secretary, Starace, whose activities in office, by creating an elephantine bureaucratic machine, has been as disastrous as his own. The police report continues: 'Starace has recognized Farinacci as the leader, so that the tiny group of the followers of Starace (consisting exclusively of Party bosses favoured by him), has gone over bag and baggage to the Farinacci group.'

Apart from attending to his relations within the Party machine, Farinacci must seek support in military circles. Here he had no choice. He had conducted a standing feud with the whole military caste, as anti-Fascist, anti-German, inefficient and disloyal. The only figure who had shown himself willing to fall in with the German conception of the struggle was the Chief of the General Staff, Marshal Cavallero. But the latter had achieved this reputation rather out of passivity of character and fatalism than deliberate intent, and his position was also under mounting attack from Ciano and in Army circles.

It might be that, as Farinacci may have calculated, an alliance between himself and Cavallero, backed by the Germans, provided the other possible alternative solution to the eventual collapse of the régime. But there is no evidence to show that Cavallero was prepared to commit himself to such a desperate plan. Farinacci was a disaster candidate, and Cavallero had observed too long and closely the march of political events in Italy in recent years to compromise himself with such a perilous companion.

Of the several legends which have grown up round the person of Cavallero, one of the most persistent is of such an alliance between the two men. In the interests of Italy such action was allegedly forced upon them in view of the conpiracy of Ciano, Grandi and Ambrosio to overthrow Mussolini and make a separate peace with the Allies, thus bringing the country to disaster. The Farinacci-Cavallero 'plot' was also a later alibi for the others and might have been in part at least originated in another camp. The atmosphere was charged with mutual fears and suspicions, and talk of disloyalty and treason. For instance, in a conversation with Ciano, Galbiati was told that Cavallero 'will betray because he does not believe any more in victory. He must be replaced, because he is intelligent and will betray well.'[18]

Caviglia's comment is rather a noting of rumour than evidence: 'Farinacci and Cavallero seem to be in close accord. The other Fascist chiefs are worked up against Farinacci, and they fear him because he has the Germans with him. They are all men who are solely concerned with their own personal interests and would like to put Farinacci in a position of not counting for anything, but he knows how to make use of Hitler's support.'[19]

In so far as there is any evidence of Cavallero's activities at this time, it points to a somewhat modified and more cautious sounding, in keeping with his temperament. General Hazon, of the Military Police, told Puntoni already at the end of October 1942 that 'the illness of the Duce has let loose the appetites of the competitors for his succession, some of whom have revealed their hands to Cavallero to find out what he thinks and how he would behave if Mussolini should disappear or in event of a coup d'état'. Cavallero, according to Hazon, had replied that 'his attitude would be that just as he had also loyally served the Duce so he would be prepared to serve the head of the government who would be appointed by the King'.[20]

During November Cavallero voiced his fears in a talk with the commander of the Fascist Militia, General Galbiati, and sounded him on the possible attitude of the Militia and the Party in event 'of the take-over of power on the part of the Germans'.[21] Or was Cavallero rather thinking in terms of his own personal position? The version of this episode given by Puntoni in his diary on November 26 is somewhat different in emphasis and more in this latter sense. The Undersecretary of War, General Scuero, was his source. 'He told me of the conversation which had taken place between Cavallero and Galbiati, and which had ended in the latter's refusal of the request by the Chief of the General Staff to put at the disposal of the Army Corps in Rome several battalions of the Militia to preserve internal order. Galbiati had replied that he had studied the proposition on his own account.'[22]

In his 'Memorandum' dictated after his arrest by Badoglio in August 1943, Cavallero gave his own version of these moves made by him, and part at least is confirmed by Hazon's remarks to the King's military secretary. 'In November 1942, when Mussolini was seriously ill, it was necessary to consider the worst eventuality. I was anxious about this, and gave instructions in such an event to General Magli, to General Ambrosio, Chief of the Army Staff, and to General Scuero, Undersecretary for War. There were two meetings for this purpose; I said clearly that they must be prepared to ensure a co-ordinated solution for the country, and first of all for Rome, in order to hand it over to the Sovereign, who had decided to whom to entrust both the Government and the High Command. I foresaw that the person would be Marshal Badoglio at whose orders, I said to my subordinates, we would all place ourselves.

'An unexpected intervention of the Militia in the affair slightly spoilt things. The situation was however overcome by the recovery of the invalid.'

There is significantly no evidence from German sources of a Farinacci-Cavallero conspiracy at this stage. Such a political solution could only be considered to be the result of a German-planned coup backed by military intervention, and the assessment of the present crisis by the Germans was similar to that of everyone else.

* * *

Amid the rumours of plot and counter-plot, the most positive activity that could be attributed to Ciano were his moves, particularly in Army circles, to secure the fall of Cavallero. Towards the end of October to this end he had already sought personal contacts in Army circles, and within the Army General Staff. In his function as Foreign Minister dealing with the Balkans, he had been brought in contact with General Ambrosio as commander of the Italian army in Croatia until January 1942, when he became Chief of the Army Staff, and also with General Roatta, who succeeded the latter in the same command. At the same time Ciano came in touch with two young and ambitious Generals, Carboni and Castellano, and a small circle formed to promote the candidature of General Ambrosio as Cavallero's successor.

According to Castellano, he first met Ciano in the latter's office at the beginning of April 1942, and 'the meeting had been prepared by General Carboni'. The purpose of the meeting was to bring Ciano into direct touch with Ambrosio to whom Castellano was a kind of private military secretary. But Ambrosio was not anxious to make the first move. On Ciano's return in November from the Munich Conference, he saw Castellano again, and the question of Cavallero's successor was mentioned. Roatta, the predecessor of Ambrosio as Chief of the Army Staff, was considered as a candidate, but Mussolini was hostile and it was agreed to press for Ambrosio, though nothing was to be said to him.[23]

On November 12 General Puntoni noted, 'Cavallero has gone to Tripoli. His Majesty spoke to me of a conversation with the Prince of Piedmont who reported to him that, among other things, Cavallero was in a critical situation, as the leading representatives of the Army were against him.'[24] On November 22 the Duce appears to have told Ciano that even the King had spoken to him about replacing Cavallero, but Mussolini 'who is again optimistic these days, finds that it is not the moment to proceed to a change while we are engaged on two fronts'.[25]

Cavallero had never been popular in military circles, and the intrigues against him in the political world had their counterpart in the army: young ambitious generals like Carboni, who with his personal contacts with Ciano was a link between both worlds, and the general staff officers who resented his personal dictatorship and the planting of his own clan in the Supreme Command; Ambrosio, who although

Chief of the Army Staff, was never able to report alone either to the King or the Duce; and his old rival and enemy, Badoglio. All were awaiting him in the shadows.

Just as Cavallero had shown such reluctance to leave Rome in November to go to Africa, so he feared what might happen during his absence the following month at Hitler's headquarters. He saw the King in the afternoon of December 16 on the eve of his departure for East Prussia. The latter's comment to Puntoni was that he 'found the Chief of the General Staff more worried about his political position than about military operations'. But at least Cavallero was taking with him his main enemy, Count Ciano. It appears that the King received the Duce the same day, and repeated his impression. 'The Duce took the opportunity to attack fundamentally Cavallero, whose position appears shaken.'[26]

Ciano, who had been originally one of the latter's supporters in replacing Badoglio as Chief of the General Staff in December 1940, had long since turned against him. On returning from their joint mission to Germany in December 1942, Ciano had reported on his servility to the Germans and Mussolini had said, 'Henceforward Cavallero is finished.'[27]

Two days later, on December 24, Ciano wrote a letter to Carboni, in answer to the latter's impatient proposals for military changes, which had been prompted, it seems, by renewed cautious soundings from Ciano himself. There was speculation already on a possible successor to Cavallero, and Ciano seems to have been thinking of the Italian Commander in Russia, General Messe, as a candidate. The King seems to have been firmly against such an appointment, and Ciano thought again of Ambrosio. In his letter to Carboni, Ciano wrote obscurely 'As to the demand which you have in view (the removal of Cavallero) it is necessary to develop organic (*sic*) action. There are several difficulties and you can imagine from what quarters.'[28]

These moves were not unknown to the Court. Puntoni had noted in his diary as early as November 26: 'Ciano is said to be working in accord with a senior officer to whom he has assured his protection in the case of "great happenings".'

In the political world of Rome, consultation between Ciano and Grandi had its own special advantages. The latter was perhaps the leading 'elder statesman' of the régime in political intelligence and his knowledge of foreign affairs. The misfortunes of the Axis alliance were bringing Ciano remorselessly into line with Grandi's own appreciation of Italy's external position. There is no doubt that, particularly after the diplomatic conversations with the Germans at Munich in November and at Goerlitz in December, Ciano had few illusions as to the course of events in Africa and Russia, but 'without finding the answers'. He was now eagerly receptive to such persuasive counsel as Grandi was ready to offer. The latter was pressing for a preliminary and private sounding of the Western Allies, at least to discover on what terms, if any, they would talk. At the end of November he suggested that he himself should visit Spain in the hopes of getting in touch with the British Ambassador in Madrid, Sir Samuel Hoare, whom Grandi had known well in London. At the last minute the journey was postponed by Mussolini, who apparently told Ciano that Grandi's presence in Spain might displease 'our German Allies', and the trip was to be postponed 'until the end of the war'. Mussolini was prepared to attempt, as he did through Ciano at Goerlitz in December, to persuade Hitler to settle the Russian war and to concentrate on the Mediterranean Front and in the West against the British and Americans. He was not however ready to consider any reverse proposal of an approach to the Western Allies in order to seek a settlement whereby the united strength of the Axis could be concentrated in the East.

A discreet and preliminary approach to the Allies could henceforth only be made by individuals at their personal risk. The relations between Grandi and Ciano had never been intimate. Apart from the fact that they belonged to different political generations, Ciano had succeeded Suvich, Grandi's successor as Foreign Minister; he had been identified with the major decisions of Italian policy since 1936, intervention in Spain, the Axis Pact, Albania, the entry of Italy into the war, the attack on Greece, and all the consequences of the wartime alliance with Germany. It was true that each step taken had been the personal decision of the Duce, but whatever reserves or doubts Ciano might personally, and indiscreetly, express as to the course which events had taken, he was committed to them. If the Duce was abruptly to change course and seek a dramatic exit from the impasse created by his own now bankrupt gamble of June 1940 on triumphant and lightning military intervention, the obvious successor to Ciano as Foreign Minister to conduct such an operation would be Grandi. Whatever the latter might conceive in private cabal, such a possibility could be and was mooted in each moment of stress, possibly encouraged by Mussolini himself. Grandi might well have been both troubled and tempted by such a solution, and the thought of it inevitably increased his caution. It was both a threat and an alternative, and in either case commanded deep attention.

The lineaments of such a position had already been discussed in the first such political crisis in the winter of 1940, which was a precursor to the present one, and produced an outline pattern of it. In the diary of General Puntoni for December 6, 1940, there is the following entry:

'The radio has announced the dismissal of Badoglio and the appointment of Cavallero as Chief of the General Staff. Insistent rumours are circulating in the capital of changes in high quarters. The name of Grandi has come anew to the surface and His Majesty is favourably disposed. The liquidation of Ciano is forecast (to go as Ambassador to Berlin or as Minister of Italian Africa), and in his place Grandi as Foreign Minister. Such items are, however, hardly to be expected to be true, and it is not improbable that they have been put about deliberately by those who out of natural interest desire a radical change in the ministerial structure.'[29]

These rumours were revealing of the recurrent political climate. On January 2, 1941, Farinacci thought it necessary to write to Grandi in his usual brutal style: 'As you know, we are both at this moment the designated victims of public opinion. I am supposed to be working and plotting to set up a German government in Italy, and you, on the other hand, are working for a government favourable to all those currents which would willingly see the eclipse of Mussolini and many of us, including naturally Ciano. Your absence had aroused some criticism, as you were seen on the previous day in Rome by several people; no one believes in your illness.

'My dear Grandi, in your own interests I advise you to choose the first good occasion to come out of your reserve. You are too much on everybody's lips, and an anti-Fascism is deliberately exploiting your name. When Italy declared war on France and England, the news spread in Italy that Farinacci would replace Ciano at the Foreign Ministry. What did I do then? I went to the Duce, and asked him to send Ciano to Cremona, where I organized an impressive manifestation for him.' The warning was clear, and a repetition must be avoided.

There were also other reasons for closer association between Grandi and his friends and Ciano. He represented to them the main source of information and intelligence on the political and military conduct of the war, and, perhaps even more important, he could be the chief interpreter of the condition and moods of the Duce and the lightning shifts of his darting mind.

Ciano was also an ideally placed channel for conveying Grandi's analysis of the situation to the Sovereign. As Foreign Minister the former had constant access to the King, with whom his relations were at this time also closer. For instance, on November 19, the day of the massive Russian assault on the Stalingrad front, 'the Sovereign received Grandi and Ciano. Grandi stayed a few minutes with the King; Ciano, on the other hand, remained in conversation for more than an hour. The King told me that he found Ciano rather well au fait with the situation.'[30] According to the latter, the Sovereign 'wanted to be informed particularly about Spain, Switzerland, and Turkey. He spoke a little of what had happened and is happening in the Mediterranean, but he is particularly concerned with our lack of forces in Italy, and especially in Rome, where even the grenadiers of the Royal Guard have been withdrawn. He requested me to intervene with the Duce to recall troops to Italy from the Russian Front, advising me at the same time not to say that it was he who had spoken to me of this "so that one should not get the impression of secret manoeuvres". As always there is an anti-German touch in his words. He showed a perfunctory confidence in the development of the war, but questioned me closely on Washington and London, and advised me to hold carefully on to any thread which might be renewed "even if it is as thin as a spider's web".'[31]

The Germans were already disturbed by rumours that Ciano was seeking contacts with the Allies and there were vague reports of a secret understanding between him and the Crown Prince as to a political deal in Italy. On November 7, 1942, Admiral Canaris, the head of the German military Counter-Intelligence, circulated a report referring to conversations between American representatives and the Italian Minister and Military Attaché in Lisbon. It was stated that Ciano was 'completely in the picture'.[32] A German telegram from Madrid dated two days later referred to the Crown Prince and to Ciano as 'anti-German'.[33] The purported Lisbon negotiations were based on the evidence of the Portuguese police in a report on November 9 from the German Legation in Lisbon, and the whole affair was summarized in a Berlin telegram circulated to the interested diplomatic posts on December 3, stressing Ciano's active knowledge of these secret talks and adding that it was also intended that the Crown Prince should become King of Italy, in event of success.[34]

These reports were circulated as a routine to the German Ambassador in Rome, Mackensen, and his comments were consistently sceptical of such rumours. On December 4 he telegraphed to Berlin summarizing his impressions. He doubted whether there was any such 'anti-Fascist' circle in touch with the enemy through the Italian Legation in Lisbon. Such rumours had been rife, however, since the North African landings. In any case Ciano was the last person to initiate such feelers. 'It is possible that Count Ciano today, when he is in power, has behind him a group of Fascists . . . It is also a fact that he is by far the most unpopular man in the country. He may be unclear about the extent of his unpopularity, but he must be living on the moon if he has any illusions that he has behind him the mass of the population in whose eyes he is precisely the champion of the Axis. Count Ciano would, however, be clear that in thinking of a separate peace the German factor could not be ignored . . . The Fuehrer would take lightning counter-measures. Ciano was aware also of the size of the German forces in Italy, and was in a position to judge what it would mean if the Reich should suddenly withhold coal deliveries. A separate peace aimed at keeping the war away from the Italian mainland would automatically make it a theatre of war.'[35]

Ciano was ceaselessly chattering at the Golf Club and in the salons of Rome. Many of these conversations were reported to Mussolini. His son-in-law was not, however, the head of a planned conspiracy, but rather a symbol of defeatism and discontent, and the voluble spokesman of the anti-German sentiments of the upper middle class and the aristocracy.

Nor did Grandi and his friends constitute an active opposition group. The impressions of the German Embassy were given in a Rome telegram dated December 19. 'There are no definite plans of action behind the Fronde of Grandi. Both Grandi and Bottai, whose tendencies today are spoken of as pro-Bolshevik, are above all only seeking for an alibi later. Also the attitude of Federzoni cannot be considered otherwise. As yet there are no signs of any other plans of action.'[36]

The physical recovery of the Duce had put an end to the

Winter Crisis, but the weaknesses of the Fascist structure after twenty years of existence had been sharply and totally revealed. The future of the régime and of the Axis alliance, as Hitler had always said, depended alone on the personal survival of the Duce. The private murmurings of these months were the precursory signs of the final dissolution, which was to be prolonged until the following summer.

CHAPTER EIGHT

The Political Recovery of the Duce

'ONE RINGING of the bell, and they will all turn out down there to applaud me.'[1] Farinacci repeated this phrase of Mussolini's in mid-November after a conversation in the latter's study at Palazzo Venezia. Gathering together his physical strength, though by no means recovered, the Duce was preparing to ring the bell. On November 19 Bottai saw him. 'People want to know whether he, Mussolini, is in a position to confront the situation, and if he can do so, in what concrete terms.'[2] His first answer was to summon on November 21 the Council of Ministers. His reappearance was awaited tensely. As on previous such occasions the Minister of Public Works, Gorla, kept careful notes. 'When Mussolini entered the room, he looked like a dying man . . . who might faint at any minute. He had a number of sheets of paper in his hand containing . . . a report of the British General Staff describing the development of the Ethiopian campaign. Mussolini began by giving a summary in the following words: "A small army of not more than 40,000 men, belonging to all the Dominions of the Commonwealth, was able to deal with 100,000 Italians and 200,000 native troops . . . The report confirms brutally that the campaign was conducted with such rapidity because of the ingenious practice of the British Command in proposing to the commanders of the various Italian sectors a surrender with all honours of war . . . These facts show a deficiency in the race, which in twenty years I have been unable to change." According to Bottai the Duce added: 'I have invented a neologism, the *bracaioli*, for those who stand around holding up their trousers, and, when faced with any difficulty, babble that there is nothing to be done.'[3]

Gorla noticed that these asides provoked protestations from

certain ministers: 'It was the first occasion on which I have seen such a thing, and the confusion is such that one cannot hear what is being said, but the Prime Minister remains impassive as if the matter had nothing to do with him. He looks at certain papers, and then continues.'[4] Bottai's notes add a further picturesque touch. Presumably during the confused interruption in the course of Mussolini's extempore remarks, the latter had interjected: 'I am making a collection of all the rumours in current circulation. I have inaugurated a special file for them, or a folder as we civil servants say. And on the cover I have written "Documents of human stupidity".'[5]

A brief account followed, in the Duce's words, of the military position in North Africa. The Axis forces at El Alamein had been shattered by the enormous superiority of the enemy, particularly in the air and in artillery. But the retreat of Rommel had been 'a masterpiece' and Mussolini predicted that he would stand on the Agedabia-El Agheila line. There was also every hope of holding Tunisia.

As to the attitude of the Vichy government, 'I consider it to be definitely hostile. I have several times advised Hitler to keep his eyes open, but I fear that Germany still nourishes illusions in regard to France . . . which is now under the dictatorship of Laval, who enjoys the confidence of the Germans. I do not share this at all. I know the man, and cannot make myself see him in the guise of a dictator . . . I have constantly reminded Hitler to keep an eye on Toulon, and under the menace of his guns, as I have not the slightest confidence in the Admiral commanding the French Fleet. The future will prove me right.' Within six days Mussolini had this satisfaction. The Toulon squadron was ordered to scuttle itself.

As to the internal position in Italy, the food situation 'was better than last year. But the public spirit had been strongly affected in recent weeks by massive air bombardments to which the Northern cities had been subjected.' There followed a significant hint to those present. 'I confirm my faith in the Italian people, and regard them as too intelligent not to understand that it would be folly to think of a change of government at this moment . . . because, of whatever complexion, this could not alter our situation in regard to the British and Americans.'

The Duce finished speaking and abruptly left the room. There was a moment of silence among the ministers. 'As soon as they began to talk, the comments were sarcastic.'[6] But Mussolini had played his first card.

The first move by Mussolini to re-establish his personal authority took its physical toll. On November 26 the German Embassy reported that the Duce was in bed with a cold, and, as Bottai anxiously noted, 'he does not reveal his state of mind or a plan of any kind to anyone'. With his peculiar deceiving humour, Mussolini, speaking of oil deliveries, said to Ciano, who as usual repeated it, 'Next year, for reasons you are not unaware of, we shall need a good deal less.'[7]

It was an external stimulus and personal challenge which now jerked Mussolini again to his feet. On November 30 Churchill, speaking over the radio, announced to the world that the Axis would soon be driven right out of Africa. On the same day Gorla noted, 'Mussolini has not yet returned to work at Palazzo Venezia, but has however summoned the Chamber in plenary session.'[8] A resuscitated Duce must speak to the Italian nation and reply both to the taunts of the enemy, and to the murmurings within the gate. He must also tranquillize German doubts as to the internal situation in Italy. The same evening Goering arrived in Rome.

On December 2 Mussolini made his first public speech since his announcement from the balcony of Palazzo Venezia on Monday, June 10, 1940, of the entry of Italy into the war. On this occasion he chose the forum of the Chamber. 'After eighteen months of silence—we have now entered the thirtieth month of the war—I have the vague impression that a good part of the Italian people would like to hear my voice again.' He referred briefly and inadequately to the social benefits of twenty years of the régime only to launch into an equally cursory justification of the Russian campaign. He, Mussolini, had foreseen the need to prevent a Russian attack on Germany's back and the Eastern war had assured to the Axis vast and fertile territories, rich in raw materials. These remarks were clearly inspired by his talks with Goering.

On returning to the Palazzo Venezia he received the retiring Japanese Ambassador. The Duce was still in a state of exaltation from his speech. The only words of farewell which the diplomat could bring himself to utter were, 'You, Duce, you worn out, very worn out, too worn out.'[9] Mussolini terminated the interview with some abruptness.

That evening Mussolini telephoned to the leading Party

paper *Il Popolo d'Italia* for the latest news. The revival of this daily habit was a symbolic measure of his recovery. He had not done so for a year. He remarked to the editor, 'Tell me, does it seem to you as if I were already dead?'[10]

On December 19 the German Embassy in Rome forwarded a report to Berlin from their 'known confidant' on the Italian political scene following the Duce's speech to the Chamber. 'The first impression was very strong, but not profound.' The feeling in Palazzo Chigi was that 'a compromise peace with favourable conditions was no longer possible.' War would last at least until 1944. Belief in victory had much declined throughout the country in the last five or six weeks, although feeling in regard to counter-action in Tunisia and early successes there had been reassuring. The reaction to air bombing had been counteracted however by the news from Tunis. The importance of German anti-aircraft reinforcements was vital, but there was a growing fear of Allied victory. In educated circles scepticism was rife as to the intentions, volume, and extent of German help. The same was true in certain Party circles.

It seemed however as if the only initiative in Italian affairs still lay exclusively in the hands of Mussolini. In a less public manner, the Duce had been prodding the Party Secretary. The latter had been ordered to de-bureaucratize the Party, to reactivate the local organizations, to set aside for the moment the 'technical' activities, which were absorbing its more essential tasks, such as gathering the harvest, and to make a maximum effort 'in view of the reality of the hour'. Vidussoni, taking his cue, responded with a boy-scout enthusiasm, to defend 'the flag of honesty, which at this moment the Party must unfurl, alongside that, even higher, of faith . . . The Party cannot and must not, be a zone of influence. I allow myself to say it . . . The Party is yourself.'

Either the Party Secretary himself, or more probably the more schooled of his intimates, had sensed a contrary wind. 'I think that a broadening of the cadres of the national leaders, with the admission of members of the Old Guard, alongside the young of the new guard to which you confided the Party, would introduce a panoramic and more up-to-date vision of the Revolution, and would condense the Fascist generations in an indestructible union and continue their fusing.'

Vidussoni therefore himself proposed a reconstruction of the National Directorate, enlarging its membership to embrace the old guard and the young, the Federal Secretaries and the honorary members. 'The enlarged body will have more influence on the national leaders, more contact with the periphery; the Party will everywhere be spurring on the provincial gerarchs.'[11] Confronted with a resuscitated Duce, Vidussoni had received sage advice in the corridors, and the Young Guard was for the moment saved from dismissal.

This reconstruction of the Fascist Party Directorate was announced on December 19. It represented a limited move away from the younger generation, represented by Vidussoni, back to the Action Squad leaders of the March on Rome. The representative in Rome of the German Nationalist Socialist Party reported to Berlin on these changes in the following terms: 'From a point of view of personalities, what is important is the nomination of two new Vice-Secretaries, namely Carlo Scorza and the Militia General Tarabini. Both belong to the circle of Action Squads. Scorza is known as a journalist of the Fascist Party press. He is head of the press section of the Ministry of Popular Culture. Of the existing Vice-Secretaries have remained: Mario Farnesi, who counts as a coming man, and Ravasio. Of the remaining members of the Party Directorate, the appointment of the Federal Secretaries of the large cities threatened by air bombardment—Genoa, Milan, Turin, Palermo, Ferrara, and Leghorn—should be particularly emphasized. The Press has underlined these appointments as indicating that the Party has been summoned to special activity and immediate organizational action at threatened points on the Home Front. Also striking among the new nominations is the appearance of the older generation of Fascist fighters in contrast to the former tendency, since the appointment of Vidussoni, to place the younger generation in leading roles.'[12]

It remained for Mussolini, now strengthened and stimulated by the nervous effort of regaining an audience and a platform, to attempt to dominate and illumine by his oratory the crucial events of the past months. On January 3, he spoke, in his inimitable style, persuasive, caustic, and compelling, to the new Party Directorate.

'I chose the third of January as a date for the meeting of the new National Directorate for obvious reasons . . . The situation today has certain analogies with those of the second half of 1924. These analogies belong not to home affairs but to international. We are faced by an Aventine much more important than that of 1924, but containing the same elements and pursuing the same objects. In order to discover what we ought to do we must examine critically the development of recent events in order to draw the necessary conclusions. The first part of our present war shows the following characteristics. It took place in distant countries: in Ethiopia, in Africa (there were only three days' fighting on the Western Front), in Greece—always on the other side of the sea. The Italian people are accustomed to this war which is not too close, and have acquired the habit of indifference under these circumstances. They have come to the conclusion that war will always be far off, that it will be fought and settled in areas which are distant from metropolitan territory.

'All this changed after October 23, 1942, when the Supreme Command discussed the date on which the British would attack. I maintained that the attack would take place at the end of October, partly because the British would wish to benefit by the fact that this would spoil the celebrations of our Twentieth Anniversary . . . That in fact is what happened. In August 1942 the Italo-German offensive at El Alamein failed. Not because the soldiers failed to fight as splendidly as always. But we must remember that in war, victory is won or lost at sea rather than on land. We have lost a very large number of tankers laden with petrol and oil, both necessary fuels without which our motorized divisions cannot function . . . On October 23 the British took the initiative for the first time and obtained a success which they could never have had in the three preceding years. At the same time the terrorist ("scientific" according to Churchill) bombardment of our Italian cities began. This combination was planned so as to exert moral pressure on the Italian people at the time of the lack of success in the land war.

'But the date of November 8 is still more important. On November 8 there happened something which required no prophet but which any ordinary observer of human affairs could have foretold: North Africa was occupied by the North Americans. Only people deliberately wishing to deceive themselves could have expected any effective result from showing political favour to France. France hated us, hates us still and will do so until the end of time, hence all this policy of "petting" (as sailors call it) France is absolutely barren of results . . . This disembarkation of November 8 had certain psychological effects even upon many Italians . . . Events had made these somewhat feeble spirits lose their balance. It was thought impossible that the Anglo-Americans would not reach Ostia in a few days. Then the balance was restored because we replied to the Anglo-Saxon move. We occupied all France, Corsica and Tunisia. The occupation of France is important because at any rate in Metropolitan France misunderstandings have ceased. France no longer has its metropolitan territory; it has no colonial territory; it has no gold, it has no navy, army or air force; it has nothing. The French people does not even possess its own soul, and this is perhaps its most serious loss because sometimes this means the final decline of a people.

'How did it come about that the battle of El Alamein was decisive? Because the other arm of the pincers was lacking. The German troops should have poured down from the Caucasus. But this was not possible because anyone who has some knowledge of geography knows that the valleys there run parallel to the sea, one after the other, and we needed to get down to Batum. In the absence of this strategic manoeuvre it was clear that the battle was bound to end as it did.

'. . . Now we are facing the year 1943 which will be a year of fundamental importance in Italian history. It will be a year in which the régime must show its strength and the Italian people must pass a very serious test. There is no doubt that the international Aventine will bring its whole forces to bear upon Italy. This too could be foreseen. I have always regarded it as more important to occupy Egypt than to occupy England. If England were occupied, the problem would not be solved; but once the hinge of three continents constituted by Egypt had been occupied, and we had come down to the Indian Ocean, and had made contact with the Japanese, we should have broken the back of British Imperialism. This has not happened because each one holds ideas which derive from his historical situation. Ours has always been a Mediterranean one, the German a continental one . . . This has allowed us to take possession of huge areas rich in raw materials which we can use to prolong our resistance, but there is no doubt that at a certain moment we must throw our weight towards the West because the war will be decided in the West, in the Mediterranean.

'We are therefore privileged to foresee that an enemy attack will be directed particularly against Italy. Why? Because it is thought that Italy is the weaker of the two allies, but particularly because the enemy counts on a failure of our morale. For this reason it was thought that under enemy bombardment the people would at a certain moment show a desire for peace, any sort of peace, a separate peace. It is essential that everyone should be convinced, that every Fascist should be convinced, that this would be the most catastrophic solution and would dishonour us for centuries . . .

'I do not believe that they (the Allies) will try to open a land front against us. It is too late; we have already taken our measures. Therefore the enemy must seek a place where conditions are more favourable. I believe that it is probable that the Anglo-Saxon attack will take place in the Balkans.

'Hitherto we have seen the following situation: the great power of resistance in Germany. From time to time there have been rumours in Italy about German morale; they always start with a misunderstanding. Because there are no signs of enthusiasm in Germany, it is thought that the German people does not want victory. The German people from the highest to the lowest knows what is at stake because it is clear that the Anglo-Saxons would tomorrow impose on Germany those conditions which were imposed by the Treaty of Versailles; that is, Germany would be paralysed for generations . . . As regards the German anti-aircraft batteries which have been sent to Italy and which have already proved excellent, Fascists must be friendly to these men who have come to live with us. A certain excessive susceptibility is a weakness, a negative feature of the Italian character; Italians are unwilling to be helped by anyone. This is going too far.

'The Italian people now has the chance to show what it is made of. The problem is a serious one for us. We must ask ourselves whether twenty years of the Fascist régime have changed things only on the surface, leaving them much the same below. We shall see in the course of 1943. If you ask me "What is your opinion?" it is this: the Italian people will stand firm and astound the world . . . By the end of 1943, which will not be the last year of war but will be a decisive year during which we shall see whether the balance will fall, the Italian people will have surmounted every test.

'The Party must be the instrument through which our armed forces become steadily more politically minded. Propaganda must fit in with time and place. Then there is propaganda carried on by everyone belonging to the Party: in the family circle, in the local Party Headquarters, in the social organizations, in conversation . . . It is not necessary for the Fascists in Italy to number four millions. It is not even a bad thing, because it is impossible to govern a big country if you are shut up in an ivory tower. The important thing is that there should be a few hundred thousand well-informed, decided, ready, united Black Shirts, all absolutely dependable men, ideologically speaking. I believe that the Italian people has the qualities enabling it to resist, to hold firm and to conquer. At the end of 1943 we shall be able to say proudly that we have in fact realized our aims. At the present moment we have transformed the Italian people if not altogether, at least in part; this was the supreme task of our revolution . . . This year will decide whether the Italian people must resign itself to being a land of tourists, a large Switzerland . . . I look forward to these months with passionate interest and absolute certainty . . . These are the directives which I give on this third of January. In addition, every month a meeting of the entire Directorate, including the inspectors, will be held at Palazzo Venezia, and I will preside. Thus we will work together.'[13]

This speech, projecting the now receding image of the Duce of the triumphant days, alert and confident, taxed his physical and nervous resources. But the cycle of the Winter Crisis was closed.

CHAPTER NINE

'The Expulsion of the Discontented'

On January 11 Mussolini was due to make his weekly report to the King, but decided abruptly to break away from the atmosphere of Rome to his retreat at La Rocca delle Caminate in Romagna. He was still unable to throw off the effects of nervous strain with its accompanying internal disorders, and he was driven to yield to medical advice. He left in a special train accompanied by his daughter-in-law Gina, the widow of his son Bruno who had been killed in 1941 in an air crash; his medical attendant, Professor Pozzi; 'General' of the Militia, Ridolfi, a picturesque old gentleman who had been his fencing and riding master years before, and now at the age of seventy-four accompanied the Duce as a personal bodyguard; Professor Vigoler, who gave Mussolini daily lessons in German; and Irma, his private maid, the wife of the porter at Villa Torlonia. The Duce travelled uncomfortably, doubled up with stomach cramps, and conversing about his symptoms and politics with the doctor. On arrival at La Rocca, two specialists were called in. In simple language, their joint opinion was that their patient was suffering from acute gastritis due to nervous tension.[1]

'The Ministers and generals are trembling because usually the isolations of the Duce are a prelude to vast changes of the guard.' Whether this was or was not his purpose, the machinery of government came each time to a standstill. Now the routine royal audience had been cancelled, and the meeting of the Council of Ministers, due on January 16, postponed. In Rome there was a rash of speculation. On January 9 Marshal Caviglia wrote in his diary: 'I know from many directions that the Royal House sees a solution near, more near than one thinks. It seems that the King is studying what to do. He will probably leave the ministry as it is and put at the head of the government Federzoni, or Grandi in his capacity as President of the Chamber. It will be a caretaker government pending a normal solution through elections, but holding the balance between the pressures of various groups and of not un-numerous pretenders.' And later again, 'The situation seems to me insoluble by peaceful means, either internally, or vis-à-vis our enemies or our ally. The latter will want to have no say regarding such a government, and will probably support his own candidate—Farinacci.'

In spite of such unchained speculation and the physical absence of the Duce from Rome, his presence had returned to the centre of the political scene. Although Ciano had said that the departure of Mussolini could be explained by his ill-health, it was a reasonable suspicion that he had retired deliberately to his mountain and that his descent would be a signal for an unpredictable reshuffle. Meanwhile rumours were circulating 'of pending changes in the whole structure of the hierarchy'.[2]

On January 8 Ciano lunched with Bottai and Farinacci. 'They are exasperated. Bottai, speaking of the loss of Libya, said, "At bottom we have achieved another aim: in 1911 Mussolini declared, 'Let us get out of Libya.' He has kept his word—thirty years too late."'[3] This private meeting did not escape the notice of the Party Headquarters. On January 19 Buffarini, together with the Party Secretary Vidussoni, seems to have visited Mussolini at La Rocca to tell him of the activities of the Ciano group.[4] A minute was also sent to the Duce on the day of his departure for La Rocca. 'I have to inform you that on Friday last Farinacci invited to lunch in his Roman villa Ministers Ciano and Bottai, the Party Vice-Secretaries Scorza and Tarabini . . . I have, however, reason to think that no views of a political character were expressed . . .'[5] Nevertheless the Duce telephoned Ciano some days later to ask whether it were true that this luncheon had in fact taken place.[6]

Ciano's next move suggests more than a hint of active caballing. On January 16 he sought out the German Ambassador, in a long private conversation, ostensibly to give him news of the state of the Duce's health. He asked for his remarks to be treated in the strictest confidence. Ciano explained that he based his remarks on the assertion that 'certain rumours would certainly reach me as a result of the

Duce's recent journey to La Rocca delle Caminate, which had become known, and of the official announcement that the meeting of the Council of Ministers had been postponed *sine die*. These rumours would be full of the serious nature of the Duce's illness, and Ciano wished to place them in the right proportion.

'Foremost among his utterances—and twice repeated—was the sentence "The Duce is not very well". The pain in the intestines, which had ceased for a few days, had now come back, and the cause was unknown to the doctors . . . The first signs of discomfort had appeared in June, just before the Duce's trip to North Africa. On his return he had been treated by Professor Castellani for amoebic dysentery, which he had never had, and as a result valuable weeks had been lost. Professor Frugoni inclined to the view, which seemed plausible to Count Ciano, that the pain was in the first place of nervous origin. The Duce, as Ciano expressed it, was so constructed that he devoured all worries within himself, and even if he appeared outwardly calm he tore himself to pieces inwardly without being able to lighten the burden by talking. He had, for example, after the advance to El Alamein on the eve of the occupation of Egypt, believed a great victory to be near and, at the further development of events up to very recently, had suffered a heavy moral blow which, as usual with him, took the form of physical pain. In Ciano's view the surest remedy would be good news of decisive importance, which however could not be expected at the moment.

'The Duce's voice, from one telephone conversation which he had had with him, was strong and fresh, his interest in affairs and his delight in making decisions was lively and undiminished. Nevertheless his absence from Rome had already had a noticeably disturbing effect in certain sectors.

'What the retirement of the Duce, on whom everything rested and who was the very driving force of Italy, would mean, Ciano went on, visibly moved, I need not tell you. But we could with absolute certainty rely on the fact that if grounds for serious anxiety should arise, the Fuehrer was the very first person whom he would inform, for he would be fully conscious of the enormous extent of the consequences of a change for the worse in the Duce's condition . . . Even though in conclusion Count Ciano once again underlined the fact that, with X-rays and blood tests, and two frank medical opinions, the thought of a mortal illness was out of the question, nevertheless the emotion with which he spoke clearly showed that he was very worried.'[7]

How far Ciano's worries were of a political order is not clear. If he were actively grasping at the succession, his telephone conversation of the previous day with Mussolini might well have made him reflect. There is no evidence of a concrete private plot, but rather of a despairing and final diplomatic move as Foreign Minister aware of the familiar signs of a possible changing of the guard.

Details of disaster on the Russian front accumulated during those days in Rome, together with depressing evidence of the climate at German headquarters. On January 19 Bottai, who was in constant contact with Ciano, noted the content of certain news which the latter showed him in his office. 'Further reports on the German situation. The first of a military character . . . refers to the first break through on the Russian front, in which, through a German collapse on the flanks, our divisions have been overwhelmed. A real and proper rout with all the familiar details of such a collapse. The second, from our liaison officer at German headquarters, shows that henceforth everything is concentrated in Hitler's hands on whom the slightest initiative depends, even the most modest posting of units. The General Staff has no longer any voice in the matter, is forced to let things go and submit . . . Finally, of much greater importance, a report from our Minister in Bucharest who had been invited to talk with the younger Antonescu, President of the Council. The latter wanted Mussolini and Ciano to know that the internal Roumanian position was desperate and untenable to such a point as to require not military but political measures, and that is peace negotiations, which he thought possible, and at this moment of definite use, even to the Germans.'[8]

Since the beginning of December the Italian Minister in Bucharest, Baron Bova Scoppa, had been reporting on the increasingly nervous reactions in Roumanian political circles to the outcome of the Don battle. His personal relations with Mihai Antonescu were close, and as early as the autumn of 1941 the two men had discussed informally the idea of a 'Latin Axis' based on Italy, France, Spain, Portugal and Roumania, a bloc 'destined to contain German expansion and Slav impulses'.[9] There was no reaction in Rome to such ideas at the time. But by January 1943 the military, and therefore diplomatic, situation of the Axis was revolutionized. Both Italy and Roumania were closely linked in a catastrophe on the Russian front; the Western Powers were in North Africa, and their advance towards Italy and the Balkans was threatening. Marshal Antonescu had in his turn been summoned to Hitler's headquarters, from January 10–12, to discuss the complete reorganization and further reinforcement of the Roumanian armies in Russia. Three days later, on returning to Bucharest, the Roumanian President of the Council summoned the Italian Minister. The latter was so excited by this talk that he at once took the train to Rome, and on the journey drafted his report summarizing the conversation, and quoting extensively the words of Mihai Antonescu.[10]

The Roumanian leaders had found Hitler 'obsessed with the Russian question, and we had the clear impression of a man tortured by grave preoccupations. He spoke to us at length of his past, of his loneliness, of his revolution . . . He seemed to draw strength from the great memories of his past to neutralize the bitterness of the present hour. In his fixation on the Russian problem, he fails to take account of America and England . . . When Marshal Antonescu posed to him the problem that if one considers the Russian Front to be decisive, all forces must then be concentrated to occupy Moscow, Leningrad, and the line of the Volga, the Fuehrer answered that what counts is to hold out, to organize Russian industry and agriculture, and to neutralize the air offensive of the Anglo-Saxons.

'Faced with this nightmare conception of war in the East, which will attract all our resources in this direction, I felt that it was my duty to ask Ribbentrop if it were not opportune also to think of those gigantic problems of a moral political order comprised together under the name of Europe. Ribbentrop replied that his experience led him to believe that one could not discuss this problem "until Russia had been beaten". Europe *must* hold out—he specified—"and that is all". But in the meantime Europe is being shipwrecked, and without losing an ounce of my faith I must make it clear that our intuition is that the chaotic defence of the East at all costs and the absolute lack of comprehension in regard to all the political and above all moral problems in Europe will bring us to the abyss.

'Under these circumstances I think that one should assist the German leaders to clarify the situation. If the position in the East gets still worse, Hitler will send all his reserves to that Front, and then the state of affairs in the Mediterranean and the Balkans will deteriorate. My conviction is that England and America have no interest in letting the Russians into Europe and I have precise information to that effect. The Turkish Ambassador came specially to tell me that America and particularly England were pressing on into Europe in order to bring the war to an end, but that they wished at all costs to avoid the collapse of the European system in favour of Russia. I have received similar reports from Portugal. I have the impression that, as things are at the moment, Germany would be content to expand to the East at the expense of certain Russian territories without putting forward any other great claims.

'I base such an appreciation . . . also on the fact that the internal situation in Germany is very serious. We have noted a certain uneasiness in the High Command, a crisis of confidence. In general, a crisis in the endurance of public opinion, in the system; a crisis above all of manpower and strategic reserves. The German army is tired. The troops who have been through four or five campaigns are as if under the influence of drugs. I think therefore that the moment has come to do something by complete agreement among ourselves. Please tell Count Ciano that it is out of common interest that I justify informing him of this and that it is essential at this decisive moment for our future to make direct contacts. Germany is obsessed with her own problems, and will not see those of Europe . . . If Count Ciano thinks that such an action is not opportune, I shall for my part continue to remain loyal to my commitments . . . Do not damage Germany by indiscretions to Germans . . . If things get worse, Italy is our only point of support, and we must help each other on a mutual basis. Will Count Ciano let me know the Italian point of view through yourself, if it is impossible for him to see me?'

On January 10 Bova Scoppa delivered this document to Ciano at the Palazzo Chigi. The latter noted, 'I shall take the report to the Duce and shall make it the subject of conversation, which I have been planning for some time.'[11]

On the following day Ciano went to La Rocca to call on the Duce, who listened attentively. Ciano's first impressions were, as was often the case, optimistic. 'Naturally, he rejected Antonescu's offer, "The Danube is not the route we must follow." But he did not jump in the air when I said openly that, at a certain point, we too should try to make some direct contact.'

The next day, however, Mussolini's reaction had altered. He described Antonescu's language as tendentious and 'confirmed in even firmer terms than yesterday his decision to march with Germany to the end'.[12]

Ciano does not seem to have appreciated the import of the Duce's last remark as the rejection of the whole Ciano-Grandi political analysis.

For weeks past, Ciano had been in touch with Grandi and his circle of friends with a view to clarifying the political atmosphere. There was no question, and no possibility, of independent action in any form. The immediate issue, in their eyes, was to persuade Mussolini to raise again with Hitler the liquidation of the war in the East and to concentrate on an all-out effort in the Mediterranean, at the same time emphasizing the need to take cautious preliminary steps to reinsure against total disaster on the lines of Bova Scoppa's memorandum.

A few days later Ciano received similar impressions in a hand-written letter from his former chef de cabinet, Filippo Anfuso, now Italian Minister in Budapest. The possibility of forming a bloc of Axis satellites in the Balkans under Italian leadership in the hopes of pressing through a separate peace was the last pipe-dream of Ciano's diplomacy. Such elements of a coherent foreign policy as he had attempted to establish since the outbreak of war lay shattered in his hands. He had always been fertile in quick solutions, and always subject to sudden gusts of optimism in moments which called for cautious pessimism. And his success in any move depended in the last resort on being able to carry the Duce with him.

Having failed to move the Germans, at the December meeting in East Prussia, to consider a compromise peace with Russia, Ciano was equally unsuccessful in persuading Mussolini on his return either to intervene personally with Hitler in the same sense or to consider separate and drastic action. This feeling of personal defeat propelled Ciano into sterile cabals in the company, among others, of Bottai and Grandi. If Mussolini was not prepared to press to the utmost the German ally to negotiate with Russia, it was even more unlikely that he would listen to the similar vague proposals emanating from Bucharest or Budapest, which seemed to have so impressed Ciano and his friends. As Grandi told Bova Scoppa, the latter's report of January 19 was 'the most interesting and important diplomatic document which he had read recently. It was of capital value. Given the mentality of Mussolini, it is destined not to be followed up immediately, but it will be.'[13]

It was now clear that Ciano's credit as Foreign Minister had evaporated, and he was unable to carry the case for a negotiated peace or even secret feelers. It was equally certain that, especially since the December talks at Goerlitz, the Germans too had their reservations about him.

On January 21 the Duce had returned from La Rocca delle Caminate to Rome, refreshed and secretive. The following morning the King received him in audience, and found him 'to be positively cheerful'. He had hinted to the King at 'an imminent reconstruction of the administration'.[14] His 'political design' would soon be apparent, and Bottai's comment that 'people have the impression that there is no longer a central government' was to be corrected.[15]

Marshal Caviglia noted in his diary, 'Perhaps Mussolini will begin to feel the ground slipping under his feet; he cannot understand that his Party bosses, those most beholden to him, are falling away from him. They are all seeking to recreate for themselves a non-Mussolinian virginity.'[16] Precisely for such reasons, the Duce was contemplating an Italianate purge.

The Duce's intentions were apparently also strengthened by information from the Germans. They were aware of the activities of the Italian Foreign Minister and his friends, and not only from Italian sources. According to Mr Allen Dulles, who was at that time head of the American Office of Strategic Services in Switzerland, he learnt early in February 1943 from Gisevius, his main contact with underground resistance groups in Germany, that the German security services had broken one of the American codes in use between Berne and Washington. One of the deciphered messages gave a picture of 'the dissension in the Italian ranks and of the anti-German group which, even early in 1943, formed around Badoglio, Grandi, Ciano and others. According to Gisevius, this deciphered telegram had been laid on Hitler's desk and sent by him to Mussolini with his compliments. A few days later Ciano disappeared from his post as Foreign Minister and went to the Vatican. I was never able to discover whether this was coincidence or whether this cable was the cause.'

* * *

During the next days Mussolini gave active attention to public business. The Council of Ministers met on January 23. Each session usually coincided with ill tidings, and on this occasion with the news of the evacuation of Tripoli by the Axis, and further details of the disaster which had struck the Italian army in Russia.

The scene is described by Gorla, the Minister of Public Works. The formal agenda for the meeting was confined to the presentation of the budget by the Finance Minister, Thaon di Revel. 'This is one of the most important acts of government, but the atmosphere is poisoned.' All anxieties were focussed on events taking place in Russia and Africa. Having disposed of the agenda, Mussolini addressed his Ministers.

'While I am speaking to you, Tripoli is being evacuated. One must not however forget that our present objective is to preserve our available forces and as far as possible to concentrate them in Tunisia. For these reasons I agreed to abandon Tripolitania as proposed by the General Staff, despite the fact that I am perfectly aware of the immense repercussion which the news will have on the masses.'

Rommel had conducted 'a masterly retreat . . . Six Italian divisions and three German can be concentrated in Tunisia, representing the advance guards of the Libyan army, besides ninety thousand men already sent direct. These combined forces, and others as well, are needed there because, as all hope of breaking through to the East is lost, the objective of extending ourselves westwards may be realized in order to link up with Spanish Morocco, and to provoke the intervention of Spain on the side of the Axis . . .'

The Duce then turned to the Russian Front, where the dire implications of the Stalingrad disaster were now clear. 'I regard the situation of the German army as very serious. This negative view is not only induced by the loss of Stalingrad and the whole army of von Paulus, but above all because of the fact that the Russian Command has taken firmly in hand the conduct of operations and the Germans are not in a position to reverse the situation.' The Italian divisions in Russia had been obliged to hold too lengthy a front. The German units had given way on either flank under the Russian assault, and the Italian positions had been surrounded. The situation was 'fluid' and 'very serious', but not 'irreparable'.

The monologue terminated in an unprovoked and abrupt attack on the Vatican 'which is becoming the centre of all opposition to Fascism' and a 'revision of judgment' on Christianity itself. 'Islam has perhaps had an even greater influence.'

On this unexpected theme, Mussolini in his usual manner rose and left the room.[17] This outburst was the prelude to changes within the whole hierarchy of the Italian leadership.

It was no secret that Cavallero was marked down for removal. He had complained formally to the Duce on January 10 of Ciano's manoeuvres against him, and met with no satisfaction.[18] Ciano himself had pressed the final case against the Chief of the General Staff in his talk with Mussolini on January 20.[19]

The news of the loss of Tripoli, and Rommel's withdrawal towards the Mareth line provided the timing and the public pretext. The consequences of the disaster on the Eastern Front were as yet incalculable, but the early German reactions were to increase their control and penetration at staff level of the Italian armed forces on every front with a view to a totalitarian effort. The liaison officer of the Italian Foreign Office attached to the High Command reported to Ciano on January 25:

'The Italian Eighth Army in Russia has been practically destroyed in the recent fighting. One can, in general terms, reckon that fifty per cent of the troops can be saved, but material and supplies have for the most part been lost. On the German side, it has been proposed to our Command that the remaining elements should be sent back on the long route "eight hundred kilometres on foot" to be re-formed, while the remaining elements still able to fight should remain on the front under German command. The question will be discussed with the Germans. On our side, the so-called requests were rejected. On the part of the Duce, who has talked to Hitler about this, it has been pointed out that General Gariboldi was responsible to the Duce for his troops, that these had not been withdrawn from his command, and that the proposal to transport them to the rear can only be accepted if they go by train. I will follow up the question and report again. I have learned about it only personally and confidentially.'

Hitler was also planning to give orders to the German commander in South-Eastern Europe, General Loehr, to take over both Italian and German forces in the Balkans. And in Africa 'the authority of our Command is now very much restricted and has become an empty formula. The Germans plan a joint Italian-German staff for the African sector. The executive authority of Kesselring and the German commander in Tunis will in effect be complete, although formally staff organizations will be mixed.'[20]

On the same day, January 25, Mussolini was again received by the King, and launched another outburst against Cavallero, and in the early morning of January 31 the King learnt that the latter had been replaced by Ambrosio.

It seemed as if Ciano and his friends had scored a signal victory. The succession of Ambrosio to Cavallero was not unconnected with Ciano's ill-concealed soundings in military and political circles around the end of the year, and on the day of his appointment as Chief of the General Staff there is a note in Ciano's diary. 'In a conversation with me, Ambrosio confirms what we said the last time we met. He is an honest man who will act in the interests of his country rather than in his own.'

Mussolini's decision was characteristic. He could not bring himself to rebel against Hitler, and Cavallero would not do it for him. He could not accept responsibility for the military disaster in Africa, and the imminent collapse of the Russian front. Military defeat in Africa and Russia had now been conveniently erased by the dismissal of the Italian Chief of the General Staff. The Duce must be infallible in the eyes of the nation.

Apart from Ambrosio's divergent views from the Germans on strategy, his appointment, following the dismissal of Cavallero, must modify adversely the relations between the German and Italian General Staffs. Ciano was at pains to tell Prince Bismarck at breakfast at the Golf Club that 'the dismissal of Cavallero has no political background. It is a purely administrative measure.' And that 'Ambrosio is the best type of Italian officer'.[21] But Ciano, with all his facile arrogance, could hardly have thought that such statements would mollify the Germans, and in fact on February 3, after a conversation with the Duce, he recorded: 'Cavallero. His replacement has alarmed the Germans. He was their servant. Now they fear that with his going the whole system will be changed. I reassure Bismarck, but I think it would be well if the Duce wrote to Hitler on the matter.'[22]

On January 31, Ciano's private secretary, Marchese Lanza D'Ajeta, sent for Prince Bismarck in order to inform the German Embassy of Cavallero's dismissal, which was to be announced later in the day, and to give an explanation. Prince Bismarck reported the news to Berlin:

'The first rift in the relationship between the Duce and Cavallero had happened this summer when the Duce, on the advice of Cavallero, had gone to the Libyan front. A telegraphic code word had been agreed between them which Cavallero would send to the Duce when he judged that the moment had come for the Duce to go to Libya. Cavallero sent the code word twice. The Duce nevertheless waited, and only when Cavallero had telegraphed a third time did he go to Libya. The hoped-for military success was not forthcoming. From this time on the relationship deteriorated, and the Duce was very sensible of the fact that, during the retreat of the Italo-German forces in North Africa, Cavallero continually described the situation in too optimistic terms. Each time a new position was taken up, he represented to the Duce that it could be held against the British. Now that the whole Italian Empire has been lost, the Duce was compelled for political reasons to draw the consequences in the form of a change in the Supreme Commander. Apart from the personal attitude of the Duce towards Cavallero, the latter had always been unpopular in the Italian army in that he embodied the type of "political general" which had never existed in Italy. Cavallero's successor, General Ambrosio, had been chosen as the most senior among the Generals who came into consideration. He was a quiet, balanced military personality.'

Bismarck added his own comment: 'Cavallero's dismissal, from the German point of view, is very regrettable. Because of his energy, intelligence and gift for making quick decisions, co-operation with him was particularly smooth and characterized by the fact that he fell in willingly with the German requests and attempted to implement them with an energy unusual in conditions here . . .'[23]

General Ambrosio took up his duties as Chief of the Italian General Staff on January 31. He had been summoned unexpectedly by the Duce. 'My first reaction was this: Today I am sacked.' He declined the new appointment, but was told that 'in a Fascist régime, orders are obeyed. In any case, I shall share with you the grave responsibility of the post.' Mussolini then asked what he intended to do. Ambrosio's version of his reply was: 'Three things: firstly to bring back to the Mother Country the maximum number of divisions (Mussolini seemed to me to be vexed); secondly, to dig one's toes in with the Germans (Mussolini exclaimed "Fine"); thirdly, to lighten the High Command of all the superstructures which my predecessors had built on it.'[24]

According to Ambrosio, the Duce agreed with the last two points, but was against the first. He gave his reasons. It would be a blow to the prestige of the country abroad, would arouse German suspicions, and encourage the enemy.

The grand design of the Duce was not complete. On the afternoon of February 5, Mussolini sent for his son-in-law. The latter describes the scene in his diary. 'On entering his office, I notice that he is very embarrassed, and I grasp what he is trying to tell me. "What would you like to do at the moment?" he begins, and then adds in a low voice that he has changed the whole government. I understand the reasons, and do not intend to raise the least objection. Among the numerous solutions which he proposes to me . . . I choose the Embassy to the Holy See. It is a place of rest, which however holds many possibilities for the future. And more than ever, the future is in the hands of God.'[25]

The next day Mussolini had second thoughts and wished to suspend the nomination. But Ciano had already taken steps to ensure the agrément of the Vatican. The Duce accepted the fait accompli 'with indifference'. Acquarone, who seems to have been in touch with Ciano at this time, told him that the King did not know, when Ciano was received in audience on February 4, that he would be dismissed. 'The King is happy that I am going to the Vatican, and personally Acquarone is delighted.'[26]

At seven o'clock on February 5 the Italian radio announced the complete reconstruction of the Government. The Duce himself took over the Foreign Ministry with Bastianini as Undersecretary. Bottai was removed from the Ministry of Education. Grandi was dismissed as Minister of Justice, but retained the office of President of the Chamber. This disposed of the so-called 'Ciano circle'.

The key Ministry of the Interior was also retained nominally by Mussolini himself. He now appointed in place of Buffarini as Undersecretary, the Prefect of Naples, Umberto Albini. At the Finance Ministry Thaon di Revel handed over to Giacomo Acerbo. In order to strengthen the conduct of the war effort, a new Ministry of War Production was set up under the expert, who had already been struggling with such problems as a co-ordinating Undersecretary, General Favagrossa; and the prominent industrialist, Count Cini, was called in, with the greatest reluctance on his part, to infuse new energy and technical experience into the Ministry of Communications, whose work had come under such clumsy fire from Goering the previous December. The old 'squadrists' Ricci and Pavolini vanished from their respective ministries, the Party strongholds of Corporations and Popular Culture.

This changing of the guard in February 1943 was a supreme example of Mussolini's method and style of personal government. In two cases he had seen outgoing ministers on the day of the public announcement. Bastianini had reported to him in the morning on business regarding Dalmatia, where he was Italian Governor, and announced his departure for Zara that evening. 'Two hours later my private secretary rushed to my hotel to tell me that the Stefani agency [the official government news agency] was about to issue a communiqué on a complete change in the government. Mussolini was taking over the Ministry of Foreign Affairs with myself as Undersecretary. I regarded this news as incredible until seven o'clock that evening when the radio confirmed it.'[27]

The experience of Gorla, the Minister of Public Works, was more original.[28] He had been received by Mussolini on February 1, and instructed to go to Sicily to enquire into the whole situation on the defence works, but 'in reality to sound public opinion and present a realistic picture as he (Mussolini) needed a first-hand account from someone whom he could trust'.

On arrival in Naples, Gorla perceived that his special ministerial carriage was being unhooked from the train, and he was informed by the railwaymen that, as they had heard over the radio, he was no longer Minister. On his return to Rome he found a letter on his desk marked 'Urgent'. 'I have decided to modify the structure of the government, and would be glad if you would place your office at my disposal. Mussolini.'

When Gorla saw Mussolini three days later, the latter greeted him, 'standing and avoiding looking at me', and explained that there was nothing personal in the dismissal. 'It was a measure of a general character which I had to take and which had to include you.' And then, to Gorla's astonishment, Mussolini went on: 'You should know that, in a first moment you were exempt, but then I had to make the change to give the measure wider character.'

Naturally puzzled, the outgoing minister called on Grandi. 'The latter shook his head. The style still gives me offence. The measure has only one significance: in order to liquidate Ciano and Buffarini all the ministers were dismissed as a wrapping round the removal of the two elements which he wanted to get rid of.'

At Court, Puntoni also referred by implication to the changes in this way. 'The official news of the reconstruction of the government has been announced. Ciano and Buffarini have been liquidated.'[29]

The action of the Duce gave rise to myriad speculations, but Grandi's view was essentially correct. Ciano was not only the most unpopular figure in the public eye but had become the symbol of the war-weariness and murmuring, and his dismissal would be quickly understood by the Italian people as a sign that the Duce was again at the helm, and that the climate of defeatism would not be tolerated.

The removal of Buffarini was the subject of less reliable comment. As effective head of the Ministry of the Interior, he was responsible for studying closely the public mood, and for assembling and interpreting political intelligence and information on all aspects of the Home Front. It seems, however, that his dismissal was more a family affair, and due to feminine influence. He had long been deeply involved with Mussolini's mistress, Clara Petacci, and her family, whose financial transactions were a source of scandal in public and Party circles. 'The Petacci affair' had been the source of open comment at a meeting of the provincial secretaries of the Fascist Party in the previous October.

It was natural, therefore, that Buffarini should incur the virulent enmity both of Donna Rachele and Countess Ciano, and both had ample opportunity to bully the Duce during his recent retirement at La Rocca. As Dollmann put it: 'The chief danger zone of Buffarini's today is represented by the ladies of the House of Mussolini who are by no means taken in by him.'[30]

The removal of the other Ministers had been interpreted 'officially' as due to connections with Ciano 'and his friends'. It is clear however that the explanation of Grandi, and that given by the Duce to Gorla, expressed the real motive. The 'Changing of the Guard' was a domestic affair, and bore no relation to any impending alteration of policy at home or abroad. It was a tactic of distraction, of the liquidation of demoralizing rumours and their deliberate replacement by new ones, an exploitation of the Italian people's love of change, and a demonstration of the Duce's renewed vigour.

As Bottai put it: 'A whirl of comments and rumours; what has Mussolini been trying to do? Firstly, I think, to achieve exactly that, and to distract people from the great interrogation marks of the hour with these questionings in the gossip columns. And then, to show his power over men.'[31]

The German Ambassador learnt by chance of Ciano's dismissal. He had been asked to call on the latter at seven o'clock on the evening of February 5. 'He surprised me with the statement that he was no longer Foreign Minister. Today the Duce has carried out a changing of the guard in grand style which included practically all the members of the cabinet . . . Ciano let it be understood that he is taking up a senior post in Rome, although perhaps not at once.'[32]

On February 8 Mackensen had an interview with the Duce and the point was made by Mussolini himself, with the comment that 'he hoped that I had seen to it that the change of government had been regarded by us as a normal internal Italian event. It in no way affected our mutual relations. His completely unambiguous and unmistakable line of policy had nothing to do with the questions as to what men he worked with. For him there was only *one* way. He had destroyed all the bridges behind him. For the rest, many of the retiring ministers had borne the burden of office for five years or more, and were tired, and therefore had better be replaced with new elements. I answered that from the Fuehrer downwards there was no German who had the slightest doubt as to the Duce's clear line. I was nevertheless surprised by this changing of the guard. The Duce capped this remark, laughing, with the words, "That is once again just my way. You must gradually get to know it."'[33]

Hitler's characteristic comments on a previous occasion a year earlier are a revealing measure of the different character of the two men as displayed in such a situation.

'The changing of the guard at Rome is not good news, I think. In my view, too frequent changes of leading figures are a mistake. A responsible chief who knows that he probably will not have time to complete a job that he would like to embark on, generally sticks to routine. I don't understand why one should create such situations. In that way one merely aggravates one's troubles.

'The reason why I can carry the new responsibilities I am

undertaking is that gradually I have been freed from certain responsibilities, by colleagues to whom I have given the chance to reveal themselves, and who have succeeded in deserving my trust. It is possible that the Duce cannot find amongst his advisers the sort of collaboration he needs. For my part, I have had the luck to do so.'[34]

On February 10, the German Ambassador in Rome reported in greater detail and accuracy on the Italian cabinet changes.

The impact of bad news from the different theatres of war in recent months had undermined the Italian people's will to resist and their readiness to hold out. 'Even the loss of Tripoli had no longer produced in them the reaction for which the Duce had hoped. To these impressions were added reports which reached him from all parts of Italy of the increasing disorganization of the administration, of symptoms of inflation and a marked decline in willingness to work among the industrial workers in the North. Hand in hand with these phenomena there appeared particularly in the provinces an ever sharper criticism of the Italian government, which no longer stopped at the person of the Duce. The main complaints were directed at the lack of technical knowledge and the tight rigidity in management of those ministries which were the most important in the organization of the country—namely the Interior, Corporations, Foreign Trade and Communications. The old attacks against Count Ciano, about his way of life and his alleged financial deals also played a considerable rôle again. The attempt to tighten up the administration, which had made itself felt through the reconstruction of the Party Directorate, had not had any lasting effect owing to the impact of military events.'

The Duce was aware of this state of affairs, and he concluded that, 'in order to take the reins of government firmly in hand again and re-establish his own prestige, it was high time to show public opinion clearly that he still had power incontestably in his hands and that it only needed a stroke of the pen to replace his existing collaborators by others. It is also certain that there had recently been increasing attempts to try to influence the Duce, and make it clear to him that several of his ministers were conducting too independent a policy and seeking to create for themselves their own spheres of interest.

'A particular part in these interpretations seems to have been played by certain incautious statements made by Count

Ciano recently in the circle of his friends . . . Since the Duce did not want to dismiss only Count Ciano and two or three other ministers whom he felt he must get rid of on such grounds, he has changed the whole Cabinet with the exception of the ministers of Colonies and Agriculture.

'The decision to remove Count Ciano and the other ministers was reached by the Duce quite independently and suddenly without consulting other persons, and particularly not the newly appointed ministers. Only Count Ciano and Pavolini were informed direct of his decision—and that on the afternoon of February 5 . . . and immediately afterwards the publication of an official announcement was arranged so that the retiring ministers first learnt of their dismissal, and those newly appointed of their nomination, through this public statement—in the case, for instance, of the Minister of Education, Bottai, through the radio, and others the next day in the papers.

'The change of ministers appears from the reports reaching me to be a measure taken by the Duce to eliminate the serious crisis of confidence in which the government found itself and which threatened to direct itself against the Duce himself, by placing in the control of technical specialists those ministries which had hitherto been predominantly in the hands of Party politicians. And Count Ciano, who for a long time had been a burden to the Duce from the point of view of popular confidence, was recalled from the front of the political stage.

'It is not surprising that in Rome political circles this change of practically every Italian minister in circumstances of, for here, surprising suddenness has given rise to a series of false rumours, particularly in connection with the appointment of Count Ciano to the Italian Embassy to the Vatican. The entire Cabinet change, so runs one rumour, "is only a put-up job in which Count Ciano is nominated Italian Ambassador to the Vatican in order to be more easily in a position to establish links with our opponents". In the case of this rumour it is a question of a malicious invention of those circles who, intentionally or out of stupidity, want to throw doubt on the Axis policy of the Duce . . .

'In deciding to accept the Vatican Embassy, it may have weighed with Count Ciano that he wanted to stay in Rome in order not to lose his connections with Italian internal politics. But I think it false to assume that in making this choice he had the prior intention to conduct from this post his own foreign policy. In the circle of his personal and political friends there are certainly many who are of the opinion that he is the man to renew these relations at a given moment, and in these circles a certain satisfaction will reign that he has taken the post at the Vatican, which can offer to him as to no one else such possibilities. Only the future will show whether Count Ciano is prepared to play such a rôle or not.'[35]

Mussolini seemed to have succeeded in his purpose. By dismissing Ciano, and covering this move by eliminating almost the whole administration, he had given the impression that politically the new team of technicians would give increased efficiency to an invigorated Italian war effort as a loyal Axis ally, and remove any suspicion of a diplomatic weakening in Italian policy. At the same time the replacement of the pro-German Cavallero by Ambrosio, as Chief of the General Staff, was neatly obscured in its possible military significance by this dramatic realization of a general 'Changing of the Guard'.

BOOK II

CHAPTER ONE

The Military Scene

THE STATE of the Italian Armed Forces was seldom brought under co-ordinated and detailed review. The initiative of summoning any formal meeting of Chiefs of Staff and their advisers lay with Mussolini as Minister of the three Armed Services and as Commander-in-Chief. Such a meeting had, for example, been held on October 1, 1942. Routine arrangements were confined to the frequent contacts of the Duce with Marshal Cavallero as Chief of the General Staff, when the former was in sufficiently good health, or with Cavallero, Kesselring, and Rintelen as the immediate situation required. Mussolini had little direct relationship with the Chiefs of the three Armed Services, and indeed Cavallero strove to prevent any such contacts being established. Ambrosio appears to have seen the Duce alone on only one occasion during his time as Chief of the Army Staff. There was, therefore, no regular use of any machinery of high-level consultation on military, or on political, affairs in the system of Fascist administration. Mussolini was, however, prepared, with an effort, to listen to the technical problems raised by his professional advisers. Matters of grand strategy would be discussed as always with Kesselring, and usually in the presence of the Chief of the General Staff only, and subsequently in correspondence with Hitler. This was strictly in accordance with the facts of the situation; the Italian war effort was totally dependent on the Reich for essential war material, equipment, and military backing on the major fronts. The myth of a 'parallel' Italian war had disappeared in Greece in 1940, and with the arrival of Rommel in North Africa the following year.

* * *

The order of battle of the Italian army was approximate in the sense that the state of efficiency and equipment of each division was seldom, if ever, analysed or discussed outside the routine committees of the War Office.

After the North African landings, Rintelen had sent the following statement to Berlin, dated November 18, 1942.[1] The number of Italian divisions was listed as follows:

France, Corsica, Tunis	9
Italy and the Islands	26 (12 Coastal Defence)
Balkans and Dodecanese	33
Russia	10
Libya	12
	90

The precise state of these divisions in January 1943 was not discussed in detail at the Palazzo Venezia meeting.

The Italian Army production programme for 1943 had been drawn up in September 1942, and did feature in a document presented at this conference, which was in effect a progress report. 'The programme drawn up in September 1942 for 1943 envisages the bringing up to efficiency of thirty operational divisions of a standard type . . . tank production at maximum capacity, supplies for the above-mentioned thirty divisions.

'It should be noted that the 1943 programme is not related to the real requirements which the army needs to adapt itself to up-to-date fighting, but is a much reduced programme, geared to the amount of raw materials at our disposal, and the capacity of our industry. The programme also takes into account the scale of production which it is effectively possible to achieve in 1943, and which in certain sectors is noticeably inferior to our minimum requirements (for example, anti-aircraft ammunition, tanks).

'The Ministry of War Production has allocated up to one hundred per cent supplies of ferrous metals, tin and zinc. It has not been able to satisfy entirely the requirements for copper, aluminium, antimony and lead.

'The beneficial effects of these quotas will not be felt for at least 6–7 months. In general, production should improve as from July/August, 1943.

'Between September 1942 and today, the general situation has changed considerably. Requirements which were not then of major importance have now become pre-eminent, such as all the provisions needed for the defence of the Mother Country, which is now directly threatened, and those arising out of the Russian situation.

'The entire tank production for the next four months is commissioned for the reconstruction of the Second Army Corps in Russia with a small margin available for North Africa and Russia.

'Tank units do not exist in Italy. There are only two semimobile groups, of which one is destined for Sardinia and the other is at the disposal of the General Staff.

'Taking into account production as planned for 1943, it should be possible to satisfy totally the requirements of coastal defence, except for artillery, which can be only met by half.'[2]

These basic data set the frame within which General Ambrosio was now called on to plan, as Chief of the General Staff, the future conduct of the war by Italy.

His view of Italy's military prospects was more sober than that of Cavallero, and less liable to be swayed by gusts of German optimism. The North African front might be held for two or three months, depending on the extent of German supplies and reinforcements, and the maintaining of the sea route to the North African ports. The battle in Tunisia must be prolonged primarily in order to prepare the defence of Italy and the offshore islands against invasion, and detailed and coherent requests for German military aid for this purpose must be formulated.

Ambrosio had little confidence in a German military recovery on the Eastern Front, and had obstinately opposed the Italian commitment in Russia. He had failed to prevent the dispatch of three Alpine divisions there in the late summer of 1942, but now hoped to be able to liquidate the whole adventure and to persuade the Duce, after the Don battle and the Stalingrad disaster, to withdraw the remnants of the Italian Expeditionary Corps.

As to the Italian deployment through the Balkans, Greece, and the Aegean islands, Ambrosio was prepared, if supported, to bring back for the defence of the Italian peninsula the bulk of the thirty divisions which were scattered throughout the area, and which represented half the effective strength of the whole Italian army. His experience of antipartisan warfare in Yugoslavia had convinced him of the futility of the Italian military occupation in those regions, and he regarded the defence of the Balkans against an Allied threat of invasion as a secondary danger compared with an all-out assault on Metropolitan Italy, which was his basic concern. The fate of the continued Italian participation in the war turned on successful resistance to such a menace.

After the cabinet reconstruction which followed Ambrosio's appointment, the Duce charged Kesselring on February 13, 'to tell the Fuehrer and Marshal Goering that the recent changes in the structure of the ministry in no way modify the goal which Italy has fixed'.[3] But the Germans were bound to interpret the removal of Cavallero as a stiffening by the Italians against German supremacy in the conduct of the war. When on February 7 Mussolini referred to German disquiet in a conversation with Ambrosio, the latter had commented laconically, 'The answer to that: it is normal.'[4]

General Rintelen, as Chief German Liaison Officer with the Italian Command, was the best informed and most responsible witness. 'Ambrosio saw himself faced with a difficult situation. The Royal House and the Officer Corps required of him greater independence in regard to the Germans. The Duce too was tired of this tutelage. On the other hand, his own machine was breaking down and one had to accept and request further German help and support.'[5] In Rintelen's view, relations between the two High Commands would from now on be increasingly strained.

During the days following his nomination as Chief of the General Staff, Ambrosio paid and received a round of official calls, thus gathering wider impressions of Italy's war effort in general.

On February 4, he held a meeting with the head of the Navy, Admiral Riccardi, to review the state of the Fleet. There could be no question of offensive action. 'Operations are thus imposed by the movements of the enemy. The means at our disposal are such that we are not able to organize counter-action against all those enemy movements which have been signalled.'

Ambrosio's main concern was the reinforcement of Tunisia. Italian naval resources were glumly reviewed: twenty destroyers, thirty motor torpedo boats, thirty submarines, and six heavy cruisers which were immobilized by lack of fuel and, above all, of escorts. Eight light cruisers were under repair. The essential task confronting the Navy was to transport ten thousand German troops to Tunis by the end of February, and thirty-six thousand more in due course. Admiral Riccardi reckoned that this operation alone would take four months. Italy was totally dependent on Germany for fuel oil. The naval consumption was 65–80,000 tons a month, of which 42–44,000 had been received through Roumania and Germany. The oil had to be brought by rail to Fiume and shipped in tankers along the Italian coast to avoid burdening the railways.[6]

In a talk on February 18 with the new Minister of Communications, Count Cini, on the transport situation, Ambrosio was told that, 'if we continue with the present organization, within six months we shall be in a major crisis'.[7]

A discussion with General Favagrossa, the Minister of War Production, revealed a similar picture. That such a department was only given a ministerial head in February 1943, after three years of war, was a measure of the lack of coordination of the Italian war effort.

The Duce, however, was seldom impressed by logistics. In his excitement at the prospects of developing the bridgehead in Tunisia as a base for a westward advance, he was ready to liquidate the Libyan adventure. Everything would be concentrated on a new grand operation to the West to remove the disagreeable memories of the failure to sweep eastwards to Egypt in the previous year. Enthusiasm for novelty was a constant characteristic of the Duce, and at most times his optimism was shared by Kesselring.

On February 5, at a meeting with the Duce and Ambrosio, Kesselring had reported that the German commander in Tunis, General von Arnim, talked of the need 'to initiate as soon as possible an offensive towards the West', that is, into Algeria towards Morocco and thought that one could start in about two weeks.*

The Duce pointed out that the situation of the Anglo-Americans was not of the best: he read out in this connection a telegram from Lisbon and commented on it. In discussing enemy intentions regarding a landing attempt in the Aegean, and eventually in Italy, he expressed doubts.

The Germans were even thinking of considering the political situation in French North Africa with a view to seeking support in French and Arab circles for an eventual Axis occupation of French North Africa, and at this meeting Mus-

* There were two German armies in Tunisia: that of Rommel and the Fifth Armoured Group under von Arnim. The latter had been in North Africa since the previous December, and was to take over the whole German command from Rommel on March 8.

solini, for once cautious, agreed to allow the Germans to deal directly with the French and the Arabs without referring to the Italian government.[8]

It was this brief mirage of 'a race to Casablanca', as logistically unreal as Rommel's ill-fated dash for Egypt of the previous summer, to which Hitler referred in talking to Rommel on March 10. This mood was not shared by the latter. On February 12, Ambrosio noted in his diary, 'Duce approves of withdrawal of Afrika Corps.'[9] Such a step also removed an obstinate critic of the new 'combined operations' to be directed from Tunisia to the West. As Rommel was under the nominal command of the Italian General Staff, he was dismissed by Mussolini. There was no prior written exchange of views with Hitler.

On January 26 the last gesture of Cavallero as Chief of the Italian General Staff had been to telegraph Rommel that, for health reasons, the latter would be relieved of his command when the Axis forces reached the Mareth line. He would be replaced by General Messe who had been the commander of the Italian Expeditionary Corps in Russia. By mid-February, the last German rearguards withdrew on to the Mareth line. The retreat from Alamein to Tunisia was over. Mussolini wrote to Hitler on February 11, 'Field Marshal Erwin Rommel has laid down the Command of the Italo-German Armoured Corps. The events of the war in North Africa after spring 1941 will always be linked with his name and actions as Commander; later developments have not detracted from the importance of his repeated brilliant successes there. He always knew how to win the unbounded trust and lively affection of the troops under him; officers and men, Italians and Germans alike, admired in him the brave, just and wise Commander. The Italian forces in Africa were genuinely sorry to see him go. Field Marshal Rommel therefore also deserves credit for having done much to strengthen the bonds of comradeship between the fighting forces of our two countries.'[10]

Hitler did not reply.

Rommel was to conduct one final attack against the Americans at Kasserine, and then, on February 23, to his astonishment, he was appointed commander of a new unified Army Group 'Afrika'. This was a move by Hitler without consulting his Italian ally to support in public the reputation of one of his most popular and able generals, while rejecting in private the latter's earlier appeals for the total evacuation of North

Africa. 'For the Army Group to remain longer in Africa was now plain suicide.'[11]

At the end of February, Rommel produced his final report on the situation in Tunisia, after consulting his Army Commanders. He concluded, 'In view of the gravity of the situation, I request that an early decision be reached on the plan for the future long-term conduct of the campaign in Tunisia. We can expect the enemy's offensive to open with the next full moon.'[12]

The whole issue of joint command and future strategy in North Africa was urgently in need of review at the summit.

Ambrosio's first study of the war situation is contained in two minutes to the Duce dated February 17 and 21.

The Germans must shorten their front in the East, and organize during the thaw. Defensive operations would be more rewarding this year than offensive, 'for lack of adequate forces'. Nothing was to be gained by the conquest of space. The occupation of the Caucasus and the industrial zones of Russia was problematical, and not decisive. 'The Russians have organized their industries and oil-wells beyond the Urals. If the Germans rest on the defensive, this is to the advantage of the Mediterranean Front.

'In the Mediterranean, too, the initiative in operations cannot for the moment be wrested from the enemy.' Tunisia must be held as long as possible. 'If Tunisia goes, the enemy will attempt landings on the coast of Europe . . . This cannot happen before May or June. We have therefore two to three months to build up in Tunisia.

'The Germans must act during this period; decide to grant Italian requests for material to put the defence of their coasts and those of Greece in order; and facilitate as soon as possible the disengagement of Italian divisions operating in Croatia, permitting their withdrawal to the coast to a line enabling them to hold the key points there. These troops in the Balkan peninsula must then be set up as a strategic reserve. Mobile forces should be sent to Greece giving added flexibility, and also to watch the approaches to Salonica.

'Finally, the Italian air forces in the Mediterranean must be built up to resist enemy action adequately, and the number of Axis submarines in the Mediterranean increased. Above all, this is the moment in which the ally must give up fighting a war of his own, and understand that for his own salvation it is equally important to stand fast on the Dnieper as in

Sicily or the Peloponnese. In conclusion, the Germans must change their operational objectives and must come to our aid, *otherwise we shall not be obliged to follow them in their erroneous conduct of the war.'*

In the second memorandum to the Duce on February 21, Ambrosio elaborated in more detail this personal assessment of the war. 'There is no sign of a blunting of Russian effort. The Germans have to fight bitterly to contain enemy offensives . . . Germany is making a major effort to reconstitute her units. This will enable her to dominate the position in the East in the spring. But the troops which she will be enabled to put into the field in the summer "represent her last reserve". They must be used economically to face not only Russian attacks but sooner or later the Anglo-American Second Front.

'There are no decisive strategic objectives in the East. If the Germans attempt a reconquest of the industrial regions of the Don and the oil area of the Caucasus, they will only be back in the same position as in October 1942. Such a struggle would use up their last resources. They would not have the effectives to continue the fight in 1944.

'Committed as she is to a current offensive in the East, Germany cannot, for lack of reserves, meet simultaneously an attack in force by the Anglo-Americans, which will develop at the same time at a point as yet unknown on the European coastline, without seriously compromising the Eastern Front.

'The coasts which are most threatened are the Italian and the Balkan peninsula, to which should be added the shores of Provence . . . As a first priority one should consider an attack on the coast of Southern France, an attack which could be supported by another co-ordinated one against the North Sea coast of France. This operation could also be considered separately from the conquest of Tunisia and will develop independently of the operations in Africa. It might however involve Sardinia and Corsica. It is therefore considered dangerous to withdraw troops beyond a certain limit from France, which although provided with an effective coastal defence in the North, is not equally protected in the South . . .

'The threat to the Italian and Balkan shores . . . is further away in time, because, without the conquest of Tunis, the enemy is not in a position to mount an operation in grand style. The essential point therefore is to hold on to Bizerta as long as possible. The Italian High Command will make every effort, but . . . this is the moment to consider the position in the event of the loss of Tunisia. Should this happen, our islands, the Italian peninsula, and the Balkan coastline, are directly threatened.

'Our assessment is that Sardinia [Corsica] and Sicily are equally exposed because, if the occupation of the first is the necessary premise on the enemy side for an occupation of the peninsula, the possession of the third gives him freedom of transit from the Central to the Eastern Mediterranean and thus the possibility of action in the Balkan peninsula.

'As to an attack against the Balkans, we think that the lack of suitable ports on the Western coastline, the impenetrable nature of the hinterland, and the great distance from the principal objective—the Roumanian oilfields—could lead the enemy to act against Salonica with a view to occupying Crete and the Archipelago.

'However, since it is dangerous in war to attribute to the enemy only the most logical solution, which is often not adopted by them, we must be ready to meet all eventualities and to take into account the necessary defence measures, which are: to bring up to strength the coastal defences (of Italy); and the creation of an adequate striking force to be moved at an opportune moment.

'We cannot carry out either on our own. In this context, as we are not entering into detail as to what we require, *it suffices to state that it is absolutely necessary for us to withdraw our forces from less important fronts* (*Croatia*), *to increase the garrisons of the islands, to build up a reserve in the mother country, to bring up to strength* the Western and Eastern Alpine frontiers. In addition we cannot contribute to a strategic reserve in the Balkan peninsula.

'To complete the general picture: the Italian Supreme Command has little confidence in the support, even indirect, which Japan will be able to give the war in Europe. She will not attack Russia, and even if she did, the exhausting spaces of Siberia would form in themselves the best and most efficient Russian defence. She will not attack India because she lacks the means to get involved in such a distant and vast operation without having first eliminated the enemy in the Indian Ocean. Her action will, in the nature of things, be limited to striking at the Anglo-American fleet in her own waters, an action which however cannot bring us any effective or timely help.

'In summary: the enemy whom Germany has so far sought

to destroy, in a magnificent effort, is not beaten to the ground; in the East, we cannot see the possibility of decisive offensive action, but only the probability of holding up the Russians in a series of defensive battles which will however take a long time; the creation of a Second Front in Europe is a grave and imminent danger. If one thinks in terms of manoeuvring on inner lines from the Russian front to the French or to the Italian Peninsula, one may run the risk of not arriving in time or sufficient strength. This danger should be faced with resolute decision and timely advance planning, which must be worked out between the two Supreme Commands.

'The operational plan must be a unified one, and must take our forces and those of the Allies into account globally on the basis that, as he tightens the circle round Europe, the enemy will involve both ourselves and the Germans increasingly in the same common danger.

'The conduct of the war must in the first instance be defensive in order to recuperate our strength, must wear down the enemy and cause his plans to fail, must be able to take the counter-offensive at any moment when a favourable opportunity arises, and, in any case, when the process of attrition will place us in favourable moral and material conditions.'[13]

These two memoranda contained the essence of Ambrosio's military thought as crystallized since his appointment, and as a basis for staff talks with the Germans, now so long overdue.

For the Italians it was of urgent importance to get agreement to their demands for reinforcements and supplies for the Mediterranean theatre. The Duce had already said to Kesselring, who had been summoned to Berlin by Goering on February 13, that he was awaiting the Reichsmarshal in Italy at an early date, and briefly sketching the problem, he added: 'As for the Mediterranean front, there will be need of submarines, planes and artillery rather than tanks. The British have most up-to-date artillery whereas ours is very antiquated. Besides, numerous submarines are required for the struggle against the enemy fleet, and aircraft to protect our convoys.'[14]

But, presumably on Hitler's direct instructions, Goering's visit was to be preceded by that of Ribbentrop. The technicalities of Mediterranean strategy, as always with the Fuehrer, were secondary to those considerations on the general balance of the conduct of the war which Ribbentrop was to present to the Duce.

At five o'clock on the evening of February 23, Bastianini

called on Ambrosio to announce Ribbentrop's visit. The Italian Chief of Staff noted that Bastianini 'assumes that the general situation of the war will be discussed. He is told that the Italian point of view is: defensive on the Eastern Front and predominant importance of the Mediterranean theatre.'

CHAPTER TWO

The Diplomatic Front

BASTIANINI had learnt of his appointment to the Foreign Ministry over the Italian radio on the evening of February 5. He had been out of touch with the conduct of Foreign Affairs since his return from London in June 1940 where he had succeeded Grandi as Ambassador. His present preoccupations were understandable. He locked himself in his hotel room in Rome for two days before taking over formally from Ciano, and only on the morning of February 10 did he call on the Duce at Palazzo Venezia.

In seeking a reason for his appointment, Bastianini might well have assumed that his previous experience at the Foreign Ministry as Under-Secretary from 1936–40, and briefly as Ambassador in London, which had led him to doubt the wisdom of the whole policy of alignment with the Axis, was now in some way relevant. He was swiftly corrected in this impression. At the first official interview with Mussolini he asked whether the latter wished that he 'should examine thoroughly the situation of Italy both in regard to the ally and the enemy, take into account every factor, and determine whether, how, and for what length of time those forces which we know and would dispose of, would permit us to continue to fight this war, which I, as you well know, deprecated without avoiding my duty of participating in it'.

Mussolini replied in substance: 'It seems to me that you are making a mistake; my intentions are not those which you imagine. We are at war. I am the Foreign Minister. You have specific duties to carry out, but the direction of foreign affairs is in my hands, and my conception is very simple; when one is at war, one stays with the ally until the end.'[1]

On February 13 the Duce left Rome for La Rocca, where

he stayed for the next eleven days with a recurring bout of ill-health, and during this lull, the new Under-Secretary sought to brief himself on the diplomatic and military situation.

There seems to have been an immediate change of tone in the functioning of the Italian Foreign Ministry. There were regular meetings of the heads of departments, and frequent consultations with the retired veteran diplomats of the pre-Fascist school, in particular the former Secretary-General of Palazzo Chigi, Salvatore Contarini, who had continued to guide Italian foreign policy in the years after 1922, but had not set foot in the building since his retirement.[2] Here were the elements of a team to advise on and to formulate planning of a more professional kind, which had been lacking in recent years.

The diplomatic scene as surveyed from Rome was set and circumscribed by the passing of the strategic initiative in the conduct of the war on all fronts throughout Europe to the enemy. A drastic review must be made by both Axis powers, not only of their future strategy on each war front, but also of their failure hitherto to face the political consequences in Axis-occupied Europe, among both the neutrals and the satellite allies, of the disasters of Alamein, the 'Torch' landings, Stalingrad, and finally the loss of all Italian Africa.

On January 27, at Casablanca, the Western Allies had broadcast their communiqué on Unconditional Surrender. The implications of this fateful statement also needed careful analysis in Berlin and Rome, and heightened the need for some counter measure of political warfare and propaganda by the Axis powers to revive declining morale within the European fortress, now threatened directly for the first time by invasion.

The precarious Axis foothold in Tunisia represented the frontline of Europe. It could only be held by massive support from Germany, and at the expense of the Russian Front. If it fell, the Allies could strike in a number of directions from African bases at the southern shores of Europe, on a front stretching from Spain to Turkey, with each area involving delicate issues of diplomacy. The shadow of war now hung over the neutral capitals, involving the Allies and the Axis in grim and relentless underground competition in preserving or infringing the neutrality of these states.

The Allied landings in North Africa had in particular raised the problem of Spain, and on both sides the risks of bringing about Spanish intervention in the conflict were under active and cautious review.

So long as Tunisia could be held, it was unlikely that the Italian mainland or the Balkans would be immediately threatened, but advance precautions must be taken. With the lack of any German strategic reserve of divisions on the continent, in view of the total commitment on the Russian Front, and the need to lock up considerable forces in the West against the threat of a future Second Front based on the British Isles, an error in calculation as to the direction of an Allied assault on Southern Europe would be irreparable.

The Allied declaration on Unconditional Surrender was followed at the end of January by the visit of the British Prime Minister, Mr Winston Churchill, to the Turkish President at Adana. This could be interpreted as a move by the Western Allies to bring Turkey into the war as a first step towards the invasion of the Balkans, which would vitally affect the whole German conduct of the war in the East. A wrong analysis of the Adana Conference could have a disastrous effect on Axis planning.

The repercussions of this Turkish visit of the British Prime Minister were first felt in the capitals of Southern Europe, and together with the shadow of Stalingrad added to the series of threatening and unresolved menaces to be faced by the German and Italian leaders.

The most pressing of these issues were those concerned with the future relations of the two Axis powers with the two leading neutrals, Spain and Turkey, each placed in key strategic positions at each end of the Mediterranean, the possession of either or both of which could tip the whole balance of the war.

German policy towards Spain at the turn of the year was confused and contradictory, and as usual conducted without any close consultation with Rome.

There was alarm at the apparent success of recent Allied political manoeuvres in Madrid, and an exaggerated fear of Anglo-American military intervention in the Peninsula. Ribbentrop's personal agent in Madrid reported on January 20, 1943 that the official Allied policy of supporting Spanish neutrality was proving successful. Its visible result was the maintenance of British control over Gibraltar. The next step would however be to set foot in Spain. 'If there is no decisive change in the general war situation, the Anglo-Saxons will attempt to jump into the Spanish no-man's land, which they have prepared politically. All Red Spanish circles are well organized and determined not to let slip the opportunity offered. A second Civil War . . . would face Germany with the choice either of supporting Nationalist Spain with military help or reckoning with a front on the Pyrenees. In some Spanish circles it is thought that such an event could give the signal for a general revolt in the whole of Europe against the Axis.

'Franco's policy, which he will not alter unless he is obliged to do so, is the attempt of the Church to find a way out in Europe and bring about in an impoverished and unbelieving continent a Roman and reactionary peace. This policy could make Spain a battlefield and face Germany with new complications in the Mediterranean.' German military aid to Spain would be a condition of improvement in German-Spanish relations.[3]

The long standing operation for the occupation of Gibraltar was subject to routine review by the German General Staff. Its implementation would inevitably mean drawing on troops from France, and it was unlikely that such a move would be made unless Spain were directly threatened by an Allied assault and gave guarantees that she would resist. In Franco's letter to Hitler of January 19 no such clear assurances were stated.[4]

On January 24 Franco slyly pointed out to the German Ambassador: 'The war has lasted much longer than one had originally thought. He must also say that his information as to the state of opinion in Italy begins to give him anxiety.'[5]

The Allied declaration at Casablanca on Unconditional Surrender at the end of January seems to have encouraged Franco for a moment to consider adopting the rôle of mediator between the belligerents. But having resisted German pressure to take up a clear position, he must also avoid a similar situation in relation to the Allies. The basic attitude and interests of the latter in Spain were identical with those of the Axis. The Iberian peninsula was a no-man's land or a battlefield. Both parties shunned the prospects of another Balkan commitment, and both sought guarantees of a defined and aggressive neutrality on the part of Spain, short of which neither party would commit itself to economic and military aid.

Franco could not resist exploiting this situation by seeking supplies and equipment on both sides, neither being able to afford an absolute refusal; and by repeating the menaces and conditions of each party to the other.

By exploiting American hints that they might have to act in Spanish Morocco, Franco forced a secret agreement out of the Germans on February 9 whereby, on the basis of war deliveries by Germany, Spain would agree to oppose an Allied move into Spain or Spanish Morocco.[6] This treaty was not disclosed to the Italians, and precisely at this moment Franco turned to Rome to seek Italian backing for further military aid on the basis of the same American pressure.

On February 13 at a meeting with Kesselring, the Duce charged him 'to point out to the Fuehrer that a new element is maturing in the political situation. America is trying to force Spain to take up a decisive attitude and disagreeable facts might emerge in Morocco.' The Duce had received a letter from Franco in which the latter revealed his preoccupation at the situation and considered that American assurances towards him were formal rather than substantial. 'In any event, the Caudillo, in anticipation of a new development, is completing the efficiency of his armed forces. The Duce asserts that he has replied to the Caudillo welcoming his intentions, but pointing out that an intervention by Spain in the conflict must only take place if she is completely prepared.'[7]

If Mussolini could persuade Hitler to concentrate attention on a combined Mediterranean strategy, then the possible contribution of Spain to future Axis planning must be defined, and in the event of a German and Italian westward counter-offensive being launched in North Africa, her benevolent co-operation must be sought.

The German and Italian strategic approaches to eventual Spanish intervention were distinct. Hitler conceived of the operation primarily, and in any event reluctantly, as an advance into the Peninsula from the Pyrenees to Gibraltar. Whereas Mussolini saw it as a counter 'Torch'—a race for Casablanca from Tunisia to take the American positions in Morocco in the rear, and from Spanish African bases to launch an assault on Gibraltar. From the immediate military point of view neither plan was practical in operational terms.

In August 1942, Hitler had told the Turkish Ambassador in Berlin, that he 'regarded Turkey as the southern protective flank of Germany. The Reich had no kind of territorial interests which could bring her into conflict with Turkey, and economically relations were developing wonderfully.'[8]

Turkish copper and chrome were as vital to the German war effort as Spanish iron ore, manganese and quicksilver, and a threat of the loss of either source was a standing preoccupation of German policy.

As Hitler stressed, 'Stalin's intentions were now clearer . . . the Bolshevisation of the Balkans.' Germany could not accept this owing to her important economic interest in the region. 'This was the reason why Germany had helped Spain against the Bolsheviks . . . and equally an attempt by Russia to seize the Balkans and the Straits would be unbearable for Germany for economic reasons.'[9]

The basic assumption of both German and Italian policy towards Turkey was that the latter would seek at all costs to preserve her resources in order to face a possible Russian threat to the Straits and the Balkans, and at the same time would seize every opportunity to check by any means such a Soviet advance.

The Allied landings in North Africa in early November 1942, however, revolutionized the strategic position, and concentrated immediate attention on future Anglo-American plans equally in the Eastern and in the Western Mediterranean.

For some time past, the Allies had been discreetly building up supply dumps and improving communications in Turkey. They might attempt to go one stage further, and bring persuasive pressure to bear on the Turkish authorities for the leasing of air bases as a first step towards a Balkan campaign.

On November 20, that skilful veteran politician, von Papen, the German Ambassador in Ankara, sent to Berlin a 'report on the political attitude of Turkey after the North African landings'.

He was optimistic. 'There is now as earlier no reason for Turkey to take part in this war preventively on one side or the other . . . In the end we shall win the game in Turkey if our military position in the spring enables us to bring quick and effective help to Turkey if need arises. In this connection the potential of the unweakened Bulgarian army is of vital importance, if we can strengthen it with motorised and air units.'[10]

The situation of Bulgaria in regard to the general frame of the war had until now received little marked attention on the Axis side. Her role as a signatory of the Tripartite Pact in 1941 had been limited by tacit understandings; she would not be asked, as a Slav power, to break off formal relations with the Soviet Union; she would continue in her military occupation of Southern Serbia, undertaken after the Yugoslav campaign of 1941, and play her part in the plans of 'pacification' in that region and on the borders of Albania; her frontier disputes with Greece in Macedonia and Thrace would be shelved pending a peace settlement. In the event of major Allied landings in the Balkans, her potential military support must be mobilized and her relations with Turkey clarified. The latter might join the Western Allies, or, as Papen had hinted, take part in a long-term defensive operation in the Balkans, both against the Anglo-Americans and eventually the Russians.

Towards the end of December 1942, in conversation with the Italian governor of Albania, Mussolini had said that 'he reckoned that in 1943 the enemy would open an early Balkan front. In this connection special importance would be laid on Bulgaria at whose territorial expense the other side, according to reports here, had already given assurances to Greece. Just as in North Africa, the enemy would attempt, under the motto of liberating the oppressed Greeks through the arrival of the Americans, to cover their activities under a mantle of idealism. It appeared from a reliable source that a strong Greek division had been raised in Syria for this purpose.

'In regard to Bulgaria, one could not ask her to take part in the war against Soviet Russia, but all the more therefore to take over the defence against Anglo-American attempts at landings in the Balkans. It was therefore necessary to handle Bulgaria carefully and he instructed the Governor of Albania, in regard to Albanian-Bulgarian frontier questions, to meet Bulgaria half way.

'The position of Bulgaria in such circumstances needed study, and her War Minister was summoned to meet Hitler in early January. These talks are of particular value in throwing a revealing light on the Fuehrer's appreciation of the potential Allied threat to the whole Balkan region.

'The Bulgars had hitherto been on the fringe of the war, and had made few requests to the Germans for military supplies. But now they were disturbed by reports from Turkey of the building with British help of railways, airfields, and stores dumps. The Turkish army might move against Bulgaria. The situation in Turkey was the same in several ways as that of Bulgaria when the German army in Bulgaria planned (in

1940–1) a camouflaged march into Greece and Yugoslavia. In Iran and Iraq there was a concentration of seventy thousand Americans (*sic*). *And, in addition, Salonica had for a long time played a rôle in the strategic plans of Churchill.*'[11]

Hitler, like the Bulgars, was equally drawn to the historical pattern of British strategy in the First World War, and the shadow of the Dardanelles and the Macedonian campaign lay heavily across his thinking. It was inconceivable to him that Churchill could not be obsessed by the desire to prove in 1943 the validity of his grand strategy of 1915, of a decisive assault against enemy occupied Europe from the South-East. This was the central fear of the Fuehrer, which now coloured his planning against the Western Allies, often in defiance of the appreciations of his military experts.

In the immediate situation, the Bulgarian War Minister told Hitler that if pressed the Turks would agree to the passage of Anglo-American troops. In such an event the Bulgarian army must take the offensive and occupy Thrace. Serbia and Croatia could be cleaned up and pacified in due course. The Greek government must be distrusted. 'In the daytime they were for the Axis and at night they were for the enemy.'

Hitler was less alarmed at the threat of imminent action by Turkey. 'He thought that the most dangerous area in the Balkan region was the Peloponnese, particularly as up till then it had not been possible to pacify the hinterland.' British and American troops would only land on Turkish soil if the Turkish army actively collaborated. Nevertheless Bulgaria must have a strong army both for the present and for the future, for Bulgaria was also likely to have the future task of maintaining order in the Balkans. He had, therefore, given orders for the delivery of weapons urgently to the Bulgarian army. In the worst case Germany would take over the common defence of the area and command of the sixteen Bulgarian divisions. German units would be sent to help. As soon as the German troops could be released from other fronts they would be sent to the Balkans. They would not, in the first instance, be sent to Bulgaria; he was thinking much more of Serbia, particularly the area of Nish as well as that of Salonica. A plan of attack in the direction of Istanbul must be worked out between the two General Staffs.[12]

In the staff talks with the Bulgarian delegation, which followed the next day, they were informed of the intended action in the whole of former Yugoslav territory. This would be carried out in close co-operation with the Italians and would have the intention of moving against the rebel movements with energy. The German commander South East (General Loehr) would, in the event of the Balkans becoming a theatre of war, take command of all forces including the Bulgarians. It was not intended to send German troops to Bulgaria at this stage. Sufficient reserves lay in Germany and France; but in the event of invasion, a forward concentration area around Nish would be organized.

The Bulgarian view was that the attitude of Turkey would change either in the spring or summer, and it was clearly in their own interest to stress the point. Hitler admitted that one must be prepared for such an eventuality, but for the moment 'the German Army Staff did not think in terms of an Allied landing in Salonica, which was made impossible by the fortified position of Crete'.[13]

But the visit of Churchill to Adana at the end of the month might the prelude to the Allied invasion of the Balkans which so preoccupied Hitler. He was, in a sense, fighting a personal war with the British Prime Minister. It was vital to penetrate his thinking, and these Anglo-Turkish talks provided the occasion to probe British intentions.

On February 2 Papen reported on his first conversations with Numan Menemjoglu the Turkish Foreign Minister. The latter was a specialist in neutrality. According to him, 'the British had expressed themselves content with the present Turkish attitude, and emphasised that Turkey should strengthen this policy and be armed for all eventualities in the post-war period. No demand of any kind was made with regard to direct or indirect support to the Russians. There was naturally no question of transit through Turkey. But Numan had found it necessary to establish that Turkey in all and every circumstance stood by the treaty of Montreux in regard to the Straits, and would admit no infringement, and that if Allied aircraft in the future flew over the area one would not be satisfied with protests, but would open fire.'

Churchill was convinced that Stalin had no aims which meant 'endangering' Europe, and such Turkish fears were groundless. But as Numan told the German Ambassador, on this point Churchill could in no way convince Turkey.

Churchill had also said 'that Germany must finally be liquidated. He regarded Italy with special hatred and wished to destroy her. General Alexander's view was that one need not reckon any further with the Italians and that Tunis could only be held for a limited period . . . When asked about his conception of post-war Europe, Churchill only expressed vague views. One wanted a political community of interest between several stateless federations, which could form a balance against Russia; the Nordic bloc, the Central European (the Baltic states, Poland, Czechoslovakia, Hungary), and the Balkan bloc. When Numan replied that behind such a concept lay no real power to hinder the planned march of Bolshevism into Europe, Churchill answered that the increasing strength of the Allies in aircraft would enable them to bring the necessary support to any point. Numan remarked that he considered this view completely erroneous, and in general the Turkish attitude to the future organisation of Europe was the farthest apart from that of Churchill.

'From the Turkish point of view the conference had been very welcome. Numan was convinced that the integrity of Turkey would not be violated by the Allies and that they needed rather a strong Turkey for all eventualities against Russia. And he discerned a real mistrust of Russia.'

The purported summary of Churchill's remarks, as conveyed to the Germans, was not only deliberately coloured by Turkish thinking, but is a falsification of the record.*

Papen summarized his immediate impressions as follows: 'The programme of Casablanca to bring the remaining neutrals into the war has failed. My conviction is confirmed that Turkey will not move from her strict neutrality even in the event of a deterioration in the position of the Axis, and this has valuable implications for us in our concentration of forces.'[14]

On February 3 Papen reported further on conversations which took place at a farewell lunch for the retiring head of the Italian mission. 'One must assume that the very probable decisions taken at Casablanca include operations against the Dodecanese, Crete, and the Aegean islands, and that it must have been important for Churchill to learn the attitude of Turkey to such an operation and whether they would lend moderate assistance.' No territorial aims had been suggested by the Allies. Possibly after an Aegean operation 'an attack on

* See the account of the Adana Conference based on the British official records in W. S. Churchill's *The Second World War,* Vol. 4, pp. 623 *et seq.*

Greece is planned and possibly through the Adriatic against the Balkans. This would anyway mean more effective aid to the Russians.'[15]

Ribbentrop was not convinced by Papen's buoyant interpretation of the Adana talks, nor did he accept Numan's version of Churchill's attitude. On February 3 he telegraphed to Ankara sourly that no one had really informed Papen about the meeting. 'It is hardly possible that they only talked about the weather.

'As for Turkey's misgivings about Russia, I take it that Churchill pointed out that at the first opportunity, for example after the opening up of the Mediterranean to British shipping, a new front would be established in the Balkans. The presence of British and American troops in the Balkans in connection with later plans for a Danube Federation would also be for Turkey a guarantee against a Russian thrust into the Balkans and towards the Straits.'

As Ribbentrop conveyed to Papen, the Italian Minister in Ankara had also reported that Numan had told foreign diplomats at the same luncheon that Turkish neutrality had not been changed by the Adana Conference 'in any essential point', and had added that, 'in the event of the Axis position in Tunisia deteriorating (and it appeared that in the long run the Axis could offer no resistance), one must reflect that a serious position would arise for Turkey and that then the pressure of the British and Americans would later take a more concrete and, for Turkey, unavoidable form.'

Ribbentrop's message concluded, 'I express my view that Turkey has preserved her neutrality in these talks. Her further attitude however depends exclusively on the future development of military operations. The military position in the Ukraine and at Tunis is here decisive. If in the foreseeable future we have successes in both these theatres of war, Turkey will harden her policy of neutrality. If, on the other hand, the Axis suffers a serious set-back, either in Southern Russia or in Africa, Turkey will join the British and Americans and try through the presence of their troops to resist the threatening demands of the Russians for bases in the Straits. I cannot share your view that Turkey is not to be drawn out of her policy of neutrality even in the event of a deterioration of the Axis position.'[16]

In his reply to Ribbentrop, Papen emphasized that 'in judging the future course of Turkey one must start from the fact that the destruction of the Central European Powers and the realization of English plans for Europe would for Turkey be the most disagreeable outcome of the war. She would find herself hemmed in for centuries between a strong Britain in the Mediterranean and a Russia capable of unlimited action.' This basic assumption of German policy towards Turkey in Papen's view remained unassailable.

On February 6, Ribbentrop replied in milder terms to Papen that he too accepted this concept, and that everything must be done to strengthen Turkish neutrality. It was, after all, Germany's strength which ultimately secured Turkey against Russia.[17]

In summarizing the results of Numan's talks with neutral diplomats in Ankara, Papen noted the reasons why Churchill apparently wanted a strong Turkey. Firstly, 'the failure of Germany to obtain Russian oil means that she must try again and will march through Turkey to Iraq. The Turkish leaders disagreed. And secondly 'if the war goes against Germany, there will be chaos in the Balkans. Turkey must be in a military position to meet this problem and to play a leading part in a future Balkan Federation.'

To Numan's question: 'if, as a consequence of an Allied victory, the Soviets behave in Roumania and Bulgaria in the same manner as in the Baltic states . . . what would be the standpoint of England? Churchill was said to have answered that he was determined not to accept this.'[18]

In completing his comments, Papen added on February 8, 'I have the impression that the assault on Italy, anticipated next summer or autumn, has caused considerable anxiety there, and one would probably prefer to see the theatre of war transferred to Turkey and the Balkans. But this must not divert us from a correct assessment of Turkey's position. From a subsequent assembling of reports on Adana . . . it clearly stands out that a basic theme of discussion was the future order in the Balkans.'[19]

The present position of the Axis in South Eastern Europe had been affected by the military disaster on the Don in January 1943, which provoked a grim reappraisal among the European allies of the Axis of the whole conduct of the war by Hitler. Apart from major repercussions on relations with Italy, historically and diplomatically the senior partner, the whole future military and diplomatic position of the satellite powers was threatened, and in particular Roumania and

Hungary, whose forces had suffered so heavily in the recent battle.

The rôle of Roumania in German war strategy was vital. Geographically she dominated the whole southern front against Russia, and her defection would throw open the historic land route of invasion of the Huns and the Mongols into the heart of Central Europe, and would inexorably and swiftly lead to a collapse of the whole German military position in the East. Her military contribution to the Eastern campaign was superior to that of any other ally, including Italy. Her losses in the Don battle alone amounted to 9,000 officers and 270,000 men killed, apart from wounded and missing.

Without the oil deliveries, German industry and her armed forces would be unable to function, and with the fading prospect of seizing the Russian oilfields of the Caucasus, Germany would remain totally dependent on the Ploesti region, north of Bucharest. Italy too, in a lesser degree, relied on grain from Roumania, and the Italian Navy was totally at the mercy of arbitrary and fitful German allocations of Roumanian petroleum. A collapse or defection of Roumania would therefore inevitably cripple the German war effort.

Confronted with a deep crisis of confidence throughout the whole of German-controlled Europe, Hitler and his advisers were forced into a series of personal interventions in an attempt to restore the position.

It was logical to begin with the Roumanians, and the 'Conducator' and his Foreign Minister, Mihai Antonescu, were summoned on January 10/11 to Berchtesgaden. They were at once exposed to an excessive blast of optimism from Hitler. 'The whole region controlled by Germany and her Allies was highly organized for the struggle. There was only one open wound, and it was at the moment the triangle Rostov, Stalingrad and the Caucasus, the most important area. This main fact must be kept in mind, and in judging the situation one must not be influenced by minor phases of the great drama but, particularly in time of crisis, keep an iron nerve. If Germany were to lose two-thirds of her iron ore, 80–85 per cent of her oil, as well as her entire supplies of coke, and in addition had to overcome a shortage of rubber, the situation would be desperate. This was precisely the position in which Russia found herself today. It was true that she possessed iron ore in the Urals, but she did not have the coke necessary to produce steel from this ore.'[20]

Such a picture, in contradiction with the evidence, could hardly impress the listeners, although Marshal Antonescu, like the Duce, was convinced that there was no solution to the war other than triumphant victory in the East.

This view was not shared by either Foreign Minister, Mihai Antonescu or Ciano, and before leaving for Germany the former sent to Ciano through the Italian Minister in Bucharest his preliminary reflections on possible diplomatic action with a view to a compromise peace with the West or at least on the lines of mutual political consultation within the Axis camp.

At this January meeting in Berchtesgaden, Marshal Antonescu in conversation with Ribbentrop, brought up again an earlier proposal made by Mihai Antonescu for 'holding periodic diplomatic meetings of the Axis powers and their Allies. *Faites vivre l'Europe par l'activité des réunions.*'

Ribbentrop replied that this would be difficult while the war was on. It would raise problems in regard to France, Holland and other such countries, in which during the course of the war severe measures must still be enforced. One might examine the plan when the situation in the East improved. Mihai Antonescu repeated his proposal with the words that 'one must gather Europe together like a family'.[21]

This was precisely what Ribbentrop feared: a coalition within the frame of the Tripartite system of pacts, escaping German leadership, and eventually passing over to the Western Allies. If Italy were to give a lead to such a manoeuvre, the maintenance of the whole German position in Europe would be decisively threatened.

It was to avoid such a complete disaster that the whole diplomatic action of Germany in the early months of 1943 was directed. Before reviewing and sounding the reactions of the smaller partners, it was essential to study in careful detail the repercussions in Italy of the defeat of the Axis armies both in Russia and Africa, and also the significance of the recent government changes in Rome in regard to Italy's attitude to the future conduct of the war.

With such intentions in mind, Ribbentrop decided to make a personal visit to Italy.

CHAPTER THREE

Ribbentrop in Rome

ON FEBRUARY 19 Ribbentrop sent instructions to Mackensen in Rome to ask the Duce to receive him 'to discuss certain important current questions'. Two days later, the Italian Ambassador in Berlin, Alfieri, called on the German Foreign Minister to probe the reasons for his trip.

Alfieri, 'who was apparently carrying out instructions, emphasized that the change of ministers in Italy meant nothing more than a confirmation of the Duce's habit of changing his collaborators from time to time. The most that one could say was that the will to work with Germany had therefore been even more strongly emphasized by the Duce.'

Ribbentrop's reply was abrupt and curious. He said that 'he regretted that Count Ciano was no longer his colleague and invited Alfieri to come with him on his visit to Italy where he would talk to the Duce, to Ciano and to Bastianini'. The German Foreign Minister clearly wished to form his own view of recent events in Rome. This talk with the Italian Ambassador was a rehearsal of the forthcoming conference, and set an informal agenda for Alfieri to report to his government.

Ribbentrop would bring a letter from the Fuehrer outlining the latter's views on the general situation 'as well as explanations on specific political and military questions'. A military expert, 'in the shape of a General', would accompany Ribbentrop. These questions related 'to the Mediterranean area, and in particular the problem of Croatia'.

Hitler's 'grave anxiety' to which Ribbentrop now referred, stemmed from his chiromantic belief that the ultimate Allied assault would come from the South-East—the personal revenge of Churchill for the Dardanelles failure in 1915.

Through the Balkans lay the direct route of attack against the whole southern flank of the German armies on the Russian front, where the Stalingrad disaster had—for the moment—endangered the life work of the Fuehrer, the crusade against Bolshevism. The challenge was total, and the call to supreme sacrifice must be totalitarian. Final victory in the East was the goal, and the nightmare of a rendezvous of the three enemy belligerents on the Balkan road must be exorcised. Hence the intensity of Hitler's neurotic obsession with these regions, and of his pressure on the Italian ally on this subject. The priority of the Russian front must be absolute. The myth of a destructive and mounting U-boat war must compensate for the absence of German offensive action in Western or Southern Europe, and would furnish the main deterrent against the Allied invasion in these areas.

It was the task of Ribbentrop to translate this obsessive vision into diplomatic terms. Hitler had outlined in Wagnerian language a massive and highly personal survey of the war in the form of a letter to Mussolini. This revealing document was to constitute Ribbentrop's instructions for the forthcoming Rome meeting, which was to be a preliminary to a summit conference between the two Axis leaders as soon as the Russian situation permitted. As Hitler wrote, 'You can hardly imagine how much I want to spend a couple of days personally with you . . . For what I am to Germany, Duce, you are to Italy; and what we both are to Europe, posterity alone can judge . . . No episode on any front can be considered and examined in isolation, since they are all part of a vast chain of events which will ultimately be decisive for the destiny of the whole of Europe, decisive in the sense of those great historical upheavals like the Persian and Punic wars, the invasions of the Huns, the expansion of Islam and the Mongol raids. But I can assure you that I am happy to be alive at such a time and to be able to fight in defence of those immortal values which have taken shape on our continent from the earliest times to the present day. And not only in the narrow racial sense, but also in the comprehensive cultural sense. It does not therefore sadden me that I was chosen to bear this destiny, but I am proud and happy that it should be so.

'The struggle against the West is being fought only in part on land: but to an important degree at sea. As in almost every war, this one too is to a great extent a problem of shipping. The final collapse of such a victorious offensive in

Libya against the British was definitely due to the impossibility of solving the supply problem from Italy or from Crete to Tobruk and Mersa Matruh. The attainment of more or less temporary success is thus of little importance. It is only of decisive value if the military gains can be held from the supply point of view. America and England may achieve some sort of advantage by acquiring temporary footholds, but what matters is if they succeed in the long run in holding such points by keeping them supplied . . . The continued menacing and obstruction of their sea supply lines is bound sooner or later to lead to catastrophe. I have therefore taken all possible steps to put our U-boat warfare on a virtually indestructible footing . . . The struggle in North Africa and for Western Europe has of course an equally decisive influence on the success of the war as a whole. But the holding and extension of the Tunis and Bizerta bridgehead is obliging England and America to transport their troops and supplies to the Near and Far East by a long detour round the Cape.'

So much for the myth of German superiority at sea. Hitler then disclosed his central anxiety. 'I regard the situation in the Balkan peninsula itself with the gravest concern . . . I was told that the Italian political leaders had counted on risings in Greece in support of the Italian invading forces in October 1940. No such thing occurred. Not only did the hostile forces, at this very moment, rise as one man against the Italian troops, even the Albanians were only reliable up to a point. If a landing takes place tomorrow, Duce, anywhere in the Balkans, then Communists, followers of Mihailović, and all the other irregulars will be in accord on one thing: launching an immediate attack on the German or Italian armed forces (as the case may be) in support of the enemy landings. I consider it disastrous, Duce, that after we have conquered the whole area in battle there should still exist armed and politically organized persons ready to turn against us in any emergency . . .

'The first phase of the operations in Croatia has been successfully carried out. We did succeed in smashing a substantial part of Tito's organization and in inflicting heavy losses in men and material on the invading troops. The extent to which the insurgents had already developed their organization is both alarming and instructive. It is high time we exterminated this movement if we do not want to incur the risk of being stabbed in the back the moment the Anglo-Saxons land in the Balkans.'

Unless the Axis disarmed both the Communists and the četniks and 'neutralized' the whole area, then revolt would break out, in the event of invasion, and all communications with Greece would be cut. The German divisions in the region would then have to fight the rebels—Communist and četnik—'and Italian troops will be unable single-handed to stave off an invasion of the Peloponnese or the Adriatic.

'I would be so glad, Duce, to discuss these problems with you personally. In the first place, I am familiar with all these regions and the mentality of their inhabitants, having studied the history of the country in which I was born and bred; in the second place the monitoring of telegraph and wireless communications, which it was found necessary to institute, provides irrefutable proof of the correctness of my views.'

The Allied alternative to a Balkan landing might be an assault on the Italian offshore islands. Hitler summed up this danger, which was the principal preoccupation of his ally, in brief and offhand terms. 'I consider it by no means impossible, Duce, that an invasion of Sardinia, Corsica and perhaps even Sicily will be attempted. Sardinia and Corsica seem to be particularly threatened. I look upon it as a matter of decisive importance to reinforce the defensive capacity of these two islands.'

The danger of Allied intervention in Spain was equally dismissed with a sad backward glance to the lost opportunities two years earlier. 'If in 1941 the Spanish Government had declared itself ready to resolve the Gibraltar problem once and for all—and unlimited troops and equipment were available for the purpose—the whole course of the war in the Mediterranean would have been different. There would have been no English or Americans in North Africa today, but only Italians and Spaniards. I have tried, Duce, to assist the Spanish army, as far as our own strained situation permits, in order to help counteract a threat of this kind, at least materially. The German Army has naturally taken all dispositions itself to meet such an eventuality.'

On February 25 Ribbentrop was received by the Duce at Palazzo Venezia, in the presence of Mackensen, Alfieri, and Bastianini.[1] He handed over this personal letter from Hitler, and while Mussolini glanced through the Italian translation, read it aloud in German 'in a robust and emphatic voice'.[2] This document was his brief for the conference, and his exposition, together with Mussolini's comments, lasted for four hours.

Ribbentrop began with the central theme of the Russian front. The Tripartite Pact powers were at the most decisive moment of the world conflict. 'The war could only be lost if Germany and Italy themselves gave in.' The stand at Stalingrad 'was of decisive importance for the conduct of the war'. It had saved the German army in the Caucasus. Germany would now, 'by the introduction of total war, bring her vast reserves into play for the first time'. A new offensive might be mounted in two and a half months' time when the muddy season was over and the German plans were complete. Hitler's plan was to paralyse Russian offensive power. He had no intention 'of launching an unlimited drive into the boundless territories of Russia . . . but would take up a position which, through the occupation of the Ukraine, would assure Germany food supplies and a substantial increase in war potential'.

Hitler did not believe that a political settlement with Russia was possible. 'In any case it would not be more than an interim solution, since the Russians of course were not to be trusted, and German troops would thus have to be held in readiness for use against them should occasion arise.' The German summer offensive aimed at paralysing Russian offensive power. Then 'there would be a switch to static warfare. The Fuehrer might have more far-reaching plans, with which Ribbentrop was not acquainted in detail, but the results which he had mentioned were the least that would definitely be achieved.'

Ribbentrop now turned to the questions of the neutrals, Spain and Turkey, whose reactions to the revolutionary changes in the balance of the war had been exercising both Berlin and Rome in the previous weeks.

Mussolini was told of the 'confidential protocol' recently signed by the German government with Franco, selling arms on the condition of a pledge by the Spanish government to defend the Iberian peninsula and the Atlantic and Mediterranean islands against any Anglo-American assault. Ribbentrop asked the Duce to treat this information as confidential, 'since its widespread dissemination would lead to unpleasant consequences for Franco. There already existed a secret protocol with Spain in connection with her accession to the Steel Pact: this too had hitherto been kept secret.'

As regards Turkey, Ribbentrop summarized his views on the Adana Conference. From various secret sources Germany could form a fairly clear picture of the talks. No binding agreements had been made with the British. Turkey would remain neutral, and was 'governed first and foremost by a strong fear of the Russians, and consequently hoped in her innermost heart for a German victory over Russia.

'In his Berlin talks with the Fuehrer, in November 1940, Molotov had laid down his well-known four conditions: Finland, Roumania, Bulgaria, and the Straits for the Soviets, thereby revealing Russia's real aims. If Germany were weak, neither Britain nor America could block the path of Russia's advance. This was the reason why Turkey would stay out of the war, and hoped for an Axis victory over Russia. But just as she would not join us, neither would Turkey allow herself to be dragged into the war against us. She would remain aloof until the very last moment, and range herself with the victor only at the eleventh hour.'

A general pattern of German strategic thinking was emerging from Hitler's letter and Ribbentrop's remarks. A total effort by the Germans on the Russian front would produce conditions of static warfare by the summer, and revolutionize the economic position of Germany and consequently of Italy. The mounting submarine war would limit the power of the Western Allies to open a Second Front, and confine them to peripheral landing operations at points round the continent of Europe. In the Mediterranean theatre Franco would probably stay on the fringe of the war. In event of an Anglo-American action in Spain or her island possessions, German military aid might be increased to hold the balance. In the Eastern Mediterranean, Turkey would maintain her neutrality, and it was improbable that the British would press her further. There remained, as the threatened areas of Anglo-American operations, Italy and her offshore islands and the Axis-held territories in Yugoslavia.

Ribbentrop gave brief consideration to the former in terms which betrayed at once the perfunctory interest of Hitler in the Mediterranean war. 'Information was coming to hand according to which England intended to proceed against Corsica and Sardinia. In this connection the question of fortifying these islands became one of decisive importance. The engineer staffs, placed at the disposal of Italy, were of the opinion that the fortification of Sardinia was totally inadequate and that, in the event of a serious British landing, the island would be occupied. The Fuehrer believed that the enemy was aware of the fact that the transport problem was becoming more and more difficult for them, and they would therefore undertake landing operations as soon as possible.'

Having thus dismissed the direct enemy threat to the Italian ally, Ribbentrop felt free to concentrate on the main theme of his instructions. With the aid of a map he now explained in detail the German appreciation of the Serbo-Croat theatre. 'The Fuehrer's view was that we had to contend here with three distinct groups: the Communists, who had just suffered a severe blow, the followers of Mihailović, including also the četniks, and the irregulars. In the event of the British landing, all these groups would hasten to the aid of the invader.' The Communist forces of Tito had been driven southwards from Croatian territory in the direction of Montenegro as the result of joint winter operations by German and Italian forces, in which the latter had reluctantly taken part and had used as auxiliary troops the 'irregular' četnik bands based on Croatia. These units were nominally controlled by Mihailović whose main forces were operating in Serbia and Montenegro.

Ribbentrop was attempting to show that the 'irregulars' referred to by Hitler and the rest of the četniks were in reality one force, and the German Foreign Minister now handed to the Duce some material assembled by the Germans which showed that all these groups 'were secretly under Mihailović's command, i.e. that they were basically directed by the British General Staff'. German and Italian plans for maintaining control of the occupied regions of Yugoslavia had been sharply opposed since the initial campaign of April 1941, and it was the central purpose of Ribbentrop's present mission to sort out this sullen tangle.

The Italian military view was represented by General Roatta, now commanding the Italian Second Army in Croatia. According to him, the četnik 'irregulars' in those areas were serving a useful local purpose. They could be employed to destroy the partisans, and only then should be disarmed and disbanded. And as Mussolini retorted at this present meeting, 'German troops had also made use of the četniks in battle'.

The real intention of the Italian Command was to execute

a gradual withdrawal of all their forces on Yugoslav soil in order to hold only a coastal belt against possible Allied landings, to withdraw as many troops as possible for the ultimate defence of the Italian mainland, and to leave četnik bands, armed with Italian weapons, to foment civil war in the interior against the partisans. The Italians did not accept the concept of a large-scale operation of 'pacification' which the Germans consistently pressed on them at all levels.

Bastianini summarized the Italian view in his only intervention in the conference. 'He contested the likelihood of a unification of all three groups in the event of a British invasion. The Russian-influenced partisans had nothing in common with the adherents of Mihailović. They regarded him as a traitor. Bastianini also rejected the idea of a military operation to extirpate the partisans. The war on the Serbo-Croat front had to be conducted on a pattern entirely different from that applied in the other theatres of war. It was not a question of the number of divisions. In mountainous terrain everything would be resolved by small-scale operations.'

And Mussolini added: 'No effective methods of combating the partisans had yet been found. The German and Italian regular troops were not up to guerilla warfare. This method of warfare was highly uncongenial, involved heavy losses, and had so far brought inadequate results. Altogether there were sixty thousand partisans and četniks. Ultimately they could of course not hold out, since—at any rate up to the present—they possessed no artillery or air force, and could obtain supplies only with difficulty.'

Ribbentrop felt the absence of his military experts in such a discussion and merely replied that 'the extent of the danger could be gauged, among other things, from one of Eden's announcements in which he openly described Mihailović's men as Britain's advance guard in the Balkans . . . The question of Mihailović and of pacifying the Croatian region was not a political but a purely military one. Once the war was won, Italy could settle her own political problems in this region. Germany had no axe to grind in the matter.'

He was well aware of Italian suspicions of German economic and strategic interests in Yugoslav territory, which remained the most sensitive subject of misunderstanding between the two governments, and was anxious on this occasion to confine the debate to the military aspects of these regions, which according to Hitler represented a major potential threat to the whole Axis position in Europe.

Ribbentrop was accompanied on his visit by General Warlimont, the Chief of Operations at the German High Command, and proposed that the whole issue should be discussed further in the presence of military experts.

Ribbentrop then swerved into an illuminating digression on his personal impressions of Stalin and his analysis of the war. 'It was a mistake to assume that Stalin would change. He (Ribbentrop) had twice negotiated with him and learned to recognize in him a tough fanatic and icy realist who dominated everything in Russia, and in whose presence none of his colleagues dared open his mouth. He was undoubtedly a man of historic stature. Ribbentrop mentioned that at the end of his second démarche in Moscow in September 1939, when a communiqué was being prepared that contained a few sarcasms at Britain's expense, he had asked Stalin, who was in a fairly expansive mood, whether Russia might not support Germany militarily as well. He was thinking in terms of, say, a Russian attack on Britain via Persia. Stalin had pondered for a long time before giving his reply, and had then said that Russia would never tolerate Germany's being weak in relation to Britain and France. Ribbentrop had not rightly grasped the full implications of this reply at the time. But in the light of subsequent developments he now realized that Stalin's whole policy was expressed in these words. Stalin had been preparing for war for fifteen years, he had then shared out Poland with Germany, and imagined that the Reich would have to wage a protracted war in the West. He had assumed that Germany would gradually wear herself out in the process and would finally be obliged to turn to Russia for support. Posing as a helpful ally, and having secured the Roumanian oil, he doubtless intended to bolshevize Germany from within and with the aid of this Communized Germany to extend his supremacy over the whole of Europe.'

It now remained for Mussolini to allude to the points raised by Ribbentrop in his outline of German views on the state of the war. 'As early as December' the Duce had reviewed the present situation 'in a calm and sober spirit'. But he made no mention of his plea to Hitler at the time of the Goerlitz talks to consider a settlement in the East. Indeed he treated the present German exposition of the Russian front as cavalierly as Ribbentrop had in his reference to the Mediterranean theatre. 'What had to be done now was to erect this barrier (possibly on the Dnieper) and then await developments. The chief enemy in Russia had always been the country itself, for it was limitless. Not only was this the lesson to be learned from history, but he had also verified it by personal observation on the occasion of his visit to the Fuehrer, when he had flown over the vast plains and gained a deep and lasting impression of their unlimited extent.'

He continued: 'Until August of the previous year the Axis had held the initiative. But from that date it had lain with the enemy, both on land and in the air. This change had been brought about partly by transport and convoy problems.' Mussolini was referring to the African theatre, which had escaped attention in the German analysis. Rommel had not been able to continue his advance to Egypt because of the sinking by the enemy of his supply tankers. 'It had been a mistake not to retreat once it was clear that Rommel's offensive had failed. In particular the non-motorized Italian divisions should have been withdrawn. . . . It was incorrect to say that Rommel had left them in the lurch, but if they had been withdrawn in time and made available for later use, Cyrenaica would not have been lost.

'Italy was furthermore obliged to fight a sort of "proletarian" war. Italian troops were still fighting with arms left over from the last war. Italy had not had time to arm, having been fighting continuously ever since 1935, first in Abyssinia, then in Spain. True, her manpower losses in these wars had not been heavy, but her losses in arms and equipment had been much more severe. Spanish artillery, for example, had come for the most part from Italy. They were weapons handed over to the Spanish at the end of the Civil War, together with several aircraft.'

The Duce probed in one phrase to the root cause of the present loss of strategic initiative by the Axis. 'The Alamein offensive had misfired because the manoeuvre could not be based on the Caucasus.' In other words, there was no coordination or summit planning by the Germans and Italians, who continued to conduct and were steadily losing their 'parallel' wars, and in particular in North Africa.

Tunisia was 'the bulwark of Southern Europe'. It could be held, in Mussolini's view, on three conditions: 'First, if all the available submarines from whatever quarter were massed in the Mediterranean; second, if the appropriate artillery were made available; and third, if our air strength were at least equal to that of the enemy.' If Tunisia were lost 'the entire strategic position would be altered. An attack on Sicily, Sardinia and the Balkans would then become possible.'

As to the long-term plans of the British and Americans which Ribbentrop had so cursorily dismissed, the Duce personally did not fear an invasion of Italy, and merely thought that air attacks would increase in strength. As regards landings in Sardinia and Sicily, he thought that these would take the form only of 'commando' operations and not of a classical invasion backed by numerous warships and reinforcements.

Unlike the Germans, Mussolini placed greater emphasis on an eventual entry of Spain into the war, and such a move might restore a limited initiative to the Axis in the Mediterranean. Such was his private hope, which he now expressed with caution. 'The British might occupy the Balearic islands. This would be all to the good, as it would bring the Spanish question to the fore. He would let Ribbentrop have a copy of a letter from Franco to him, together with his reply. Franco had told him in his letter that he had no faith in British and American assurances and was making preparations for armed resistance. The Duce added that he presumed this attitude on the part of Franco was materially influenced by the fact that there were four American divisions on the border with Spanish Morocco, that the former Red President of Spain, Negrin, had turned up in North Africa and that Britain was propagating among the Arabs the notion of complete independence from Spain as well. Finally, there was still a great danger of Communism in Spain itself, since Franco had not carried through any kind of social reform and present-day Spain differed only superficially from the Spain of former days. Spain's entry into the war was unavoidable, and an enemy victory would also mean the end of Franco. Spain's entry into the war ought only to take place at a propitious moment, as otherwise she would become more of a burden than a help. He was therefore glad Germany was sending arms to Spain, the more so as he considered it out of the question that Spain should ever turn against the Axis.'

Mussolini did not expressly comment on the position of Turkey or on German confidence in her neutrality. He concluded his survey with a curt and sober note. 'The attitude of other countries towards the Axis was dependent on the situation in Tunisia and on the Russian front.'

* * *

It was agreed that the next meeting should be held together with the military experts and confined to the whole politico-military situation in Yugoslav territory.

In the interval the Duce and his advisers were able to study the contents of Hitler's letter of February 16, which Ribbentrop had delivered at the opening of the talks. To the Italians there was little new and nothing encouraging in this document. The twin disasters of Alamein and Stalingrad had not impressed on Hitler the need for that strategic revolution for which the new Italian High Command had hoped. The German war would still be essentially conducted on two main fronts: the war against Allied shipping at sea, and the destruction of the Soviet Union on land. All else was in effect secondary. There was little sign of a coherent plan of action in the Mediterranean, although the 'struggle in North Africa' was glanced at as having 'an equally decisive influence on the success of the war as a whole'. The repeated myth of wearing down the Allies on the sea route round the Cape was once again hopefully cited. And then, significantly, 'our enemies' counter-measures can, apart from the attempt to drive us out of Tunis and Bizerta, consist only in attempts at landing on the Continent itself'. And here lies the key to Hitler's thinking. He was not concerned about a major Second Front in the West in 1943, and mentions a series of possible Allied landings, or rather raids, stretching round the whole Northern and Western periphery of Europe from the Baltic to Portugal, but it is not in these areas that his interest lies; nor even in the outer defences of his Italian ally, Sardinia, Corsica, and Sicily. These are dismissed in five lines of the letter.

'I regard the situation in the Balkan peninsula with the gravest concern.' This was the historic invasion route into the heart of Europe, and the obvious point of concentration for the Allies. An enemy landing in the area, backed by local nationalist and Communist uprisings, might lead to the rapid control of the whole region, and the worst nightmare of all, to the exposing of the German southern flank in the East and an eventual gigantic turning movement—a joint Anglo-American-Russian enterprise—into Germany itself.

Mihailović and Tito, in ironic association, at the head of small bands of irregular guerillas, had become the symbol of the Fuehrer's main disquiet.

On the morning of February 26, the two delegations assembled at Palazzo Venezia. Ribbentrop was now accompanied by General Warlimont, and Mussolini was flanked by General Ambrosio and Bastianini.[3]

The Duce introduced the discussion on the central theme of the conference. Hitler had stated, in his letter, firstly that the Italian military authorities in the Balkans were supporting the četniks and delivering arms to them in order to use them against the partisans; and secondly, that the great danger lay in the 'unclarified conditions in the Balkans' in event of an Anglo-American landing on the Adriatic coast. He felt that there was no distinction between četniks and partisans, that all help should cease to the former, and that they should be disarmed. He had the impression that not many arms had been handed over to the četniks, as Italy did not dispose of many weapons. Something may possibly have happened, but the broad lines of policy, as laid down by him, were perfectly clear: to avoid substituting diplomatic solutions for military problems as long as possible, for such a move could only bring about misunderstandings and disagreeable surprises. The Duce had therefore called this meeting to clear up these matters with the help of military experts. 'General Ambrosio knew the conditions well and could be very helpful in this task.'

Ambrosio spoke with authority. He had commanded the Italian Second Army in Croatia until January 1942. There had at that time been no case for using the irregular 'nationalist' bands. 'But then the disturbances had spread, and under his successor, Roatta, certain subordinate military headquarters had accepted the četniks' offer to fight the partisans, to whom they stood in strong opposition.' It was true that the četniks hated the Italians, 'but in spite of that one had to use them, because Italy had not enough troops available to deal with the partisans who were scattered everywhere.

'As to the general objective laid down by the Fuehrer, the destruction of those groups operating in Serbia and the pacification of that region, no immediate solution was possible. As always in the Balkans, so this time too, long and bitter fighting and in addition a permanent and numerous occupation force, would be needed to pacify the area finally.'

Ambrosio agreed that the četniks should be disarmed, but by stages. Clearly both četniks and partisans were enemies of the Axis. 'But it was not possible to beat them both at once.'

The Duce interposed that an Allied landing on the Adriatic coast would be 'a very dangerous and complicated operation'. He believed however in the possibility of Commando raids, but not a regular invasion. 'The British had better opportunities elsewhere.'

Ribbentrop replied that he was not a military expert and, whether or not such a landing was feasible, 'it was in any case completely impossible to leave strong forces of četniks and partisans in the rear of the German forces, if for instance a major landing took place in Greece. The Fuehrer was particularly disturbed by the latter possibility, for he knew that the disruption of the railway connections by rebels in Croatia at the moment of a British landing would have the most serious consequences.' Unless the area were cleared at least of the large bands, 'it might be necessary to bring divisions which ought to be protecting Greece from the British back into Croatia to fight the partisans'. Time played a very big rôle in action against the bands. In a life and death struggle one could not leave great masses of troops idle. The same measures must be taken in Croatia as in the East; as many partisans and followers of other hostile groups as possible must be liquidated. 'The report which General Warlimont had with him showed that more or less all the groups in Croatia were led by Mihailović, that is by the British General Staff.'

Ribbentrop then went on: 'To take the view that the area could not be pacified seemed to him to be a form of resignation that we could not allow ourselves in this war. It was possible that perhaps the whole region could not be cleared, but at least the larger bands . . . must be destroyed.'

General Warlimont was now called on to summarize the German military case. 'It was a matter of safeguarding the further requirements of 200,000 tons of bauxite, on which the carrying out of the German Air Force programme was dependent, and above all by destroying the main centres of resistance in the country to prevent the outbreak of a general revolt in event of a British landing . . .' He then described on a map the various operations in progress, and estimated the strength of the partisans at 15–20,000 men. 'Operation Weiss I' in the western part of Croatia had led to the liquidation of 5,000 men. 'But the Tito State (*sic*) had a considerably larger and wider woven organization than one had at first assumed. Most of the 15,000 men had got away in the direction of Mostar. Previously this situation had seemed very dangerous, but now certain advantages appeared. For the first time it was possible to surround and destroy the whole Communist force so that they could not take evasive action again.' He was prepared to agree that the četniks should take part in these coming operations, but not in contact with German troops. After the Communists had been destroyed, the četniks would no longer be needed, and could be at once disarmed. 'Then action could be taken against the centre of the Mihailović movement, namely in Serbia. The Fuehrer had therefore requested that firm directives should be agreed upon in Rome whereby these operations should ensue.' Warlimont then gave up to the Duce a draft of such orders which he had prepared in Rome on instructions from Ribbentrop.

While Mussolini was reading this document, Ambrosio continued the debate. The disarming of the četniks, 'which the German Foreign Minister had described as urgent, need not be precipitated so long as no actual British landing had taken place in Greece, and while Tunis still remained in German and Italian hands . . . a joint Italo-German military operation in Croatia would in Ambrosio's view not be successful. He thought that within a fortnight the same disorder would break out again. It was not possible, in the circumstances prevailing in Croatia, to mount long-term operational plans.' In any event, new Italian divisions were not forthcoming. 'They were needed for the defence against an eventual British landing in Italy itself.'

Ribbentrop retorted that it was not feasible to postpone or even not carry out all operations 'against the British auxiliary troops of Mihailović in Croatia simply out of fear that the British might perhaps carry out an operation somewhere else'.

The Duce remarked that the četnik problem was more political than miltary, and Ambrosio agreed that this was the case with 'the whole Croat question in general'. Ribbentrop had no intention of being drawn on to this delicate and contested ground, and he sharply countered. 'It was a purely military problem. Political questions could easily be settled when the war had been won.'

The tone of the meeting had risen, and Mussolini adjourned the discussion by agreeing with Warlimont's proposals, and instructing Ambrosio to work out with the latter the details at a separate military conference.

* * *

Even the dry official tone of Schmidt's record of these talks does not conceal the frustrated irritation of Ribbentrop. He had received categorical instructions from Hitler to reach a military agreement with the Italians to take joint operational measures to remove the menace of possible partisan activity in Yugoslav territory against economic targets and lines of communication in an area of vital concern to both allies. The Duce knew the problem, which needed no further explanation or exposition. He had been told by Goering in October and again in December. Ciano and Cavallero had been lectured on the same subject in the same month. The Fuehrer had now written a long personal letter as well, and sent Ribbentrop expressly to Rome to put an end to the delay and to clear up the matter once and for all. Yet there was clearly obstruction if not sabotage, both on the spot in the Balkans, and in Rome by the military authorities. Why should Ambrosio be so obstinate about abandoning Italian support to a few četnik bands operating on Croat territory?

Ribbentrop's exasperation exploded in a private talk on February 28 with that admirable listener, Alfieri.[4] The German and Italian military experts had met in the course of February 26. Early the following morning Warlimont had told Ribbentrop that full agreement had been reached, and the Italian High Command was preparing a joint memorandum. This document had now been received. 'It contained provisions about the Command arrangements, which did not coincide with the verbal agreements, whereby the German and Italian forces would operate separately, but with liaison staffs and the most precise co-ordination of joint plans. And further, the document—and this was the gravest point—omitted any mention of Mihailović.'

Ribbentrop 'expressed emphatically his astonishment at the activities of the Italian High Command. He must explain quite openly that during his meeting with the Duce he had detected a certain resistance on the part of the military gentlemen, which gave the impression that they were not convinced of the need for operations in Croatia, and they expressed the view that they did not have enough troops. Perhaps in many circles of higher officers the connections between the different theatres of war were not well enough known . . . In the Italian High Command there were tendencies which one could not exactly describe as Fascist.'

Was this a veiled warning? Ribbentrop's view of the Italian

military leaders had been marked by the demoralizing collapse of their armies on the Russian Front, and by what he regarded as the inability of the senior officers to fight an ideologically Fascist war. Sharing with Hitler the contempt and distrust of senior officers in Nazi circles, Ribbentrop, seemingly for the first time, began to reflect seriously upon the political consequences of military defeat, both on the structure of Fascist Italy, and upon the Italian High Command itself.

The final session was held on February 28 at Palazzo Venezia. Neither Ambrosio nor Warlimont was summoned and, presumably to give it an exclusively diplomatic character. Only Mackensen, Alfieri and Bastianini were present. This was curious, as all decisions in regard to the Balkans—much to Ciano's annoyance in the past—had been taken exclusively by the Italian High Command.

Mussolini started the conversation with the 'question of Mihailović', and explained that 'he too regarded him as a dangerous and bitter foe of Germany and Italy'. Ambrosio had been given orders in regard to the necessary operations. 'Ambrosio was an excellent man who would make no promise that he could not keep, but who would in all circumstances carry out the Duce's orders.'

In reply to a query by Ribbentrop, the Duce said that in South-East Europe between Ljubljana and the Dodecanese, there were twenty-five to twenty-six Italian divisions. Ribbentrop pointed out tartly that 'once Mihailović had been liquidated, Italy would free a large number of divisions so that the destruction of Mihailović would bring great advantages to the Italian High Command'. He did not add that this figure of Italian forces represented nearly half the total Italian army, and might point to the original importance which the Italians gave to their Balkan interests.

At this point the Duce and Ribbentrop withdrew from the meeting to talk in private and without witnesses. There is no written record of this conversation.

There had been no mention in these talks of Bastianini's plan to sound the Germans on the advisability of some public declaration on the European 'New Order', both with the purpose of encouraging the occupied and allied countries of Axis Europe, and to test the reactions both of the neutrals and the enemy. According to Bastianini, however, the Duce in the course of the conference, and presumably during this last private conversation, obtained Ribbentrop's reluctant consent to the publication of an official communiqué which mentioned for the first time the ideals of liberty for all peoples and active collaboration between the nations. 'It was in substance the first and last official declaration of the basic principles of that New Order which the Axis up to that moment had avoided defining in any way.'[5]

In the event, the Germans suppressed any public comment, and the main effect of this preliminary show of independence by Bastianini seems to have been the neglect of Ribbentrop in making any protocol call at Palazzo Chigi at the end of his visit.

Mussolini himself showed little enthusiasm for the plan. As Prince Bismarck stated later: 'It is rumoured in Berlin that at the last meeting with Ribbentrop, Mussolini turned the discussion on to the problem of Europe. It was all limited to a few very vague phrases, and . . . my impression is that he has no clear ideas on the subject.'

On February 27 Ribbentrop has been received by the King of Italy. The German Ambassador, Mackensen, accompanied him, but did not enter the royal study. After the audience, General Puntoni noted: 'the German Minister is full of optimism. He has no doubts about the success of the war in Russia, where, he says, the Germans will take the initiative as soon as possible. Hitler is placing his main cards on submarine warfare. According to Ribbentrop, the internal situation in Great Britain and Russia is far from cheerful. Turkey will not enter the war on the Anglo-American side, and Spain, in the event of her suffering any aggression by the Allies, will come in on our side. Germany understands the importance of Tunisia and will undertake the impossible to come to its defence and facilitate a rapid counter-attack. The content of these statements, made without any request on my part, makes me think that Hitler is disturbed at the lack of confidence which now reigns in many circles here.'[6]

CHAPTER FOUR

Spring Tensions: Russia and Tunisia

'FROM WHAT I could understand, the Duce had succeeded in putting across our point of view in regard to three questions of fundamental importance: no more soldiers in Russia; Tunisia is of capital importance to us; it is essential to strengthen the air forces in the Mediterranean and the islands.' Such was the King's account to Puntoni of the audience of the Duce on March 1 on the talks with Ribbentrop.

These matters would be clarified in Mussolini's reply to Hitler's letter of February 16, and Ambrosio in particular hoped to influence this forthcoming statement of Italian policy. He had drafted a note for the Duce on the same day as the royal audience.[1]

'I think it advisable to bring again to your attention two concepts, already set out in previous memoranda, because of their basic importance, and because from the military point of view it is of the highest interest to write them to the Fuehrer.

'To hold Tunis and defend our coasts we need German help in artillery, light naval craft, technical equipment, aircraft, and oil supplies in the measure as requested also through General Warlimont. This aid is all the more necessary in that we have agreed to the operations in the Balkans, which will prevent us withdrawing from this region the troops we had counted on to reinforce the defence of the Mother Country.

'The German conduct of an offensive war cannot, in our opinion, lead to decisive results, at least unless the Germans succeed in pinning down and destroying the Russian army. This possibility is very chancy, while it is certain that offensive operations will lead to an enormous wastage of men and material. We also maintain that the Germans, being totally committed to an offensive in Russia, cannot effectively oppose the Anglo-Americans in other parts of Europe for lack of adequate reserves.

'The Ally must revise his plans and pay more attention to the Mediterranean theatre, because the danger does not come only from the East, but may well appear at any moment on the flank or rear of the German army.

'The Germans are not greatly worried about an Anglo-American attack because, in the first instance, it would take place far away from their territory. We are in the opposite position. One of the most likely objectives in the Mediterranean is Italy, and we shall end by bearing the weight of the struggle alone, a battle which will put our country to fire and the sword, and expose her to major damage. It may be that this thought forms part of the German plan, namely that they want to commit us to bear the brunt of the initial Anglo-American assault, with little regard to the fate of our population and cities.

'If we receive aid in respect of the necessary and indispensable flow of supplies, and if the operational views of the Germans both towards Russia and in regard to the vital Mediterranean theatre will be in conformity with a more positive vision of the strategic position of Europe, there will be more chance of holding Tunisia as long as possible . . . Otherwise the prospects cannot be equally hopeful and Italy will then have to consider how to avoid the consequences of irreparable mistakes which are not of her making.'[2]

This memorandum of the Chief of the Italian General Staff, written under the impact of the Rome talks, marks the first signs of his open revolt against the German attitude to the conduct of the war and of his anxiety as to the future of the Axis alliance. The meeting with Ribbentrop and Warlimont had been his first official contact with the German leadership. His reactions are revealed in this note. The last paragraph of the memorandum contains an early hint, as yet apparently unsupported from other quarters,* of the need of an independent Italian solution.

* It is perhaps significant that in the days immediately following Ribbentrop's visit, Ambrosio saw the Prince of Piedmont (March 1 and 3): Badoglio (March 2), Caviglia (March 5), and Bonomi (March 5). (Italian Collection. Ambrosio diary.) Was he seeking cautious support for such future action in the event of Mussolini refusing to face the realities of a war to the finish?

But for the moment the Duce, and he alone, could persuade Hitler to modify his position. It might even be that these common anxieties about the Russian war in certain German and Italian circles during recent weeks, of which Ambrosio was directly aware, in a sense delayed the elaboration of any counter action with the Italian Army Command against the continuation of the Axis alliance. On February 28 Ambrosio saw the head of the German Military Intelligence, Admiral Canaris. It is not known what passed between the two men.

The rôle of Mussolini as a possible arbitrator with Hitler had not yet been exhausted even though his performance with the German Foreign Minister had not been encouraging. The present concern of Ambrosio, however, was to press the Duce with every argument available in the direction of increased German aid to Italy in order to meet the enemy on more effective terms than hitherto in the Mediterranean theatre.

On March 8 Mussolini replied to Hitler's letter, giving his comments on the recent Rome talks. It followed the same general order of subjects as set out by Hitler, opening with North Africa.

'I am glad to note that you too regard Tunisia as an essential factor of the strategic campaign . . . We must remain in Tunisia, whatever the cost: in any case we must stay there as long as possible, since this will interfere profoundly, and perhaps decisively, with the execution of the plans drawn up by the Anglo-Saxons at Casablanca. In order to hold Tunisia, we must extend our bridgehead and not shrink it as Rommel wanted, since this would mean being overwhelmed and–in short–driven towards the sea, without means of escape, given the superiority which the enemy would gain from linking up his armies and being able to use all the airfields abandoned by us in Tunisia.

'I am convinced that we must resist on the Mareth Line. But in order to resist, and perhaps even counter-attack, our forces must be provisioned; and above all guns, tanks, and petrol must reach them. Shipping on the short but compulsory route of the Sicily channel must be safeguarded. To obtain all this, Fuehrer, I will never tire of repeating it: the Axis air forces in the Sardinia, Sicily, Tunisia zone must be at least equal to the enemy aviation.

'As to the operation in Croatia . . . I find that the results, if not decisive, are at least satisfactory.' The 'četnik-partisan theme' had been discussed at length with Ribbentrop. The local Italian Generals in Montenegro had been summoned to Rome and instructed to cease deliveries of arms to the četniks, who would be disarmed 'as soon as the partisans have ceased to be a dangerous armed movement'. Agreement with the German commander in Yugoslavia would be reached 'on the subsequent action to be taken in regard to the movement of General Mihailović'.

As to possible Allied landings, 'it is henceforward axiomatic that the Allies must try to set up a Second Front in Europe. The demands of Russia are imperious. And when, as I firmly believe, the Russian initiative will peter out, the Anglo-Saxons will have to honour their engagements and land at some point in Europe . . . I foresee, and particularly if Tunisia were definitely lost, the following operations against Italy: mass bombing in the northern and southern regions of Italy; commando and parachute landings in Sicily and Sardinia, to improve the naval position of the Allies. A serious invasion of the peninsula is an operation which the Anglo-Saxons cannot carry out. Faced with these eventualities, all our defence preparations in the two islands have been stepped up.

'Spain is still a card in our game, in spite of the oscillations of Franco's policy, and I feel that she could play a most important part the day on which she would allow us across her territory to take the whole Anglo-American position in North Africa from the rear. I get the impression that the enemy fear a move of this kind.'

On the subject of the Russian front, the Duce displayed unusual caution, and seems to have allowed his comments deliberately to be strengthened by Ambrosio's arguments, perhaps sensing too the opportunity to exert that element of personal persuasion on Hitler which, Mussolini realized, was expected of him in various quarters, both German and Italian.

The wording of this paragraph was sybilline. 'I have never doubted for a single moment that the armed forces of your Reich would restore the situation . . . I am sure that at a certain moment the Bolsheviks will find themselves up against an unsurmountable wall.

'But, Fuehrer, on the day when you accomplish the East Wall—with troops and fortifications—Russia, exhausted, will no longer represent the mortal danger of two years ago, and unless you are absolutely certain that you can destroy her forces once and for all, I wonder whether it is not too risky to repeat the struggle against the boundless space of Russia which is practically impossible to reach and grasp, while the Anglo-Saxon peril is mounting in the West? The day when, one way or another, Russia will be eliminated or neutralized, victory is in our hands. But I hope to discuss this thoroughly with you when I have the good fortune to meet you again.'

Finally, the future of the Italian contribution to the Russian war, which the King was so anxious to liquidate, was settled by the Duce's decision, apparently communicated to Warlimont by an unwilling Ambrosio during the Rome talks, that 'Italy cannot remain absent from the Russian front', and that the Italian Second Army Corps should stay in Russia. 'It must however be reformed and re-equipped with effective weapons, since with a threadbare deployment, like the Italian 8th Army on the Don, without reserves and with antiquated weapons, things could not turn out any differently from before . . . But allow me to express the wish that the Italian Army Corps will be used, not in duties in the rear, but in battle.'

Behind this cussed insistence by Mussolini on retaining Italian military presence in Russia lay an intricate set of pressures. He was aware that such a contribution could only be symbolic. He could sense the catastrophic effect on Italian public opinion of the news of the military disaster in Russia in the previous January and the dissolving influence of the reports of the Italian soldiers repatriated from the Eastern Front.

Under the weight of the massive Soviet winter offensive the whole Italian front had collapsed. There had been no defence in depth, and the promised German reserve support of an armoured division behind the Italians never materialized, nor had the Italian transport received any supplies of petrol before the battle.[3] In many cases the Germans, like Rommel's forces in Africa, seized Italian lorries and left the shattered units to face a death march to the West.

On March 14, in a dispatch marked 'Behaviour of the Italian Army in Russia', Alfieri wrote to Bastianini that the tendency on the German side was to make one believe in the unworthy behaviour of certain units of the Italian Expeditionary Corps in the last Russian offensive and to insist that the disaster had happened solely owing to the fault of the Italian and Roumanian troops. This attitude of course was not new, and Ciano had complained of it at Goerlitz in the previous December. Alfieri, however, felt that there was need for a temperate reply, showing the failure of the Germans to produce reserves and supplies. This position could not of course be concealed from the Italian people and indeed the Germans themselves emphasized the point with every publicity. They had even ordered their cinematograph units to take films of the Italians in full flight.[4]

In Innsbruck, the Italian Consul-General reported in February that there were 'unsympathetic reports of the military conduct of the Italians on the Don and that there had been attacks on Italian shops in the Tyrolese capital'.[5]

In spite of this situation, Mussolini could not, for reasons of prestige, bring himself to recall the whole Italian armed expeditionary corps. He withdrew the shattered units, and, regrouped with reinforcements, this somewhat smaller military contingent remained, which the Germans now showed marked reluctance to equip.

At a military conference held by Hitler at the 'Wolf's Lair' at Rastenburg about this time, Jodl reported that the Italian High Command had sent a memorandum on the reconstruction of the Italian Army Corps in the East, stating that no more Alpine troops could be sent there. Perhaps, said Jodl, one should follow their wishes. There was need for a good Alpine division in Tunis.

As to rearming the existing Italian divisions in Russia, Hitler intervened, 'I shall tell the Duce that it makes no sense. We give them weapons and it is the same self-deception . . . If we want to equip our twenty-one divisions, we need our weapons . . . We cannot again equip 700,000 Italians . . . I shall tell the Duce that it would be much better to take these units away . . . and get them into shape here in Germany . . . It is no use giving the Italians weapons for building up "an Army", which will lay down its arms at the first opportunity in front of any enemy. It is equally no good equipping an army if one is not sure of its internal security . . . (text illegible) the Duce needs two, four, six, eight divisions gradually to be put at his disposal as a guarantee that nothing will happen internally in Italy. They will be no use outside Italy. I shall not let myself be taken in again.'

The Don disaster was a turning point in the relations between the two countries and indeed the decisive psychological failure in 'Fascist' warfare. The lack of comradeship with the Germans was of course widely felt throughout the Italian armed forces, in particular after the North African campaign of Rommel, but the situation on the Eastern Front was more deep and grave than that. The Germans were fighting a fanatical crusade against Bolshevism, a concept which never really penetrated the Italian military mentality, and the lasting effect of contact between the Italian troops and the Russians was both to give the former a marked respect for the industrial potential of a society with which they were not familiar, and, as the Italian Consul-General in Innsbruck put it (in a dispatch of April 7) 'a feeling of increased consideration for the (Russian) army and possibly even for Russia'.[6]

The point was even more forcibly made by a private letter written from the Russian front to Bastianini and read and initialled by Mussolini. 'Among the officers of both higher and lower rank a general feeling of rancour and distrust against the Germans as responsible for every mistake is generally predominant here. A dangerous anti-Fascist spirit lurks and creeps . . . The majority do not understand that our frontier is today on the Don.'*

The recriminations between the two countries were not only confined to the Don disaster. 'Evidence has mounted as to the deterioration of the climate between the two allies' as Bastianini wrote to Alfieri on March 17. 'I am sending you a note† which speaks of the bad atmosphere towards us in Germany. I am sending it to you because it is not the only one of its kind, and it is in direct contrast to the idea we had here of Italo-German relations; or rather, of the German state of mind about us. What is the real truth?

'On the other hand we must note . . . that scarcely any of the war materials we asked for have been sent. Now comparing this with the situation in the enemy camp, where material is sent in bulk from the U.S.A. to Russia, and to England, this extreme parsimony about material in the face of our need, and in the common interest, does serious moral and material harm.'

The Germans tended to belittle the successes of their allies. 'I know very well that telling you all this is very like sending "coals to Newcastle" but I only heard these things half an hour ago. I have not yet read your latest reports on this subject, but they seem to be arcadian in comparison

* Italian Collection. Private letter to Bastianini, April 10, 1943. (Signature illegible.) It is not perhaps without significance that many of the officers and men, particularly from the Alpine divisions in Russia, appear as the leaders of partisan bands in northern Italy at the end of the year.

† Not included.

with many similar ones I am sending you, so that precise information on this score is particularly desirable.

'Think how very difficult it is to un-poison the minds of our comrades returning from the Soviet battle fields, who tell horrible tales of their sufferings during the full retreat, when they were retreating on foot and fighting, and the others were flying to safer places in motor vehicles (some belonging to the Royal Italian Army)—if, in fact, there was a flight . . . Anyway, I am sure you will know how to use your tact and the necessary sincerity in time to smooth out the atmosphere.'[7]

There was worse to come. On his return from Rome Ribbentrop had conveyed to Hitler the extent of his disquiet at the attitude to the war of the Italian High Command, even to the extent of hinting at the possibility of treason in certain Italian military quarters. It was indeed in part to meet such a threat that a summit meeting of the Fuehrer and the Duce must be held without undue loss of time, and on March 8 Ribbentrop summoned Alfieri to tell him that Hitler wished to meet the Duce 'as soon as possible, namely as soon as he could leave the Eastern Front; which would be in ten to fourteen days or a little later if need arose. The Fuehrer wanted to talk to the Duce on those specific subjects, which had sharply struck him, Ribbentrop, during his stay in Rome. . . .

'He (Ribbentrop) wanted to tell the Italian Ambassador quite openly that he had formed a very negative impression of the attitude and mentality of the Italian High Command. Certain other things had also struck him. The Fuehrer was of the opinion that the situation could only be remedied by the Duce if he carried out exceptionally drastic measures. In certain moments the Fuehrer also had bowed to such a necessity in regard to Germany . . . The mentality of the High Command was the incubus of the Italian Army. The Duce had talked about this in confidence to Ribbentrop, and he could tell Alfieri as an old Fascist and collaborator of the Duce that apparently also the Duce appreciated the situation. The Fuehrer understood even better, as he had found himself in similar circumstances. In the winter of 1941, certain of his generals had come to tell him that it was impossible to hold the occupied regions, to which he had replied that the Army must stay at all costs where it was, but that the generals must return at once to Germany. One general, who did not obey the order, and who did not hold on to his position with his Division, was brought before a court martial in Germany and shot.

'In regard to the Italian army one must not be unfair, in spite of disappointments. The Italian soldier was fine if well led. The deficiency lay in the senior officer corps . . . This matter was of vital importance, and Ribbentrop asked Alfieri to raise the question with the Duce of drastic measures to be taken after the meeting with Hitler. The old generals must be replaced with young Fascist officers, even if the latter had not such a good military experience and training. Alfieri remarked that the Duce had often had such thoughts. But the question was a very difficult one.'

Ribbentrop then revealed the subject of his main anxiety. 'It was only a step from such a bad military spirit on the part of the generals to a bad political state of mind. Failed generals mostly wanted to play politics . . . A general, who is not spiritually one hundred per cent behind the Duce and does not do everything to bring about the military triumph of Italy, is a traitor.'[8]

There was also both humiliation and resentment on the Italian side. On March 17, in a minute recording an interview of Alfieri with Steengracht in Berlin, the latter noted that: 'From the conversations which the German Foreign Minister had had recently both with the Duce and also with Alfieri, it might be that the Duce would raise with the Fuehrer the subject of the Italian army and its achievements. Quite apart from the remarks of the German Foreign Minister, it should be stated that the feeling of the German army and public towards their Italian comrades in arms was subdued. The Duce was considering what could be done to re-establish complete and comradely confidence.'[9]

The 'Russian problem' between the Axis partners must now await discussion at the summit. The parallel issue of Tunisia, however, needed urgent review by military experts. It had been generally agreed, during the Rome talks, that this last African bridgehead must be held and that German aid, probably in the air, might be forthcoming. Mussolini's own conception was broadly that the Mareth line must be held, and the Axis forces built up for an eventual strike westwards in the direction of Morocco with the general hope of Spanish intervention on the Axis side. Rommel, who was still gloomily present in the North African sector, had never subscribed to such a strategic plan. On March 1 a report by him to his commanders was discussed at a meeting in Rome between the Duce, Kesselring, and Ambrosio. Rommel's general view was 'in favour of abandoning the Mareth Line, and retiring to a line further north'. Kesselring was opposed to this, and Mussolini was convinced that 'the loss of Tunisia would be a very grave blow and enable the Anglo-Americans to land on one or other of our own islands'.[10]

But the 'Tunisian problem' was to be discussed on a higher level. Just as Ribbentrop had been sent to Rome to raise the issues arising out of the Russian war, and in particular a possible Allied threat to South-Eastern Europe, now the visit of Goering was announced, presumably to initiate like discussion on the war in Africa.

The first Italian reactions to this familiar visitor were cool. At five o'clock on the afternoon of his arrival on March 8 he had an interview with Mussolini. The latter reported to the King that 'in substance Goering had neither added nor detracted from what Ribbentrop had promised. He (Goering) says that, by March 10, a German motorized regiment with much anti-tank equipment will reach Leghorn to be sent to Sardinia, and thence, as soon as possible, to Tunisia.'[11]

On March 13 the Duce mentioned to Kesselring rather cryptically: 'We have had a long talk with Goering on all problems on the agenda, distinguishing clearly between politics and the conduct of operations. At certain moments in fact the conduct of war should not be touched by politics.'

Goering had always regarded himself as the Italian specialist in high German circles, and apart from the problems of the war in Africa, he, like Ribbentrop—whom he had hoped to precede and not to follow in Rome—was anxious to form a first-hand view of the Italian political scene, particularly after the 'changing of the Guard' in February.

He seems to have had at least one private talk with the Duce during this March visit, of which there is no record. The subject of Russia was mentioned, as a letter of March 26 from Mussolini to Hitler shows. 'I have discussed this at length with the Reichsmarshal.'

But the open purpose of Goering's visit was again to hector the Italians into a total war effort. As on previous occasions, a meeting was held with Italian technicians, with Goering in the chair. His usual protests against the failure to construct airfields, to repair bomb damage in the ports, to arrange convoy escort, were met 'with timid objections' on the part of the Italian military representatives. It fell to Count Cini, the new

Minister of Transport and Communications, to answer sharply by listing the promised German supplies of war material, none or little of which had been sent.[12] Cini himself referred drily to this incident at a conference of ministers a day or two later. It had been 'an inconclusive meeting except for a few points of secondary importance'.[13]

On March 9 Rommel flew to Rome. At a meeting alone with the Duce he expressed his pessimism. 'The situation was very serious.' Enemy preparations against Mareth were far advanced, and the British attack could be expected after March 15. The Duce reiterated that, 'Tunisia must be held at all costs: it is the fortress of Europe and if this falls, the world situation can be definitely altered. The supply situation is first in importance, we are making every effort to get them there. I agree with the Fuehrer that Tunisia must be held. It may be that the enemy will attempt a landing in Sardinia, but more probably in South-East Europe: the enemy is making preparations also in Palestine and Syria. We must therefore resist. If we can improve the supply position, we shall improve the whole situation.'

According to Rommel, the Duce offered another Italian division for Tunis, but the former declined saying that it would be better to equip the existing troops. There were already 300,000 troops (of whom 116,000 were German) and 40,000 air force in Tunisia.[14]

The tone of the interview was cordial, if a little acrimonious at the end.[15] Mussolini repeated that one must hold on, 'otherwise an American landing in the South-East—in Greece—may be inevitable'. It was a minor irony that Rommel himself, on the basis of such appreciations, would be sent to Greece at the end of the following July.

Rommel bore no rancour towards the Italian leader. 'Actually, I had always had a great regard for the Duce. He was probably a great actor, like most Italians. He was certainly no Roman, though he tried to act the part. Although of a high intellectual capacity, he was far too dependent on his emotions to be able to carry through his ambitious plans . . . Now the Duce saw his dreams crumbling, it was a bitter hour for him, and he was quite incapable of shouldering the consequences. Perhaps I should have spoken differently to him at the end, but I was so heartily sick of all this everlasting optimism that I just could not do it.'[16]

At the end of this interview, the Duce asked Rommel if

he had seen Goering. 'I have to call on him later, but I want to leave at once unless I receive orders to the contrary.' But Goering wanted to see him. 'He seems noticeably anxious to come with me to the Fuehrer's Headquarters. I declined the offer as I wanted to make my report without Goering's continual interjections, which, being invariably of an optimistic tinge, were too attractive.'

The meeting between Rommel and Hitler took place on March 10 at the latter's advanced headquarters in Russia. The Fuehrer lay under the shadow of Stalingrad, and defeat increased his delusions. He rejected without discussion Rommel's guarantee to defend 'our southern European flank' with the 'African' troops re-equipped in Italy. 'I would beat off any allied invasion in Southern Europe. But it was all hopeless. He instructed me to take some sick leave and get myself put right so that I could take command later for operations against Casablanca.'[17] Hitler had been reluctant to remove the most popular German Field Commander, even though the conflict of policy in North Africa rendered the decision imperative.

On March 14 Hitler wrote to Mussolini that he had sent Rommel 'on leave for reasons of health as, in the opinion of the doctors, and it is also my personal impression, he needs this urgently . . . I want however to give you, Duce, a personal explanation of the definite reconstruction of the command in Africa. In any case I would ask you, Duce, especially that, on the sending on leave of Marshal Rommel and on the temporary changes in the African command, absolute secrecy is maintained . . . And specially in this case it would be very dangerous for us to divulge the news. I would ask you therefore, Duce, to give instructions in this sense to your various headquarters.

'What is more tragic is that this man, who is among my bravest officers, with exceptional gifts of bearing and courage, should have failed in the problem of supplies, which can only be solved by a massive increase in sea transport.'[18]

It is difficult to appreciate how such a problem at any stage was the responsibility of Rommel. But Hitler seems to have accepted such an unworthy judgment. A month later he told Admiral Horthy at Salzburg, 'The best German General has lost his reputation in Africa through lack of supplies.'[19]

The removal of Rommel had the indirect effect of forcing the unwilling Duce's attention back to the critical issue of supply convoys to North Africa. At the instance of Count Cini, the Minister of Transport and Communications, who was still ruffled at Goering's blustering on the state of Italian ports and communications, a special meeting of the Italian Service Chiefs on March 10 was held at Palazzo Venezia to review the state of the Italian Merchant Navy on which depended the future of not only the last foothold in North Africa, but also the maintenance of the Italian war effort itself. This was the first attempt of a technical civilian minister of the February Cabinet to press for the efficient management of public affairs. Italy was facing a supply crisis, which, as Mussolini said in opening the discussion, 'can in practice paralyse the defence'.

The ensuing debate not only revealed the desperate nature of Italy's position, but also the rumblings of discontent, particularly of Count Cini, at the chaotic and amateurish direction of the war with an implied criticism of the Duce himself.

Cini's task was to open the review of the situation. The state of the merchant navy 'which constitutes the central problem of the war situation, is very grave'. It consisted of 3,300,000 tons in 1940; 560,000 was subsequently acquired from France; the losses as at March 1 stood at 2,200,000. This left 1,470,000: leaving out of account those ships which were laid up or under repair, and also tankers, 595,000 tons remained, and those were mostly slow ships.

'The number that can effectively be used is very small owing to lack of escorts, enemy air and submarine attack, lack of port installations, loading berths, warehouses and railway sidings, of loading and unloading due to the situation of the workers. Military requirements affect this by requiring irrational use of shipping. Sometimes ships have to leave half loaded and return empty. In such a situation we are further faced with an alarming rhythm of sinkings. The average of the last eight months is 50–55,000 tons a month. That of the last two months is 80,000. One should add to this rhythm, an increase in demands for shipping. There is also a transport crisis in being, or rather, should I say, it has been in being for some time.'

In the next four months it was hoped to replace the merchant fleet at the rate of 100,000 tons monthly, and taking into account sinkings, by June 30 the total figure available would be 450,000 tons. By more rational organization this estimate might be improved, but 'the situation cannot be substantially changed. One must consider it in its reality; one must relate programmes to possibilities. This, however, is the concern of the man conducting the war.'

The Duce commented on this survey that 'he is gratified for the clear and explicit exposition which only today, March 10, 1943, is shown in its full reality in contrast to the vague figures which have been hitherto given. We must also not forget that we have been at war for 33 months and have had to supply nearly 300,000 men in Libya. Our losses would have been smaller if we had been able to neutralize Malta . . . In February we carried out only three operations against Malta; these led to a concentration of enemy forces there with a consequent rise in our losses.'

The situation was now reviewed in relation to Italy's military commitments. There were nine theatres to be supplied, of which in present circumstances Tunisia and Sardinia were the most important. The total armed forces involved were 1,250,000 men, and they needed supplying at the rate of 337,000 tons monthly.

'The problem is most serious in Tunisia. 120,000 tons a month are required. Taking into account sinkings at a rate of about 30,000 one should dispatch 180,000 tons . . . Thinking in terms of convoys of ten ships each, we ought to send one convoy every three days, which is impossible.'

In Greece, transport was much delayed because the Balkan railways made a minimum contribution. They also had to supply Crete and the Aegean. They were run by Germany. There was no joint Axis agreement. The result was that the main burden fell on supply by sea.

The Duce interposed that one should increase convoys on the North African run and cut down on the Adriatic run. Use of Balkan railways must be improved. 'One must bear in mind that the forces in Greece will have to be increased.' The new problem was that of labour force and raw materials.

Cini spoke as an experienced leading industrialist. No revolutionary change in the situation could be expected. 'It would be interesting to hear, after these comments, who is responsible for the conduct of the war.'

The Duce 'insists again that one should not think of a revolution in the situation; that would be a dream; it is a matter of keeping afloat, of holding out. He quotes a minute which he had kept, in which figures are given showing that in June, or the latest July, we would have remained without a drop of petrol and fuel. After which date we should have had to seek an armistice. On the contrary, we have remained afloat.

'At the worst today we dispose of 600,000 tons of shipping, and with a loss of 100,000 a month in six months we shall be left with only fishing boats. The essential is to protect our patrimony now while preparing to safeguard what we shall have later. Anyway no one can state that our losses will be at the rate of 100,000 a month.'

Cini 'points out that the present situation is already at the limit of our possibilities'. It had taken the major disasters of the previous winter to bring about one such revealing meeting.

A series of contacts between the Fuehrer's headquarters and Rome now took place as preliminary soundings on which a summit meeting between the two leaders would be based. Following Goering's return to Germany, Kesselring was also summoned to report to Hitler. On March 13 Kesselring had a meeting with the Duce.[20] The pending conference at Hitler's headquarters was to review the whole position in regard to preserving the Tunisian bridgehead and in particular to overhaul the vital machinery of convoys. As Kesselring told the Duce, 'Admiral Doenitz has also been summoned. He will then return to Rome with him on Monday or Tuesday. Given the presence of Admiral Doenitz, he assumed that the present Mediterranean situation will also be discussed. Before taking leave, Kesselring stressed once again the necessity of increasing by every means shipping for Tunisia.' He also asked whether the Duce had any message for Hitler and was told that it had already been suggested by Mussolini in his letter of March 8 that a meeting might take place at the end of the month or the beginning of April and that Mussolini wanted to discuss the whole situation.

'For my part,' he told Kesselring, 'I consider that the possession of Tunisia is a question of vital importance, and equally the problem of building up Sardinia as a defensive position. Here the Duce stressed his anxiety about an eventual Anglo-American landing in that island; reports from Gibraltar showed that preparations included 4,000 parachutists and other troops, the total of which corresponded roughly to the forces assembled at the time for West Africa.'

A further Italian division had been sent to Sardinia, which the Duce thought was the most threatened of the islands. The enemy would 'in the next few weeks' launch their offensive in Tunisia. Kesselring's estimate was 'at the next full moon'.

The meeting at Hitler's headquarters took place on the following day, March 14. He gave a concise summary of the 'African problem'.

'Tunisia is strategically of prime importance. The conquest of Tunisia means a saving of four to five million tons and more to the enemy . . . The 80,000 tons per month cited as necessary by the Italian Supreme Command are entirely inadequate; rather, 150,000 to 200,000 tons monthly are needed. We estimate for each division about one train—500 tons daily. For the eight divisions in Tunisia, inclusive of the Italians . . . a total of 4,000 tons daily. It is impossible to supply armies by air . . . Protection of convoys by the Air Force alone is not possible; ships continue to be required. The Straits of Sicily must teem with patrol and escort vessels. Good organization is essential. Only the German navy can organize this . . . It is therefore necessary at the present time to confront the Italians boldly with the alternative of either making an all out effort to get through supplies regardless of personnel considerations, or to lose Tunisia, and with that also Italy.'[21]

Doenitz was to be authorized to present these views to the Duce, and they were embodied in a personal letter from Hitler, which Kesselring was to deliver before the German Admiral arrived. The letter, dated March 14, dealt both with the military situation in North Africa, especially the central nagging question of convoys and supplies.

'. . . Among the questions of great importance which engross me at the present time, the first, Duce, is the preservation, and possibly also the extension of your positions in North Africa . . . On the other hand I cannot refrain from holding the view that all this can succeed and is only possible if the supply problem is faced and resolved in a truly radical manner. This is the decisive factor, Duce; not so much the air weapon as the organization of escort protection . . .

'The solution of this problem, Duce, is of such importance that on it depends the fate of your North African possessions, and that, at the same time, is also an important condition for the victorious conclusion of this war. I am therefore sending to you perhaps the best naval officer that the German Navy has ever had, Grand Admiral Doenitz, to make proposals to you, Duce, which I would ask you to examine solely from the point of view of the necessity of adopting whatever measures are appropriate to settle this most important problem.'[22]

Admiral Doenitz's mission to Rome was to deliver an ultimatum. If the Italians were unable to handle the North African convoys effectively and independently, the Italian naval machine was to be penetrated by German 'experts' and in reality taken over.

The situation was reviewed at a meeting held by the Duce at Palazzo Venezia on March 15. Doenitz approached the subject cautiously by suggesting an exchange of experiences with the Italian navy on convoy work by attaching German naval advisers to the Italian General Staff and in certain ports. German anti-aircraft crews could be installed on Italian escort vessels. It was proposed to hand over seven or eight ex-French vessels now in Bizerta or Toulon, and Doenitz wondered whether they should not be grouped into an all-German convoy escort as an experiment.

The thought of German control by stages of the Italian navy, even though in the last resort the latter was totally dependent on German oil supplies, was inconceivable. Rather than produce counter-arguments, the Duce embarked on a glorious alternative. 'In event of an enemy attack on Sardinia, which I regard as more probable than that against Sicily, I want to bring out the fleet, including the battleships. There is however one great difficulty, lack of fuel oil. I would be very sorry if we were not given this opportunity of attacking the enemy naval forces . . . From reports received it seems that the Anglo-Americans want to land in Tunisia and therefore they will have to protect their convoys and accept battle when our ships appear on the scene. I am prepared to run this risk.'

Doenitz's only limp reply was, 'I will get in touch with Berlin immediately; as I do not know exactly what we have available.'[23]

The Duce was suffering from a fit of optimism. Provided that 'the Russian chapter could be liquidated in some way or other', the Axis would turn to the West and regain the initiative lost the previous autumn. As he wrote to Hitler on March 26: 'It should be realized that the Anglo-American landing in North Africa has been a fortunate move in that it has created a new strategic situation, which allows them to think of carrying out plans which earlier would have appeared fantastic—

namely, the invasion of the Continent. That such plans exist and that the enemy is preparing to carry them out, I have not the slightest doubt. Now we have the possibility of converting what was a happy conception and a lucky, not to say easy, enterprise into a catastrophe which could have incalculable consequences on the development of the war, especially in the United States. The Allied expedition to North Africa would become a disaster if the Axis resisted in Tunisia to the end. And it is to make this resistance possible that I have sent you an urgent request for air reinforcements . . .' This must be coupled with a major operation in the rear of the Allies across Spain and into Morocco. The Balearic Islands were to be occupied to give the Axis control of the Western Mediterranean.

The revival of the discarded operational plans of 1940–1 on the creation of a Spanish theatre of war was now to be the magic Italian contribution to a revised Mediterranean strategy, though the mention of a practical Italian military contribution to such an extension of the war is not touched upon.

Mussolini's letter continued: 'The day when the first German armoured unit arrives in the rear of Gibraltar, the English fleet must move out and cannot go to Alexandria (if we still control the Sicily channel). Even without conquering the Rock of Gibraltar we would have—with long-range artillery—control of the straits, and from the air also of all the Atlantic ports which today serve the Americans. Cut off from supplies, the fate of the Anglo-American troops would be sealed. What I propose to you is a bold move, but you have given too many proofs of your audacity for this not to interest you. And after all—since Roman times it has been said—fortune favours the bold.

'It remains to consider—what will Spain do? Nothing. She will not oppose because she cannot, and because such a move is also to her advantage. Spain will let well alone. This manoeuvre, which should of course be like lightning, would restore to the Axis the initiative in that sea which will be decisive for the fate of the war, and will allow Italy to march with Germany to the end.'[24]

The mirage of Malta in the previous summer was now replaced by the illusion of a successful operation against Gibraltar, which would decide the war in the Mediterranean.

At least one German witness however was sceptical of the Duce's powers of advocacy. Prince Bismarck, Counsellor at the German Embassy in Rome, told a senior visiting German official, who was preparing the ground for the forthcoming summit talks, 'I do not foresee, on the part of Mussolini, any particular embarrassing request. His fleet does not exist, his army is problematical. His future is even more so. He feels himself to be weak. Even in the past he has avoided raising questions of principle in his various meetings with Hitler, and it is unlikely that he will do so now. Hitler only thinks and talks of military matters, and this is not a favourable platform for Mussolini. One can say of Hitler that he has and does make mistakes, but he has also ended by being competent in military questions. Mussolini has remained a dilettante. Even in this field he sticks to generalities. I can say, since I have seen the minutes of the talks between Mussolini and Hitler, that the Duce has never taken the initiative and never raised general questions as to the political line to adopt.'

The long awaited meeting with Hitler had to be postponed 'as a result of the opening of the Anglo-American offensive in Tunisia', but as the Duce explained in his letter of March 26, he ought to be able to get away 'during the coming week'.

CHAPTER FIVE

The Home Front

'THE ITALIAN situation must be carefully examined as far as the Home Front is concerned, since we can only go on fighting if it holds. Moreover, any new serious military blows can be borne only if the whole nation is fully prepared for them.'

One of the Italian informants of the German Embassy in Rome began with these words a long and comprehensive report on internal conditions in Italy in February 1943. The 'Changing of the Guard' at the beginning of the month had but briefly affected the scene. 'It was with a real feeling of relief that true Fascists heard of the ministerial changes, while anti-Fascists did not hide a certain interest in the affair.' This dramatic move by Mussolini was intended to demonstrate the strengthening of government action at the centre, but his solicitude for the retiring ministers, who were all provided with honorary posts, 'gave rise to the comment that if the Duce had wanted to throw them overboard he had not the courage to condemn them, and this strengthened the belief that either he put up with them through weakness or they really were implementing his wishes and commands'.

The Duce, as was his habit, had shelved responsibility for the darkening scene at home. The situation was comparable to that of 1917, after the grim military defeat at Caporetto, but with instructive and basic differences. During the crisis of the First World War the country was governed under a parliamentary and party system; in the Second, by a totalitarian régime. Fascism alone would be responsible for a collapse on the Home Front, and equally only the 'system' could take steps to prevent such a disintegration. The Duce 'still enjoyed prestige in many circles', and if he adopted 'a more energetic conduct, as the lower classes in particular demand', he could regain 'a respect which today is completely lacking'.

In 1917, military defeat had led to the occupation of three Italian provinces and a direct threat to the vital industrial areas of the North. A million refugees from those territories brought the reality of war to the country as a whole. The disasters of 1942 at Alamein and in French North Africa were the decisive events in the loss of Italy's imperial position on the African continent. The war had not reached the shores of Italy whose metropolitan territory was still intact, and, apart from the demoralizing air bombardment of the main Italian cities, the ordinary Italian was relatively protected from the effects of the war. In 1917 the country was exhausted by general mobilization and her last military reserves and hopes lay in one age group—that of 1899. In early 1943 the bulk of Italy's man-power had not yet been called up.

'Since Fascism is a totalitarian régime it leaves no room for spontaneous patriotic reactions as in 1917. Therefore the régime alone can bring about a recovery, just as it alone can make the collapse of the Home Front fatal, and final defeat inevitable.'

The official war propaganda and measures of Fascist government had signally failed in their purpose. There had been no organized building up of morale. The uncertainties of the period of non-belligerency in 1939–40, the lack of clarification to the public of Italian war aims, the deliberate and hectoring underestimation of the strength of the enemy, and the late introduction of food rationing, together with its corrupt and ineffectual administration, created a general climate of absence from the conflict, and a lurking sense of unalarmed defeatism.

As Mackensen's informant wrote: 'People are saying that this is a transition government, and that Mussolini is going to choose better men. This is the wishful thinking of true Fascists. But they themselves cannot fail to wonder whether while the house is burning, anyone has thought of how to extinguish the blaze once the house is burnt down. For their part, anti-Fascists are taking advantage of the ever-increasing decay in the country, of the lack of authoritative intelligent leaders at the Ministries and in the Party, of a general slackening of public order, to raise a threatening head. And those who do not do so are spreading everywhere the corrosive poison of their defeatist, pro-democratic, anti-German campaign.

'Vidussoni's nomination only stirred a unanimous wave of

ridicule from Fascists and anti-Fascists, who found themselves in agreement for the first time. In a country which has been making wars since 1911—the Libyan war—it is quite normal for an Italian to be a veteran, and the heroic loss of an arm is something worthy of great respect but not of political reward. What is more, after Fascism has preached the need for preparing men for posts of leadership however small, the sight of the supreme Party position in the country being entrusted to a young man who has not even taken his degree, as the communiqué announcing his nomination said, and who appears increasingly lacking culturally and mentally, has been and continues to be a cause of very great weakness to the Party. This boy, whom even true Fascists persist in not taking seriously—and therefore the Party whom he impersonates—is surrounded by other young men of no political colour, devoid of ideas and above all out of touch with the present moment . . . Their propaganda is of schoolboy standard, and leaves Fascists unmoved while producing quite contrary effects in other circles.

'The Party today is not respected, its strength is only superficial; Fascists of the old school or those who would like to bring it back to fighting condition are kept at a distance, and sometimes not even intentionally, but because young men who have become party leaders do not and cannot know anything about the Revolution and the men who made it. When the rumour was spread that not even the Duce is satisfied with Vidussoni, that he has been a disappointment to him, the Party Secretary lost his last follower, and with him the Party passed into the second rank, while it still keeps all the organizations which should today be functioning at full strength, so that Italy is facing the battle for the home front with no political organization at all. The regional situation reflects that at the center. Everything leads one to suppose that at this rate the Party will shortly not even be in a position to keep its own members loyal, and discipline itself, superficial and choreographic, is tolerated with more and more impatience and less and less respect.

'Since the country's political and social activities are entirely incorporated in the Party, it is easy to imagine what an abandoned and decadent state they are in, with very obvious detrimental effects to resistance on the home front.'

This devastating analysis reveals the basic failure of Italian Fascism to capture the loyalties of the second generation. The same writer also gives a revealing picture of the effect of this cardinal weakness of the system as it affected in particular the élite of the 'second wave', the student youth, of whom Vidussoni, in spite of his academic failings, was intended to be the symbol. Despite their incorporation in the Fascist youth and university para-military organizations, which had been the pride of Starace and Ricci, these young men displayed 'very little Fascist feeling. The older classes up to 1910, whether called up or not, show a certain amount of seriousness and understanding. The really young, the students, are easily influenced by the atmosphere, which just now is not over-favourable to Fascism among the middle classes to which these students belong. When the figure of the Duce appears on the cinema screen, only the proletariat, young men in their thirties, and one or two from the lower middle classes, applaud. The very young are silent, more indifferent than hostile, even if that morning they were wearing Fascist uniforms. The widespread opinion of these youngest generations is that Fascism should be purely profitable: this mentality does not make for willing sacrifices. There are brilliant exceptions, but against these the mass of the young is at least detached from Fascism when it does not adopt—even if on the Party registers—Bolshevik tendencies favoured by the climate in intellectual circles.'

The responsibility for the maintenance of order and morale lay, however, with the machine and leadership of the Party rather than with the heads of the various ministries, and in the former sphere there was spreading a climate of frustrated alarm under the lengthening shadow of military disaster. Increasing reports of discontent in high Fascist circles reached Palazzo Venezia. The Duce was never short of information or informers. The files of his secretariat had accumulated, since the beginning of the régime, an indiscriminate mass of intelligence and gossip. The human game involved, and the individual weaknesses exposed, appealed to his sardonic humour, and his own intuitive judgment of men was rarely affected by the flow of denunciation and hearsay which passed daily across his desk. The Party dossiers, and the police reports which from an independent angle supplemented them, were among the most revealing comments on the climate of the régime.

On February 16 one such report was sent to Palazzo Venezia, drawing attention to disquiet in Party circles at Vidussoni's 'lack of capacity, which each day is further emptied of any meaning'.[1] The Party Directorate was the centre of strife: 'The poetaster Ravasio (one of the Party Vice-Secretaries) leaving Rome every now and then like an hysterical woman . . . making no mystery of the fact that he declines all responsibility, seeing that the Party comes to no decisions and is lost in idle chatter. The effect of this attitude of a Vice-Secretary, who was believed by all to have the confidence of the Duce—(he was the Dictator of the official Fascist review *Gerarchia*)—has a bad effect even among intransigent Fascists. Ravasio spends his time denigrating Vidussoni. His accusations are met with approbation and in effect they correspond to the truth. Vidussoni limits his functions to visiting the wounded in hospital, football and boxing matches. He does not know the business or the personalities of the Party. The questions which people are asking are: "Why does the Duce, who has so much human material at his disposal . . . keep at the head of the Party a boy of twenty-six, who does not know men or business or can make speeches or organize, and who has no ability of a political character?"

'Why doesn't the Duce place in positions of leadership men who have already had a following in the provinces and in the nation? The Federal Secretary of Naples, for example, has no hold on the masses. He is one of the young men transferred from one province to another "like railwaymen". A possible answer has been the nomination of Tarabini and Scorza, both old members of the action squads, at the centre of affairs. But independently of the fact that Tarabini is regarded among the old leaders as a nullity, and Scorza has been given a secondary sphere from a political point of view, their inclusion has made a bad rather than good impression. Vidussoni and Farnesi, the senior Vice-Secretary, regard the two as possible candidates for their succession, especially Scorza, and are out to sabotage them. The picture presented is the reason why the Party does not exist.'

On a sterner and more practical note, another 'Memorandum for the Duce' referred to the Party directive of November 1942, calling on members to help with the grain harvest.

But the passive resistance of the agricultural masses was matched with the failure of the Fascist industrial confederations to control the industrial workers. Although wages had been nominally blocked in 1940, labour was short, particularly in the war industries, and employers would pay illegal rates. The workers tended to ignore the syndicates and make their own terms.[2]

The whole structure of the Corporate State, so pompously advertised in the 1930's, was coming apart at the seams, and together with the failure of economic regulation of prices, productivity, and supply at the ministerial and Party level provoked the internal crisis on the Home Front parallel to, and accelerated by, the successive disasters in the military conduct of the war.

It was such a situation which was characterized even by the Political Police as 'the progressive degeneration of the State'.[3]

Intensive Allied bombing of the Northern industrial cities added to the disruption of economic life, and to the general spirit of defeatism and discontent. There had been rioting at the departure of certain troop trains for the Russian front, and, between August 1942 and February 1943, sporadic strikes throughout the industrial centres of Northern Italy.

The rationing situation, placed fatally in the hands of the Party and its organizations, was alarming. Food prices had risen from an index of 100 in 1939 to 172 in 1942. At a private meeting of the Fascist Syndicate leaders in October 1942 in Milan, their leader Malusardi said, 'Wages are lower by not less than 5.80 lire a day in relation to the official cost of living.' And at the same period the Duce himself had telegraphed to the Milan authorities: 'In the great industrial centres the hardship from the point of view of food supplies is becoming increasingly acute.'

At the beginning of March there was a sudden explosion. At 10 o'clock on the morning of March 5, the workers at the large Fiat Mirafiori factories downed tools. The prearranged signal was to be the daily testing at that hour of the air-raid sirens. The management had however been warned, and no test took place. But within a few minutes all work stopped throughout the plant, and the news spread through Turin. Although Fascist militia units had been standing by since dawn, as the authorities expected some planned demonstration, no immediate counteraction was taken. By that evening the strike had spread to seven other factories in Turin. On March 8 the local secretary of the Fascist Confederation of Industrial Workers had cabled the new Minister of Corporations in Rome, Tullio Ciannetti, that token strikes at 10 o'clock that morning had involved between 30–35,000 workers. By March 12 over 100,000 had come out. The following day, secret meetings of the strike leaders were held in Turin at which economic demands of the strikers were discussed, and the drafting of leaflets decided, calling for a continuation of the movement and its extension to other regions. On March 14 the underground committee of the Italian Communist Party for Lombardy met in Milan to hear a report on the events in Turin and Piedmont. In the following days the agitation ranged through Lombardy. The call to strike was announced in Milan on the 24th, and the Pirelli and Falk works followed the example of Turin. Over 130,000 workers seem to have been affected, and the key war industries of the country were temporarily disorganized.

Behind the economic demands for a paid 192-hour month, a cost of living bonus, and increased rations, lay traces of concerted political agitation. The Fascist authorities had been aware of the increasing activities of clandestine groups during the course of the previous year. Although the main leadership of the illegal Communist Party was either in exile or under arrest, cells had been strengthened, and the underground press re-established.[4] The attention of the police had been particularly drawn to the intensive leaflet propaganda circulating in the previous January and February in the industrial areas of the North, and the Communist paper *Unità* had reappeared since June 1942. It was also logical that Turin should be the historic centre of a revival of political action against Fascism, with the memories of the civil conflicts of 1920. A National Action Front had appeared there at the end of 1942, and an appeal was published in *Unità* on December 27 calling for a separate peace and directed particularly towards 'soldiers, officers, militiamen and honest Fascists'. This Front was in effect a liaison committee linking together the small groups of the old anti-Fascist parties, the Communists, Socialists, and 'Justice and Liberty'. (The Socialist-Liberal group in exile in France founded in 1929 by Carlo Rosselli.)

The frame was established on Communist initiative, and their few cadres planned the militant strike action of March. The Front itself held no regular meetings and played no part, as such, in the strikes. It was primarily a symbolic signatory of leaflets, and an intermittent secret forum for exchanging ideas and programmes. The Italian Communists were particularly concerned to act as the initiators, and indeed organizers of a Popular Front, but not as an isolated group. Although the myth of these strikes appears in Communist historiography as an exclusive achievement, the figures from their own sources are a striking endorsement of their own tactical intentions at the time. The key strike, initiating the whole movement, which broke out at the Fiat Mirafiori works had been planned the previous month by the leader of the Communist cell there. Out of 21,000 workers, there was a cell of 80 members, none of whom paid regular party subscriptions until the following May, and in three other leading Turin factories the cell membership at that time was 30, 72 and 60 respectively.[5] The essential significance of the movement was that by the action of such small cadres a mass explosion was generated, with decisive effect upon the structure and prestige of Italian Fascism.

The reaction of the Fascist authorities revealed even more faithfully than the phenomenon of the strike movement itself the weaknesses of the régime. The Chief of Police, Carmine Senise, describes the situation in his memoirs: 'The strikes were proclaimed for economic motives, but with political aims, particularly as the factories where the workers folded their arms were all engaged in war production. We had wind of this strike some twenty days previously, as I had got hold of certain instructions issued by the Communist Party. I took these personally to the Duce, who read them carefully and kept them . . . Although forewarned, it was obvious that the Police could do nothing to forestall it. I do not know what action the Corporative organs took, but can only think that the Duce must have given some instructions, if only to observe the attitude and state of mind of the workers, all of whom belonged to the syndicates. The notable fact was that everyone took part in the strike, Fascist and non-Fascist, even those who were members of the Militia. At the Fiat in Turin there was a special Legion composed entirely of workers in their factories, set up by agreement between the Party and the management with the aim of controlling the political behaviour of the masses. These militiamen took part in the strike like all the other workers, and one cannot possibly imagine that they did not understand the aims of a movement which had an obvious political character and was opposed to the war.

'The Head of the Government never summoned me to report during the strike, but only telephoned me every morning to ask for the latest reports from the local chiefs of Police . . . I do not know what instructions he gave.'

Such instructions as were given were not draconic. As the Vice-Secretary of the Party, Scorza was sent to Turin on

March 17 and visited the party sections at Fiat, but had no contacts with the workers as a whole. All Fascist Party members were now ordered to wear black shirts at their places of work. On March 27 the leaders of the Fascist syndicates met in Milan, and were addressed by their local head, Malusardi, who stressed the political character of the agitation, and threatened the strikers that they would be treated as mutineers. In fact they were technically under military law. But the official attitude was 'soft'. Some strikers were mobilized and sent to Sicily. Some 300 were arrested in Milan. 164 were likewise picked up in Turin, and 87 charged. Directions to the Prefects were concentrated on Communist activities, and the police were instructed to keep watch on what lay behind 'the pretext of economic concessions', and to observe with particular attention military circles where the Communist movement 'hoped to set up armed groups'.[6]

The leader of the original Fiat strike was caught with some thirty companions. The police realized that they were facing an organization directly working for a collapse of the Home Front. In the report to the Chief of Police in Rome, the head of the Public Security in Milan stated:[7] 'The results of the operation, both from the capture of propaganda material, and from the confessions of the majority of the accused, prove objectively that the reconstruction of the Turin Communist Party has taken place, personally directed by an emissary of the party so far unidentified, and that the subversive work undertaken by it aims at destroying the national structure, inciting the working masses and even the army against the war and the German ally, to rouse the people against the régime, and against the powers of the State.'

This emphasis on the role of the Communists in popular agitation was both a familiar tactic of the Fascist authorities, and an expression of the fear of a historic bogey created in the past by themselves to justify the original take-over of power. The response of the masses to action by a handful of conspirators was in reality more alarming than the party allegiance of that minority, and the consequent revelation of the weakness of the hold of the Fascist Party on those masses revealed more effectively than ever before during the history of the régime, the hollowness of the achievement of the Corporate State. Cianetti, the Minister of Corporations, and as such the most actively challenged of the members of the government, later described his visit to Milan:

'When as an old syndical organizer I confronted thousands

of workers who immediately went back, although the Fascists showed themselves to be completely passive in the workshops and in some cases had even fomented the strikes, this latter phenomenon impressed me enormously and made me see that there was something which was wrong, and I returned to Rome with the precise conviction that one must put on the brakes a little.'[8]

But the significance of these March strikes is perhaps most harshly and clearly stated in a letter from Farinacci to Mussolini on April 1: 'I have seen the demonstrations of the workers in Milan though naturally standing in the background. I have remained profoundly embittered both as a Fascist and as an Italian. We have not been capable of taking either preventive or repressive action, and we have violated the principle of authority of our régime. In Milan events have deprived the local Party Secretary of any authority, though he is a fine comrade and brave fighter, but without the strength to dominate that situation. And then there is Liverani of the industrialists, and Malusardi of the workers who did not know how to avoid what has happened, and then were unable to get themselves taken seriously by the workers.

'If they tell you that the movement has assumed an exclusively economic aspect, they are telling you a lie. The attitude of the workers at Abbiategrasso (a small industrial town near Milan) in front of Cianetti is eloquent, as also the flowering of leaflets clandestinely printed, which give the demonstrations a deliberately and preordained anti-Fascist character. The few arrests do not count. One must have the courage to make an example which will give the workers in other factories and cities something to think about. We must not worry about what Radio London or Moscow may say, but about how to maintain the solidarity of the internal front and the prestige of the government.

'As to the State administration, you will admit that it does everything to make trouble for you. For the last three months the industrialists themselves have been saying how necessary it is to do something for the workers and you yourself were aware of this. But the Confederations, and the whole machinery, have moved at a snail's pace. And now I . . . take the liberty of proposing to you that you make an example both at the top and the bottom, but at least fairly high up, and do not always take on yourself the responsibilities for the mistakes of others.

'And do not rebuke me if once again I repeat to you that the Corporative experiment with all its innovators, improvisers, doctrinaires and demagogues has not succeeded in the spirit of our political faith and according to our aims. One must leap to the defence, and force the organizers of the war effort away from their grand ministries, among their secretaries, typists and assistants, into contact with the masses. Naturally for this we need capable and honest people who are able to make speeches and have a certain physical bearing. You know from experience that the masses want to receive a certain magnetic influence from their orator . . . If *you* were talking to a crowd of Bolsheviks or priests, you would get them to clap before you opened your mouth.

'The Party is absent and impotent . . . And now the unbelievable is happening. Everywhere, in the trams, the theatres, the air-raid shelters . . . people are denouncing the régime, and not only this or that party figure, but the Duce himself. And the most serious thing is that no one reacts. Even the police do not function, as if their work was now useless. We are facing a period when military events may become agonizing. Let us defend our revolution with all our strength . . .

'My dear Prime Minister, why do you not summon the Grand Council? Let everyone give vent to his feelings, speak his mind, and come away comforted by your words.'[9]

Here was the first call to a review by the Fascist leadership at the summit, above the Party secretariat, of the internal scene in Italy. The 'system' was facing the greatest political crisis in its history since the murder of Matteotti and, as in 1942, Farinacci incarnated within the higher ranks of Fascism the demand for harsh measures.

His proposal for the summoning of the Grand Council was the first such move in 1943, and it was not until three months later, when the military situation reached the final edge of disaster, that Mussolini yielded to the request.

The National Party Directorate met on March 11 under the direct shadow of the strikes in Piedmont and Lombardy, of increased allied air attack on Italian cities, and of vague but verifiable signs of overt criticism of the régime. The Duce's traditional opening speech was more truculent than usual, and deliberately played down the unrest in the industrial North. He was perhaps not yet aware of its extent and implications. It was not a pungent oration, as he was not yet convinced of the need of another purge in the Party secretariat, and he was anxious to avoid drastic public changes, following so soon on the ministerial reshuffle of the previous month. He was also anxious not to increase still further the already lively preoccupation of the Germans with the Italian Home Front.

His speech was, however, as always a subtle amalgam of the gusts of public opinion, as seen through the prism of the gossip, rumours, and police reports which represented the information, scanned and selected by the Duce, and on which he based his political judgment.

'Some people complained recently of the Party's lack of activity in various manifestations of Italian life. Evidently many of these critics forget that 1,387,000 of the enrolled members of the Party are in the forces. It is clear that if these members were at home the general activity of the Party would be more intense. On the other hand, at times like the present the Party must have only one simple essential object —to keep the home front steady.

'At our last meeting [on January 3, 1943] the main points of discussion were the following: the Russian campaign and the bombing of Italian cities. The Russian winter campaign has had various psychological effects, so have the American landings in Algiers. There were some people with weak nerves, and some people who are the scum of the earth, who thought that when the Americans disembarked they would be much nearer us in four or five days.

'Thus when the Russians overran first the Roumanian front, secondly the Italian, thirdly the Hungarian, and each time the German front, these people thought that Stalin would arrive at Longatico [a small seaside resort near Rome]. This was absurd. I never doubted that the Germans would succeed in first halting the Bolsheviks and secondly taking the initiative . . . What happened then? A large number of Italians, who at first were afraid that the Germans would win, showed a remarkable instinct for self-preservation . . . Some Fascists wished to belittle the work of Fascism during this war; they seemed to say "this is not a Fascist war, that is an accusation brought against us by our enemies, this is Italy's war". We must react energetically against this attitude . . . It has been said that this is Italy's war because it is Fascism's war, and that it is Fascism's war because it is Italy's war. I reject distinctions of this kind. Even if they are made, do not believe that they will have any effect on our enemies: they will continue to say that this war was desired by me, Mussolini, because I am a friend of Hitler . . . As regards the spiritual attitude of Italians, if you look for enthusiasm among any of the people engaged in this war you will not find it. This war is one which goes behind individual feelings and thoughts . . . This demand for enthusiasm is idiotic. We must rather see that discipline prevails. It would be absurd to lament a few scattered events.

'Organized movements of any kind have only recently taken place. One at Milan was slightly serious because attacks on the régime were planned. Finally one was liberal-communist in character. Some people realized that a people cannot be content, consequently they invented a name, "liberal socialism" or "social liberalism". Anyhow, just recently there appeared in Turin the first sign of a combined workers' movement. Here are the reasons for it. Evacuation pay was given to the families of evacuated workers. At a certain point workers who remained demanded an equal increase of wages. In general I have always been opposed to doing this, and at present I assert firmly that we must not give a single cent. We are not a liberal state which can be blackmailed by one hour's stoppage of work in a factory. I consider such payment as real treachery . . . Thirty years ago the programme which we have quietly carried out for the Italian workers was considered to be an extreme socialist programme. We do not ask for any gratitude for this . . . but if these men abandon their work at a time like this, when the whole life of the nation is at stake, if they do not pull themselves together in the shortest possible time, they will be treated as one treats those who leave their post of duty at the front.

'The Secretary of the Party has given the figures of enrolled members. Members are one thing, Fascists are another . . . We must purge the Party, because now, as in 1924, individuals who have no courage think they win merit by disappearing so that they may be forgotten. However, it is certain that we do not forget them.

'As regards the young, we must be very careful. The great mass of young people is all right, but there are certain tendencies which demand our attention; for instance, this lack of interest in the history of world events and this listening to foreign voices. Further, it is essential that during and immediately after air attacks the Party should be present. Fascists must regard themselves as soldiers or rather as fighters . . . As for criticism, Italy is an extraordinary country. Newspapers can say what they like . . . Recently an article appeared in which attention was drawn to the possibility of a compromise peace with remarks addressed particularly to the Anglo-Saxons . . . This article made a great impression, and made people think that the Italian people were tired and hoped for a compromise peace. In peacetime I am indifferent to anything that may be said of me, of the régime, of Italy and of Fascism. But in war it is a different matter, because what is said may raise the morale of the enemy . . . The newspapers talk about everything; I do not object, but they must be intelligent. The Government does not consist of infallible beings . . . We sometimes make mistakes in our planning. Sometimes the people wait a long time for interesting plans of ours to be put into effect.

'What I wish to stress is that there is no substitute for the Party which constitutes the necessary link between State and People . . . The State must keep in touch with the People, for our State is not a police or absolute state, not a monarchy which says "This is my pleasure" . . . In war-time the people have justifiable susceptibilities, and non-fighting Fascists must not lay themselves open to criticism from the people who are suffering . . . That which belongs to the State is one thing, that which belongs to its citizens is another. Now there is a tendency among many people to confuse these things, to indulge in some small profiteering, making use of one's political career. This is a very bad thing. Sometimes it is not a negligible matter. For instance, there is this mania for trafficking . . . It is bad enough when it is carried on in Italy, but much worse when done by soldiers abroad as it was in Croatia, Dalmatia, Albania, and now is in France. It is very bad for the country's prestige . . . As a country we still suffer from the common phrases used to describe us three centuries ago . . . We have fought, we have built the swiftest ships in the world, we have built whole cities and produced heroes who would honour the greatest peoples, but we cannot free ourselves from the old epithets of sellers of statuettes and organ-grinders.'

The impression of Mussolini's speech and of the situation which it reflected was less comforting to some at least of the Party leaders. Bottai noted in his diary on the same day, March 13: 'Rumours and more than rumours of an imminent crisis in the Party. One asks what man could, at the point which we have reached, restore life and movement to this heavy and cumbersome body. "Both too late and too soon" was the answer of someone to whom I talked. And it is so;

too late in regard to the war-time crisis, which does not allow those profound changes of direction and structure capable of persuading the country of the existing political and moral validity of Fascism; too soon for the post-war crisis which will involve a total transformation of men and ideas.'[10]

The German Embassy in Rome had for some time received a prompt if truncated report on each occasion of this valuable first-hand evidence of the Duce's appreciations of the moment. In so far as he ever expressed to an audience his unfettered thoughts, he seems to have done so on these occasions, and this series of speeches seems therefore to represent the most valuable evidence of all the current mood and preoccupations of the Head of the Italian Government.

On the next day, March 12, Mackensen sent the following telegram to the German Foreign Office: 'In spite of the strong rule of silence, a member of the Directorate of the Fascist Party, solely because of his friendly attitude to the Reich, has transmitted some information from yesterday's meeting of the Directorate on the improvised statements made by the Duce on Italy's internal and external position . . . The Duce's remarks are a clear proof that he has expressed, not only for us Germans, but also for that circle of men on whose co-operation he is primarily dependent his unbending will to fight the war to the end on our side, and his unshaken faith in a common final victory . . . In view of the absolute necessity to avoid giving this strictly confidential communication any office circulation at all, I ask that as an exception it should be transmitted as a direct report.'

This telegram was shown to the Fuehrer personally by Ribbentrop the next day, and the latter minuted by hand in the margin. 'The Duce is still the only *man* in Italy.'[11] But this unexpected phenomenon of the March strikes came as a disagreeable reminder to the Germans of the fragility of the Italian political front. Hitler, at a Military Conference, expressed his dismay at the stoppage of work in Turin, 'Yes, and note—for wage increases'. Jodl interjected: 'Communist manoeuvres'. Hitler exploded: 'But that it is possible for people to stop work firmly in eight factories is for me unthinkable. And then no one dares to intervene. They have put a stop to it—but even so, after hesitating whether or not to intervene in a radical manner. I am convinced that if one shows the slightest weakness in such a case, one is lost. But that is what I am saying the whole time.'

If the Fascist régime in Italy collapsed, were there extreme elements loyal to the Axis on whom the Germans could depend to maintain the war effort?

German penetration of Italian Fascist circles, and indeed intelligence on Italian political affairs, was superficial and uncoordinated. Himmler's organization, as represented by Dollmann in Rome, nurtured a circle of 'friends', mutually disloyal and of secondary importance in the hierarchy. It was not until the spring of 1943, and conceivably as a result in part of the March strikes, that the German Security Service was allowed to operate directly on Italian territory and was able to report from its own secret wireless station from Rome on the spreading signs of conspiracy against the personal régime of the Duce.[12]

CHAPTER SIX

The Royal Secret

'As from January 1943, I took the definite decision to put an end to the Fascist régime and to dismiss the head of the government, Mussolini. The carrying out of this precaution was made more difficult by the state of the war, and had to be both prepared in the smallest detail, and conducted in the utmost secrecy, which was also respected by the few persons who came to talk to me of the discontent of the country. You were aware of my decisions and personal directions, and you know that these alone, from January 1943 onwards, led to the following July 25.'

In theory it should be possible for the King to dismiss his Prime Minister without disagreeable consequences, but although the constitutional myth of the Monarchy had survived the successive violations of Fascist legislation, no one knew in practice what would follow such an assertion of the royal prerogative. The Prime Minister was also the Duce of Fascism. The dyarchy of Monarchy and Party marked the point where the political revolution had stopped, and it was this dualism of loyalties which generated the confusion of the Italian scene.

If, when all else failed, the Crown should be forced to take political action, would the Party accept the decision? If the Monarchy was driven by external events into the centre of Italian political life, from which it had withdrawn in 1922, the whole balance of forces in the régime would be inevitably changed, and the beneficiaries of Fascism might in their turn revert, as twenty years earlier, to the panaceas of illegality. The retired revolutionaries might find themselves called up. This eventuality was ever present in the calculation of the entourage of the King, and the shadow of a Fascist counter-coup lies henceforth over each move and sounding of the Court.

Nor could the internal political scene be considered separately from the military. The fate of the régime was conditioned by the course of the war. The very problem of the intervention of the Crown was posed by the mounting threat of the greatest national disaster since the collapse of the Italian front at Caporetto in 1917. Only extreme circumstances, threatening military collapse and political chaos, which would involve the monarchy itself, could induce the King to act.

So long as there was any hope that the war situation could be restored, no such action would be envisaged. But in an atmosphere of rising pessimism, the whole range of possible solutions must be studied, and each related to the peculiar structure of the régime as conditioned historically by twenty years of Fascism. The historical significance of the present crisis was the undoing of the consequences of the March on Rome.

The political future of Mussolini depended on the successful conclusion of hostilities, which was remote unless, at least as a first stage, Hitler could be induced to liquidate the Eastern Front; or on the even more improbable negotiation of an acceptable compromise peace with the Allies, with or without German consent. The development of the internal political scene in the coming months would be governed by these postulates, and every move must be observed and studied within the privileged enclave of the Royal circle.

The Minister of the Court, Duca Acquarone, as the King's main adviser and confidant, would have to be the most accurately informed on the intricate interplay of political affairs both within the Fascist Party and machinery of government, among the retired elder statesmen and Army marshals, and to be aware of the lineaments of a clandestine opposition. And in particular he must keep in close touch with the General Staff and the governing circles of the Armed Forces. It might be that military events would force brutally on the Crown a decision in adverse internal circumstances, and some elementary precautions would have to be taken. In this sense it is possible to trace the rudimentary frame of an emergency royalist coup d'état.

Ambrosio, as Chief of the General Staff, reported daily to the Duce, on whose reactions everything depended, and there was always a hope that a top-level solution of the war might still be found.

In a subsequent statement after the event, Ambrosio said:

'It is not completely true that in the early days of my appointment as Chief of the General Staff I had already drawn up a plan for immediate action, or shall we say, forcible action. I certainly knew our military situation well: I realized that it was desperate. But my initial hope was to be able to persuade Mussolini to make a rapid "disengagement" from the Germans.'[1]

Among the officers attached to the Supreme Command was General Castellano. He had been involved in routine military planning since February 1942, but with the changes following on Ambrosio's appointment he undertook, in part on his own initiative, the task of keeping in touch with the world of politics. He already knew Ciano, with whom he had been in contact through another politically-minded young General, Carboni. After the February changes, Castellano came in closer touch with Acquarone.

Shortly afterwards the former drafted a plan for the removal of Mussolini, listing the measures to be taken to avert a Fascist counter-coup, the action to arrest Mussolini and the Party leaders, and the military plans to be put into effect against a German reaction. According to Castellano, both Ambrosio and Acquarone saw a copy of this draft, and Ciano knew of its contents. Castellano's superiors seem to have advised caution, and he settled down to cultivating political and diplomatic circles in Rome.

The corridors of the Fascist Senate in these weeks were the scene of active speculation. Here was one of the few places where the small group of ageing survivors of former governments and the commanders of other wars, the remnants of the political élite of the days before the March on Rome, could meet with impunity and exchange impressions of the increasingly fragile Italian scene. Outside the circle of the Court, here was perhaps the only place where a discreet club vintage anti-Fascism could be audibly voiced, although the open debates were unanimous in their sycophancy. Here in a fragmented prism could still be discerned the historical shape of an earlier political world, that of the Ultras of a future Restoration.

On February 23 the King received a survivor of this generation, General Zuppelli, who had been Minister of War in 1915, and was now a Senator. 'He is an old man of eighty-four, and a little afflicted with age. He spoke to the King in an excited and agitated manner, advising him to support a coup d'état and chase Mussolini out "on his two feet".' At the end of the audience, the King was 'rather annoyed' and told General Puntoni, 'The situation is serious, but not desperate . . . A new element could intervene and radically change situations from which there appears to be no way out. In any case a coup d'état at this moment against the Duce and the régime, with Germany in the house and at the gates, is completely inopportune.'[2]

Constitutionally, the Senate was the only surviving organ of the pre-Fascist State, and in theory could be the focus of a potential National Front. But behind the outward forms of an inviolate enclave within the 'system', lay the broad reality of senile subservience. The body had long been in the main infiltrated and packed by beneficiaries of the régime.

As Marshal Caviglia noted in his diary: '. . . The present situation can be managed either within the Party or the Senate. If the Senate were more independent, if it were not so subservient to Mussolini, it could easily settle the situation. But as it is not independent, one would have to find a hundred senators, more concerned with the fate of Italy than of Mussolini . . . Let these hundred senators make a collective request to the President of the Senate to call on the government in plenary session to expound the conduct of the war, and to define what are the national interests which inspire the administration, for there is no doubt that the interests of the State must be clearly separated from those of Mussolini. But perhaps it will not be possible to persuade a hundred senators to adopt with courage such an attitude.'[3]

The possibility of a rift within the Fascist Party played an early part in royal calculations. An ideal but improbable solution would be the rejection of the Duce by the Fascist Party, thus enabling the King to act constitutionally, and untrammelled by a hint of illegality. It was more likely that leading elements, particularly those who had played a role in the events of 1922 in helping to establish the original compromise between Fascism and the Monarchy, might seek in declining circumstances the arbitration of the Crown.

A 'constitutional' Fascist administration might provide a temporary makeshift, or individual figures from such a grouping might strengthen an eventual coalition. Such a solution would cause the least disturbance of the political scene. The personal role of the Duce would be replaced by a 'National' government including 'moderate' Fascist elements—a reconstruction of the 'compromise' of 1922 without Mussolini. But it depended essentially on the eventual attitude of the Western Allies, and also on the co-operation of at least certain leaders of the pre-Fascist parliamentary groups, who still survived either in the Senate or in retirement.

The 'Changing of the Guard' in February 1943, however, was in effect the expulsion from the government of those very moderate elements of the Fascist movement, who might fit into such a royal design. Their acknowledged leader was Grandi, and, although dismissed from his post as Minister of Justice, he remained as President of the Chamber, and was thus strategically placed in a central position to initiate discussions with the politicians of the Party.

On February 12 Grandi was received by the King in audience on his retirement as Minister of Justice. On leaving he entered into conversation with General Puntoni, the King's military secretary. 'One must not have any illusions,' Grandi said. 'Italy should attempt little by little to unhitch her wagon from that of Germany to make the crash less painful. I have always been a supporter of a policy of understanding with Great Britain, and within the limits of my power have always sought to oppose the thrust in the direction of Germany . . . On the home front, in face of the apathy of the great mass of the people, a general lack of confidence in their leaders, there is the resentment of many of the old Fascist elements, who have been frustrated in this desire to make and serve the country. For them, Fascism should be an instrument of redemption. At any moment, in face of military disaster, a political movement could take shape with a social basis which the Communists would at once exploit. Only the King at the right moment could restore things in their place. It would, however, be a most difficult and dangerous operation. For my part, I am with the King.'[4]

The following month a more significant move was made on Grandi's initiative. In February he had sought the support of Mussolini in approaching the King on his behalf as a candidate for the highest Italian order, the Collar of the Annunciation, which made its holder the symbolic cousin of the Sovereign.[5]

The first reaction of the monarch was cool. The honour would have to be conferred in Grandi's capacity as President of the Chamber. The King would therefore be obliged to bestow it also on Suardo as President of the Senate 'and there is no chance of doing that after the recent gossip about Senators giving information to the Police'.

Within forty-eight hours, however, Victor Emmanuel abruptly changed his mind, and the order was bestowed on Grandi. 'Was the conferring of the Collar a part of the conspiracy, by any chance?' This honour did however give Grandi, in principle, unrestricted access to the Crown.

The ministerial dismissals of February had, as was intended, outwardly dispersed the Grandi-Ciano circle. The former spent much of his time between Bologna and Rome. Ciano did not come out of the Vatican Embassy until the summer. Bottai busied himself with the Roman scene. Little or no continuous contact between these men can be traced until July. Ciano's removal from political office threw him into the shadow and his future role, if any, would be subordinate to that of Grandi.

In event of an open political crisis, and constitutional action by the Crown, the Army would inevitably be involved directly in politics. Not only would internal law and order have to be maintained, but the issue of the conduct of the war and relations with the German ally would have to be faced. The new administration, whatever the details of its composition, must be headed by a military figure. The ultimate choice of the Crown was limited to the thinned ranks of the surviving figures of the First World War, and in effect to two: Badoglio and Caviglia. The events of the previous winter had already posed in general terms the problem of the succession to the Duce.

Both men had long been rivals and enemies, and each sought in private to strengthen his personal following in military circles and in the Senate.

Badoglio had not seen the King since his dismissal as Chief of the General Staff in December 1940, but he had for some months been increasingly active behind the political scenes. In December 1942 his 'proposition' had been made to Ambrosio, then Chief of the Army Staff. At the turn of the year, the Marshal had made his own private soundings in British circles in Switzerland, which were presumably not unconnected with recent developments in Vichy France. The concept of transitional governments by reliable Marshals might have an appeal in certain Allied circles.

In January Marshal Caviglia noted in his diary: 'Badoglio too is actively promoting his own succession to Mussolini. He has apparently prepared his ministry and indicated the ministers for the different portfolios.'[6] In the Senate, and in the military clubs of Rome, he had already been sniffing the atmosphere. According to Cassinelli, Badoglio had expressed on several occasions his anxiety at the lack of suitable candidates for a 'National' administration. 'Several times he consulted the list of senators, and the parliamentary year books. The good ones were over seventy and the young have not shown themselves.'[7]

The dismissal of Badoglio's rival and personal enemy, Marshal Cavallero, now gave rise to much speculation and there were few candidates on the top level for military appointments. Badoglio had already been in touch with the new Undersecretary of War, General Sorice, and, when consulted, had shown a direct interest in the appointment of a 'reliable' Commandant-General of the Military Police. In the event of internal political tension, the importance of this post, controlling the forces of public order, was considerable. It was with Badoglio's approval that General Hazon, who had served under him in Africa and was already in the confidence of the Court, was appointed.

The German Ambassador had been warned by an anonymous informer that Badoglio 'is busy bringing together individuals who do not see eye to eye with the government, and carrying on anti-Fascist activities in those sections of the army still loyal to him'.[8] Sorice had also alerted Badoglio that the King was displeased with him 'because he was creating a Fronde'.[9] This deliberate note of caution preceded a summons to the Quirinal. The royal audience appears to have taken place on March 6, and it is perhaps significant that four days previously Ambrosio, in his new capacity as Chief of the General Staff, had called on Badoglio.

The latter had not seen the King since December 1940. He explained his impressions to the Sovereign in very general terms. 'When a war is made on the explicit calculation that it will be short and if the preparations are for a lightning war, it is lost as soon as the opposite happens. When the country is against war, the war is lost. Every month we descend one step more towards defeat.' The King answered: 'I am also of this opinion,' and here the conversation came to an end.

The police reports reaching Mussolini gave a different impression. Badoglio had been received by the King 'last Saturday'. The conversation had lasted one and a half hours. It was rumoured that the King had asked him to take over the Supreme Command, and that the Marshal's terms were that there should be no interference in military affairs by the

Duce, nor by the Commander of the Militia, which must come under the direct control of the Army.

In any event the King had made a significant personal link with one of the few military leaders with a national, if controversial reputation, and an active following in Army circles.

General Ambrosio told Puntoni after a royal audience on March 13 that the Duce ought to retire in favour of Badoglio. The King remarked: 'He (Ambrosio) is a gallant fellow, who does not mince words. He says what he thinks, but this is not always a good method.'[10]

On March 15 Caviglia sent a private memorandum to the King written, it would seem, under the influence of the March strikes. 'Politically what should one do? The duties of the people are distinct from the will of the Crown. It is not for the King alone to handle the situation, but Italians. It is they who forcibly brought Mussolini to power, thus violating the laws of the State. The King, in order to avoid civil war, accepted the revolutionary solution . . . At the most he gave his consent and advice. Today the question can only be resolved by Italians . . . One should not pay too much attention to the activities of various groups which have sprung up at this moment as a natural reaction, and which often show little historical or common sense. The conflict of views between parties was after all no less serious during the Risorgimento when they were struggling for the unity and independence of Italy. So long as the situation is handled under the aegis of the dynasty, its solution will have a legal orderly character, and the troops will still obey their leaders. But if events take a different course and the troops do not obey, if there is an internal revolution with or without Soviet influence, there is no predicting what might happen. But, in order to avoid excesses, there should be twenty or thirty divisions in the country itself, the Militia must be incorporated in regular regiments and divisions, the organization of the Fascist Party must be handed over to the Military Police, in the early stages the senior officer in each province must take over the Federal Secretary (the regional head of the Fascist Party), and equally a non-commissioned officer in the place of the political secretary.'[11]

Caviglia, too, had his supporters among the survivors of the First World War. On March 16 the King had received Admiral Baistrocchi, who wished to hand to the King a memorandum. It was received with some scepticism. Baistrocchi proposed the setting up of a military government headed by the Prince of Piedmont, with Marshal Caviglia as Vice President.[12]

The ties between Caviglia and the heir to the throne may well have militated against the former. The Prince was not in the close confidence of his father, and his household was at times regarded as the source of a possible rival political solution.

Although the whole machinery of the opposition parties to Fascism had vanished after the totalitarian legislation of 1925, a number of politicians, particularly of the former Socialist and Liberal parties, remained in the country on the fringes of retirement, or with one foot in the Senate.

The military reverses in the winter of 1942 gave a spurt to these survivors of an anti-Fascist parliamentary opposition, and brought some of them together in secret conclave. By the end of the year regular meetings were being held in Bonomi's house at No. 4 Piazza della Libertà in Rome.[13] A discreet series of consultations took place between former colleagues. Their names recall a whole political world. The three leading Liberals in Rome were Alessandro Casati, the representative of his party in Mussolini's second cabinet, who resigned, after the acceptance by the Chamber of the legislation of January 1925 setting up the machinery of dictatorship; the Marchese Tomasi della Torretta, Minister of Foreign Affairs in Bonomi's own government in 1921 and afterwards Italian Ambassador in London; and Senator Alberto Bergamini, a former director of the *Giornale d'Italia.* The group met each Sunday in the latter's apartment in Rome. These men formed an elementary 'shadow cabinet' maintaining links with other survivors, with Vittorio Emmanuele Orlando, the Prime Minister of the First World War, together with Marshal Caviglia and others.

In the Via Cola di Rienzo in Rome, in the office of one of the former secretaries of the Catholic Popular Party—also dissolved in 1925—the group held frequent meetings with Alcide de Gasperi and Meuccio Ruini, the acknowledged leaders of Christian democracy in event of a major political change, through whom discreet relations with the Vatican were established. The Socialists too, represented by Giuseppe Romita, came to meetings at this address, and an embryo coalition front came into being, representing the historical currents of constitutionalism and a party system. Here were the Guizots of an Italian Restoration, innocent of any revolutionary intent.

Early in their discussions, it became clear that any initial action against Mussolini could only be taken on the initiative of the Crown, and that these clandestine political groups could only represent isolated and unorganized traditional currents of opinion.

With the organs of political control exclusively in the hands of the Fascist Party, an effective opposition could act only under cover, as yet inviolate, of the Monarchy, and through the prestige of an Army with its traditions of loyalty to the Royal House. Unless such a line was pursued, the alternative would be a popular revolution, sweeping away not only Fascism but also the vestiges of a constitutional monarchy.

The Monarchist solution, to which Bonomi and his group were instinctively and temperamentally bound, met with obstinate opposition from the younger generation of anti-Fascist intellectuals, whom Bonomi and his friends in Rome now sought to approach.

In recent months another centre of private discussion appeared in Milan, grouping together businessmen, writers, and university professors round two young Southerners, Ugo La Malfa and Adolfo Tino. From this group emerged a strong element of suppressed republican Radicalism, latent in Italian politics since Mazzini. As Bonomi put it: 'This current saw no other solution except a Republican one and deludes itself that a popular rising at one blow would rid Italy both of Fascism and Monarchy, setting up a democracy with anti-clerical tendencies, determined to punish the Church for its approaches to Mussolini enshrined in the Lateran treaties.'[14]

The Rome and Milan groups established regular links, and the debate between them initiated in clandestinity early in 1943 was to become the central political theme of the Resistance movement in Italy. By April, with external events moving fast, Bonomi felt it imperative to sound the Royal House, at the same time grouping as far as possible on a united programme the democratic elements in Rome and Milan with whom he was now in touch.

His first approach to the Court had already been made in the form of a secret meeting with the Princess of Piedmont in a villa near Rome. Bonomi gained the impression that the Crown had decided to remove the Fascist régime, and that the Army would follow the King. Clearly the second condition was decisive and, at the Princess's suggestion, he saw the Undersecretary of War, General Scuero whom she had indicated as a leading anti-Fascist in military circles. The latter was less optimistic. 'The Army was not prepared for a coup against Fascism and its then head, Marshal Cavallero, was still closely tied to Mussolini.'

At the same time, through intermediaries, Bonomi was kept in touch with the views of Acquarone, and although discouraged by what appeared to be an absence of any military preparation, these contacts remained in being.

At the beginning of April, two reports from the Vatican caused alarm in the Rome group.

'1. The British Minister to the Vatican, ably questioned by Professor Gonella, a friend of De Gasperi and a discreet and serious person, let it be clearly understood that England would prefer a monarchical solution and that the withdrawal at this moment of Italy from the struggle would lead to notable compensations from the Allies. But action must be quick and there should be no delays in seeking for more radical solutions.

'2. The efforts of Grandi and Ciano were not being rejected out of hand by the British Minister Osborne. This showed that the Anglo-Americans, in order to come to an early solution, would not only accept proposals from the Monarchy, but also the mediation of elements of Fascist origin, even if they were now dissident.'[15]

Bonomi and his friends feared that this information might signify the beginning of an understanding between the Monarchy and Grandi and Ciano, and they hastened to try to restrain their Republican friends, now grouped in the clandestine Action Party which had been formed in Milan in January.

The March strikes in the North had accelerated the formation of anti-Fascist groups, representing the varying strands of historical resistance to the régime, and in particular the Communists, in the Northern industrial cities. Some time later the first clandestine meeting to include a Communist delegate was held at a palace in the Piazza del Popolo in Rome. He was Professor Concetto Marchesi, Professor of Latin at the University of Padua. His intervention, on party instructions, was directed towards supporting for tactical reasons any decisive proposals which the Crown might make towards the overthrow of the régime. The Communists were ready to enter a 'new government even with a minister without portfolio'.[16]

It was now essential to have some first-hand impression of

the intentions of the Crown. Apart from Acquarone, the King was rarely available to anyone. His two conversations with Marshals Caviglia and Badoglio had therefore been an eager subject of discussion among these elder statesmen, but revealed no hint of the King's thoughts.

At a meeting at Bonomi's house early in April it was decided to approach the one man who had automatic access to the King—apart from the officials of the Court itself. As Chancellor of the Orders of Knighthood, the Duca del Mare, Thaon di Revel was alone in such a position. The old Admiral, Commander-in-Chief of the Italian Navy in the First World War, was a traditional Piedmontese aristocrat with an almost religious respect for the person of the Sovereign. With great reluctance he agreed, and having gone to church to pray for divine strength, he sought a royal audience. This led to no result. 'The King entrenched himself behind the usual constitutional fictions, asserting that only the Chamber and the Senate could provoke his intervention.'[17]

There was nothing to do but wait for a sign. The King had told Puntoni of his conviction that henceforward it was not a matter of concealing from oneself the need of a decisive gesture in regard to men and affairs. But he said that one must choose the right moment and avoid in the most absolute manner any headstrong action. 'A mistake in the choice of the moment,' he said, 'could be fatal to the country.'[18]

CHAPTER SEVEN

The Axis and the Shadow of Stalingrad

DURING THE February talks in Rome Ribbentrop had been instructed to oppose any 'political' solution of the Russian war. Hitler was determined at all costs to bring his anti-Bolshevik crusade to a successful conclusion. There could be no European community or a common political programme prior to a decisive military victory. Although any open opposition in high German circles to this rigid approach to the European situation could but vaguely be discussed, the Italians began to receive reports which showed that cautious doubts existed in diplomatic and military circles in Germany.

How far Ribbentrop himself shared these anxieties at the time is beyond precise analysis. If he felt any such hesitations, he was careful never to put any such hints on record. But at his post-war trial at Nuremberg, and in his posthumous memoirs, fragmentary references do occur, suggesting that he may have held at moments such a view:

'During the sad days which followed the end of the battle of Stalingrad I had a very revealing talk with Hitler . . . On this occasion and in a later memorandum I again suggested peace feelers to Moscow, but the document suffered an inglorious end. The Fuehrer would have nothing to do with it, and had thrown it away. I mentioned the subject once again during a personal conversation, but Hitler replied that he must first be able to achieve a decisive military success; then we could see. Then and later he regarded any peace feelers as a sign of weakness. Nevertheless, I did make contact with Madame Kollontay in Stockholm through my intermediary, Kleist, but without authority I could do nothing decisive.'

Bastianini has since stated that he discussed privately with Ribbentrop in Rome the possibility of sounding the enemy with a view to a separate peace. He attempted to persuade the German Foreign Minister to make contact with the Russians, while he would seek to approach the British and possibly the Americans. Ribbentrop did not categorically dismiss the suggestion.[1]

At the end of the Rome talks, one of his advisers, Megerle, had a private discussion with Babuscio Rizzo, Bastianini's chef de cabinet. This seems to have been the first hint to reach the Italians that, behind Ribbentrop's official attitude, certain such hesitations existed. Although none of the German leaders could oppose Hitler openly on the issue of the Russian war, some of them thought, and possibly Ribbentrop himself, that the only person who could persuade Hitler to seek a compromise solution with the Russians was Mussolini. Goering also, during his visits to Rome, appears to have hinted in the same direction.

Megerle seems to have taken a calculated risk in his talk with his Italian colleague. According to him, the German people, although sorely tried by the war, were resolved to support unreservedly the Fuehrer's orders to mobilize all the material and spiritual forces of the country, so as to organize a formidable resistance to the bitter end in all areas. But Europe would never collaborate effectively in Continental resistance by the side of Germany unless not only German methods but her whole vision of the Europe of the future were profoundly and radically altered.

'It is impossible to think of continuing to govern with bayonets and violence, and it is essential to associate the people of Europe in the future order of the Continent through terms and forms which are roughly acceptable to each, or at least to the majority of them. This, in his opinion, is the central problem that the Axis has to face and solve today, in order to make resistance into something virile and active, capable of creating those material and spiritual foundations without which concepts of a "New Order" would be vain and sterile, since until now, all the European peoples without exception have associated it with undisputed German dominion.'

According to Megerle, the task to convince not Germany, but her rulers, 'of the absolute necessity of profoundly modifying their present vision of Europe, belonged and now belongs more than ever, to Italy, under pain of falling completely short of what has always been and continues to be her specific and extraordinarily important mission within the

Axis, and which is, above all, the most valid justification of her presence in the Axis.

'Since the possibility of a total military victory of German arms is compromised, he knows that the actions of Fascist Italy are automatically destined to rise in the estimation of friendly European peoples, who have in effect now transferred their hopes from those arms to the spiritual and political resources, possibilities, and capacities, of the Italians. And Fascist Italy must profit from this in order to speak to Germany with words now no longer solely Italian, but European, and therefore of much greater weight and importance, and to interpret those tendencies and demands which are the only living and vital things on the Continent today, and which alone can undo those *idées fixes* which move the peoples of the hostile coalition, and consequently diminish their capacity to create offence and resistance.

'Megerle did not know what the Duce had said yesterday or proposed to say to Ribbentrop, but he ardently hoped that he would speak with his authority, prestige, and wisdom. He said in these explicit words: "The Duce is the only man who can do it. Even we Germans think of him in our minds as our most effective interpreter with the rulers of Germany, who, too immersed and absorbed in the cruel war, are perhaps of necessity driven to see and appreciate only the military side of the problem too vast and too complex to be reduced exclusively to these narrow limits." There are many men who think in this way in Germany, but they have not yet reached the highest positions of command, although they are near them. At any rate, they are from now on building up around the German rulers that atmosphere which will facilitate every work of persuasion to this effect. Ribbentrop has certainly a strong personality. He is obstinate and stubborn. It is difficult for him to listen to other people. To exert an effective influence over his mind, it is necessary to choose the right moment, words, and circumstances. But, under these conditions, he is open to persuasion—this is what Megerle and his friends will continue to do.

'Megerle earnestly and repeatedly recommended that the source of these impressions should not be revealed in any circumstances: that is, that his name should in no event be mentioned. For this reason, it would seem that the time is not yet ripe enough. He spoke with conviction; and, at times, with an emotion which he did not trouble to hide.'[2]

A cryptic confirmation of such an attitude in certain German circles appears in a brief record of a talk between General Ambrosio and the head of the Italian military intelligence, General Amé, on the afternoon of March 6. The latter reported on his conversation held recently in Venice with his German colleague, Admiral Canaris, who pointed out how the morale of the German population had been affected by recent events. 'In the main the situation on the Russian Front is still viewed with pessimism.' The fall of Tunisia was inevitable, and the submarine campaign could not produce decisive results.

What subtle ultimate motives Canaris may have had for his defeatism have not been clarified, but the future of an opposition forming within the German leadership to Hitler's insistence on a war to the finish in the East might well depend directly on the future intervention of Mussolini with Hitler.

In this intricate and menacing climate, the rôle of Goering was obscure but not absent. Hitherto, the only shred of evidence as to his attitude had been his remark in private to Mussolini during his previous visit to Rome in December 1942 that the Duce's proposal of 'a new Brest-Litovsk' would be 'Hitler's ideal'. And this was prior to Stalingrad.

Early in March 1943, following on Ribbentrop's *tour d'horizon*, Goering came again to Rome. Although it is not clear what was said in the talks between the two men, it was at this moment that Mussolini re-opened the whole subject. At a luncheon at Palazzo Venezia, Bastianini noted Goering's 'reserve' when the Duce stressed that the Russian front must cease to exist in order to concentrate an all-out effort against the British and Americans in the Mediterranean.[3]

A few days later, in his letter of March 8 to Hitler, Mussolini in a carefully worded paragraph repeated these arguments: 'I ask myself whether it is not too risky to repeat the struggle against the boundless space of Russia, which is practically impossible to reach and grasp, while at the same time in the west, the Anglo-Saxon peril mounts.

'The day when, one way or another, Russia will be eliminated or neutralized, victory is in our hands. But I hope to discuss this thoroughly with you when I have the good fortune to meet you.'

On March 17 the Italian Ambassador in Berlin, Alfieri, was instructed to press for such a meeting, and this prompted him to review in a revealing personal letter to the Duce three days later certain relevant aspects of the German political scene relating to such a solution. 'I have been able to put together the reactions in those circles of the immediate advisers of the Fuehrer and Minister von Ribbentrop to your letter of March 8, which has made a strong impression on the Fuehrer, and which has been received in responsible circles with deep satisfaction; it is particularly the paragraph relating to the war on the Russian front which has aroused the greatest interest . . . You have thus fed the hopes that your view, listened to by the Fuehrer, may influence radically his decisions.'

Before attacking Russia 'the Fuehrer had to overcome resistance to his plans from both the politicians and the military, the latter stressing the inexhaustible reserves of men and material at the disposal of Russia, and the former the spectre of the feared "Second Front".

'This resistance reappeared, particularly on the part of the generals, during the campaign regarded by the Fuehrer as a war between two ideological imperialisms which could not be ended except by the annihilation of one or the other, and in which successes of a political or moral character ought to have an importance much superior to purely strategic results.

'The will to carry through his plans triumphantly, the increasingly violent clash with the reality of things, and the mounting resistance of the enemy, gradually led to an increasing rigidity in the Fuehrer's spirit and a great inflexibility and intransigence, fixing his mind on one sector of the immense theatre of the war, making him forget perhaps that the Russian was not his only mortal adversary.

'The lack of success of the plans worked out by the generals in the first phase of the war, drove Hitler to impose the offensive against Moscow; the negative results of this action led him to take over personally the supreme direction of operations. The campaign of 1942 culminated in the episode of Stalingrad, which Hitler had conceived of as a clamorous political success and around which he subsequently wished to create a legend of epic military sacrifice.

'This series of operations, worked and carried out by the Fuehrer, the practical results of which have not come up to expectations, have made a noticeable dent in the German war potential and have ended in weighing down the strategic situation on the Russian Front . . . Hitler, feeling himself personally and gravely committed and compromised in the eyes of his people, does not know how to bring himself to give up his design of avenging, by victory of arms, the disillusion and suffering of recent months, and on the other hand, he cannot see any other objective than the Russian one.

'The lively interest, with which responsible circles here have received the doubts expressed by the Duce as to the expediency of a total offensive effort on the Eastern Front, is clearly a reflection of the doubts present in the minds of not a few German leaders. They hope that on the occasion of a meeting, which it is hoped here is imminent, the Duce talking alone with the Fuehrer with complete clarity and precision, will drag him out of this fanatical atmosphere which has made him lose the correct vision of things, and will liberate him from the goad of the Soviet sphinx which dominates totally his thought.

'If the Fuehrer would give up, at least for the moment, the idea of an all out offensive in the East and could be induced to concentrate on the sector in the Mediterranean, the forces thus available could possibly obtain, with infinitely smaller means, and with results probably even greater for the entire war economy, that decisive success which he conceives possible only on the Eastern Front.'[4]

The hopes of an Axis summit meeting before the end of March were however dashed by a general Allied offensive in North Africa. But Mussolini persisted with his arguments about Russia, and wrote again on March 26 to Hitler: 'In the meantime, permit me to return to the subject which I hold to be decisive at this moment—Russia. I have discussed it at length with the Reichsmarshal. When we met at the Brenner on June 1, 1941, I told you that, with Russia, one had to choose between alliance or war. After the long and tormented meditations of which you have often spoken to me—and which few are better placed to understand than myself—you chose war, informing me of your decision a few hours before your troops crossed the border. History has proved that you were right. Russia had deceived Europe and the world, in the campaign against Finland too, and constituted a formidable threat in the rear of the Axis. In almost two years of war, through heavy sacrifices and acts of heroism such as have never been seen before, you have succeeded in weakening Russia to such an extent that she cannot, at least for a long time to come, constitute any real threat.

'For this reason I tell you that the Russian chapter can be closed. By a peace if possible—and I think it is—or by a systematic defensive—an imposing Eastern wall—which the Russians will never be able to cross . . . The summer advances and winter retreats cannot be repeated without leading to exhaustion, even if mutual, to the exclusive advantage of the Anglo-Americans. I would add that relations between Stalin and the Allies are really bad and that the political moment is somewhat favourable to us. In my opinion Russia cannot be annihilated, not even through the improbable intervention of Japan, given the enormous distances. The Russian chapter must therefore be liquidated in some way or other. On that day, we can put out our flags as victory will definitely be within our grasp. Having deprived England of the last continental army—and the most powerful—on which she has counted, the Axis, with all its strength, will turn to the West and regain the strategic initiative which since last autumn has passed into the hands of the enemy both on land and in the air.'[5]

At last the Duce seemed prepared to face the menacing issue at the heart of the Axis conduct of the war. On March 30, on the eve of the forthcoming talks, he reviewed the situation with Mackensen in Rome, who reported the following day: 'The Duce concluded his survey, which he made with great calm and with no trace of nervous tension or anxiety, with the remark that victory would indubitably be ours if we succeeded in liquidating the Russian Front. As to "how?" he did not vouchsafe further. However, I had the impression that particularly on this question he was thinking of talking to the Fuehrer.'[6]

A private and cautious sounding, similar to that of Megerle in Rome in February, was reported two months later by the new Italian Ambassador in Ankara, Guariglia, in the form of a conversation between a German diplomat on military service in Russia with a member of Guariglia's staff, who had been a former colleague of his in Moscow.

This memorandum throws a rare light on certain circles of German opinion, and of a latent opposition in Germany to the Fuehrer's conduct of the war.

'I am taking the liberty of summarizing for you the conversation which I had with a German official just returned from the Russian front, where he had spent two years with various military headquarters. He is a member of the German diplomatic service, whom I had occasion to meet in Moscow in 1929. It appears that he is at present concerned with Russian questions, and is awaiting demobilization. According to what he told me, he had come to Ankara "to pay a visit to his colleagues"; but before returning to Berlin, he will wait for Ambassador von Papen's return from Istanbul.'

After stating firmly that he was expressing his own personal opinions, he said: 'My stay at the front, my study of Soviet problems, and of the fortunes of the war, convinced me as long ago as last winter that a military solution in Soviet Russia is impossible. The war production of the Soviet Union is in good working order, and perhaps even increased, compared with the pre-war period; the difficulties of supply, and those relating to the civilian population, are not such as to worry the Soviet Government: the human resources have been severely tried, but can still feed the Red Army, and are in any case superior to the German ones. The defensive possibilities of the Soviet Union are inexhaustible, and if ever the German army wanted to undertake another summer campaign, the Red Armies would repeat their tactics of retiring to the East, making the German advance beyond a certain point difficult and dangerous. Even if the Russians were driven to the Urals, their powers of active defence would not be broken, while Germany would still have to face a front of several thousand kilometres. The maintenance of such a front would demand a number of men exceeding German manpower. The numbers used in active defence on such a front would be greater than that of the annual military intake into the German Army.

'In such conditions we must pose clearly before us the problem of finding some other solution than the military one. Is it possible to come to an agreement with Russia? The political prerequisites for it, and the conditions which we must or could offer the Russians in order to reach agreement, exist. I think that Stalin would be satisfied with the old frontiers, or rather with the line of demarcation fixed with Germany before the conflict, with the annexation of the Baltic republics, and with eventual loss of interest by the Axis in the Straits. We could moreover push the Soviet Union towards Iran, and find in a programme for the industrial reconstruction of the Ukraine, those reciprocal compensations which should appear as the basis of the agreement. It would be a question of knowing whether Moscow would be willing to negotiate on these lines, since in holding out such a possibility to the German ruling circles, we would be taking a very grave responsibility on ourselves. I think, however, that we must do it; and I think that we should not put off sounding the temper of the Russian rulers any longer than the autumn.'

The Italian diplomat interjected that, 'knowing the political mentality of the men in the Kremlin, and particularly Stalin's, I had not excluded the possibility in the course of this war of an agreement with Moscow in certain defined circumstances. For some time past the Soviet attitude towards her Anglo-Saxon allies had confirmed my suppositions. In my opinion, however, these circumstances needed to ripen still further, and the Russians needed to feel the real impossibility of breaking German military power. Then, perhaps, Stalin would be willing to negotiate. As far as the Soviet territorial hopes were concerned, I shared his opinion: Stalin was dreaming of ending his political career by making Russia the dominant power in the Euro-Asian continent. As to the Straits, however, I had to point out that the Russian presence in the Dardanelles would mean, to a greater or lesser degree, her predominance in the Mediterranean, i.e. in the Balkans and all the region washed by that sea. Since Italy lives—literally speaking—on the Mediterranean, such a solution would visibly affect her. For the rest, Russian entry into that sea would mean, later on, the encircling of Western Europe, and therefore also a threat to Germany.

'My colleague then tried to explain that the offer of the Straits to Russia would only be a move in the political game. In his opinion, the Soviet Union would not realize this dream because she would automatically line up against her not only Turkey, but those same Balkan states which now look on Russia as an elder sister. The Anglo-Saxons would moreover feel bound to prevent the Soviet advance towards the Middle East. Germany must now consider if her blood-letting is not to the advantage of a third party. Let others think of building dams against the Bolshevik danger in their own areas.

'Without going into the merits of these political forecasts, I want in conclusion to express some personal impressions which might help your Excellency to judge the value of the conversation. From the way my colleague expressed himself, and from his reiterated requests to keep the exchange of views secret, I became convinced that he was not only expressing his own thoughts, but that he wanted to establish general ideas on a subject already discussed in responsible (German) quarters. His repeated references to the necessity of resorting to political action at a certain moment in the war, a need which, according to him, is now understood and demanded even in German military circles, seemed to me important. Moreover, he denied all possibilities of scaling down the national structure of the Soviet Union, judging useless even the attempts made to such an end at Berlin with Caucasian elements. When I asked him finally what were the possibilities of convincing certain German circles of the expediency of what he had disclosed to me, he remarked that *"only narrow circles of the Party now rejected such ideas, but that they were already understood and admitted by the majority of the German ruling clan"*.'

On this remarkable document, Guariglia made certain comments in his covering letter to Bastianini:

'Two points seem to me especially worthy of your attention. (1) The doubts which Germany has about reaching a military solution in Russia, now or later. These doubts are also distinctly present in German circles in Ankara, especially military ones, and they are not hidden from me in intimate conversations with my German colleagues, except naturally, by those tied to Ribbentrop, whom, by the way, the others blame most for the errors committed in Germany. (2) The desire for a political agreement with Russia, who would be offered "Axis disinterestedness in the Straits".

'When Relli informed me of this extraordinary idea of his German interlocutor, I instructed him to give the latter an effective picture of the consequences which Russia's entry into the Balkans and the Mediterranean would have not only for Italy, but also for Germany herself.

'In fact the threat which Russia, as a Mediterranean and Balkan power, would then constitute to our country would at the same time menace Germany, not only as Italy's ally, but as making her liable to encirclement, in her turn, round her central European borders.

'The German diplomat replied to these observations that it was simply a question of a political "move", and that Turkey, the Balkan states, and . . . England, would see to stopping Russia! These ideas of German diplomats, and of Ribbentrop's "systems", are the very ones which have brought Germany to her present plight.

'Once Russian military power were firmly settled on the Straits, neither the Balkans nor Turkey would be a serious bulwark, while by closing the Straits, Russia would no longer be vulnerable to the British Navy. That leaves America—and although the North American penetration of the Mediterranean, the Middle East, and Iran, is being accelerated, it is now and probably will be for many years to come, only a primarily economic penetration, profiting from the present political and military contingencies, and completely indifferent to eventual Russian hegemony, provided that the latter leaves the ports open to American traffic.

'The Germans need to understand once and for all that they are making a great mistake in formulating war propaganda only round the Bolshevik dangers, and that they ought to make all Europeans and even the English see the Russo-Slav danger, of which Bolshevism is only the ideological disguise.

'If this mask were torn away, the Russo-Slav danger would no longer enjoy all those sympathies and assistance which the Communists of all European countries are freely offering at present, or she would enjoy them to a lesser degree.'

The immediate fears, on the part of the Germans, were however of a defection of the satellites as part of general Allied offensive action in the Balkans, and possibly with Italian connivance. This possibility played an increasing part in German calculations in the spring of 1943. Stalingrad had broken the myth of German infallibility, and given substance to a general desire among the Axis partners for a negotiated peace.

The rôle of Turkey in developments in South-East Europe must always be of special importance. Her major consideration was simple: the ultimate danger was the spread of Russian influence into the Balkans and up to the Straits, and the defence of these regions against such a threat was paramount. In this sense the success of Germany's campaign in the East was in the direct interest of Turkey, but it was the danger of a German military collapse on the Russian Front after Stalingrad that caused the Turkish leaders to reappraise the whole Balkan position, and accept the exploratory talks with the British at Adana.

As Papen later reported to Berlin. 'As previously reported, the possibilities of a preventive defence against a Russian thrust into the Balkans were discussed at Adana. The Turks took the view that the line of the Danube must be defended in time.'[7]

The Anglo-American commitments to the Soviet Union circumscribed any advantages, from the Turkish side, of safeguarding their vital interests by entering the war on the Allied side, and their realistic appreciation of this situation, as confirmed by the Adana conversations, led them to consider cautiously a line of action independent of either warring camp.

Since January, the Turks had begun soundings particularly

with the Yugoslav and Greek governments in exile, with a view to resurrecting plans for a Balkan Federation under Turkish leadership in order to preserve the whole area from Great Power control. Such a project, concerning an area of vital strategic importance, must affect all the belligerents.

The Germans were at once aware of these moves through intercepting the messages of the Yugoslav and Greek representatives in Turkey to their respective governments in London. From similar secret sources, they also knew that this Turkish plan had been communicated to Churchill at Adana.

The British were less alarmed than the Germans and Italians by such a project, being solely concerned with accelerating the early break up of the Axis positions in South Eastern Europe. According to Papen, Churchill had pleaded 'for a Turkish-Bulgarian rapprochement, as Bulgaria is the only Balkan state intact for the protection of Turkey and Near East in event of a German collapse on the Eastern Front'.[8] And again: 'Numan told Churchill that in all circumstances he recommended that the British should work with King Boris, as he was the only guarantee against the growing bolshevization of Bulgaria in event of a German defeat.'[9]

Such intelligence caused immediate and common concern in Berlin and Rome. The Bulgarians represented the only mobile reserve for the Axis in event of an allied landing in the Balkans. If the British influenced the building of a Balkan bloc under Turkish leadership in a neutralist and anti-Axis direction, a critical situation would ensue.

Mackensen reported from Rome after talks with Bastianini. 'As I have learned in confidence from the Italian Foreign Minister, the development of Bulgarian-Turkish relations is being watched at the moment with special care in regard to rumours from an English source that there may be a question of Bulgarian-Turkish negotiations for a non-aggression pact.'[10]

The scare of a possible Bulgarian defection, however, was temporarily dispelled during the course of the month.

A German Foreign Office memorandum noted that the 'Bulgarian Ambassador in Berlin reports that in Sofia one is convinced that at the moment Turkey is not up to any intrigues. One noticed the anti-Russian tendencies at Adana. The English went as far as they could to the limit permitted without directly compromising themselves in Moscow.'[11]

There was always, however, the danger of communist penetration into Bulgaria, and of a Russian-organized coup. Such a threat was the decisive element in the adherence of Bulgaria to the Axis, and indeed, by common agreement, formal diplomatic relations were maintained between Sofia and Kuibychev.

At the end of March, King Boris was summoned to Hitler's headquarters. His visit heralded a further general series of conversations with the heads of the satellite states of the Axis, reviewing the post-Stalingrad scene. He was shown in confidence the Adana military protocols, which had been obtained by the German Intelligence. The Germans seem to have been reassured by the King's reactions, and he was not subjected to any pressures. 'The question of breaking off relations with Russia had been discussed during the King's visit in 1942, and the King had asked for the break to be postponed. This point of view was also supported by the German Legation in Sofia.'

The Turkish plan for a new Balkan bloc was also raised with him, 'but without any concrete results'.[12]

Although the fears consequent on a Turkish-Bulgarian understanding had been dispersed, approaches were made in March by Ankara in the Hungarian and Roumanian capitals. These moves were regarded with renewed anxiety, as a precursory sign of a possible defection of the minor satellites.

The Hungarian Prime Minister, Kallay, informed the German Minister in Budapest on March 10 of the Turkish démarche, and Ribbentrop immediately sought Papen's comments in Ankara.

'The Turks have approached Kallay with the suggestion of an anti-Bolshevik pact—to include also Roumania, Greece, Bulgaria, Serbia and Croatia.' It was difficult to approach Greece and Serbia formally as they are occupied territories, 'but Kallay told Turkey that he was very interested and asked for further details. Kallay thinks that the proposal might bring Turkey nearer to the Axis and strengthen Roumania internally.'

Ribbentrop added that, from secret sources, the Turkish project of resurrecting a Balkan Union, and of attaching Hungary to it, was already known. But no clear picture emerged from Kallay's statements. 'In regard to Greece and Serbia, is the exiled or the local government envisaged in the Turkish project?'[13]

On March 19, Papen replied after consultation with the Turkish Foreign Minister. The latter denied disingenuously that any instructions had been given in the sense reported by the German Minister in Budapest. But Turkey would leave nothing undone to prevent a Russian move to the south-east. 'The best means would be an agreement between the Balkan states.' Papen's own thesis was that 'if the idea of a Balkan Federation was conceived as a protection against Bolshevism, it could only be considered in closest co-operation with us'.

Numan thought that 'given the tension between the Anglo-Americans on the one side and the Russians on the other, this worldwide conflict held within itself all the elements of surprise. One could not overlook that one or other of the Anglo-Saxon partners might strengthen itself by a separate alliance with the Russians, or that one day Germany might come to terms with Russia. Turkish policy must take into account every eventuality, and remain friendly with all warring parties.'[14]

On March 23 Papen telegraphed again, that Numan had told the Hungarian Minister in Ankara that in the days of growing Bolshevik danger he had wanted to discuss Balkan federation, but there was no need now to 'activate' the question. Things were much better on the Eastern Front. The British Ambassador had also asked for the talks not to continue, even at the request of the London exiled governments.

There was a momentary and general retreat on all sides from the Balkan field.

These suspicions were the subject of an enquiry when, later in the year, the Germans seized the Italian Foreign Office archives. These files were analysed, and one report refers to these Turkish efforts to build up a Balkan bloc.

'On the soundings made by Turkey in Budapest and Bucharest directly after the Adana conference with a view to setting up an alleged anti-bolshevik Balkan bloc, in which also Hungary should be included, we were already informed by the middle of March through communications from the Hungarian Government and from secret sources. On the basis of these reports Ambassador von Papen discussed the subject thoroughly on March 19 with the Turkish Foreign Minister, who attempted to play down the Turkish initiative. The matter was also raised with the Bulgarian Minister in Berlin.

'The assumption that the Italian Government did not discuss with us at the time the Turkish initiative, is not borne out by our own archives. These show rather that, on March 23 and April 8, extracts from the relevant reports of the Italian representatives in Bucharest and Ankara were transmitted to us . . . and that the Italian Embassy in Budapest kept our Minister there informed in detail on Hungarian-Italian talks on the Turkish démarche.'

Italy's relations with Hungary had always been specially close, and this had been the personal achievement of Ciano. German pressure on Hungary after Stalingrad to increase her war effort led Kallay, with the consent of the Regent, Admiral Horthy, to turn for support to Rome.

The German reactions in Budapest had also been sharply hostile to any Hungarian participation in Turkish plans. Kallay had professed astonishment at this attitude, and told the German Minister that he 'would seek clarification in Rome' during his forthcoming visit.[15]

On April 7, the Italian Ambassador in Budapest, Anfuso, telegraphed an account of a talk with his German colleague just after Kallay's departure. The German Minister 'read me a long sermon on the Hungarian Government's attitude which he defined as continually shifting and somewhat far removed from the complete war aims of the Axis. Hungary's latest attitude was not liked by his Government, and perhaps for the purpose of getting Hungary to collaborate more satisfactorily, it would be wise to invite the Regent to Salzburg to meet the Fuehrer who could reveal to him the expediency of replacing the present President of the Council by Imredy, who was noted for his strictly pro-Axis political ideals.'[16]

Anfuso added that in his view Imredy was under German orders; he had practically no political following, the Regent openly opposed him, and his possible nomination would provoke a grave internal crisis.

This German pressure on the satellite allies reveals a certain coherent pattern. Hitler had decreed a total war against both the Russians and the Anglo-Americans, and having set the example of a complete mobilization of the resources of Germany, he directed, in the spring of 1943, that the same policy should be extended, if possible, by diplomatic pressure to the other Axis countries. This might even imply radical changes in the political structure of each ally, and either the dictatorship of the extreme pro-Nazi elements, such as the Arrow Cross in Hungary and the Iron Guard in Roumania, or direct military rule through a reliable officer of high rank. But the conditions for such a revolution did not exist in practical terms in any of the countries concerned.

It was partly therefore to resist such pressures by the Germans on Hungary, and also to discuss the common possibilities of seeking at least a limitation of the war, that the Hungarian Prime Minister came to Rome on April 4.[17] The visit was originally fixed for January, but had then been postponed in view of the military setbacks in North Africa.

According to Bastianini, the Hungarian Prime Minister 'begged Mussolini to undertake two operations: first to put himself at the head of the minor allies, and to bring decisive pressure on Hitler to bring him back to reality; and second to undertake in their name some diplomatic initiative in the event of Hitler persisting in his plans of an all-out war, seeking a victory by now unobtainable . . . Mussolini promised him to speak frankly to Hitler about the situation and to propose a conference of the heads of all the allied governments.'

Kallay also had an audience with the Pope and alleges that the latter indicated that he was prepared to offer his services as a mediator at an appropriate time. Mussolini was informed of this conversation and said that everything depended on his forthcoming meeting with Hitler, but he 'clasped his hands and rolled over and over on the sofa' adding that he did not feel physically up to a row with the Fuehrer.[18]

CHAPTER EIGHT

The Salzburg Meeting

(April 7–10, 1943)

ON THE AFTERNOON of April 6 Mussolini left Rome for Salzburg by 'the last special train of the real Duce'.[1] He was accompanied by the German Ambassador in Rome, Mackensen, Ambrosio and Bastianini with a team of Italian Foreign Office experts.

The last summit conference between the Axis leaders had been held a year before at Salzburg.[2] The setting in April 1943 in the Castle of Klessheim was the same, but as Ribbentrop now told his Italian colleague on arrival 'much has happened' since the previous meeting. Behind this laconic understatement lay the brutal unfaced reality that a decisive Axis victory in the war could no longer be won. The hammer blows of Alamein, 'Torch' and Stalingrad had marked the turning point of the conflict. The strategic initiative now lay with the enemy on all fronts, and the survival of the Axis depended on a basic revision of military policy. The issue was stark. There was no way back for Germany and Italy to the favourable balance of forces of 1940–1; the conception of a 'Blitzkrieg' was dead; the menace of a Second Front in Western Europe, derided by the Axis leaders in 1942, was now a strategic possibility; the loss of all Italian North Africa, and the mounting threat to the fragile Axis foothold in Tunisía brought the war close to the Italian mainland. The continued presence of Italy in the war coalition depended on a decisive reinforcement by Germany of the Mediterranean theatre. Such a strategic revolution could only be carried out at the expense of the Eastern Front, which must either be reorganized on a defensive basis or closed down following the negotiation of a separate peace with Russia. If this crucial move could be made, an all-out effort against the British and Americans might lead to a negotiated settlement which would preserve something of the Axis position at least in Europe.

Such an analysis of the war situation in the spring of 1943 was in general shared both by German and Italian circles—with the cardinal exception of Hitler. The pervasive fear of total defeat had seeped into the leadership of both countries, and the awareness that salvation lay uniquely in the relics of personal prestige which Mussolini still held in the eyes of Hitler. Only the Duce could persuade him to consider the necessity of a strategic revolution by liquidating the anti-Russian crusade. In such a move lay the last opportunity of the Axis to avoid defeat, and all depended on the person of Mussolini. At such a decisive moment, all defeatist caballing in high circles both in Rome and Berlin was stilled. Such was the significance of this Salzburg meeting.

Throughout the journey northwards, Mussolini was doubled up with severe stomach cramps, but nevertheless spent some three hours with Bastianini discussing the agenda for the conference, 'repeating his suggestion to seek from Hitler a complete explanation on all points. I suggested that he should propose that two feelers should be put out; to the Soviet Union through one of those agents who had already been used by him for such a purpose in Stockholm; and by ourselves to England.' The Duce replied that the matter 'could be considered'.

On the following afternoon the train drew up just beyond Salzburg, near the Castle of Klessheim. The meeting of the two delegations took place with the familiar ritual of martial music and press photographers. Those present were startled by the physical appearance of both leaders. Mussolini's doctor wrote in his diary: 'Hitler looks tired, his face is pale, he has great pockets under his eyes.'[3] His own patient had little reserve of strength. Mussolini was lodged in the pavilion of the Castle, where Mozart had once played for the guests of a former Cardinal prelate.

The Italian delegation had drafted a political plan before leaving Rome. Three days prior to the conference, Bastianini had proposed that Mussolini, during the forthcoming talks, should develop with the Fuehrer the theme of the Axis communiqué issued after the February talks with Ribbentrop in Rome on the future of Europe, as a preliminary move to the central issue of the Russian front. 'He instructed me to make a draft of a European Charter, which would be like a Declaration of Rights of the constituted European nations. . . . Three days later I took the document for which he had asked to him. It consisted of five points assembled together in some twenty lines. He read and re-read it, pondering each word and amalgamating two points. Then he asked me to have it recopied on official notepaper.'[4]

Mussolini was now half persuaded by Bastianini that, if the Germans could comprehend and co-operate, he and only he could rally the Axis powers in Europe, together with some of the neutral nations, into a political community, an answer to the Allied pronouncements at Casablanca on Unconditional Surrender and to Churchill's speech of March 21, and give some meaning and a programme to an Axis-controlled Europe. There should be a joint pronouncement on the rights of small nations and the principle of nationalities directed to the occupied territories in Western Europe, in the East, in the Balkans, to the satellite Allies and to Vichy France—a European charter as opposed to an Atlantic Charter.[5]

Having rallied a European front on such a diplomatic basis, the Italians would seek for military agreement with the Axis partner on a defensive strategy on the Russian Front, and, in order to redress the political and military balance in the Mediterranean, a renewed and pressing approach to Spain should be made to enter the war on the Axis side. These combined moves might then create the conditions in which peace negotiations on a compromise basis could be opened with Russia, America, and Great Britain. Italy was possibly better equipped diplomatically to initiate such negotiations through the Balkan states or the neutrals.

If Germany would not consider such a programme, she must urgently come to the military aid of her ally by a major reconstruction of the Southern Front. A new Army Group South must be formed, an effective air defence of the Italian mainland be built up.[6]

Such was the programme of the new Italian Foreign Office team, drawn up largely by Bastianini and his experts and in agreement with Ambrosio. The latter had also raised with Mussolini the subject of a separate peace with Russia during the previous month. It had been however 'a simple subject of conversation without any ulterior development'. But there was now a tacit understanding between the Italian diplomatic and military leaders to force the issue at Salzburg, and Ambrosio took part in last minute discussions on the train.

The forthcoming private talks between the Duce and the Fuehrer were reviewed in a preliminary three-hour conversation between Ribbentrop and Bastianini on the afternoon of April 8, in the presence of Mackensen and Alfieri.

The German Foreign Minister based his comments on Mussolini's letter of March 26 and the 'Italian Memorandum'. Ribbentrop touched at once on the Russian theme, voicing the obsessive determination of his master. There 'can be no compromise in the world battle'. The main aim was to destroy Russian military power and not occupy more territory. 'Germany had never expected Russia to collapse at once. She had never intended to occupy the whole of Russia, but to destroy her military and national power so that there could never again be a threat from the East. This has been and still is the aim of the war against Russia, and this will certainly be achieved.'[7]

A captured Russian general had given the figure of Russian losses as 11,300,000. Out of 190 million Russians, 70 were in German occupied territory; out of the remaining 120 millions, 14 had been destroyed. The military potential of a country was ten per cent of its population; therefore 12 million soldiers were still available, but this presented a severe manpower problem for the Russians.

When Ribbentrop had been in Rome, the Russian Front had not been 'stabilized'. Now the German armies were in the Donetz basin and the Russians had been pushed back two hundred kilometres. 'In any case the Russian problem could only have a military and not suddenly a political solution.' Perhaps as the consequence of a liquidation of the military problems a political settlement could find a place. Germany could not leave the Russians near her frontiers without running the danger of one day being bombed from the air. 'Besides she needed the Ukraine. Stalin was also not ready to make peace.'

There were now two objectives; the remaining third of Russian manpower must be destroyed; and then troops and air-force moved from the Russian Front and committed against the British Isles. Allied losses in shipping had been 1,100,000 tons in the last month alone. 'The Germans wanted no peace with England until the latter begged for it.'

Bastianini countered with an outline of the Italian thesis,

stressing the danger of playing the opponents' game. The Duce took the view that the 'continuance of war with Russia was a source of great satisfaction to the British and Americans, as they felt that Germany would then have no strength left to fight England.

'As for the position on the various fronts, Italy was compelled to supply nine armies by sea. This provisioning was becoming more and more difficult. Not one convoy, large or small, reached its destination, so that ammunition had now to be flown to Tunis.

'The general food position is so serious, because of the Anglo-American submarine war, which is now directed against motor sailing vessels which one had hitherto not thought worthy of torpedoes, that Sicily, for example, had wheat supplies for only five days, and Sardinia for only three . . . Italy had only 400,000 tons of shipping available, since in March alone 180,000 tons had been sunk; she would soon come to the end of her shipping capacity. . . . How in these circumstances could one ensure the maintenance of 1,374,000 troops in the nine areas dependent on supply by sea? . . . In two to three months the Russians would again be beaten. But in the meantime what would happen to Italy in view of the difficulties just described?'

Mussolini was also concerned that the Italian army could no longer take any initiative, and must confine itself to a defensive rôle. 'One wondered how long that could go on, for an army without initiative is in the end condemned. In these circumstances therefore it was understandable that a wave of pessimism was passing through Italy . . . which must not be underrated, nor must one overlook certain manifestations such as the unofficial strikes in Turin and Milan. One always talked of the good old Italian people; but their good nature had its limits. He knew these splendid Italians, as for example after the last war when Fascists, among others, had been flung into boiling water.' Ribbentrop's supposition 'that the strike had been contrived by British agents' was energetically contradicted by Bastianini. It had been the work of Italian Communists, 'who still existed in Italy and who received their instructions from Moscow'.

The strikes in Northern Italy had cast doubts on the internal security of the Fascist régime. The whole matter would be discussed between the Duce and the Fuehrer. Ribbentrop stressed the general need for drastic measures in such cases. This had been successful in Norway and failed in Denmark.

There was a special case for such action in France. The implied parallel with Italy, if tactless, is an unconsciously startling revelation of the German Minister's inner view of his ally. He continued by stressing the need for harsh measures in Greece! 'The dynamism of those nations conquered by the Axis was naturally directed against the victors. An understanding between Italy and Greece, for example, was simply not possible. One must confine oneself to setting up a government which would as far as possible be at the beck and call of Germany and Italy. Wherever independent governments were set up in countries occupied by Germany and Italy, they would immediately conspire with England.'

These remarks led Bastianini to bring forward his European programme. 'He wondered whether Germany and Italy were not attempting simultaneously to do two mutually contradictory things, and therefore delivering new propaganda material to England. The English set themselves up as the defenders of the small and weak nations, while Germany was branded as an oppressor at a time when she was in fact fighting Bolshevism in the common interest of all.'

Ribbentrop replied that he had discussed this problem at length with the Fuehrer, and had also written him a memorandum. The recent speech of Churchill had caused great unrest. 'But if the Axis were to make a declaration it could only happen at a moment when the military situation was one hundred per cent in its favour, otherwise the following difficulty would arise. The Fuehrer would have to take drastic measures in the occupied countries to mobilize their labour force . . . If one set up governments in these countries, such measures would be continually thwarted by them. If one were to promise independence to the occupied states at the present moment, the effect of such a declaration would disappear into thin air in a fortnight. One would have to offer clear and substantial concessions . . . If for example one had allowed Laval to rebuild in part the French Army . . . these French divisions would have marched with the Axis so long as things went well. But they would go over to the enemy in twenty-four hours if the situation changed. One had to be very careful in these matters.'

Bastianini agreed, but 'after Churchill's declaration a new political situation had arisen. The German Foreign Minister closed the subject with the remark that one would never again get rid of the ghosts which had been called forth.'

At this point Ribbentrop was summoned by Hitler at the conclusion of the latter's first talk with the Duce.

No direct records of the private conversations between the two Axis leaders during the Klessheim Conference have yet come to light. According to Bastianini, the first talk between Hitler and Mussolini took place in private in the former's apartments almost immediately after the arrival of the Italian delegation.

The conversations continued during the afternoon. Ribbentrop had meanwhile reported to the Fuehrer the substance of his talks with Bastianini that morning, and later told his Italian colleague 'that Hitler hoped to go into the political gesture proposed by me together with the Duce'.[8]

That evening Bastianini hastened to call on Mussolini. He was in constant pain, but refused to see a doctor. He had attempted to talk to Hitler, but, as he told Bastianini: 'Hitler only played the same old record. I let him go on, but tomorrow I shall do the talking and very clearly. The affair of the European Charter doesn't work. He told me that it was premature. He has given orders to the German Air Force to send massive reinforcements to Italy, which I will in due course distribute. He will also send anti-aircraft batteries, and as to the rest of our military requirements, our General Staff must define their requests and naturally on an acceptable scale.[9]

'I insisted that he should find a way of putting an end to the war in Russia . . . He agreed, but as he is convinced that he will be able to deliver a decisive blow against the Russians in the very near future, I could not raise with him peace feelers of any kind.'

Ambrosio was summoned by Mussolini on the evening after the opening of the Conference and told that there would be no further discussion of a German offensive on the Eastern Front as Hitler had given way to all the Duce's arguments.

Ambrosio heard from Ribbentrop an opposite version of this conversation: 'I learnt later that Mussolini, having referred with Hitler to the situation in Russia, provoked a lively reaction on the part of the latter who intended to demonstrate to him that Russia, in view of enormous losses, was on the eve of final collapse and to this end therefore the German offensive was directed.'[10] There was to be no further talk of a separate peace.

These statements are however somewhat modified by the following indirect evidence. That Mussolini did raise with Hitler the proposal of seeking some compromise with Russia appears from the following confidential report to Ribbentrop later in the month.[11] The Japanese Ambassador, General Oshima, had been instructed to call on Hitler and seek information on the results of the Klessheim talks. 'The closest collaborator of Oshima claims to know that Mussolini, in his talk with the Fuehrer, pointed to the possibility that Japan could under certain conditions mediate at Kuibychev between the Axis powers and Russia, if Stalin had to be convinced of an absolute military deadlock in the course of this year. The Japanese diplomat believed that this view of Mussolini's was shared in Tokyo. He even hinted that Mussolini had possibly been strengthened in this view . . . from the Japanese side.'

On April 22 Oshima had told Alfieri that he had sounded the German Foreign Minister on the possibility of peace negotiations with the Soviet Union at a later stage, but that Ribbentrop had replied that the conditions proposed by Germany would not be acceptable to Stalin.[12]

That such conditions had been proposed is stated in one unique piece of evidence. Towards the end of April the Italian Military Intelligence forwarded a report to the Duce allegedly giving a summary of the Klessheim talks as transmitted by Oshima to Tokyo as a result of his interview with Hitler.[13] The latter is reported to have said: 'I am convinced that notwithstanding the fact that in Italy the people are fed up with the war and public opinion is hostile to us, Mussolini is decided to continue the struggle at all costs. We cannot in reality consider the two years of war against the Soviet Union as a success, and in order to save ourselves being dragged towards defeat we must this summer turn to a new "system" not from a technical standpoint, but a general one. To tell the truth, this war was begun too soon from our point of view. It should have been started five years later, so that we could have completed our preparations, especially at sea. We expect major help from Japan in this latter respect. I cannot ask you to launch your armies against Siberia. In the first instance, however, we need you to block the arrival of American supplies to the Soviet Union via Vladivostok. In addition, we need Japanese submarine activities in the Atlantic. As to the war in North Africa, we find ourselves in the situation of not being able to decide anything except the withdrawal of our troops.

'Oshima asked Hitler if Germany had made any peace offers and Hitler replied that one had been made to the Soviet

Union only at the end of last year. It was proposed that the Germans should evacuate all occupied Soviet territories except the Ukraine, but the Soviets energetically turned down the suggestion.'

It is not impossible that this account, which is not confirmed by other existing evidence, was 'planted' on the Italians by Admiral Canaris, the head of the German Military Intelligence, as part of an attempt by certain German quarters to press and encourage Mussolini in his personal efforts with Hitler to seek a way out of the Russian war.

Both among the political and military members of the German delegation at Klessheim there was a climate of defeatism and doubt as to the successful issue of the Russian war, and this attitude was deliberately conveyed to their Italian colleagues.

The Italian Foreign Office officials, whom Bastianini had brought with him, 'had ample opportunities to talk at length with their diplomatic colleagues in Ribbentrop's entourage, and they formed a united impression that the bellicose and rigid intransigence of their chief found no wholehearted response in their minds. Some of them even expressed a completely contrary view and they all stated that they expected, as a result of Mussolini's visit, that there would be a change of direction based on the realities of the situation . . . The military men also expressed the hope that Mussolini, by speaking openly and even threateningly, might succeed in bringing Hitler back to the path of reason.'

Bastianini reported the gist of the conversations to the Duce 'who told me that even Goering appeared to him to be very pensive'.[14]

There does seem to have been apparent, during these Klessheim talks, a definite and significant body of opinion on the German side in favour of a negotiated peace with Russia, and even a conscious feeling that the personal intervention of Mussolini was the only means of bringing Hitler to accept such a solution. The rôle of Goering is unclarified, but he had at least one meeting with Mussolini alone in the Castle of Klessheim on the evening of the first day of the conference, and the latter told Bastianini at the time that they had discussed the Russian war 'which must be terminated at all costs as Goering himself affirmed'.[15]

The failure of the Duce to persuade Hitler to consider such

a course meant the disintegration of such a climate in high German circles.

Even before the discussions between the military delegations had got under way, the Germans had drafted their communiqué for release to the press on the talks ostensibly in progress. On coming out of the Duce's room on the first afternoon, Bastianini was met by Ribbentrop, who handed him a verbose and meaningless statement to be given to the press on the talks hitherto conducted between the two leaders. Bastianini rejected the draft, and the issue was postponed until the military conversations had been held.[16] In the meantime, Mackensen minuted to Ribbentrop: 'Under-Secretary Bastianini spoke to me early this morning about what he had discussed in my presence with the German Foreign Minister regarding the communiqué to be given out on the Fuehrer-Duce meeting. He wanted to point out to me once again that in the present circumstances it was difficult for the Duce to return to Rome with a fulsome communiqué in the form drafted by us, but otherwise more or less empty handed. One must be clear that at this moment the whole Italian people had very special expectations about the present meeting. He, Bastianini, personally thought that the statement as drafted by us could be accepted by the Duce without further ado, if at the same time it brought with it the five hundred aircraft for which the Duce had asked in his telegram to the Fuehrer some five weeks previously. He asked me to have yet another word about these questions with the German Foreign Minister. They seemed to him to be of really considerable importance in the present critical time.

'I then brought the matter to the German Foreign Minister, who in my presence immediately raised it with the Fuehrer. The latter answered that the Italian request could not be met since, according to reports in front of him, the concentration of aircraft on the Italian airfields in Southern Italy, Sicily, and Sardinia was such that a single bombardment by the British or Americans would be enough to destroy fifteen, twenty or even thirty aircraft on the ground.'

Mackensen reported this decision to his Italian colleague, who answered that these conditions were not known to him. On the contrary, he seemed to think that these airfields were capable of receiving further aircraft, at least up to the quantity now requested. He was asked to obtain reliable evidence from the Italian air force.[17]

After such an episode it hardly seemed as if the Germans had any serious intentions of sending effective assistance to the Mediterranean theatre.

The general impressions gained during the course of the meetings of the military delegations, and the round table conference under Hitler's chairmanship, as recorded in Ambrosio's notes,[18] reveal the lack of any real progress at these talks, and of any co-ordination in Italo-German planning.

'On the German side insistence on the need to liquidate the Russian problem. It is hoped to succeed in this—given the state of exhaustion of the Russians after the effort made —by adopting the method of trying to annihilate the enemy forces rather than occupying territory.

'As to the Mediterranean problems, German concern is limited to what one might have for a theatre of secondary importance. They see the need of holding Tunisia at all costs; to pin down enemy forces as long as possible; they fear a landing in Sicily and in Sardinia, and are prepared to ensure all possible aid, but they have a tendency not to allot the available means to passive zones which are not expected to be attacked.'

The Italian proposals about Spain had last been raised in preliminary fashion by Mussolini in his letter to Hitler of March 26, and then embodied in the formal Italian memorandum to the conference, as part of a general set of proposals on the Italian side for an overhaul of the whole Axis position in the Mediterranean.

The subject was raised in the informal talk between Ribbentrop and his Italian colleague on the afternoon of April 9 at Klessheim. 'As to the question of Bastianini about Spain, the German Foreign Minister remarked, with reference to the Duce's letter, that Franco by his attitude in making impossible the operation against Gibraltar had done the Axis a bad turn. He had not only shown himself ungrateful to the Duce and the Fuehrer, but had also proved that he did not possess very great foresight. Whether one could now work out something with the Spaniards was dubious. It was not clear how this could happen, and there was always a great risk that the Spaniards would turn against the Axis. Historical examples showed how strong such a Spanish resistance could be. The Spaniards were also very good and able soldiers in defence.'

The Italian delegation were firm in pressing talks with the

Spaniards, perhaps by offering them concessions in Morocco. Ribbentrop answered, 'If one could persuade Franco that his régime would be endangered unless he allowed Axis troops into Spain, perhaps one could embark on something with that country. But it seemed doubtful whether Franco could be thus convinced. One only had to reflect on what experiences one had had with him on an earlier occasion. He had already once let a favourable opportunity slip, when everything had been prepared to the last detail for the conquest of Gibraltar.' The Italians had however received a reliable report that Franco had been surprised that, after the Anglo-Saxon landing in North Africa, the Axis had not requested the right to march troops through Spain.

'The German Foreign Minister commented that he was not at all sure. Perhaps the Spaniards would not have opposed an Axis entry. Franco was a wavering man, who had no power of decision, such as the Duce and the Fuehrer possessed.'[19]

The Spanish problem was also raised at the formal sessions of the conference. The Italians hoped to implicate the German leadership in joint pressure on Franco 'to obtain, if not the military co-operation of Spain, at least authorization to cross her territory'. Italy would take part in such an operation with at least one division together with naval and air forces. The objective was not the capture of Gibraltar. Such a plan could only be conceived with Spanish agreement. Mussolini had already proposed a meeting with Franco to such an end, and was counting on the presence of Hitler. But the latter had not forgotten the rebuff of Hendaye in 1940, and had little confidence or interest in an extension of the existing German commitments in the Mediterranean theatre, which he was already unable to honour.

It was agreed at Salzburg that this Spanish conference 'was first foreseen as Tripartite—Fuehrer-Duce-Franco, and then at a later stage it was decided to make it a *tête-à-tête*—Duce-Franco'.[20]

Whatever military solution might be reached at Klessheim, Bastianini was determined to air his political programme of a European union which he and his advisers had been working on for weeks past. The Germans had already received a hint of such an Italian move when Alfieri had pressed in March for the Salzburg meeting. A German Foreign Office minute recorded at the time: 'Since the incident of Casablanca, and in view of the imminent major Allied conference in Washington, a counterweight on the side of the Tripartite powers would be of value and importance. Alfieri gave one to understand that he was not only speaking on his own initiative, but rather that the Duce was thinking in terms of a kind of European conference, without it as yet having any concrete conception.'[21]

It seems that the Duce had been almost convinced by Bastianini that, in a position of military stalemate, and as effective propaganda against the Allies, he could now play a diplomatic rôle in Europe 'as in 1938 he had been able to prevent at the Munich Conference the outbreak of war'.[22]

On the morning of April 9, therefore, Bastianini renewed with Ribbentrop those arguments, which had been abruptly cut short on the previous day. He began by taking up 'the theme of the small states', stressing in the case of the occupied countries their fear that in the event of an Axis victory 'they would become German and Italian provinces'. Ribbentrop's counter-view, as before, was that a decisive military victory must be the prerequisite of any such consideration.

'As to the question of some sort of European Declaration, he, Ribbentrop, supposed that the Duce and the Fuehrer would deal with it in their talks. He would today raise the matter with the Fuehrer . . . He however "had the intuitive feeling that such declarations, as the example of the Atlantic Charter now clearly showed, if they were not well thought out, only caused damage, and their success was anyway problematical". The Fuehrer was of the opinion that a military success must be aimed at, and, particularly with a view to the situation in Tunis, a premature publication of such a declaration would be exploited as a weakness and have the opposite effect.'

Bastianini made a vain and final effort at a private talk over the tea-table, without Alfieri or Mackensen being present, on the afternoon of April 9. Ribbentrop told him of the attempt of Laval 'to obtain a declaration from Germany on France and Europe'. Hitler had answered that he was busy with military matters, and did not think that the time had come for such a statement. 'Laval pulled out every stop in order to get concessions . . . European co-operation was to be understood in the sense that the small states, when the war was won, must understand that they have to follow the leadership of Berlin and Rome. For Italy and Germany had undertaken great duties in regard to Europe, and had therefore claims to the right to make major decisions. They had had to defend Europe, and the others must therefore follow them.'

Bastianini replied that 'in international affairs the enemy has sought to throw sand in the eyes of the world through the Atlantic Charter, and has stated that Germany wants to destroy everything. Politically therefore the moment is favourable to repeat that the war waged by Germany and Italy is revolutionary in character. Bolshevism and plutocracy must be beaten . . . and it must thereby be visible that Fascism and National Socialism have not given up. This fight is against plutocracy, not against Europe.'

Behind this verbal fencing lay a more practical disquiet on the German side. The Italians had already hinted, and even threatened, as Bastianini had done at their first talk, at the 'wave of pessimism passing through Italy'. But the present suggestion of a European declaration might well lead not only to organizing the war weariness of the satellites, the Roumanians, the Hungarians, and the Finns, but might lead further to rally the whole bloc to seek a compromise peace, and even under Italian leadership. This was exactly what Bastianini had ultimately in mind.

The Roumanians had already nearly maimed such a plot, if it existed, by making vague soundings of such a nature in Madrid, which had been reported by certain Spaniards to Ribbentrop. He had taxed Bastianini on this subject, and the latter promptly minimized the incident. 'The Duce does not believe it, and the papers are filed away.' And as if abruptly to change the subject, Bastianini drew attention to 'certain Turkish efforts apparently originating at the Adana Conference. It was a question of building up a kind of Balkan entente under the cover of a common protection against the Russians, but with the aim of loosening certain states from the Tripartite Pact. In Greece, Bulgaria, and Roumania people were convinced that in the long run Turkey could not stay out of the war, but must at least take part in the same form as Bulgaria, i.e. through making available airfields and other indirect assistance.' And Bastianini then remarked noncommittally, 'One must regard the present position of Turkey with certain question marks.'

Ribbentrop added that from reliable sources it was known that Turkey had made 'agreements in certain contingencies' with England, and remarked that 'if Turkey entered the war one must act very quickly. Both Germany and Bulgaria were agreed that one must then take preventive action beforehand.'

Ambrosio's notes of the general and military conferences showed however little immediate anxiety: 'A landing in Greece is not thought to be imminent, and to be related to the attitude of Turkey. It is thought that the latter will wait long before making a move, inasmuch as Bulgaria, after the recent statement of King Boris, would enter the war against her. Besides Turkey is an element of manoeuvre in British hands against eventual excessive and dangerous Russian claims.'

In a conversation with Ribbentrop on April 10, Bastianini illustrated by an anecdote the attitude of Churchill to Italy in 1940 'which he had learnt about from four different sources, for example, from an Italian head waiter at the Savoy Hotel who had overheard a conversation of Churchill's at a meal. The British Prime Minister had then taken the view that if Italy and Germany succeeded in conquering Egypt before America came into the war, England was finished, but that the Axis could be broken if they did not succeed before the American entry. One would then wear down Italy and finally, after three or four weeks, stir up civil war in Italy. Then the British, as in his time Allenby in Egypt, would be welcomed as saviours bringing law and order after a considerable bloodbath caused by the Fascists.'

Bastianini regarded such a programme as still feasible 'unless one could succeed in cleaning up the most serious situation in the Mediterranean and prevent the war reaching the island and leaping on to the mainland'.[23]

General Ambrosio and his staff had come to Klessheim prepared for orderly technical discussions, both on the future joint conduct of the war and on the lists of urgent requirements in materials and supplies to enable the Tunisian bridgehead to be held. Previous interchanges of correspondence, the visits of Warlimont with Ribbentrop in February, and Goering and Doenitz in March, as well as frequent discussions with Kesselring and Rintelen in Rome, led the Italians to believe at last, after a year since the last summit meeting and in view of the recognized critical phase in Tunisia, that the pending talks would constitute a thorough review of the situation.

* * *

The tenor of the military conferences at Klessheim mirrors the reluctance of the German High Command either to consider a combined war strategy with their Italian ally or to face the supply issues involved in maintaining her armed forces in being for the defence of Tunisia, and, in the end, the Italian mainland.

German fears of the political collapse of Italy, and their distrust of Bastianini and Ambrosio, deepened. Sensing this atmosphere, and also wishing indirectly to sound the Germans on their views on the internal situation in Italy, Mussolini shrewdly appealed for advice from an unexpected quarter. He asked to see Himmler. The conversation is summarized by the latter's representative in Rome, Dollmann.[24]

Mussolini was particularly concerned with the internal effects of a prolonged war on the political structure of both countries. Himmler, while expressing satisfaction with the system of forced labour and concentration camps as a prophylactic against political disorder, did not recommend similar measures in Italy. He thought rather that special militia units should be formed on the model of the S.S. for security duties, and offered to send instructors and the latest equipment to set up a complete division. He considered that the actual commander of the Italian Fascist militia, General Galbiati, was probably not up to his task. Himmler had met him in 1942 in Berlin, and had rated him 'as a good Fascist, but in my S.S. at the most a non-commissioned officer'.[25]

This proposal of Himmler's was almost the only practical result of the whole meeting. It aroused Hitler's renewed interest, and he also discussed with the Duce the position of the Fascist régime in Italy, and such possible safeguarding measures.[26] As he had expressed it, at a military conference during the previous month: 'The Duce once said to me, "I did not myself know how. I only know that if, in Italy, Fascism is not victorious, Italy is lost" . . . It is roughly similar in Austria and the Sudetenland, where the National Socialist movement never came to anything. Only in Italy . . . (text illegible) the personality of the Duce spans everything, and then there is the courage of his own actively Fascist military organizations. There is no doubt about that. But of course the ideological basis is not there. I have it in a letter from Farinacci.'

Jodl interposed: 'A personal bodyguard is important,' and Hitler retorted, 'I only hope that the guard does not string him up!'

There is also a subsequent reference by Hitler to the private conversations between the two leaders. 'At Klessheim the Duce made a remark while we were having dinner together. He suddenly said, "My Fuehrer, I don't know; I have no successor in the Fascist revolution. A chief of state can be found to succeed me, but no one will continue the Fascist revolution." '[27]

On the morning of April 10, after a breakfast of milk and biscuits, Mussolini was able to attend a closing plenary session on the military situation. There was no further news from the Eastern Front. Hitler warmed to his departing guest. 'Duce, I guarantee to you that Africa will be defended. The situation is serious, but not desperate. Recently I read the story of the siege of Verdun in the First World War; Verdun resisted successfully the attacks of the best German regiments. I do not see why this should not happen also in Africa. With your support, Duce, my troops will make Tunis the Verdun of the Mediterranean.'[28]

The formal meeting was closed; the two dictators led the way down the staircase of the main hall of Klessheim Castle where the members of both delegations were assembled. Some of them saw Mussolini for the first time since his arrival, as he had not left his room except for this one brief public appearance. Both leaders 'were livid, with contracted features, and vacant eyes'. The Italian delegates saw them with alarm. 'They seem like two invalids,' said one. 'Rather like two corpses,' said Dr Pozzi, Mussolini's personal doctor.[29]

A private lunch was held in Bastianini's apartment, at which, apart from the Fuehrer and the Duce and their respective Foreign Secretaries, only Goering was present. The only point of conversation recorded, apart from the familiar comparisons made by Hitler between himself and Frederick the Great, was the Fuehrer's offer of a free hand to Mussolini in dealing with Franco in an attempt to bring him into the war on the Axis side. But as Hitler remarked, in getting up from the table, 'I do not believe that he will do it.'[30]

The two leaders then went through the formalities of leave-taking at the train. The Duce was in intense pain on the journey back to Rome, though a further radiographic inspection on his return yielded no new symptoms. He said to Alfieri before leaving: 'My illness has a name: "convoys".'[31]

* * *

The Duce had arrived at Salzburg in an exhausted physical condition, and for one entire day all talks had to be suspended 'as he was not in a state to participate in them'.[32] Hitler failed to persuade his guest to be examined by German doctors. The egregious Dr Morell flitted expectantly in and out of the public rooms of the castle, dispensing pills. 'A face like a full moon, with gold pince-nez, a green jacket and long grey trousers. He gives me,' wrote his Italian colleague, 'the impression of an unsavoury person.'[33]

Both dictators seem nevertheless to have been satisfied with their encounter. The familiar, indefinable and mutual hypnotism generated at such moments had reasserted itself once again. 'The Fuehrer told me,' Goebbels wrote in his diary, 'that the Duce had been really restored to his old form during their four days' discussion. The Fuehrer did everything he could, and by putting every ounce of nervous energy into the effort, succeeded in pushing Mussolini back on the rails. In those four days the Duce underwent a complete change at which his entourage was also amazed. When he got out of the train the Fuehrer thought that he looked like a broken old man; when he left again, he was in high fettle and ready for anything. We can see by the policies which he is now pursuing that his regeneration is continuing . . . The Duce understands clearly that there can be no further salvation for him except to win or die with us. The Fuehrer is very happy that he will now adopt a tougher tone in Italy.'[34]

The Duce was, as always, susceptible to this treatment. Hitler had lectured him about Stalingrad, and of the need to stay in Tunisia 'until quarter past twelve'. His advisers, however, political and military, came back from the Klessheim talks in a sharply contrasting mood of frustration and distrust.

The tipstaff and [illegible] for [illegible] an [illegible] conditions [illegible] that [illegible] table [illegible] [illegible] of the table [illegible] for which he [illegible] to be [illegible] electors. The [illegible] Dr [illegible] out of the [illegible] the table [illegible] [illegible] with gold [illegible] green jacket and [illegible] grey trousers [illegible] impression [illegible]

It [illegible] order. The [illegible] [illegible] The [illegible] [illegible] [illegible] [illegible] [illegible] [illegible] [illegible] [illegible] the [illegible] the [illegible] he [illegible] [illegible] the [illegible] in the [illegible] [illegible] [illegible] [illegible] that he [illegible] [illegible] [illegible] The [illegible] that he [illegible]

The [illegible] was [illegible] about [illegible] [illegible] [illegible] [illegible] back from the [illegible] [illegible] and [illegible]

BOOK III

CHAPTER ONE

The End in Africa

On his return from the Klessheim conference, Mussolini reported to the King that 'he had found much understanding on the part of Hitler, who had promised help in the form of tanks and planes for Sicily, and had undertaken to send back our Second Army Corps from Russia'.[1] On the same day the Duce also told Kesselring, 'On my visit to the Fuehrer I saw the unanimity of everyone, . . . as to the importance of Tunisia. All possibilities are open to us if we resist and therefore we shall hold on.' Kesselring could hardly appreciate this note of optimism, and replied that 'nevertheless we need men, munitions and precisely at once'. The Duce added more realistically, 'We have sacrificed our fleet in the African war. The merchant navy has lost threequarters of its strength.'[2] Allied attacks on shipping and ports were increasing. Two Italian cruisers had been sunk in harbour. It was clear from the attitude of the Germans at the conference that they were unable to supply the Italian battle fleet to enable it to put to sea. The Italians equally rejected any German control of the North African convoys, and Doenitz had concluded that the only solution of the naval war lay in an intense concentration on the submarine campaign. This had been put to the Italians during the conference as one of Germany's main strategic objectives.

Neither Ambrosio nor Bastianini shared the Duce's optimism over the summit talks. As the former told Puntoni after an audience with the King on April 16: 'The Salzburg agreements have served no useful purpose. Germany is only thinking of "her" war and not of Italy's interests, which are henceforth decisively compromised . . . Only on the repatriation of the Second Army Corps from Russia has there been not too much argument, but the formula worked out for the return of our units seems to be somewhat vague. There is talk of a "reorganization to be carried out in Italy rather than Germany". I am not substantially in agreement with the euphoria of the Duce. We have got and shall get nothing.'[3]

Bastianini had already told the German Ambassador two days earlier that he 'had come away with the impression, and he could confirm that the Duce had too, that as things were the result was very reassuring, but now he heard from many different sides, and particularly from General Ambrosio, that in the question of fulfilling Italian military requests practically nothing had happened. The Duce took the opposite view, and was satisfied also on this matter. But he (Bastianini) had gained no clear picture of exactly what had come out of it.' Mackensen admitted that, on the German side, 'we ourselves had run up against certain differences of view and lack of clarity, which perhaps had not been tidied up'. In other words, the German High Command had no intention of fulfilling any programme of military deliveries to Italy. The German Ambassador hedged. 'These were military matters, and on our side, jurisdictions were sharply drawn.' He admitted however that since Bastianini had raised the subject it became a political question, and it was important that his Italian colleague 'should know exactly what had been done at Klessheim in the military sphere'. He had talked to Kesselring and it was proposed that a meeting of German and Italian political and military representatives in Rome should be held to reach 'complete clarity'.[4]

Bastianini summoned this conference at five o'clock on Sunday, April 18, at Palazzo Chigi. Ambrosio asked drily whether the meeting would simply duplicate the recent discussions, to which his political colleague replied: 'Today it is a matter of establishing exactly what was the outcome of the Salzburg talks.' Kesselring expressed his regret at not having been present 'as with his particular knowledge of the Mediterranean, many things could have perhaps been simplified'. Ambrosio then summarized the results of the previous military discussions; the written negative reply by the Germans to the principal request for tanks. 'All this in regard to a request for 1,250 tanks.'

Kesselring's attempted defence made the fundamental point of the German situation: 'If we had not had the disaster of Stalingrad a great part of the requests could have been satisfied, but the German General Staff has instead had to throw in all its reserves to stop the Soviet steam roller.'

Ambrosio pointed out that the Italian demands represented needs, and, with a thrust at Cavallero, 'the former Chief of the General Staff let them pile up and hence today the figures of the requests are so high'. Kesselring undertook to support all Italian requests during his next visit to Germany.

There was no response from Berlin.

On April 30 Mussolini himself telegraphed to Hitler: 'If, as I have already several times represented, the air problem in the Mediterranean is not solved at once by sending air support to counterbalance the shattering air superiority of the enemy, it will no longer be possible for any warship, or supply-ship, or plane, to arrive in Tunisia. This means losing Tunisia at once, without saving anything. Attempts to use destroyers for transport are also doomed to fail. Three destroyers, two of which were laden with German troops and one with ammunition, were lost today as the result of continuous air attacks by huge enemy air formations escorted by 70–120 fighters.

'Fuehrer, the question is one of the utmost urgency. The troops in Tunisia are fighting splendidly, as the enemy himself is forced to admit, but if we cannot supply them their fate is sealed.'[5]

Hitler replied on May 2. 'The Second Air Corps had a strength on March 1 of 1,012 front line aircraft. During March a further 574 planes have been sent. Stronger reinforcements were sent in April. Last month alone 669 front line planes were dispatched. This number only includes the normal consignments of planes without counting those attached to the detachments transferred to Italy, and the transport planes. I am studying at the moment what can be done to strengthen our air forces further. For this purpose Marshal Kesselring will call on you today.'[6] The Italian Embassy in Berlin, who transmitted this telegram, saw at once its implications. 'The Germans today are not in a position to conduct a struggle on two fronts. They regard the Tunisian one as lost. They will not send again a single plane. The Fuehrer naturally does not say so, but it is easy to understand from his reticence.'[7]

The discontent within the Italian High Command at the lack of a consistent direction of the war by Mussolini, which was a leading element in the gathering opposition to the whole structure of his leadership, is seen in an unsigned and unheaded minute, dated May 2, and initialled by Bastianini.

'The order of the Duce to reinforce Tunisia at all costs with warships has produced a sharp reaction in the Italian High Command. The reaction at Navy Headquarters has been the most open and lively, and has in this regard clearly and insistently expressed a contrary view to the use of naval vessels for transporting troops.

'The three warships loaded with troops sunk recently by the enemy in the Sicily channel have naturally exacerbated the discussions and criticisms of the person of the Head of the government, who in his capacity as Commander-in-Chief of the Armed Forces, issues directives on the conduct of the war and orders which are often contrary to the opinions expressed by the competent General Staff Officers.

'Lively resentment has also been provoked by the direct interference of Marshal Kesselring, whose influence on the Duce in the conduct of operations is a subject of open comment. The conduct of the war, which is a pre-eminently amphibious one, is confided to the exclusive direction of the General Staff Officers of the army, whose incompetence in such matters is well known.

'For some days, with the increasingly critical situation in Tunisia, unfavourable comments at the expense of the Duce and Marshal Kesselring have been openly, and often violently, expressed, and with a significant solidarity between Generals and Admirals, to such a point as to give rise to a suspicion that a "common attitude" between the leaders of the Armed Forces is under way, and also in agreement with certain German elements.'[8]

On May 4, at a meeting between Mussolini and Kesselring, there was still talk of reinforcing Tunisia, though no reference to the Fuehrer's message. The Duce pointed out that to use any further destroyers for such a purpose would prevent the main battle fleet putting to sea. But, as Kesselring said, the Duce must decide on the use or not of destroyers as emergency troop transports. '1,200–1,300 troops could be sent in ten days by air to Bizerta. But the three ex-French destroyers will not be ready till mid-May. Less than 200 men a day is much too few. At least a battalion and its equipment must be sent daily.' The Duce added plaintively, 'One sees clearly the value of control of the sea. If we could send two armoured divisions, we could revolutionize the situation in Tunisia. The crisis will be grave during the next eight to ten days.'[9] He was optimistic. Four days later, on May 8, Allied forces entered Tunis and Bizerta, and the last foothold in Italian Africa was lost, together with more than 200,000 German and Italian troops killed, wounded, or taken prisoner.

The loss of Tunisia, 'the front line of Europe' as Mussolini had called it, heralded an early threat by the enemy to the Italian islands and mainland. The Allies would certainly strike in the first instance either at Sicily or Sardinia as a move to an assault on the Italian peninsula, either as a single operation or geared to an all-out offensive against the southern coasts of Europe at a number of points, ranging from Spain to France and the Eastern Mediterranean.

Whatever the direction of the ultimate Allied strategic objective, both Sicily and Sardinia were now the immediate outposts of the Axis defences of the Southern coasts of Europe. Their protection must fall to Germany, and indeed the loss of Tunis forced on the German High Command the whole problem of the Mediterranean War, at a moment when a major German offensive in the East was planned to change the whole balance of the war.

The Fuehrer's prime concern in the Mediterranean theatre was to keep the war as far away as possible from the borders of Germany, and towards this end the territory of metropolitan Italy must be regarded as a key strategic area to be defended, which might at any time become an operational zone. Such a defence implied the strengthening of the German military position, and this in turn raised issues, hitherto muted, of an integrated Axis command in Italy. Hitler had by now realized that he might have to go further and even 'take over the Italian positions with German forces, and keep —and this point was the decisive consideration—the war as far away as possible from the heart of Europe and thereby from the frontiers of Germany'.[10]

On May 5 General Rintelen reported from Rome on the state of the Italian Army which 'has up till now in the war not carried out its appointed tasks and indeed has failed everywhere to do so. The main reasons for this are its completely inadequate armament and equipment, the faulty training of the officer corps, the insufficient psychological preparation of most of the other ranks and the lack of enthusiasm owing to doubts as to the favourable outcome of the war.' The Italian troops fighting alongside the Germans in Russia and Africa were glaringly inferior both in weapons and equipment. 'This lowers the will to fight and the Italian soldier must regard himself only as a camp-follower and a second line soldier except for certain deeds of individual bravery . . . There was no question of any inner participation in the vital battle of our time. The mass of the Italian people, as well as the soldiers, had on the average little understanding of an "Italian Great Power" or a "Mare Nostrum". The inner driving force to carry through such an idea is lacking.'

The High Command under Marshal Cavallero 'has got the best out of the army and war industry', but, given their structure, not much could be done, and the effort would probably deteriorate. There had been no improvement in the production of arms and equipment for the Italian army during the course of the war, but only through German deliveries. 'It has been hindered by Allied air attacks, lack of organizing ability, and an economic system which is dishonest and considers only private gain.

'The core of the Italian Army has been destroyed in Africa, Greece and Russia.' Italian troops were now 'not up to the burdensome problems of a major struggle: they are only of value as a weak stop-gap of a strong ally. The main question-mark will be the reaction of the Italian Army to the invasion of the Motherland. The result of the first days of the battle will have a real importance.' If the first invasion wave were successful, 'most unpleasant consequences may follow in view of the atmosphere of reigning fatalism'. The weakest point was the absence of any Italian mobile reserves. There was only one armoured division in existence in Sicily, and that equipped with old French tanks.

'In summary, it must be said that the Italian army alone is not in a position successfully to ward off a major assault on its metropolitan territory. This can only be expected with strong German support and central mobile reserves.'[11]

In spite of the warnings of Rintelen, Hitler continued to underestimate Italian susceptibilities, now pathologically sharpened by the realities and implications of the loss of Africa. On May 6 Kesselring informed his Italian colleague that three German divisions would be re-formed within a few weeks out of the survivors from, and reinforcements destined for, Tunisia, and would be available for the defence of Italy. Mussolini expressed an instantaneous reluctance. 'We need first of all tanks and planes . . . As to our defence, the three divisions will change nothing.'

On May 9 the Germans offered two further divisions. Four

days later, Mussolini sent a message to Hitler thanking him for the German offer, 'but pointing out that the commitment of three German divisions in all in Italy would be sufficient, and asking instead for heavy air force reinforcements in Italy'. In a reply to the Duce, explaining to him the position, it was stressed that the divisions to be formed out of the elements from Tunis would be organizationally, and in numbers, so weak that one could not compare them with regular divisions. For this reason, as well as the two divisions now in Sicily and Sardinia (the forces available were lacking for the third), the 16th Armoured and the 'Hermann Goering' divisions would be sent to Italy.

For the first time a note of personal alarm and mutual suspicion had been sounded between the two Axis leaders. In the presence of Rintelen, Mussolini declared that three divisions would be sufficient, that he would make use of the hitherto undeployed German units in Italy, and would not accept further troops in the country. There were increasing rumours and indications pointing to a deep crisis impending in Italian affairs. The German High Command had no confidence in either Ambrosio or Roatta. Mussolini had recently and inexplicably refused to accept German training personnel for the 'M' division now being formed, as a result of the agreement at Klessheim in April, for purposes of internal security.

In order to study these developments, to attempt to mobilize Italian resources, and gain their consent to joint defensive planning, Hitler decided to send Admiral Doenitz again to Rome. Control of the sea by a joint Axis effort might still delay the Allied assault on Italy and the off-shore islands.

He arrived on the afternoon of May 12. In a preliminary conference with Admiral Riccardi and the Italian naval chiefs, they stressed that an attack on the Italian islands must be expected 'any day'. Enemy air attack had destroyed rail communications with Sicily, which must now be supplied by sea from Naples, and the island had reserves for only seven days. A similar situation existed in Sardinia. The Italian navy estimated that Sicily would not be under attack until the enemy could clear and utilize the ports of Bizerta and Tunis and sweep the minefields between North Africa and Sicily, and that therefore the threat to Sardinia was more urgent. 'An enemy invasion of Spain or Southern France is not being considered. The main objective of the Western Allies is a free line of communication through the Straits of Sicily. To attain this objective, the Balearic Islands and Southern France are not essential; however, Sicily and Sardinia are important. The Italian Admiralty therefore believes that Sardinia will be the first to be invaded. An invasion of Sicily may be expected some time after June 22. If the supply system fails,' Doenitz interjected, 'the islands cannot be held. However, a defeat at sea would not be decisive for us.'

All kinds of craft might have to be used, including submarines and cruisers. Harbour facilities must be ruthlessly exploited. As Doenitz said, 'The responsible Italian officer must have the right to draft civilians for this task. It must not happen, as it did in North Africa, that we are defeated because our supply system failed.' Air cover and support were vital, and he promised to support the previous and unsuccessful Italian requests for increased air power.[12]

On the following morning he called on Ambrosio. 'A polite but formal reception.' Doenitz repeated the thesis of the Italian navy that it was more important 'to supply transport than to engage the enemy in battle'. Ambrosio, whose relations with his naval colleagues were increasingly distant, commented that 'he felt that submarines and cruisers should fight'. To which the German Admiral answered, 'The naval forces have already ceased fighting.' Ambrosio disagreed with the Italian naval thesis, and thought that 'the problem of Sardinia will arise after that of Sicily. At Salzburg it was said that Sardinia would be more in danger than Sicily. I think however that today the latter is the more threatened.' He also disagreed that the main task of the Navy was a supply one. The enemy must be held away from the Italian coast, the defences of which were weak, unlike those constructed by the Germans on the Atlantic shores of France.

Later that morning Doenitz was received by Mussolini, who appeared 'well, optimistic, composed, very frank, sincere, and amicable'. The Duce at once made it clear, to Doenitz's surprise, that he was opposed to Hitler's offer of May 9 of five German divisions for the defence of Italy.

'Since August of last year I have had the conviction that the battle has been lost at sea. I have always been aware of the problem of the air. In recent days our inferiority in this field has been strong. I look on all this with the greatest calm. However, we do not know the Anglo-American plans . . . But I maintain that with the air superiority of the enemy a landing is one thing; an invasion another. In the latter case one has to supply divisions fighting on foreign soil. As regards troops, we do not need men; we have them. The Fuehrer has suggested five divisions. I think this is too many; three are enough, provided they are well equipped and mobile, and armoured. In my telegram of yesterday evening (May 12) to the Fuehrer I have put down the details.' He then asked the German Admiral for the main reason for his visit, and was told that it concerned the problem of supplying Sicily. 'I am ready,' said Doenitz, 'to place at the disposal of Admiral Riccardi all the German naval forces in the Mediterranean, including all the units at Marseilles, and submarines when bases would be available.'[13]

That evening a final consultation took place between Doenitz and Kesselring. The latter referred to Hitler's offer to send the two further divisions to Italy. 'The fact that the Italian High Command had partially refused the Fuehrer's offer of five divisions was reported directly to the German High Command, without informing the Commanding General South (Kesselring himself) or General Rintelen. Kesselring considers this an act of political importance inasmuch as it proves that the Italians want to remain masters in their own house. Relations between him and General Ambrosio are not very cordial.'[14] But like Ambrosio, he felt that Sicily was more in danger than Sardinia. The Italian and German naval forces together were so weak that their role in an invasion attempt would be minor. Kesselring was going to recommend reinforcing the second German Air Fleet.

Doenitz returned to Germany on the afternoon of May 14 and reported to Hitler on these Rome conversations. He had concluded that 'the plan to hold the Italian islands will result in a purely defensive operation. It will consume much energy without getting the Axis out of its defensive position.' The only hope of breaking the deadlock on the naval side would be a drastic stepping up of the submarine war. At present the only outbound route for submarines was a narrow lane in the Bay of Biscay.

Hitler then voiced his central suspicions. He believed that 'the Duce partly rejected the offer of several German divisions under the influence of the Italian High Command in order to keep a free hand'. The Fuehrer asked also whether Doenitz thought 'the Duce is determined to carry on to the end'. The reply was that Doenitz 'accepts this as certain, but he cannot be sure, of course. He has gained the impression that the primary failing of the Italians is their lack of initiative.' Hitler added that 'he does not trust the Italian upper classes. He believes that a man like Ambrosio would be happy if Italy could become a British dominion today.'[15]

Kesselring had already stated on May 13 that 'he considers an attack on the Iberian peninsula the best way of bringing relief to the Mediterranean situation and intends to submit such a plan to the Fuehrer'.[16] Doenitz again pressed the same case at this conference at the Fuehrer's headquarters. In view of the critical situation in the submarine war, the occupation of Spain, including Gibraltar, would be the best strategic solution. This would constitute an attack against the flank of the Anglo-Saxon offensive, the Axis would regain the initiative, and a radical change would take place in the Mediterranean, and submarine warfare would be given a much broader basis.

Hitler answered: 'We are not capable of an operation of this kind, since it would require first-class divisions. Occupation of Spain without the consent of the Spaniards is out of the question, since they are the only tough Latin people and would carry on guerilla warfare in our rear. In 1940 it might have been possible to get Spain to agree to such a move. However, the Italian attack on Greece in the autumn of 1940 shocked Spain. The Axis must face the fact that it is saddled with Italy.'[17]

This conference at least showed that there was no separate naval solution to the Mediterranean theatre. Equally, the defence of Italy could no longer be treated as an exclusively military problem. In reinforcing the German units in Italy account must henceforth be taken of their ultimate role in the event of Italian defection or collapse, and in supplying the Italian armed forces one must reckon on their ultimate use against Germany in event of a political coup d'état in Rome, followed by the withdrawal of Italy from the war. On May 9 Keitel referred cryptically to 'approaches to the Duce in Italy, if the situation in Italy becomes grave'.[18] On May 10 Rommel called on both the Fuehrer and Goebbels. 'I took the opportunity to stress the small capacity to fight and readiness for battle of the Italians, and thus the very serious position in Italy.'

Between May 10–16 a 'Survey of the position in event of the withdrawal of Italy from the War' was drafted for consideration by the German General Staff. The dilemma would be how 'to hold the fronts on the southern periphery of Europe, how far German forces were sufficient for the task, and what allied forces could be employed'. Italy, the Balkans, and Southern France would have to be regarded as operational zones.[19] At the same time, under the code names 'Alaric' and 'Konstantin', detailed planning began to prepare the necessary counter-measures; the former to deal with the occupation of Italy, and the latter to take over the Italian positions in the Balkans. The original General Staff directives for these two operations do not seem to have been authorized explicitly by Hitler, who preferred to give top secret verbal instructions to the two commanders concerned. General Loehr, commanding the German Army Group South-East, was summoned to Hitler's headquarters for this purpose immediately after the fall of Tunis.

At a conference of advisers on May 15, Hitler spoke of probable developments in Italy and Greece. 'Prospects for an early commitment of forces exist.'[20] In regard to Italy, Hitler decided to entrust Rommel rather than Kesselring with this task, and by the middle of May the former was established with a skeleton staff in Austria.

The forces for 'Alaric' and 'Konstantin'—and these two operations to take over military control of Italy and the Balkans were closely linked—could only come from the German Army Groups in the West and the East. Any premature allocations of such forces would mean the postponement of Hitler's Grand Design of seeking a solution of the war in Russia by the summer. The Russian operation was held up, and, for the first time since the outbreak of war, the Germans gave their full attention to the Italian scene, and to the assessment of future Allied strategic moves in the Mediterranean theatre.

CHAPTER TWO

Diplomatic Interlude

(*April–May 1943*)

THE KLESSHEIM talks in April between Hitler and Mussolini marked the opening of a renewed German diplomatic offensive in Europe. The Stalingrad disaster had not only immediate and fatal military repercussions on the conduct of the war, but cracked the prestige of the Axis, weakened German morale at home, and encouraged the Italians to seek support among the minor satellites and the neutrals to challenge German supremacy in controlling occupied Europe, and to explore the possibilities of a 'political' solution to put an end to hostilities. Hitler now moved to reassert German authority within the continental fortress and stifle any such Italian initiatives.

Following the departure of Mussolini from Salzburg, first Marshal Antonescu and then Admiral Horthy were called to the presence of the Fuehrer. To the former he delivered a requisitory on the subversive intrigues of the Roumanian Foreign Minister in hinting at alleged German moves for a separate peace with Russia, adding that his last peace offer had been made to England in July 1940, 'since when the Germans had initiated no further negotiations'.[1]

To Horthy, the theme of total resistance was expanded with a highly personal touch of historical rhetoric. In 1918 the German collapse had been grave, 'but in spite of this, the essential substance of Germany as well as that of Hungary, Bulgaria, the Baltic States and Finland had been saved and thereby the Baltic countries and the Finns had been rescued by Germany from Russian domination'.

This collapse could not be exploited by anyone. In the West, Germany's enemies were at the end of their strength.

'This the Fuehrer had learned from Lloyd George personally in a conversation at Obersalzberg (in September 1936). It would have been inconceivable for them to have continued the war. In the East—and this was decisive—there was no power left . . . The Bolsheviks had unfortunately control of the Ukraine, but on the other hand they were driven out of the Baltic region. If there had been a firm government in Germany at the time, an energetic drive would have dispersed to the winds the completely unorganized Red forces.

'Today a collapse of the Central Powers in the East would no longer create a vacuum but the mighty strength of Bolshevism would immediately press westwards. It was very important that as a result of this situation, all the allies should be clear that at the moment it was a question of total war, and that there was no distinction between the East and West, Russian and Anglo-Saxon. No Balkan alliance of Turkey, Roumania and Hungary could hold out against Russia in the same way as the German Reich with its 240 divisions. It was therefore urgently necessary that there should be no distinction between East and West.

'One could say perhaps that one could go over to the defensive in the East but this would merely mean that the Bolsheviks, who had already been severely mauled, could recover. Also the proposal to build an East Wall was pure theory.'

Bolshevism represented a permanent danger. Strong leaders like Horthy, Hitler, Mussolini and Antonescu would one day no longer be alive; then the danger of Bolshevism, if it had not already been liquidated, would remain and bring with it severe consequences. 'This mighty struggle might go on for decades as with the Huns and the Turks in the past.'[2]

The main purpose of these April talks was to impress on the minor allies the determination of Germany to make no concessions and to fight to the end. The alarm expressed at Klessheim by Ribbentrop to Bastianini about Roumanian feelers in Madrid and similar Hungarian moves in Ankara took the form of bringing pressure on the Roumanian and Hungarian heads of state to dismiss Mihai Antonescu and Kallay, their respective Foreign Ministers, and to seek Italian backing to such an end. But a further if more deeply concealed cause of German anxiety lay in the signs of an Italian 'design' for Europe. The Germans were, for instance, not clear what had passed during Kallay's visit to Rome early in April. Just as the Roumanians had hinted at impending peace feelers by the Germans in Madrid, the Hungarians had apparently, and perhaps on surer ground, insinuated similar intentions on the part of the Italian government. On April 14, therefore, Ribbentrop had instructed the German Minister in Budapest to give a formal summary to the Hungarian President of the Council of the Klessheim talks with the Italians. Both Axis partners were decided to pursue the war in the East to the end. Ribbentrop attached 'importance to informing him of this message because it would be clear from it that Kallay's communications to you on his talks with the Duce do not seem to convey the real attitude of the Duce'.[3]

Ribbentrop energetically sought evidence of a concerted conspiracy against German hegemony in Europe. Did the clues all lead to Rome?

The German Foreign Minister sent Dr Paul Schmidt to Italy to hand personally to Mussolini alone—and significantly not in the presence of Bastianini—the list of complaints presented by the Germans to the Roumanians and Hungarians, at Klessheim.

Schmidt reported, on his return, that he had explained verbally to the Duce that Hitler 'had spoken seriously to Marshal Antonescu about Mihai Antonescu and that we would keep the Duce informed of the results. I also spoke of the mistrust which Hitler had expressed to Horthy in regard to Kallay. The Duce remarked that he regarded Mihai Antonescu with great reserve. Kallay had made a particularly bad impression on him, because during his visit to Rome he had appeared as "the apotheosis of Hungarian parliamentarianism". In addition he had reported on his reception by the Pope, who had complained that the Axis powers had not made any peace proposals, to which the Duce had replied that there was no question of such a move. Kallay then reported further that the Pope had stated that he himself was not in a position to forward such peace proposals so long as Germany acted as harshly as she had done up to the present in the occupied territories. The Duce answered that this was not his business, but that soft measures were pointless as he had learnt from his own experience in Greece, Slovenia, and elsewhere.'[4]

Mussolini's pliant and evasive tact brought little satisfaction to Ribbentrop, who was further concerned at the forthcoming Roumanian visit to Rome, which was already long overdue. At the end of April Ribbentrop asked the Italian Government to postpone such an invitation. If the Roumanian

Foreign Minister came at this juncture to Italy 'it will appear that Hitler's comments to the Marshal (Antonescu) are not taken seriously . . . Could not the Italian government make the excuse of the war situation in Tunis to postpone the visit? In a roundabout way the point could also be made that Hitler naturally would not receive any foreign statesman who did not possess the confidence of the Duce.'[5] Mussolini told the German Ambassador that it would be 'delicate'. He found Mihai Antonescu 'perhaps even more unattractive than the Fuehrer does', but this would be the fourth postponement, and further there was the question of oil supplies.

The Duce bowed however to the Fuehrer's wishes, and in Mackensen's presence sent a cable giving the pretext of the battle in progress for Tunis in order to postpone the visit.[6]

On the same day as Ribbentrop approached the Duce on the Antonescu visit, Goebbels noted in his diary: 'From the Research Office's reports, I learn that the Roumanians were by no means as enthusiastic about the meeting at Salzburg as we had imagined. They felt the clear lack of aim in our policy and our war effort. Mihai Antonescu seems to be especially busy pointing this out. He is very unreliable. In a diplomatic report, I read about a conversation of his in which he emphasized that the Italians knew all about his aims and plans. It looks as though Bastianini were playing a somewhat dubious game.'[7] The suspicions entertained by Ribbentrop during his February visit to Rome of the political reliability of the Italian High Command were extending to the circles of Palazzo Chigi.

In a discussion with Mackensen on April 22, Bastianini reverted to his arguments put forward during the Italo-German conference at Klessheim earlier in the month. The Allies were waiting for the Russians and Germans to wear themselves out. 'We must not take part in this game, but must try, by political means, to counter it. In answer to my question as to how, in view of the Fuehrer's clear and effective statements at Klessheim, he conceived of the practical possibilities of a political solution, Bastianini confined himself to referring to Ribbentrop's summer talks in Moscow in 1939, which had really brought about a miracle.' The German Ambassador pointed out how conditions had changed. 'Bastianini then enlarged on the theme that the position of the Axis powers today was different from their former one in so far as the initiative had been taken from them and was on the other side. There was also no prospect in the foreseeable future of winning it back, for that could only happen, if Africa had to be completely evacuated, either by operations in the West, in the direction of Spain; or in the East through Turkey.'[8]

The brief illusion of Mussolini, fostered during the Italo-German talks at Klessheim, that the military deadlock in the Mediterranean could be broken by Spanish intervention on the Axis side, was soon dissipated. Hitler had at this time suggested that the Duce should take the initiative in seeking a meeting with Franco. It appears however that, after his gust of optimism at the end of March, Mussolini had lost interest. His enthusiasm for the problematical Spanish operation wavered with the extent of his immediate fears of the end in Tunisia. The Fuehrer's harangue at Klessheim also temporarily restored the Duce's nerve.

When Schmidt visited Rome in mid-April, on Ribbentrop's instructions, he asked whether the Duce would meet Franco. He answered that 'he had in mind a conversation at the end of April at the Spanish border, and had proposed this in a letter to Franco. The Duce did not think that Franco would be able to leave his country and therefore he was prepared to go to the Spanish frontier. But he was not certain that Franco would accept the proposal of a meeting, for he had recently become very cautious in these matters. Spain was on the way from "non-belligerence" to full neutrality, and the improvement of the internal economic position in Spain had increased the people's dislike of warlike undertakings.'[9]

On April 20, the new Italian Ambassador to Madrid, Marchese Paolucci de' Calboli Barone, presented his credentials to Franco, and presumably the letter from the Duce proposing a meeting. Franco opened the conversation by stressing Spain's economic dependence on the Allies. From the military point of view he was primarily interested in whether the Axis powers would succeed in holding Tunis, which he described as being at this time the most important strategic key position. When the Italian Ambassador assured him that the Axis forces were determined to defend Tunis, Franco was visibly gratified. 'He himself had no doubt that Tunis would be held. What the Bolsheviks had succeeded in doing at Stalingrad the Axis would find possible in Tunis . . . As to imminent landing operations in the Mediterranean, these would be aimed in the first instance, according to Franco, at Sicily and Sardinia. He did not believe in an attack on the Balearics.

'In authoritative circles in England, there was an almost

panic fear that Germany and the Soviet Union might come to terms. Franco expressed only indirectly his well-known desire for a peace, by saying that perhaps in the autumn a situation might arise which would show that between the Axis and the Western Powers no final decision could be reached, while on the other hand the Soviet Union could be played out as a military factor.'

In view of Franco's mood, it is not surprising that the Italian proposal for a meeting between him and Mussolini was politely shelved.

'At this point in the conversation . . . I had the opportunity to suggest how much a frequent exchange of ideas between the Duce and himself would be of value to both countries. Franco made a polite comment of assent, as if he shared my view, but stressed that the international situation made personal meetings very difficult for him.* He could not forget the repercussions which his journey to Bordighera had occasioned, and which had taken the form of a hostile attitude by America and England. The delivery of raw materials essential to Spain had been stopped . . . At that time it had been possible to meet these difficulties and in due course to surmount them; but today the reaction would be stronger and more dangerous.' Spain only possessed reserves of petrol for road transport for a few weeks, and for aviation spirit for fourteen days. 'On the other hand, Spain could not count on deliveries from Europe, which in effect had not been fulfilled in spite of assurances and promises from Germany, who it is true had not great export possibilities, as could also be confirmed in regard to deliveries to Italy.

'"My heart is with you", continued the Caudillo, "and I desire the victory of the Axis. This is also in my interest and that of my country, but you must not forget the difficulties which I face both in the international sphere and in internal politics."'[10]

The German Embassy in Madrid reported on May 5 a hint that Franco would accept a proposal for a meeting with Hitler 'but not with the Duce'. Two days later, Ribbentrop gave instructions only to encourage the proposal if Franco himself took the initiative. On May 8 the Allied armies entered Tunis, and Franco promptly made a pacific speech. As the German Ambassador in Madrid wrote, 'It is not impossible that developments in Tunis have strengthened ideas about the bal-

* To meet Mussolini in February 1941.

ance of power.'[11] When, on May 19, the Japanese Ambassador in Berlin, General Oshima, pressed for the occupation of Gibraltar by the Axis, Ribbentrop replied that 'Germany had had such a plan in mind for some time, but that Franco's policy of neutrality and peace makes it more difficult to carry out'. As Oshima observed, 'Spain judges the intentions of the Tripartite Powers with scepticism.'[12]

The last of the cycle of diplomatic encounters at Klessheim in the spring of 1943 was with the most wily 'European' of all, Pierre Laval. At least in the field of German and Italian relations with Vichy, Ribbentrop had some expectation of support from Rome. The maintenance of an actively neutralist and collaborationist administration at Vichy was a central and joint Axis interest, now heightened by the possibility of Allied landings in Southern France as one direction of an assault on the European mainland. The political position of Vichy must be strengthened before such a military crisis might break.

Reports of spreading opposition to Laval in Vichy circles had prompted the summons to this meeting. According to Bastianini's account, however, he received this unexpected invitation to Salzburg through the German Ambassador in Rome without any indication of the purpose of the summons, and he learnt of the presence of Laval at the forthcoming meeting only on arrival at the railway station.[13]

Ribbentrop and Bastianini met at Klessheim on April 29 before Laval's arrival. The former told his Italian colleague that he had 'been invited to come to Salzburg at such short notice because news had come in from France that certain elements were working for the retirement of Laval, just as on December 13, 1940 . . . Pétain was very old and therefore he was very easily influenced by his entourage as he did not any longer survey the scene. He was, however, not only very old but also an old fox . . . One could not therefore ignore the cross currents and intrigues in the entourage of the Marshal because this could lead one day to Laval being kicked out again, and for the purpose and aims of the Axis in France, there could not be a better man. He was shrewd, and . . . convinced that only an Axis victory could preserve France from Bolshevism.' From a French point of view there were perhaps better patriots with whom one could have more sympathy, but Ribbentrop favoured those who were of use to Germany and Italy. Hitler had therefore sent a letter to Pétain which contained a warning in no uncertain terms that

Germany would not permit such a repetition of the events of December 1940. Reports from French intermediaries had indicated that Pétain intended to withdraw his confidence from Laval. The latter, on his side, had definite and confidential evidence that close friends of Pétain had contacts through Switzerland with enemies of Italy and Germany. 'In the long run Germany and Italy could naturally not put up with this. Ribbentrop believed that it would be better if it were somehow possible to leave Pétain in his present position. They must watch the above-mentioned contacts very carefully, and if necessary sever them at a later stage. If it were necessary to remove him in the end, they would in this way have collected decisive evidence against him which would justify a sudden move. They need take no action against his collaborators . . . At the moment it would be more useful to keep Pétain than to 'lance the boil at Vichy'.

The underlying German fear was a repetition, not so much of the internal events in France which led to the previous dismissal of Laval, but of the impact on French affairs of another Allied landing such as had followed in November 1942 at the time of 'Torch', and which, if repeated, might lead to a loss by the Axis of any semblance of political control of France. Pétain could be the symbol of collaboration or resistance.

If necessary the Germans and Italians would have to act overnight. 'For example, they could inform Pétain that they had heard of English plans whose aim was to assassinate him and they would therefore place him in German and Italian protection. The German Foreign Minister added that this question was, however, not yet urgent. Under no circumstances could they let Pétain leave France; therefore all his movements were very carefully watched, and the Germans had already arranged for him to be continually under the surveillance of the German security services wherever he went. He had recently protested a little against this action, but then gave way to the proposed German arrangements. In no case could they afford to trust Pétain. This Ribbentrop had never done.'

Laval was now due at Salzburg. 'He seemed rather nervous and wanted to know if Germany and Italy would still back him up.' Germany relied on him. Hitler would express this directly and personally, and Ribbentrop now wanted to know whether Laval also enjoyed the confidence of the Italians. He had naturally a whole list of requests. Above all, he wanted a declaration on the future of France. 'In this connection there was nothing to be done. Everything was too fluid. Until the war was won, in the German view no declaration about France could be made. What would one say for example about Tunis? Tunis, Corsica and Nice would go to Italy, but Ribbentrop thought it imprudent to make any such statement.

'In general the French had a kind of touching naïveté . . . On the evening of Montoire, de Brinon [the Vichy Minister representing the Pétain government with the German authorities in Paris] had said to him in all seriousness that the French had in no way lost the war because they had not fought properly and had not wished to fight. If a statement about France were put out today, within fourteen days the French would come up with fresh demands . . . Under such circumstances one must regard the relationship with France in a very sober light. The real basis lay in the occupation of France by German and Italian troops as well as in the fact that Laval was shrewd enough to know it was also in France's interests to wish for an Axis victory. He was bound hand and foot to the Axis and there was no way back. In general the French police were strongly committed to the Axis. This was in a certain sense an ideal situation. Anything else was Utopian and led nowhere.'

Bastianini thought that Hitler's letter would be effective. Laval must be clear that he could count on German and Italian support. Italy 'was against any declaration on France's future position such as he was seeking. It would be impossible to make such a statement at the present moment until the position of France was assured. In addition the future position of France could not be established alone through an outside act of will. France must work out her own moral fate. At the moment she did not seem to appreciate the position. The French loved neither the Germans nor the Italians, but they had also not understood that they had been beaten by Germany and that their country was occupied by German troops. If they had understood the meaning of these facts they would not run over to a Giraud or a de Gaulle. In this respect the views of the leaders of the new Europe, namely the Fuehrer and the Duce, fully coincided.'[14]

According to Bastianini, Ribbentrop also added that Hitler had wished for the presence of an Italian representative that morning to show Laval that there was complete Italo-German agreement and 'to discourage him from repeating again the effort already made with Ciano to play on the imaginary possibility of a difference between the Axis powers'. Laval would however certainly press for concessions and the Fuehrer thought that 'one ought to move very cautiously, and keep Italian claims out of the discussion'. Any increased Axis support for Laval, or any concessions to France, must be at the expense of Italy, particularly if the remaining part of the French fleet was handed back.

Laval arrived late that morning at Salzburg. He first met Ribbentrop alone. The German authorities at Vichy had just been instructed to confirm to Pétain that Laval possessed the confidence of both the German and Italian governments, 'but on the German side it was thought necessary that this fact should be officially known in Vichy, and the Fuehrer had therefore last night sent Marshal Pétain a letter clarifying the German attitude in unmistakable terms'. In this letter, which Laval had learnt about on his journey, the Fuehrer 'had made it clear once and for all that Germany would never again bow to intriguing elements, and would never again accept a change of government. Such a game of intrigue would have catastrophic results for France.' Laval would be received by the Fuehrer that afternoon, and Bastianini would also be present. The Italian attitude to the situation at Vichy was identical with the German. Laval then said that 'in order to forward his present policy, a clearly recognizable goal must be put in front of the French. The struggle against Bolshevism was not enough. One must give France an aim and security, and take French national sentiment into account. Germany wanted to create a new Europe. He wanted to help in this, but France must be accorded a place which suited her.'

Ribbentrop replied: 'At Montoire the Fuehrer had made France an offer of the closest collaboration in order to beat England and America. This offer had not been accepted. France had handled the situation with reservations. This had led to the greatest betrayal in history. North Africa had seceded, although France had always maintained that she would defend it, and had sought and received arms for its defence. Whenever the question of France's future appeared, he (Ribbentrop) could only reply that the sole way to secure this future was Laval's policy. After all Germany and Italy shed their blood to the end also in order to protect French culture.'

Laval answered that 'he would not persist in his desire to obtain a declaration on the future of France. But he must stress that he had reached the limit of his capacity. The Germans must for once see the situation from a French point of view. He had mobilized one age group after another for labour service in Germany, without being able to tell these mobilized Frenchmen why this was happening.'[15]

The two foreign guests were received that afternoon in Hitler's study at Berchtesgaden, where Laval was subjected to a catalogue of the Fuehrer's resentments against Pétain. 'For a Germany at war, France constitutes no problem. Two gauleiters would do the job; a German in one zone, and an Italian in the other.'[16]

Laval began at once with an outline of his central political thesis: by creating a new Europe, Germany and by opposition, the Allies, would be forced to define their war aims, which would narrow to questions of frontiers which could be easily settled. 'In order to construct Europe you assume that first the war must be won. In my opinion it would be preferable to organize Europe in order to win the war.'

Hitler's reply was that he needed no Declaration of a European Order 'but 20,000 planes and 20,000 tanks'. Laval riposted, 'A Declaration of twenty lines would be worth 20,000 planes and 40,000 tanks. You ought to take me on as secretary, set me up in a corner and I would write it for you.' The dialogue petered out round the tea-table in front of the Fuehrer's fireplace in the 'Eagle's Nest'.

A truncated communiqué 'recognising France's place in Europe' was the only result of this Franco-German dialogue. Laval returned with the renewed assurances of Axis support for a policy of collaboration with him, a repeated threat that the Germans would not tolerate his removal from power, and no concessions to make his tenure of office viable.

That evening Ribbentrop gave a dinner for the Italian and French delegations. Bastianini wrote later that Laval held the conversation. 'You talk of a New Order to be set up in Europe after your victory. There is a need to do so, but people are asking what you intend and you do not tell them . . . Explain what this New Order consists of. Maybe people will like it. Begin to install it, and for the first time the French will be convinced of your good faith. I wager that if I go to Rome and talk to Mussolini we will reach agreement on how to define it. But if you don't do it, the enemy will have an easy time with their propaganda against you.'[17]

Late that night he and his advisers returned in Goering's special train to France. Ribbentrop's parting words, according to de Brinon, were, 'Now you must get rid of your opponents.'[18]

Bastianini had also used the occasion of this visit to press once more his own European plan. He had been, as he explained to his advisers, 'for some time seeking to convince the Germans to make some gesture . . . which would have the concealed purpose of preparing a "European Charter" fit to serve as a basis for possible peace negotiations'.

If he had been alarmed at the German attitude at the first Klessheim talks early in April, he received even less comfort from the second. 'The Germans suspect Pétain in France, they suspect Kallay in Hungary and Mihai Antonescu in Roumania. They suspect Franco and fear Turkey. Naturally they suspect us. And they are right. The whole of Europe is in revolt against the German attempt at hegemony, conducted with such bestiality. And Italy, to whom so many peoples are turning, hoping that a voice of common sense will reach them from that quarter, is allowing herself, like the others, to be drawn into the vortex of this madness. Throughout the whole day a leaden atmosphere weighed on our group, isolated from the Germans, in the halls of Klessheim.'[19]

According to his own account, Bastianini had gone so far as to lecture Ribbentrop not only on the need for the reconstruction of Europe, but also for the inclusion of France. It was pointless to exasperate her national feelings. And on May 1 the Duce went so far as to instruct the official Stefani News Agency to issue a statement in this sense. But even if a mild collusion—and it is very doubtful—existed between Laval and Bastianini at this moment, the rancours and frustrations in Italo-French relations lay too deep for any mutual understanding. As Bastianini told Mackensen some weeks later: 'It was laughable that Laval should now talk of empty hands, when at taking leave in Berchtesgaden he showed himself fully satisfied.' The argument had been that Laval's position should be strengthened by a continuation of the policy of collaboration. Mackensen added: 'As for so-called collaboration today, it was rather that the whole of France was only waiting for an enemy landing to throw off the mask.'[20] And what of Italy?

* * *

The Italians had no illusions as to the German reception of their European programme. As Alfieri reported from Berlin on May 14: 'I asked Steengracht whether the idea of a "European Charter" had by chance made any progress in the minds of the German leaders, since, I added, I had the impression, which was confirmed by the last meeting at Salzburg, that, on the German side, one had accepted with extreme difficulty a small part of the Italian thesis and only to please the Duce. The respective positions remained unchanged. Steengracht admitted loyally and confidentially that my impression corresponded to the reality.'[21]

But more significantly, those German circles which had looked cautiously for the Duce's intervention with Hitler in regard to the Russian war, both in the previous March and in timid conclave at Klessheim in April, were now stilled. Hitler had dispersed the shadows of Stalingrad on the German home front, and none of his advisers would risk any form of criticism of his obsessive pursuit of the Russian adventure.

As Steengracht declared to Alfieri, 'Hitler is intimately and deeply convinced of having the equipment, weapons, and men, and sufficient possibilities to inflict the gravest blow on the Russians. Perhaps this is the reason why none of the direct collaborators (Goering, Ribbentrop, Himmler, Bormann, Goebbels), who could have some influence on him, dare talk to him about such a problem and of the negative possibilities which are inevitable in all human affairs.' Alfieri felt therefore that 'at this point . . . it is useless to insist. It only remains to await the results of the first German military successes and to choose a good moment to exploit the favourable situation, and then to take another step towards the formulation of a European Charter.'

The worsening of the Italian military position after the fall of Tunis in May was as usual marked by an extension of her diplomatic and political campaign independently of her German partner. At the instigation of Bastianini the Italian Senate became a brief forum of discussion on foreign affairs. The debate was harshly viewed in Berlin. On May 19 Mackensen reported the leading speech of Senator Salata, 'which as I learn reliably is based on Foreign Office material, and has been agreed with Bastianini'. It represented a full dress review of Italian foreign policy, and called for 'joint Axis action in the political and military fields'. In regard to Spain, although she remained a non-belligerent, she 'was anything but indifferent to the present phase in the Mediterranean'. The so-called Iberian Union met with great sympathy in Italy because of its influence in Southern Europe, Africa and South America.

Italian relations with Turkey were unchanged. They shared a common anxiety at the renewal of Soviet aspirations towards the Dardanelles, and Turkey could not remain indifferent to the future New Order in the Mediterranean. In the Balkans Italy must secure the Eastern coastline of the Adriatic and control the Ionian Sea. Italian claims on France, Tunis, Nice, and Corsica, were markedly stressed. These conditions for Italy's entry into the war had always been recognized by Germany, and 'confirmed in the last talks between Hitler, Bastianini and Laval'.

Salata drew attention to the Eurafrican aims of the Axis against the imperialist and bolshevik powers. The policy of Britain was anti-European. Casablanca had shown the Allied intention 'to set up a dictatorship of four basically non-European powers'. On the other side, since the Hitler-Mussolini meeting at Klessheim, the programme of the independence and unity of Europe and co-operation of European peoples had been stated anew. Italy had set herself two historical aims: to create again the position in the Mediterranean which belonged to her, and 'to offer to the small peoples the leadership of Rome'. The Duce was 'the European'. 'The Europe of the Axis, which was resisting the assault on its fortress, must make every effort to see that the direction of Europe does not slip from the grasp of Europeans. This is the meaning and the commitment of the last meeting of the two statesmen and their mission to Europe.'[22]

On the following day, May 20, Bastianini made his contribution to the debate. He referred to the period of the previous three months during which he had been at the Foreign Ministry. Senator Salata had rightly stressed the meeting between the Duce and the Fuehrer which took place at Salzburg in April. 'But further emphasis should be laid on the importance of the basic problem stated at that meeting, to which Italy and Germany intend to cling, to prepare the conditions and premises for the future order of the world: no aggression on small states by the Great Powers, no elimination of the national individuality of the smaller states, but a guarantee of the free development of all nations, with their spontaneous collaboration assured. It was in this framework of firm decision and sincere European collaboration that last month's meeting with Laval took place. The principles laid down by Germany and Italy as the basis of European and world order are also at the basis of Italy's relations with France. No wish to destroy or humiliate France, and understanding of her vital necessities. But to take part in the work of reconstructing Europe, France must understand the need to make sacrifices and contributions not only to Axis production and war efforts, but also to settling the questions which still remain outstanding with her conquerors. This is the essential condition for Italo-French relations to find, in a framework of mutual understanding, their place in greater Europe.'[23]

This speech enraged Hitler, who read the text aloud at a military conference on May 20. He took exception in particular to the concluding remarks about France. 'How can he say such a thing! The French say that they were not beaten by the Italians . . . a very rotten speech and it strengthens my feeling that a crisis of the type which we have discussed can develop there at any moment.'[24]

CHAPTER THREE

The Italian 'Political Design'

'THE TWO military requisites for successful Italian diplomatic activity are: German destruction of Russian strength, and the defeat of the Allies in the Mediterranean. Such hopes however are tenuous . . . Today it is unreal to suppose that Stalin would make peace with Hitler, or Churchill and Roosevelt with Mussolini.'

Such was the view expressed in an Italian War Office minute written by one of Ambrosio's staff after the Klessheim Conference. During the summer months of 1943 in Rome, as the military situation of the Axis deteriorated in inexorable stages, the Italian Foreign Office headed by Bastianini and his professional advisers sought with mounting desperation their own diplomatic solution to the war. The first stage in such a 'plan' was to be a firm private agreement with the satellite allies in Southern and Central Europe, Roumania and Hungary, before taking soundings in the West as to the chances of a negotiated peace. The opportunity for such moves seemed to appear after the visit of Churchill to Adana at the beginning of the year, and was based on reports that the British Prime Minister had expressed views which could be interpreted to mean that the Western Allies, in particular Britain, were anxious about the future post-war extension of Russian influence on the Straits and in the Balkans, which would bring the Soviet Union to the shores of the Mediterranean.

This thesis, on which the hopes of Italian diplomacy came to be exclusively centred, is set out in a document transmitted to Berlin later in the year by the German Ambassador in Bucharest. 'Immediately after the Adana Conference the Turkish Minister here, Tanroier, made a contact with the

Italian Minister, which was strengthened in numerous talks. The plan of building up a bloc consisting of Italy, South-Eastern Europe, and Turkey was discussed, and Tanroier developed the idea, to which Bova Scoppa rallied, that these states should seek a way to an agreement with England and then, rifle in hand, take the defensive against an eventual Russian attack on the Balkans.'

This conception was carried further in talks between Mihai Antonescu and the Italian Minister. 'The need to find a political solution to the war compelled these powers grouped round the Axis sooner or later to reach an understanding with England. The bridge to such an agreement would be built up on Turkish-Roumanian relations. The aim of this activity must be to persuade the Duce, and through him the Fuehrer, of the necessity of such a way and its feasibility.'

Italian leadership must be the prime element in such a scheme, which might also be extended from Eastern Europe to the neutrals of the West, Spain and Portugal, and even perhaps to the France of Pétain and Laval. This chimera lies henceforth at the centre of Italian diplomacy. In timing any further moves, much depended on the German military situation in the East. The reports of Bova Scoppa from Bucharest since the beginning of 1943 proved to be not only invaluable in this sense, but also the only direct source of such intelligence; the Italian Embassy in Berlin being able in effect to comment only on such reports as the Germans chose to pass on them.

On May 12 Bova Scoppa wrote a private letter to Bastianini, based on such confidential information from the Roumanian Military Attaché in Berlin, General Gheorge, as to German intentions on the Russian Front, and passed on to him by Mihai Antonescu under pledge of secrecy.

'The Germans do not intend to begin a large-scale offensive against Russia this year . . . At the German Headquarters they maintain that Germany will only be ready to launch a decisive offensive against the Russian Army in 1944, when the total mobilization of all the forces of the nation has borne fruit. . . . The Fuehrer and his colleagues speak of "the new Seven Years War"—affirming that after the Soviet Army is destroyed, two more years will be necessary to deal with and wipe out the Anglo-Saxon offensives on European soil. The Fuehrer likes this historical parallel, because during that war, Frederick II was in a very similar position to the present one, and made a later come-back.'

As Mihai Antonescu pointed out to the Italian Minister, 'If the German General Staff proposes to wait another year before launching a decisive offensive against the Russians, we must bear in mind that this year will be used by our enemies, and that the time factor is certainly not on our side . . . And if this winter the Russians begin another offensive like this year's, what will become of our armies, if at the same time we have to deal with the Anglo-Saxon threat in the West?'[1]

On May 14 Bova Scoppa wrote again to Bastianini, on this occasion to summarize the views of the very active Turkish Minister in Bucharest, who had been pressing hard from behind the scenes for a 'diplomatic' solution of the war. The excessive optimism of Tanroier in regard to an eventual British attitude to peace feelers was to exert an unfortunate and misleading influence in the future.

'As each day passes, the Allies' morale rises a stage, while that of the peoples of Europe falls. Germany thinks she can win the war with the submarine war, but in many people's opinion this is a dangerous illusion. The Allies feel in a position to cope with the serious threats of the battle in the Atlantic.' There was one more dangerous illusion: Russia. 'By now the war on that front has changed from a battle against space to a battle against time. It is almost certain that the Russians will move against the Germans as soon as a second front can be established in Europe. The possibility of Russia collapsing must therefore be discarded, and, in my opinion, so must that of a separate peace between Germany and Russia.'

In such conditions, the struggle in the Mediterranean became of decisive importance. 'You are not unaware that the Allied programme is to put Italy out of action, as the first act of the final battle against Germany. Now that you have lost Tunisia, a violent air offensive will be launched against your country: your cities will be destroyed, and my European heart cannot think of this prospect without shuddering . . . It is now probable that the Allies will try to land quickly in Sicily and Sardinia, and will seek to engage your fleet. If ever they get hold of your islands' gigantic air bases—Italy would be changed into a sea of ruins. Think too of the possibility of Italy herself becoming the battlefield of the Allied and Axis Armies . . .'

Tanroier stressed that he was speaking personally. 'I am certain that, if you were ready to negotiate peace, England would give you honourable conditions. The reason is very simple. England is not unaware that Italy is an essential balancing and stabilizing element for the Europe of the future. Could you ever imagine that, having won the war, the English and Americans would stay on guard in Europe to prevent suffocation by the Slavs, and the rebirth of Germany? Italy must have her place in Europe and in the Mediterranean, and land for expansion. We Turks too want this to happen, and we have not hidden it from the English. I am sure of what I am saying, that if you agree to negotiate peace, with that historic courage which must be shown in face of certain untenable situations, and if in doing so you emphasized the essential function Italy could have in the Europe of tomorrow, and you came to an anti-Bolshevik union with England, then Italy would save her fate, and perhaps her régime as well.

'Her régime as well?

'I think so. The Anglo-Americans will never negotiate with Hitler and the Nazis, but it is very probable that they will treat with the Duce and the Fascists.'[2]

These dispatches stimulated Bastianini's long maturing 'political' design.

On May 29 Bova Scoppa came to Rome to report and was instructed to draft a memorandum on the Roumanian attitude to be sent to the Duce. On June 5 the document was handed to Bastianini, who now presented the whole case to the Duce in a minute dated June 14, enclosing both this memorandum, and an equally significant dispatch from Anfuso in Budapest.[3] The covering note was headed 'The Collaboration between Italy and the Danubian Countries in seeking a political solution of the War'.

The dispatch from Anfuso showed clearly 'the irrevocable decision of the Hungarian government to cling tight to Italy in any future eventuality . . . and to place henceforward their full and definitive trust in the loyalty of our friendship. We have also had recent proof of this from other quarters. 'You will remember, Excellency, the ready and, I would say, almost impatient support which Hungary gave to the idea of a Balkan bloc outlined by the Turkish representatives in some of the Balkan capitals. Even before identifying it as an English manoeuvre, or as an attempt to detach countries from the Axis, she saw in it the possibility of reinforcing her position in the Balkans by securing herself beforehand in an anti-Soviet direction, against possible Axis military disasters. This Hungarian position is not greatly changed; her need for assurance about the future is only increased and strengthened.

'The ups and downs of her relations with Germany are, in this light, only episodes, and if the Hungarian government today decided on definite concessions, this is with the sole object of not compromising the most vital interests of the near future in impulsive and ill-timed decisions. This is why Hungary has listened to the advice of her friend Italy, but it is also for the same reason that she is still waiting for those directives which she declares herself ready to follow from this very moment.'

Bastianini recommended therefore that the moment had come to clarify to Kallay Italy's policy in the Danube basin 'which coincides precisely with that of our (Hungarian) ally. The general lines of direction of our political conduct . . . which consisted above all in the strengthening of existing friendships with the Danubian countries, Hungary and Roumania, and in seeking closer ties with Bulgaria, are confirmed for the first time in the attached report of Minister Anfuso.'

It was equally important to consolidate 'in a precise manner our friendly relations with Roumania'. From Bova Scoppa's memorandum it appeared that 'the political line' of Antonescu fitted in many respects that of the Duce. 'In any case, it appears to be indispensable to keep him in his prearranged course of conduct in such a way that Roumania does not make any compromising gesture, not even in reaction to certain excessive and harsh pressures on the part of the Germans.'

Antonescu's visit to Rome should therefore at last take place. 'These talks could be decisive for a comprehensive exchange of views on the present situation, and the future, and for the stabilization of the second link in that close political chain binding Roumania to Italy and thus to consolidate that transversal Danubian-Balkan Axis, which should be headed by yourself and should follow your directives, not only in our interests, but for the same reasons of the war which imposes the closest solidarity between the adherents to the Tripartite Pact.'

Bastianini asked for detailed instructions for such a visit both in political and economic terms. There was also the urgent question of Roumanian oil and wheat deliveries to be discussed.

The memorandum by Bova Scoppa represented a wide-ranging survey of the war as seen from a Balkan capital, and in particular by the Roumanian Foreign Minister. 'After winning innumerable battles, Germany is reduced to defending the European fortress: a similar situation to that of 1918 apart from the scale of the defence. Since she attacked Russia while she still had to conquer England, Germany is powerless to destroy the Soviet Army. Great Britain and America are defended by the sea; Russia by land. Without an internal revolution, which seems unlikely, Russia is invincible in the present state of affairs . . . All the reports we have had at Bucharest are agreed on this aspect of the problem, and it appears too that they are in entire accord with those from Turkey and even from Japan.

'Germany is going through a profound crisis due to lack of man power, to a crisis in war production both because of the lack of some essential raw materials, and because of errors in aircraft construction, and to the general conditions of the masses who are sorely tried by the increasing bombardments . . . German supremacy in the air has ceased on all fronts. You cannot with impunity hold a front of 10,000 kilometres from the North Pole to Salonika—says Antonescu—without reducing your defence to a minimum, nor can you hold down a mass of 90 million men—the population of the occupied countries—without denuding the war fronts, as happened in the Eastern theatre last winter. The German hope of winning the submarine war is belied by the results of the Atlantic battle in the last few months. With her industries bombarded without respite, her cities bombed ruthlessly, a Russian front which shows no signs of being decided soon, and where the Germans are suffering continued attacks, with her occupied peoples in ferment and ready to rebel, with tired and discouraged public opinions which have lost faith in victory, the "Festung Europa" offers—according to Antonescu—a tempting spectacle to the Anglo-American war leaders.'

The results of the Tunisian campaign, where superiority of planes and tanks was decisive, left Antonescu in no doubt that the Allied General Staffs could dictate their will through an enormous concentration of materials and men at given points on the European coast. 'Even if a first and second attempt to invade the "Festung Europa" did not succeed, the Axis successes would be temporary, and whatever happened our attitude would always be negative, i.e. that of defenders, not of conquerors imposing peace . . . It is a question of a mathematical calculation. It is a question of time, and time is against us.' Militarily the war could no longer be won. According to Antonescu, 'this is the last hour for returning to the political method. It is therefore the hour of the Duce; he could be immortalized once more in a "Munich of the War".'

In addition the frequent contacts which Antonescu had with German military and diplomatic circles in Roumania convinced him 'that this idea is by now widely held in Germany too, and within the Nazi Party itself. In some occupied countries, certain S.S. elements regard a change to political strategy as indispensable and urgent. Because of this, he considers that, if the Duce took the initiative through a shrewd, very cautious diplomatic action, he would not only save the Axis countries from a dramatic situation, but would render a signal service to Germany herself.'

The reaction of Mussolini to this evidence in support of a political solution of the war by joint action between Italy together with the satellite allies, Roumania and Hungary, is described later by Bastianini. 'The effect which I was seeking was achieved in part. Mussolini declared that he agreed that Hitler should be placed with his back to the wall, that a close understanding should be established with Bucharest and Budapest, that a conversation should be held with Mihai Antonescu. Within two months, he (the Duce) said, the position would be clarified.'[4] But as Bastianini added to Bova Scoppa, Mussolini 'says however that it is still too soon to take the diplomatic initiative'.[5]

Bastianini sought what advantage he could from the Duce's long delayed approval to the first step of a meeting with the Roumanian Foreign Minister on Italian soil, and on June 21 he felt able to tell Mackensen that he was planning to meet the Roumanian Foreign Minister in Venice.

'A further postponement, now the fifth, was no longer possible' in view of the importance of trade negotiations. 'Bastianini intends to discuss Roumanian-Hungarian relations in the sense of the policy of the Axis powers. If sufficient reason appears, he will take Mihai Antonescu incognito to meet the Duce.'[6]

On June 29 Bastianini received his Roumanian colleague in Venice. The economic questions between the two countries were discussed. The conversation with the Duce took place at La Rocca on July 1. The discussions lasted for five hours, both before and after lunch. Mihai Antonescu 'wanted the Duce to know, first of all, how the Conducator and himself since 1941 had been concerned to define in a way which would be clear to all, allies and foes alike, the political war aims of the Tripartite Powers. Since that time, on the several visits which he had made to the Fuehrer and Herr von Ribbentrop in Germany, he had spoken with complete frankness of the evident need to conduct the war not only by military but also political weapons, both to strengthen the will to fight of the Tripartite Powers and to show the European peoples that the Axis New Order represented a "substantial improvement" for the future of the Continent and based on "fair and just principles" to which the neutral nations could also subscribe.'

According to Antonescu, these ideas had been accepted in general terms by Ribbentrop, and therefore the former had had a certain 'exchange of views' with Salazar on general questions arising out of a common Latin tradition shared by Roumania and Portugal and the 'function of a common Latin heritage in this war and after the conflict'.

Roumania was not preparing for a separate peace, 'which also from all evidence seemed geographically impossible', but rather hoped to define 'certain political issues on which . . . the adhesion of the largest possible majority of the European peoples could be assured, and against which in effect extra-European forces were fighting'. Antonescu therefore appealed to the Duce to further the action begun by him. 'Roumania intended to bind her destiny entirely to that of Italy, and he was stating this to the Duce in the name of the Conducator.'

Mussolini was cautious in his reply. 'He noted the wishes of Roumania, and the firmness which she showed . . . He would not fail to speak to the Fuehrer at their next meeting. The view that the war must also be fought with political weapons had led him to make a proposal to the Fuehrer. This had been put aside two months ago, but he intended to take it up again as soon as the military situation had had that indispensable clarification which was now in progress. The Duce assured Antonescu that he had no intention whatever of abandoning this line which he had begun some months ago, and indeed it was his precise view that this line should be repeated and defined at a meeting of all the governments of the Tripartite countries.'

In Bova Scoppa's phrase, Mussolini must be persuaded that 'it is the Duce's hour: he could be immortalized once more in a "Munich of the War"'. All hopes were focused to this end in the present meeting, but they were modestly fulfilled. As was his habit, Mussolini accepted the basic views of his audience, and promptly defined an escape clause. He agreed to the principle of a general conference of the Tripartite Powers, and would make such a proposal to Hitler, but within the next two months. In spite of Antonescu's pleading, both at the two formal meetings and during luncheon, Mussolini would not yield, nor listen to the Roumanian argument that Hitler in any case would never agree and that their two countries must in any event seek their own solution. He did however imply that after two months, if Hitler had not listened to him, he would call such a conference 'including the neutrals'. He made no reference to Mihai Antonescu's hints 'at eventual peace feelers towards negotiations' with the Western Allies.

After luncheon the party adjourned on to the terrace of La Rocca, and looking across the plain of Forlì, the Duce remarked with little relevance that this was the area 'where he had fought Socialism'. During the afternoon the talks were resumed and on taking leave Mussolini turned to Antonescu saying, 'I hope that this meeting may have an historical significance.' Bova Scoppa assumed that the Duce had given way on the time limit of two months, but on the train to Rome learnt that Mussolini had insisted that 'one could not negotiate when one was under the blow of a military defeat like that in Africa'.[7]

At the end of the conversation Antonescu had asked whether during this two months' interval he could continue to act on his own account, and the Duce had 'authorized' him to do so.

Eight days later the Allies landed in Sicily. The slim chances of any such diplomatic initiative vanished.

Bastianini accompanied his guest to Forlì station. 'Antonescu told me that he had understood that, while the Duce had shown the most cordial comprehension and had promised to raise with Hitler questions of minor importance concerning Roumania, he had avoided undertaking commitments of major significance. There was however no time to lose as Bolshevik Russia was at the gates, and one could assume that America and England shared with us the common interest in preventing Bolshevism being established in half Europe. I said that I agreed—and we were both to be proved wrong—and he assured me that I could count on total Roumanian support for whatever initiative that I had taken . . . I did not tell him that when I begged Mussolini to let me act on my own and on my responsibility he had replied that it was too soon.'[8]

The only positive result of this meeting was that Bastianini knew that henceforward he could count on the Roumanians if he could persuade Mussolini on a last gamble to seek terms from the West. Before initiating any such action, he must give some explanation to the Germans of these talks with the Roumanians and, if possible, blunt their inevitable suspicions.

On July 4 Mackensen reported: 'Bastianini took advantage of my evening call . . . to inform me in general terms of the meeting with Mihai Antonescu. The first talks took place according to plan in Venice, where above all, economic matters were raised and experts called in. In regard to commercial affairs there had been only a modest success in breaking the marked deadlock because Roumania could not deliver those raw materials particularly needed by Italy—he quoted in the first instance oilseeds. Also in regard to grain deliveries, things did not look good, and this in particular was of the greatest importance for Italy, for according to yesterday's report from the Minister of Agriculture to Bastianini, in spite of a normal harvest in Northern Italy, the results in the Centre and the South would be small, so that the total average would be far behind that of last year.'

In Venice, Antonescu had expressed the same views on political matters as at the subsequent meeting with the Duce at La Rocca delle Caminate. He had given formal assurances that Roumania would and must follow with the Axis powers to the end. There had been no question of any kind of peace feelers. 'For Roumania it was and could only be a question of going with the Axis powers to the end. The danger for the country was as always Russia, whether it was a Bolshevist Russia or another, behind which for Roumania the dangerous Panslav idea lay.'

The assurance given by Bastianini that there would be 'no separate peace feelers' might well be received with scepticism by the Germans. It is however significant that there had been no German reports of any such moves by the Italians since the previous spring.

On March 26 Mackensen had reported to Berlin that in his view the very concept of an 'Italian Government' engaged in secret negotiations was false. 'The Italian Government is the Duce; to attribute such a thought to him is absurd.'[9]

The German Ambassador was formally correct in this view.

Mussolini had never permitted his Undersecretary to make any such soundings. But from the German point of view the danger still existed of a secret understanding between the Italians and the satellite allies sanctioned by Mussolini. It seemed however from Bastianini's account to Mackensen of the talks with Mihai Antonescu that the Duce had not encouraged any such move, and again this was strictly accurate.

From these discussions held by Bastianini with the Roumanians during the late spring and summer of 1943 had emerged a clear and erroneous image of the Western Allies, of their relations with Russia, and their strategic conception of the war. A set of misleading assumptions was produced, which coloured irrevocably the belated Italian approach to peace feelers towards Britain and the United States.

Within the circle of the Italian Foreign Office a certain mirage had been conjured up. The Western powers, fearing above all else the post-war domination of Europe by the Soviet Union, were planning as their major assault on the Axis-controlled continent a landing in South-Eastern Europe in order to contain in the last resort the advance westwards of the Russian armies. In such an operation the support of the Roumanian and Hungarian forces, together with the resources of Italy, would be of decisive value. If Italy as the senior member of such an Entente, and speaking also in the name of Bucharest and Budapest, could approach the Allies with the offer of military assistance in such an event, and thus escape the consequences of the Axis commitment, salvation might still be won. In spite of the Casablanca formula, the British would treat with a Fascist Italy but never with Nazi Germany.

The diplomatic activities conducted in these assumptions between April and July 1943 had led to the point at which Bastianini was now able to speak, in any secret talks with the Western Allies, on behalf of Roumania and Hungary. It now remained, as a final manoeuvre, to secure the approval of the Duce to undertake such a move.

CHAPTER FOUR

The 'Last Wave' of the Fascist Party

DURING HIS visit to Klessheim the Duce had been reflecting on the creeping fissures in the Home Front and relating them to the international scene. The leadership of the second generation of Fascism, the young men who had fought in Abyssinia and in Spain, of whom the Party Secretary Vidussoni had been groomed as the symbol, had not revolutionized the position, much less halted its disintegration. The Party had also been noticeably 'absent' during the March strikes.

On his return to Rome Mussolini struck simultaneously in different quarters. His first act was, on April 14, to dismiss the Chief of Police, Carmine Senise, who was officially accused of neglect of duty in not taking effective action against the strikers in Northern Italy.[1] The German agencies in Rome had been reporting against him to Himmler, and the Fascist Party machine was also out for his head. He was replaced by Renzo Chierici, a career officer in the Forest Militia, and a former companion of Italo Balbo from Ferrara. Bastianini informed the German Ambassador of Senise's dismissal on the following day, April 15. He described Chierici 'as an old Action Squad member and specially trustworthy. A first step has now been taken.'

After 'an intense gestation of rumours and indiscretions', three days later, on April 17, Mussolini now summoned the Party Directorate to Palazzo Venezia. The Duce issued his latest confidential directive. 'The applause with which you have greeted Vidussoni's report shows your opinion. It is with great regret that I have decided to accept his resignation from an office which he has carried on faithfully for fifteen months. Vidussoni is not an orator. In normal times this would be meritorious, for I am not of those who believe in talking, but in times like the present the man who is number two in the régime must have this gift as well, because he must be able to get in contact with the masses, especially when there is uncertainty . . . I have chosen Carlo Scorza as his successor. I have known him for twenty years and perhaps more. I am certain that he will carry out my directives in a true fighting spirit . . . In order to indicate what these directives will be, I must refer to recent happenings—to be precise, to the happenings of March 10, the date of the disturbances among the workers in Turin, Milan and other smaller cities of Piedmont and Lombardy. This unpleasant and deplorable episode has suddenly plunged us twenty years back. We must relate these happenings to the general international situation, that is, to the fact that the Russian advance at that time seemed irresistible and that it appeared that the moustachioed man, which is what the workers call Stalin, would shortly arrive to "liberate" Italy . . . The importance of these events is not only due to its character but to the fact that it at once involved political speculation. The motive of economic discontent seemed to justify the disturbances, but this motive was adopted as a pretext by Communist cells and by other cells which were more or less liberal. The old questions of "a separate peace", "an increase in the bread ration" (as if we did not all want to increase the bread ration if possible), "release of prisoners" and other similar desires came out into the open. This is a rough account of the facts; it is not enough; now we must consider whether all the organizations worked as they should have done. I do not believe it. First of all an upheaval of this kind does not fall from heaven like a thunderbolt. It is clear that there must have been signs to warn us of what was brewing, signs which would give the alarm and would tell us to be on our guard as something was about to happen.

'On the contrary, Rome got no warning. This raises the question of the close connection between the syndical organizations and the working masses. This connection is essential, otherwise we shall find ourselves faced by these unpleasant criminal surprises which convince the workers that if they go back to the old methods they will get what they want. It is useless to create large numbers of press offices, it is useless to rack our brains over statistics and to organize legal offices; all these already exist . . . The syndical organizer must live in daily contact with the masses whom he claims to represent, he must have courage to uphold their interests if they are justified, and to oppose them when he sees that behind economic discontent there exists political speculation. At Turin a most extraordinary thing happened. The workers were asked to return to work through a printed pamphlet. The impression was that no one had the courage to sign it, neither the Federal Secretary of Turin, nor the Mayor of Turin, nor the Prefect of Turin; some form of signature was necessary to assume the responsibility. This pamphlet was a pathetic document not only in its contents but in the way in which it was handed out at Turin. When it was known that these people were going to strike at 10 o'clock, it was suggested that the siren should not be sounded; as if these people had not got watches. These are small tricks, but I call them serious deceptions by means of which people hoped to avoid existing difficulties. On the contrary, they must be resolutely confronted.

'Once again, the Party. We must recognize that the Party was not in command of the situation either at Turin or at Milan. Why not? Because the Fascists themselves were not unanimous in their behaviour. Some went on strike, some did not, some made an agreement with the strikers. We got the impression that the whole local Party apparatus had been taken by surprise. At a certain point an announcement was made: "All Fascists are to put on their Black Shirts." But nothing was said about for how long, or whether this was compulsory . . . Some put on their shirts, some did not. This also gave the feeling of there being a serious division of opinion. The Federal Secretaries went to their posts, both the Federal Secretary of Turin and the Secretary of Milan, but I have not got the impression that they succeeded in getting control of the situation. Why? Because at a certain moment recourse was had to the disabled service men. It seemed that the situation was so uncertain that only the disabled could go into the factories and recall these gentlemen to their duty of producing munitions while our comrades were fighting in Tunisia, and that only these disabled men had sufficient prestige to restore the situation.

'Therefore do not be surprised that I have given draconian orders to the Police Chiefs and Prefects. There is another sector to be examined: I did not get the impression that the police forces were sufficiently alert, they did not act sufficiently severely to make an end of the troubles. You do not get any result by saying to the workers "you must go and be a soldier", as if that was a punishment, "you will lose your exemption, you will be sent back to your own districts". All this showed lack of obedience to the directives from Rome. If they had fired at the workers, I would have taken the responsibility. When Italian workers murder other Italians who are fighting, I have them shot. All this explains the change of the Chief of Police. We must have a Fascist police; not policemen who are Fascist, but Fascists who are policemen. This will make many people think again. This is only the first step in the direction of a policy which for the moment I will call a rigid policy, while reserving the right to adopt a word with a more severe meaning. As it has always been said that we did not have a revolution (although we did have a very real revolution which has left a mark on the country) because we did not resort to terrorism, these persons will obviously force us to adopt it. Then they will not be able to deny that our revolution has had all the attributes of a revolution.

Carlo Scorza, the new Party Secretary, was a foundation member. Born in Paola di Calabria in 1897 of a poor and numerous family, in 1916 he joined an elder brother in Lucca, where he settled until he was swept into the war, and like many of his generation came back from the front uprooted and restless. He studied accountancy for a time at a technical institute, but by 1920 was wholly active in extremist politics, and became the founder of the Fascist organization in Lucca. His career followed the pattern of a regional Party official. He was political secretary, and editor of a weekly newspaper *Intrepido,* giving French lessons to supplement his resources. The Lucca Action Squads occupied Civitavecchia during the March on Rome. Scorza rose in the normal ranks of hierarchy to be Federal Secretary of his province, when he also commanded the Militia. He was alleged at this time to have been responsible for the fatal manhandling of the Anti-Fascist leader, Amendola. In 1924 he was elected deputy, and entered the national machine of the Party as inspector and in 1929 as member of the Directorate. After 1930 he played a leading part in organizing the Fascist youth movement and its para-military organization.

His newspaper widened its range, and, as the *Popolo Toscano,* became a leading extremist organ of regional Fascism. But, as elsewhere in the Fascist machine in the provinces, Scorza's local control was contested by rival ambitions. Between 1926 and 1932 he was the subject of five Party enquiries, ending in his dismissal from all offices and the closing down of his paper in 1932. His main enemy was Achille Starace, the Party Secretary, who in spite of the backing of Scorza by Farinacci and Ciano, succeeded in keeping the boss of Lucca out of national affairs. After 1940 Scorza joined the army, and began to work his way back into Party affairs, specializing in questions relating to the Militia. In December 1942 he returned to Party Headquarters as Director of the Press Office, and one of the Vice-Secretaries. This nomination had already been a hint that the younger generation was under fire. His present appointment indicated by implication the bankruptcy of the 'second wave', the second generation of the Fascist élite typified by his predecessor, Vidussoni. He represented the action squads of the early 20's, the pretentious world of provincial Fascist journalism, and the Party machine of the 30's.[2]

Scorza now charged into his task. The Party cadres were shaken up, and in the following weeks four senior Party officers and twenty provincial secretaries had been changed. He also had plans for an internal emergency, and pressed on Mussolini to create special squads, under the direct control of the Party, to be attached to each party office in the provinces. It seems that the Duce first agreed and then retracted. He had already discussed such eventualities with Himmler at Klessheim in April, and embarked on another solution—the Armoured Division of Blackshirts which the Germans had offered to equip.

On May 3 the new Party Directorate was summoned to Palazzo Venezia to receive the directives of the Duce. The phrases were familiar.

'We must look after the best sections of the people, while the police deal with the lower elements which can weaken the resistance of the entire Italian people. You have certainly noticed that from the moment a new direction was given to the life of the Party, the atmosphere cleared immediately. I am convinced that if we hold to this line of absolute moral and political intransigence we shall obtain concrete results. It is not that the Italian people is estranged. We must remember that the best part of the population is not on metropolitan territory. There are 1,300,000 Fascists fighting in Tunisia, in the Balkans or in lands which will one day belong to the mother country. All Fascists must be convinced—and they must convince the people—that the destiny of Italy for the next generations is now at stake. And there must be no arbitrary, superficial distinctions between Fascism and Italy, because there is absolute, perfect identity between them.'

The mystic power of the Duce's oratory faded with the dispersal of the audience. The continuous flow of comment on the political scene, which reached Mussolini daily in the form of reports from various agencies and individuals, had for so long marked the gulf between rhetoric and reality. A report on his directives of May 3 underlined this phenomenon.

His speech was described as 'a supreme appeal to the whole structure of the nation to strengthen our resistance, and, as such, a sign of the danger which hangs over the country'. It was also 'a recognition of the bankruptcy of the system, political, industrial, and economic hitherto adopted. People found it strange that the main heads of accusation are apparently directed against the masses, when the responsibility of the deficiencies mentioned weighs on the spheres, which up till now have directed all national activities.' The appearance of Scorza, however, had not been ill-received. He had shown courage in raising certain matters, which involved the responsibility of people in high places. His warnings to the youth and their harmful and illogical interference in affairs, had also been regarded as pointed.[3]

On May 5, two days after the Duce's speech, the new Secretary of the Party held a mass reunion of Fascists in the Teatro Adriano. Unconsciously it was to be the final appeal of old guard Fascism on the edge of political disintegration, but it was momentarily, by its very recognizable familiarity, to give a brief sense of security, that all was well, and Scorza's words were greeted with a show of genuine enthusiasm.

This last set piece of Fascist rhetoric lasted from noon, with one hour's break, until four o'clock that afternoon. 'The first attribute of the Fascist must be honesty . . . He is a temperament, a definite individuality, unmistakable, clear, precise. The Duce said one day that the Fascist should also look physically different from others.' There was now a need to resurrect the 'figure of the old Fascist as created by the Duce . . . For long years we have made rhetoric and anti-rhetoric . . . And we have made such use of this rhetoric that we have reached a real form of inflation. If we merely did our duty, we immediately assumed the right to exceptional rewards.' The Party needed higher standards. Scorza had extended the closing date by which one could withdraw one's membership card to June 10. He hoped however that people would not do so . . . There was an old argument: should the

Party be a mass or minority one? This was an idle discussion. 'The question is one of quality: an aristocracy of the masses, selected in the spirit of minorities.' The Party cannot be reduced to a caste or a clan because of its vast tasks. The question of cadres is the central problem of Fascism. The test is competence. There must be no improvisation. Another point to clear up: the profession of Party leader should be abolished (applause). Professionalism has lowered the level of the leadership.'

Purges must also be instituted against irresponsible denunciations. There would be no question of sacrificing innocent victims, but the authorities would be implacable against the unworthy. 'The necessity of defending the country has delayed the Fascist construction.' There was now a need to return to the origins of the Revolution. The Party was the link between the State and the people. 'As defender of the State, the Party reserves the right to supervise and control and intervene in all organs and institutions of the State.

'If we must die, let us swear to fall in style.'[4]

The inevitable police report mirrored mercilessly and vividly the content of this general internal malaise. Although Scorza, in his speech, had returned to the basic postulates of Fascism, 'everyone says that not even he can bring the Party back to that original creed, because he can do nothing against the camarillas, which have formed in the bosom of the Party itself, headed by this and that Party boss . . . The Party has in twenty years lost the confidence and esteem of even its own followers, because of the excessive robberies of the bosses and the patent injustices which have been committed.' The activities of war profiteers attracted universal attention. 'Enormous progress has been made by Communism, which is undermining all branches of production.'

The report closes with the quip of a Roman working woman, 'But no one asked him whether he eats with the Party card.'[5]

Later in the afternoon of May 5, and as if to complete the circle, the Duce addressed the crowds from the balcony of Palazzo Venezia for the first time since June 1940. It was the anniversary of the entry of the Italian troops into Addis Ababa. The square below him was crowded with exalted citizens many of whom had come from Scorza's speech on the new spirit of the leadership of the Fascist Party in the Teatro Adriano. The joint celebrations, with their familiar pattern of heady oratory, was the last public expression of the twenty-year dialogue between the dictator and the crowd. When the Duce withdrew from the balcony, the tall windows would never be opened for him or for such an occasion again.

Outside Party circles the reaction to Scorza's appeal to a Fascist Golden Age dissipated in general frustration. Dollmann reported one typical episode to Himmler: 'The latest and grave internal crisis of the country has been without doubt influenced in a positive sense by the new and extensively felt wave of energy from Palazzo Venezia.' With the nomination of Scorza 'a fresh wind has been blowing among the Fascists themselves'. This was noticeable at the recent celebrations of the twenty-fourth aniversary of the founding of the Roman Fascio. The usual well-worn phrases of the Federal Secretary of Rome about 'in the name of the People, everything for the People' etc. were interrupted with enraged shouted interventions of the old bemedalled party members. 'We want deeds not chatter. What have you done for the People? Only what remains over from the millions which have poured into your pockets.' Amid stormy applause, proceedings against Volpi, Cini, and Morgagni (the director of the official Stefani press agency and a well-known profiteer) were called for. Bottai, the Minister of Education, wishing to defend his own kind, who for years had fed with him at the trough, entered the fray, and the meeting broke up in confusion.[6]

There was no escape from the established workings of the 'system'. The Fascist Party reigned by an uneasy shifting balance of forces within the hierarchy of rival clans.

An anonymous report, or summary of reports, presumably from the central offices of the Party, forms a sour commentary on the inescapable functioning of the machine from which Scorza too, as an early beneficiary, had no chance of dissociating himself.

'The nomination of Scorza as Secretary of the Fascist Party was no longer regarded so favourably as it had been for the following reasons: It had been proved that either from fear or friendship he was under Farinacci's orders. His actions were in complete contrast with his famous twelve points and with the tenor of his speech in the Teatro Adriano.

'He had attacked political professionalism and then copied former Party Secretaries who had installed the system. For instance, he had transferred federal secretaries from one province to another as if they were civil servants. Further, while it was clear from his speech and his twelve points that the Party Secretary, the Federal Secretary, and the Secretary of the Fascio were alone to form the backbone of the Party, he still nominated Party Inspectors. Their names showed clearly that he did this to find jobs for Party bosses turned out of other posts.

'The Fascist Directorate, although partly composed of true, and proved, Fascists, was completely the creature of Farinacci. Cucco, one of the new vice-secretaries, though most worthy of respect, must be grateful to Farinacci who insisted on his re-admission to the Party from which he had been unjustly expelled.' Tarabini, also a vice-secretary, was notoriously a Farinacci man, and in constant touch with the latter, who kept him informed of his wishes on changes of personnel so that he could stir up Scorza to make these changes. 'The opinion of Fascists, who had hoped much of Scorza, had consequently completely changed because he had set his course towards that favoured by Farinacci. Everyone said that in a few months' time they would pay heavily for faults once again committed.'[7]

Although expelled by the Duce's persistence from the centre of power in the Party machine, Farinacci, who had destroyed the pristine provincial enthusiasm of the 'first wave' of Fascism, possessed the classic style of a Party boss, and, although himself the prophet of that centralized Party bureaucracy which he himself had built, had through the years become by skilled management the more powerful of the clan leaders precisely because he had sought his support among the regional elements of Fascism, which he had weakened and attempted to destroy when Party Secretary.

Scorza was undoubtedly committed to the whole style of Fascist Party rule, but, though circumscribed in action by his own past, he strove at least to assess the situation in realistic terms.

On June 7 he produced a private report for the Duce, written in the familiar style and tone of twenty years of Fascist political vocabulary, and cognisant of at least some of the causes of present discontents.

Among the rich, anti-Fascism and hostility to Mussolini was only limited by the fear that the eventual triumph of such an attitude might favour a negative outcome of the war, and thereby, with a Bolshevik triumph, the loss of their material belongings. Among the middle classes in general, 'there is neither anti-Fascism nor any open attitude against Mussolini, but neither is there any exalted Fascism. There is only a diffuse and apathetic resignation, aggravated by economic restrictions which face them with the elementary problem of having enough food. Among the lower middle class and including the working class, there is a genuine honest Fascist feeling and absolute devotion to you. This enormous mass is really the one on which we could work by a lively operation of penetration and conquest.'

As to the Party, Scorza had no illusions that in the few days that he had been Secretary any radical transformation had taken place. Drastic measures were needed as to the necessary time to carry them out.

The Party suffered from several diseases: firstly, 'an elephantiasis, not only numerical but also spiritual, which dissipates the will to fight and aggravates the spirit of preservation. In general everybody tries to preserve something, a position either in the Party hierarchy or finance. Such conservatism has transformed the dynamic earlier "offensive" into a concept which I can call modestly and even miserably "defensive". Even if one talks of heroism it is not the heroism of the Arditi,* who despise their own trenches in order to take those of the enemy, but the defensive heroism of the besieged.'

Secondly, a distrust between Party leaders in and out of office 'who, rather than consider matters from the national, and consequently Fascist viewpoint, are more concerned with their personal relations and rather than yield a jot of their positions and prejudices, ruin everything'.

Thirdly, the exaggerated enrichment of certain leaders. 'The distrust of the Fascist masses towards the leaders derives from this, as they have naturally lost any substantial credit, even if they retain any formal one.'

The youth had 'a somewhat limited belief in Fascism for various well-known reasons. But in their vast majority they represent material which can be recaptured (only a few months more, Duce!) as soon as we have changed the climate of the Party.'

Scorza now turned to the flaws in the structure of the administrative machine of government: 'The various Ministries are today a real tangle of seldom defined and even more often overlapping functions, which complicates the enforcement of the simplest measure. I would add that this overlapping is

* The front line commandos of the First World War.

frequently eliminated, and the measures decided on the basis of a common, and nowadays current, private deal: which means that personal favours are exchanged and money is circulated. While the lower ranks of the bureaucracy are in general both honest and Fascist, the higher ranks are in general neither honest nor Fascist: with the result that while the Party penalties are applied to petty infringements, the major sins of the big men go unpunished. And this not so much because these men know how to "organize" their affairs better than their inferiors, as because they are defended, often in good faith, by the politicians. . . . The upper ranks of the bureaucracy are not to be feared only because they are not Fascist, but above all because, by means of their own experience and the subtle and often captious interpretation of the law, they dominate the men and therefore the affairs of the régime. . . .

'This is not flattery, Duce, because you know I am a soldier not a flatterer, but at this point in my reflections I cannot help thinking that simple obedience to your orders and directives in East Africa, North Africa and Greece, would have produced different results. When the history of this war is written, documents, some of which I know personally, will give incontestable proof of your intuitive foresight of necessities, dangers, possibilities. . . . Now the organs directing the war have failed. Since the tasks have changed, it is only natural to change the organs.

'Our war was and is directed not by one but by five bodies. By a confused High Command, whose strategy is uncertain, and which has neither panoramic vision, nor connected or co-ordinated plans; by an Army General Staff which has gradually swelled out with cumbrous powers; by a Ministry of War with reduced functions, or interfering in functions no longer within its competence; by a Ministry for the Navy and a Ministry for Air who often act, in the technical field, without co-ordinated contacts with the other Armed Forces, and without taking into account, in estimating supplies, the time factor, the terrain, enemy progress, or our productive capacity. . . .

'Everything can be remedied, Duce, but on one condition: that you begin from the top, not only by substitutions in the ranks. Two-thirds of our generals are old, sour, and incompetent. They need support, or hierarchical procedure, or red tape before they will take the slightest step. They are armchair not horseback generals.'

Under such conditions it was not surprising that the Germans had 'no respect for us at all . . . We were not able to show—during these three years, either that we knew how to organize ourselves for what we needed, or that we were strong. And it is permissible to think today that without you, without the weight of your will, Italy, involved just the same in the war which she could not avoid, would be occupied by German troops, and with our Military Authorities themselves convinced and happy about it. . . .'

These brave words bore much truth. The real crisis of the régime was, however, that the power and the will to act and reform had long since atrophied.

This report by Scorza might be regarded as a comprehensive and perceptive round up of the defects of the 'system'. It might have been written by the Germans. In directing his main attacks on the Civil Service and the Ministries of the Armed Forces, Scorza failed to pursue the implication that it has always been conceived to be the duty of the Party to act as the nosing watchdog of the régime in all spheres of government. The Party, however, had already exhausted its prestige and its cadres.

Italian Fascism had never succeeded in being totalitarian, and its fate in the end was to be decided in those enclaves which it had failed in twenty years to penetrate and control —the Court, the Army, the Civil Service, and even the Police.

On the day when he dispatched his analysis of the Home Front to Mussolini, Scorza initiated a series of disciplinary measures. The immediate reaction was one of general approval, but as forecast in his own report, the higher officials aimed at were protected by the Minister concerned and 'gently admonished'. In general, if Party members were denounced to the judicial authorities they received Party protection and suspended sentences.[8]

The Party was now, in the eyes of its hierarchy, a law unto itself, and the very root from which the growing demoralization of the nation had blossomed. Far from being the vanguard of resistance, it was from the ranks of the Party itself that the precursory signs of a national collapse could be envisaged.

The Director-General of Public Security sent a brief marginal note to the Duce headed 'Signs of alarmism and defeatism'.

'It has been reported that the group of persons composed

of Party leaders, various senators and industrialists opposed to Fascism are of the opinion in favour of seeking a separate peace.'

Scorza seems to have had the fitful backing of the Duce in such isolated gestures. On June 11 twenty-four prefects were dismissed, a further nineteen retired, and twenty new appointments made in the provinces. These moves presumably were made on Mussolini's personal instructions as Minister of the Interior.

On the same day the news of the fall of the Italian naval and air base of Pantelleria brought the reality of enemy invasion to the approaches to Sicily. In the Duce's words, 'Pantelleria is an alarm bell; I might almost say, a warning ring at the gate.'[9] As Mussolini later put it in his Memoirs, 'Following the perturbation caused by the staggeringly unexpected surrender of Pantelleria, there was born in high circles an attitude of mind tending towards capitulation. There was a fresh chorus of defeatism.'[10]

The shadow of imminent invasion pervaded the whole internal scene. Not only were strategic considerations under hasty review, but the dangers of political and administrative collapse loomed. Scorza even exceeded his functions. Following on the strictures in his report of June 7 to the Duce on the Service Ministries, he took it upon himself to hold at Party headquarters on June 15 a meeting of the three Under-Secretaries of the Armed Forces, harangued them on the menace to the Home Front, and the need for military command to take anti-sabotage precautions. Ambrosio was furious at this interference by the Party and instantly complained to Mussolini, who characteristically did not support his Party Secretary but scolded him. Scorza's reply was a plaintive minute to the Duce:

'We talked of the repercussions in the country of the fall of Pantelleria and Lampedusa. I made it clearly understood to the comrades present that the "directive" of the Directorate, approved by you, was definite in the sense that it was up to the Party to determine a new phase in the conscience of the country and in the evaluation of military information; that in effect Pantelleria and Lampedusa were to be considered as the lowest point of major depression in the descending curve and not as the continuation of a mentality of surrender.

The 'alarm bell' also rang for the civilian ministers. De Marsico, Minister of Justice, and Count Cini, the leading industrialist, who since February had been Minister of Communications, both members of the new government team nominated in February 1943, had for some time felt the urgency of forcing the lurking political crisis into open discussion among their colleagues. In particular, the efficiency of the country's military resistance depended clearly on the maintenance of the interior lines of communication on the mainland of Italy. 'After Pantelleria, Cini and myself,' said De Marsico later, 'agreed to press Mussolini for a complete report on the effective possibilities of this country in face of the war, and to seize the first occasion of a meeting of the Council of Ministers to put forward our own views.'[11]

This opportunity came on June 19, and both men spoke out. This was the first and last independent expression of view within the governing clan. Both Ministers appealed to the Duce, in this hour of crisis, to accept 'a more open and frank division of responsibility' and to take his collaborators into his confidence. 'The series of failures are the consequence of irrational and inappropriate use of the few means at our disposal.'[12]

Mussolini merely commented, 'Any discussion is useless. Italy has only one alternative: to conquer or fall at the side of Germany.' And he closed the meeting.[13] In his eyes, this inner Cabinet had never assumed a collective action or responsibility. It was never summoned again during the following weeks of mounting crisis.

Three days later Count Cini wrote to the Duce to explain his initiative at this meeting, and to resign.

'I meditated at length and hesitated before taking the decision which I now submit to you. I am putting forward certain rash doubts which I could not express at the Council of Ministers of June 19 which ended before I had the time to speak a second time.

'At that meeting, I pointed out the gravity of the moment and stressed the need for changing those methods which had produced such unfavourable results. I proposed that one should make a profound study of the general situation in its various aspects and warned that I did not intend to anticipate solutions which could and should only result from an objective examination of the situation itself.

'You, Duce, did not accept my proposal. You dismissed its practical value by referring to it as "academic". On the other hand you lingered over the theme of "peace", as if I had started the discussion, whereas not only did I not raise the issue, but said clearly that no solution could be reasonably considered without the necessary elements on which to form a judgement. My reference to peace was made with the sole aim of giving a warning that we must not find ourselves unprepared as we were when war broke on us.

'You likewise rejected the value of the discussion as you viewed the situation as such that it did not permit any possibility of release, summarizing your thoughts in the resolute and peremptory phrase "Burn our boats behind us". I permit myself to think that such an imperative is valid only for individuals: one does not burn boats for whole peoples unless every alternative is excluded and one is at the point of desperation. But this is not our case.

'In any event, I repeat, my proposal was not aimed at opening a discussion on peace, but to find out whether you would admit at least your colleagues to that examination of general policy which I regard as indispensable for any conscious responsibility.

'But your intention was clear, to limit collaboration only to the technical field. I do not disagree, but I would be overreticent if I did not express my dissent on this essential point. Almost everyone thought as I did. But no one dares to say so. But I prefer to displease you rather than to betray your trust.'

Cini ended by asking to be relieved of his post. His wish was not granted until July 24.

According to one source, Scorza broached a similar view at this time to Mussolini on behalf of the Party. In the general uncertainty, Fascist circles in Rome were pressing for a lead from the Duce. Scorza apparently wrote two letters on the theme of transferring to other hands the military direction of the war, thus placing the person of the Duce 'above criticism', but on both occasions was met with contemptuous rebuff. Instead, the national Party Directorate was summoned to an informal meeting by Scorza, who drafted its last expiring autocriticism. This document was sent to Mussolini to await a sign from him.

On June 23 Scorza felt it necessary to write to Mussolini, who had summoned for the next day the monthly meeting of the Party Directorate, which had been delayed by military events.

'I am under the impression that tomorrow you are going to put a brake on my activities. I say "impression", but I should say more exactly "I am afraid", for I have been afraid of it since hostile comments began to be made against the Directorate's "directive".

'In every case I have acted in accordance with the directives which you laid down for me in your speech at the time of my appointment: you read and approved my speech made at the Adriano; you read and approved the Directorate's "directive". What has been the result of all this? The nation and the Fascists understood clearly that acting through the Party you were imparting an atmosphere of greater severity to the régime, or rather, were creating an extraordinary, wartime attitude everywhere. The Party is much stronger in consequence, and the results are truly considerable, for in scarcely two months the Party has not only returned to its position as the central motive power of national life, but it is valued, and what is more important, feared.

'You say that you are first and foremost Duce of Fascism and only secondly Head of the Government. It follows logically that everyone must be first Fascists and secondly hierarchs of every grade and office. But this must be clearly laid down. You alone can do this and make it a command. It is a strange law, Duce, and yet it must now be defined as being a real law, that a Fascist who enters the Government, or a Bank, or the Civil Service, or the Army, inevitably becomes a slave and succumbs to the environment in which he functions. . . .

'I have told you, Duce, of the anxiety which precedes the summoning of the Directorate, which in my opinion will be an important date in the history of the Revolution.'[14]

On June 24 the meeting was summoned to Palazzo Venezia. Scorza read what was to be the last report on the state of that Party, which had been the central organ of Italian political life for twenty years. The statistics were impressive. 'These are the figures,' he concluded, 'but they will have no absolute value if they do not represent spirit and will. The will and the spirit which animate the forces mobilized under the banner of the "Littorio" are called—loyalty, discipline, resistance, and victory.' Such was the vacuous epitaph of twenty years.

The Party representatives awaited the commentary of the Leader. In his customary address, the Duce referred to the criticism of the Party which had been aired at the last meeting in May. He admitted that it had been too bureaucratized, but it was the spirit that mattered. The mass of the people were behaving well, and should not be confused with an unreliable minority.

'Those relics of the old parties will never be those who will succeed in ousting the régime . . . One should pour ridicule on the authors and distributors of such detective stories, the product of a sick imagination.'

There was no way out of the war, and no question of a 'dishonourable' peace. 'The enemy must play their card. They have talked too much about the necessity of continental invasion. They will have to attempt it, for otherwise they will be beaten without having fought. As soon as the enemy attempts to land, he must be blocked at the line which the sailors call the foreshore, the sand line where the water ends and the land begins . . . The duty of Fascists is this: to give that feeling, and, more than a hope, the absolute certainty, which comes from an iron unshakeable granite sense of decision.'[15]

Breaking with tradition, this speech was published in the Press on July 5, and with unfortunate results. It was intended to raise public morale on the eve of the Sicily landings.

CHAPTER FIVE

Royal Hesitations

THE SURRENDER of the Italian First Army in Tunisia on May 12 closed the imperial episode of Fascism and the penultimate phase of the drama of the régime. The loss of the last foothold in Africa meant inevitably that unless a compromise peace, or an armistice, were negotiated with the enemy, an Allied invasion of the mainland of Italy would follow, bringing with it the certain collapse of the Fascist state and possibly the end of the Monarchy.

On May 19 the King said to the head of his military household, General Puntoni: 'I am afraid that at any moment the British government or the King of England may approach me direct in order to negotiate a separate peace. Such a move would cause me grave embarrassment. If it should happen, I would act without subterfuge. I would speak to the Duce and agree with him on a line of action.'[1]

By the end of May, Acquarone had established direct relations with Bonomi and his friends. He was also anxious that these politicians should not gather too closely round the alternative focus of the heir to the throne, the Prince of Piedmont. 'Let us leave aside the young ones,' was his remark to Bonomi at their meeting on May 26. But the main purpose of this preliminary talk was to indicate the readiness of the King to receive at first hand the views of his surviving advisers of the days before the March on Rome.

This audience took place at the Quirinal on the morning of June 2. The two men had not met for some twenty years. Bonomi recorded the conversation. 'Passing to the present situation . . . I underlined the need for overturning the Fascist régime, the cause of all evil in Italy. The King, who alone possessed the prestige of supreme power and had the support of the Armed Forces, could, whenever he wished, dismiss the Prime Minister and Head of the Government . . . Naturally if the Duce were dismissed, he would have to be placed under arrest to avoid the chance that, backed by the armed Militia of the Party, he might plunge the country into civil war. The first act then must be to turn to a military government. The King had but to choose between his military chiefs. In this respect I put forward three names: General Ambrosio, Chief of the General Staff, Marshal Caviglia, and Marshal Badoglio. The King did not reply, except to observe that Ambrosio is a professional soldier only, and that Caviglia is too old.'

The second act must be the denunciation of the pact with Germany. On this subject the King had no wish to comment. Bonomi however pressed on, pointing out that the Axis pact was not an alliance between states, but as drafted in the preamble, 'between two régimes and two revolutions'. 'With the fall of the Fascist régime the alliance is no longer valid.'

The King followed the whole exposition in silence, and only added, 'The nation always has the right to what it chooses.'

Bonomi reported to his friends, 'I think it unlikely that such a design will be accepted. It may be that the King will decide to act at the last minute.'[2]

As Puntoni noted in his diary: 'His Majesty, who does not miss a note of what is happening, is not what he was a month ago. He is conscious of the gravity of the situation, and is reflecting on what to do, but I think that, at least for the present, he is still decided to support Mussolini's action. The plan which His Majesty is elaborating in his head is a mystery to everybody, and I think that not even Acquarone is informed.'[3]

One possibility had already occurred to the King: a 'constitutional solution' arising from a political crisis within the ranks of Fascism and along the lines feared by Bonomi and his friends, already in April. This may have been the reason why, on the day following his talk with Bonomi, June 3, the King received Grandi in audience. According to the latter's account he repeated to the Sovereign the arguments which he had used on previous occasions. 'Your Majesty, there is no choice: either Novara, namely abdication; or a change of front in the style of Victor Amadeus II who, when he realized the mistake of the alliance with the King of France, saved

Piedmont and the dynasty at the last moment by going over to the Imperial camp.' The King replied: 'The moment will come. I know that I can count on you. Leave your King to choose the opportune moment and in the meantime help me to obtain the constitutional means.' Grandi assumed that the King implied a vote by the Chamber or by the Grand Council, and that presumably it was in his capacity as President to the former body that he was being received.[4]

As from this moment Grandi carefully avoided the Roman scene, and retired to Bologna as if awaiting a second March on Rome.

The fall of Tunis in May had also re-opened speculation round the choice of a possible military figure, the indispensable leader of any action in the name of the Crown. Caviglia's name was mentioned more frequently in the clubs and corridors, but his personal contacts with the General Staff of the Army, apart from Ambrosio, were, because of his age, impersonal and distant. Badoglio felt that he could count on the inner group, who effectively controlled the Army: Ambrosio, Roatta, and Sorice.

Another former minister of the 1920's, Marcello Soleri, who was then living in dignified retreat in Piedmont, was received by the King at this time. Acquarone had a particular regard for him and had already held a preliminary discussion with him on the afternoon of May 31.

'He did not conceal from me,' Soleri wrote in his Memoirs, 'that he was engaged in trying to persuade the King to substitute for Mussolini's administration a military government entrusted to one of the Marshals Badoglio or Caviglia or to General Ambrosio.' According to Acquarone, it was conceivable that the King might act at the weekly Thursday audience with Mussolini on June 8. In any event Soleri was asked to stay in Rome, and await an urgent summons. He then called on Bonomi, with whom he had already been on several occasions in contact, and learned of the latter's unsatisfactory audience with the King. On June 7 Soleri met Acquarone again and was told that the monarch had been disappointed in Bonomi and that 'the King had decided not to intervene at once: and that without a new political or military fact, this would not come about, as it seemed to him otherwise to be committing in cold blood an act of treachery towards Mussolini'.[5]

Soleri had also been in close touch with Caviglia. On the

same day the latter's aide-de-camp had called on General Puntoni to say that the Marshal had hoped to seek an audience of the King, but was obliged to leave Rome immediately, but also that 'the Marshal had expected a gesture from the King which would right the situation, and that he was against coming to Rome because he felt that the King had no desire to discuss with him urgent matters of moment'.[6]

Early on the morning of June 8 Soleri was received by the King for the first time since the outbreak of war. His theme, that of the need to give back to Italy her freedom of action by a withdrawal from the war and by setting up at once 'a political anti-Fascist government' to treat with the Allies, took more than half an hour to deliver to the Monarch. Soleri was then thanked, and without further comment asked to come and see the King in Piedmont.

In reflecting on his two talks with Acquarone and his audience with Victor Emmanuel, Soleri wrote later: 'Subsequent events made one think that the "new fact", political or military, to which Acquarone referred, as necessary to determine the intervention of the King, could only be precisely that inner split in Fascism and that rejection of Mussolini which would necessitate the King, thus given no choice and in no danger of making a mistake, dismissing his Prime Minister. It is perhaps this "new fact", during the first week of June, the possibilities of which may have been glimpsed, if not its preparation begun, and thus for this reason the operation—if ever conceived at this stage in practical terms—was postponed.'[7]

Badoglio was already aware of the views of Bonomi and his political associates. The first meeting between the two men took place on June 30.[8] Badoglio had been Chief of Staff a quarter of a century earlier when Bonomi had held the portfolio of Minister of War. They both knew that, in five days' time, on July 5, Ambrosio was proposing to put before the King documented evidence showing that the military situation of Italy was no longer tenable.

On July 5 Ambrosio was received by the King, who had returned to Rome for this audience. Puntoni records that 'it was on this occasion that His Majesty spoke to me for the first time of the action which the Chief of the General Staff was developing in order to achieve the substitution of Mussolini. It seems that he has talked of this openly with the King and suggested the appropriateness of the military dictatorship with either Caviglia or Badoglio at its head. His Majesty, however, has not received either of these schemes with much enthusiasm. My impression is that he thinks the carrying out of such a plan both premature and dangerous, especially in so far as the military situation is concerned. He tells me, too, that the arrival in power of Caviglia would mean a decisive return to Freemasonry and a consequent drawing nearer to the Anglo-Americans. His Majesty is however of the opinion that in approaching the problem of removing Mussolini, Fascism will not allow itself to be overthrown at one stroke. Instead, one will have to modify the system by stages and in order to change those attributes which have proved damaging for the country. On the other hand, he admits that Badoglio, although he has a character which he does not like, has a certain following among the masses and this following could be the unique catalyst of the situation. "I have the impression," His Majesty stated, "that Ambrosio is uncovering himself too much and has too many contacts with elements outside military circles."'[9] Two days later, on July 7, the King told General Sorice, the Undersecretary of War: 'In the other war (1914–18) one did not feel this sense of isolation. For example, the Central Powers, although engaged in fighting did not lack official contacts with the powers in the other camp. And I have no Prince Sixte of Bourbon-Parma.'[10] [Prince Sixte attempted to negotiate in 1917 a compromise peace between the Central Powers and the Allies.]

By the beginning of July, according to Castellano, pressure increased on military circles for action against the personal rule of the Duce. 'Albini, Bastianini, Cini, and Volpi, were among the most disturbed, and all turned to Ambrosio.'[11] Castellano was again in touch with Ciano. The latter had been under observation, and they had ceased to meet for some months. The General was in good relations with General Chierici, Senise's successor as head of the Police, and the Carabinieri were now under the command of General Hazon, who was both loyal to Ambrosio, and had formerly served under Badoglio in Africa.

During the course of the month Ambrosio instructed Castellano to redraft the project for Mussolini's arrest. The previous memorandum had been destroyed. This had contained a statement that one month's preparation was required before any plan could be carried out. The period was now reduced to twenty days. Certain general considerations had to be faced. Both Palazzo Venezia and Villa Torlonia, the Duce's personal residence, were heavily fortified, and his personal police guard, a special unit, was an unreliable element. The arrest must therefore take place elsewhere. Ambrosio took a draft plan, as drawn up by Castellano, to Acquarone, but both men thought that it was premature and hoped till the last moment that Mussolini would act against the Axis alliance. Acquarone would only concede that the King would decide soon 'and that from that moment not more than twenty-four hours would elapse during which Acquarone himself, Ambrosio, the future head of the government, the Commander of the Military Police, the new Chief of Police, and myself must remain locked in a room in the Quirinal so that no one should let out a word'.[12]

An important personage in this list would clearly be the new Chief of Police. Although Chierici was on good terms with Ambrosio's staff, he was a Militia general and was not taken into confidence. The civilian technician to be employed in such an event had already been chosen by Acquarone. He was Chierici's predecessor, Carmine Senise, who had completed plans for an eventual coup d'état before his sudden dismissal from office after Mussolini's return from Klessheim in April.

Senise seems to have continued his activities unofficially with the connivance of the Undersecretary of the Interior, Albini, and with the 'supine acquiescence' of his successor. During these weeks, he made a series of visits. He warned Ambrosio that the Germans also were manoeuvring against him. He saw Castellano, who discussed with him details of the central telephone exchanges, an essential element in event of any coup, and he called on Ciano, who hinted that he might be required later.[13] He also appears to have met Acquarone frequently, and the latter's personal stenographer, who had been placed in this position by Senise the previous winter, continued to act as a private link.

According to a later report, Senise was received by the King at least five times between April and July, 'staying at least one and a half hours'.[14]

CHAPTER SIX

Operation 'Mincemeat'

THE GERMAN and Italian military intelligence services provided their respective General Staffs with a reasonably accurate picture of the build-up of the Anglo-American forces in the British Isles, and of Allied troop movements and concentrations in the Mediterranean. Any developments at Gibraltar in particular were well covered, and both Axis staffs were confident, and indeed complacent, about their ability to identify the enemy order of battle. The interpretation of such intelligence was less sure, and indeed there was no coordination on a technical level, and the available historical evidence consists of arbitrary and discordant statements at irregular intervals by Hitler or Mussolini or by their immediate military advisers.

Mussolini's general analysis concentrated on the imminent threat to Sicily or the gateway to the Italian mainland. Hitler, on the other hand, saw the main danger in Sardinia. His interpretation of future Allied strategy was more consistent than that of the Duce. He foresaw that from Sardinia the enemy could threaten Rome and the main ports of Genoa and Leghorn, strike simultaneously through Upper Italy and at Southern France, and thence at the heart of the European fortress. A logical consequence of such a move on the part of the Allies would then be to attempt to turn the South-Eastern flank of the German position in Europe by a large-scale landing in Greece and the Balkans. Such was the essence of Hitler's strategic thinking during these weeks on the Mediterranean war and future enemy intentions in that theatre.

On May 9 a startling and dramatic confirmation of this interpretation reached the German High Command. On April 30 the body of an unidentified British officer had been washed ashore at Huelva in Southern Spain. Attached to the wrist of the corpse was a briefcase, containing confidential documents. The local German intelligence agent was able to extract photostat copies from the Spanish authorities, and it was a tribute to his efficiency that a telegraphic summary reached Berlin so rapidly.

The appropriate section of the German General Staff produced an appreciation of the material on the same day. The British order of battle in the Mediterranean, contained in one paper, was accepted as genuine. On May 11 the German Commanders of Army Groups South and South-East were informed of the existence of the documents, which were accepted in Berlin as genuine, and warned that a major attack on Sardinia, timed with a feint against Sicily and a secondary landing in the Peloponnese, was to be expected. On the same day a detailed analysis of this material was presented to the German General Staff.

On May 12 the German General Staff sent a signal to Kesselring: 'From a source which is regarded as absolutely trustworthy, an enemy landing attempt on a grand scale will be made in the Eastern and Western Mediterranean in the very near future.' A summary of the material followed, together with a message for Doenitz, at that moment in Rome. 'Army Group South is requested to inform Doenitz at once of this report so that he can formulate his requests in his talks with the Italian High Command with increased emphasis.'

Meanwhile, a confirmation of this startling intelligence came through German Foreign Office channels from Dieckhoff, the German Ambassador in Madrid. His telegram was dispatched at 11.20 on the evening of May 12, and received in Berlin ten minutes later. 'According to information just received from a wholly reliable source, the English and Americans will launch their big attack on Southern Europe in the next fortnight. The plan, as our informant was able to establish from English secret documents, is to launch two sham attacks on Sicily and Dodecanese, while the real offensive is directed in two main thrusts against Crete and Peloponnese and against Italian mainland. The enemy's chief rallying-point in Eastern Mediterranean will be Alexandria, in Western Mediterranean, Algiers. It is clear from the document that the attack in Eastern Mediterranean will be launched mainly by British, and that on Italy mainly by Americans.'[1]

An hour later a second message followed. 'Information from confidential source . . . largely tallies with that just communicated to me in strict confidence by Jordana (the Spanish Foreign Minister) . . . He also spoke of wholly reliable news of impending sham attacks and major offensives; as regards the latter he did not refer to Italy but only to Crete and Peloponnese. Jordana begged me not to mention his name, especially as he wanted to exchange further information with me in the future. He emphasized that having regard to his source he considered the information wholly trustworthy, and felt it his duty to pass it on to us.'[2]

There is no record of the German General Staff meeting on May 11, or of Hitler's immediate reactions. But the next day he issued a general military directive in the following terms: 'Following the impending end of fighting in Tunisia, it is to be expected that the Anglo-Americans will try to continue the operations in the Mediterranean in quick succession. Preparations for this purpose must in general be considered concluded. The following are most endangered: in the Western Mediterranean, Sardinia, Corsica, and Sicily: in the Eastern Mediterranean, the Peloponnese and the Dodecanese islands.

'I expect that all German commands and offices which are concerned with the defences in the Mediterranean will co-operate very closely and quickly to utilize all forces and equipment to strengthen as much as possible the defences in these particularly endangered areas during the short time which is probably left to us. *Measures regarding Sardinia and the Peloponnese take precedence over everything else.*'

This document represents a summary of the British document, which was promptly subjected to further expert analysis in two further German Intelligence summaries, both dated May 14.[3] 'The genuineness of the captured documents is above suspicion' is the opening of the first report, and the second contains an analysis of the material on receipt of the originals from Spain.

On May 19, Dieckhoff again telegraphed from Madrid, summarizing the most recent intelligence available through Spanish sources in Gibraltar and North Africa: 'The Navy Minister, Moreno Fernandez, with whom I had detailed discussion today, seems convinced that an Anglo-American offensive against Southern Europe is about to be launched. He told me that all his information indicated that strong forces would be concentrated in Alexandria, Benghazi, Tripoli, Biserta, and Algiers in preparation for an attack on Greece and Italy. In the past few days specially large convoys, heavily guarded by battleships, had sailed into the Mediterranean from the Atlantic and continued in an easterly direction. He could scarcely imagine that the operation would be long delayed, the more so as a powerful force of enemy battleships was now assembled that would hardly be kept in Algiers etc. unless an early operation were being planned.

'The Navy Minister regards an attack on Greece as especially likely, since, owing to the conduct of the Greek population, a landing there would probably entail fewer difficulties than an attempted invasion of Italy; but he thinks it by no means ruled out that a simultaneous attack might be launched on Italy as well, and in this case one ought also to be prepared for sham attacks.

'Jordana, who dined with me last night, also confidently expects an early start to the enemy attack on Southern Europe. He again yesterday insisted that there were still no grounds for inferring any threats to the Iberian peninsula; everything pointed to the fact that operations would be directed against Greece, and possibly Italy as well.'[4]

This intelligence was confirmed in part by a patchy and verbose summary passed by Kaltenbrunner to Ribbentrop, and placed before Hitler on the same day. 'Reports from reliable sources show that the enemy have collected in the Algiers area 800 transport vessels of every kind with a total tonnage of about 1½ million. This leads one to suppose that preparations for a landing are already far advanced. In contrast to the reports for March and April which spoke in particular of operations planned against the French coast and the Iberian peninsula, reports now mention as the targets of enemy operations Italy and her islands as well as Greece.

'The head of the American Intelligence Service for Spain and Portugal has stated that for the moment a landing in Spain was not being considered. After the occupation of Italy, this country (Spain) would climb down of her own accord and freely let through the Allies.

'Generally speaking in American Embassy circles the view is that as soon as Tunis has fallen, the enemy will attempt to land in Sicily, Sardinia and the Italian peninsula. Italy will be attacked from two sides, in order to cut off the southern part. The British Embassy reports from Madrid confirm this information . . . The attitude towards Spain must depend on the position taken up by the Reich towards that country.

'A confirmation of the enemy intention to land in Sicily

lies in the great interest shown by the American Military Intelligence in assembling reports from their European representatives on the political and economic state of Sicily and the morale of its population.

'The above reports also indicate that a second pincer movement against Italy will be mounted via Crete and Greece. The Turkish Ambassadors in Washington and London reported similarly at the beginning of May that the Allies wanted to advance into the Balkans through Greece. Italian reports give further details of the landing planned in Greece. The landing would be in Kavalla in order eventually to thrust up into Roumania. In this connection the Americans intend to occupy Roumania to prevent a further advance of Soviet Russia into the Balkans.

On May 14, at 5.30 in the evening, Hitler received Doenitz's report on his Rome visit, and referred for the first time directly in conference to the British material. 'The Fuehrer does not agree with the Duce that the most likely invasion point is Sicily. Furthermore, he believes that the discovered Anglo-Saxon order confirms the assumption that the planned attacks will be directed mainly against Sardinia and the Peloponnese.' These judgments were 'not new at this time', but it is clear that they were considerably strengthened by 'the papers found on the body of a British courier washed up on the southern coast of Spain'.[5]

Hitler's strategic appreciation of the future course of operations in the Mediterranean now assumed a sharper outline. Allied plans for occupying the Italian islands and Southern Italy were but a prelude to a wide ranging landing operation against the western coasts of the Balkans in the Adriatic. If this analysis was correct, the consequences of an Italian collapse would have direct, grave, and early consequences in South-Eastern Europe, and a stage later on the southern flank of the German armies in Russia. This situation was debated by Hitler on the afternoon of May 19 at a military conference, and the movement of German troops to Italy to counter such an event was for the first time reviewed in practical terms. 'In the last few days, and particularly last night, I have again been giving much thought to the consequences which would follow if we lost the Balkans, and there is no doubt that the results must be very serious.' Keitel interjected 'And certainly much more difficult if we have to protect ourselves against this front from anywhere in Italy.' The satellite allies would be 'shaken', and the vital supplies of Roumanian oil, and Yugoslav bauxite and copper would be lost.

Hitler's first proposal was 'as a precaution to take a further preventive measure against an eventual attack on the Peloponnese'. There was only one division readily available in the West, and it was from this zone only that troops could in principle be withdrawn as 'at the moment I have no fears that anything will happen in the West'.

Hitler assumed that Italy could always be managed. 'The Italians are not to be relied on, while on the other side I am convinced that, with relatively small forces, in the event of any mess in Italy, we can handle it, particularly if the first advance guards arrive within ten days . . . Zeitzler says that these fighting units will be there within ten days for he will lay on sixty trains a day. One can therefore say, one division will arrive in two days.'

According to the calculations of the German Operations Staff, the Parachute Corps from the West, and the main body earmarked for Operation 'Gisela' to move into Spain were available for Italy from the resources of Army Group West. 'Naturally I want to send to Italy first of all the three S.S. divisions, because they know Fascism best.' Hitler was against sending young troops to Italy. 'They have not the experience, politically speaking too, nor the adroitness of my old S.S. divisions, who are propagandists. I am convinced that, if the three best S.S. divisions are sent there, they will very quickly achieve the closest fraternization with Fascism.'

The nagging problem was how to divide the armoured reinforcements in an emergency as between the Italian and Balkan theatres. And harping back to the conviction obviously based on 'British courier' documents that the immediate Allied plan was a combined assault on Sardinia and the Peloponnese, Hitler again stressed 'the danger is that they will establish themselves in the Peloponnese'. Two armoured divisions from the Eastern Front had already been earmarked for transport to Greece in an emergency.

On the basis of the memorandum which Hitler had received from the Italian High Command, he had 'come to the conclusion that, even more dangerous than the problem of Italy, which in the worst case we can always somehow tidy up, is that of the Balkans. If a landing takes place in the Balkans, let us say in the Peloponnese, then in a foreseeable time Crete will go. We have now supplied it for six months

. . . If we lose the Peloponnese, then any further supplies are out of the question. . . . There are two German formations now there. . . . The nearest other units are in action in Montenegro. If we run into any trouble, particularly if we have difficulties with the Italians, we cannot depend on these units. They will be lost and we shall never get them out. Then we shall have to occupy the Montenegrin-Dalmatian coast, and disarm the Italians.

'I have therefore decided whatever happens to transfer one armoured division to the Peloponnese. As things are, it can only be taken from the West. For naturally I want to attack only in the East, if no other situation arises and even if an Italian crisis breaks. I mean to say, I do not want to attack her only on account of a landing. So long as the Italians sit on the fence I do not want to attack in the East. But as soon as the Italians show signs of folding up or of internal collapse, we must attack in the East . . . If the enemy are going to attack anywhere they will do so only in Italy and naturally the Balkans. . . . If anything should happen in Turkey, and we shall have in any case to move forces from the East, I have only one reservoir there, and that is the Bulgarians.'

Warlimont appears to have made a separate report at this conference in his capacity as Deputy Chief of the Operations Staff, summarizing the Italian position, and elaborating in particular on the necessary counter-measures to be taken in event of an Allied attack on Sardinia (the first priority, according to the 'British Courier' documents). 'The task of the German Army Group South is the defence of Sardinia, Sicily, and Southern Italy.' The harbours are menaced by air attack. 'Sardinia is particularly threatened. . . . the state of the defences of Sicily is better. . . . The Italians jealously claimed control and sovereignty. There is no full mobilization, no authority, no sort of civil defence, and no workers in the ports.' He went on to explain in his report that, with the present 'system of alliances' the task was insoluble. The influence of German leadership and troops as a 'heavy corset' was the prerequisite for the defence of Italy.

'In the event of the loss of Sardinia, the threat to Northern Italy is extremely acute. This is the key point for the whole of Italy, "the Balkans", Southern France and the base for an allied air offensive against Southern Germany. The invasion gates are Genoa and Leghorn. Their defence by German forces must now be prepared. The build-up of supplies for the defence of Northern Italy in the area of Verona and Milan must now be got under way. The early move of an armoured division to the area of Genoa seems to be required.'

This conception of Allied intentions plays an increasingly central rôle in future German planning for the Italian theatre. If Sardinia was the first Allied objective, this must imply, as the next stage, a threat to Northern Italy, through the Gulf of Genoa along the main lines of communication, and aimed ultimately at the southern borders of the Reich. The eventual plan of the Allied Command of climbing up Italy, punctuated by tactical landings 'of little operational or political advantage', was the least expected by the German Command.

During this military conference Hitler mentioned the memorandum from the Italian High Command which had been recently received in Berlin. It concerned the joint anti-partisan operations in progress in Montenegro. On the previous day, May 18, the German military representative in Rome, General Rintelen, had been instructed to protest to General Ambrosio at the continued lack of Italian co-operation in this theatre. Ambrosio was evasive and surly. These views had already been expressed in discussions with Ribbentrop in the previous February. There had been talk then of pacifying the region in two months. Operations were now in progress 'but one need not have excessive illusions as to the results'. The dialogue became unfriendly. Rintelen remarked that 'it had been reported from Montenegro that there is "no co-operation between Italians and Germans"'. To which Ambrosio retorted: 'In practice your troops act independently . . .' there was 'no question of disarming nationalists in Montenegro unless we wish to augment the rebels by 100 per cent'.

Rintelen could only repeat the German thesis expounded by Ribbentrop in Rome. 'The formations of Mihailović should be liquidated as soon as possible simultaneously with action against the partisans.' Ambrosio's reply was unambiguous. 'This appreciation is my business.' Rintelen answered that the Fuehrer was sending a letter through Kesselring on the subject, adding, 'We have a maximum interest in the pacification of the Balkans.'[6]

This document, dated May 19, is the sharpest ever written by Hitler to Mussolini during the course of their relationship.

Rintelen was so alarmed at its tone that he asked for confirmation that he should deliver it. The order was repeated.[7] The immediate occasion of the letter was the copy of the report of the Italian High Command on the operations in Montenegro. Hitler considered that the views which it expressed 'are entirely off the point, and for Germany militarily untenable. . . . I am anxious to send you these lines. . . . as it is not a question of the problems of the High Command, nor of the (Italian) Second Army, nor of the Governor of Montenegro, but of the common struggle for our future destiny.' The Italian command was now using a new expression for the irregular bands protected by them, namely, 'Montenegrin national formations'. Hitler had passed on numerous intercepted radio messages proving that 'without exception all these formations were collaborating with England'. It had already been agreed that if this were the case they should be disarmed after the destruction of the partisans. Instead the Italian authorities had deliberately favoured these bands, had failed to prevent the Communists from penetrating Montenegro, and in some areas Italian units were cut off and asking for German help.

The Italian High Command had completely misunderstood the situation. 'The observations which we have made from the air leave no doubt that the Allies are planning a large-scale invasion of the Mediterranean basin.' Hitler went on to allude to the British Courier material but without disclosing what it was. 'It is also clear from documents which have been found that they also intend to invade the Peloponnese and will in fact do so. Neither the High Command nor the Governor of Montenegro will be in a position to prevent such invasions single-handed. The Second Italian Army (in Croatia) is in no position, either from the point of view of equipment and armament or from that of training, to protect the Peloponnese and Greece in general from similar invasions. If the British attempts are to be prevented, as they must be at all costs, this can only be done by German divisions. To allow these troops to fight in an area exposed to the danger of losing its supply lines would, however, be a crime against soldiers who are risking their lives in the front line. This is true of Italian soldiers as much as of Germans. However, as long as the fighting there has to be done by German soldiers, I am not in the least interested in General Pirzio Biroli's views (the Italian Governor of Montenegro), which might well lead us into a situation identical with that which we saw end in such terrible catastrophe in the Mediterranean. The fact that, in spite of our exertions, we did not succeed in assuring supplies for North Africa resulted not only in our disaster, but also in the repeatedly established heroism of Italian and German soldiers being in vain. To let our troops in Crete, in the Dodecanese, in the Peloponnese and southern Greece be put in the same situation through the blindness and incapacity of the military leaders would be a crime against the human lives engaged there. However, if banditism and all this "Comitadji atmosphere" is not immediately and ruthlessly put down, this situation will inevitably develop. We have little time to lose in this situation.

'As soon as any real danger of invasion appears within the next few days or weeks, a large number of German divisions must be sent immediately to the Peloponnese. It is, therefore, absolutely necessary for the areas behind the lines of communication to be cleared up in the meantime, so that our formations can pass into the areas where they will have to be used. It is, in fact, the last possible moment for restoring order with the greatest urgency throughout this territory. Moreover, by exercising truly angelic patience I have frequently and repeatedly succeeded in arriving at real collaboration in the conduct of the war in this region. But my efforts have failed in face of the repeated sabotage–I must use this hard word–of the agreements reached on operations, and of the insufficient desire to establish order in a territory which is of vital importance to both of us. Without German intervention there would be no more talk of bauxite supplies, and besides, the Italian High Command desperately needs German aeroplanes. The economic supplies which you should be able to obtain yourself from this territory have become unobtainable solely because of the behaviour of the Italian military posts, since instead of providing promptly for the security and tranquillity which are indispensable to economic life, they have allowed the territory to degenerate steadily under bandit activity; and this need not have happened, for this relatively small country cannot be compared with the huge spaces of the Orient.

'If, however, the High Command wishes to conclude from this that Germany has no intention of collaborating with Italy, I reject such a charge with the utmost indignation. Even before General Ambrosio made his historic appearance, I had long left no possible doubt about my desire to collaborate with Fascist Italy. General Ambrosio and the Governor of

Montenegro were unknown to me when Italy was at war with Abyssinia. But already at that time I led Germany to support Italy. Since then this collaboration—which began on the battlefields of Spain and continued until recently—has been sealed both by Italy and Germany with the blood of tens of thousands of men, and the present operations in the Balkans have no other significance than that of preparing the ground for German formations to bring immediate help in case of an Allied invasion, and therefore to shed their blood again in the common cause.'

Unless order was restored in Yugoslav territory 'a crisis as grave as that of North Africa must ensue', and Hitler begged that the Duce should give clear instructions which complied with the spirit not the letter of previous written agreements. He added that he was transferring an armoured division to Greece.

Hitler barely concealed his distrust of the Italian General Staff, not only in regard to their 'sabotage' of joint Axis operations in Montenegro, but in the general conduct of the struggle. 'Let me say once more that the German and Italian Generals were not all behind us at the beginning. . . . Whether this will recur in the future I cannot say, but at least I can and must reassure you, Duce, that whatever happens I will always stand by you.'[8]

The alarm expressed in this letter was heightened in the following hours. Kesselring, who had been present at the Fuehrer's military conference of May 19, asked for an urgent interview with Mussolini on returning to Rome. He bore an invitation to an immediate summit conference between the two Axis leaders to discuss the situation arising out of the loss of Tunisia, but also to enable Hitler to sound the Duce on the present attitude of the Italian military leadership. Kesselring was summoned on May 20 to Palazzo Venezia. In replying to the proposal of a meeting, Mussolini replied evasively that 'there is always a host of problems which deserve handling' and made no further comment. He then asked: 'What do they say at the Fuehrer's Headquarters on the possibilities of an enemy landing?' Kesselring answered: 'They consider one possible in Sicily, Sardinia, or Corsica.' The Duce agreed, particularly in the event of a German offensive on the Eastern Front. 'Stalin insists on the opening of a new front (in the West), but this time a proper one, and not a secondary front.'[9]

Mussolini's cautious question to draw out Kesselring at this meeting may have been tinged with sly humour. On May 20, the same day as this talk and probably before it took place, the Duce himself was in the secret of 'the British Courier'. As Mackensen telegraphed to Berlin: 'Bastianini asked me to call on him on instructions from the Duce in order to inform me of the following and with the request to send an immediate report.

'Ambassador Paolucci in Madrid, has information from an absolutely unimpeachable source that the enemy intend landing operations in Greece in the very near future.' There was no doubt as to its reliability. Bastianini added that the Ambassador had sent the information through his wife 'who had come by plane as he did not wish to entrust it to anyone else'.[10] The Italians must have known of this 'information' some days before passing it on to Mackensen, and the Germans seem to have had no intention of reciprocating this gesture.

In replying to Hitler's letter of May 19, Mussolini summarized in temperate and factual terms the discussions on the Yugoslav issue between himself and Ribbentrop in Rome in the previous February. It had been agreed that the četnik bands would be disarmed after the defeat of the partisans. 'As is known, the "Weiss" operations, whose aim was the annihilation of the partisans in Croatia, did not lead to any decisive results, in that the main body of the Communists fleeing from the jaws of the trap set by the Italian and German troops succeeded in escaping to Montenegro. The necessary conditions . . . for proceeding to disarm the četnik formations are thus lacking . . . Given the present state of affairs, it seems to me appropriate that we should reach speedy agreement on the further prosecution of our joint operation. . . .'

'What really matters in these hard times, Fuehrer, is to keep up the prestige of our armed forces, and concentrate the efforts of the Axis on striking down our common enemies and bring victory to our peoples.' Mussolini had therefore ordered the Governor of Montenegro to clarify the situation regarding 'all those who were, are, or would be our enemies. We cannot run the risk of having rebel zones in our rear at a moment when the possibility of an enemy landing in Greece might be imminent.'[11]

This last sentence of Mussolini was the only oblique reference made to the source of 'information' shared jointly with

Hitler, and which the latter seemed so reluctant to disclose to his ally, a reticence which marked the extent of the spreading distrust in high German circles of the Italian will and intention to resist.

CHAPTER SEVEN

The Military Crisis of the Axis

HITLER WAS waiting for news from Rome of Mussolini's acceptance of the proposed conference, and had left East Prussia to be near a meeting point. But on May 21 Mussolini told the German Ambassador, who had been instructed to repeat the Fuehrer's invitation, that 'owing to the latest extraordinary and extensive shipping movements in the Mediterranean, as the Fuehrer would understand, he could not leave Rome'.[1] The Duce also insisted on a 'rendezvous' in Italy, and as Hitler's advisers feared for the latter's personal safety in such an event, the idea of these talks was dropped. As the precursory signs of an Italian defection mounted, Italo-German relations had reached their lowest point since the signature of the Axis Pact. Reports that the Italians were fortifying their Alpine border (as at the time of the assassination of Dollfuss in 1934) increased the tension, and Hitler was not convinced by Mussolini's explanations.

But in the Fuehrer's thesis of treason in high circles in Rome the Duce was not the villain but the victim of the Italian military leadership, and poised in the wings stood the figure of the Sovereign. Within the Court and the High Command lay the elements, as yet unmobilized, of an alternative régime. This threat lay at the heart of the Italian scene, and at each crisis in the struggle it drew the anxious attention of the German leaders: after Alamein the visit of Himmler was directed in the main to probing the shadows of the Court and seeking for traces of a Royal conspiracy; in the days following 'Torch' Goering searched for further evidence; and after Stalingrad, Ribbentrop detected furiously the lurking dissidence of the Italian High Command. Hitler's own alarm was constantly reviewed in discussion with his advisers.

On May 2, while awaiting Mussolini's reply to his proposal for a private consultation, he reflected on an earlier talk during the visit of the Duce to the Russian front in the winter of 1941 'down in the Galician area where the big tunnel was'. The two men were discussing the Soviet 'system'. 'At night we spoke about the Russian commissars; how there could not be two powers . . . Then he became very thoughtful, and while I was eating with him on the train, he suddenly said to me: "What you say is true, Fuehrer, that one should not have two powers in one army; but what do you think, what can you do if you had officers who entertain reservations towards the régime and its philosophy of the state? They say they have reservations because they are officers, and the moment you reason with them by appealing to the idea of the state or the interest of the state they say: We are monarchists and obey the King. That is the difference." That was already his problem in 1941. And it was even more pronounced on October 28, 1940 . . . Suddenly he said to me: "You see, I trust my soldiers but not my generals; I can't have confidence in them." The man told me this on the very day on which he started his offensive against Greece.'

By May 1943 this tension had mounted to a danger point. Hitler continued: 'The question is how he feels physically. If the Duce were fifteen years younger today the whole thing would be no problem, but at the age of sixty it is more difficult. But in my opinion those two worlds have always existed. The one world was not removed and so continued to spin its web.'

This conference revealed in still sharper outline the progressive undermining of the Italian scene. The meeting had been called to comment on a report from Baron von Neurath, the son of the former German Foreign Minister, who had been on a special mission of inspection in Italy. He had been told by the commander of the Italian army in Sicily, General Roatta, that 'he did not have too much confidence in the possibility of a defence of Sicily'. If the island fell to the Allies and a general Italian collapse or defection followed, the bulk of Kesselring's Southern Army Group might be trapped in the peninsula and the southern frontiers of the Reich directly threatened. If the Italian armies deserted the Axis, the vital Alpine passes would be the first point threatened. Their main defences were anti-aircraft units, and Hitler gave orders that their supply of ammunition 'must be handled in such a way that it can be stopped at any time'.

When Rommel, who was present at this meeting, suggested that Italian troops should replace the Germans in Sicily, Hitler's answer was: 'What does worry me is that they do not want to defend it: we can see this lack of determination. The Duce may have the best intentions, but they will be sabotaged.' Hitler's 'definite opinion' was that the war had been sabotaged from the beginning 'by a certain group' in Italy. 'Every memorandum I wrote to the Duce immediately reached England. Therefore I only wrote things I absolutely wanted to get to England . . .' Neurath pointed out that 'this sort of trafficking with England is still going on. The night before last, on the train, the submarine commanders based on Spezia told me that they had proof that every morning from 8 to 10 o'clock there was contact between the battleship Vittorio Veneto and Malta . . . The Italian Crown Prince is there as commander-in-chief of the Italian troops. It is significant that he holds frequent inspections, and that General Roatta spends a lot of time with him . . . Personally I am convinced that Roatta is up to something. Officers down there agree that it has become noticeable how he increasingly makes use of the Crown Prince, how he tries to find some common basis with him that would be acceptable when the English descend on Sicily.'[2]

The rôle of the Prince of Piedmont at this time baffled the Germans. Their information was fragmentary and contradictory. Mussolini himself had persistently defended him, but from what motives was less clear. He had pressed Hitler to invite the Crown Prince to visit Germany. This proposal had been aired in April when Schmidt had been sent privately to Rome. According to the latter, the Duce welcomed such a suggestion 'because it would in a certain sense "compromise" the Crown Prince with the Axis . . . although I had told him beforehand on the grounds on which I had been instructed, that the Fuehrer put no store by such an interview'.[3]

A month later, however, the proposal was renewed by Kesselring, and it was coupled with the invitation on May 20 to the Duce to a summit meeting. The latter asked 'When would this be? Before or after my visit?' Kesselring answered, 'Rather before: possibly after.' The German intention was not clear. Were they seeking a hostage from the Royal House or even an alternative figurehead in opposition to the King in the event of basic changes in the régime? But Mussolini was equally emphatic in encouraging the plan. On June 11 he asked Mackensen for news of the planned visit which he would welcome.[4] An entry in the War Diary of the German General Staff reads: 'The attitude of the Crown Prince of Italy, whose visit to the Fuehrer was repeatedly proposed by the Duce, was completely puzzling.'[5] Yet the one consistent theme which German reports from Italy in June underlined was the loyalty of the Royal House to Mussolini. Rumours that the Crown Prince was anti-German or anti-Fascist were discounted. On June 23, for example, Colonel Berger of the German Army Staff on a special mission in Italy reported that any such rumours were not true, and General Rintelen told him that he was in favour of the Crown Prince's visit to Germany which had been so often postponed. 'The Duce is the decisive factor and is loyal to the alliances. There is no question of disloyalty among the upper ranks of the Army to the Duce, so long as the Royal House is loyal to him. Any cleavage between the Officer Corps and the Duce is not to be feared. But he still over-estimates the fighting capacity of his people.'[6]

But if the identity of the 'certain group' to which Hitler had referred on May 20 was not as yet satisfactorily clarified, the extent of their sabotage activities was increasingly documented. On June 3, for example, the head of the German counter-intelligence, Admiral Canaris, informed the German Foreign Office that he had acquired an intercept of a cable from the American Embassy in Berne revealing that the measures promised by Hitler to Mussolini for increased military aid had leaked. The German Army Command intended to report to Hitler that 'such information has reached the enemy from the immediate entourage of the Duce'.[7]

Evidence was accumulating that the group of high officials in the Italian Foreign Office, including Bastianini's closest advisers, were active in private intelligence with the enemy. This leakage was regarded by the Germans as an example of this alarming development, which, as a further German counter-intelligence report stated, was 'the main organization of treason which exists in Italy', and with which Ciano himself was closely identified.

Against such a background the Italian government pressed with a deliberate air of innocence for the increase of German military support for the defence of Italy. As Mussolini had told Kesselring on May 15, 'Tell the Fuehrer that I have written to him. The principal theme is always that of the defence (tanks: anti-aircraft: anti-tank). I think that with three basic German divisions we can be tranquil about Italy, Sicily and Sardinia.'

The Duce relied on Kesselring to press for these requests with Hitler, and at the same time Bastianini invoked Ribbentrop's backing. Alfieri was given instructions to this effect on May 20, stressing that the essential requirement was reinforcements for anti-aircraft defence, and with Ribbentrop's support was considered by the Duce to be 'of special importance'. Little did the Italians realize that on that day Hitler had given instructions to keep down the supply of ammunition to the A/A batteries in Italy to a minimum. The Italian Embassy in Berlin was also showing signs of agitation at 'the startling flexibility in German supplies to Italy. If we remonstrate, they take refuge behind difficulties owing to air bombing. If we insist, they say that our workers in Germany do not work. If we stick to it, they let us understand that they regard Italy henceforth as written off.'

The formal requests from the Italian side however were maintained. On May 26 Alfieri delivered to the German Foreign Office a further note from Bastianini. Heavy enemy concentrations were reported in the North African ports. The air effort requested from Doenitz during his visit to Rome was now needed to stop or delay a landing in Italy. Would Ribbentrop also back this up? 'Thanks to his intervention last time three armoured divisions were on their way to Italy.'[8]

These notes from Bastianini were perhaps also intended for the record in order to show that every effort was being made to persuade a reluctant ally to produce the means to defend Italy against invasion, and to document a possible withdrawal from the war if the situation arose. 'Bastianini is assuming in regard to the Germans an increasingly tough and intransigent attitude. We have the impression that he is seeking intentionally to poison relations between the two countries in order to provoke an incident which would justify an eventual breach.'[9]

The issue on the German side was deceptively simple. If aid to Italy ceased her collapse would be accelerated, and the military consequences for Germany would have to be faced. If limited supplies were sent, the Fascist régime of the Duce might be preserved temporarily, in spite of the increasing signs of treason in military and diplomatic quarters, but equally even among those elements still prepared to fight a marked sensitiveness to an extended German control of the Axis war effort must be expected. There was no absolute solution, and the Germans could only play for time.

Hitler had already decided to give effect to the planning of German counter-measures in the event of a military breakdown on the Italian front. During May and early June, transport arrangements were made, as a result of the Fuehrer's military conference of May 19, for three S.S. divisions to be moved if necessary to the Italian Alpine border. One of these units was the crack S.S. 'Leibstandarte' which was to be assigned to the special political rôle as outlined by Hitler. A similar movement plan was worked out to transfer the armoured divisions from the East. It was calculated that the move to Northern and Central Italy would take eight to ten days. Part of this group might have to be switched to the Balkans. For a complete German operation in Italy, fourteen infantry divisions would be needed, including those already in Italy, and the remainder could only be withdrawn from the West.

On May 31 the German Army Group West offered two armoured and six infantry divisions for operation 'Alaric'. In addition, two parachute divisions were to be alerted in the event of an Italian coup to control the central Alpine passes. On June 4 there is a laconic note in the German General Staff files: 'The Fuehrer has agreed in general to the intentions and proposals of Army Group West for "Alaric".'[10] It was to be the duty of this command to occupy the Western Alpine passes in event of an emergency, and to watch and disarm the four Italian divisions in France. But this German Headquarters in France was faced with technical complications in planning for such an eventuality since, on Hitler's orders, they were not kept informed of any general strategic plan. At no stage did Hitler relinquish personal control over these operations ('Alaric' and 'Konstantin'). Indeed, direct orders in event of an Italian collapse would be given by Hitler verbally in order to prevent any leakage.

As Hitler had stated on May 19, his prime objective, subject to military and political conditions in Italy, still lay in the East. On June 18 he gave orders to launch operation 'Citadel' —the long-planned offensive against the Kertch peninsula. This decision meant the end of any armoured reinforcements for eventualities in Italy and the Balkans. On June 19 the Operations Staff pointed out that, in view of this operation, it would be impossible to defend in an emergency the coastlines of Italy and the Balkans. The only troops now available to this end were the infantry and parachute divisions earmarked in the West. The modified proposal of the German High Command was to move as soon as possible the infantry units for plan 'Alaric' up to the Brenner and to consider a defence line in Northern Italy, withdrawing in the event of a crisis from the South to such a prepared position.

This had always been Rommel's view, but he immediately pointed out that he had no forces at his disposal for such a move. The troop reinforcements from the West would certainly be committed in the event of an Allied assault on Italy, and would not be available for the 'special task' confided to Rommel. Apart from his skeleton staff and the designation of Army Group B as his future command, he had in fact no troops immediately available. There were also no plans for reinforcing the German Second Air Fleet, in spite of promises to the Italians, and no adequate anti-aircraft defence of the vital Alpine passes. Nor had any preventive action yet been planned against the Italian fleet.

Hitler hesitated. He had realized the extent of such a commitment in Italy. Pending the summer outcome of the offensive in the East he must continue to keep the Italian army in the field by limited doses of military aid, and seek every opportunity to reinforce the political position of the Duce on the Home Front.

At the beginning of May, Dollmann had sent from Rome an alarmist report to Himmler headed 'The Situation'. 'In these recent days requests have reached me from the circles among the older Fascist generation asking that German military equipment now in Italy . . . should not be handed over to Italian army units but held as an iron reserve to be available when the crisis breaks.' In event of a crisis the Duce had at his disposal about 150 private bodyguards armed with revolvers; the Militia, 'very badly led and ill equipped, who will go as a faithful flock to the slaughter'; the old Fascists 'who are hardly organized at all, but whose leaders now at last, even if hesitatingly, are aware of the danger of the hour, and of the vital need for mutual understanding; and a Police force, which is inadequately armed, overbureaucratized by Senise, and very badly paid.

'On the other side the King . . . has at his orders the well organized, disciplined, and reasonably armed military police. And then the Army: that is almost the whole of the higher and middle-ranking Officer Corps, which was always hostile to the Axis . . .' The Fleet and the Air Force would obey blindly from above. There was widespread passive resistance to any co-operation with the Axis.

The ultimate threat to the maintenance of internal order in Italy was in theory the special concern of Himmler. But with Mussolini's deliberate procrastination over the arming and training of the 'M' division, proposed at Klessheim, a well mounted political conspiracy could no longer be suppressed by a simple police operation. Nor, in spite of Farinacci's continual offers to organize a counter-coup, were 'the old circle of friends of the Reichsfuehrer SS', whom the latter had sounded during his Rome visit of the previous October, confident that they could ever produce an alternative Fascist government. Nor were they a united group. As Dollmann reported: 'Everyone is clear and agreed about the size of the danger. I have been able to confirm that under the pressure of the moment old differences are being overcome, the worst being between Ricci and Buffarini. All these are faithful to Himmler.' Buffarini was particularly committed 'personally and practically. His fanatical hatred of the Ciano clique has contributed to this', and he had kept Dollmann informed in detail on everything within his range. He wanted urgently to meet Himmler and was very pessimistic at the internal situation. The present Ministers were 'a Cabinet of God-forsaken mediocrities.

'Ricci has specially undertaken, in the sense of the Reichsfuehrer's suggestions, to work for a reconciliation among the older Fascists, which I have carefully explained to him in three visits . . . From a human point of view Ricci is of all Germany's most unreserved friend in Italy. Unfortunately the Duce will not bring himself to decide to entrust to him again one of the great commanding posts, for example, the Party or the Militia.'[11]

While the German Intelligence authorities handled the discontented Fascists, the Embassy analysed the more official reactions of the Roman scene.

On May 22 Mackensen reported in a contrasting vein to that of Dollmann. 'However, the deliberate and thorough measures adopted recently by the higher authorities have met with a considerable response . . . in the government changes of February 5, the disappearance of Ciano was considered to be crucial, since in the eyes of Italian public opinion his name was linked with many unfortunate aspects of the régime. In contrast to him is the lucid personality of its new Foreign Secretary, Bastianini, who embodies the best type of old Fascist, entirely loyal to the Duce, and who above all does not avoid expressing his opinion openly to him. Equally fortunate is the designation of Albini as Undersecretary at the Ministry of the Interior, the nomination of Chierici as Chief of the Italian Police with the task of making this body a safe political instrument in the hands of the Duce, and the appointment of the new Fascist Party Directorate and the replacement of the weak and completely a-political Party Secretary, Vidussoni, by the energetic Scorza.

'In general one can say that internal politics in Italy are passing through an indisputably critical phase. The population increasingly questions the purpose of the war following on the heavy defeats and the loss of the African empire, and in critically reviewing the situation, inevitably judges the régime's achievements negatively. The Party, which was earlier the driving force, has become in recent years a free-wheeling engine. Nevertheless one can say that it is not too late for a change for the better.

'We must in future organize our own measures so that, in the event of an increasingly probable local collapse of a separate Italian resistance, we can stifle the beginnings of anti-Fascist revolts at the threatened points, and in this respect too be of real assistance to the Duce. Naturally any further developments depend on his personality. His disappearance or a noticeable decline in his health would have unforeseeable consequences.'[12]

The Duce had already tuned to Hitler's more receptive mood. On June 5, in a conversation with Kesselring, who had again been summoned to Hitler's headquarters, Mussolini asked him to tell the Fuehrer that 'as regards the divisions which should be sent to Italy, I am content with three. They are enough to defend the islands and the peninsula. As to the situation, today it has been altered. The Anglo-Americans have bombed La Spezia and hit two battleships. To repair them up to full efficiency will require a few months. Perhaps I am a little optimistic. This new situation means that we must reinforce our air strength. It has always been my idea that the best defence of Italy can be achieved with a strong air force. Only if we have at our disposal such a force can the danger of an enemy invasion of the peninsula be lessened . . . Tell the Fuehrer that as to the bombing of our cities, the morale of the population is good . . . But 70,000 tons of shipping have been damaged.'

To add to the confusion, and perhaps the intention was deliberate, General Roatta, who had relinquished his Sicilian command at the end of May and was now Chief of the Army Staff, pressed on his own initiative for an extensive scale of German military support on Italian territory. Rintelen reported to the German War Office that 'on June 6 General Roatta expressed his views on the need for German aid as follows: for the defence of Italian home territory ten German divisions in all would be required, namely two each in Sardinia and Sicily, and three groups of two Armoured divisions in South, Central and Northern Italy. He particularly stressed that this request arose from a strictly military point of view.'

Both Ambrosio and Roatta told their German colleagues that the Duce would accept reluctantly the sending of the two further divisions for which the German High Command had been pressing and provided only that they were armoured. This would mean a total reinforcement of the Italian theatre by five divisions. When Kesselring proposed on June 18 that an additional two divisions should be requested by the Italians he was told that 'the Italian Chief of the General Staff had just had to intervene with the Duce to get his consent for the two further armoured divisions, and was not inclined to raise a new request with him, as he would counter with more hesitations and objections. General Ambrosio stated that the Duce had after lengthy resistance agreed to the sending of these two only because Italy possessed no armoured divisions.'[13]

Axis speculation on the direction of the overshadowing Allied strategic assault was unco-ordinated and groping. On June 1 Mussolini told the German Ambassador in Rome that the enemy 'will next go for Pantellaria, then West Sicily, and finally Sardinia, so as to attack France simultaneously or shortly afterwards'.[14] On June 7, General Marras, the Italian Military Attaché in Berlin, had a talk with Keitel which summarized the latest German appreciation of Allied strategic intentions in the Mediterranean theatre.

'The Anglo-Americans are ready for one or more landing operations. In order of probability, the German Command considers that these landings could take place in Sardinia, Sicily, Greece, and the Dodecanese. The main probability is Sardinia, after the occupation of which the enemy will probably pass on to Corsica . . . The possession of Sardinia, completed by that of Corsica, would give the enemy, as has been repeatedly stated, an excellent air base from which to hammer Italy and Southern France. The German Command then considers that a landing operation could be carried out in the Peloponnese, in Aetolia, Epirus, and the Gulf of Patras. A landing in Crete is thought to be too difficult. The occupation of the Peloponnese and the Dodecanese would permit the isolation of Crete. But the principal aim of the landing in Greece would be to secure an air base whence to operate into the Balkans: the main objective would be the Roumanian oil fields.'

The first disclosure of Allied intentions was the attack on the Italian naval and air base of Pantellaria on June 10, in accordance with the Duce's intelligent guess of ten days previously. Rintelen was in Ambrosio's office when the Duce telephoned instructions to telegraph Malta to inform the enemy that owing to shortage of water resistance had come to an end. 'It is astonishing that the Duce, without further enquiry, should have ordered the surrender.'[15] Mussolini never referred to this action on his part.

The Germans still maintained their view that Sardinia, and not the Italian mainland, would be the next objective.[16] But the abrupt fall of this defensive outpost of Sicily sounded the alarm. On June 12 Ribbentrop telephoned to Alfieri that the Fuehrer was sending Air Marshal Richthofen to Rome 'with a strong air unit'. But on arrival the latter announced that he was on a tour of inspection and that 'the High Command had not the slightest intention of sending any air group, big or small, to Italy'.

The Italian requests for increased military aid as formulated at Klessheim had never been met beyond a token degree. They could not have been satisfied except at the expense of the Eastern Front. The wrangling between the two allied Staffs between April and June 1943 is therefore primarily of interest in revealing German suspicions and Italian intentions.

The crisis of Italian military demands now broke. On June 21 Ambrosio told Rintelen, in presenting him with a detailed memorandum, that he realized that Germany could not fulfil Italian requests, but that he must present the maximum needs to make the Italian army capable of fighting to its full capacity. As Rintelen said later, 'Keitel, to whom I forwarded these requests, saw in this list a pretext for giving up the war.'[17]

Colonel Berger, of the German Army Staff on a special mission to Italy, wrote in his report dated June 23 that the three arms of the German forces in Italy came nominally under Italian High Command, and as he put it, 'the more modest the achievements, the more important for the Italian matters of prestige'. His mission was to report on the readiness of the German units in Italy in the event of an Allied assault. His alarming conclusion was that for the next six weeks no German unit would be fully on a war footing. On June 30 Rintelen pointed out in a dispatch that the core of the Italian army had been destroyed in Greece, Russia, and Africa, and with an essential loss of equipment. Out of eighty-five nominal divisions, only twenty were effective. The Italian army was not capable of supporting the burden of a major war as an independent commitment. And yet, as Italian military strength declined, the High Command increased their demands to control the Mediterranean war.

On July 6 General Roatta made a formal request for the two German armoured divisions to be sent to Italy. Four days later, according to the War Diary of the German Army Staff, instructions were given that this demand was not to be met.

BOOK IV

'Conspiracies are not made without the association of others, and are thus most dangerous; since most men are imprudent or evil, one runs too great a risk in being involved with such people.'

GUICCIARDINI

CHAPTER ONE

Sicily: 'The Water's Edge'

'I HEAR on reliable grounds that information has reached the Spanish General Staff that major offensive operations by the Americans out of Algeria and Tunis are imminent. Direction of attack probably Sicily.' The German Ambassador in Madrid telegraphed this report to Berlin on June 18, and it was confirmed six days later by the German Security Service. 'From a very reliable Spanish source comes another supplementary report that very strong Allied convoys have passed the Straits during the last week, and are steering a course along the African coast.'[1]

On July 9 the Italian Military Intelligence produced an evaluation of enemy intentions, which hardly clarified the situation. 'An Anglo-Saxon offensive in the Mediterranean is imminent. The enemy attack with massive quantities of equipment and men will be directed most likely against our islands, especially Sardinia, in the Aegean, on the French coast, the Spanish peninsula, where Portugal will only make a token resistance, and on the coast of northern Europe while Russia will launch a major offensive.' A landing in Greece was less likely owing to Axis reinforcements.[2]

Confusion as to the precise direction of the Allied assault obscured the Axis scene until the last moment. During the night of July 9/10, however, Allied forces landed in strength at several points on the southern coast of Sicily.

The Duce was inspecting the 'M' division near Lake Bracciano, just north of Rome. The King was at his private estate of San Rossore near Pisa. Both men hastened back to the capital to study the first bulletins from the front. The drawn-out crisis of the Mediterranean war was about to break, and both men would be faced in the next days with decisions involving not only the military position of Italy in the war. The loss of Sicily would inevitably provoke the crisis of the régime.

At noon on July 12, Bastianini telephoned to Alfieri in Berlin, in an excited voice, instructing him to approach Ribbentrop at once with a renewed demand for aircraft. 'We cannot hold on any longer in Sicily.' Ribbentrop was ill, and the Undersecretary of State, Baron Steengracht, was not available. At 2 p.m. a telephone call from Rome came through again to say that 'we will try to seek aid through other channels'.[3] A personal message from Mussolini to Hitler was therefore sent through General Marras, the Italian Military Attaché in Berlin. 'This morning (July 12) I asked Marshal Kesselring to inform you of the absolute necessity of an urgent and important reinforcement of the German air force to defend Sicily. Imposing naval convoys, tanks, and artillery in increasing numbers would constitute precious objectives for enemy air attack, whose intervention would be decisive. The existing air strength although exposing itself generously, is not sufficient either to hinder landings or oppose the enemy air force which is inflicting ever mounting losses on our divisions. The figure of available aircraft is infinitesimal in relation to requirements, and is increasingly diminishing. The moral and military effect of any enemy reverse at the first attempt to invade Europe would be incalculable.

'The state of the game is such that every effort must be made to end it in our favour, and this is only possible by a maximum and immediate German air reinforcement. The attack on Sicily can be cleared up in the briefest possible time, after which the air formations will be available for other tasks.

'I would ask you, Fuehrer, to give attention to the above, and give the maximum air support to the defence of Sicily, particularly with fighters. If adequate support is not forthcoming, the land, sea, and air strength of the enemy is such that the defence of the Sicilian theatre will be extremely difficult. I would add that one cannot exclude that the enemy will launch his attacks elsewhere, against which the operations of the air force, in its present condition, would be nil.'

Mussolini had deliberately refrained from seeking direct German military aid at this critical hour. Hitler had already been forced to issue orders on July 11 for the immediate reinforcement of Sicily as a result of the Allied landings, although even as late as July the Italian High Command thought fit to ask that any such armoured units which might be sent to Italy should be incorporated in Italian divisions. A week later, Rintelen made a shrewd analysis of this attitude. 'The opposition to a further spreading of German forces throughout Italy comes from the Duce himself. The reasons for this are probably the following: the maintenance of Italian prestige in the country itself; the excessive economic burden through having many German troops; a considerable overestimation of battle-worthiness of Italian troops. In contrast to this, the Duce for months has been asking for a substantial increase of the German air force.'[4]

In the meantime, news from Sicily reaching German headquarters provoked a violent outburst. The immediate cause was the surrender of the naval base of Augusta, where the Admiral in charge blew up the coastal batteries without a shot being fired. Rintelen was ordered to convey to the Duce the indignation of the Fuehrer at this incident and at other examples of Italian military conduct. Rintelen saw Mussolini on the evening of July 12, and handed him a copy of the most savage of the German telegrams from Sicily. The Duce told Rintelen that he would have an enquiry held into the Augusta affair, but in private he appears to have made the cryptic comment: 'For me this telegram is at least a fifty per cent alibi.'[5]

On July 12, the same day, Alfieri sent a personal letter to Bastianini describing the first German reactions to the Sicily invasion. 'Shorn of side issues and polemics, the Italian-German situation, after the landing of the enemy in Sicily, can be summarized as follows: Germany is fully committed in her engagement with Soviet Russia, against whom she has offensive plans of a grand style, although actual needs have forced her to postpone this operation until next year. In the meantime she proposes to preserve her forces intact, to build up new ones, and put off as long as possible any eventual assault on the territory of the Reich. This is why she considers friendly and occupied countries as bastions of the German fortress, and nothing more.

'Italy constitutes in effect just one of these bastions. Anglo-American power, let loose against her, finds thus an outlet and an obstacle; otherwise this power could threaten areas more closely linked to the territory of the Reich. Germany cannot commit herself fully in Italy against the Anglo-Americans, because she must reserve her main effort against Russia. . . . One has the impression that she intends to aliment the heroic Italian resistance with limited concessions.'[6] As the

Italian Minister in Berlin noted, 'the impression is forming that the Germans, by leaving us unaided to fight in desperate conditions, are pursuing a plan aimed at provoking a collapse in Italy in order to install a new government completely subservient to them'.[7]

Even Kesselring, who during recent months had almost alone pressed the military case to keeping the Italian ally in a position to continue the war, was not prepared to maintain with any confidence his attitude any longer. His hesitations were a measure of the hopelessness of the situation. On the evening of July 12 Mackensen called on him. The position in Sicily had 'sharpened'. There had been 'a complete collapse of the Italian coastal divisions. The Fieldmarshal had asked himself yesterday the question whether, under these conditions, he cared to be responsible for the further transport to Sicily of German troops, which might be more urgently required elsewhere, but nevertheless had answered this question in the affirmative, as the politico-military importance of withdrawing from Sicily was of extraordinary significance. He had therefore decided on a further strengthening of his forces there.'[8]

On the following day, July 13, at a meeting with Kesselring, the Duce reviewed the situation in Sicily. The former was prepared to recommend the transfer of two German divisions from the mainland to Sicily, but there was not even any question of holding the whole island, and in any event 'new forces would arrive too late'. The Italian commander on the island, General Guzzoni, however, had confirmed on the telephone to the Duce that with the two divisions he could hold on. Mussolini added: 'I consider the situation serious and delicate . . . but not desperate. From the political point of view, if we lose this large island the success for the enemy will be too great. The repercussions on the morale of the Italian people, and also the German, would be too grave . . . During the course of this week the situation will be decided.'[9]

On July 14 Ambrosio minuted to the Duce on the intervention by Rintelen two days previously. 'General Rintelen, on the evening of the 12th, told you, Duce, in the name of the Fuehrer, that certain Italian troops in Sicily had not fought adequately, and added that if the Italians did not intend to fight, the Fuehrer would send no further troops to Italy . . . The hypothesis advanced by the Fuehrer is unjustified, and must be rejected.'[10]

On the same day Ambrosio drafted his own appreciation in a 'Note to the Duce'. A covering minute in the file states tersely: 'The High Command outlined to the Duce the gravity of the military situation and the impossibility of continuing the struggle with honour, without a notable and immediate allied intervention with land and air forces.'

This memorandum was a bleak survey of the operational prospects in the event of the loss of Sicily. 'The fate of Sicily can be regarded as sealed with a more or less brief delay. The essential reasons for the rapid collapse are: the absolute lack of naval opposition and feeble resistance in the air during the approach to the coast, the landing, the advance of the enemy, and our counter-offensive reactions; the inadequacy of equipment and grouping of the coastal divisions; the scarcity and weakness of defensive works; and the lack of efficiency, in weapons and mobility, of the main Italian force.

'It is useless to search for the causes of this state of affairs. They are the result of three years of war, begun with scanty means, and during which the few resources have been burned up in Africa, in Russia, and in the Balkans. The same serious situation exists in Sardinia, in Corsica, and in the whole peninsula. Once Sicily had been occupied, the enemy could operate, either against the Italian mainland methodically in a series of operations within the range of fighter aircraft from South to North, or strike a single blow aimed at dividing the peninsula in two, or in Sardinia and Corsica as a preliminary operation to one against the peninsula or the coast of Provence.' Ambrosio judged that the first hypothesis was more likely, it would be strange to attack Sicily 'in order to reach Leghorn, Genoa, or Toulon, with the prospect of facing three landings rather than two'.

In any event the Italians were not 'in a position to face the situation alone. After the experience of Sicily, the problem of Sardinia and Corsica was more or less insoluble, given our inferiority at sea and in the air.' The defence of the Italian mainland required 'immense quantities of equipment and of land and air forces, which we are not capable of getting ready ourselves. One must however consider the need to organize the flow into Italy of German land and air forces (motorized units other than those already arrived, and 2,000 aircraft), even at the cost of interrupting temporarily operations in progress in the East, in order to defend Italy, and reconquer a relative air superiority in the central Mediterranean.'

For this, the Axis must operate massively 'against the more dangerous enemy, represented now by the Anglo-Americans, who, through the occupation of the Italian peninsula, would create the conditions whereby they would reach a decision above all in the Balkans (Roumanian oil).

'It is urgent to break from the outset the attempt to create a stable Second Front on which, in a more or less brief space of time, the Anglo-Americans will succeed in having an absolute superiority.

'The very slight chances, outlined above, of our being able to resist at sea, which appear from the recent operations, may induce the enemy to accelerate his timing. It is therefore indispensable that the above-mentioned forces are concentrated at once in the peninsula.

'On the other hand, the ally cannot persuade us that victory for the Axis is probable if the constitution of a second land front is prevented as long as the war in Russia drags on.

'If one cannot prevent the setting up of such a front, it will be up to the highest political authorities to consider whether it would not be expedient to spare the country further sorrow and ruin, and to anticipate the end of the struggle, seeing that the final result will undoubtedly be worse in one or more years.'

As an analysis of the possibility of further Italian resistance, Ambrosio's memorandum would have met with approval at German Headquarters.

On July 13, the Fuehrer had already issued a military directive on Sicily. 'After the bulk of the Italian forces are eliminated, the German forces alone, even if grouped together, are no longer sufficient to push the invading enemy forces back into the sea. In addition, further enemy landings in the west of the island must be expected. It will now be the task of our forces to delay the enemy advance as much as possible and to bring it to a halt.'[11] Hitler was now reducing his commitment on the Italian front as far as possible without precipitating the inevitable.

On the same day he replied to Mussolini's request for aircraft in the following terms: 'I completely share the judgment of the situation contained in your telegram which has reached me on July 13, 1943. The loss of Sicily would represent for the enemy the definite control of traffic across the Sicily channel and a base for the further assault on the Italian mainland.

'After the unexpected and rapid folding up of the forces employed in coastal defence, which, as I communicated to you through General Rintelen, at least in one of the most important sectors did not even accept battle, the principal task of the air force must be, in an even greater degree than previously, concentrated on the maximum destruction of enemy shipping. This can be of decisive importance for the subsequent development of the fighting in Sicily and for the beginning of further landing operations in the Mediterranean. In spite of all difficulties, I have decided to continue maintaining the potential of the German air strength in Italy. In July, 220 machines were dispatched, and a further 250 bombers and fighters will follow, as foreseen, by the end of the month. And in addition I have arranged for a further strengthening of the Second Air Fleet by one fighter and seven bomber groups. Two bomber groups recently assigned are specially equipped for action against naval objectives. To reinforce the battle against the enemy forces which have landed, I have in the first instance given orders that the First Parachute Division shall be transported by air to Sicily and that the 29th Armoured Division shall be transferred to the Reggio area.

'Allow me, Duce, to beg you to take immediately the necessary measures to remove such obstacles and further to ensure that your forces stationed in Sicily give their utmost in the defence of the island which can only be held by the joint efforts of our troops.'

The letter was delivered to Mussolini on July 15 at a meeting at Palazzo Venezia with Kesselring. He had precise instructions. 'The Fuehrer has said that he is opposed to sending equipment and troops to Sicily until supplies of ammunition, petrol, and rations can be assured.' It was more important to defend the lines of communication in Calabria.[12]

The reluctance of Hitler to move German troops to Sicily led to worried speculation on the Italian side. As Mackensen reported on the same day: 'From an unprejudiced source, I know that in a conversation today the Duce referred with some seriousness to the effect which the abandonment of Sicily would have in the country. Similar remarks in front of Germans have been made by Ministers Cini and Albini, linked with earnest requests for the strongest air support. The loss of Sicily would produce in the Italian people a quite different effect from that noticeable in the surprisingly calm acceptance of the news of the loss of Libya or later the surrender of Tunis.'[13]

Kesselring's proposal to send two German divisions from the mainland to Sicily, which he had made two days previously, had been overruled. He now announced, 'on Hitler's orders, that no movements of troops will be undertaken until supplies are assured in Sicily . . .' The pretext was also given that 'the Fuehrer is concerned about the Leghorn zone' at the moment covered by one of the two German divisions concerned. Kesselring added: 'I don't understand why the Fuehrer sees a danger in Tuscany. I don't know the reasons.'

Kesselring was not yet aware that an intrinsic part of the planning of operation 'Alaric' was the building up of a reserve supply base in Northern Italy, and on July 13 the German War Office had drawn attention to the need to send at least one German division to Northern Italy 'on the grounds of the danger of an Allied landing or assault in the area of Genoa and Leghorn'. From the military point of view there might well be a risk of sabotage and Allied air attack on the main lines of communication through the Alpine passes. Marshal Rommel, with his embryo planning staff, was to move at short notice into Northern Italy, with the responsibility of assuring the German Front in the peninsula in event of a crisis. This advanced headquarters had been set up near Munich early in July, and with instructions that its existence must not be discussed in writing.

Hitler's own interpretation of future Allied plans on the Italian front was that they would make a series of landings in the Genoa-Leghorn region. Mussolini, in his talk with Rintelen on July 15, took a different view, perhaps in accordance with Ambrosio's judgment in his memorandum of the previous day. He felt that 'the enemy has a greater interest in liquidating the whole of the South'.

There is indirect evidence of Ambrosio's reaction to this meeting. 'He was astonished at the contemptuous tones used by the German and that the Duce puts up with it. Rintelen complained, among other points, that the German divisional headquarters were badly received everywhere and not given facilities in their tasks of deployment. When he left, the Duce instructed Ambrosio to prepare the reply to Hitler. Ambrosio did so at once, but now fears that he has let himself go in strong language. The letter ends by saying that if our allies do not hurry to support us in the air . . . we will have to open negotiations with the enemy. Ambrosio will take the letter to Palazzo Venezia this evening, but is very much afraid that the Duce will not sign it. He has told the Duce . . . "that the war is lost because Germany is not in a position to bring us immediately the necessary aid (Russian front etc.). Whether from this hypothesis follows the enemy occupation of Italy, preceded by the destruction of our cities, will be seen in a matter of weeks. One must talk clearly, honestly and clearly, to Germany. Italy cannot accept the use of her territory, with no hope of salvation, as the outer defence of the Reich. All Italy is convinced of this. Even if the armed forces would attempt it, the country would not submit to it, seeing the uselessness of this terrible effort. Germany is, on the other hand, for geographical and industrial reasons, able to hold out against the enemy for another year, perhaps longer. In these conditions it is better for both sides that Germany allows us freedom of action, thus safeguarding by common agreement, and in the best way, German interests too . . . One must not hesitate but cross the ditch before it is too late. And if the Germans want to make Italy their battlefield, one should not altogether exclude the possibility that Italy should fight against these allies who have systematically failed in their word."

'Ambrosio is seeing the Duce this evening between 8 and 10 p.m. to give him the reply to Hitler, drafted along these lines. Ambrosio says that the Duce has not reacted in any way to this verbal stand of his. Ambrosio is keeping the King informed. It is a pity that Mackensen has left before the Duce received this draft telegram. Ambrosio feels like resigning if the Duce does not agree with these conclusions.'[14]

On the evening of July 17 the Duce redrafted Ambrosio's version of the telegram to Hitler with many watered down 'corrections', and it was presumably sent off the next morning. 'The rapid initial success of the enemy landings in certain sectors of Sicily is not due to the lack of combative spirit by the troops assigned to coastal defence, but to the preponderance of equipment which the enemy has been able to put ashore with the help of strong naval forces which have been employed with impunity close to the coast owing to the limited possibility of opposition from our weak air force, and our artillery. The coastal defence has done all in its power given its equipment and emplacements.

'My directives assigned to the air force, in event of the enemy landing, as a principal task the assault and destruction of enemy shipping. The air force has always operated accordingly, acting beyond the limits of human possibility.

'But it is not with the modest forces available, faced with an air concentration of overwhelming strength, that one can expect results of a decisive importance against the Allied battle fleet and transports, which have been concentrated in the Mediterranean for an operation in which England and America have committed their prestige in the eyes of Russia and the world.

'In view of the importance and continued aggravation of the war in the Mediterranean, your aid, even if generous, has not been enough, and at times has been subjected to impediments which have vitiated its employment with a unified vision. The 29th (German) division has lost and is losing precious time.

'I cannot accept your observations regarding the conduct of the Italian authorities, who have always done all in their power to assist their German comrades.

'All possible ground arrangements have been made, but enemy air attacks on our landing grounds have assumed an intensity which has seriously affected the efficiency of the organizations. This too is due to enemy air preponderance to which alone are due the losses on land. The ground organization in Calabria is rapidly being set on foot.

'I assure you, Fuehrer, that the Italian forces in Sicily, in accordance with my orders, have always been and still are firmly decided to defend the island to the last.

'The enemy has opened the Second Front in Italy, concentrating there the huge offensive resources of England and America in order not only to conquer Italy, but to open up the road to the Balkans at the very moment when Germany is engaged on the Russian front.

'The sacrifice of my country cannot have as its principal aim the delaying of a direct attack on Germany.

'Germany is economically and militarily stronger than Italy. My country, which entered the war three years earlier than had been foreseen, and was thus unprepared, has progressively worn itself out, bringing up its resources in Africa, in Russia, and in the Balkans.

'I think, Fuehrer, that the moment has come to examine the situation together, in order to draw the most appropriate conclusions to the interests of both countries.'

* * *

Meanwhile, on July 15, at a meeting at Hitler's headquarters, Jodl produced a challenging report on the Italian front and proposed urgent measures to be taken to avoid a further disintegration of the military and political scene.[15]

'On any admission Sicily cannot be held any longer. It is not clear what the next aim of the enemy will be; Sardinia and Corsica, the Italian mainland or Greece. Large landings in Norway and France are not to be expected. The higher leadership of the Allies is centrally constructed, and their political leadership is geared to military requirements. Anti-Fascist elements in Italy want to capitulate and are active in wide circles of the Italian officer corps but at the moment treason is still camouflaged. It may be the object of the Italian traitors to request more and more German support and in such a situation to bring about their destruction.

'If we wish to take into account southern Italy, which is indispensable to us for the defence of Greece, then we must have strong striking forces ready in Apulia and Calabria. But so long as the cleaning up of the Italian military command apparatus is not carried out and the strongest measures taken . . . against all signs of decomposition within the Italian army, one cannot be responsible for keeping German troops south of the Apennines. It is therefore necessary that this internal political decision should be implemented. As a pretext could be used the need to oppose to the united command of the Anglo-Saxons a strict and unified Axis command in the Mediterranean. As the Italians do not possess the necessary leadership, German commanders must be placed at threatened points. These proposals will certainly meet with opposition from all anti-Fascist elements, and this in itself is a reason for a general clean up in Italy as a second stage of the Fascist Revolution. This must be prepared by placing in all Italian higher military positions reliable commanders, and must end with the removal from the Italian High Command and the local Commands of all opposition personalities in Italy. German commanders must be placed at all important points in the Mediterranean area. Marshal Rommel seems to be the only leader in the Mediterranean under whom numerous officers and other ranks would willingly serve.'

Preparations had already been made for setting up German military administration in those areas of Italy under Axis control, in other words, the whole metropolitan territory and the islands, excluding Sicily.

At the same time direct German administration in certain

areas of the Balkans, in particular Montenegro and Albania, was also planned. On July 15, Hitler gave orders to strengthen the German military forces throughout the whole of South-East Europe, and on the assumption that the whole area might have to be occupied.

These military decisions assumed an imminent political collapse in Italy. Hitler alone however favoured caution at the last minute, and summoned a meeting on July 17 in order to 'have a clear picture of the political situation in Italy'. Mackensen was summoned hastily from Rome for this conference, which was to consider the 'far-reaching proposals' which Jodl had made two days earlier. 'The main question was to back up the Duce in his efforts to bring into leading military positions in Italy hard and in every way reliable men who are ready to fight to the end.'

At a conference on the same day Doenitz agreed with Jodl's appreciation. From the naval point of view 'if we want to hold Italy, German troops and German naval coast artillery must take over the mainland ports. Otherwise Taranto and Naples may meet the same fate as Augusta.'

Hitler said that 'he himself has been pondering the question how this might best be done. The greatest problem is the demoralization of the Italian army about which nothing has been done. Only very severe measures, like those applied by Stalin in 1941 or by the French in 1917 will be of any avail. If only individual units were affected, we could appeal to their sense of honour by offering medals etc., but the whole army is in a state of collapse and only barbaric measures can help to save the nation. He believes that a sort of directorate, tribunal, or court-martial should be set up in Italy to remove undesirable elements. Some capable people must be left in Italy, for everything could not suddenly have turned evil.'

Mackensen, who had left Rome after collecting a set of pessimistic reports on the internal position from Scorza, Farinacci, and others, could 'suggest no one capable of taking over the leadership'.

Doenitz believed 'that either we have to do without the Italian army altogether, or we must try to strengthen it with German troops'. Hitler replied 'that without the Italian army we cannot defend the entire peninsula. In that case we would have to withdraw to a relatively short line' and this move, as Jodl added, 'would have very serious repercussions in the Balkans'. Doenitz pressed for the infiltration 'of our men into the Italian army'. But who could take over the task?

Rommel then entered the meeting and was asked 'whether he knows of any really capable persons in the Italian army who are fully co-operating with Germany'. He replied that 'there is no such person'.

Hitler ended the discussion: 'Everything depends on a radical change in the Italian situation. If this can be brought about, it will be worth the risk. If not, there is no point in throwing in additional German troops and thus engaging our last reserves.'[16]

On July 17 Alfieri reported despairingly in a personal letter to Bastianini. German air reinforcements were clearly not arriving with the necessary speed. Alfieri proposed that the Italian High Command should ask the German authorities to indicate exactly and in detail how many aircraft had been sent to Italy, to what airfield and on what dates. 'All this in the form of a precise commitment. In military and political circles in Berlin (very confidentially for the moment), one is saying that if Sicily must be abandoned, an impregnable line of defence must be established on the Continent . . . I have not yet found out to what line they are referring; but putting together certain rumours and remarks, I have come to the view that they are thinking of the Apennines.'[17]

The Italian Minister in Berlin wrote later: 'The German plan in Italy, barely indicated in Alfieri's last letter to Bastianini, is taking shape in the form of a defence organized throughout the length of the peninsula, aimed at stiffening along the line of the Po. Marras (the Italian Military Attaché in Berlin) declares that, faced with such an eventuality, Mussolini, whether he likes it or not, will be forced to get out of the war. In the meantime we are noting alarming signs: the German divisions in Italy no longer obey the Italian commands; they manoeuvre on their own, with the evident intention of carrying out this plan.'[18]

On July 18 the German General Staff informed the Italian Military Attaché's office in Berlin that the major Russian offensive had begun along the whole Eastern Front. Any chance that the Germans might even be in a material position to aid Italy must now vanish.

On the same day, there is a laconic note in Rommel's diary: 'At the Fuehrer's at midday . . . In the East the Russians are attacking along the whole front. They are held for the moment. But no chance of withdrawing a few divisions. I gather that the Fuehrer has been advised not to give me command in Italy because I would be ill-disposed towards the Italians . . . My mission to Italy has therefore been postponed. The Fuehrer is probably going to meet the Duce.'[19]

APPENDIX

The Epilogue to Operation 'Mincemeat'

Ribbentrop was not slow to realize after the Sicily landings that the top secret information reported in May 1943 from Spain in regard to Allied strategic intentions in the Mediterranean had been a brilliant fake.

On July 29 he cabled Dieckhoff in Madrid, 'for the personal attention of the Ambassador exclusively. Upon considering the remarks of Foreign Minister Jordana, which you report in your telegram of July 15th, 1943, I am struck by his emphasizing that we must certainly have been prepared for the Anglo-American attack on Sicily, as the Spanish had repeatedly pointed out to us what was about to happen. Jordana apparently meant this as a reminder of the report you telegraphed to us in your telegram of May 12, 1943. But in this report it was stated that the English and Americans were only going to launch sham attacks on Sicily and Dodecanese, the intention being to launch the *main* offensive against Crete and the Peloponnese.

'This report has meanwhile been proved false, since the operation directed by the English and Americans against Sicily, far from being a sham attack, was of course one of their planned major offensives in the Mediterranean. It is therefore reasonable to assume that the report passed on to you by Jordana, which tallies with the information (referred to in your telegram of May 12) you received direct from a "wholly reliable source", was deliberately allowed by the enemy to fall into our hands in order to mislead us as to the military plans.

'I would add that about the same time as we received your telegrams, mentioned above, we were also apprised by another source, though again via the Spaniards, of the content of certain English military documents pointing in the same direction as the information communicated to you by Jordana and your informant. This information can apparently be traced back to familiarity with these documents. We should therefore reckon with the possibility that these documents are consciously misleading and were deliberately allowed by the enemy to fall into Spanish hands.

'In the light of this, I would ask you to undertake a most careful reappraisal of the whole matter, particularly of your earlier reports, and to consider in so doing whether the persons from whom the information emanated are directly in the pay of the enemy, or whether they are hostile to us for other reasons, by virtue of their Catholic affiliations for example.

'Kindly telegraph your reply.

RIBBENTROP.'

Dieckhoff took immediate refuge behind his correct forecast of the Sicily landings, contained in his telegram of June 18.

'I do not think there was any intention to mislead. What I learned on May 12 from the Spanish Foreign Office regarding the imminence of a major Anglo-American attack on Southern Europe was based on documents which had been found some days previously on the body of a shot-down English officer, and handed over in the original to our Counter Intelligence here by the Spanish General Staff. The documents were investigated by the Abwehr and I have not heard that their investigations cast any doubt on their authenticity.

'When Jordana referred me on July 15 to the Spanish warnings he no doubt chiefly had in mind the communications from the Spanish General Staff of which I notified you as follows on June 18: "It is reliably reported to me that the Spanish General Staff tonight received news of a major offensive operation about to be launched from Algeria and Tunisia. Objective: Sicily."

DIECKHOFF.'

Ribbentrop was not content with this, and his suspicions ranged further afield to the possibilities of Spanish complicity in the whole operation:

'In your telegram of July 30 you express your conviction that there was no desire to mislead us by passing on the English documents dealing with English invasion plans; you say that these documents were also examined by the Counter Intelligence without any doubt being cast on their authenticity.

'Here again it is taken for granted that the documents really emanate from the British. But the fact that they say that only a sham attack on Sicily is planned and the main offensive was launched against Sicily, permits us to conclude with certainty that the documents were deliberately intended to mislead us. The idea was presumably that we should not adopt any defensive measures in Sicily, or that we should adopt only inadequate ones. It is thus practically certain that the English purposely fabricated these misleading documents and allowed them to fall into Spanish hands so that they might reach us by this indirect route. The only question is whether the Spaniards saw through this game and deliberately led us out on a false trail, or whether they were themselves taken in by the Intelligence Service.

'In order that we may judge of this will you kindly let me know whether those persons in the Spanish Foreign Office who originally circulated the information evidently derived from these documents are, in your opinion, directly in the pay of our enemies or whether they have themselves fallen victims to this British deception manoeuvre from some other cause, perhaps by reason of their informant's Catholic affiliations.

RIBBENTROP.'

Dieckhoff refused to be chastened:

'I have no reason to suppose that Jordana and Doussinague (the Secretary General of the Spanish Foreign Office), who on May 12 provided us with the information derived from the English documents, are in enemy pay, nor have I any reason to suppose that these two persons have themselves fallen victim to a British deception manoeuvre from any other cause such as their Catholic affiliations. Both the Navy Minister and General Munoz Grande spoke to me at the time, shortly after May 12, about the documents and pointed out their significance. Like the Spanish General Staff, which notified our Abwehr, they too evidently lent them full credence.

'In my view this was not a case of an English deception manoeuvre. I gave very close consideration at the time to the question whether the documents might not have intentionally been allowed by the English to fall into our hands in order to mislead us; but the circumstances in which they were found overwhelmingly refuted such an assumption.

'It is my belief that originally (i.e. at the end of April or beginning of May) the English and Americans had every intention of acting as laid down in the documents. Only later did they change their minds, possibly regarding the plans as compromised by the shooting down of the English bearer. The operational plans must have been finally settled at the Washington Conference at the end of April; this is evidently where the attack on Sicily was decided upon; the Spanish General Staff, acting on their own North African intelligence, gave us accurate forewarning of the attack on May 18, and it actually took place on July 10.

DIECKHOFF.'

On August 4, in exasperation, Ribbentrop terminated the argument, through a subordinate:

'The Reich Foreign Minister has instructed me to inform you that the British Secret Service is quite capable of causing forged documents to reach the Spaniards, by whatever means, with the object of deceiving us. He therefore concludes once for all that the possibility of a forgery exists, it being merely open to question whether all the Spaniards through whose hands the documents passed believed in their authenticity.'

The head of the Italian Military Intelligence, General Amé, has added later his sibylline comment. 'It was not false documents written in the hand of the Vice-Chief of the British General Staff which served to give credit to our faulty appreciations, as a recent British publication would have it, but the concepts of the same Vice-Chief of Staff expressed in an authoritative manner, which came to the knowledge of the Italian Military Intelligence, and confirmed our exact valuation.'

CHAPTER TWO

The Roman Scene

ON JULY 10 the Duce inspected the 'M' division, armed and trained by the German S.S. as the mobile striking force of Fascism guarding the centre of government in event of internal disorder. The main precaution taken on the Home Front had been the creation in May of this Division. The equipment for which the Duce had asked was delivered punctually by the end of that month. The skeleton division, which had been forming near Chiusi, was now to be brought south to the lake of Bracciano.[1] The parade was held at Sette Vene about twenty miles from Rome on the Via Cassia, and was attended by military leaders and German representatives, curious to see an exercise conducted with the latest military equipment provided by Himmler. It made a good impression, but a brief one.

The previous night, and throughout the early hours of July 10, the Allies landed in force in Sicily. In the confusion of events, Mussolini handled in characteristic fashion the local issue of the 'M' division. General Ambrosio, during the manoeuvres at Sette Vene, had already suggested sending these 'Security' troops to the front, and before witnesses the Duce agreed. On the following day the commander of the Militia Galbiati and Ambrosio met and argued. The latter wanted to get these 'political units' away from Rome, and proposed sending the division to Messina. On July 14, making use of the Duce's name, Ambrosio ordered Galbiati to move his troops. That afternoon the latter went with a written protest to Mussolini, and it was settled that it might be technically impossible to move the division, at least until July 21. But Ambrosio achieved one decisive gain: as from that date, the division came under the direct command of the Army—a point of decisive significance in the following days.[2]

The machine of the Fascist Party had reacted in its turn to the invasion of Sicily. An emergency meeting of Prefects and Federal Secretaries from Southern Italy was held at Palazzo Wedekind, the Party headquarters, at midday on July 13. Scorza also invited, among others, Bottai, Albini, Bastianini, and Chierici. As Bottai commented, 'I immediately had the impression of being at a small council of war.' The Party Secretary had a plan; to carry the Duce's message of a 'granite sense of decision' to the provincial capitals of Italy through a speaking tour of Party bosses. Scorza had particularly hoped that Grandi would take a lead, and had telephoned him in his capital at Bologna. Grandi refused. Scorza now approached Bottai with a request to go to Bologna to persuade Grandi to change his mind, for without his support the oratorial ranks of the senior Party leaders would thin rapidly. Bottai too was sceptical. 'You must put me in a position to tell Grandi what line to give to the speeches. A few days ago Mussolini said that the enemy would never set foot on Italian soil. People have long memories. What are your instructions to justify this tragic reversal of the situation? And what *is* the situation? So that at least those of us who have to illustrate it are aware of it in its true light.' Scorza made no reply.[3]

The Party meeting then listened to the reports of the regional officials, scattered incoherent fragments which gave no clear summary of events. Scorza broke up the debate, and hurried to Mussolini. He returned in half an hour. The regional reports were to be deferred, the list of orators was to be drawn up, and the Roman group of Party bosses would be summoned to the Duce before the end of the week. The course of military events might make this their last meeting, and final opportunity to propose a 'radical' solution to Mussolini.

Bottai stayed on in Scorza's office. The whole structure of the régime was rumbling under the approaching earthquake. The Party, if it were to survive, must be given a lead and a programme. Now was the supreme testing of its élite. But Scorza had on his shoulders the dead weight of past errors, and an increasing sense of operating in a void, out of all touch with the realities of a situation, the details of which were unknown to him, with a Party machine scarcely turning over in a vacuum, and a leader beyond reach in self-imposed and total isolation.

On the following day Bottai drafted a note interpreting his own thoughts in view of the forthcoming meeting of Party leaders with the Duce. There were two possibilities: first, on the assumption that the political situation was completely in the hands of Fascism, and that Mussolini would act as head of the government within the rules of the Fascist constitution, he should nominate military ministers, allow the Chief of the General Staff to fulfil his duties unhampered, make the civilian ministers actively responsible for their departments, permit the Cabinet to function properly, summon the Grand Council, and propose a message from the King to the Nation followed by a manifesto of the Duce and the Grand Council. Second, in the event of a situation considered untenable partly or wholly by Fascism, this would fall within the competence of the Crown. 'It is up to the latter to decide on a form of Government: military? civilian? military and civilian? . . . Including Fascist civilians? or solely with non-Fascist civilians? or both? These are the two alternatives.'

Bottai took this note on the afternoon of July 14 to Scorza's office, and a discussion followed. The latter agreed that there was no third solution. 'Either everyone with Mussolini, even if he were forced to act with us, in a close and frank solidarity of intentions and acts, for the final attempt to produce a government for the defence of Italy: or everyone with Mussolini in leaving it to the King to attempt such a defence.

'We both say together: then there are the Germans. Mussolini, and he alone can do it, ought to obtain from them *in extremis* an undertaking not to torment the country; the King to do the same with the others, the Allies. To achieve a kind of neutrality. To get us out of everything . . . A risky operation whose outcome is uncertain.'[4]

Scorza now felt it essential to convey to the Germans the rising alarm in Party circles. He asked Bastianini to arrange an urgent interview with the German Ambassador for that evening. The two men went together. The conversation was reported by Mackensen to Berlin. 'Scorza thanked me for receiving him and asked me if he could speak openly and in confidence, as both of us were convinced of the indissoluble alliance of the Axis powers. Above all he wished to make the formal declaration that the Fascist Party was determined to fight in the common cause to the last man. So long as one

Fascist remained alive, nothing else was thinkable. The loss of Sicily would have unforeseeable consequences for Italy.' In the name of the Fascist Party he begged both the Fuehrer and the National Socialist Party for help 'to the bounds of possibility in the battle for Sicily, which would be decisive not only for the future of Italy, but also for that of Germany, and even of Europe . . . The Italians alone had not the necessary means. To ask for such means from the Axis parties at this decisive hour was his sacred duty as Party Secretary, and was independent of all the military departments. This was not the moment in which to go into the why and wherefore of Italian weakness in armaments. But the Fuehrer could be assured that, if the next critical fourteen days could be overcome, he, Scorza, by ruthlessly exploiting the intrinsic full powers of his position would set in motion with every means at his disposal a basic revival of the Italian people, which would bear comparison with the year 1793 in France. Nothing would be untouched by such a revival; neither the Army, nor its leadership, nor war industry.'

Mackensen answered that the Fuehrer was certainly following events in Sicily with the same attention. 'I stated personally to Scorza that we were fully aware of his services in bringing new life into a party which had lapsed into a complete free-wheeling, but that we were also clear that in wartime the omissions of years could not be made up from one day to the next.' Scorza did not deny this, but emphasized that he would act 'with an iron broom'.

Mackensen was impressed: 'With him (Scorza) and through him we should be able to achieve that change in the exercise of the powers of command, which hitherto seemed unrealizable.'

Ribbentrop replied with a personal telegram the following day. The Fuehrer had noted with interest Scorza's appeal. 'Already all available units are on the move, and war material is rolling every hour in the direction of Italy . . . All our thoughts and wishes in these days are with the Italian people and the Fascist Party, on whom the future of Italy depends.'[5]

But the Party Secretary, eager in his rally for the last stand, like other actors in the scene, created his own vacuum round him. At such a moment, inexplicably, he had abolished the liaison officers between the units of the Militia and the machinery of the Party. It would therefore in a supreme crisis be impossible to organize common action on a political level. And for the next ten critical days, Scorza was 'unavailable' to the Militia commander, General Galbiati.[6] The body of the Party had a tail, but no teeth. As the Chief of Police, Chierici, told Bottai, '"One must act quickly", and then he told me of the landslide of the Party in the provinces. It would be ingenuous, he said, to reduce the present crisis to a police problem, even supposing that the forces available were sufficient to maintain order.'[7]

On the morning of July 16, Scorza summoned to his office at Party headquarters certain of the leaders designated for the grand tour of the provinces. He wished to go over the arguments to be put before Mussolini that evening at a meeting of the orators to which the Duce had reluctantly agreed. It was important to present a united front. The discordant note was as always sounded by Farinacci 'thundering as if at a political meeting, giving vent to his uncontainable rage against the Leader'. But the majority were agreed that Mussolini must accept to govern within the limits of the existing Fascist constitutional legislation 'and the proper working of all the organs of consultation, control and decision'—in particular of the Grand Council—must be demanded of him. The meeting was temporarily interrupted by a visit from the German Ambassador to tell Scorza that he was leaving by air for Berlin to press for immediate reinforcements for Sicily.

At 5.30 that afternoon Scorza and the orators, with the exception of Federzoni and Grandi who both refused to come from Bologna, called on the Duce at Palazzo Venezia. There were fifteen Fascist leaders in the group. 'He turned his head to us, one by one, slightly aslant as if he wanted, by looking at us sideways, at the same time to defend himself and to penetrate our intentions. I know so well this attitude of the fencer ready for the parry and the thrust. How well I know that smile which now twists his lips; it is born of a nervous twitch which tries in vain to become an open courteous smile and remains half way between a diffident grimace and dissimulated ease.'[8]

Farinacci spoke first with his usual violence, soon losing the threads of his discourse and plunging into detailed complaints, exposing himself to the favourite game of the Duce of involved interruptions. Why, for example, should the Duce deal with matters of detail such as the price of bread? The retort is swift: 'Napoleon . . . stated that there were no such things as details.' But Farinacci's argument was clear. In his own words, 'I began by saying that the situation was serious because I had no faith in the General Staff and particularly in General Ambrosio, who had told me some days previously that the war was lost, and that within fifteen days we would have to shut up shop. I asked Mussolini that all those present should be put in a position to assume total responsibility along with him, by summoning the Grand Council.'[9]

Another speaker 'brought the subject back to the theme which we had set ourselves: it was not a matter of neglecting details, but of passing them to . . . those responsible organs whose actions the Leader should co-ordinate. This had not happened, there were only institutions which did not function, and laws which were not applied.' Mussolini opened his eyes wide. 'What's that? What then have we done in twenty years?'[10]

Bottai pointed out that the constitutional organs of Fascism must be allowed to function. This was no formal matter. 'The clash between the spirit of the law and the conduct of government shows a crisis of authority and of command, harmful at the best of times, and at this moment dangerous. Convinced of such a danger, we are here to enunciate in constitutional terms a question, which is simply and solely political . . . We are asking that the régime puts its apparatus in working order again. We are not here to ask that your powers or power should be diminished or to divide or fragment your responsibilities. We are here to share those responsibilities. The constitution provides that you should be "the first" but not the only minister: the first in a Council of Ministers really operating in each sector.' He also suggested that a reformed Grand Council should be created, capable of debating and deciding on the problems involved in a major overhaul of the structure of government. The two Chambers must also be made to function and with them the syndicates and corporations.

'From Mussolini's expression it appeared that he had made up his mind for some time. After a moment of silence he said, "Very well, I shall summon the Grand Council. They will say, in the enemy camp, that it has been assembled to discuss the surrender. But I will call it together." And he dismissed us. Nothing else. No taking into consideration of any one of our proposals; and we wanted something more than just this announcement.'

The idea of a Mussolini collaborating cheerfully with a

happy and united band of loyal collaborators in making Fascism work ignored the whole historical experience of twenty years, and of the Duce's character.

The following day he said to Bastianini: 'Scorza in a little more than two months has brought me with his Secretaryship two speeches, one directive, and one pronunciamento.' And Bottai commented in his diary: 'The "pronunciamento" is our move of yesterday. To such a point is the situation destroyed. Talking to others he (Mussolini) sneered: "Who were those badly dressed gentlemen? What did they want? What authority had they? The authority of a speaker which lasts just as long as his speech."'[11]

Mussolini wrote later: 'I did not much welcome this gathering, as I did not care for meetings not prepared in advance with a regular agenda . . . All the speakers, or nearly all, insisted on the necessity of convening the Grand Council if only to enable me to inform the members of the highest assembly of the régime of certain facts which could not be given to the general public. At the end of this discussion, which not having been prepared revealed nothing but a sceptical frame of mind all round, I announced that I would convene the Grand Council in the second half of the month.'[12]

Although the deliberate absence of Grandi and Federzoni weakened this Party deputation, its significance was clear. This meeting in the Duce's office had been the dress rehearsal. The arrangements, and in part the initiative, lay now in Scorza's hands.

Ciano also had been absent from this gathering. On the pretext of ill-health, he retired during these crucial days to his family house at Leghorn. That day, however, Mussolini summoned him to Rome. The news of his return raised alarm in German circles. The Germans feared above all that Ciano was the main link between a Grandi-Bottai-Federzoni group and the Court.[13]

Dollmann wrote two notes for Mackensen on his own contacts with 'the circle of Villa Torlonia', which signified his main informant Buffarini, with whom he had been until three o'clock in the morning of July 16. As Dollmann reported: 'Villa Torlonia sees its salvation only in the taking over by us of at least combined military responsibility and leadership and has the greatest mistrust of Count Ciano.' That afternoon Dollmann had talked with Donna Rachele. 'I would like to stress the clear and pressing warning from her side against her son-in-law and his plans.' Ciano had arrived from Leghorn and 'has had a long talk with Bottai, and other members of his circle'.[14]

Ciano then sent a message to Mussolini saying that 'he had never felt so close to the Duce as at this moment, and that whenever the Duce thought it necessary he could come and talk to him'. He seems however to have hesitated and pleaded ill-health, and only on July 20 added in a further note that he was well enough to call 'at any time'.[15] It does not appear that the Duce sent for him.

The shock of the Sicily landings was also felt in the field of foreign affairs. Military defeat was now inevitable and the search for a compromise peace could not be postponed. Bastianini hoped that at last the opportunity had arrived to act on his own initiative. If Mussolini were to allow him such latitude, there was no time to lose and a plan must be ready. As Bastianini wrote later, 'Supreme decisions are not taken by an Undersecretary, but I can at least try to put them into effect rapidly.'[16]

On the evening of July 17, Bastianini called on the Vatican Secretary of State, Cardinal Maglione. It is revealing of the absence of consultation between the Vatican and the Italian Government that the two men had not met since 1924. In any soundings towards the Western Allies, a logical and historical starting place would be through the diplomatic channels of the Papacy, whose nuncios in neutral and belligerent capitals were in a sense the professional representatives of peace.

For months past, rumours of peace moves initiated by the Vatican, and supported by the Portuguese, the Spaniards, and the Swiss, had circulated in European capitals, but no reliable evidence appears of any interest in such soundings on the part of the Italian Government. There seems equally no reason to believe that Ciano at the Italian Embassy to the Vatican had made any formal approaches either to the Cardinal Secretary of State or to the British, American, or neutral Legations in the Vatican City. There are equally few records of his private activities in this direction. He was reported, for example, by the German Legation to the Vatican to have remarked cryptically to a Cardinal in April 1943 that the war would not last long and that 'new developments might take place on the Eastern Front'.[17] A month later a vague German report from Berne mentions evidence supplied by the Swiss

Minister at the Vatican that negotiations were in progress between Ciano and the Allies, who, however, were insisting as a preliminary condition on the resignation of Mussolini. The Italian King feared apparently that there would be public disorders in such an event and on this issue negotiations were suspended.[18]

But these rumours lacked any confirmation, and if accurate seemed to relate to a personal initiative. Bastianini's present move was the first to come belatedly from the Italian Foreign Office.

As the basis of an exploratory discussion he handed a memorandum to Cardinal Maglione. This was a bald statement of Italy's position. The war might last 'for an undetermined period of time'. Germany was still strong, and, with each shortening of the front, she could concentrate her military resources. But Italy was the main target, and thus the whole of her position must now be examined within the general frame of the war. 'Rumours have reached us of steps which the Pope would not be unwilling to take, if he had the prior assurance of Italian and German concurrence.

'Italy cannot take any initiative on her own, both for moral reasons as she must safeguard the honour of the country, and for practical reasons as she must take into account that any unilateral move in drawing away from Germany would automatically transform her territory into a battlefield. If the military situation in Italy should deteriorate even further, the only person in a position to persuade Hitler to withdraw troops from Italian territory is the Duce. It was therefore essential that England and America should not raise the immediate issue of the removal of the Duce, as this would not be in their own interests. The Germans would withdraw first to the line of the Po, where the Anglo-Americans would confront them, and then to the line of the Brenner. The intervention of Mussolini with Hitler would thus save them having to engage the Germans twice on our territory.'

The formal purpose of this note was to seek Vatican initiative in sounding the Western Allies on their political intentions in Italy. With what persons would they be prepared to treat? Were they planning to set up an Italian government-in-exile?[19]

But there was also a more urgent and practical request. On the assumption that he would obtain the Duce's agreement, Bastianini had conceived of sending a trusted envoy to contact the British, and placed his remaining hopes of a political solution on this one mission.

He had in mind for this delicate task a leading Roman banker, Luigi Fummi, who was connected with J. P. Morgan and Company, New York, and also with the administration of the property of the Holy See. Bastianini's plan was that Fummi should travel on a Vatican passport to Lisbon, and apply for a British visa there in order to go to London on financial business for the Vatican, but in reality to get in touch with the British Foreign Secretary, Anthony Eden, with a personal message from Bastianini.

Cardinal Maglione agreed without comment to issuing such a passport, but when Bastianini explained the task to be given to Fummi, namely to attempt to negotiate, on Bastianini's responsibility, the exit of Italy, Roumania, and Hungary from the war, the Cardinal 'looked at me with a paternal expression, and certainly thought that I was deluding myself'.[20]

The next morning Bastianini went to Mussolini in a last attempt to persuade him to sanction such a diplomatic initiative. He proposed that he should take certain steps, and if they failed, and were discovered by Ribbentrop, the Duce should disown his Undersecretary. Mussolini did not reply in either sense, and this was the best that Bastianini could expect. He left hurriedly and returned to Palazzo Chigi. There was no telephone call from the Duce for the rest of the day.

Fummi was now briefed and sent by direct plane to Lisbon. Some months earlier, Bastianini had secured the appointment of three experienced career diplomats in the key neutral capitals of Lisbon, Madrid and Ankara for precisely such an eventuality.

There had been inconclusive contacts with British agents in Lisbon at the end of 1942, which had been severed on Ciano's instructions. The Italian Minister, Prunas, was now hastily instructed to try to renew these links. Fummi was explicitly told to conduct no discussions in Lisbon, but to insist on access to Eden in London. His mission was to convince Eden that Italy was in a position to answer both for Hungary and Roumania in seeking peace terms from Britain and the United States, on the assumption that the withdrawal of these three enemy powers from the German alliance would be a decisive element in Allied plans for an invasion of the Balkans, on which indeed the whole project depended, so as to bar eventually the Soviet occupation of South-East Europe.

Fummi left Rome on July 17 or 18, and waited in vain in Lisbon for the British visa. He was still there on July 25.

In reply to his request to Cardinal Maglione, Bastianini was told that, after enquiry, the Allies did not seem to be planning to set up a 'puppet' Italian government. This augured perhaps well for Fummi's mission. Bastianini now informed Acquarone, and through him the King, of this démarche.

The final step was to create an alibi with the Germans in the event of a favourable Allied reaction. Ribbentrop was to be told that Italy could not continue the struggle unless immediate and total satisfaction of Italian requests for military aid were immediately fulfilled. On July 17 Alfieri received instructions in this sense.[21]

The Germans were not unaware of these moves in Rome. On the same day, July 17, Dollmann reported to Mackensen: 'During the last two days, the Duce has been under pressure from various quarters, in particular from members of the government, in the direction of an "honourable capitulation".'[22]

During the first week of July the King was away from Rome at San Rossore, but he had returned in haste on receiving the news of the Allied landings in Sicily. Anticipating the long awaited political crisis, Badoglio and Bonomi met again on July 14 to draw up a joint shadow cabinet, which the former would attempt to urge upon the Sovereign. Bonomi was alarmed at news that Acquarone was hesitating. 'One must go by stages; bring down Mussolini, yes, but not attack the whole Fascist movement frontally.'

The two men now agreed on a provisional skeleton plan of a politico-military administration which would carry out two simultaneous operations, the overthrow of Fascism and the withdrawal of Italy from the German alliance. Badoglio would be the head of the new government, and Bonomi Vice-President of the Council. They arranged that Badoglio should seek an urgent audience with the sovereign to 'draw the conclusion of these clear premises already outlined by Ambrosio'.[23] There was a certain element of historical irony in the situation. It had been in October 1922 that the then Prime Minister, Facta, had summoned Badoglio to his office to discuss the possibility of military action against the imminent Fascist March on Rome.

The King received Badoglio on July 15 at Villa Savoia. He was, as Puntoni noted, 'about to take grave decisions'. On the following day Bonomi wrote in his diary, 'The King has not accepted Badoglio's scheme. He objected that prearranged action fixed for a certain date had no chance of succeeding. In Italy people were not good at keeping secrets; after a few hours the whole thing would be widely known, and the plans at the disposal of anyone who had any interest in them.

'In addition the King did not believe that if he intervened —an eventuality which he did not even yet admit—it would be well to form a political ministry; it would offend too many people and things, and as it would consist of old men, would give the impression of a pure and simple return to the past.'[24] Here at last was the essence of royal counsel.

The following afternoon Bonomi called on Badoglio to hear the latter's account of the audience. The discussion opened with the presentation by the Marshal of a brief memorandum on the military situation showing that with sixteen ill-equipped divisions in Italy and practically no Air Force, there would be no effective resistance to the Allies. The thirty-four divisions in France and the Balkans could neither be withdrawn at once nor without German consent. To this picture, the King showed little reaction, but only responded in clear opposition to the proposal to consider a political ministry. The elder statesmen from Bonomi to Casati, from Soleri to Einaudi, from Rodinò to Ruini, were all ghosts, the King said in Piedmontese dialect. To which Badoglio answered: 'Sir, we two then also are ghosts.'[25]

The German Intelligence received another and perhaps more accurate version of this audience: 'A completely reliable informant and well-known political personality reported to me yesterday the following, which he had been told by Marshal Badoglio with whom he has close relations. The King has turned to Badoglio with regard to eventually taking over the administration in Italy. Badoglio has explained to the King that he is in no way inclined to take over in any way the succession of Mussolini. He would be prepared to exercise the powers of government on the orders and full responsibility of the King, and would carry out to the letter his instructions. If the King ordered that one should continue to fight on the side of Germany, he would carry this out loyally; if the order was to initiate peace negotiations, this he would also undertake; and so on. In any event let the King bear the responsibility: he, Badoglio, was only prepared to carry out the latter's orders, whatever they might be, in the most loyal manner. The King wept, and has not yet come to any decision.'[26]

The same afternoon, July 16, Acquarone asked to see Soleri, and confirmed, what the latter already knew from Bonomi, the King's insistence on a 'technical' administration of civil servants. This royal decision was firm, and Soleri was asked to propose names. Acquarone seemed nervous and uncertain. 'It seemed to me that the excessive power which Badoglio would concentrate in his hands was a source of preoccupation to him, and he particularly did not like the idea of the Marshal being also Minister of the Interior . . . A phrase escaped him (Acquarone), "If all goes well for him, who will stop him?" Perhaps ill-natured gossip had also reached Acquarone that Badoglio resented that the King had not backed him in the quarrel with Farinacci at the time of his dismissal in December 1940, and had let him resign as Chief of Staff and that the Marshal aspired, in the not unpredictable event of the Sovereign's abdication and that of Prince Umberto, to become the regent of the little Victor Emmanuel.'

Soleri reported this talk to Bonomi and his friends. He found them excited and, in face of the King's refusal to agree to a political ministry, prepared to disown the monarchy. Before taking such a step, however, they would wait to confer with the Prince of Piedmont, 'to clear up definitely certain preliminary understandings which had been reached with him in a conversation held some days previously'.

The discussion ended inconclusively, and Soleri left that evening for his home in Piedmont. This was the end of a parliamentary solution of the Italian crisis. Everyone reassumed his liberty of action. Badoglio would not resist the alternative suggestion of an administration of civil servants and experts, and as the King determined to move by stages, such a government headed by a military figure was to remove Italy from Fascist control before facing the issue of withdrawing from the war.

According to General Cerica, the future Commandant of the Military Police, the King wrote a private memorandum about July 12. 'They have proposed to me a lottery of three names: Badoglio, Caviglia, and Thaon di Revel. Caviglia has close Freemasonry links and must be kept out. Thaon is too old. One, Badoglio, is left, whether I like it or not.'[27]

CHAPTER THREE

Feltre

'ON THE NIGHT of July 17 Hitler had received an alarming report on the situation in Italy. Things were going so badly that they might seriously endanger the programme of the German High Command, who were counting on holding the enemy as far distant as possible, and above all to bar the road to the Reich.' Such was the information available at the Italian Embassy in Berlin.[1]

On Sunday, July 18, the German Ambassador in Rome, who had just returned from the crisis discussions on Italian affairs at the Fuehrer's headquarters, transmitted an urgent invitation to a summit conference. Hitler was prepared to come to Italy, and the meeting might last three days. This message seems to have been conveyed to Bastianini by Mackensen late that morning. The former enquired as to the agenda for such a conference, and was told by the German Ambassador that he did not know.

The Duce seems to have made a brief display of anger at Hitler's message. He accepted, however, the rendezvous, and telephoned Ambrosio at four o'clock that afternoon instructing him to leave within three hours for the North.[2] Hasty protocol arrangements had been made for the two delegations to meet at the seventeenth century villa, with its magnificent park, belonging to Senator Gaggia, near Feltre, in the province of Venice.

On the late afternoon of July 18 Mussolini left by air for the coastal resort of Riccione with his doctor and secretary, without holding any meeting with Bastianini or Ambrosio as to the policy or procedure to be followed at the forthcoming talks. He would spend a few solitary hours of reflection before facing the ultimate crisis of the Axis alliance. Bastianini met Ambrosio at Palazzo Venezia, when delivering Hitler's message to the Duce, and suggested 'that he should be ready to leave with documentary material which would be useful in sustaining a somewhat heated discussion'.

Meanwhile, on the German side, a last minute discussion was held at Berchtesgaden on the evening of July 18 to draft the headings which would form the basis of discussion at the conference. This document had been drawn up by General Warlimont, and was starkly concise.

The situation in the Mediterranean area urgently required unity of direction. This could only be placed under the command of the Duce. In view of a strengthened military commitment in Italy, a German Command, under the Duce, must be set up, to which the Italian armies would be subordinate. If German units were to be sent to Southern Italy, further Italian divisions must also be moved from the North. The Italian High Command and the other Staffs must be so constituted that complete and trusting co-operation could be ensured. The Air Command must be transferred to the head of the German Air Force in Italy, Marshal Richthofen.[3]

The essence of the German plan was thus to preserve this nominal authority of the Duce to cover the assumption of total military control by Germany in the Italian theatre.

The two delegations now converged on the rendezvous at Feltre. On the morning of July 19, Bastianini and Ambrosio arrived by train at Treviso, the nearest railway station. Alfieri, who had flown from Berlin, sought anxiously for a short briefing from the Foreign Undersecretary. The latter told him in the car between the station and the airport that both internally and militarily the position was serious. 'Mussolini no longer shows any external reactions. He has shut himself up in an impenetrable silence, and it is impossible to guess his thoughts.'[4]

At 8.30 a.m. Mussolini arrived in his personal plane at the airfield of Treviso. None of his advisers had as yet been able to brief him on the latest developments, and Alfieri now attempted to give him a hasty summary of events as observed from Berlin. The scene was dominated by the violence of the Russian assault on the Eastern Front where the main attention of the German leaders was inevitably engaged, and the effect of which could only be to reduce to vanishing point any willingness on the German side to send aid to Italy. 'I also stressed the anxiety of the German High Command as to the Italian situation. Bastianini interrupted to say that during the journey he had attempted to get confirmation from Mackensen and Rintelen as to the veracity of the confidential information that Hitler was proposing to place the Italian armies under the control of the German High Command, on the specious pretext of greater unity of direction and action.'[5]

Before Mussolini could react, the German delegation headed by Keitel interrupted the dialogue to pay their formal respects to the Duce. As he descended from his plane a few minutes previously, Keitel gave Rintelen a brief clue as to German intentions: 'All power to the Duce, elimination of the Italian Royal House, stronger German intervention under German command.' As Rintelen began to express his astonishment at Keitel's remarks, saying that the Duce had indeed all power in his hands but could no longer exercise it, the conversation was cut by the arrival of Hitler's plane.[6]

Alfieri describes the scene. 'At eight minutes to nine appeared in the sky the profile of the large machine carrying the Fuehrer: the plane made one large sweeping circuit of the airfield, as is usual, and then another . . . Someone murmured "What could be the reason?" Mackensen who was next to me observed, "It is three minutes to nine and the arrival is fixed for nine o'clock precisely." '[7]

According to Mussolini's own account, 'the meeting was, as usual, cordial, but the entourage and the attitude of the higher Air Force officers and troops were chilly'. It appears that Hitler had announced that he had to return that afternoon to Germany, and that therefore 'the time had to be used to the best advantage'.[8]

The two leaders travelled alone by train to Feltre and thence by car to their destination, and 'merely exchanged trivialities'.[9] Meanwhile the Italian and German delegations, in anticipation of the meeting, were sparring in the same train, which took them from Treviso to Feltre. The unusual absence of Ribbentrop and Goering emphasized the strictly military concern of the Germans with the meeting. A brusque dialogue developed between Keitel and Ambrosio. The former was 'confident that the Russian drive will be held'. The latter retorted 'in effect you are reduced to the defensive. What are the chances of victory? And your plans for the future?'

Keitel answered that on the Russian Front the Germans would succeed in wearing down and weakening the enemy; in the meantime they would prepare new forces which would enable them to operate actively next winter on the Southern Front, in the Balkans, and in Italy. To Ambrosio this was not an active programme, 'but a renunciation of operational initiative. The Axis is under siege, closed in a circle. One must get out of it. What proposals have you for doing so?' This question was evaded. Ambrosio then examined the situation in the Mediterranean where, in view of the commitment in Sicily, the enemy would presumably persist in his operations against Italy, and not only by aerial bombardment. 'The Second Front has been opened in Italy, and one must provide for her defence; the Italian forces are not sufficient.'

Keitel accepted the view that the enemy would seek to cross from Sicily to the peninsula and agreed that it was necessary to take measures to defend Italy. Germany, however, could not send any air reinforcements other than those promised in the recent message of the Fuehrer, nor had she any armoured divisions available. He maintained that the coasts must be defended on the shore, with infantry divisions ranged behind. Above all, one must have recourse to the Italian infantry divisions, which were nearer and more easily available. German reinforcements could not be available for a couple of months. As it was above all essential to defend the southern coasts, the Italian divisions now in Central and Northern Italy must be sent to the South, including the Alpine divisions and those being re-formed, and then one would make provision to send German divisions gradually into the North. Ambrosio objected that, for the defence of the peninsula, infantry and motorized divisions were needed. As the Italian army only possessed infantry divisions, it was for Germany to contribute motorized divisions. The Italian units would cover all the coasts, including those troops in the Centre and the North; while the German mobile divisions must move to the South as well as the North, but particularly to the South which was more exposed. This dialogue at least clarified the extent of German assistance which might be forthcoming. It remained to discuss the conditions.[10]

Villa Gaggia—a labyrinthine edifice described by the Duce as 'a crossword-puzzle frozen into a house'—was now the scene of this confused, ill-organized meeting, confined by Hitler's time-table to a single formal session. The two delegations assembled at eleven o'clock; on the Italian side, Ambrosio, Bastianini, and Alfieri; and on the German, Keitel, Warlimont,

Rintelen, and Mackensen. Apart from the last, no representative of the German Foreign Office was present.

The company, sitting in a circle in the main lounge, was confronted with a sweeping review of the war in a two-hour monologue from Hitler who held a large file of documents on his lap. 'Mussolini, perched on the edge of an armchair too broad and deep for him, listened impassively and patiently, his hands clasped on his crossed legs.'[11]

The Fuehrer began 'with some remarks on the war situation'. The present conflict 'was no isolated war like the Franco-German War of 1870–1, but a struggle to determine the fate of Europe'. Control of vital raw materials, 'the material aspect of the conflict', lay at the centre of the struggle. As regards iron and steel production, this was thoroughly assured in those territories controlled by Germany. Iron-ore supplies would suffice under all circumstances. Extensive deposits existed on German Reich territory, particularly in Lorraine. Coal was likewise plentiful, and there was also at the disposal of the Reich the additional supply of coal, steel and iron ore from the East European countries. Just as important as iron, however, was the large number of raw materials, particularly metals such as molybdenum, nickel, chromium and the like, supplies of which had to some extent been assured for the Axis armaments industry in sufficient quantities only during the war by occupation and annexation. These raw materials were quite indispensable to the conduct of the war. There was no particular need to stress the immense importance in this respect of the Balkans, with their important sources of raw materials. Equally important was oil. Hitler had intended for this reason to seize the oil resources of the Caucasus. 'This operation had unhappily not succeeded.' Roumanian oil was thus all the more essential.

The paramount importance of these basic raw materials made it necessary to move in troops to guard those regions whence they came. One must have some understanding of the industrial basis of warfare. In military circles this was often lacking. Hitler had, for example, had to explain in detail the importance to war industry of the Donetz basin before having it properly understood that no heroism could make up for the coal deposits won there should the Donetz basin once be lost. Without nickel and without chromium, production of aircraft engines would come to a complete standstill.

As to the problem of food supplies, this could only be overcome with the aid of the Ukraine, which was helping to feed the army of a million deployed in the Eastern territories. The Ukraine could also export more if more petrol were made available for agriculture, particularly for tractors.

'If we could safeguard all the regions containing raw materials of military importance that were now in our hands, from Northern Norway to the Balkans and from the Ukraine to France, the war could be carried on indefinitely. Its continuance would then be simply a matter of mobilizing the necessary manpower. *This was a question of willpower: if we were to save the nations from ruin we must shrink from no hardship. We should not adopt the totally mistaken attitude that present-day defeats could be made good by future generations.*' Hitler 'was sacrificing the whole of his time and personal comfort to the task of bringing about a settlement in his own lifetime'.

At midday the conference was interrupted. The Duce's secretary came into the room, holding a paper, which he handed to his chief. Mussolini read, translating aloud into German, a brief communiqué. 'At this moment the enemy is engaged in a violent bombardment of Rome.' But even this news was but an irrelevant interruption to the strident voice.

There would soon come a turning-point in the U-boat war, especially when the new types, equipped with the latest technical devices, were brought out. As regards the Air Force, mass production of aircraft had only just got into its stride. Hitler then mentioned 'two new weapons he preferred not to enlarge upon, which would be used against the British at the end of the winter and against which they would have no way of defending themselves. Even Germany possessed no means of defence against them apart from her geographical position.

'Turning to the military operations, the Fuehrer stated that the question on the Eastern Front was to weaken the opponent as much as possible before winter set in. The twenty-one divisions lost at Stalingrad and several others besides had been re-formed. In the past year 32 divisions, including 8 light armoured divisions, had been earmarked for an attack on Mesopotamia (*sic*). They had unfortunately had to be used during the winter in Russia to relieve the crisis there, so that the project for which they were originally intended had had to be shelved.

'Germany was also having to supply an air force on a vast

front, beginning in the North, where cover had to be provided for the convoys transporting iron ore from Sweden to Germany. If there were no more iron, no more aircraft engines could be built. These communications had therefore to be protected. But this was done chiefly by means of first-rate ground organization of the airfields.

'If—as had happened in Italy—300–400 out of 500–600 machines were destroyed on the ground, it meant that organization was simply bad. One just could not afford to pander to private interests in such matters. Every hardship imposed now would be a minor matter compared to what would happen if we lost the war. Germany had drawn her conclusions. Private considerations would be entirely swept aside. Airfields would be enlarged, runways for the aircraft constructed and protective walls, to shield individual machines against bomb splinters, erected wherever this might be necessary, and without regard to objection from private persons. Nor should the question of compensation play any part. If the war were won, then compensation could be paid. But if it were lost it would no longer be necessary, since the claimants would no longer be alive.'

It was quite inadmissible that in Sicily and Southern Italy 27 machines should have been destroyed on the ground on one day, and 52 on another day, owing to the unprofessional, unmilitary conduct of the ground personnel. Italy herself must find the personnel to staff these airfields. A labour force of this kind could of course not be sent from Germany—there were simply not enough men. With proper organization losses through the destruction of machines on the ground could be cut to a small percentage. 'In Germany and the West it was generally only 1 or 2 machines per raid. If the German Air Force had lost as many aircraft on the Eastern Front as had been lost through ill-organized airfields in Italy, it would have succumbed to the Russians long ago.'

As to the strategic problem of convoys at sea, Hitler recalled that the German Navy had needed strong pressure on his part before consenting to use warships for transport purposes. He emphasized the need for using cruisers, too, as troop transports, since they were fast vessels and as such less vulnerable to air attack. He pointed to the example of the British mine-laying cruisers that had supplied Malta in the most difficult days of the struggle. All the arguments of prestige advanced by the Navy must be silenced. Fast transport craft of the type just mentioned were needed for Sardinia,

Corsica and the Dodecanese. Emotional arguments should be dismissed.

'Turning to the question of Sicily, the Fuehrer said he was in two minds. If reinforcements could be ensured Sicily would have to be defended, and, at a given moment, defence would have to revert to attack. But this presupposed that the hinterland was safe. If this were not the case then it would be better to withdraw from Sicily, though it was clear to him that this would mean a heavy blow to morale. The best solution of course would lie in defending the island. This postulated the complete protection of supply lines, and in particular the safeguarding of the crossing from Messina.

'Strong and excellently equipped infantry divisions would be far better as a defence force than armoured divisions, which were suitable for attack but not for defence. What was involved here was the fundamental decision as to whether we should actually fight. If so we would have to bear all the consequences of our decision in a fanatical spirit. If we did not want these battles, every man we sent to Sicily would be sent in vain.' Reichsmarshal Goering was ready to concentrate a large number of anti-aircraft batteries at Messina to cover the reinforcements. Additional supplies could then be moved up from other parts of Italy, where they would of course have to be replaced immediately by equipment from Germany. 'What was definite, however, was that every soldier and every officer who deserted an army or naval battery while there was still so much as a single shot left in it, must be shot. This was a question of training, and as experience showed would take some time to inculcate. To begin with, therefore, Germany would accompany the batteries she supplied with tough, proven German personnel.

'For the purpose of warding off attacks on Southern Italy, far more Italian units must be also concentrated in the "toe" than there were at present.' Hitler was following closely the proposals of his military advisers.

'It was therefore of fundamental importance to establish whether we believed that the decisive battle would preferably take place on the Italian mainland itself. If so, then every man we sent to Sicily would be wasted. Armoured divisions took a very long time to replace once lost, for tank warfare was largely a matter of routine and experience, demanding lengthy troop training and exercise. If, however, we wanted to hold Sicily, we must bear all the consequences, down to the very last. In that event, Germany would send in crack units. But such a decision would entail considerable re-casting of plans. What had happened now in Sicily must not be allowed to happen again! Several German units had had to be sent down, to establish first a defensive front, then a full-scale offensive front . . . If we held the position in Sicily and concentrated the attack on the British supply lines, in a few months' time the British would find themselves in the greatest difficulties as a result of the renewal of submarine warfare mentioned before. The Sicilian operation might then turn out to be a catastrophic defeat for them . . .'

Hitler was opposed to saying that the Axis would not hold Sicily but only Southern Italy. That way they would end up by only being able to hold Central Italy, and in the end only the North. The more advanced the defence position, the more effective it would be, and it would also have favourable repercussions on those parts of the interior which were threatened by air attack.

'If we decided to hold out we must steadfastly abide by the consequences of such a step, in the same way as he (the Fuehrer) had intervened in Germany with the utmost severity. Fifteen-year-old youths had been posted to anti-aircraft batteries as Luftwaffe auxiliaries. The fire brigades in areas threatened from the air were composed of elderly and very young persons. Women had been enlisted for productive labour on a far-reaching scale; since peasant women were needed on the land, and many women were in any case already working in industry, these measures had affected all women, even those from the middle and upper classes of society. At the same time he had also intervened at the front, and personally dismissed any proven officers who had temporarily lost their nerve. Italy, too, had a fundamental decision to make: it entailed the most drastic consequences and made it necessary to overcome all obstacles.'

As regards Italian requests for war material, Hitler said that a demand for 2,000 aircraft was of course impossible for Germany to honour in practice, and in view of the airfield situation was quite pointless. Nor could air force units be simply transferred from the Eastern Front, as owing to the completely different tactics obtaining there they would need a month's training first. 'The war would be won in the first place by men, and then by tanks, anti-tank guns, aircraft and anti-aircraft weapons.'

Hitler turned to the situation in South-East Europe where

he had just reorganized the German commands and was dispatching Rommel to Salonika. He announced that several more German divisions would be moved to the Balkans, particularly to Greece.

'Before lunching alone with the Duce, the Fuehrer once again stressed that Sardinia and Corsica could only be held if defence got under way the moment the landings took place. The Fuehrer expressed concern as to the behaviour of the Corsican population. At this point the Duce spoke for the only time during the meeting. He stated that the Corsicans were now reasonably quiet. He had been showing signs of uneasiness, shifting in his armchair, wiping his forehead, and appearing to be in pain.'

The delegations dispersed for luncheon. The Italians were indignant and frustrated. They gathered round the Duce in a last attempt to persuade him to counter Hitler's stand in private. As he joined the group—Ambrosio, Bastianini, and Alfieri—his first remark was: 'I am very upset to be away from the capital at such a moment. I would not like the Romans to think . . .' As Alfieri commented: 'In the position in which he was, his only thought was that the Romans should not imagine that he had gone away on purpose! I must admit that at this instant my devotion for Mussolini was put to a severe test.'[12]

His advisers pressed for a frank and final approach to the Germans to seek a way out from the alliance and the war. Ambrosio in particular 'used stronger language to Mussolini probably than he had ever heard'. Having listened to Keitel on the train journey, the Italian Chief of the General Staff was certain, if he needed such a confirmation, that the Germans would not be able to reinforce the Italian front. According to Bastianini who was listening, Ambrosio now delivered without any introduction an 'ultimatum' to the Duce, to get out of the war within fifteen days.

Mussolini controlled a brusque gesture of impatience, and told everyone to sit down. 'Perhaps you think,' he said, 'that this problem has not been consciously in my mind for a long time. Under a seemingly impassive mask there is a deep torment, which tears my heart. I admit the hypothesis: to detach ourselves from Germany. It sounds so simple: one day, at a given hour, one sends a radio message to the enemy . . . But with what consequences? The enemy rightly will insist on a capitulation. Are we ready to wipe out at one stroke a régime of twenty years and the results of a long bitter effort, to admit our first military and political defeat, to disappear from the world scene? It is so quickly said: detach ourselves from Germany . . . What attitude will Hitler take? Perhaps you think that he would give us liberty of action?'[13] In this last phrase lay perhaps the wisps of a solution.

The Duce's secretary came to tell him that Hitler was awaiting him for luncheon. The only direct record of what passed between the two men appears in Mussolini's notes written down a month later. 'After the Fuehrer's speech, we had our first discussion in private. He gave me two most important pieces of information. (1) That submarine warfare was about to be resumed with new means. (2) That at the end of August the Reprisals Air Fleet would commence operations against London, which would be razed to the ground in a few weeks. Among other things, I told him that, in anticipation of reprisals, the air defences of Italy would have to be strengthened. I was again called away to the telephone, and in the meanwhile the time of departure had arrived.'[14]

According to Rintelen, the Duce had promised Ambrosio to make a final attempt during the train journey to describe to Hitler Italy's desperate situation. 'He (Mussolini) only asked for further German help, especially in the air. He could not bring himself to admit that Italy could not fight any longer.'[15]

The two leaders travelled alone on the train to Treviso. Mussolini wrote later: 'It was only in the train on the way back that I was able to make quite clear the following points: Italy, I said, was at the moment being called upon to bear the full burden of the onslaught of two empires, the British Empire and the United States. She was in danger of being overwhelmed; the air attacks were not only undermining the morale of the people, but were also causing grave damage to war production and to the whole social fabric of the nation's life. I repeated that the African campaign would have taken a very different turn if we had had superiority, or at least parity, in the air. Finally I told him that the moral tension in the country was very great. He replied that the crisis in Italy was a phase, and that he would send further reinforcements to strengthen the air and land defences of the peninsula. The defence of Italy, he declared, was of the utmost importance to Germany. The tone of our conversation was very friendly, and we parted on the best of terms.'[16] The only recorded remark of Hitler was that 'during our last meeting at the station, the Duce suddenly remarked: "I do not know how my generals reason, where they want to defend Italy, and why they keep such strong forces in the North." '[17]

On the return journey in the train from Feltre to Treviso, Ambrosio and Keitel held a second discussion in the presence of Warlimont and Rintelen. Keitel raised again the possibility of reinforcing Southern Italy 'in the sense that the Italians should eventually contribute at least two more divisions'. Perhaps these could be withdrawn from the Italian Eighth Army in France, but, as Ambrosio pointed out, 'the withdrawal of divisions from France would have political repercussions, and such a question should be consequently put in the first instance to the Duce'. Keitel continued, 'It now remained to decide if one wanted to defend Sicily to the last. The Fuehrer has said that in Sicily one is defending Italy. Naturally if one accepts to defend Sicily to the end, the actual forces are not sufficient. At the present time the Germans have not the means to make a unilateral effort. In order to move eventually troops from the West, they will first have to be replaced and the divisions earmarked for this purpose are still re-forming.' Ambrosio asked how long it would take for them to arrive.

Keitel replied, 'As quickly as possible. As soon as the decision about Sicily has been taken.' He then produced the final ultimatum of the German High Command.

(1) From the tactical point of view: increase of forces to enable the setting up of a robust line, withdrawing the mobile units to a second position. (Two divisions.)

(2) From the operational point of view: the assurance of supplies and the creation of strong defence in Calabria and Apulia in Southern Italy.

(3) From the organizational point of view: a rigorous application of measures to give full liberty and control to the military authorities in Southern Italy, in order to organize and make full use of the airfields, railways, roads, depots, etc. The war must be totalitarian, suppressing all private interests and everything devoted to the war and to defence.

Ambrosio added a fourth point. 'We have need of an adequate air force.' Keitel retorted, 'Only after everything has been directed in the sense of the above three points, can all the necessary material be sent to this sector.' But as regards the air force, seven air groups were on their way. In Southern Italy everything must be organized on a military basis and all civil activity placed under the command of the Italian Seventh Army. This was a necessary contribution towards victory. To facilitate the task of this organization the Germans were prepared to set up a liaison staff with the Seventh Army. It was naturally assumed that all orders were an Italian affair.

'If there is a perfect agreement on these three points, I do not doubt that the Fuehrer will make available as much as possible.' Here lay the essence of the German plan.

Keitel went on: 'There are only two alternatives: either to fight with every means to hold our positions in Sicily with the prospect of going over to the offensive, or if we do not intend to do this, it would be better not to send further reinforcements. This point must be cleared up as soon as possible . . . We can dispose of our two infantry divisions for the defence of Calabria, if the Italians do the same. But I repeat I cannot commit myself to obtain from the Fuehrer the dispatch of such divisions unless I have a formal undertaking from you on the three points which I have outlined.'

Ambrosio's answer was sharp. 'We have not such a luxury of divisions. Moreover I believe that we are considering possibilities too far ahead, while our situation requires absolute and urgent measures . . . I make the reservation of examining the question of the availability of our forces. As to the measures of a general and civilian character, the decision rests with the Duce.'

Keitel concluded by saying, 'It is necessary, however, for you to do everything to persuade him to take these measures. We too have had to make grave sacrifices: they are however needed on an even greater scale.'[18]

Rintelen has a summary account of this exchange between the two commanders. He describes Ambrosio as 'unforthcoming and monosyllabic', and adds that he protested again that the Italian Command was not allowed to dispose freely of the German divisions in Italy.[19]

The two leaders took leave of one another at Treviso airport at five o'clock that afternoon. They were not to meet again until the following September and then in revolutionized circumstances. The main cycle of the Axis closed with this encounter.

Mussolini's only later comment was: 'On parting from Hitler I said to him, "Ours is a common cause, Fuehrer." '[20] He then turned to Keitel and remarked, 'Send everything we require as quickly as you can and remember that we are in the same boat.'[21]

As Hitler's plane took off, the Duce stood with his arm raised at the salute and remained thus until the machine was out of sight. His advisers approached him on the runway. 'I had no need to make that speech to Hitler,' he said, 'because, this time, he has firmly promised to send all the reinforcements which we need.' And turning to Ambrosio, 'Naturally our requests must be reasonable and not astronomic.'

Ambrosio and Bastianini travelled in the same car from the airport to Treviso railway station. The former suddenly burst out, 'Did you hear what he said to Hitler after my warning of this morning? He asked him yet again for that war material which they will never send. He still deludes himself, and did not take my words seriously. He is mad, I tell you, mad. What I told him is serious, very serious.'[22]

All last minute hopes that Mussolini would take issue with his ally, demonstrate that Italy was at the end of her resources and seek an exit from the war with German consent, had now vanished. The Italian delegation had been subjected to a two-hour period of instruction in German, a language which they imperfectly understood. No simultaneous translation was made, although the familiar figure of Paul Schmidt, Hitler's personal interpreter, was present. He commented later on the conference: 'This meeting of July 20, 1943, was one of the most depressing in which I have ever taken part. Mussolini was so overwrought that on his return to Rome he asked urgently for my report: we were told that he had not been able to follow the conversation, and could therefore only consider the defensive measures agreed upon when he had my text before him. After Hitler had gone through the report in East Prussia, it was dispatched to the Duce by special plane.'

Rommel was present at these talks, and had spoken with the Duce. He noted that the latter gave no clear decisions, and 'cannot act as he would like . . . The Duce is aware of the political intentions of his collaborators.'[23]

This cryptic remark may throw some light on Bastianini's comments on Ambrosio's attitude at Feltre. 'This brusque change of front by the Chief of the General Staff, from the decision expressed in writing to fight to the finish to the fixing of a delay of fifteen days to withdraw from the conflict, did this neither alarm Mussolini nor make him suspicious? . . . Did it not cross his mind that this threatening ultimatum revealed the existence of an atmosphere of "pronunciamento" in high military circles?'[24]

Such an interpretation may be too subtle, and the fragmentary evidence which exists of these events does not show that, prior to the Feltre meeting, a date had been settled by the King for the dismissal of the Duce and his replacement by Badoglio, although this might have happened at the royal audience of July 16 or shortly afterwards.

But the general significance of the Feltre meeting is clear. The Duce in person bore the historical responsibility for the entry of Italy into the war. The Sicily landings marked the approaching end of that Italian participation. Unless, within a matter of days, a tidy formula could be devised releasing Italy from her obligations under the Axis alliance, approaching military defeat would be followed by the collapse of the régime. Only Mussolini could conduct such an operation with German consent. As he had said to Alfieri during the talks, 'Perhaps you think that he would give us liberty of action?' Indeed, it might be possible to convince the Germans that their own strategic interests lay in withdrawing their divisions intact from the whole Italian theatre, concentrating on the defence line of the Alps, and allowing Italy to treat with the Allies on the basis of neutralizing Italian territory. The future of the Duce's position in Italy depended on some such solution. The significance of the Feltre meeting was that no such formula could be reached or even discussed with Hitler. With this failure vanished any illusion about a tidy exit from the war.

APPENDIX

'The Politico-Military Conduct of the War by the Axis.

The politico-military conduct of the present war is characterized on the German side by a completely continental strategy and a total incomprehension of the decisive importance of the Mediterranean theatre.

In fact, apart from the episode of the air assault on England, and the battle of the Atlantic—to which can probably in the main be attributed a secondary role in favour of the battle for Northern Europe—the whole German effort has always and only been directed against the continental Powers (France—Norway—Russia).

A like tendency is shown by numerous points of fact which are briefly recapitulated:

1. *Armistice with France.*

The armistice with France was accepted only by taking into account the military necessities of Germany; this has been clearly admitted even in German circles. In fact, General Guderian in a *confidential* conversation with General Marras in April (1943) expressed himself thus. "In 1940 I had urged the Fuehrer to postpone the armistice: I could then have marched on Gibraltar and occupied North Africa with a couple of armoured divisions."

The occupation of French North Africa in 1940—a problem not difficult to solve, given the total lack of preparation of the British and the overwhelming superiority of the Germans—would have permitted the unbarring of the western door of the Mediterranean with the consequent incalculable advantage for the Axis of:

– having the maximum liberty of action in Africa (the possibility of occupying Egypt and of operating in the Middle East and Italian East Africa, and also of exploiting the anti-British ferment in Iraq, and among the Arab peoples.

– being able to save the main part of the forces and equipment committed to the defence of the southern frontiers of Europe, and avoiding the burdensome operation of conquest and subsequent occupation in the Balkans.

– exploiting all the resources of North Africa and the Middle East along the most economical sea route of the Mediterranean and without appreciable enemy interference.

– obtaining, perhaps, unforeseen developments of the conflicts in the direction of the Caucasus and India.

The justification (of the German view) that once France had fallen one could foresee the imminent conclusion of the war with England, and at least in a very brief space of time, does not hold. Official German circles, in fact, notwithstanding that they held this erroneous view, equally and rightly were concerned with occupying all the French Atlantic bases, up to the Pyrenees, for the requirements of an eventual continuation of the conflict.

2. *Armour for Italian North Africa.*

From 1940 onwards armoured equipment was requested for the Italian troops in Italian North Africa to put them in a condition to undertake a rapid offensive against the British forces in Egypt. The requests for material were not conceded, in spite of the fact that during the whole of the second half of 1940 and the first quarter of 1941 the German army was not engaged in any operations of war.

A few hundred tanks at that time would have probably been enough to occupy the zone of Suez.

3. *Relations with France.*

The relations with France, given the territorial conditions of the armistice (Mediterranean coast of France–Corsica–and French North Africa not occupied by the Axis) could but have direct and important repercussions on the conduct of the war in the Mediterranean theatre.

The attitude taken up by the Germans in such relations was sharply in contrast with that of the Italians, and often in contradiction to a rational conduct of the war: in fact,

(i) the various haphazard concessions in rearming French North and West Africa were made by the Germans in the main without taking into account the necessities of war in the Mediterranean theatre, and in opposition to the Italian point of view, which initially maintained the need:

– to strengthen Dakar to enable the French to defend themselves against British attacks, but without giving them the eventual possibility of using such material against the Axis;

– to be sparing, on the other hand, of concessions in favour of French North Africa, and especially of Tunisia;

– to pursue simultaneously a direct action to ensure the proper use of the material conceded: (removal of disloyal leaders, and principally of Weygand, for whose removal the Italian Armistice Control Commission had to fight a real battle against the German).

(ii) In December 1941 Italy, having realized that the attitude of wait-and-see which characterized the situation of France after the armistice could not last indefinitely, accepted at face value the good intentions of the French government to turn decisively in the direction of the Axis (Darlan-Vacca Maggiolini conversation in Vichy; declarations of Pétain: Ciano-Darlan meeting in Turin), and after careful consideration of the situation and of the French demands, decided to arrive at a regularizing of relations with France. (Verbal instructions from the Duce to Excellency Vacca Maggiolini.)

Such a solution, which must have brought about within a

short space of time the alignment of France on the side of the Axis powers, would have reversed the position in the Mediterranean, and eliminated the harm done by the conclusion of the armistice in 1940. (Contribution of the French fleet, completely loyal to Darlan—use of the first-class bases of French North Africa—liberty of movement in the Mediterranean.)

The German side, to whom the question was put by the Duce, not only refused to accept the Italian point of view, but with a sudden and completely unjustified change of course, adopted an attitude of rigid hostility towards France, making the continuation of negotiations impossible and bringing about the fall of Darlan and probably also, in the long term, his defection.

(iii) In examining the successive demands for strengthening French North Africa, the Italian side, who were henceforward convinced that the French, after the failure of their attempt to draw closer to the Axis, would never again collaborate with the Axis itself, logically took up an attitude, which if not decisively negative, was at least procrastinating. The Germans, however, sought by every means to meet French requests, declaring themselves convinced of the loyalty of the troops and commanders in French North Africa, notwithstanding the opposite Italian view . . .

4. *Occupation of Malta.*

In the winter of 1941–2, in order to resolve the burdensome problem of the Mediterranean and of supplies to Africa, Italy tackled the planning of the landing on Malta, notwithstanding her modest industrial potential.

The German side accepted the Italian point of view, and collaborated in a responsive manner in the air preparations for the operation and promised a notable assistance in the form of units and material to build up an Expeditionary Corps.

In May 1942, when faced with the chance of carrying out an offensive in Cyrenaica, the Italian Command tenaciously clung to the view that any initiative in Italian North Africa must be subordinated to the occupation of Malta with the aim of ensuring supplies for certain and being in a position to exploit to the full in the strategic field the eventual success of the initial battle.

The German side did not agree, and authorized Rommel to begin offensive operations which, after a brilliant initial victory, ran to ground at El Alamein, precisely from the impossibility of ensuring the necessary supplies.

In consequence of the advance on El Alamein, the German Command, in spite of the contrary view of the Italian, persisted in the conviction that the occupation of Malta was no longer necessary and that one must persist in the effort to reach the zone of Suez.

The Italian side, lacking the main air support which was part of the Expeditionary Corps (for Malta) and the petrol supplies, was obliged to accept the decision of the Ally and postpone *sine die* the operation for occupying Malta, the preparation of which was by then complete.

5. *Supplying of Italian North Africa.*

(i) In July 1941 Italy asked Germany for a loan of a milliard francs to be used mainly in buying various material in Tunisia for supplying the troops operating in Italian North Africa.

Germany, notwithstanding the fact that she was receiving 500,000,000 francs daily for expenses of occupation (in France), saw fit to refuse.

(ii) During the second British offensive against Libya, Italy began negotiations with the French regarding the use of Tunisian bases to supply the expeditionary force in Italian North Africa.

On that occasion also the Germans hindered the course of these negotiations by underhand manoeuvres, and openly declared that they did not wish to take part, although the question was also of interest for supplying the German troops.

(iii) And again, in order to avoid the serious consequences of failing to occupy Malta, the Italian side, following also on the experience of the El Alamein battles, insistently sought from Germany at least enough aircraft to gain sufficient control in the Mediterranean to keep within tolerable bounds the shipping losses between Italy and North Africa. The demands put forward in October, November, and December 1942 had no result.

6. *Reaction to the Anglo-American occupation of French North Africa.*

(i) During the Salzburg conference, in examining the counter-measures to be taken:

(a) Germany reverted to the mistaken idea . . . that a

threat to occupy the so-called "free" zone of Metropolitan France would be sufficient to compel the French in North Africa to resist eventual Anglo-American aggression and proposed as a solution to occupy the Free Zone and eventually Corsica, but completely neglecting Tunisia; only as the result of the clear and peremptory Italian attitude was it decided to occupy Tunisia, the firm possession of which, apart from allowing us to continue the war in Africa, would evidently also resolve automatically the problem of the other two theatres.

In actual practice, however, the Germans raised various difficulties and tried to obtain the constitution of an expeditionary corps, consisting only of German troops, with the evident aim of damaging Italy in a region clearly the object of our claims. Such a manoeuvre had the sole effect of delaying the Axis landing in Bizerta and Tunis by 2–3 days, with the consequent and considerable reduction of the initial bridgehead, all to the advantage of our opponents.

(b) The Duce also proposed and tenaciously stressed the expediency of seeking Spanish intervention to cut off at Gibraltar the supplying of the Anglo-American expeditionary force in Algeria.

The Germans, not being able to deny the appropriateness and sense of the operation from a military and political point of view, agreed in the first instance to the Italian proposal suggesting a meeting between Mussolini, Hitler, and Franco. At a second stage they changed their attitude, and came round to the idea of a meeting of two—Mussolini and Franco—which was the equivalent of a polite but clear refusal.

(ii) On a series of occasions (November and December '42, March and April '43) Italy renewed her urgent requests to Germany for air reinforcements to feed the battle in Tunisia. No request was completely and satisfactorily met.

7. *Defence of Italian Metropolitan territory. Second Front.*

As the course of the battle for Tunisia took shape, Italy became increasingly concerned with the strengthening of the defence of the Mother Country, and as the Anglo-American intention of attempting operations on a vast scale in the Mediterranean became apparent (opening of Second Front), she sought German aid in:

– aircraft, to balance the growing enemy air superiority;
– arms (tanks, artillery, trucks, etc.) and troops to put the

coastal defences of Italy in a state to face up to the expected massive enemy assault.

On such occasions we repeatedly pointed out to the Ally:

(a) the importance of the Mediterranean theatre, where having concentrated their main resources the Anglo-Americans were trying to open the Second Front, which if it succeeded would not only have deprived the Axis of the main chances of victory, but even of resistance;

(b) the need to put the defence of the sea frontiers of Italy in such a state as to meet the enemy attack even temporarily, to give time to the Axis reserves, which were ready in Germany, to hasten when needed to the battle zone (manoeuvre on interior lines).

Germany not only agreed partially and tardily to the request for troops and material to strengthen the coastal defences but, in spite of the specific appeals made personally by the Duce, took the initiative of new commitments in Russia whence she was obliged to send the reserves built up at home at the very moment when signs of an imminent landing in Italy were completely clear.

The decisions of the German High Command seem absurd even from a strictly military point of view. Indeed, on the basis of the experience of the campaigns of 1941–2, no decisive successes were foreseeable; whereas a victory in Sicily —an eventuality not improbable to achieve—would have inflicted such losses on the enemy as to make impossible another attempt in strength before the winter season or even the spring of 1944. To such a result must be added the favourable repercussions—also calculable in military terms—on the resistance of the home front, in occupied countries, in the neutral and in the allied countries themselves, repercussions which would be all the greater in view of Anglo-Saxon propaganda and the anxious awaiting of the announced Second Front.

8. *Various.*

(i) The responsible German agencies declared on numerous occasions that the solution of the actual conflict is bound up with the Russian—not with the Mediterranean—theatre.

(ii) In dealing with the problem of Spain, the Fuehrer asserted that he preferred to give arms to countries already fighting for the Axis (Roumania) rather than to those who might be able to fight in the future; which does not alter the fact that concessions of reinforcements to Italy, who was already fighting, were always a subject of haggling.

Arms and equipment were, however, conceded to Turkey, evidently because the Turkish problem directly impinged on the continental theatre.

(iii) The Germans neglected no opportunity to compete with the Italian economy in exploiting the occupied countries, and in utilizing the contribution of the minor allies, thus contributing to the weakening, if indirect, of the military possibilities of the Axis in the Mediterranean.

Although conclusive evidence is lacking, it is not to be excluded that Germany has, partially at least, followed an organic plan of despoiling Italy herself, by systematic purchase of valuable goods by troops in transit or stationed in the peninsula, who have been deliberately and generously supplied with Italian currency.

9. *Conclusion.*

It appears clear and indisputable, from what has been set out, that the Germans, in the conduct of the war, have never had a realistic and panoramic vision of the Axis war, but have let themselves be guided prevailingly by one particular aspect: namely, the German war.

The incomprehension and deliberate lack of appreciation of the importance of the Mediterranean theatre:

(a) can be explained, if not justified, in the politico-military situation of the years 1940–2, when the lack of preparation of the Anglo-Americans could leave out of account decisive enemy operations in the Mediterranean while the possibility existed of liquidating once and for all the Russian danger before the Anglo-Americans completed their preparations.

(b) find no explanation or justification in 1943, when the enemy preparations allowed one to foresee without difficulty that the Anglo-Americans would attempt an attack on the European fortress in the Mediterranean to open that second front whose realization implied almost certainly the military defeat of the Axis.'

CHAPTER FOUR

'Five Minutes to Twelve'

The Eve of the Grand Council

ON HIS RETURN from Feltre on the evening of July 19, Marshal Ambrosio drafted a summary of the military questions raised with the Germans at the meeting and on the train journey.

'The Fuehrer does not intend to send the 29th Armoured Division to Sicily, or the 3rd Motorized Division (which anyway is not ready) to Calabria or to move further German forces to Italy unless Italy undertakes a greater commitment in the war. She must therefore dispatch her infantry divisions to Sicily so that the German mobile forces, the 15th and Goering Divisions, can be withdrawn and placed in reserve; send two infantry divisions to Calabria to secure its defence; and, above all, remove all obstacles placed by civilian and private interests in the way of military action, concentrating all authority in Southern Italy in the hands of the Commander of the Italian Seventh Army. In such an event Marshal Keitel takes the view that he can get the Fuehrer to send two German infantry divisions.

'In more general terms, given the fact that the German forces will not be ready for two months and seeing that it is urgent to build up the defence of Southern Italy, it will be necessary to transfer at once the forces available in Northern Italy to the South, and namely Italian divisions, including the Alpine and those re-forming. They will then be replaced in due course by German divisions moving in.'

Ambrosio concluded his report. In answer to the 'well-known Italian point of view . . . the German side recognizes that the Second Front has opened in Italy, but has stated that it cannot send considerable air or armoured reinforcements, and has even made conditions for the dispatch of the minimal reinforcements available'. Ambrosio had already pointed out to Keitel that these conditions were for the Duce to decide.[1]

At noon on July 20, Ambrosio made his routine report to Mussolini, and the situation created by the Feltre talks was reviewed. A rejection of the German ultimatum, for such it was, would inexorably lead to a collapse of the whole Italian front, and with it the régime. An acceptance would imply ultimate German control over the threatened areas of Southern Italy, the *de facto* German military occupation in due course of the North on the pretext of organizing the defence of the Po Valley and the Alpine regions against an Allied landing in the Gulf of Genoa, and the inevitable infiltration of German influence into the Italian High Command and government itself. The decision was stark in its simplicity.

At Feltre, Ambrosio had pressed for the course of rejection and a withdrawal from the war in fifteen days. Mussolini told him calmly, 'I will now write to the Fuehrer to tell him what you in your aggressive statement yesterday represented as being in the interests of the country,' and took a sheet of notepaper to draft a letter asking to be released from the alliance. Ambrosio interjected that 'this could only have been achieved verbally at the Feltre meeting, and pressed his resignation. This was curtly rejected, and Ambrosio withdrew to his work.'[2]

That afternoon Rintelen called on the Duce at Palazzo Venezia, having received instructions from the German High Command to demand an answer to Keitel's 'three points' made on the train journey from Feltre. Ambrosio was present. 'Both had dark looks. The demands of the German War Office were accepted by the Duce. As we left Mussolini's study, Ambrosio explained to me that he had asked to resign.'[3] On the evening of July 21, Rintelen reported to Berlin that the Duce, in the presence of Ambrosio, had said that Sicily would be defended to the last man, but that 'those questions are still open'.[4] As Rintelen reported a few day later, 'In all authoritative military and political circles since the conversations of July 19 exists the overriding doubt whether Germany is in a position to give sufficient aid to Italy in her defensive struggle against invasion.'[5]

If Italy continued as a member of the Axis, the Germans could not prevent her military collapse. The Feltre meeting had demonstrated beyond doubt that Hitler would not discuss the withdrawal of Italy from the war. The essence of his ultimatum was the maintenance of Mussolini as the figurehead of the existing Fascist régime to cover the temporary and limited reinforcement of the Italian theatre, militarily to gain time to organize an orderly withdrawal to a tenable front against the Allies in Central Italy, and politically to take counter-measures against a threat of a coup d'état in Rome. Having thus forced certain military measures on Mussolini after the Feltre meeting, which might serve to delay the Allied invasion of the Italian mainland, what political precautions, if any, did the Germans take in the event of the threat of a coup d'état against the Duce?

On July 19 Himmler had written to Bormann a letter enclosing a message from Rome. 'I have received the following report from reliable sources. It comes with absolute certainty from the circles of the Committee of Five and I would ask you as soon as possible to bring it before the Fuehrer . . . Thanks to Italian circles friendly to the Axis, a counter-movement to resist these developments has been set up in a loosely organized form . . . Riccardi has been designated as the leading figure. The movement is directed by a Committee of Five. . . . This counter-movement aims at setting up a War Cabinet to carry out an anti-Freemason, anti-Jewish, and pro-German policy, the radical exclusion of traitors of every kind, the reconstruction of the Fascist Grand Council in permanent session, the creation of a unified military command for the Axis forces. They seek German support for putting the Duce completely in the picture, with the aim of immediate granting of full powers to Riccardi, together with one of his above-named collaborators.'[6] The name of Riccardi occurs frequently in German Intelligence reports from Rome. As Minister of Exchange and Currency from 1939 to February 1943, he had been involved heavily in financial dealings with the German authorities. After his dismissal he seems to have been one of the leading German informers in Italian circles, but in event of an extreme Fascist administration he had not the stature to head a government. The leading specialist in crisis situations, and also a member of this group, was Farinacci, as at the time of the murder of Matteotti in 1924.

On the afternoon of July 21 Farinacci requested an interview with the German Ambassador. He wished to 'speak out openly on the internal situation' and inform Mackensen 'about certain inner political events which have happened here during the last week'. Marshal Cavallero accompanied Farinacci 'as a friend . . . and almost exclusively as a listener'. Farinacci began by describing the meeting of the Party leaders with Mussolini on July 16. Joint proposals had been made to the Duce 'on the inadmissibility of the present methods of government, and at the same time pointing out that it was five minutes to twelve'. Farinacci and the others had been assured by Mussolini that the three Service ministries, in Farinacci's view the most important, 'would be filled with their own ministers, and that the Grand Council would be summoned by the end of the week'.

The conversation with the German Ambassador turned to the Feltre talks. Farinacci had learnt the results in general terms from Scorza, who had been told by Mussolini, but 'his information referred only to that part in which there had been talk of the extent of eventual German aid'. At this point Mackensen interrupted to say 'that in view of the confidence which I enjoy of the Duce and Bastianini, which is the . . . basis of my work, I must naturally inform Bastianini of the content of this conversation, and also I must ask him (Farinacci), when criticizing the person of the Duce, not to forget that I was not only his personal friend but in the first instance the representative of the Fuehrer'. Farinacci answered that he would take this into account, but that in the situation in which Italy found herself today, he must nevertheless speak openly, as he wished the Fuehrer to see clearly the real attitude of Fascism which he and his friends represented. Mackensen then added his version of the Feltre meeting. 'The Fuehrer had not made any "conditions" to the Duce, but had sketched out plainly the prerequisites which must be fulfilled before German military help would make any sense, and only after that could it naturally be achieved. And in the first instance, that our troops stationed in Italy should not have difficulties placed in their way in regard to their installations, air bases, quarters, etc. from the Italian side by Prefects, Federal Secretaries, or mayors. Only a radical change in this respect, a removal of all bureaucratic frictions, and a rigorous supervision of the Duce's orders could bring about a change.' In developing his thoughts on this theme, Farinacci spoke in a manner 'which almost word for word corresponded with what the Fuehrer told the Duce at Feltre, and what the Fuehrer mentioned to me at his Headquarters'.

The main purpose of the interview was now unfolded. Farinacci 'produced the idea, not of a directorate, but of one man, with absolute powers to issue decrees, a sort of Minister of the three Armed Forces . . . My conception of what we would call a battle headquarters he seized on with enthusiasm and thought that this was the only right solution.'

In a swift analysis of the political scene Farinacci scattered a handful of judgments. The King was 'indissolubly bound to the Duce by conviction'. Next to the Crown Prince was 'a small question mark'. Badoglio was 'absolutely against the Duce'. Grandi 'hoped to count for something by holding back', and Ciano was 'politically finished'. Farinacci then attacked the Italian Army and in particular the officer corps in a destructive way which was 'completely in line with that of the Fuehrer'. Up to this point Cavallero had not uttered a word, and now made his only contribution to the dialogue. He 'thought, although he was hesitant, that one must make reservations, but this did not alter anything, for he too recognized that in this matter much, if not all, needs overhauling'.[7]

From this conversation, and from other reports, Mackensen formed a particular impression of the Roman crisis, namely that an energetic group represented by Farinacci in the higher ranks of the Party, and in league with Cavellero, had forced a meeting of the Grand Council which would call for the same basic military and administrative reforms as Hitler had pressed at Feltre. This action would be the decisive element in the next days, and, if all went according to plan, might provide the political counterpart to the military measures now being taken by the German General Staff.

A curious passivity henceforward overtakes German action in Italy, almost as if their plans were prepared for every eventuality. A strange leaking of Hitler's thoughts at this moment reached the circles of the clandestine German opposition. Just after Feltre Goerdeler wrote to Field Marshal von Kluge, 'Hitler has told his entourage that his aim is the partition of Italy. In the end, he said, Mussolini will be forced to turn to him and perhaps he will make him governor of Northern Italy and make the Apennines the German Frontier.'[8] This was a startling and unconscious prophecy.

The troop movements requested in Keitel's ultimatum on July 19 to Ambrosio would provide the immediate delaying action against Allied invasion in the South and, in the second stage, lead to the transfer of Italian divisions to Calabria from the North where they would be replaced by Rommel's new Army Group now in formation with the ultimate task of reconstructing the German front in Central Italy. Such measures would also ensure the taking over of Italian military commitments on Italian metropolitan territory in the event of a sudden collapse or coup d'état. It is also significant that 'for reasons of the impressions gained at Feltre' Jodl had ordered that the preliminary alert for operations 'Alaric' and 'Konstantin' should be called off.[9]

This complacency seemed justified when on July 22 Ambrosio formally requested the dispatch of the two German divisions to Northern Italy and the transfer of the 29th Motorized Division from Calabria to Sicily, stressing that 'it is indispensable that the German reinforcements sent into Italy be freely employed by the Italian High Command'.[10] These German troop movements began on July 23.

On July 21 Rommel had been suddenly switched from his skeleton command in Southern Germany, pending the setting-up of the German Army Group in North Italy, to take up the defence of Greece and the Aegean islands. The general assumption of German military planning had been that a major crisis in Italy would be followed on the Allied side by a landing in South-Eastern Europe.

'Already on July 19 the King conveyed to us (*sic*) the decision to liquidate Mussolini.'[11] Ambrosio had returned from Feltre only that evening, and had driven from the station with Colonel Montezemolo, the liaison officer of the Italian War Office with the High Command, to his office in the War Ministry. There is no record of any audience with the King that evening. It is however significant that the King later stated that when he received Mussolini to hear his version, he 'already knew of the conversation at Feltre from what both General Ambrosio and Colonel Montezemolo had reported to me'.[12] The mention of the latter suggests that the two men drove direct from the station to be received by the King on the evening of July 19, and that during the conversation the latter did make at least a preliminary decision, and that in any event he seems to have made up his mind to act by the time he saw the Duce on July 22, and had planned to arrest him after the next routine audience on July 26.

Before going to report to Mussolini the following morning, Ambrosio received a visit from the Prince of Piedmont, and, perhaps more significantly, in the late afternoon Acquarone came to the War Ministry.[13]

On July 19, the day of the bombardment of Rome and the return from Feltre, in Anfuso's words, 'the conspiracy took definite shape: each character put on his mask and came onto the stage'.[14]

The news had seeped round Rome that the summit conference had produced no lightning and magic formula. A buzz of activity followed. Early on July 21, Bottai called on Farinacci at his hotel and both men went to seek out Bastianini in his office to learn what had been the outcome of the meeting with the Germans. The description was discouraging. 'An atmosphere of embarrassment, uneasiness and ambiguity had hung over the talks.' There was no sign from above. Bottai, who saw Scorza later in the day, records that the Party Secretary 'is waiting for Mussolini to confirm the meeting of the Grand Council and fix the date. He tells me that the boss has shown no critical reaction to the démarche of the sixteenth.'

Grandi had hitherto kept aloof in Bologna from the Roman arena. He had refused to attend the meeting of Party leaders on July 16 in spite of an angry telegraphic summons from Mussolini 'to justify his refusal to obey'. While in Bologna Grandi had drafted a series of papers. He first sent a private letter to General Puntoni after the Sicily landings. 'Almost a hundred years to a day since a great King of Piedmont promulgated the Statute of the Realm and drew his sword to give Italy liberty, unity and independence, the fatherland is running towards defeat and dishonour.' He then wrote two letters 'of equal tenor' to the King and to Mussolini enclosing the substance of his ultimate motion submitted to the Grand Council, whose summoning had been accepted by the latter on July 16.

The essence of Grandi's 'Programme' as now outlined was twofold: firstly, a thorough reform of the conduct of national affairs by reconstituting and resuscitating the existing organs of government. The Chamber, the Council of Ministers, the various Ministries, and above all the Grand Council itself must be allowed to function. The personal rule of one man had destroyed the administrative process, as both Cini and De Marsico had already pointed out at the meeting of the Council of Ministers on June 19. Secondly, the military conduct of the war must be separated from the control of political affairs and must revert to where it theoretically lay, until usurped by the Duce in 1940, to the Crown.

Federzoni was also at that time in Bologna, and the two men consulted together before leaving for the capital. Grandi now decided to return to Rome and enter the political arena which he had been avoiding since June.

On the morning of July 21 he called on Scorza, who told him that Mussolini, 'descending from the train' on his return from Feltre had ordered the Party Secretary to summon the Grand Council for July 24. During this talk at Scorza's office it seems that Grandi gave him the draft text of his motion, for according to Mussolini the latter received the Party Secretary the same morning at the hour of the usual report, and was handed a copy. 'I read the document—a pretty long one of more than three pages—and handed it back to Scorza declaring that the document was inadmissible and contemptible. Scorza put it back in his briefcase and did not insist further. It was on this occasion that Scorza made me a rather ambiguous speech in which he spoke of a "shocker" or "super-shocker" which might be in store, a speech to which I did not attribute great importance.'[15]

Grandi's document was in no sense revolutionary, and his solution was deceptively simple. It was the spirit of application, not the structure, of the Fascist State which was at fault. The régime was out of joint because of the political method, or lack of method, of the Duce. If he could not be persuaded of this, the only incalculable and untried sanction was the royal prerogative, and for its use there was no precedent in the twenty years of Fascist history. And here Grandi was as much at a loss as everyone else, and in the end equally deluded. With deliberate calculation, and using all his political capital, he set to work to rally support for his project, not as a conspirator, but essentially as a politician. He left Scorza's office at midday, and went first to Federzoni's house where he also found Bottai. 'We all three thought alike. There was no need of discussion.'

Grandi's next move was to make a final attempt to persuade the Duce to accept his proposals, either after debate in the Grand Council, or without summoning that body at all. Grandi had never pressed for its summoning, presumably because of the danger of giving a focus to the Party machine either under the leadership of Scorza or Farinacci or both. The Grand Council was also the traditional forum where Mussolini asserted his personal authority over the leaders of the régime. Grandi's later thesis was that the final summons was only sanctioned after Mussolini had talked to Hitler and that it was the latter who provoked this step by referring to the 'treachery' of many members of the Grand Council. It was thus the Germans who were ultimately responsible for the meeting, and their real motives were to supply the setting for a dramatic move by Farinacci to initiate the German 'plan' for Italy as conceived at the Feltre meeting, and face the Duce with a *fait accompli*.

At five o'clock that afternoon (July 24) Grandi was received at Palazzo Venezia. The formal pretext for the interview was for Grandi to hand to the Duce a copy of a book on the London Non-Intervention Committee during the Spanish Civil War. On arrival, Grandi was shown by the usher the list of appointments: he was allotted twenty minutes. As he passed through the ante-room, which was the Grand Council room, and where the chairs were already arranged for the forthcoming meeting, Grandi was aware of a senior German officer seated. The usher explained that he was Field Marshal Kesselring, who would be received next by the Duce for a lengthy interview.

According to the Duce, in this conversation 'Grandi touched on various points, but said nothing of what was to come'.[16] Grandi has recorded that the ensuing conversation, which lasted 'at least three-quarters of an hour' was not stormy as subsequently alleged. 'I told Mussolini everything that I had to tell him, and which I later repeated to him in front of the Grand Council.' He listened patiently and at the end said in quiet tones, 'You would be right if the war had been lost.' The Germans would produce a secret weapon which would revolutionize the situation. Grandi then asked him to renounce the idea of summoning the Grand Council, and to carry out of his own free will the proposals put forward in the draft motion. At this point Mussolini hardened. 'I will not hand over the reins of command to anyone.' Grandi took his leave. It was the last time the two men were to meet alone.

There is little further evidence of this key conversation. Giacomo Acerbo, Minister of Finance, stated that 'at Palazzo Venezia I met Grandi just as he was leaving the Duce's office, and he confirmed to me that the latter, albeit with clenched teeth, had authorized the presentation of the motion'.[17] That evening Bottai noted in his diary: 'I returned to see Grandi who had just come back from Palazzo Venezia, where he had found Mussolini "roused like a lion but not too much so". He was able to talk to him and say some tough things. He had above all narrowed him down to the argument of a national government, and the complete return of the King to the command of the Armed Forces.'[18]

The next day Kesselring informed the German Ambassador of Grandi's visit. 'Field Marshal Kesselring tells me that when he called on the Duce yesterday (July 21) he had to wait a long time as Grandi was with him. This latter interview lasted at least three-quarters of an hour. The Duce apologized for the delay due to receiving Grandi, whom he described as a "trustworthy man". In connection with what Farinacci told me yesterday, although Grandi has been called upon by him to take part in a joint approach to the Duce, he had kept away and excused himself on the grounds of ill-health. This interview of Grandi with the Duce seems to me to be highly significant.'

This 'significance', and the danger from the German point of view, might well be a repetition of Mussolini's tactics of a 'Changing of the Guard', as in the previous February, but with the contrary object of forming an administration to seek a 'political' solution of the war. Grandi in such a case might be the obvious Foreign Minister.

Action by Farinacci and his friends was a matter of increasing urgency. In concluding his telegram to Ribbentrop, Mackensen wrote perhaps rather plaintively, 'The summoning of the Grand Council has, as far as I know up to the present moment, not yet taken place.'

It does not appear that Mussolini asked for, nor had the King proposed, a special royal audience after his return from Feltre, and he was received as a matter of routine on the morning of Thursday, July 22. Since coming to power twenty years before, he had been received in audience by the Sovereign at the Quirinal every Monday and Thursday. During recent months both men seemed to have avoided the mutual embarrassment of a serious discussion of the looming crisis. As Alfieri wrote, 'In such a manner a neutral zone between the King and the Duce had come into being which each for contrary reasons did not wish to cross.'[19]

Mussolini found the King 'frowning and nervous. "A tense situation," he said. "It cannot go on much longer . . . We must tell the Germans our dilemma."' The King stated later that Mussolini 'came to talk to me . . . I listened to the account of the Prime Minister. At Feltre Hitler had done almost all the talking in order to prove that the war was not lost. I observed that the Germans in Russia, in Africa, and also in

Sicily, without any regard to the Pact or to honour, had retreated and left us in the lurch whenever it seemed to them the right moment. The situation in Italy was such that the dilemma must be put to the Germans . . . I prefer to avoid ruin and distress to my country, rather than sacrifice everything to a now useless resistance . . . Mussolini started talking to me of the German secret weapons. I interrupted him: "The best secret weapons are those which are best known." He took leave of me. The rest is known.' Puntoni records that he found the King, after Mussolini's departure, 'dark in the face and frowning. At first he seemed to find it difficult to speak and then finally, as if to free himself from a weight which oppressed him, he said: "I tried to make the Duce understand that it was his person, which was not only the target of enemy propaganda, but also was aimed at by public opinion, which prevented an internal recovery, and called in question a precise definition of our military situation. He did not understand or did not wish to do so. It was as if I was talking to the wind."'[20]

The formal invitations to the Grand Council for Sunday, July 24, had been issued the previous day from Fascist Party headquarters, and Grandi and his friends had exactly two days to complete their political action. The intention was to gain the support of the majority of the members of the Grand Council before the meeting. The inner group agreed on a more simple draft of the motion, and the collection of signatures began. Grandi went from his meeting with the Duce to call on Scorza. He announced that he would present his motion, and returned to his friends, Ciano, Bottai, Federzoni, and others. Scorza was kept informed of their conclaves and their intentions. De Marsico, the Minister of Justice, called on Grandi that evening, and brought his legal knowledge to bear on the redrafting of the document.

On the morning of July 23, there was much coming and going at the Party Headquarters in Palazzo Wedekind. Towards midday Grandi arrived with Bottai, and there they found Ciano in discussion with the Party Secretary. Ciano stated later, during his interrogation before his trial, 'I found him (Scorza) somewhat preoccupied and depressed; he thought that the situation was grave, but believed nevertheless that on the home front the Party had sufficient forces and means to control it. During the conversation Grandi arrived and spoke of the need to raise national morale and referred to a motion which he had drafted and to which in principle several comrades had agreed, among them Federzoni.'[21]

The arrival of Farinacci at Party Headquarters struck a different note, and brought back memories of past internecine strife within the Fascist ruling clan. The boss of Cremona had always been an untouchable. His conception of Fascism as a permanent revolution had nothing in common with the 'constitutional' version of Grandi, Federzoni, and Bottai. His presence was embarrassing at this moment, as his close connections with the German Embassy and agencies in Rome were no secret, and, for tactical reasons, Grandi and his friends were not anxious to reveal in their present political move any hint at this stage of disloyalty to the Axis. Their formal programme was one of political and military reconstruction in order to carry on the war. As Bottai notes: 'We all sensed the meaning and limits of his (Farinacci's) approval, which was understood as solidarity *jusqu'au bout* with the Germans.'[22] Farinacci was not fooled, and in any event had his own solution. At his house on July 22, after his talk with the German Ambassador, he had, together with Cavallero, drafted a motion which he in his turn intended to produce at the Grand Council.[23] He was by now aware of the text of Grandi's draft and may even have agreed to sign it, perhaps as a deception. There is no evidence to show that he revealed his present intention. The wording of his draft, which followed that of Grandi in nominally calling on the King to assume command of the Armed Forces, concentrated on 'standing fast in the observance of the alliances concluded, and the restoration of all the organs of State', including the Party and Corporations, omitted in Grandi's draft.

Farinacci's private tactics were planned in advance. He would force the dismissal of Ambrosio and the recall, on the very evening of the Grand Council meeting, of Cavallero as Chief of the General Staff. Farinacci himself would be nominated as Minister of the Interior, and the 'defeatist' Party bosses, or at least Grandi, would be arrested.

On July 17 Ciano had returned, like Grandi from Bologna, from a diplomatic retreat at his family home in Leghorn. The two men now spent that afternoon together with Bottai, retouching the draft, first in Grandi's office and then at Bottai's house. It was there that Ciano formally adhered to their plan of procedure. He thought that the Grand Council was not the effective place for such an ultimatum 'as its composition was not purely political', but realized that 'the day would be decisive for us all'.[24] His rôle during these hours is not clarified by the available evidence. Anfuso, who had arrived in Rome during the Allied bombardment of July 19, called shortly afterwards on Ciano, who had been watching the air attack. 'He was at home with a political ailment, attached to the many threads of numerous conspiracies.' The house was invaded by numerous Princesses and Countesses. At one point Cini arrived and disappeared in private conclave with Ciano. On departing, the former—by way of explanation—said that Mussolini was mad, and that one must have the courage to remove him. Amid the bustle of visitors, Ciano took Anfuso to one side. 'You don't understand that everything is finished. I cannot tell you anything, but you must understand.'[25]

The final meeting of the group was at Grandi's office on the following morning, July 24. Scorza had been sent a copy of the final draft of the motion. Farinacci arrived, and appeared to agree with everything except freer powers to the King. Alfieri, the Italian Ambassador in Berlin, had been summoned by Scorza to Rome. He too accepted without reserve the line taken in Grandi's document. Other signatures were canvassed. Cianetti, the Minister of Agriculture, came and expressed his agreement. Cianetti's later account of this scene reads: 'Grandi said to me textually, "Dear Cianetti, it is a matter of liberating the Duce from the total responsibility of the conduct of the war; the monarchy to which *we* have given lustre and ornament must be implicated."'[26] Federzoni had sounded out the 'Old Guard', De Vecchi and De Stefani. They too agreed, but did not actually sign.

Shortly after his arrival in Rome, Grandi was invited to call on Acquarone, but decided that he would not do so until after the meeting of the Grand Council. Grandi now sent his friend, Mario Zamboni, to explain his refusal. 'What we are preparing to do in the Grand Council is most dangerous, and for that reason we do not wish to expose the Crown. Our aim is to furnish the King with the "constitutional clue" which the Sovereign has always declared to be the indispensable condition to induce him to act. We do not intend to "conspire" with the Court, still less with the Army. The generals will never take any initiative except after the King has ordered them to do so. The key to everything is the King alone.'

On July 24, an hour before the meeting of the Grand Council, Zamboni again called on Acquarone to hand him a letter from Grandi to the King, and a copy of the text of the motion to be presented at the session. 'I have the honour to inform your Majesty that I shall be leaving shortly for Palazzo Venezia to submit to the Grand Council the enclosed motion, the text of which I would ask Your Majesty to read . . . I do not know whether the initiative, taken in agreement with other members, will have a majority of those assembled. We have thought fit to undertake the extreme attempt to postulate the constitutional conditions for a restoration of the statutory guarantees and of the prerogatives of the Sovereign.'

The events of July 23, culminating in the discussions at the Party Headquarters on Grandi's draft motion, had created a deceptive atmosphere of unanimity in the higher circles of the Fascist Party. Scorza found himself sponsoring a political move of national importance, which reached far beyond the responsibilities of the Party secretariat, and had given the impression to the younger Party bosses, such as Bignardi, that the official leadership of the Party was backing Grandi, and even with Mussolini's knowledge.

About 8.30 p.m. that evening, he called to his office the four Vice-Secretaries of the Party and one of them has put down the gist of his remarks: 'You have seen in these last days that there has been much coming and going of Party bosses and high personages here at Party Headquarters. I tell you at once that some of them are thinking in terms of replacing the Duce. Well, I have told Grandi, who is the exponent of this group, that I do not take any part in their plan. To me, the idea of replacement of the Duce only aggravates the situation. For the moment they have all kept away from Party Headquarters, and from me. You will have noticed that since yesterday morning none of them has been seen here. Now as in the face of every eventuality it is as well if each of us assumes his own precise responsibility, I have prepared my own motion which nobody knows about, not even the Duce, and I shall take it on myself to present it tomorrow at the meeting of the Grand Council. I shall read it to you as I want to know the opinion of each of you.'[27]

This text, the third now to be presented at the forthcoming meeting, was composed in the vacuous phraseology of Party manifestos, but is of perplexing interest as throwing some light on Scorza's own reactions to the pending crisis of the régime. 'The Grand Council is convinced that the new situation created by the events of the war must be faced by new methods, and means.' It was urgent to carry out 'these reforms and innovations . . . in the Government, in the Supreme Command, and in the country's internal life'. The Grand Council 'salutes in His Majesty the King . . . the symbol and strength of the continuity of the nation'. There was in Scorza's draft, and most significantly, no reference to handing over military powers to the Crown.

The four Party officials expressed unanimous agreement and the following morning (July 24) signed a declaration to that effect. In the meantime Scorza had apparently seen Mussolini, who said that he was prepared to announce during his opening report at the Grand Council the reforms and innovations which Scorza had in mind.

The ultimate defence of the régime had lain for twenty years with the Party and its armed embodiment, the Militia. The rumours of plots were everywhere. Scorza himself told the Duce of one particular report of a secret meeting of generals at which it had been decided to arrest Mussolini and place Badoglio in his stead. The Duce had commented, 'Don't produce detective stories.' It was nevertheless the duty of the Party to take counteraction, and make recommendations to the Duce.

Reliable evidence pointed to Ambrosio as the central figure in the coalescing conspiracy against Fascism. At a secret meeting of selected Party bosses on July 22 his removal was discussed. Scorza had suggested the name of Graziani, Badoglio's predecessor as Chief of the General Staff in 1940 to replace him. One of those present, Alessandro Melchiorri, was instructed to sound the Marshal through the latter's private secretary. It appears that Graziani came to Rome on the morning of July 24, and through these intermediaries it was agreed that he should hold himself at the disposal of the Duce. Melchiorri drafted a letter to be sent to De Cesare, the head of Mussolini's private office, before the meeting of the Grand Council. The pretext of this approach was that the writer 'had heard mention of Graziani visiting the King and meeting or coming to some agreement with Badoglio'. This information had probably been given to the Chief of Police in good faith because one of the very few persons whom Graziani visited lived opposite Badoglio's house and another near the royal Villa Savoia. Graziani denied that any such meetings had taken place, and Badoglio he 'considers as his worst enemy.' He also told Melchiorri that should the Duce think it necessary or suitable, Graziani would always be at Mussolini's orders, and in a postscript hastily added to this letter Melchiorri wrote that Graziani 'still hopes that the war might be brought to a favourable conclusion', but it must be 'an honourable one'.

The nomination of Graziani to succeed Ambrosio may have been the main item in Scorza's 'plan', and Mussolini was aware of this possible card before the meeting and also that Scorza intended to propose it under certain conditions at the Grand Council.

Each party had in fact his military figure: the King with Badoglio, Grandi with Caviglia, and now perhaps Mussolini with Graziani.

The Duce was aware of the manoeuvres developing around him. He knew of Grandi's motion and of the currents of opinion within the Party. On the evening of July 23, Chierici, the Chief of Police, informed him of the contacts between the various members of the Grand Council and gave his opinion that Grandi's motion had probably already the support of the majority of the votes. He had been warned of conspiracies round every corner, at Court, within the General Staff. He had received similar reports for twenty years from the police, old Party members and by anonymous denunciation. The history of Fascism is shadowed by the perpetual theme of treason within and outside the régime. In such admonitions the specialist was Farinacci, with his favourite theme of 'the traitors of the General Staff'.

As Melchiorri had also written in his letter of July 24, 'Marshal Badoglio has declared that he is not a Mexican General and will not act as such. This statement should be taken to mean, according to Graziani, that Badoglio will not carry out a piazza revolution in Mexican style, but will act or attempt to act constitutionally since most of the General Staff are for him and he hopes for the support of the House of Savoy.' This proved to be an accurate forecast.

It seems that, according to the Duce, Grandi was hesitant and alarmed during the last hours. 'There was much coming and going in Piazza Colonna, where the Party Headquarters was housed in Palazzo Wedekind, on Thursday and Friday (July 22 and 23). At a certain point Grandi put forward the idea of postponing the Grand Council—a clever move to look like an alibi. Scorza telephoned to know if this were a possibility. I replied that it was now absolutely essential to reach a general clarification of the position. The date had been fixed. The invitations had been issued. Of all the constitutional organs the convening of which was envisaged that week, the Chamber or the Senate, the Grand Council was the most suitable for reviewing the problems of the war in the light of recent events such as the invasion of national soil.'[28]

Mussolini himself was calm, and as always at such a moment, in splendid isolation. The German Ambassador saw him for what was to be the last time on July 23. 'My interview with the Duce, in order to hand over the transcript of the Fuehrer-Duce conversation (at Feltre) only took place at midnight owing to the Duce's heavy commitments with the recent political crisis and then owing to an air-raid alarm. The Duce thanked me for transmitting the text, read through several passages, and then remarked that he thought that it was an almost exact stenographic record of the Fuehrer's remarks. He then embarked on a long explanation, referring to a map of Sicily, of the military situation which showed clearly how much the statement of the Fuehrer had impressed him. In describing . . . the prerequisites for a successful stand in Sicily he used expressions which were identical with those employed by the Fuehrer on this theme. This time his still very exaggerated estimate of the fighting value of the Italian divisions was noticeably different. The calm, assured, and confident way in which the Duce spoke in no way revealed that in internal politics he was in the middle of the gravest crisis with which the régime had been faced since Matteotti.'[29]

In the early hours of the same morning, Mackensen sent another telegram. 'In connection with the grave crisis through which the Fascist leadership is passing, the far-reaching importance of which is confirmed by Farinacci's communications to me, and from other reliable quarters, it seems to me highly significant that the Duce should receive Grandi in a long audience. He is a man whose attitude for a long time has been deliberately impenetrable in a situation which has been resolved by the collective move of Farinacci, Bottai, etc. He will not identify himself with the Farinacci group, although no lesser person than the Party Secretary, Scorza, belongs to it. It is not only my own opinion that the Duce under certain conditions wants to make use of Grandi in order to try to get out of a highly unpleasant situation, otherwise than by yielding to the Farinacci group. One of the main demands of this group he has in the meantime fulfilled. I hear from the best sources that he has summoned the Grand Council for tomorrow, Saturday.'

The German analysis assumed throughout that the initiative at the coming critical meeting of the leaders of the régime lay in the hands of Farinacci and his friends. 'The efforts of the group extend to producing not only ministers who will think and act for themselves, and not simply carry out the Duce's orders, which are not always based on complete information and thus lead to wrong decisions, but also who will administer their departments in a responsible manner on the basis of expert knowledge and the use of all sources of information.'[30]

The same day Rintelen telegraphed to the German War Ministry: 'The Fascist Grand Council meets on July 24. This session is being held under circumstances of great importance. It is rumoured that a group of the Council will demand a stronger and more energetic leadership of the State. There is talk that the Duce will be obliged to give up the personal control of the Ministries of the Armed Forces.'[31]

In the closed circles of the Italian Court and the High Command the preliminary technical plans to meet the possible consequences of the dismissal of the Duce by the King had reached their final phase.

According to the former Police Chief, Senise, he had received a summons to call on Acquarone, apparently on the afternoon of July 19. For his own personal curiosity Acquarone asked for his view 'of the evident aspirations of the opposition Fascists like Grandi, Ciano, and Bottai, to take over the succession of Mussolini'. Senise thought that there could be no question of such an administration. Acquarone then asked how the Party and Militia would behave when faced with a Royal decision. The answer was that 'as for the Party, it would be enough to proceed with its dissolution without fear of any eventual resistance by the Fascists . . . The state of mind of the Militia was roughly that of the Party, but it would be dangerous to disperse armed men to their homes, and the best plan would be to incorporate all units into the Army under an energetic general.' Acquarone enquired what attitude should be adopted towards Mussolini at the moment of his dismissal from office. Senise replied that the King must summon the Duce to the Quirinal where the latter must be arrested 'within the Palace itself'. To allow him to leave the building 'would constitute a serious threat to public order and the security of the country'.

It appeared from this conversation that Acquarone touched on the composition of the administration which would replace the Duce. Senise claims that it was he who at this stage suggested consulting the veteran Prime Minister of the First World War, Vittorio Emanuele Orlando. Two days later, on July 21, Acquarone again sent for Senise, and told him that the King had decided 'to carry out the coup d'état'. Badoglio would head the new government, which would consist of senior officers and civil servants. The Germans were to be told that Italy would continue the war. The King wished Senise to take over the Ministry of the Interior, but the latter refused and it was agreed that he should resume his old post of Chief of Police.

The technical planning of the coup d'état, which had already been studied for months past, was to be the responsibility of Senise. This was to include measures for the arrest of the Duce, the occupation of the Central Telephone Exchanges, the dissolution of the Fascist Party, the incorporation of the Militia in the Army, and the possible call-up of the railway and postal workers. Senise, however, insisted that the arrest of the Duce must be carried out not by the Police, 'being still under the order of Chierici, who certainly cannot be brought into things', but by the Military Police, as this must be the responsibility of the new government, and technically Senise was not even an official on active duty. The list of Fascist leaders to be arrested had been drawn up for some time, and the other measures also envisaged could be handled by the Police. It was agreed that the two men should meet again 'within a few days'. That afternoon Senise received a message from Acquarone telling him to be ready by July 25.[32]

According to Castellano, Acquarone had told him on July 20 that the King had decided to bring in Badoglio 'within six or seven days'. The Duce would probably be arrested at the customary royal audience on Monday, July 26. With a delicate sense of legality Senise would not, as he had explained to Acquarone, have this operation carried out by the Police.

The element of force must therefore be found in the Military Police, the traditionally monarchist and Piedmontese body linked to the structure of pre-Fascist Italy. Their commander since February–General Hazon–had been close to the Court since the outbreak of war. He was however killed in the Allied air-raid on Rome on July 19. There was a hasty search for a successor. General Angelo Cerica from the Forest Militia was nominated. The new commander, who was on leave near Florence, only took up his duties on July 22. He was immediately approached by Ambrosio the following morning, and according to Castellano, the details of the Duce's arrest were worked out.

In addition to the rôle of the Military Police, certain precautions against a possible Fascist counter-coup were taken by the Army. General Roatta, the Chief of the Army Staff, had already been warned by Ambrosio at the time of his appointment in early June, of an imminent change of government. 'Just before the meeting of the Grand Council, he was taken on one side by Ambrosio after a conference of the Chiefs of Staff, at which he made no reference to such questions, and ordered to bring into Rome certain mobile units "already designated".'[33]

On July 21, General Carboni, the enterprising and ambitious young General who had been 'launched' by Ciano in the campaign preceding the dismissal of Cavallero, was appointed to command a Motorized Corps in the process of being formed near Rome, with the mission to defend the capital against any German-inspired Fascist counter-measures. The following evening, at the routine meeting of the Italian Chiefs of Staff, Ambrosio gave the following formal order: 'To ensure the defence of the capital against eventual landing attempts, certain units in Lazio (the province adjacent to the capital) are to be brought nearer to Rome.'[34] For reasons of security Ambrosio had been giving verbal orders since July 10 at these meetings. After Feltre it was planned to concentrate the three divisions which constituted the Motorized Corps, now under Carboni, round Rome, and this move had precedence over all others 'including defence against the Anglo-Americans'.[35]

The news that invitations had been issued to a session of the Grand Council at 5 p.m. on July 24 electrified the whole political scene, and just as Grandi and his friends had two days in which to decide their course of action between the announcement and the meeting of the Grand Council, so Acquarone and his military contacts in the General Staff had to complete in the same period and quite separately their precautionary measures. The result of Grandi's action might well enable the King to dismiss Mussolini 'constitutionally', but the risk must be considered of revolutionary outbreaks by the Fascist Party Militia, to say nothing of hostile action locally by the Germans.

On the morning of July 24, Senise and Castellano visited Cerica, the new Commandant of the Military Police. It was agreed to call on the support of the police officer commanding the 'Internal Group' in Rome, and of the head of the Transport Centre. The technical details were left to Cerica, while Castellano and Senise checked together the list of Fascist party bosses to be arrested. These arrests should coincide with that of the Duce.

The same morning Castellano accompanied Acquarone and Ambrosio to the house of Marshal Badoglio. They announced that the King had decided to remove the Duce, and call on the Marshal. He was shown a copy of the proclamation of the new government drafted by Orlando, on which he made no comment.

Later in the morning Castellano saw Carboni. 'As Cerica had not sufficient forces to parry an eventual move by the German S.S., I decided with Carboni to entrust to the Military Police only the task of the arrests, while Carboni would carry out the military occupation of the City with his troops.'[36]

It now remained to await the outcome of the Grand Council.

CHAPTER FIVE

The Meeting of the Grand Council

'I INTENDED the meeting to be a confidential one,' Mussolini wrote later, 'in which everybody would have the chance of asking for explanations and receiving them; a sort of secret committee. In expectation of a long discussion, the Grand Council was convened for 5 p.m. instead of the usual hour of 10 p.m.'[1]

Both the setting and the hour were unusual. This inner cabinet of Fascism had always been held throughout its twenty-year history with full ceremony. The standards and insignia of the Party were brought under Militia escort to Palazzo Venezia, where the Musketeers of the Duce, the personal bodyguard, were on duty. But on this occasion even the outward trappings of power and unity were absent. De Cesare, the Duce's private secretary, telephoned in the morning to General Galbiati, the Commander of the Militia, with orders not to place the Musketeers on ceremonial guard. Only the private police squad was present at Palazzo Venezia, and four sentries of the Militia paced outside the building. There was no Party banner on the balcony. The square in front of the palace was almost deserted on the hot summer afternoon except for a few plain clothes detectives. Many citizens had left the capital after the bombing of July 19. The last act of the régime was concluded austerely and without accompaniment.

The members of the Grand Council* began to arrive shortly before the appointed hour, parking their cars in the inner courtyard in order to avoid public attention. Several of them expected a violent outcome to the session. Some, like Feder-

* For a list of members attending this meeting of the Grand Council see Appendix to this chapter.

zoni and Grandi, had been to confession; others appeared to have concealed weapons on their persons. Grandi admitted later that he carried two hand grenades, and passed one to De Vecchi under the table.

The members gathered in small groups in the Council Room where the seats were placed in their usual order; that of the Duce on a raised dais covered with red brocade at the end, with De Bono on his right as the Senior Quadrumvir of the March on Rome; next to him De Vecchi the other surviving holder of this title; Scorza as the Party Secretary on the Duce's left, and beside him Suardo, as President of the Senate. The others were to sit at two long tables opposite each other and at right angles to that at which the Duce presided. There was no stenographer, and the stool in the centre of the room was empty.

As those present waited, Grandi was to be seen hurrying from group to group canvassing last-minute signatures to his motion. At five minutes past five the chief usher, carrying a briefcase, appeared in the doorway and announced the Duce. He entered, dressed like all those present, in militia uniform. Scorza called for the ritual salute to the leader. The members moved to their places.

Mussolini opened a bulky file of documents in front of him, and began to speak. He had summoned the Grand Council at the express desire of those orators designated by Scorza on his orders to tour the provinces, and several of them had explained to him the significance of this move as 'a manifestation of conscious responsibility'.

'Let us first of all consider the history of the High Command.' Political and military circles aim their sharpest criticisms at those who bear the responsibility for the military conduct of the war. 'Let it be said once and for all that I did not in the least desire the delegation of Command of the Armed Forces in the field given to me by the King on June 10. That initiative belongs to Marshal Badoglio.' Mussolini then read out three memoranda written by the latter dated May-June 1940, showing the proposals made on this subject. How did these arrangements function? 'Falsehood has dominated the conduct of this war', partly because of the difficulty of checking reports and details sent in from various fronts, all overseas. The strategic decisions in these far distant theatres of operations could only fall on the local commanders on whose initiative one had to rely. The action of the High Command was more of a technical nature.

And then with a faint emphasis of pride, 'Only once—in Cavallero's absence—did I personally direct a battle: the naval action off Pantelleria on June 15, 1942. That decisive victory was due to me . . . When I fell ill in October 1942, I contemplated giving up my military command, but I did not do so because it seemed to me unseemly to abandon the ship in midstorm. I postponed doing so until after a "sunny day", which has not yet appeared.' There was nothing further to be said on the subject of the command.

There followed a catalogue of errors: Alamein and the blunders of Rommel in North Africa, the premature evacuation of Tripoli; the shameful surrender of Pantelleria where Mussolini had to give the final order. And now the scene in Sicily, the flight of the troops to their homes, and the dispersal of units in rout all over the island, the first signs of anti-Fascism in the villages and hamlets. 'And what does the General Staff forecast for the immediate future? Perhaps an enemy attack on Sardinia where there are one hundred and sixty thousand men, or in the Dodecanese and other Mediterranean islands, in order to prepare not for a landing on our peninsula, which is thought improbable, but a long-range manoeuvre either in France or the Balkans.'

What about help from Germany? The extent of her aid had been questioned in certain circles. It was generous and substantial. And Mussolini recited a list of figures showing the raw materials imported into Italy from German sources since 1940.[2]

The Duce had reached the end of his military exposition, and turned to the essential point of this meeting, the challenge to his authority in the Grandi motion. Bottai watched him. 'Up till then he had been speaking with his head bent over his papers . . . But now he looked up in the strong light which shone on us all from above. The mask fell. His real face appeared on which I read the signs of a will resigned to the final settlement of accounts. His voice no longer had the provocative sneering tones of aggressive polemic. It was strangely quiet, and his usual form of phrase for effect sounded inert and without the warmth of conviction.'[3]

Mussolini continued: 'Another point of the capitulationists is that "the people's heart is not in the war". Now the people's heart is never in any war. Not even in those of the Risorgimento, as can be proved by unimpeachable documents. We need not disturb those great shades; let us remember more recent events. Was the people's heart in the

1915–18 war, by any chance? Not in the least. The people were dragged into the war by a minority which succeeded in winning over three cities—Milan, Genoa, and Rome—and some minor towns such as Parma. Three men launched the movement—Corridoni,* D'Annunzio, and myself. Even then there was no sort of "sacred unity". The country was divided into neutralists and interventionists, and this division continued even after Caporetto. Was the people's heart in a war which produced five hundred and thirty-five thousand deserters in the country? The "people's heart" seems to have been far less in that than in the present one . . . War is always a party war, a war of the party which desired it; it is always a one man's war, the war of the man who declared it; if today this is called Mussolini's war, in 1859 it could have been called Cavour's war. This is the moment to tighten the reins and to assume the necessary responsibility. I shall have no difficulty in replacing men, in turning the screw, in bringing forces to bear not yet engaged, in the name of our country whose territorial integrity is today being violated. In 1917, some provinces of the Veneto were lost but no one spoke of "surrender". Then, they spoke of moving the government to Sicily; today, if we must, we shall move it to the Po Valley.

'Now Grandi's motion calls upon the Crown. His is an appeal not to the Government so much as to the King.' The latter had two choices: either to ask Mussolini to carry on, or to take over complete executive power in accordance with the Constitution of 1848, still nominally in force, and liquidate the régime. 'Reactionary and anti-Fascist circles, the elements devoted to the Anglo-Saxons, will press for the latter. Gentlemen, beware. Grandi's motion may place the very existence of the régime in jeopardy.'

The Duce had been speaking for nearly two hours, and without one reference to the recent talks with the Germans at Feltre.

Marshal de Bono followed, in order of precedence, with a brief unconvincing defence of the Army and its leaders in halting and emotional phrases. He was quickly interrupted by Farinacci, who observed that no technical discussion was possible unless General Ambrosio, as Chief of Staff, were summoned before them. Mussolini appeared to agree, but let the matter drop.

* Filippo Corridoni. One of the syndicalist leaders who followed Mussolini in the interventionist campaign. Both men were expelled from the Italian Socialist Party in November 1914.

As De Bono sat down, he whispered to De Vecchi, the other surviving Quadrumvir of the March on Rome, 'Give me a hand.' The latter claims that he defended the Army against the Duce's slighting remarks, and blamed the failings of the Fascist education of the youth and the 'political appointments' of senior officers. 'Mussolini showed no reaction, merely shrugging his shoulders, and motioning with his hand to pass on down the table.'

Grandi now rose in his turn and read the final text of his motion. It was already known to most of the members present.

'The Grand Council declares . . . the immediate restoration of all State functions, allotting to the King, the Grand Council, the Government, Parliament and the Corporations the tasks and responsibilities laid down by our statutory and constitutional laws.

'It invites the Head of the Government to request His Majesty the King—towards whom the heart of all the nation turns with faith and confidence—that he may be pleased, for the honour and salvation of the nation, to assume, together with the effective command of the Armed Forces on land, sea and in the air, according to Article 5 of the Statute of the Realm, that supreme initiative of decision which our institutions attribute to him and which, in all our national history, has always been the glorious heritage of our august dynasty of Savoy.'

He was heard in silence. He then continued with a bitter requisitory against the personal rule of one man, which 'having lasted too long and with its degeneration has changed the face of its leader, has destroyed and killed Fascism. The real enemy of Fascism is the dictatorship. From the day when the old motto "Liberty and Fatherland" inscribed on the banners of the Action Squads was replaced by the other "Believe, obey, fight", Fascism was finished. The narrow absurd formula of the Fascist war has brought the nation to ruin. The responsibility for this disaster lies not with Fascism, but with the dictatorship. It is the latter which has lost the war,' and, turning to the Duce, 'It is not enough that you assume the responsibility. We are also in it, and so is the country . . . In the fifteen years in which you have held the military offices of state, what have you done? The initiative of the Crown has been suffocated and its prerogatives manhandled.'[4]

He attacked the administration of the Party by Starace and was disillusioned with the rule of Scorza, 'which had begun in promising fashion'. His own order of the day aimed at creating an 'internal national front, which until today has not existed in Italy because the Crown has taken up an attitude of prudent reserve'. Let the King assume his historic responsibility.[5]

Grandi had been speaking for nearly an hour. He concluded his attack by reminding Mussolini of the catchword of 1924: 'Let faction perish so that the Fatherland may live.'[6]

While he was talking, Mussolini sat aslant on his chair with his hands shading his eyes and showing little sign of reaction, except a sarcastic interjection: 'Tonight we can also debate that the Revolution is finished.'[7]

Bottai followed. He, like Farinacci, thought that the presence of General Ambrosio at the meeting would be helpful to the military discussion. He was not talking as a military expert but as a politician, and as such had three points to make: 'First, the thesis of the General Staff, according to which the enemy, having occupied Sicily, will not direct his attention towards the mainland, does not seem to me plausible. The enemy will face a choice between a widely ranging strategic operation which would bring him either into the Balkans or Southern France, or alternatively, a strategic-political plan which would lead to an occupation of the Italian mainland. The first would doubtless be more profitable strategically, but longer term. The second would be quicker in results and more profitable politically. Will the enemy be able to resist the immediate advantages to his prestige of this latter move when not even Hitler, when his armies reached the Channel, was able to resist the attraction of Paris. Italy means Rome. And in a war which you have defined as "a war of religion", this would offer him the right to occupy the leading capital of the opposing political religion in the field.'

Was Italy prepared for the shock? 'The question by itself gives concrete meaning to the other one asked by you: war or peace? . . . To the question which you have put to us you yourself have given a negative answer. Your report has been a sore blow to our last illusions or hopes . . . You have expounded to us, on the one hand, a series of mishaps, mistakes, and malfunctioning which characterize the structure of the General Staff, and the whole of our military machine; on the other, a succession of your judgements, proposals, and orders regarding those projects of construction, and for war materials or operational plans which those technically responsible have not carried out or taken into account. This means that between the two lobes of the brain of the nation at war there is no organic link, no accord or harmony, and the political section of the Command has not the necessary ascendancy to impose its decisions on the technical. And thus a worm is boring at the very fibres of our system of command.'

Bottai concluded: 'In addition to a manifest technical inability to meet an enemy attack against the peninsula we are confronted with an inefficient machinery of command.'

The next speaker was Ciano, who quietly and measuredly described the background of the alliance with Germany, the Pact of Steel, and Hitler's undertaking 'not to raise matters which might lead to war until 1942'. But he had already decided to occupy Poland before signing the Pact. 'In any event we are not the betrayers, but the betrayed.'

There was a moment of silence, and Farinacci followed. He first read the text of his motion. Its main emphasis lay on close collaboration with the Axis, on the duty of all Italians to stand fast in the observance of the alliances concluded.

The following clause is almost identical with Grandi's wording, except for the significant inclusion of the Party in the list of ruling organs. 'It declares that the urgent necessity for this purpose is the complete restoration of all State functions, allotting to the King, the Grand Council, the Government, Parliament, the Party, and the Corporations the tasks and responsibilities laid down by our Constitution and legislation.' Finally, and also as in Grandi's motion, the King should be pleased 'to assume effective command of all the Armed Forces'.

Farinacci went on: 'In my motion I call for an even closer union with our ally Germany in the conduct of the war. And now since the Duce, in his statement, has undertaken such a commitment, all those present have let it pass, although they say that both in internal and external affairs they all know that he alone does everything himself. But at this grave hour it is a question of everyone committing himself in the face of the world, of backing up our leader, and sharing with him a common fate . . . I am convinced that in this room one could count on the fingers of one hand those who are ready to commit themselves to a moral and political pact with the Duce to the end, whatever may happen, and although we are convinced that our cause is really just, as up to a few months ago even comrade Grandi showed that he thought so.'

Farinacci continued violently, and closely in tune with the German 'programme' for Italy. 'In the second place, my motion calls for a severe enquiry into the military leadership, into the unheard of collapse in Sicily, into the conduct of Ambrosio, Rosi, Roatta, and Guzzoni. I demand that General Ambrosio be heard here in the Grand Council and that we, the political leaders, can at least this once judge as to the means, the men, the weapons and the methods adopted by the General Staff to defend our policy and our country. I also call for the resignation of Ambrosio, a supplementary enquiry into the Generals' plot, and for an effectual amalgamation of the High Command with the Germans. In this war our enemies, first the Anglo-French and then the Anglo-Americans, have set up a unified command and politico-military direction of the war. The Axis has reached this position in the political field, thanks to the Duce and the Fuehrer, but in the military sphere we are completely sovereign and independent and with the results which we see.

'I also ask, as comrade Grandi has also rightly requested, that the King and the Royal Household be brought onto the stage, and called upon to share the honour and burden of the war, which, if it proves victorious, will serve to make the House of Savoy one of the most glorious reigning houses of Europe. I agree, comrade Grandi, about Article Five of the Statute. But I would want to see in your motion, where it said "His Majesty should assume the supreme decision of initiative for the honour and safety of the country", that one word should be added—"Fascist". To put it clearly and bluntly to Victor Emmanuel: "For the good of the nation we Fascists return to Your Majesty the powers and prerogatives which belong to you under the terms of the Albertine Statute, but only because you are fighting at our side for the greatness of Fascist Italy."'

At this point Ciano interrupted: 'Subtleties unworthy of the moment.'

'That is not true,' Farinacci went on. 'With Grandi's motion today, if it is approved, the King could say: "The Fascists at the Grand Council have placed Mussolini, and with him the Fascist Government, in a minority. It follows that I can form a new government, even of anti-Fascists, since by your vote you have not bound me to Fascism, but only to the good fortune of the country." But, with one qualifying adjective, you would prevent the monarchist clique from creating this alibi.'

This was a curious refuge in the wording of a formula.

Farinacci continued, turning to Grandi: 'You have provoked the crisis of Fascism with the enemy invading national soil. You cannot continue this underground and cannibal war against us. Besides, in this supreme Fascist gathering, accusations have been raised not only against previous Party Secretaries, but also against Scorza and the Party in general. Such attacks on the Party are also against the Duce, the methods, the system, the doctrine, and the rank and file. I demand that the Party be given means to defend itself, and its leader, and that it be given absolute powers up to six months after the end of hostilities. Only the Duce and the Fascist Party can have the responsibility and guidance of the Home Front.'

As Farinacci sat down, Mussolini intervened briefly in the debate. He deprecated the corrosive attack on Fascism and on the Party. And what was the meaning of this 'return to the Statute'? It was not with such criticisms and revisions that one confronted in war three imperial powers.

These remarks brought the Minister of Justice, De Marsico, to his feet. He had played an active part in drafting Grandi's motion, which he now supported. He argued that in effect 'the Italian State is in a crisis, and that the actual state of the war itself demanded a speedy overhaul of its structure, which culminated in the powers of the King and in his complete initiative of decision'.

While De Marsico was talking, the Duce was consulting in whispers with Scorza, and at the end of the speech he announced that the Party Secretary had proposed an adjournment of the Grand Council until the next day.

This brought an outburst from Grandi. 'On the Charter of Labour you kept us here for seven hours. Today, when it is a question of the life of the Fatherland we can, if necessary, go on discussing for a week.'

The Duce yielded, and Federzoni rose to support Grandi's motion.[8] He took issue with the Duce on the latter's remarks about the unpopularity of all wars. This had not been true of the Libyan campaign or of the 1915–18 war. If the present war was unpopular 'this was due in great part to the formula of the "Fascist war" which divided Italians more profoundly than had already been done by the Party with its policy of organization'. Federzoni's speech was in effect repudiating that alliance of the nationalist middle classes with Fascism, which had made possible the March on Rome.

A short maiden speech by the President of the Confederation of Agricultural Workers, Bignardi, followed on the isolation of the rural masses from the administration of the economy of the country.

It was a few minutes to midnight. Mussolini brought the session to a temporary break. For the next quarter of an hour the Duce remained in his study 'to read the latest telegrams from the battle areas'.[9] He was joined successively by Alfieri and Scorza.

Alfieri had followed Mussolini from the conference room into the study. 'What is happening in Germany?' was the rather surprising question from the Duce. Alfieri gave a short version of what he had already said to Mussolini at Feltre, emphasizing the particular interest in Berlin in the internal situation in Italy and the impression created by the Allied bombing of Rome. He repeated the argument pressed at Feltre by himself, Ambrosio, and Bastianini that the Duce must make one final effort to persuade Hitler that Italy had reached the limits of loyalty.

Mussolini sat in distant silence, drinking slowly from a glass of milk, and after remarking. 'And you, the Ambassador in Berlin, talk like that,' Alfieri was dismissed 'coldly'. He was followed into the study by Scorza. Outside he found Grandi, who handed him, with neat timing, a copy of his motion with the signatures appended. Alfieri now signed. It was the nineteenth and last name on the list.[10]

Buffarini, according to his own account, was also summoned and pressed for drastic action. 'Arrest them all. It is a plot. There will not be even twenty to put inside. And outside here we should pick up Badoglio and a dozen more . . .' Mussolini's only response was to tell Buffarini to keep calm.

In the Council room, Grandi had been passing from group to group adding to the list of signatures to his motion. The tension relaxed a little, but there was as yet no atmosphere of decision. The intervention of the Duce in the debate following his speech had been brief. Most of those present felt that his auto-defence was yet to come.

* * *

The session of the Grand Council now reopened. Albini referred to the grave internal position, pointing out that the conflict of tendencies in the Grand Council reflected the situation in the country.

Bastianini, although not a member of the Council, was called on by Mussolini to speak. 'You have invited us to talk frankly and accept our responsibilities, and I will do so and not without saying first of all that everything I am about to say I have already brought to your attention on different occasions, either verbally or in writing . . . Today there is a profound division between the country and the Party. To the constant and progressive decline of our war production, to the tremendous deficiencies of our armaments must be added the spiritual inefficiency of the nation.'

Mussolini interrupted with the retort that perhaps this division was due to the enrichment of certain individuals.

Bastianini went on that whatever the causes, the present need was to rally the nation. 'In these twenty years, you, Duce, have given to the nation deeds, words, ideas which have raised it high in its own estimation, and all cannot be lost in a few months. Even if Giolitti had been in your place the work of twenty years could not melt away in an instant. Ideas are not canaries to be kept in a cage.' All national forces must be rallied. 'Let the King speak to the people as in other grave moments of history. The enemy must be given proof of our will to resist.'

Bastianini wrote later that he also stressed the need to 'form a bloc of those forces which would raise the flag of the united Fatherland against the invader. I said that the King, placing himself at the head of the army, would restore publicly the feeling of total solidarity between the régime and the Crown, and would establish that sense of duty wherever it was lacking. I said this, and had the certainty that it would be promptly realizable from your own words which you uttered just before I spoke, and which I reproduce textually: "My relations with the King are perfect; no later than last Thursday the King said to me: my dear Mussolini, you are being attacked from all sides, but I am at your side to defend you."'[11]

Bottai recorded in his notes that Bastianini spoke of the diplomatic scene in the following terms: 'Abroad there could only be a political solution of the conflict, as had been proposed in vain to the ally at the last Salzburg meeting. One way or another: but it is only politically that a solution is possible. And indeed it still is possible. Those contacts must be revived, which it was our mistake not to keep alive.'[12]

There followed an intervention by Galbiati. 'I have not signed and will not sign Grandi's motion and will state the reason. The situation is so serious that no motion can mend it even in the slightest degree. All those statements which we have so far heard condemn the lack of preparation for war, the conduct of operations, and the incapacity of the generals. As to the failure to prepare for war, it is all too clear that the fault does not lie in the fact that Mussolini has been Minister of War for seventeen years, as has been insinuated here, but in the unforeseeable development of the conflict, which has assumed proportions absolutely unequal to the resources of our country . . . The conduct of operations is a problem closely linked with the gigantic one of the availability of logistic means.' As for the capacity of the commanders, one must be circumspect in judging. 'Why did we enter the war? Let us consider this. We entered the war, at the side of Germany, confident of winning . . . Who would have doubted our victory last September when our divisions stood opposite Alexandria? . . . Today it is evident that, with the enemy in Sicily, with the enemy staring down from our skies and threatening our coasts, Italy cannot talk of successes. But it is also true that Italy, like any other nation, must still exert herself to the full.

'You have spoken of the rupture between the Party and the country, between Fascism and the Nation. This is not true; no such break exists. It may be that there is a rupture between you and the country, between Fascists and many Party members . . . If there were a schism between Fascism and the Nation, it would also be more visible and crude in regard to the Militia, which is the armed element of the Fascist Party. On the contrary, the Militia enjoys high prestige in the country and, incorporated as it is in the other armed forces, has fought and is fighting in close comradely solidarity with the soldiers of the other services . . . The schism, if it exists, and I must repeat, is between Fascism and Party members infiltrated into its ranks, ever ready to betray; it is between the mass of good Italians and those who are soft in character, capable of every renunciation, even of honour.'

The tone and direction of Galbiati's remarks gave the signal for Mussolini to intervene again in the debate. He made no effort at sustained argument, but lapsed characteristically into personal invective. If there was a rupture it was among the Party bosses themselves. 'There should be a searching of conscience. If there was a schism, it should be said that it was caused by the financial situation of many party bosses, whose economic standard is too high in relation to their political activity.' An outburst followed. 'And further, this motion raises the gravest problems of personal dignity. What does the expression mean "The head of the government requests His Majesty . . ."? And again, what will the King reply? Let us admit that he accepts the restitution of the delegated military powers. It is then a question of knowing whether I accept to be beheaded. I am sixty years old; and I know what certain things mean. It is better to talk quite openly.' And as a note of final confusion, 'And what is more, I have in my head a key which will resolve the war situation. But I will not say what it is.'

These remarks of the Duce produced a natural and momentary hesitation. As Bottai noted: 'Artifices are not without effect on tired minds.'

This was the moment chosen by Scorza to speak. During the brief interval at midnight he had been in the Duce's study, but there is no reliable record of what passed between the two men, nor does there exist any complete and dependable text of the short speech which he now delivered. If he had given Grandi and his friends previously the impression that he accorded them a circumspect support, he now attempted to assert a limited and somewhat fictitious independence. Perhaps, as Bottai seems to have thought, he was stung by attacks on the Party into a lame and brief defence.

Scorza announced that he too had prepared a motion similar in tone to that of Grandi, but at variance on certain essential points. In particular, there was no mention of the reassumption by the Crown of control of the Armed Forces. The essence of his text was to stress that 'the new situation, created by the events of the war, must be faced by new methods and means'. He called therefore upon the Grand Council to proclaim 'the urgent necessity of putting these reforms and innovations into effect, in the Government, in the Supreme Command, and in the country's internal life, which, through the full functioning of the constitutional organs of the Régime, may bring victory to the united effort of the Italian people'.

Scorza's further recommendations were outlined in vague and cautious terms. 'I do however wish to put forward certain demands in my capacity as Secretary of the Party. First, the position of the General Staff must be entirely overhauled. It is clear that there has been treachery, sabotage, and negligence, and lack of preparation in what should have been the brain of the Armed Forces. A severe enquiry will be undertaken.' Secondly, a Front of National Union must be realized, as has happened in Russia at the moment of supreme danger, and it must be based on the Party, the responsible guide of the future of the nation. 'In regard to the plots which have been mentioned here tonight, any reliable evidence has already been previously passed by me to the Duce.' Bottai apparently interrupted: 'we also should be told about it'. But he obtained no reaction.

Scorza concluded his speech by a defence of the conception of the Party, calling for a purge of unreliable elements, and a rallying of all groups and classes, the Army, the middle classes, the peasants, the ecclesiastics, possibly by declaring martial law and handing over full powers to Fascism.

At this point Ciano interrupted: 'For goodness sake do not touch on the Church. We have had enough trouble with the Vatican over our recent policy.'

It was nearly one o'clock in the morning of July 25. A ragged and imprecise division of opinion between those in favour of total support for the Duce, and those giving varying degrees of support to Grandi's motion had been clear for some hours to those present. There was also a growing, if dim, awareness, that each of them would be judged in remorseless fashion for his stand in this debate on the future of the Fascist régime itself. Even while the speakers followed each other round the Council table, there were last-minute shufflings of allegiance in the corridors, adjoining rooms, and in the adjacent small salon, turned into an orangeade bar for the occasion. Beyond this area of the Palace, access to the outside world was cordoned off by plain clothes detectives.

Galbiati describes the scene: 'I met other members who had absented themselves briefly and with whom I attempted to exchange ideas, but they all belonged to the group who opposed my point of view, and I felt myself being shunned. When I walked back the first time into the Council room, I noticed outside the door and comfortably seated were

Chierici, De Cesare, Stracca, Agnesina (the complete staff responsible for the Duce's safety as well as the command of the Italian police and detectives attached to his person) and possibly others. They had evidently been following the entire session.'[13]

Round the table the debate spluttered on. Having tried twice in vain to attract the Duce's attention, Alfieri now obtained leave to speak. 'In my view those decisions, which are both desired and awaited, and which the head of the government will see fit to take at the conclusion of this debate in the interests of Italy, must be in the first instance brought to the knowledge of Hitler. This is a precaution which seems to me to be indispensable in order to avoid our being taxed with treason. Since one has been insisting here on aid from Germany, I must confirm to the Grand Council what I have emphasized often in my detailed and precise reports, of which the Duce has certainly been aware: Germany will not send to Italy again either timely or effective reinforcements. It is therefore useless to continue deluding oneself . . . Quite apart from the manifest ill-will in helping us, she is too heavily committed on her various fronts to dispose her forces. What Germany wants is to make Italy her bastion in order to delay the occupation of German territory, and only that. There can be no doubt as to this programme. And yet one has been talking here of an Italian resistance at all costs, against everything and everybody. These are noble and generous plans, which however err in not taking into account the real situation in which our people find themselves. Every sacrifice has a limit. At the recent conference at Feltre, General Ambrosio declared to the Duce in my presence that the Italian army could at the maximum resist only for another month. Albini for his part has outlined the extreme gravity of the internal situation. In such conditions, it is absolutely vital to our country to find a solution. Only the Duce can do so, by dealing directly and personally with Hitler.'[14]

This intervention produced a visibly divided effect on the audience. The President of the Senate, Suardo, announced, sobbing, that he withdrew his signature from Grandi's motion. In this momentary confusion Bottai saw the need to rally the other supporters, and in particular the uncommitted. 'I sensed the ambiguity which such oscillations could bring to the vote which was so imminent. I asked to speak. I pointed out that Grandi's motion, to which I adhered, was divided into three parts. The first, consisting of four paragraphs is a complete and proud affirmation of the will to resist; on this point one cannot admit doubts or speculations. With differences of emphasis, motives, and phrasing, everybody is agreed, from us to Farinacci and Scorza, in their motions, that we want to resist. As to the ways and means, the responsible organs will decide. Everyone has his own rhetoric and uses words in his own "scholastic" sense. It may be that ours do not coincide with that of General Galbiati or that of the Secretary of the Party . . . Nevertheless we are all in agreement in calling for the "revival" as we and Farinacci say, or the necessary "reforms" as Scorza puts it, of those institutions capable of guaranteeing united and responsible action by the government. It is not a matter today of reforms, but of applying laws which exist.

'Now I come to the last part of the motion: the appeal to the King. Broad and complete in ours: unacceptably confined to the military sphere in that of Farinacci. This is a considerable difference, which however seems to cancel out when one considers that, having turned to the Sovereign, even a half appeal becomes total, embracing the sum of his prerogatives. Scorza, on the other hand, shows that he thinks a crisis involving the whole nation in its historic interests is soluble within the frame of the Party and régime, and cannot be looked upon as a whole by the supreme decision of the Crown. We want to see visibly and appreciably in this grave hour the realization of that unity of directives between the King and the Duce which is the guarantee of the combined safety of the nation and the régime.'[15]

Grandi followed, briefly. He then handed his motion to Mussolini. The names of the nineteen signatories were appended. The Duce put the paper in front of him 'with affected indifference'.[16] And then 'without another word or gesture and in a relaxed and resigned manner' he called on Scorza to put Grandi's motion to a vote.

Scorza stood up, and starting in order of priority round the table with De Bono, he called the roll of the names of those present. In an oppressive silence, he counted. Nineteen in favour; seven against. Suardo abstained; Farinacci supported his own motion, on which no vote was taken. The Duce gathered his papers, and stood up. According to his subsequent account he said: 'You have provoked the crisis of the régime. The session is closed.'[17] Scorza attempted to call for the ritual salute to the Duce, who checked him, saying, 'No, you are excused,' and retired to his private study.

It was 2.40 a.m. on Sunday, July 25. The debate of the last meeting of the Grand Council had lasted, with a brief interval, for nearly ten hours.

APPENDIX

List of members of the Grand Council

(July 24, 1943)

The Duce of Fascism	
De Vecchi	Quadrumvir of the March on Rome
De Bono	Quadrumvir of the March on Rome
Scorza	Secretary of the Fascist Party
Suardo	President of the Senate
Grandi	Member. President of the Chamber
Acerbo	Member
Pareschi	Minister of Agriculture
Polverelli	Minister of Popular Culture
Galbiati	Commandant of the Fascist Militia
Ciano	Member
Farinacci	Member
Albini	Under-Secretary at the Ministry of Interior. (Present by invitation of the Duce)
Rossoni	Member and Minister of State
Frattari	President of the Confederation of Agriculture
Gottardi	President of the Confederation of Industrial Workers
Bignardi	Secretary of the Confederation of Agricultural Workers
Balella	Secretary of the Syndicalist organizations
Marinelli	Member
Buffarini	Member
Alfieri	Member. Italian Ambassador in Berlin
De Stefani	Member
Bottai	Member
Tringali-Casanova	President of the Special Tribunal

Bastianini	Under-Secretary at the Ministry of Foreign Affairs. (Present by invitation of the Duce)
Cianetti	Minister of Corporations
Federzoni	Member. President of the Italian Academy
Biggini	Minister of Education
De Marsico	Minister of Justice

CHAPTER SIX

The Coup d'État

The Duce returned to his study at the close of the meeting, where he was joined by a group of those members of the Grand Council who had supported him in the voting; Scorza, Buffarini, Tringali-Casanova, Biggini, and Galbiati. 'The question was raised as to whether all that on which we had voted was legal, but I did not take any particular interest in the matter.' This was Mussolini's only recorded comment on this desultory discussion. He had allowed the Fascist hierarchy to speak their minds. But he had not deigned to disclose his own views on the critical situation confronting them. He seemed interested neither in the manner nor the outcome of the vote. He had been prepared in the past to summon the Grand Council at a decisive historical moment and to permit an informal debate on high policy. He had done so in February 1939, when he himself made a considered review, drafted in advance, of Italian foreign policy, precisely because he regarded the Grand Council as the appropriate body to place his views on record, and as he said in the course of his speech on that occasion: 'An autocratic and totalitarian régime—that is, without opposition parties—should have the courage of autocriticism.'[1] The body had last met in December 1939 to accept the decision not to enter the war and to declare Italy's non-belligerency.

The attitude of Mussolini to the rôle of the Grand Council was clearly stated in a letter to Farinacci in October 1925. 'My orders are not voted on, but are accepted and acted upon without any chatter. The Grand Council is not a small parliament: never, I repeat never, is there any question of voting in it.'[2]

It was consistent therefore with this attitude that now, in

his study in the early hours of July 25 nearly twenty years later, he should pay scant attention to the disjointed counsel of the small groups gathered around him. Scorza nevertheless felt impelled to contest the constitutionality of the vote. As Buffarini noted with a touch of malice: 'He thought of it afterwards.'[3] But Buffarini himself, with the original texts relating to the function of the Grand Council in his head, pressed the argument that such a vote was in fact unconstitutional.[4] Grandi's motion was purely an internal affair of the Council, and need not be disclosed to the outside world.

Those present also seemed to have urged the Duce to order the immediate arrest of Grandi and his supporters. Mussolini did not trouble to answer, but picked up the telephone and spoke to the Prefect of Bologna ordering the publication of a message of encouragement to the people of that city, which had been heavily bombed some hours earlier. He then put down the receiver, and dismissed those in the room without a word.[5] Scorza stayed behind. He asked to accompany the Duce back to Villa Torlonia, and the two men left the building together, just after three o'clock.

'The streets were deserted. But one seemed to feel in the air, now almost clear in the morning twilight, that sense of the inevitable which comes from the wheel of destiny when it moves and of which men are often the unconscious instruments. In the night which has come to be known as the "Night of the Grand Council" the discussions lasted for ten hours . . . It is quite likely that the crisis would have broken out even without the session, the debate, and the order of the day, but history does not take into account assumptions which are not confirmed.'[6]

Mussolini had apparently mentioned before leaving his study that he would seek an audience with the King 'the next day, and ask him to appoint "the military ministers", and to issue a royal message strengthening the union of all Italians'.[7] According to Farinacci, the Duce told him after the meeting, 'I accept your advice about Ambrosio and have contacted Graziani—I think he will accept.'[8] He was confident that the King would not demur at whatever political solution of the crisis might be suggested to him. Mussolini was without doubt thinking of such a private design. His natural secretiveness has covered any trace of his intentions.

'I was up at seven o'clock,' Mussolini wrote later, 'and at eight in Palazzo Venezia. My working day—the last one—began regularly, as for the last twenty years. There was nothing very important in the official mail, except an appeal for clemency for two Dalmatian partisans, who had been condemned to death. I telegraphed to the Governor in a favourable sense.' About 9.30 Scorza 'gave a sign of life' and telephoned to say that 'many of those who had voted for Grandi's motion were beginning to regret it. I answered that it was now too late. Almost at the same minute a letter from Minister Cianetti was brought to me, in which he informed me that he withdrew his vote. I did not attach the slighest importance to this fact.'

The Duce now sought to find Grandi. 'I wanted in fact to ask him why, when he came to see me on Thursday (July 22) . . . he had asked and even beseeched me not to summon the Grand Council. An alibi or a manoeuvre?'[9] Mussolini was told that Grandi had gone to the country, and had left no message as to his whereabouts. Subsequent speculation has not produced any valid explanation of this move by the Duce.

Albini came into the study at eleven o'clock to make his daily report from the Ministry of the Interior. He was told that he had no right to vote the previous night, and answered by profuse demonstrations of loyalty 'which left me indifferent'.[10] Indeed the morning was devoted to routine business, and Mussolini showed no concern in seeking advice from his collaborators.

Scorza seems to have appeared at Palazzo Venezia at the customary hour at noon, and bearing a draft letter to be sent to each member of the Grand Council over the Duce's signature. It stated merely that, having summoned in conformity with the law that body 'to consult it on the actual political situation, he had noted the various orders of the day and statements'. As Mussolini commented laconically, 'It seems, from this communication which was not in effect sent and which it would have been useless to send, that Scorza envisaged a normal development of the situation.'[11] If he too had a private solution, it has as yet not been clarified. He returned to Party headquarters about quarter to four in the morning, where the Vice-Secretaries of the Party were awaiting him with impatience. Scorza first described the conversation in the Duce's office after the end of the session of the Grand Council. He stressed that there was no doubt that the vote had no validity, and that the Council was legally only a consultative body. He also told those present that, in the car on the way home, the Duce had thanked him for his intervention in the debate, and that he, Scorza, had replied: 'You left me alone,' meaning that Mussolini had not publicly referred to 'the important events which they had agreed together'. This obscure hint seems to be an oblique reference to a last-minute move, instigated just before the meeting of the Grand Council. In event of a crisis at that meeting over the military command, the question would inevitably arise as to the possible substitution of Ambrosio as Chief of the General Staff, or even of a military figure as head of a new government. In fact each interested group was already considering a candidate. Grandi had in mind Caviglia; Farinacci was thinking of Cavallero; Scorza of Graziani.

For the moment, however, Scorza did not pursue this last-minute plan. His immediate concern seems to have been to minimize the effect of the vote of the previous night. He telephoned Farinacci to seek a meeting, but the latter was untraceable. He then seems to have gone to his office as President of the Chamber at Montecitorio where among others he met Bastianini and Cianetti.

Bastianini, in his letter of November 9, 1943, to Mussolini, relates that Scorza told him that 'as a result of the vote of the Grand Council you were about to make changes in the government' and that Bastianini suggested certain names.[12]

On this fateful morning Mussolini, as head of the Government and of the Armed Forces, made no move to summon the Chief of the General Staff, General Ambrosio, to receive the latest reports from the war fronts. Nor did he conceive of the need for taking exceptional measures in relation to any threat to internal security. General Galbiati however appeared—and unannounced—with a memorandum.[13] He had thought of a series of solutions: to summon the Party Directorate, or the senior personalities of the Party and Militia, or to send himself to make unofficial contacts with Himmler in Germany. Again Galbiati, who had heard that Grandi was unavailable, pressed for his arrest, and that of the group who had voted with him. The Duce would not hear of it, and added rather obscurely: 'In a few hours I shall go to the King, and examine the position with him. Measures against a particular person must be preceded by his being first replaced in the office which he holds. It is a question of Ministers and Undersecretaries whom I cannot change without royal assent.

And then there are the Collars of the Annunciation whom I cannot treat in the same way as an ordinary citizen.'

In his secretive way Mussolini was moving towards his own solution of the crisis as so often in the past. He would minimize the implications of the events of the previous night, and would make no extraordinary move. For the past twenty-one years he had been received by the King at half-past ten every Monday and Thursday morning. As a small concession to the untowardness of the present situation, the Duce asked his secretary, De Cesare, to seek instead an audience at Villa Savoia 'or elsewhere' for that afternoon at five o'clock, and to add that he would appear as usual in civilian clothes. The appointment was confirmed with Puntoni by telephone. It would almost appear to be a visit on routine business.

Scorza knew of this move, and was possibly present when the appointment was made. Shortly afterwards he received Tarabini and Host Venturi, both leading and long-standing Party members. The latter suggested that there was no point in wasting time with repentant members of the Grand Council, but that he must act. Scorza told him that 'the Duce will see the King the next day, and that everything would be settled quietly'.[14] Such was Scorza's interpretation of the Duce's intentions. According to his later account, Host Venturi insisted that the 'M' division must be brought to Rome, and asked what Galbiati was doing with the Militia. Scorza replied that he did not know. Indeed he had no contact with Galbiati during these hours, nor had he been available when the latter asked to see him for the last ten days. And it was Scorza himself who had abolished the liaison officers between the Party and the Militia, thus making impossible any organized common action on a political level.[15]

It was clear that Scorza had no intention of instigating any precautionary move by the Party. There is no evidence that he was aware of any measures being taken by the Court, or of the need to take any revolutionary move in defence of the régime. He was not in the close confidence of the Duce, and the latter's subsequent comment is drearily relevant: 'When I think back on the attitude of Scorza to many things, strong doubts occur to me.'[16]

Whatever he may have known about impending events he was probably, like the Duce, immune to rumours of plots and counter-plots, and by instinct a believer in political solutions.

* * *

At noon the Duce received his next visitor, the new Japanese Ambassador, Hidaka, who had arrived in Rome late in June. He had already attempted to have an audience with Mussolini before the Feltre meeting. 'Without any connection with the interview which his government had asked him to seek, he was to have called on the Duce personally to gather information on the general situation in Italy. The audience was finally fixed for midday on July 25.'

Bastianini, who was present, made a record of the interview.[17] 'The Japanese Ambassador asked the Duce, in the name of the President of the Council, Tojo, to give him as precise a picture as possible of the political and military situation of Europe, which Japan regarded with some disquiet, adding that the Japanese Government was ready to collaborate with the Italian Government in whatever way was thought to be the most opportune in leading towards an improvement. The Duce replied that . . . he approved of the policy followed by Japan in the Far East because he himself held the view that when armed force was not sufficient to deal with a situation one must revert to politics. He had repeatedly attempted, on various occasions, to make the Fuehrer understand this, but nevertheless had not succeeded in persuading him . . . The Duce had therefore decided that in the course of the coming week, he would undertake an energetic approach to the Fuehrer to draw his most serious attention to the situation which had recently developed, and to induce the Fuehrer himself, as he had already attempted to do on previous occasions, to cease hostilities on the Eastern Front, and thus arrive at a settlement with Russia. Once this had been obtained, the Reich would be able to bring the whole weight of its military potential to bear against the Anglo-Americans in the Mediterranean, and thus restore a situation which today was undoubtedly compromised.

'The Duce asked the Japanese Ambassador to inform the President of the Council, Tojo, that it was his earnest wish that he (Tojo) should do all he could to support such a démarche with the Fuehrer, with a view to arriving at a cessation of hostilities against Russia. In the present situation it was in fact no longer a matter of thinking obstinately of holding on to the Ukraine, which could not represent for the Reich a complete solution of her economic problem and her food supplies. The Duce addressed such a request to President Tojo because only in this way did he think that the situation could be modified in favour of the Tripartite powers.

Otherwise the conditions in which Italy was fighting were such that she would, and in a short space of time, find herself absolutely unable to continue hostilities, and would be obliged to examine a solution of a political character.'

Hidaka later commented to his German colleague: 'The Duce had thoroughly put him in the picture and in half-an-hour's conversation in no way gave the impression of a man who was not sure of his position.'[18]

A few days later Mackensen was told by Bastianini, who also spoke of this meeting between the Duce and the Japanese Ambassador, that, 'in answer to the Ambassador's request for information on the situation, the Duce had in reply mentioned—as Bastianini says, for the first time in his presence—the possibility that Italy might not be able to hold out come what may, but, should sufficient support be lacking, might be forced to give in. The Duce added that in the course of the next days he would approach the Fuehrer and bring it home to him that he must make peace with Russia and that the possibility of doing so existed.'[19]

It seems that, under the impact of the events of the previous night, the Duce was confidently—and as always in impenetrable isolation—conceiving a dramatic formula which would liberate him this time from the gravest impasse of his career, and enable him to reassert abruptly his personal domination over the Italian scene. In order to do this, he must clearly find a lightning solution simultaneously on the disintegrating military and home fronts. In relation to the former, he seized swiftly on the opportunity given to him by the Japanese Ambassador's request at such a moment for an interview, in order to press once more as his own the formula of a separate peace between the Axis and Russia as a central and immediate solution for the future conduct of the war, and to place this aim squarely if belatedly as the main and urgent issue in relations with the Axis partners.

The 'possibility' which presented itself, and which fitted tidily with that occasioned by the talk with Hidaka, was that on July 29 Mussolini would be celebrating his sixtieth birthday. It had been suggested previously that this occasion should be marked by a ceremonial visit from Goering. It would not be the first time that the envoy of the Fuehrer had arrived, and opportunely, on a personal mission to Rome. The relations between the two men remain unclarified. There may well have been some mutual understanding between them. The records which exist of their previous meetings strengthen such a view. Goering's position in Germany was to some extent bound up with his personal relationship with Mussolini, and with his own predominant interest as head of the German Air Force in the Mediterranean theatre of war. And, most striking of all, there is more than a hint that Goering shared the Duce's attitude to the Eastern Front, and that each needed the other in campaigning in the Fuehrer's circle on this theme. Goering had never dared to raise the subject with the German leadership, nor had the Duce, when faced with Hitler in person, been able to press the argument. But Mussolini must have realized that by now such a move was the only and ultimate possible one, and Goering's co-operation might prove decisive in a final approach to the Fuehrer. But in view of the internal crisis provoked in the Grand Council, and the challenge to the Duce's leadership at home, Mussolini could not afford to wait four days. Co-ordinated timing between two solutions—abroad and at home—was vital.

On returning to the Italian Foreign Office from the meeting between the Duce and the Japanese Ambassador, Bastianini was telephoned by Mackensen to enquire 'regarding the visit of the Reichsmarshal for the Duce's birthday. He immediately transmitted it by telephone to the Duce and suggested that perhaps it was desirable, particularly at the present moment, to have an opportunity of talking to the confidential envoy of the Fuehrer. It should not be regarded as a visit for his birthday, but July 27 or 28 had already been mentioned as dates. The Duce at once agreed, for it would then be a matter not of congratulations, but of a talk which might be really useful. He could then talk to the Reichsmarshal about his ideas on a solution of the German-Russian question.'[20]

The promise of such a solution of the external crisis of the war must have strengthened the Duce's optimism in his abilities to handle the internal deadlock when he saw the King later that afternoon. Faced with the supreme dilemma of his career, Mussolini was both subtle and simple. The pattern of his behaviour is familiar, but sharpened and clarified more than ever before by his feline awareness of the consequences of failure during the next hours ahead. If he could persuade Hitler to cease fighting on the Eastern Front, the Mediterranean theatre might still be held and stabilized. And if he could convince the King to resume command of the Armed Forces, 'a command which I had for some time past been thinking of relinquishing',[21] and to accept yet another routine reshuffle of Ministers, the Duce would again emerge triumphant, supreme, and alone at the summit of power. In the meantime there would be no private consultations, no clues as to pending dismissals or promotions, only the maintenance of impenetrable and even unnerving secrecy.

Before returning to Villa Torlonia, the Duce summoned Galbiati back to his office to accompany him on a tour of those quarters of Rome which had been heavily damaged in the Allied air bombardment of July 19. It seems that the Duce sought instinctively at this moment some psychological refreshment in a direct contact with the crowd such as he never gained in private and personal discourse. 'In the neighbourhood of the church of San Lorenzo, groups of young people who were engaged in their preliminary service training for the Navy organized a spontaneous demonstration for me.'[22]

On their way back in the car to Villa Torlonia, the two men discussed the memorandum which Galbiati had given him that morning and they went over, one by one, the members of the Grand Council. 'These lily-livered creatures who accuse me of having replaced them from time to time in commanding positions, and of summoning them back too late.' Galbiati replied, 'They need to be sent to Chianciano (a spa in Central Italy for liver complaints) for a cure, and under strict supervision. And then one would see, and take further steps. In itself, Grandi's order of the day merely provides an alibi for tomorrow.'

Mussolini interrupted, 'They have sniffed the contrary wind, and felt the approaching storm, as happens with certain species of animals, and they fool themselves into creating an alibi. It never occurs to these pusillanimous creatures that when he who raised them up on his own shoulders is no longer here, they will feel pretty miserable in the mortal dust.'[23]

Galbiati left the Duce at the gates of Villa Torlonia. Mussolini insisted that he had complete confidence in the King. 'I have never done anything without his complete agreement. For over twenty years I have been to see him once or twice a week, and have consulted him on every matter of State and even private questions. He has always been solidly with me.' The Duce referred again to the memorandum which

Galbiati had brought to him that morning, and said categorically: 'As to our own riff-raff, do not do anything to aggravate matters. There is always the Party or the Police to deal with them. Make a detailed study instead of eventual clandestine military action.'[24] The Duce then promised that he would telephone after the royal audience.

It was already three o'clock. 'An oppressive sultriness weighed on things and people. It sank down on Rome from a motionless sky . . . I lunched as usual, and then spent an hour talking to Rachele in the music room. My wife was more than depressed. She was deeply disturbed in expectation of something which must happen in the next moment.'[25]

Meanwhile Scorza was trying urgently to reach the Duce by telephone, and succeeded only as the latter was leaving for his audience with the King. Scorza had met Graziani's secretary in the early afternoon, and seems to have pursued the proposal of considering the Marshal as the successor to General Ambrosio. The Duce merely replied: 'All will be well. Afterwards I will summon you either to Palazzo Venezia or to Villa Torlonia. Bring with you *that person*.'[26]

The Duce seems thus to have imparted to his collaborator the same illusory optimism which he himself dispensed around him.

The night's work at the Grand Council held a very different significance in other circles. As soon as Acquarone received Grandi's message on the late afternoon of July 24, he had appreciated that the circumstances which he and Ambrosio had been awaiting in order to achieve the palace revolution, which had been so quietly and actively planned in recent weeks, might be now created by an adverse vote in the Grand Council itself against Mussolini. The latter would be forced to consult the King, who would demand his resignation. Prompt action must be taken, in such an event, to ensure against any counter-coup from the Party or the Fascist Militia, and a technical operation to this end must be mounted immediately.

The first step was to learn the outcome of the session of the Grand Council with a minimum loss of time. The obvious informant was Grandi. Having instigated the crisis, he would certainly have his own political solution to propose. Its essence lay in his motion, the draft of which Acquarone already had in his hands, and if this had been carried at the meeting, Grandi would inevitably have a more detailed plan to submit to the King. Not that the latter had ever shown any special concern or interest, in his confidential talks with Acquarone or Ambrosio in recent weeks, in a 'Grandi solution' in political terms as an alternative administration. Grandi's rôle in the eyes of Acquarone was to provoke a crisis of the régime from within, which if successful would thus place the King in a position to act constitutionally and decisively in removing Mussolini, and restore the Crown to a historic position from which it had been excluded since the March on Rome.

On leaving Palazzo Venezia, Grandi had gone to his office in the Parliament buildings. Here Acquarone went to find him and to hear at first hand an account of the session. It was 3.30 in the morning. The two men left at once for the house of Grandi's confidant, Mario Zamboni, in the Via Giulia, and stayed there talking for nearly three hours. Grandi handed to the Minister of the Royal Household the text of his motion bearing the original signatures of the nineteen supporters. Everything now depended on the royal will. In these early morning hours the whole structure of Italian government was in suspense. The man who had provoked the crisis of the régime had considered also its solution. His version of this conversation exists in summary form.[27] The King must forthwith accept complete responsibility and form a new administration. Grandi's candidate for the head of the government was Marshal Caviglia 'the only one of the old Marshals of the 1915–18 war who had preserved an attitude of dignity and pride in face of Mussolini and the dictatorship. His prestige with the Army is very high and he is the only person who can negotiate with head high with England and the United States.' Caviglia should form a transitional ministry of experts, both Fascist and anti-Fascist. Orlando, as the veteran leader of the nation in 1918, should draft a manifesto to the country appealing for a sacred union of all patriots. The King should issue a royal decree transforming the Fascist Chamber into a Chamber of Deputies. Grandi assumed that as its President he should guarantee a two-thirds majority for a vote of confidence in the new government. Most Fascist Party members would follow the royal action, but no member of the Grand Council should serve in the new administration.

Acquarone asked about Badoglio, hinting that the Marshal might be summoned to power, and received the answer that he was unsuitable 'for obvious reasons' and in particular as bearing major responsibility for Italy's entry into the war.

'And yourself?' asked Acquarone. Grandi explained that all he wished was 'to leave tonight on my own responsibility for Madrid, and to make contact with my old friend Samuel Hoare . . . to explain to him the situation with a view to a peace offer, which can be handled by whomever you wish to designate'.

The Minister of the Royal Household listened and made little comment. He asked one final question. How would Mussolini now react? 'I would not be surprised', answered Grandi, 'if he considered the voting tonight as a trump card in the disengaging manoeuvre which he intends to carry through on his own with Hitler. The only thing which would astonish me would be to see him oppose any decisions of the King.'[28]

Acquarone left to report at the royal villa. Extreme measures must now be set in motion. Plans had already been drafted to arrest Mussolini at the customary audience which was due on Monday morning, July 26. But events might now be precipitated.

At about seven o'clock Acquarone joined General Ambrosio at Supreme Command Headquarters. It was now only a matter of putting into action a preconceived plan. As Ambrosio stated later, it had been suggested that the summoning of the Grand Council had taken him by surprise and upset arrangements. 'This is not correct. I would say that Grandi's action . . . and the decisions of the Grand Council complemented our plan; besides, the verdict of the Grand Council offered the King the constitutional weapon for removing Mussolini.'[29] Ambrosio had already been told by the King on July 19 that he had decided to take such action at an opportune moment.

Acquarone now told him, after talking to the King in the early hours of Sunday, July 25, that this moment had arrived.

At 10.50 a.m. Puntoni went to the Sovereign. 'I found him quiet and serene. We discussed the situation, and from His Majesty's words it was easy for me to understand that the replacement of Mussolini had been decided. The King will tackle the Duce tomorrow, Monday, at the usual audience.' At 12.15 Puntoni was telephoned by Mussolini's secretary, and this upset the King's programme. 'De Cesare asked for a private audience for the Duce at 5 o'clock at Villa Savoia. I immediately telephoned to the Sovereign and replied to the Duce's private secretary that His Majesty agreed to Mussolini's request. I also warned Acquarone, and told him that the King wished to see him at four o'clock.'[30]

Acquarone immediately telephoned this news to Castellano, and seems to have admitted that the King was still reluctant to give the actual order to arrest the Duce. Both men agreed to meet at Ambrosio's house. The detailed preparations for the arrest of the Duce were made in the early afternoon. It had already been agreed by the inner circle of the palace conspiracy that the arrest must be carried out by the Military Police. Their new commander, General Cerica, who was then on leave near Florence, had only been appointed on July 22. On the morning of July 25 he was completing his formal calls, when just after midday he received an urgent summons to go to Ambrosio's office in Palazzo Vidoni.[31] According to Cerica's own account, he was told that the King was about to dismiss Mussolini and appoint a new President of the Council. 'After the audience you must take steps to arrest Mussolini, who may try to contact his people and put himself at the head of a subversive movement.' In reply to Cerica's question as to whether 'we are acting constitutionally or outside the law', Ambrosio answered: 'Constitutionally. The order comes from the Sovereign.'

At this point Acquarone was announced. He was 'anything but preoccupied'. After repeating certain details of the meeting of the Grand Council, he turned to Cerica. 'You must act at once, as there is no time to lose. As Ambrosio will have told you, the two radio stations at Prato Smeraldo and at San Paolo must also be occupied, the offices of Italian Radio, the central Post Office, the telephone exchanges at the Ministries of the Interior and of War.' Cerica then took his leave. He wanted to go at once to General Puntoni in order to arrange the entry of the Military Police into the gardens of Villa Savoia. Acquarone interrupted. 'His Majesty has given orders that, apart from the commander of the Military Police, no one will be told of the plan. The personnel chosen for the operation will make contact with me direct.' As Cerica was leaving, he remembered the presence of the Fascist 'M' division with their thirty-six Tiger tanks sixteen miles away on the outskirts of Rome, and mentioned to Ambrosio that if they intervened, he could do little to press the plan. 'You think of the part of the operation which concerns you. I have already studied the military question,' was Ambrosio's reply. At the door of the office, Cerica met General Carboni, who had been summoned for this very purpose. The latter's assignment was to take over the Rome garrison after the Duce's arrest.

It was, according to Cerica, precisely 12.25. It was essential to prevent the different groups of Military Police in the city dispersing on Sunday leave. He hurried to the main headquarters in the Viale Liegi, and sent out orders to all barracks in the Rome area that leave was suspended until 4.30 that afternoon, as he intended to review each unit as their new commander. Cerica had at his disposal some eight thousand men. Then he picked three officers to carry out the operation, and also consulted a senior police official, Marzano, who was not only the liaison with the Police, but also commanded the motor transport section of the Ministry of the Interior.

Together this small group worked out a technical plan. It was decided to use a motor ambulance, escorted by fifty Military Police in a truck. It was probable that the Duce would be accompanied by a personal escort, and there was a disagreeable risk of a scuffle in the open street outside the royal villa unless there was a clear decision to carry out the arrest within the precincts. It was essential to receive precise orders, but this final point would have to be left until the last moment. The senior police official attached to the royal household now appeared at headquarters to co-ordinate arrangements. The ambulance would be parked in the drive of Villa Savoia, and the truck with fifty men concealed in the bushes inside the grounds facing the main staircase.[32]

The King was preparing to receive Mussolini in this unusual audience. General Puntoni had been summoned shortly after three o'clock, and was told by the King that at the conclusion of the interview he had authorized the arrest of Mussolini 'outside Villa Savoia'. The King then added: 'As I do not know how the Duce will react, I would ask you to stand by the door of the drawing-room where we shall retire to talk. You can then intervene if need arises.'[33]

While the two men were talking and pacing up and down the drive, Acquarone joined them. He explained that Cerica was pressing to be allowed to carry out the arrest inside the grounds of the villa 'to avoid compromising the operation'. The King made a gesture of annoyance, and an obstinate dialogue followed. Mussolini was due at any moment, and the King reluctantly gave the verbal order for which Cerica was waiting.

Just before five o'clock the Duce's car drove up. He was accompanied by De Cesare. Three cars, with his personal detectives and escort, remained outside the gate. The King received the Duce on the steps of the main entrance.

There are several versions of their last meeting. The Duce was anticipating an uneventful discussion. He merely needed the formal approval of the Sovereign in order to solve in his own familiar way the temporary crisis provoked the previous night. 'I took with me a book containing the Grand Council Act, Cianetti's letter, and other papers from which it emerged that the Grand Council's resolution was not binding on anyone, in view of the consultative function of the organ itself. I thought that the King would withdraw his delegation of authority of June 10, 1940, concerning the command of the armed forces, a command which I had for some time past been thinking of relinquishing. I entered Villa Savoia therefore with a mind completely free from any forebodings, in a state which, looking back on it, might really be called utterly unsuspecting.'[34]

It was a shuffling and embarrassed dialogue. The Duce began, in a low voice, to give a short account of the military situation, and of the meeting of the Grand Council. He did not reach the point of offering any recommendations. The King did not propose to argue, or to prolong the interview. In a few disjointed sentences, interspersed as was his habit with phrases in Piedmontese dialect, he announced that the developments of the last few hours had forced him to take certain steps. He now asked the Duce for his resignation. He had already arranged for Badoglio to succeed him as head of the government. 'He was in fact practically in office.'[35] There was a silence in the room, 'broken only by a phrase which the King had repeated several times during the course of the conversation: "I am sorry, I am sorry, but the solution could not have been otherwise."'[36] The audience ended in silence. The King accompanied the Duce for the last time to the front entrance. 'The conversation had lasted half an hour. As the King said good-bye to me on the threshold, he shook me by the hand with great warmth.'[37]

During the course of this short interview, the preliminary steps for the Duce's arrest were put in motion. His chauffeur was quietly taken in charge in the telephone room of the villa, and his car removed from the main entrance.

The Duce appeared on the front steps. 'My car awaited me on the right side of the palace. As I was walking towards it, a Military Police captain barred the way, and said to me: "His Majesty has ordered me to protect your person." As I made a gesture to get into my car, he forced me into an ambulance which had been standing there for some time.' His secretary, De Cesare, insisted on accompanying him, and the incongruous party drove at high speed to a Military Police barracks in the Via Quintino Sella. Mussolini was put in the Colonel's office, and an armed guard mounted outside the door. In such a manner the ruler of Italy for over twenty years was abducted abruptly and without trace from the public scene.

The arrest of the Duce was the essential prelude to the 'legal' revolution. The brisk execution of the long-prepared technical details formed a muted epilogue. Cerica had completed his appointed tasks by about five o'clock. Senise, with a body of some five hundred police had appeared at the Ministry of the Interior about an hour earlier, and all government communications passed into safe hands.

Buffarini arrived at Villa Torlonia just after five o'clock. Donna Rachele was awaiting the return of her husband from the royal audience. In mounting disquiet Buffarini telephoned round Rome. None of the numbers answered. Finally a call came through that Mussolini had been arrested. Buffarini stayed through the night in the isolated villa, and was placed under arrest the next morning.[38]

About five o'clock Scorza summoned the Vice-Secretaries to Party headquarters to await the results of the royal audience. A message was sent to Farinacci to join them. The time passed, and there was no news from the Duce. Scorza failed to get through on the telephone to Palazzo Venezia, and this seems to have been to him the first indication that an abnormal state of affairs had abruptly arisen. Panic spread rapidly among the small group at Party headquarters. He then telephoned to the central exchange at the Ministry of the Interior, and was heard to exclaim, 'Oh God: not that.' After an excited discussion with two of his subordinates, he left by car for Palazzo Venezia, giving instructions that if he did not return, the Rome headquarters of the Party should be alerted and mobilized.[39]

Scorza did not attempt to enter Palazzo Venezia, but drove to the headquarters of the Military Police, where he was received by General Cerica. Scorza explained that he had come to seek help in tracing Mussolini, but Cerica interrupted quickly that he was obliged with regret to place his visitor at once under arrest. 'I explained to him that Mussolini was no longer President of the Council but was under detention outside Rome, and that he, Scorza, was the first on the list of persons to be arrested, which had been given to me by my superiors.'

Both men were at a loss. Scorza, according to Cerica, argued that his arrest would 'leave the Fascists without orders or a leader, and unleash civil war'. If he were allowed to leave, he would issue instructions 'so that Italians would not slaughter each other'. Cerica released Scorza on parole, and the latter 'gave such orders'.

Scorza left, and instead of returning to Party headquarters went into hiding.[40] It is not clear whether he telephoned any instructions to his subordinates following his talk with Cerica. When Scorza did not return, the Federal Secretary as head of the Party organization in Rome, who had already been summoned to headquarters, was told of Scorza's mobilization orders. This official replied that, being Sunday, he could not raise more than twenty comrades. At this moment the private secretary of one of those who had left the building with Scorza, returned with the news. The Duce had been arrested and removed to La Rocca delle Caminate. Scorza was also apparently detained, and a similar fate awaited the leading Fascist personalities. The telephone rang, and it was answered by Tarabini who was now the senior Party official present. It was General Ambrosio on the line. 'Tarabini replied: "Good. I will see to it at once." And he took down notes of a text, dictated verbatim on the phone. At the end of the conversation he said so that all could hear: "This telegram has to be sent to the Federal Secretaries." He sat at a desk to copy out the text. When he had finished, he added: "It is better to sign it 'Scorza'." As it was a Sunday, the Party telegraph office was closed; an official was sent to the central Post Office, and paid in cash for the cables at the counter.'

The group in Scorza's office had completed their work, and dispersed. Later that evening, the building was occupied by the Army. Tarabini went home, where Host Venturi called on him at eleven o'clock that night, and was told what had happened at Party headquarters. In the early hours of the morning, the latter walked through the streets to the city headquarters of the Party in Palazzo Braschi, 'to see whether the Party had made any move. Everything was deserted and complete calm reigned.'[41]

Meanwhile Galbiati seems to have decided on his own initiative to consult Himmler's representative, Colonel Dollmann, whom he summoned to his office at five that afternoon. He did not give Dollmann much information about the meeting of the Grand Council, but said that he had been ordered by the Duce to prepare for eventual military action, and asked for an appointment with Marshal Kesselring to co-ordinate such activities. Dollmann undertook to fix this for the following day as Kesselring was out of Rome.

Then, like Scorza at the Party offices in Palazzo Wedekind, Galbiati, surrounded by his staff at Militia headquarters, awaited further enlightenment from the Duce. As time passed the tension mounted. There was no reply to telephone enquiries at Palazzo Venezia. Dispatch riders reported no sign of the Duce's car at Villa Savoia. There was evidence of troop movements in the city. Buffarini telephoned repeatedly from Villa Torlonia but with no news, and mounting suspicions. Galbiati sent his chief of Staff to Chierici at police headquarters. The officer returned about seven-thirty with the news of Mussolini's resignation and apparent removal to La Rocca delle Caminate. Shortly afterwards, Tarabini arrived and repeated the description of the scene at Party headquarters.

At seven forty-five that evening the militia command in the working-class quarter of Trastevere reported that they were under fire from regular troops. Evidence of attacks by civilians on isolated militiamen in the streets began to come in. Galbiati gave instructions to all militia commands to avoid provocation but defend themselves if attacked, and then, in a despairing final attempt to keep some control over the situation by telephone, Galbiati attempted to put through calls to the headquarters of the 'M' division still idle at its base at Sette Vene, to Bologna, and to Milan. He was told by the operator that the exchange had cut all lines on orders from the Ministry of the Interior.

For the next two hours a chaotic dialogue followed in Galbiati's office. Everyone took part: staff officers, militiamen, drivers, and civilians. There was loose talk of another March on Rome. Galbiati was not prepared to consider any move. The 'M' division was dispersed on manoeuvres round Lake Bracciano to the north of Rome, and since early July was under the direct orders of the General Staff.[42] There were no

Militia battalions on a war footing in the city of Rome, and the anti-aircraft units, formed by the Militia, were dispersed over an area of one hundred kilometres.

On the other hand, visible counter-measures by the Army were mounting, and the square in front of Galbiati's own headquarters was already occupied by tanks. After the arrest of Mussolini, Roatta received orders by telephone from Ambrosio to bring the 'Piave' division into Rome. By the following morning the capital was heavily garrisoned by motorized units.[43]

At 10.10 that evening, Galbiati managed to speak on the telephone to Albini, who was still at his desk at the Ministry of the Interior. He dictated a brief minute. 'I request you to inform whoever at this moment is responsible for the government that the Militia remains faithful to its principles, which are: to serve the Fatherland in the joint names of the King and the Duce.'[44]

Shortly afterwards Ambrosio telephoned to say that he had received this message, and that Badoglio, who had taken over as head of the government, requested to see him. Galbiati said that he did not wish to stay at his post, and asked for a successor to be appointed. At midnight he received a letter signed by Badoglio, telling him to hand over in due course. This exchange of messages completed the history of the rôle of the Militia in these events.

The technical counter-measures planned by Ambrosio and Acquarone thus unfolded without resistance. The formal protocol arrangements proceeded equally smoothly. Shortly after five o'clock Acquarone telephoned to Badoglio, summoning him to the royal presence. He had received a preliminary warning in the morning, and had spent the afternoon prudently playing bridge. Badoglio arrived at Villa Savoia in Marshal's uniform. The King told him briefly of the Duce's arrest and of the nature of the task ahead. The immediate measures were the formation of an administration of military and civilian technicians, the maintenance of law and order, the issuing of the proclamation of continuing the war on the Axis side, which had been drafted by the veteran Orlando. Badoglio departed in the car which had brought the Duce to the previous audience.

The first step was to ensure that all measures to avoid a Fascist counter-reaction had been completed. The immediate responsibility had already been assumed by Ambrosio in consultation with Acquarone, and for the following hours the precarious seat of power lay at the headquarters of the Supreme Command. By seven o'clock the operation was completed. It was not until 11 p.m. that evening, however, that Badoglio cautiously appeared in Ambrosio's private office.

The three radio messages to the nation announcing the acceptance by the King of Mussolini's 'resignation', the appointment of Badoglio, the direct assumption by the King of command of the Armed Forces, and the continuance of the war, had been drafted by Acquarone and Orlando by 6.30 that afternoon.[45] They were broadcast at 10.45 p.m. just before Badoglio's carefully timed arrival at Palazzo Vidoni.[46]

Such was the style of the transfer of power.

Perhaps the most pertinent comment is in an intercepted telephone call the following day from a senior Party official to a lady. 'We have avoided civil war; we have submitted to insults without firing a shot, and without reacting. Tomorrow we shall dissolve the Party, and all will be over. Order will have been re-established by the Army.'[47]

EPILOGUE

'This is my eighteenth Brumaire.' It is said that these words were murmured by the King walking in the garden of the Villa Savoia after the arrest of the Duce. It was in the same residence that he had received other Prime Ministers; Salandra at the time of the intervention crisis in 1915, and Facta in the hours before the March on Rome in 1922. On the present occasion, as previously, the shape of events was decisively marked by the personality of the Sovereign. The coup d'état which led to the fall of Mussolini was a personal and dynastic operation.* The prime objective was the preservation of the House of Savoy in its traditional rôle of the defender of those Italian constitutional liberties that had been successively violated during the years of Fascist rule. It seemed that after the successive humiliations of twenty years, the King could now hope to establish his personal rule. The nature of the action against the Duce also mirrors his personality, diffident, cautious, and secretive, and aimed at a minimum disturbance of public affairs. In its preparation 'there was perhaps more distrust of others than self-assurance'.†

* The interpretation of these events, central to the history of modern Italy, is the basis of extensive controversy among Italian historians. Professor Salvatorelli, for example, has stressed in particular this personal dynastic aspect of the crisis, while the Communist spokesman Professor Battaglia seeks to eliminate the individual element. To the latter the Italian crisis of 1943 is essentially the result of a long-matured mass action against Fascism as exemplified by the March strikes and the reaction of Italian industrial and financial interests seeking a way out of the war, in order to forestall Socialist revolution. For a preliminary discussion of these points, see the reports of the Conference of the Italian Liberation Movement ('The Italian Crisis of 1943 and the Beginnings of the Resistance' in their periodical 1955, Nos. 34–35). Professor Battaglia has also developed his thesis in more detail in an article in the Communist Party fortnightly review *Il Contemporaneo* Anno II, No. 5, January 29, 1955.

† Leopoldo Piccardi *La Storia Non Aspetta* (1957) p. 42. A book

In the maze of rumour, gossip, and delation in Italian political circles it is possible to discern two separate and opposing conspiracies, or perhaps rather private cabals, against the régime. The idea of a coup d'état originated around the personality of the Princess of Piedmont in the summer of 1942 in an atmosphere of pre-Fascist Liberalism and drawing-room politics. From this restricted circle extended the network of clandestine consultation between the leaders of the traditional parties of order of the Giolittian system, and the leader and co-ordinator of these personalities and programmes was Ivanoe Bonomi. By the summer of 1943 the elements of an historic anti-Fascist opposition emerge with a plan of political action. As he wrote later, his house by mid-1943 had become the centre of all anti-Fascist circles, including not only extremist elements whose views and intentions were known, but those from the old 'parties of order' which could properly set up a government 'capable of resuscitating the physiognomy of the demo-Liberal cabinets preceding the March on Rome'.

These groups had established 'occult and assiduous contact with the live forces in the country'. Their programme depended, like that of any other pretender or pretenders to the succession of the Duce, upon the ultimate action of the Crown. Bonomi's plan was in essence simple: the King must get rid of Mussolini's government, carry out his arrest and internment to prevent a counter-Fascist revival, place a general at the head of the new administration for a very brief period, and then nominate a civilian cabinet of the older statesmen to negotiate with the Allies for the withdrawal of Italy from the war. It is significant that even the Communists were prepared to accept such a solution, and in particular with regard to the monarchy.

In the eyes of the King, such a political manoeuvre was open to certain basic objections. The circle of anti-Fascist figures was connected in origin with the Princess of Piedmont, whose political activities had always been regarded with distrust by her father-in-law. Just as on the eve of the events of 1922 family feuds within the Royal House, at that time between the King and the Duca d'Aosta, had their significance,

---

of collected political writings. See the first brilliant essay on 'The Twenty-fifth of July'. See also his intervention at the Conference of the Italian Liberation Movement cited in note (*) above. The author was the civil commissioner for Corporations in the Badoglio administration.

so too in 1943. The connection of the Princess with these anti-Fascist personalities in part alienated the Sovereign but also forced him to meet their representatives. His confidence in these men was slight. His experience led him to believe that those forces that had failed to stop the rise of Fascism in 1922 could hardly form an effective alternative government in 1943. As he told Badoglio, who had originally acceded to Bonomi's plan and undertaken to press it upon the Sovereign, 'They are ghosts.' They had also never been able, in the prevailing climate of Fascist rule, to maintain the elements of an underground skeleton of a party organization. The only exception, and that a limited one, was the illegal Communist Party which had agreed to work with this embryo anti-Fascist opposition, and even in their case and in spite of their subsequent inflation of the significance of the strikes in March 1943, the real structure was modest. They had planned to move their organizational centre into Italy in August 1939 at a secret meeting held in Paris at which twenty-one delegates were present. The collapse of France destroyed the plan, and the first emissary arrived only in July 1941.

Indeed, if such mass organizational support for an anti-Fascist government had existed, the King would have displayed even greater suspicion of such a political plan, which might not only provoke civil war and a Fascist counter-coup, but could well undermine in the course of the explosion the existence of the monarchy itself, thus creating a situation which the King was at all costs determined to avoid—the setting up of a republican régime. By the middle of June 1943 the King had, however, made it clear that the Bonomi programme was not acceptable, and that any royal action would be concentrated on the setting up of a military government, strengthened by civilian technicians for the take-over of power. The details of such an operation remained guardedly in the hands of Acquarone and Ambrosio.

Any overt move against the authority and control of Mussolini had to be preceded by the undermining and fragmentation of the Fascist system itself. With the mounting tide of military disaster, the elements of a second Fronde took cautious and probing shape within the official ranks of Fascism. There was no conspiratorial group as such, nor organized plot against the régime. The leading elements of moderate and 'revisionist' Fascism, represented by Grandi, Federzoni, and Bottai, met from time to time in private conclave to seek another solution. It was these elements that opposed the entry into the war in 1940, and had played, each in its own way, a restraining and moderating part in the political compromise which emerged out of the March on Rome in 1922. The activities of these politicians—they could not be described as an organized political group—sought to define a programme in which the monarchy would resume its constitutional prerogatives violated by twenty years of Fascist rule, and in which a national front would be constructed, governing through the revived powers of the Senate and the Chamber, of which Grandi was President, producing the semblance to the outside world of a constitutional régime and including all men of good will—among them the moderate elements within the Fascist Party who, whatever opinion others might hold of them, regarded themselves as uncompromised by the errors of the personal rule of the Duce, and in particular by responsibility for the war itself.

Like Bonomi and his friends, the Grandi circle possessed no mass organization upon which it could rely and through which it could become a political force. The ultimate value of any proposals from such a quarter could lie only in the possible services to the Crown which the individuals themselves might render. Federzoni, as the elder statesman of the Italian Nationalist groups, still commanded considerable but completely unorganized support in certain Fascist circles. Bottai, the prime mover in the setting up of the Corporate State and a tireless campaigner for Fascist revisionism, which aimed at creating the licensed opposition within the ranks of the movement itself, seemed also on his past record to be an influential figure. Grandi possessed perhaps the strongest qualifications of all. Apart from being known at home after 1922 as a moderate in internal affairs, he had an undeniable and marked reputation as such in circles abroad. He saw himself, and not without reason, as the most acceptable negotiator between an Italian government reorganized on the initiative of the monarchy and the Western Allies. His constitutional programme, which he elaborated in private conversation with Federzoni and Bottai in the spring and summer months of 1943, was essentially linked with a concerted peace feeler towards the Western Allies.

There is no evidence as yet to show that at any stage the King was prepared to consider the Grandi plan as a political solution. In regard to eventual negotiations with the Allies, following the historical precedents of the First World War upon which the Sovereign's education was based, the only hope of working out a compromise peace lay within the circles of the Court, and it would be perhaps with the King alone, if at all, that the Allies might ultimately treat. There could be no question, in the Royal view, of any peace negotiations prior to the overthrow or collapse of the personal rule of Mussolini. The activities of Grandi and his circle were rather of immediate value to the Crown and to the Minister of Court, Acquarone, in accelerating the fragmentation of power of the Fascist system itself, and increasing the isolation of Mussolini within the Roman scene.

By the beginning of July the King seems to have agreed reluctantly to limited planning for a technical coup in Rome to be organized by the Army and the Military Police, to carry out the arrest of Mussolini and the leading Fascist Party bosses, and to set up an emergency military government under Badoglio. The timing had to depend upon events, and until the last minute he felt obliged to await the outcome of Mussolini's last moves towards Hitler in the hope of securing by diplomatic means Italy's withdrawal from the war with German consent. Everything turned on this now almost hopeless enterprise. It was the ultimate failure of Feltre which precipitated the crisis, but not its shape. It was to be left to the élite of Fascism itself to initiate the destruction of the system.

The summoning of the Grand Council, for which Scorza issued official invitations on July 21, as Mussolini put it at the meeting, 'precipitated the crisis of the régime'. In the view of most interested parties, and because it was the only form of effective and high-level debate which could be called into existence, the meeting of this body was the signal for intense and expectant agitation. But seldom has such a vital session been held in such confused circumstances. From the point of view of the Crown, the summoning of the Grand Council, if concluded with an adverse vote against Mussolini, gave the King the one weapon he was seeking—namely, the constitutional means to dismiss his Prime Minister, thus reducing direct and violent action to a minimum. To Grandi it was a supreme risk and challenge, and it is hardly surprising that at the last minute he seems to have hesitated. If all went well at the session, Grandi could go to the Crown with the majority vote which would mirror the strength of his personal position within the ranks of the Fascist movement and perhaps his ability to lead them in a 'constitutional' direction. If he were outvoted, he would be the first victim of repressive measures.

The attitude of Mussolini throughout these critical days of June and July 1943 as yet defies accurate analysis. In a bland understatement he wrote later: 'Everything came down to understandable expressions of discontent.' With his brilliant instinct for turning unpromising events to his advantage, he might derive positive results from the session. An adverse vote —and he never regarded the Grand Council as a voting body but a sounding-board—might give him the pretext to put sufficient pressure on Hitler to agree to the tidy withdrawal of Italy from the war which he had not been prepared to discuss at Feltre. On the internal front, Mussolini as Prime Minister would be able to go to the Sovereign, as he confidently did, with routine suggestions for the reconstruction of the government to carry through such a plan, and if he could transfer back to the Crown its military prerogatives, the burden of a break with Germany might perhaps be alternatively shouldered onto the King.

In the event, this historic meeting of July 24–5, 1943, voted unconsciously, and without conspiratorial intent, the fall of the régime. Its real significance was to obscure and confuse the ultimate responsibilities of power as wielded under Fascist rule. There were no organized parties within the Fascist system, as the result of the deliberate technique of the Duce's personal rule. The Grand Council itself was neither a cohesive body nor held together by strong group loyalties. The effect of this summoning in a supreme crisis was to blunt any possible rallying action by the Fascist Party and its armed embodiment, the Militia, in the defence of the régime. Everything was discussed in an air of bogus cabinet deliberation which was alien to the tradition of Fascist rule. The decision of the Grand Council, even if formally unconstitutional, seemed to absolve the Fascist leadership from its responsibilities, and the debate of the night of July 24–5 represents a complete abdication of the leadership, involving each individual member, including Mussolini himself.

Even the Germans awaited with complacency the outcome of this meeting. To what extent they had planned in practical and detailed terms either to support Mussolini forcibly in event of open opposition to his rule, or to replace him in event of political defeat, is not clear. The political atmosphere of Rome during these months is shadowed by ghostly threats, and the subsequent search for historical alibis further confuses any attempt to analyse the scene. The German Embassy seems to have overrated the activities of Farinacci and his extremist circle. It may be that they assumed that the latter possessed the stature of a Stellvertreter in event of the collapse of the Duce's position, or at best could with ultimate German support inject a final dose of resistance into the crumbling system with the Duce as a nominal figurehead. In any event, a strange quiet pervades German official circles in Rome during the critical hours. It was not until July 24 that reports reached Berlin of the summoning of the Grand Council for that evening, and the events of the subsequent days seem to have caught the Germans by surprise. The general view on the following morning that there would be some routine reshuffle of the government seems to have stilled any anxiety.

Whatever manoeuvres or intrigues or plots possessed any political reality during these hours, the shape of the crisis must in the last resort be dominated by military events. Both Bonomi and Grandi, from their very different analyses and attitudes, shared the same view that the removal of Mussolini from office, and the re-transfer of all constitutional powers to the Sovereign, must be linked with negotiations to put an end to Italian participation in the war. Such a decision must lie, however, exclusively with the Crown, and that far the King was not prepared to go. Having been forced by events to decide upon the arrest of Mussolini as a minimum operation, and to take certain precautionary measures against a Fascist rising, the King seems to have instructed the veteran statesman of the First World War, Vittorio Emmanuele Orlando, to draft the controversial radio announcement that 'the war continues', with its fateful consequences leading to the events of September 8, 1943, and circumscribing brutally the actions of the Badoglio administration.

The justification, however, in historical terms of such a decision depends upon the analysis of German strength and intentions in Italy in the event of the removal of the Duce. The opinion of the Italian military leaders must have been decisive here, together with the temperamental caution of the Sovereign. General Ambrosio's main concern, when pressing forward with the technical arrangements for the coup d'état on July 25, was with a possible German reaction.

During the course of July 24, Ambrosio, who had now made what military dispositions lay within his power to protect the capital, heard rumours of certain suspect German troop movements. At 5.30 p.m., just after the Grand Council had opened its session, Ambrosio asked Kesselring to come to his office. The latter announced that 'I wanted to inform you that it is agreed with Reichsmarshal Keitel that the two German divisions—the 305th and 76th—are ready to be transported to Southern Italy.' This move had been the subject of discussion between Keitel and Ambrosio on the train from Feltre to Tarvisio, and an uneasy and sibylline agreement had been obtained from Mussolini under pressure from Rintelen in Rome after the conference. It is not clear from the minutes of this present meeting between Ambrosio and Kesselring that the Italian Chief of Staff expressed any comment or agreement on this proposed move of German troops, which might have decisive implications in the pending crisis in Rome. But one thing must have been clear to Ambrosio: he could not answer for the military consequences of an immediate breach with the Germans, whether or not he expressed any view about Kesselring's announcement. And this decision must lie behind Orlando's draft radio broadcast on 'The War Continues.' Thus any possible plan for a simultaneous desertion of the Axis alliance at the time of Mussolini's arrest vanished.

Such was the military background to the establishment of the Badoglio administration in Rome on the evening of July 25. The technical coup d'état had taken place between the hours of 5 and 7 p.m. and in an atmosphere of apathetic calm. The expected reaction from the Fascist Party and Militia never came. The slow erosion of Fascist morale had reached the point of collapse, and the edifice toppled in a cloud of dust with no loss of life. The ultimate responsibility of the Duce was total.

After his arrest at the Villa Savoia on July 25, Mussolini was taken to the Carabinieri barracks in the Via Legnano. That evening he was visited by a doctor, to whom he described his medical symptoms at some length. He refused to take any drugs, adding, 'My physical person interests me no longer, but only my moral personality.'

Shortly after one o'clock on the following morning, a senior officer of the Italian General Staff called at the barracks with a personal letter addressed to 'His Excellency Cavaliere Benito Mussolini.'

'The undersigned Head of the Government wishes to inform Your Excellency that what has been done in your regard has been done solely in your personal interest, detailed information having reached us from several quarters of a serious plot against your person. He much regrets this, and wishes to inform you that he is prepared to give orders for your safe accompanying, with all proper respect, to whatever place you may choose.'

Mussolini promptly dictated to Badoglio's envoy the following reply, which the latter wrote down in his own hand.

July 26th, 1943. 1 a.m.

'I wish to thank Marshal Badoglio for the attention he is according my person.

'The only residence at my disposal is Rocca delle Caminate, whither I am prepared to go at any moment.

'I wish to assure Marshal Badoglio, if only in remembrance of the work we have done together in the past, that not only will I raise no difficulties of any sort, but I will co-operate in every possible way.

'I am glad of the decision to continue the war together with our allies, as the honour and interests of the country require at this time, and I express my earnest hope that success will crown the grave task which Marshal Badoglio is assuming by order and in the name of His Majesty the King, whose loyal servant I have been for twenty-one years and shall continue to be. Long live Italy!'

The historical significance of this letter has often been evaded, and has hitherto received little comment. Mussolini himself published them both in 1944, but Badoglio, during his period of office, never released either text. The tone and import of Mussolini's letter is identical with that of similar missives sent to Badoglio, by both Galbiati and Scorza, and shows a total moral abdication and acceptance of the King's action in dismissing the Duce, thus ending twenty years of Fascist rule and appointing a new administration. Mussolini's letter would appear by implication to absolve from all political responsibility those who had voted against him at the meeting of the Grand Council.

Throughout Sunday, July 26, Mussolini was under the impression that he would be exiled, as he had requested Badoglio, to his own house at Rocca delle Caminate. It seems, however, that for security reasons the new government hesitated to make such a concession, and that the Prefect of Forlì had indicated that he could not answer for public order in the event of Mussolini's being interned in the Romagna. It was decided, therefore, at the first meeting of the new Council of Ministers, to transfer the former Head of State to the island of Ponza off Naples, which Mussolini himself had established as a penal colony.

From the moment of his departure from Rome under escort on the evening of July 27, Mussolini disappeared from the public scene. He was taken from Caeta to Ponza in a corvette under the command of Admiral Maugeri. The party reached the island on the following morning. The Duce was treated as an ordinary internee. He was without funds with which to buy simple necessities until his family sent him 10,000 lire a few days later. He was installed in a small dwelling where the Abyssinian Ras Imeru had been similarly housed. On arrival the military police escort made off to lunch without making any such arrangements for their prisoner. The wife of one of them prepared a rough meal while the Duce rested in his whitewashed room on the bare springs of his bed with his greatcoat as a pillow. During the ten days of his stay on the island the fire was never lit to cook hot food. He remained isolated from the other internees and guarded by two military police, who also acted as batmen. Orders were given that no one was to speak to him.

Mussolini seems to have thought of compiling a Napoleonic memorial in exile, and he clearly had no thought of a Restoration. As he had said to Maugeri on the brief sea voyage to Ponza, 'I am politically dead'. His ill-fortune dated 'from June 28, 1942 [on his return from Africa]. One ought after all to give a man who had lost his chance the time in which to recover it.'

Hitler, however, was already mounting a special rescue operation for just such a purpose. This was not the chance which Mussolini was awaiting. He was content with his St. Helena. But the burden of power was not to be lifted from him so easily, and there was to be no escape from the strait-jacket of 'the brutal friendship' with his Axis partner and friend, Adolf Hitler.

After the spurious tranquility of only a few weeks' interlude of oblivion and isolation, he was to be jolted back into the political scene by his indefatigable German ally, without any chance or means to redeem the failures of the past, and chained to a hopeless future as an Axis satellite. The Duce was not to be spared one final act, and the only abdication was to be his own death by shooting.

BIBLIOGRAPHY

(A) Unprinted Documentary Sources

1. *Italian Collection.* Owing to the historical circumstances of the Second World War, in particular of the Armistice signed with Italy in September 1943 and the establishment of the Republic of Salò, only fragmentary collections of the Italian government archives fell into Allied hands. From the point of view of the historian, there is therefore no comparable set of records such as those of the German Foreign Office and Admiralty which ended in English custody, and of the German High Command and War Office which were deposited in the United States.

This Italian material, which is deposited at the present time at St. Antony's College, Oxford, and is referred to in this volume as the Italian Collection, falls into the following categories:

a) A series of documents, for the period up to July 1943, containing such valuable items as the correspondence between Mussolini and leading Fascist personalities dating back to the early period of Fascist rule. In particular, some of the Farinacci correspondence was found in the German Embassy in Rome in June 1944, where it was presumably deposited before his flight to Germany in the previous July. Other files throw new light on the workings of the Fascist Party, enlightened by numerous police reports on individuals. The minutes of frequent military conferences between the Duce, Field Marshal Kesselring, and General Ambrosio (including the latter's diary) have also been preserved.

b) A separate set of documents which contains certain papers of Ciano, and copies of the correspondence between Hitler and Mussolini, have been added to the above collection. These files were removed surreptitiously from the Italian Foreign Office in August 1943 on the orders of the then Foreign Minister, Baron Guariglia, and transferred to the Italian Legation in Lisbon, where they were handed over to the Americans at the end of the war. Much of this material has been printed either in the Diplomatic Papers of Ciano or the Italian edition of the Hitler-Mussolini Correspondence. But certain unpublished documents from this source have been published in the present volume.

The originals of all the above material have been returned to the Italian Government, and are deposited either in the Foreign Office or the State Archives in Rome.

2. *German Collection.* The documents referred to under this heading are from four sources:

a) *The German Foreign Office Archives* from which selected files have been deposited in the Public Record Office. None of this material has been previously published, and the author has drawn heavily on this collection, particularly for the German minutes of the Axis summit conferences of the war, minutes and memoranda of the German Foreign Office on Italian affairs, and the records of the German Embassy in Rome. The originals of this whole collection are now in the German Foreign Office.

b) *Himmler Files.* These are fragmentary and small in bulk, and are of interest only as containing certain reports to Himmler from his agents in Italy. Copies of this material exist in the Institut für Zeitgeschichte in Munich.

c) *Archives of the German War Office.* These are deposited in Alexandria, Virginia, and have been used primarily in relation to the military records of certain conferences and reports, in particular from General von Rintelen, German Military Representative in Rome.

d) *The Hitler Military Conferences.* Most of these records have been published in Gilbert: *Hitler Directs His War* (Oxford University Press, 1950), but certain unpublished extracts have been used in this book. The original documents have been deposited in the Library of the University of Pennsylvania, U.S.A.

(B) Printed Documentary Sources

1. *Italian*		
Ciano, G.	*Diary* (1939–43) (English translation)	Heinemann. 1947
——	*Diplomatic Papers* (English translation)	Odhams. 1948
Hitler e Mussolini	*Lettere e Documenti*	Rizzoli. 1946
Mussolini, B.	*Opera Omnia.* Volumes XXXI & XXXII. (Edited by Edoardo e Duilio Susmel)	La Fenice. 1960
2. *German*	*Fuehrer Conferences on Naval Affairs* (Edited by the Admiralty)	1947
	The Goebbels Diaries (Edited and translated by Louis Lochner)	Hamish Hamilton. 1948
	Hitler Directs His War (The stenographic records of certain Military Conferences. Edited and translated by Dr. Felix Gilbert)	Oxford University Press. New York 1950
Hitler, A.	*Table Talk* (1941–1944) (English translation)	Weidenfeld & Nicolson. 1953
	Nazi Conspiracy and Aggression (Documents presented at the Nuremberg Trials. 10 volumes)	Washington, D.C. (1946–8)
	The Rommel Papers (English translation. Edited by Captain B. H. Liddell Hart)	Collins. 1953

(C) Secondary Sources

1. *General Works*

Begnac, Yvon de	*Palazzo Venezia. Storia di un Regime*	La Rocca. 1950
Bullock, A. L. C.	*Hitler*	Odhams. 1952
Canevari, E.	*La Guerra Italiana*	
Churchill, W. S.	*The Second World War*	Cassell (6 volumes)
Faldella, E.	*L'Italia e la Seconda Guerra Mondiale*	Cappelli (Second edition). 1960
Gigli, G.	*La Seconda Guerra Italiana (1939–1945)*	Laterza. 1951
Germino, D. L.	*The Italian Fascist Party in Power*	University of Minnesota Press. 1959
Hinsley, F.	*Hitler's Strategy*	Cambridge University Press. 1951
Salvatorelli, L. and Mira, G.	*Storia d'Italia nel Periodo Fascista*	Einaudi. 1956
Tamaro, A.	*Vent' Anni di Storia (1922–1943)*	Tiber, Roma. 1953
Wheeler-Bennett, J.	*The Nemesis of Power (The German Army in Politics, 1918–1945)*	Macmillan. 1953
Wiskemann, E.	*The Rome-Berlin Axis*	Oxford University Press. 1949

(C) Secondary Sources

2. *Memoirs, Monographs, and Special Studies*

Abshagen, K. H. *Canaris* Union Deutsche Vertagsanstalt. 1949

Alfieri, D. *Due Dittatori di Fronte* Rizzoli. 1948

Amé, C. *Guerra Segreta in Italia* Casini. 1954

Anfuso, F. *Da Palazzo Venezia al Lago di Garda* Cappelli. 1957

Badoglio, P. *L'Italia nella Seconda Guerra Mondiale* Mondadori. 1946

Bastianini, G. *Uomini, Cose, Fatti* Vitagliano. 1959

Benigno, Jo di *Occasioni Mancate (Roma in un Diario Segreto, 1943–1944)* S.E.I. Roma. 1945

Bolla, N. *Il Segreto di Due Re* Rizzoli. 1951

Bonomi, I. *Diario di Un Anno: 2 guigno 1943–10 guigno 1944* Garzanti. 1947

Bottai, G. *Vent' Anni e Un Giorno* Garzanti. 1949

Bova Scoppa, R. *Colloqui con Due Dittatori* Ruffolo, Roma. 1949

Brinon, F. de *Mémoires* L.L.C. Paris. 1949

Canevari, E. *La Fine del Maresciallo Cavallero* Latinità (Collection: Documenti per la Storia)

Carboni, G. *Più che il Dovere (Memorie Segrete 1935–1948)* Parenti. 1955

Catalano, F. *Storia del CLNAI* Laterza. 1956

Cavallero, U.	*Comando Supremo, Diario* 1940	Cappelli. 1948
Caviglia, E.	*Diario* (1925–1945)	Casini. 1952
Cucco, A.	*Non Volevamo Perdere*	Cappelli. 1940
Dollmann, E.	*Roma Nazista* (Trans. Zingarelli, I.)	Longanesi. 1951
Favagrossa, C.	*Perche perdemmo la Guerra*	Rizzoli. 1947
Galbiati, E.	*Il 25 luglio e la MVSN*	Bernabo. 1950
Gorla, G.	*L'Italia nella Seconda Guerra Mondiale*	Baldini e Castoldi. 1959
Guérard, J.	*Criminel de Paix*	Nouvelles Editions Latines. 1953
Hagen, W.	*Die Geheime Front*	Niebelungen Verlag. 1950
Hillgrüber, A.	*Hitler, König Carol und Marshall Antonescu*	Steiner, Wiesbaden. 1954
Kallay, N.	*Hungarian Premier*	Oxford University Press. 1954
Kesselring, A.	*Soldat bis zum Letzen Tag*	Athenaum, Bonn. 1953
Kleist, P.	*Zwischen Hitler und Stalin 1939–1945*	Athenaum, Bonn. 1950
Kordt, E.	*Nicht aus den Akten*	U.D.G.S. Stuttgart. 1950
——	*Wahn und Wirklichkeit*	U.D.G.S. Stuttgart. 1948
Leto, G.	OVRA	Cappelli. 1951
Macartney, C. A.	*October Fifteenth. A History of Modern Hungary 1929–1945*	Edinburgh University Press. 1956
Mallet, A.	*Pierre Laval* (2 volumes)	Amiot-Dumont. 1955

(C) Secondary Sources

Massola, U.	*Marzo 1943. Ore dieci*	Edizioni di Cultura Sociale, Roma. 1950
Maugeri, F.	*From the Ashes of Disgrace*	Reynal and Hitchcock. New York. 1948
Messe, G.	*La Guerra al Fronte Russo*	Rizzoli. 1947
——	*La Mia Armata in Tunisia (Come Finì la Guerra in Africa)*	Rizzoli (Second edition). 1960
Monelli, P.	*Roma 1943*	Migliaresi. 1946
Mussolini, R.	*La Mia Vita con Benito*	Mondadori. 1948
Napolitano, V.	*25 Luglio*	Vega. 1944
Pansa, R. C.	*Marcello Soleri*	Garzanti. 1948
Pini, G.	*Itinerario Tragico*	Omnia. 1950
Pini, G. e Susmel, D.	*Mussolini l'Uomo e l'Opera* (four volumes)	La Fenice. 1953–5
Pozzi, A.	*Come li ho visto Io*	Mondadori. 1947
Puntoni, P.	*Parla Vittorio Emmanuele III*	Palazzi. 1958
Ribbentrop, J. von	*The Ribbentrop Memoirs* (Trans. Watson, O.)	Weidenfeld & Nicolson. 1954
Rintelen, E. von	*Mussolini als Bundesgenosse*	Leins. 1951
Roatta, M.	*Otto Milioni di Baionetti*	Mondadori. 1946

Senise, C.	*Quando Ero Capo della Polizia 1940–1943*	Ruffolo. 1946
Silva, P.	*Io Difendo la Monarchia*	de Fonseca. 1946
Simoni, L.	*Berlino, Ambasciata d'Italia*	Migliaresi. 1946
Soleri, M.	*Memorie*	Einaudi. 1949
Tamaro, A.	*Due Anni di Storia, 1943–45* (Three volumes)	Tosi, Roma. 1948
Vailati, V.	*Badoglio Racconta*	Ilte. 1956
——	*Badoglio Risponde*	Rizzoli. 1958

(D) Articles

1. *Bibliographical*

Rava, F. and Spini, G. — 'Fonti documentarie e memorialistiche per la storia della crisi dello stato italiano' (1940–1945)
Rivista Storica Italiana LXI

Toscano, M. — 'Fonti documentarie e memorialistiche per la Storia Diplomatica della Seconda Guerra Mondiale'.
Questioni di storia contemporanea, 1952

2. *Articles from reviews and interviews in newspapers*

Ambrosio, V. — 'La parte dei militari nel 25 Luglio e nell' 8 Settembre'. Interview in *Il Corriere della Sera*, March 11, 1955.

(See also a further interview with General Ambrosio in *Unità*, October 22, 1953.)

(D) Articles

Cerica, A.	'Sull' arresto di Mussolini'.	*Tempo*. July–August, 1956
Farinacci, R.	'Diario'	*Il Giornale* (Naples). Jan–Feb, 1947
Federzoni, L.	'L'Ultima Seduta'	*Quadrante*. October 19, 1946
——	'Memorie'	*Indipendente*. May–July, 1946
Grandi, D.	Interviews in *Incom Illustrata* July–August 1952; in *Il Corriere della Sera*, 9–10 February 1955; and in *Oggi* May–June, 1959.	
Maugeri, F.	'Mussolini me ha detto'	*Quaderni di Politica Estera*. 1944
Pellicano, I.	'I superstiti del Gran Consiglio si sono decisi di parlare'	*L'Elefante*. 13–20 October, 1949
Vecchi, de	'Mussolini Vero'	*Tempo*. November 1959–March 1960

APPENDIX

The German authorities and the Italian Foreign Archives (1943–1944) *

(a) *The Seizure of the Archives.*

During the course of researches into the German Foreign Office Archives and certain documents in the Italian Collection for this study, a number of references has come to light revealing in part the fate of those files from Palazzo Chigi, which were impounded by the Germans after the Italian armistice.

On September 12, 1943, Ribbentrop sent instructions to Ambassador Rahn in Rome to take all necessary steps to seize the archives of the Italian Foreign Office.[1]

At 10.30 on the morning of September 14 the senior official in charge at Palazzo Chigi, Ambassador Rosso, noted in a memorandum drafted on the following day,[2] that the personnel at the entrance to the building warned him that it 'was about to be surrounded by a cordon of German military armed with sub-machine-guns, who were taking up positions at the corners of the edifice'. An S.S. officer, accompanied by an armed escort, was announced in Rosso's office and introduced himself as Major Kappler, the German Police Chief in Rome. He declared that he had instructions from the Fuehrer 'to take charge of all documents which could be of interest to the Anglo-Americans if they should fall into their hands', Major Kappler appeared to be well informed of the lay-out of the premises, and made an immediate search of certain private offices. He then announced that he must impound and remove certain files. As Rosso cryptically noted in his memorandum of September 15, 'In fact one succeeded in avoiding that Major Kappler should take away a great part of the archives', but he did show particular interest in the papers of Minister Vitetti, and those of Minister Pietromarchi from which he also removed a portable radio transmitter.

Three lorry loads of documents in all were taken away that evening from Palazzo Chigi. It was noted by the Ger-

* Professor Mario Toscano has published an article entitled 'Le Vicende degli Archivi Segreti di Palazzo Chigi' in 'Nuova Antologia' (No. 1923 March 1961), which is based in great part on the original draft of this appendix.

mans 'that the shelves and the filing cabinets in the Secret Archives Section were empty'. Considerable funds were found, and Rahn suggested that these should be transferred to a new Italian government.[3] On September 17, 41 packing cases of files were dispatched under armed guard to Berlin.[4]

(b) *The preliminary study of the material by the German authorities.*

On September 23 Dr Stieve, of the German Foreign Office Archives, was instructed to set up a team to study these Italian papers.[5] The preliminary report was sent to Ribbentrop from Berlin on September 28. The 41 cases contained some 2,000 files with 15,000 documents in 200 series. There had been an 'unbelievably disordered keeping of the documents', which were barely in chronological order, in loose folders, many of them not even tied up. They consisted broadly of (1) Cabinet papers of the Foreign Minister (filed under subjects) (1932 to August 1943). (2) Papers of the Directorate-General of European and Mediterranean Affairs (1936 to August 1943). (3) A collection of ingoing and outgoing 'non secret' telegrams (1940 to 1943).

On about September 4, according to enquiries made subsequently by the Germans in Rome, Guariglia had ordered each section of the Ministry to destroy their secret files.

The papers in (1) above contained the main files during Suvich's period of office as Undersecretary at the Italian Foreign Office (1932 to 1935) including records of his political conversations. 'For the period of Ciano and Bastianini all papers are missing. It appears that these were kept in a secret collection, and have either been destroyed or taken away.'

There was almost nothing of value on the period after the fall of Mussolini, or on the Lisbon negotiations with the Allies after August 15, and only one secret telegram revealing that these messages did not pass through the Foreign Ministry.

On general points Stieve reported:

(1) *Of immediate propaganda value.* Very little, except on Italo-Roumanian relations. This would be worked up at once. A few interesting details regarding Spain and Portugal. Fairly full reports from Italian missions in Germany and German-occupied territories. Conversations with Japanese diplomats and in Turkey.

(2) *Historical.* One could reconstruct in detail Suvich's period of office.

(3) *Personal.* A few individual notes of interest.

Stieve then summarized the first impressions of his team. The Italian reports from Germany after the autumn of 1942 were 'extensively negative, mistrustful, and unfavourable'. There was no sign of any reproving action by the Duce. Alfieri's dispatches 'in this respect are unbelievable'. Throughout 1943 there was a daily increase of defeatism in the Italian Foreign Ministry.[6]

On October 1, 1943, Steengracht, the Undersecretary at the Foreign Office, minuted that the file of Hitler's letters to Mussolini had been found in a folder made up for the use of Guariglia. The last letter was dated May 19, 1943, and two letters are missing–March 11, 1938 and February 5, 1941.[7] Ribbentrop showed great personal interest in this file and gave orders to look for copies of Mussolini's letters to Hitler.[8] On October 6 a Foreign Ministry telegram was dispatched to Rahn asking him to find out from the Duce if he has copies of the two missing Hitler letters, and also to make a further search.[9] On October 11 Rahn's subordinate, Moellhausen, reported that such a search had proved fruitless.[10] On October 23 a further report from Rahn stated that the Duce did not know where the missing letters were.[11]

(c) *Detailed reports by Strohm on Italian Archives*

A more thorough survey of the material was now undertaken by Consul-General Strohm. It appears that he drafted 16 reports numbered in order. These were passed to Ribbentrop by Dr Hencke of his Private Office with covering minutes. The German records contain three of these minutes, based on Strohm's third, sixth, and fifteenth reports and dated October 18, October 21, and November 20 respectively.[12] There is no trace of Strohm's original reports.

The three surviving Hencke minutes are:

(a) October 18, 1943.

'Herewith is submitted the enclosed report No. 3, which has been drawn up by Consul-General Strohm. It is concerned with the efforts made by Turkey to build up a Balkan bloc in early this year and certain steps taken by Roumania in the same sense in August 1943.

'As to the content of the Italian archives submitted herewith, attention is drawn to the following:

(1) 'On the soundings made by Turkey in Budapest and

Bucharest directly after the Adana Conference with a view to setting up an alleged anti-Bolshevik Balkan bloc, in which also Hungary should be included, we were already informed by the middle of March through communications from the Hungarian Government and from secret sources. On the basis of these reports Ambassador von Papen discussed the subject thoroughly on March 19 with the Turkish Foreign Minister, who attempted to play down the Turkish initiative. The matter was also raised with the Bulgarian Minister in Berlin.

(2) 'The assumption that the Italian Government did not discuss with us at the time of the Turkish initiative, is not borne out by our (own) archives. These show rather that Minister Baldoni transmitted to us on March 23 and April 8 extracts from the relevant reports of the Italian representatives in Bucharest and Ankara, and that the Italian Embassy in Budapest kept our Ministers there informed in detail on Hungarian-Italian talks on the Turkish démarche.

(3) 'On the conduct of the Roumanian Government in early 1943 and the rôle of the Italian Minister Bova Scoppa, we were already informed through the reports of the former Stefani representative in Bucharest, Trandafilo (the correspondent of the Italian official news agency Stefani, and an informant of the Italian legation) . . . These reports are fuller than the only fragmentary Italian archives. The extracts from these documents also confirm Mihai Antonescu's readiness to respond to Turkish prompting, although he expressed his conviction that this could not have been made without British agreement.

'We know anyway from secret sources that the Undersecretary of State, Bastianini, warned the Roumanians some weeks later against following up the Turkish proposal, since he regarded it as an intrigue inspired by England.

(4) 'From these Italian documents, Turkish motives are clear. The Italian Minister in Ankara compares two alternatives:

(a) Turkey is pursuing the plan of building up a definitely defensive line within the sphere of her special interests in the event of an Axis withdrawal from the Balkans becoming necessary.

(b) The Turkish initiative is merely one link in a series of British attempts to drive Hungary, Roumania and Bulgaria out of the Axis.

'Ambassador von Papen has expressed the view that the Hungarians and Roumanians had attributed an exaggerated importance to the more theoretical Turkish démarche. The Bulgarian diplomats have also a similar impression. It is not firmly established in our documentation how far England has in fact inspired in detail this action by Turkey.

'The British Ambassador in Ankara has told the Yugoslav emigré representative there that, a week before the Adana Conference he had given Turkey information on British plans for the post-war organization of Europe and for the various federation projects. On the basis of this move it seems therefore that the planned Turkish initiative was discussed in general terms at the Adana Conference. In any event, only a few weeks ago the Turkish Foreign Minister told our Ambassador that the British had put forward at Adana the idea of a Balkan Federation. Anyway, the British did not this time openly support the amalgamation of the small states of Europe into groups of states, as Churchill's broadcast of March 21, 1943, shows.

'Whether Churchill agreed to the Turkish proposals in every detail is doubtful. For example, the inclusion of Hungary does not seem to correspond to British intentions. The reports of the Yugoslav and Serb (*sic*) emigré representatives give the impression that England was rather thinking of an extension to the various Balkan states of the agreement of January 15, 1942, of the Greek and Yugoslav Governments in exile. One can also probably assume that London was not quite in accord with Turkish activity, since rumours soon appeared in the press which only stressed the anti-Bolshevik side of the plan. It appears from our archives and from secret sources that the Turks had already dropped the subject by March 22, and had never officially taken it up again. The Turkish Foreign Minister told the Hungarian Minister in Ankara that the British Ambassador had asked him not to continue conversations. From the reports of the Yugoslav and Greek emigré representatives in Ankara one can see likewise that the English had put the brake on the Turks as from mid-March, as they had to take into account a foreseeable opposition from the Soviet Union.

(5) 'As to the Roumanian initiative in Sofia in August 1943, we were immediately informed by Minister President Filov. According to the latter's communication to us, this initiative went further than the Italian archives reveal. Apart from a co-operation of the Balkan states, it was proposed in the event of a German collapse to bring in British and American troops, so that they could protect the Balkan states

against Russia. The only new point for us is that Mihai Antonescu informed Bova Scoppa of his successful move in Sofia, and explained already on August 21, 1943, that the political action of Roumania must seek its inspiration in that of Italy. It is also noteworthy that Bova Scoppa gained the impression from a talk with Mihai Antonescu that the latter looked to an intervention by Turkey in the Balkans precisely in order that this would hold up the dreaded Soviet advance.

'I cannot join in the view that Bova Scoppa's telegram of August 21 (not quoted) offers proof that the Roumanians were informed of the Italian armistice negotiations.

'It might be expedient to inform our Minister in Bucharest of the content of these extracts as they are of interest to him for the attitude of the Roumanian Government in recent months. A corresponding draft is attached.

'These Italian reports, set out in the first pages of the report, on Churchill's efforts of the Adana Conference to induce Turkey to prepare an anti-Bolshevik advance post in the Balkans, could be exploited to disturb Anglo-Soviet relations. I would therefore suggest that these passages are transmitted to Ambassador von Papen with instructions to play them, without revealing their source and in so far as he sees no objection, to Soviet agents with the comment that such information as is already known as to Churchill's attempts to whip up Turkey against the Soviet Union receives further proof.'

(b) October 21, 1943.

'The report No. 6 on the Italian archives drawn up by Consul-General Strohm is herewith submitted, together with an appendix belonging thereto. The collection of documents contains particularly interesting extracts from reports and minutes of conversations between Japanese and Italian diplomats and statesmen, above all in the summer of 1943.

'Attention is drawn to the following points contained in the Italian documents under review:

'The extracts show that Japanese and Italian diplomats have repeatedly referred to a joint or parallel influence on German policy. This joint action is above all based on the fact that they were only in effect interested in Germany's war against England and America, and judged Germany's struggle against Russia primarily from the standpoint that it could hinder or endanger a victory over England.

'It thus resulted that:

(1) 'Both powers wanted a strengthening of the German war effort on the Mediterranean front. As, for example, the Japanese Ambassador in Rome, Horikiri, explained in a conversation with the Italian Ambassador in Madrid on June 15, 1943, it was a grave error that the Germans would not regard the Mediterranean as the main military theatre. On the other hand, Bastianini assured the Japanese Ambassador on July 23 that Italy had never failed to stress in Berlin in every possible way the importance of the Mediterranean front.

(2) 'Both powers are interested in the conclusion of a separate peace between Germany and the Soviet Union, and seek to influence Germany in this sense. Already in a conversation on October 21, 1942, Oshima spoke to Alfieri of the possibility that Japan would formally guarantee such a separate peace. On April 22, 1943, Oshima informed Alfieri that he had sounded the German Foreign Minister on the possibility of peace negotiations with the Soviet Union at a later stage, but that the German Foreign Minister had replied that the conditions proposed by Germany would not be acceptable to Stalin. On June 16, 1943, the Japanese Minister in Madrid told the Italian Minister there that Japan had already made attempts at mediation, which had failed because of Germany's refusal to consider the condition of handing back the occupied territories to the Soviet Union. Horikiri complained, in the above-mentioned conversation of June 15, of the alleged refusal by Germany to give up the annexation of the Ukraine and the Caucasus, and remarked that "not enough pressure had been brought to bear on Germany to move her to give up the occupied territories."

'This Japanese standpoint finds a certain parallel in the statements of Bastianini and the Duce shortly before the latter's fall. On July 23 Bastianini stated to the Japanese Minister that already several months ago the Duce had outlined to the Fuehrer and to the German Foreign Minister his views on the necessity of a political solution in the East. The Duce himself informed the Japanese Minister at noon on July 25 that he had decided in the course of the following week "to undertake an energetic démarche with the Fuehrer . . . with the intention of moving the Fuehrer to cease hostilities in the East and reach a settlement with Russia". Mussolini requested the Minister in a very pressing manner to inform the Japanese Minister President that "it was his earnest wish that Japan should support with all her strength such an approach to the Fuehrer".

'It should be mentioned in this connection that at the beginning of September the Japanese government, following a telegram from the Italian Minister in Tokyo of September 5, considered as unlikely the possibility of a separate peace between Germany and Russia in view of the increase in Soviet aspirations.

(3) 'As a result of this pressing desire for the conclusion of a separate German-Russian peace, there appear various expressions of regret as to German territorial demands on the Soviet Union. This regret takes the form of unfriendly criticism of the above-mentioned remarks of Minister Horikiri. Also in the minute drafted by Bastianini on the draft statements to the Japanese Minister on July 25 there is a note of criticism.

(4) 'There is also a parallelism in Japanese and Italian policy in seeking from Germany greater concessions towards the small states of Europe. Thus the Japanese Minister in Rome reports on June 8, 1943, that Oshima had recommended to the German Foreign Minister "a policy in favour of the small states". Horikiri welcomed the well-known speech of Bastianini to the (Italian) Senate on the problem of Europe, and expressed himself in critical terms of Germany because she had not, like Japan in the Far East "given back to the small states their political and economic independence". On the other side, Bastianini assured the Japanese Minister on July 23 that the Duce had already repeatedly drawn attention in Berlin to the "fruitful and intelligent" organization by the Japanese of the New Order in the Far East.

(5) 'The extracts from the documents show that many Japanese diplomats regard German foreign policy with a certain reserve and criticism. In particular this applies to the former Minister in Rome, Horikiri. On the other hand, it is clear from the documents under review that Minister Oshima is regarded by his Japanese colleagues as an unconditional supporter of collaboration with the Reich. This is expressed by Horikiri in the remark: "Oshima is a soldier, and has completely fallen for the German military."

(6) 'Bastianini stated as late as July 23 that no other purpose existed in Rome other than "to resist in every way and by every means in our power, great or small". The Duce, however, two days later, said that, unless one arrived at the cessation of hostilities with the Soviet Union for which one was striving "the conditions under which Italy is fighting *her*

war are such that in a short time it will be absolutely impossible for her to continue hostilities. She will therefore be compelled to examine a solution of a political character."

'It should of course be realized that this statement was meant to emphasize above all the urgency of the request to Japan to support the planned démarche to the Fuehrer.'

(c) November 20, 1943.

'I attach Consul-General Strohm's report No. 15 on the Italian documents, in which he has put together all the findings about Italy's conduct at the outbreak of the war and during the French campaign. Report No. 16, also attached, examines on the basis of the evidence in report No. 15 the Foreign Minister's question as to whether the Italian documents give any indications that perhaps "Mussolini's conduct towards us was at certain moments doubtful." In conclusion the following should be noted on the contents of the report:

(1) 'The documents we have for 1939 and 1940 are so fragmentary that no reasonably definite picture of Italy's policy can be formed from them.

(2) 'The reports confirm, as we knew already and as was also apparent from the documents captured in France, that England had since the beginning of 1938 taken immense pains to cultivate her relations with Italy. Through these she was not only pursuing the aim—increasingly apparent in the Italian records—of effecting through Italian action in Berlin some postponement and modification of Germany's political initiatives, she was also striving in the long run to detach Italy from her friendship with Germany and to preserve Italian neutrality in the event of war. Therefore, as we know from the French documents, England sought during the winter of 1938–9 and right up to summer 1939 to induce France to make concessions towards Italy's Mediterranean aspirations —naturally without success. Italy must have welcomed England's conduct, since first of all it brought about recognition of the conquest of Abyssinia, and then opened certain prospects of realizing her aspirations *vis-à-vis* France on a peaceful basis. That the Italian government in return, so to speak, for English recognition of the Empire definitely promised in spring 1938 to exert constant influence in Berlin for "modifications" in England's favour, seems to me to be an inference which so far is not fully borne out by the available material. (That on several occasions the Italians let English

confirmations of their "peace-promoting" activity pass uncontradicted, is understandable for reasons of propaganda.) At any rate the Italian documents show, as Consul-General Strohm also concludes, that in spite of all England's efforts, under the Duce's personal influence the Italian government put friendship with Germany more and more before relations with England, although these were welcome in themselves. This led, as early as the beginning of June 1939, to Mussolini's unambiguous question to the British Ambassador in Rome, whether considering England's isolationist policy "the Anglo-Italian agreement was still worth anything".

'After the outbreak of war England continued in markedly friendly language to try to hold Italy to her neutral course, and even at the beginning of September 1939 with a reference to Italy's efforts at mediation held the prospect of playing the rôle of European peace-bringer before the Duce's eyes. The documents give no evidence that the Italian Government was influenced in determining its policy by such enticements. Rather, at the turn of the year 1939–40, Mussolini refused to receive the former Dutch Minister President Coljin whom the Dutch Government sent to Rome to sound out possibilities of peace. He informed the Dutch Foreign Minister explicitly that he did not intend "to make any peace initiatives in the present circumstances". Finally, the British Government's attempts at the end of May 1940 to induce Italy to preserve her neutrality, by being willing to start immediate negotiations on the basis of English and French political concessions, were wrecked: already in the middle of May, as is apparent from the American White Paper "Peace and War", Mussolini had given Roosevelt clearly to understand that he had decided to enter the war on the side of Germany. We already know from public explanations given by the British Prime Minister that these last English efforts took in part the form of letters from Churchill to Mussolini. It is merely new that on May 26, under the pressure of the defeats in France, Halifax told the Italian Ambassador in London that he was definitely prepared in Italo-English negotiations "to take Italy's special connections with Germany into account, i.e. in the comprehensive framework of a lasting and just European settlement for which the Duce had worked ceaselessly and untiringly". This basic readiness for general peace negotiations was however qualified by the corollary "as soon as a favourable and decisive opportunity for this should arise". Finally, moreover, on May

30 Daladier suggested to the Duce "making a peace initiative through a universal settlement of European conditions on a new basis".

(3) 'Since the end of 1939 Roosevelt had played an increasingly large part in the attempts to keep Italy neutral. Already on January 6, 1940, the American President had suggested common "effective action" by the United States, Italy and the Pope "for the restoration of peace in Europe" and had even expressed the desire for a personal meeting with the Duce in the course of 1940. The Americans obviously expected that Sumner Welles' tour of May 1940 would open the way for further efforts in Italy; it appears that the results of the North American Undersecretary of State's visit to Rome did not come up to these expectations. We already know from the American White Paper "Peace and War" all the details of the four messages by which Roosevelt sought in May 1940 to hold Mussolini back from intervening in the war, and the Duce's answers.

(4) 'The Italian documents confirm the impression that in the first month of the war Ciano and Italian diplomacy strove to complete Italian non-belligerence with a policy of fundamental neutrality, and to place Italy at the head of a "Neutral Bloc", through which Italy's position especially in the Balkans and Spain would be decisively strengthened. Berlin should be made to infer from this that such an attitude was also in Germany's interests, since a "Neutral Bloc led by Italy" would hinder England's policy of extending the war. It was obvious, however, as the attitude of the Italian Ambassador in Berlin, Attolico, shows, that this influential Italian diplomatic representative considered that she should adopt this policy even without Germany's approval. At the same time a closer mutual friendship with Japan was being considered which, according to the documents, appears partly attributable to initiatives made by the Japanese Government of the time, under the first impact of the German-Soviet Treaty.

'All these plans for an independent Italian neutral policy were however obviously very soon dropped again. In any case as early as October 6, 1939, Ciano had explicitly informed the Spanish Government that he had never said that Italy would make a declaration of neutrality. In the documents at our disposal there are no indications of a later return to such tendencies.

(5) 'Apart from the theme of Italian policy towards Ger-

many and the Western Powers, the contents of the documents contain the following notable details:

(a) 'Already on February 21, 1938, Chamberlain explained to the Italian Ambassador, Grandi, that the British Government looked upon Austria as lost and had no intention of making proposals or suggestions to other states in relation to the Austrian situation.

(b) 'A Polish attempt to urge Italy through the Vatican to use her influence in Berlin was answered as early as May 2, 1939, by Ciano, with instructions to the Italian Ambassador in Warsaw to make it clear to Beck that in the event of a crisis Italy would "take her stand clearly at the side of Germany".

(c) 'From a Spanish minute delivered in Rome on August 30, 1939, it appears that at the end of August Bonnet implored General Franco to call for a 10-day "armistice" in which to continue negotiations, France and England being willing. Franco asked in the minute for Mussolini's opinion, since he "was in direct touch with the Fuehrer". How the Italian Government reacted to this suggestion is not clear from the documents; probably it was superseded by the well-known Italian initiatives.

(d) 'This sentence from Ambassador Bastianini's report of October 24, 1939, on his first impressions in England should be noted: "Halifax, Vansittart and Cadogan have made no secret of their preoccupation about the progress Communism might make during and after the war."'

There is no further reference to this study of these Italian documents in the microfilmed records of the German Foreign Office except, in a minute of March 21, 1944, the German War Office appear to have instituted a detailed study of documents relating to Badoglio's 'betrayal'. Field Marshal Jodl instructed Professor Major Schramm to undertake the research, and the latter asked to see the material held by the German Foreign Office, and Steengracht in the above minute recommended that he should have such access.[13]

The subsequent fate of these Italian archives is unknown. One version states that they were destroyed in an Allied bombardment of Berlin. If this is the case, the three memoranda drawn up by Dr Hencke of Ribbentrop's private office constitute the sole surviving evidence of their contents.

NOTES

Book I

1: 'The Fourth Punic War'

1 Italian Collection. Speech of the Duce to the Grand Council, February 4, 1939
2 Quoted in Pini e Susmel, *Mussolini: L'Uomo e L'Opera,* Vol IV, p 161
3 *Hitler's Table Talk,* p 592
4 *Ibid* p 614
5 Nuremberg Trial Documents (German edition) Vol XXVI, D.798, p 339
6 German Collection
7 Italian Collection. Mussolini to Hitler, May 30, 1939. (Also printed in Toscano, *Le Origini Diplomatiche del Patto D'Acciaio,* pp 362–5)
8 *Ibid* Telegram from the King to Mussolini, September 17, 1939
9 *Ibid* Memorandum by the Duce, March 31, 1940
10 *Ibid* Minutes of meeting of the Duce with the Chiefs of Staff, May 29, 1940
11 Italian Minutes of the Munich meeting June 18, 1940, in Carboni, *Più che il Dovere* (Second Edition, 1955), pp 95 ff
12 Italian Collection. Mussolini to Hitler, June 22, 1940
13 Carboni, *op cit*
14 *Ibid*
15 German Collection. Rintelen report, September 11, 1940
16 Rossi, *Mussolini e lo Stato Maggiore,* p 21
17 Graziani, *Processo I* (stenographic record), p 132
18 Italian Collection. Memorandum by General Ambrosio (undated, but probably drafted for the Feltre meeting July 19, 1943), 'The Politico-Military Conduct of the War by the Axis'
19 Printed in Graziani, *Africa Settentrionale* (1940–1), p 279
20 Messe, *La Guerra al Fronte Russo,* pp 177–8
21 Quoted in Rintelen, *Mussolini als Bundesgenosse,* p 21
22 Rintelen, *op cit* p 165
23 See Faldella, *L'Italia e La Seconda Guerra Mondiale,* p 428
24 Cavallero, *Comando Supremo,* p 251

25 e.g. 2,700 tons of stores unloaded at Benghazi on May 13. Cavallero, *op cit* p 256
26 Quoted in Cavallero, *op cit* pp 274–6
27 Kesselring, *Soldat Bis Zum Letzten Tag*, p 169
28 Italian Collection. Hitler to Mussolini, June 23, 1942. An abbreviated version in Cavallero, *op cit* pp 277–8
29 *Ibid* Mussolini to Hitler, July 22, 1942
30 *Ibid* Hitler to Mussolini, August 4, 1942
31 Cavallero, *op cit* p 282
32 *Ibid* p 283
33 Alfieri, '*Two Dictators Face to Face*' (French translation), pp 255–6 (August 5, 1942)
34 German Collection. Hitler-Vidussoni conversation, October 7, 1942
35 Cavallero, *op cit* p 321
36 Official Italian War History. *Seconda Controffensiva Italotedesca in Africa Settentrionale*, p 388. Quoted in Faldella, *op cit* p 459
37 Italian Collection. Hitler to Mussolini, August 4, 1942
38 German Collection. Rintelen report, March 26, 1942
39 *Ibid* Rintelen report, February 13, 1942

2: Twenty Years After

1 Italian Collection. Duce memorandum, July 22, 1942
2 Quoted in Dante Germino, *The Italian Fascist Party in Power*, p 13. The author is indebted to this recent American study for background information in this chapter
3 *Ibid* p 85
4 German Collection. Anonymous Italian report dated February 1943
5 Bottai, *Vent' Anni e Un Giorno*, p 96
6 Gorla. *L'Italia nella Seconda Guerra Mondiale*, pp 103–4
7 Ciano, *Diary* pp 515–6
8 *Ibid*

3: The Problem of the Succession

1 Ciano, *op cit* p 504
2 Bottai, *op cit* p 231
3 See the biographical articles on Ciano by Susmel published in '*Tempo*' October 1960–January 1961
4 German Collection. Dollmann to Wolff, February 16, 1942
5 Puntoni, *Parla Vittorio Immanuele III*, p 31
6 Ciano, *op cit* p 226
7 *Ibid* p 242
8 Grandi, Dino Grandi Racconta p 36
9 Bottai, *op cit* pp 200–1
10 Grandi, *op cit* p 37
11 Bottai, *op cit* p 6

12 *Ibid* p 233
13 Puntoni, *op cit* p 40
14 *Hitler's Table Talk*, p 594
15 Puntoni, *op cit* p 34
16 *Ibid* p 96
17 Italian Collection. Police reports. September 1939
18 *Ibid* Farinacci to Mussolini, November 9, 1940
19 Italian Collection. Personal letter of Alfieri to D'Ajeta, Ciano's private secretary, September 30, 1942
20 Ciano, *op cit* p 510
21 German Collection. Dollmann to Wolff, November 1, 1942

4: 'TORCH'

1 German Collection. Rome telegram, October 17, 1942
2 Italian Collection
3 German Collection. Rome telegram, October 23, 1942
4 *Ibid* Goering-Duce conversation. Schmidt minute and two Rome telegrams (Bismarck) October 23, 1942
5 Rintelen, *op cit* p 177
6 Cavallero, *op cit* p 368
7 *Ibid* p 371
8 German Collection. Rome telegram, November 7, 1942
9 Rintelen, *op cit* p 180
10 Cavallero, *op cit* pp 371–2
11 German Collection. Rome telegram, November 8, 1942
12 Cavallero, *op cit* p 377
13 Ciano, *op cit* p 521
14 *Ibid*
15 German Collection. Hitler-Ciano conversation, November 9, 1942
16 Ciano, *op cit* pp 521–2
17 German Collection. Hitler-Ciano conversation, November 10, 1942
18 For details see Mallet, *Pierre Laval* II, p 108 and footnotes
19 Ciano, *op cit* p 522
20 German Collection. Hitler-Ciano-Laval conversation. November 10, 1942. Afternoon
21 Ciano, *op cit* pp 522–3
22 Cavallero, *op cit* p 384
23 *Ibid* p 387
24 Ciano, *op cit* p 523

5: THE AXIS AND NORTH AFRICA

1 German Collection. Mackensen memorandum, November 13, 1942
2 *Ibid* Rome telegram, November 13, 1942
3 Italian Collection. Hitler to Mussolini, November 26, 1942
4 Hitler e Mussolini, *op cit* pp 120–1
5 German Collection. Madrid telegram, November 16, 1942

6 *Ibid* Note for German Foreign Minister, December 3, 1942
7 *Ibid* Rintelen telegram, November 14, 1942
8 Ciano, *op cit* pp 533–4
9 Rommel, *The Rommel Papers,* p 349
10 Italian Collection. Hitler to Mussolini, November 20, 1942
11 Rommel, *op cit* pp 361–2
12 *Ibid* pp 365–6
13 Ciano, *op cit* p 529
14 Cavallero, *op cit* p 403
15 *Ibid* pp 404–5
16 Rommel, *op cit* p 367
17 Ciano, *op cit* p 531
18 Rommel, *op cit* p 366
19 Ciano, *op cit* p 532
20 Rommel, *op cit* pp 368–9

6: 'The Beresina Wind'

1 German Collection. Duce-Goering conversation, October 23, 1942
2 *Ibid* Rome telegram, November 7, 1942
3 Ribbentrop *Memoirs,* pp 168–9. See a slightly different version in the Nuremberg Trial Documents, Supplementary Volume B, p 1204
4 Bottai, *op cit* p 239
5 Ciano, *op cit* p 533
6 *Ibid* p 535
7 Italian Collection. Unsigned and undated note headed 'Policy 1943'.
8 Gilbert, *op cit* pp 4–5
9 *Ibid* p 12
10 German Collection. Schmidt minute
11 *Ibid*
12 Italian Collection. Ciano minute
13 German Collection. Schmidt minute
14 *Ibid*
15 Ciano, *op cit* p 536
16 Simoni, *Berlino Ambasciata d'Italia* p 299
17 Italian Collection. Ciano minute
18 Ciano, *op cit* p 537
19 *Ibid*

7: The Winter Crisis

1 Puntoni, *op cit* pp 193–4
2 *Ibid* p 104
3 See Dollmann's portrait in his book *Roma Nazista* (Italian translation) pp 71–5
4 Leto, *OVRA* pp 231 ff
5 Ciano, *op cit* p 392

6 Senise, *Quando Ero Capo della Polizia,* pp 51–3
7 *Ibid* p 238
8 Puntoni, *op cit* p 109
9 Italian Collection. Militia report dated March 6, 1943
10 Puntoni, *op cit* p 107
11 Vailati, *Badoglio Risponde,* p 76
12 Caviglia, *Diario, 1925–42,* p 341
13 German Collection. German War Office minute, November 1942
14 Italian Collection. Farinacci to Mussolini, November 19, 1942
15 *Ibid* Farinacci to Mussolini, January 20, 1932
16 *Ibid* Farinacci to Mussolini, November 9, 1940
17 *Ibid* Farinacci to Mussolini, January 22, 1933
18 Galbiati, *Il 25 Luglio e la MVSN,* p 177. Some time in December 1942
19 Caviglia, *op cit* p 388
20 Puntoni, *op cit* p 98
21 Galbiati, *op cit* pp 176–7
22 Puntoni, *op cit* p 107
23 Castellano, *Come Firmai l'Armistizio di Cassibile,* p 25
24 Puntoni, *op cit* p 103
25 Ciano, *op cit* p 527
26 Puntoni, *op cit* p 111
27 Ciano, *op cit* p 537
28 Carboni, *op cit* p 176
29 Puntoni, *op cit* pp 30–1
30 *Ibid* p 105
31 Ciano, *op cit* p 526
32 German Collection. Canaris minute, November 7, 1942
33 *Ibid* Madrid telegram, November 9, 1942
34 *Ibid* Weizsaecker telegram to Rome, December 3, 1942
35 *Ibid* Mackensen telegram, December 4, 1942
36 *Ibid* Bismarck telegram, December 19, 1942, quoting a report dated December 12 and presumably from Buffarini

8: The Political Recovery of the Duce

1 Bottai, *op cit* p 233
2 *Ibid*
3 *Ibid* p 234
4 Gorla, *op cit* pp 378 ff
5 Bottai, *op cit* p 235
6 Gorla, *op cit* p 380
7 Bottai, *op cit* p 235
8 Gorla, *op cit* p 381
9 Pini e Susmel, *op cit* IV, p 196
10 *Ibid* p 100
11 Italian Collection. 'Note for the Duce' from Vidussoni, December 5, 1942
12 German Collection. Himmler Files. Report from Dr Ehrlich,

the Rome representative of the German National Socialist Party, to gauleiter Bohle and forwarded by the latter to Himmler with covering note dated January 11, 1943

13 Italian Collection and *Opera Omnia op cit* XXXI, pp 34 *et seq*

9: 'THE EXPULSION OF THE DISCONTENTED'

1 Pozzi, *Come li ho visto Io,* pp 122–8. See also Ciano, *op cit* p 544
2 Gorla, *op cit* p 388
3 Ciano, *op cit* p 544, January 8, 1943
4 Pini e Susmel, *op cit* IV, p 205
5 Italian Collection. Report to Duce from Party Headquarters, January 11, 1943
6 Ciano, *op cit* p 546, January 15, 1943
7 German Collection. Mackensen telegram, January 16, 1943
8 Bottai, *op cit* pp 246–7. See also Ciano, *op cit* p 530, December 1, 1942. The liaison officer was Scamacca, an Italian Foreign Office official.
9 See the long and interesting letter from Bova Scoppa to Ciano dated August 6, 1941, in the former's book '*Colloqui con Due Dittatori*', pp 42 ff
10 This report is dated January 15. A copy exists in the Italian Collection of Ciano's papers, and it is also printed in Bova Scoppa, *op cit* pp 72–5. The latter's text differs from the original in several passages, and the summarized translation here is based on the former.
11 Ciano, *op cit* p 548, January 20, 1943
12 *Ibid* p 549
13 Bova Scoppa, *op cit* p 80
14 Puntoni, *op cit* pp 115–6, January 22–3, 1943
15 Bottai, *op cit* p 250, January 27, 1947
16 Caviglia, *op cit* p 388, January 26, 1943
17 Gorla, *op cit* pp 389 ff. See further details of this meeting in Bottai, *op cit* p 248
18 Canevari, *La Fine del Maresciallo Cavallero,* p 17
19 Ciano, *op cit* p 548. On January 23, the Italian Foreign Office liaison officer at the Italian High Command reported that, among his colleagues on the General Staff 'a final decision on Cavallero's dismissal was awaited'. (Italian Collection, Scamacca to Ciano.)
20 Italian Collection. Scamacca to Ciano, January 25, 1943
21 German Collection
22 Ciano, *op cit* p 554
23 German Collection. Rome telegram (Bismarck) January 31, 1943
24 Interviews in the newspapers *Il Corriere della Sera* March 11, 1955, and *Unità* October 22, 1953. For a slightly different version of this conversation see Castellano, *op cit* pp 22–7. See also Jo di Benigno, *Occasioni Mancate,* p 37

25 Ciano, *op cit* p 554
26 *Ibid* p 555
27 Bastianini, *Uomini, Cose, Fatti,* p 79
28 Gorla, *op cit* p 397
29 Puntoni, *op cit* p 118, February 6, 1943
30 German Collection. Himmler Papers. February 16, 1943
31 Bottai, *op cit* p 253
32 German Collection. Mackensen telegram to Ribbentrop, February 5, 1943
33 *Ibid* Mackensen telegram 'For the Foreign Minister only' February 8, 1943
34 *Hitler's Table Talk, op cit* p 186. January 6–7, 1942
35 German Collection. Political Report of Mackensen, February 10, 1943, 'Reconstruction of the Italian Cabinet'

Book II

1: The Military Scene

1 German Collection. War Office Archives. Rintelen report, November 18, 1942
2 Italian Collection. Army Programme for 1943, January 28, 1943
3 *Ibid* Duce-Kesselring-Ambrosio conversation, February 13, 1943
4 *Ibid* Ambrosio diary, February 7, 1943
5 Rintelen, *op cit* p 191. Ambrosio's first audience with the King as the new Chief of the General Staff was on February 2. See Puntoni, *op cit* p 117
6 Italian Collection. Ambrosio-Riccardi meeting, February 4, 1943
7 *Ibid* Ambrosio-Cini meeting, February 18, 1943
8 *Ibid* Duce-Kesselring-Ambrosio meeting, February 5, 1943
9 Italian Collection. Ambrosio diary, February 12, 1943
10 *Ibid* Mussolini to Hitler, February 11, 1943
11 Rommel, *op cit* p 416
12 *Ibid* p 417
13 Italian Collection. Memorandum for the Duce, February 17, 1943, and 'Evaluation of the General Military Position by the Italian High Command' February 21, 1943. The text of this document also exists in German, and one can assume that a copy was passed to the German military representative in Rome
14 Italian Collection. Duce-Kesselring-Ambrosio meeting, February 13, 1943

2: The Diplomatic Front

1 Bastianini, *op cit* pp 80–1
2 *Ibid* p 83

3 German Collection. 'Memorandum on the possibilities of the future implementation of policy towards Spain.' January 20, 1943 (Hoffmann Memorandum)
4 *Ibid* Ribbentrop telegram to Madrid, January 25, 1943
5 *Ibid* Madrid telegram, January 24, 1943
6 *Ibid* War Diary of the German General Staff
7 Italian Collection. Duce-Kesselring-Ambrosio meeting. February 13, 1943
8 German Collection. Hitler-Arikan conversation. August 14, 1942
9 *Ibid*
10 *Ibid* Papen political report, November 20, 1942
11 *Ibid* Bismarck telegram, December 20, 1942
12 *Ibid* German Foreign Office memorandum on Jodl's report of conversation between the Fuehrer and the Bulgarian War Minister January 6, 1943
13 *Ibid* January 7, 1943
14 *Ibid* Papen telegram, February 2, 1943
15 *Ibid* Papen political report on the Adana Conference. February 7, 1943
16 *Ibid* Ribbentrop to Papen. February 3, 1943
17 *Ibid* Ribbentrop to Papen. February 6, 1943
18 *Ibid* Papen telegram, February 6, 1943
19 *Ibid* Papen telegram, February 8, 1943
20 *Ibid* Hitler-Antonescu conversation. January 10, 1943
21 *Ibid* Ribbentrop—conversation with the two Antonescus. January 11, 1943

3: RIBBENTROP IN ROME

1 German Collection. Ribbentrop-Duce conversation, February 25, 1943
2 Bastianini, *op cit* p 272
3 German Collection. Ribbentrop-Duce conversation, February 26, 1943
4 *Ibid* Ribbentrop-Alfieri conversation, February 28, 1943
5 Bastianini, *op cit* p 85
6 Puntoni, *op cit* pp 121–2

4: SPRING TENSIONS: RUSSIA AND TUNISIA

1 Puntoni, *op cit* pp 122–3, March 1, 1943
2 Italian Collection. Ambrosio 'Note for the Duce', March 1, 1943
3 *Ibid* Report of the Italian Consul-General in Odessa
4 *Ibid* Minute of the Italian Ministry of Popular Culture to the Italian Embassy, Berlin. April 17, 1943
5 *Ibid* Report of the Italian Consul-General in Innsbruck, February 22, 1943
6 *Ibid* April 7, 1943
7 *Ibid* Bastianini to Alfieri, March 17, 1943

8 German Collection. Ribbentrop-Alfieri conversation, March 8, 1943
9 *Ibid* Steengracht minute, March 17, 1943
10 Italian Collection. Duce-Kesselring meeting, March 1, 1943
11 Puntoni, *op cit* p 125, March 8, 1943
12 Dollmann, *op cit* pp 132–3
13 Italian Collection. Ministerial conference, March 10, 1943
14 Rommel, *op cit* p 418
15 Italian Collection. Duce-Rommel meeting, March 9, 1943
16 Rommel, *op cit* p 419
17 *Ibid*
18 Hitler e Mussolini, *op cit* pp 146–7
19 German Collection. Hitler-Horthy meeting, April 16, 1943
20 Italian Collection. Duce-Kesselring meeting, March 13, 1943
21 Fuehrer Conferences on Naval Affairs 1943, *op cit* pp 13–15, March 14, 1943
22 Hitler e Mussolini, *op cit* pp 146–51
23 Italian Collection. Duce-Doenitz meeting, March 15, 1943
24 Hitler e Mussolini, *op cit* pp 151–4

5: The Home Front

1 Italian Collection. National Fascist Party. Report by Angelo Caruso, February 16, 1943
2 *Ibid* Fascist Party office. Memorandum for Duce
3 See, for example, Leto, *op cit* p 245
4 Massola, *Marzo 1943. Ore dieci* pp 50–1
5 Vaccarino, *op cit* pp 20 ff
6 Vaccarino, *Aspetti della Resistenza in Piemonte,* p 28
7 *Ibid* pp 31–2
8 Deposition of Cianetti. In Cersosimo *'Dall Istruttoria alla Fucilazione'* p 97
9 Italian Collection. Farinacci to Mussolini, April 1, 1943
10 Bottai, *op cit* p 255
11 German Collection. Mackensen telegram, March 12, 1943
12 Hagen, *Die Geheime Front,* p 392

6: The Royal Secret

1 Ambrosio interview in *Il Corriere della Sera,* March 11, 1955
2 Puntoni, *op cit* p 121
3 Caviglia, *op cit* pp 396–7
4 Puntoni, *op cit* p 119
5 Mussolini, *Memoirs,* pp 141–2
6 Caviglia, *op cit* p 385
7 Cassinelli, *op cit* pp 17–19
8 German Collection. Anonymous report to Mackensen. Undated
9 Cassinelli, *op cit* p 16
10 Puntoni, *op cit* p 125
11 Caviglia, *op cit* p 395

12 Puntoni, *op cit* pp 125–6
13 For the following see Bonomi, *Diario di un Anno,* (passim)
14 *Ibid* p xxv
15 *Ibid* p xxviii
16 For details see Catalano, *Storia del CLNI* pp 18–19
17 Bonomi, *op cit* p xxxvii
18 Puntoni, *op cit* p 126

7: The Axis and the Shadow of Stalingrad

1 Bastianini to the author
2 Italian Collection. Babuscio Rizzo to Bastianini, March 1, 1943
3 Bastianini, *op cit* p 108
4 Alfieri, *op cit* pp 290–1
5 Hitler e Mussolini, *op cit* pp 151–4
6 German Collection. Rome telegram, March 31, 1943
7 *Ibid* Papen telegram, March 9, 1943
8 *Ibid* Papen memorandum, February 6, 1943
9 *Ibid* Papen telegram, February 8, 1943
10 *Ibid* Mackensen telegram, February 17, 1943
11 *Ibid* Weizsaecker memorandum, March 3, 1943
12 *Ibid* German Foreign Office 'Notes for the visit of King Boris to Berlin', March 29, 1943
13 *Ibid* Ribbentrop to Papen, March 12, 1943, repeating Jagow's telegram from Budapest of the previous day
14 *Ibid* Papen to Ribbentrop, March 19, 1943
15 *Ibid* Budapest telegram, March 29, 1943
16 Italian Collection. Anfuso telegram, April 7, 1943
17 For a detailed study of Kallay's visit to Rome, see C. A. Macartney *October 15. A History of Modern Hungary,* Vol II pp 147 ff
18 Kallay, *Memoirs* (English translation by C. A. Macartney) pp 144 ff

8: The Salzburg Meeting

1 Dollmann, *op cit* p 144
2 April 29–30, 1942. The Italian record of this meeting is in Hitler e Mussolini, *op cit* pp 119 ff. The German minutes are published in English translation in the Department of State Bulletin July 14, 1946, pp 57–63
3 Pozzi, *op cit* p 139
4 Bastianini, *op cit* p 92
5 Rintelen, *op cit* pp 192–3
6 Dollmann, *op cit* pp 145 ff
7 German Collection. Ribbentrop-Bastianini meeting, April 8, 1943
8 Bastianini, *op cit* p 95
9 *Ibid* pp 96–7
10 Italian Collection. Notes by Ambrosio

11 German Collection. Confidential Report, April 19, 1943 'From an informant in Oshima's closest entourage'
12 German Collection. Minute to Ribbentrop on Strohm's report No. 6 on the captured Italian Foreign Office Archives (dated October 21, 1943). For an account of these papers see Appendix (b) at the end of this volume.
13 Italian Collection. Military Intelligence report, April (the day is illegible) 1943
14 Bastianini, *op cit* p 96
15 *Ibid* p 97
16 *Ibid* pp 98–9
17 German Collection. Mackensen memorandum, April 9, 1943
18 Italian Collection. 'Memorandum on the Klessheim Talks' dated April 12, 1943. 'General Conduct of the War, Impressions derived from the various discussions April 7–10, 1943.' These appear to be Ambrosio's own notes
19 German Collection. Ribbentrop-Bastianini talk, April 9, 1943
20 Italian Collection. Notes by Ambrosio on the Klessheim talks (see 17 above)
21 German Collection. Steengracht minute, March 17, 1943
22 Rintelen, *op cit* p 192
23 German Collection. Ribbentrop-Bastianini talk, April 10, 1943
24 Dollmann, *op cit* p 146
25 *Ibid* p 148
26 Rintelen, *op cit* p 193
27 Gilbert, *op cit* p 37. Hitler Military Conference, May 20, 1943
28 Dollmann, *op cit* p 151
29 Pozzi, *op cit* pp 147–8
30 Bastianini, *op cit* p 100
31 Simoni, *op cit* p 331
32 *Ibid*
33 Pozzi, *op cit* p 139
34 Goebbels, *op cit* pp 274–5, May 7, 1943

Book III

1: The End in Africa

1 Puntoni, *op cit* pp 128–9. April 12 and 16, 1943
2 Italian Collection. Duce-Kesselring meeting, April 12, 1943
3 Puntoni, *op cit* p 129
4 German Collection. Mackensen telegram, April 19, 1943
5 Hitler e Mussolini, *op cit* p 154
6 *Ibid* p 155
7 Simoni, *op cit* p 334
8 Italian Collection. Foreign Office minute, May 2, 1943
9 *Ibid* Duce-Kesselring meeting, May 4, 1943

10 German Collection. War Office Archives. War Diary of German Army Staff, July 25, 1943
11 Rintelen report. May 5, 1943
12 Fuehrer Conferences on Naval Affairs 1943, *op cit* pp 22 ff, for Doenitz's Rome visit
13 Italian Collection. Duce-Doenitz meeting, May 13, 1943
14 Fuehrer Conferences on Naval Affairs 1943, *op cit* p 32
15 *Ibid* p 38
16 Italian Collection. Duce-Doenitz-Kesselring meeting, May 13, 1943
17 Fuehrer Conferences on Naval Affairs 1943, *op cit* p 39
18 German Collection. War Office Archives
19 *Ibid* War Diary of German General Staff. Entry for July 25, 1943. There is as yet no trace of the Survey
20 *Ibid* War Office Archives

2: DIPLOMATIC INTERLUDE

1 German Collection. Hitler-Antonescu conversation, April 12, 1943
2 *Ibid* Hitler-Horthy conversation, April 16/17, 1943
3 *Ibid* Ribbentrop to Jagow, April 14, 1943
4 *Ibid* Schmidt report, April 20, 1943
5 *Ibid* Ribbentrop to Mackensen, April 22, 1943
6 *Ibid* Mackensen to Ribbentrop, April 23, 1943
7 Goebbels, *op cit* p 265, April 23, 1943
8 German Collection. Rome telegram, April 22, 1943
9 *Ibid* Schmidt minute on his interview with the Duce, April 20, 1943
10 *Ibid* Rome telegram May 1, 1943. Extract of report of the Italian Minister in Madrid handed to Mackensen by the Italian Foreign Office
11 *Ibid* Madrid telegrams, May 5, 7, and 10, 1943
12 *Ibid* Ribbentrop-Oshima conversation, May 19, 1943
13 Bastianini, *op cit* p 160
14 German Collection. Meeting between Ribbentrop and Bastianini, April 29, 1943. Alfieri and Mackensen were also present
15 *Ibid* Ribbentrop-Laval meeting, April 29, 1943
16 Guérard, *Criminel de Paix,* p 117
17 Bastianini, *op cit* pp 290–1
18 De Brinon, *Mémoires,* p 164
19 Simoni, *op cit* p 333
20 German Collection. Rome telegram, May 18, 1943
21 Simoni, *op cit* pp 335 ff
22 German Collection, Rome telegram, May 19, 1943
23 Bastianini. Speech in the Senate. Summary in the newspaper *La Stampa,* May 20, 1943
24 Gilbert, *op cit* p 35

3: The Italian 'Political Design'

1 Italian Collection. Bova Scoppa to Bastianini, May 12, 1943. This is the complete text. See also Bova Scoppa, *op cit* pp 96 ff
2 *Ibid* Bova Scoppa to Bastianini, May 14, 1943. Also partly in Bova Scoppa, *op cit* pp 90 ff but under the date of May 7
3 Tamaro *Due Anni di Storia* I, pp 66–8, prints the minute of Bastianini to the Duce and the memorandum of Bova Scoppa. (See also the latter's book, *op cit* pp 102 ff.) The dispatch of Anfuso is to be found only in the Italian Collection.
4 Bastianini, *op cit* p 113
5 Bova Scoppa, *op cit* p 110
6 German Collection. Mackensen to Ribbentrop, June 21, 1943
7 Bova Scoppa, *op cit* pp 114–5
8 Bastianini, *op cit* p 324
9 *Ibid* Mackensen telegram, March 26, 1943

4: The 'Last Wave' of the Fascist Party

1 Senise, *op cit* pp 176–7
2 Much of this information on Scorza's career is contained in Mackensen's two telegrams of April 20 and 23, 1943, in the German Collection
3 Italian Collection. Police Report
4 *Ibid* Text by the official Stefani news agency
5 *Ibid* Police Report, May 11, 1943
6 German Collection. Dollmann to Himmler, May 9, 1945
7 Italian Collection. Police Report
8 *Ibid* Police Report, June 12, 1943
9 Cucco, *Non Volevamo Perdere,* pp 84–5
10 Mussolini, *Memoirs,* p 32
11 Pellicano. Articles on the Grand Council published in the review *Elefante* in October 1949, No. 5
12 Bottai, *op cit* p 263
13 Pellicano, *op cit* Article 5
14 Italian Collection. Scorza letter to the Duce, June 23, 1943
15 See a summary of the text in Pini e Susmel, *op cit* IV, pp 233–4

5: Royal Hesitations

1 Puntoni, *op cit* p 132
2 Bonomi, *op cit* pp 3–8
3 Puntoni, *op cit* p 133, June 1–3, 1943. Puntoni does not mention Bonomi's audience
4 Grandi Interview in *Il Corriere della Sera,* February 9, 1955
5 Soleri, *op cit* pp 231–2
6 Puntoni, *op cit* p 133
7 Soleri, *op cit* p 237
8 Bonomi, *op cit* pp 15 ff

9 Puntoni, *op cit* p 137
10 Benigno, *Occasioni Mancate* p 62
11 Castellano, *op cit* p 45
12 *Ibid* p 52
13 Senise, *op cit* pp 191–2
14 Italian Collection. 'Personal Note' on Senise's activities compiled for the Duce's Secretariat. September 14, 1943

6: Operation 'Mincemeat'

1 German Collection. Madrid telegram. May 12, 1943. 21.20 hours
2 *Ibid* May 12, 1943. 22.30 hours
3 See Montagu. *The Man who never was, passim*
4 German Collection. Madrid telegram. May 19, 1943
5 *Ibid* War Office Archives. May 14, 1943
6 Italian Collection. Ambrosio-Rintelen meeting. May 18, 1943
7 Rintelen, *op cit* p 202
8 Italian Collection. Hitler to Mussolini. May 19, 1943. Hitherto unpublished
9 *Ibid* Duce-Kesselring meeting. May 20, 1943
10 German Collection. Rome telegram. 'For German Foreign Minister personal.' May 20, 1943
11 Hitler e Mussolini, *op cit* p 156

7: The Military Crisis of the Axis

1 German Collection. Rome telegram, May 21, 1943
2 Gilbert, *op cit* pp 29–38, May 20, 1943
3 German Collection. Schmidt minute, April 20, 1943
4 *Ibid* Rome telegram, June 11, 1943
5 *Ibid* War Office Archives. War Diary of the German General Staff, July 25, 1943
6 *Ibid* War Office Archives. Report by Colonel Berger, June 23, 1943
7 *Ibid* Steengracht minute, June 3, 1943
8 *Ibid* Steengracht minute, May 26, 1943
9 Simoni, *op cit* p 343, May 30, 1943
10 German Collection. War Office Archives. Staff memorandum, June 4, 1943
11 *Ibid* Himmler papers. Dollmann to Himmler, May 9, 1943
12 *Ibid* Rome telegram, May 22, 1943
13 *Ibid* War Office Archives. Rintelen report, June 19, 1943
14 *Ibid* Rome telegram, June 1, 1943
15 Rintelen, *op cit* p 206
16 Simoni, *op cit* p 346–7
17 German Collection. War Office Archives

Book IV

1: Sicily: 'The Water's Edge'

1 German Collection. Schellenberg to German Foreign Office, June 24, 1943
2 Italian Collection. Military Intelligence report, July 9, 1943
3 Simoni, *op cit* p 358
4 German Collection. War Office Archives. Rintelen report, July 19, 1943
5 Extracts from the diary of an Italian Staff Officer at the Ministry of War quoted by Tamaro, *op cit* I p 186
6 Alfieri, *op cit* pp 298–9
7 Simoni, *op cit* pp 359–60
8 German Collection. Rome telegram, July 13, 1943
9 Italian Collection. Duce-Kesselring-Ambrosio meeting July 13, 1943
10 Tamaro, *op cit* I p 190
11 Fuehrer Directives, 1942–5 p 83
12 Italian Collection. Duce-Kesselring-Ambrosio meeting July 15, 1943. This is the last document in the series
13 German Collection. Mackensen telegram, July 15, 1943
14 Tamaro, *op cit* I p 186
15 German Collection. Report by Jodl July 15, 1943, and summarized in the War Diary of the German General Staff
16 Fuehrer Conferences on Naval Affairs 1943, *op cit* pp 59–62
17 Alfieri, *op cit* pp 300–1
18 Simoni, *op cit* pp 365–6
19 Rommel, *op cit* p 430

2: The Roman Scene

1 German Collection. Rome telegram, June 1, 1943
2 Galbiati, *op cit* pp 192 ff
3 Bottai, *op cit* pp 269–70
4 *Ibid* pp 272–4
5 German Collection. Ribbentrop to Mackensen, July 15, 1943
6 Galbiati, *op cit* pp 214 ff
7 Bottai, *op cit* p 276
8 *Ibid* pp 281 ff
9 Farinacci deposition in Cersosimo, *op cit* p 5
10 Bottai, *op cit* p 282
11 *Ibid* p 287
12 Mussolini *Memoirs, op cit* p 49
13 Hagen, *op cit* p 391
14 German Collection. Dollmann to Mackensen, July 16 and 17, 1943

15 Italian Collection. Ciano to the Duce, July 17, 1943
16 Bastianini, *op cit* p 115
17 German Collection. German Legation to the Vatican to Berlin, April 14, 1943
18 *Ibid* Berne telegram, May 15, 1943
19 Printed in Tamaro, *op cit* I, pp 70 ff
20 Bastianini, *op cit* p 117
21 Simoni, *op cit* pp 362–3
22 German Collection. Dollmann to Mackensen, July 17, 1943
23 Bonomi, *op cit* pp 17 ff
24 Bonomi, *op cit* p 22
25 *Ibid* p 23
26 German Collection. German War Office Archives. Abwehr telegram, July 14, 1943
27 Cerica. Article in *Tempo,* July 19, 1956

3: FELTRE

1 Alfieri, *op cit* pp 318–9
2 Italian Collection. Ambrosio diary
3 German Collection. War Diary of the German General Staff, July 19, 1943
4 Alfieri, *op cit* p 305
5 *Ibid* pp 306 ff
6 Rintelen, *op cit* p 212
7 Alfieri, *op cit* p 316
8 Mussolini, *Memoirs, op cit* pp 50–1
9 *Pontine Notes, op cit*
10 Italian Collection. Tarvisio file. Minute dated July 20. 'Summary of first conversations, Excellency Ambrosio-Marshal Keitel (in the train).' Extracts are quoted by Rossi, *Come arrivammo al armistizio* pp 335 ff
11 Alfieri, *op cit* p 309
12 *Ibid* p 313
13 *Ibid* p 315. See also Rintelen, *op cit* p 214
14 *Pontine Notes, op cit*
15 Rintelen, *op cit* p 214
16 *Pontine Notes, op cit*
17 Fuehrer Conferences on Naval Affairs 1943. P 81
18 Italian Collection. Tarvisio file 'Summary of second conversations. Excellency Ambrosio-Marshal Keitel (in the train)', dated July 20, 1943
19 Rintelen, *op cit* p 215
20 Mussolini, *Memoirs, op cit* p 51
21 *Pontine Notes, op cit*
22 Bastianini, *op cit* p 121
23 German Collection. Rommel Diary, July 20 and 21
24 Bastianini, *op cit* pp 122–3

onta,

ler-

man

sio

this

ry-

re

4,

he

at

35 Italian Collect
1943. 6 p.m.
36 Castellano, *op*

5: The Meetin

1 Mussolini, *M*
2 *Ibid* pp 58—
3 Bottai, *op cit*
4 *Ibid*, pp 307
5 Mussolini, *M*
6 Grandi, *op*
7 Federzoni, *M*
from May 30
8 Bottai, *op ci*
9 Mussolini, *M*
10 Alfieri, *op c*
11 Letter from
in Cersosim
12 Bottai, *op c*
13 Galbiati, *op*
14 Alfieri, *op*
'L'Ultima S
15 Bottai, *op*
16 Alfieri, *op*
17 Mussolini,

6: The Coup

1 Text in the
2 *Ibid* Musso
3 Spampanat
4 Galbiati, *o*
5 Pellicano,
6 Mussolini,
7 Spampanat
8 Farinacci,
9 *Pontine N*
10 *Ibid*
11 Mussolini,
12 Bastianini,
op cit pp
13 Galbiati,
14 Host Ven
pp 125 ff
15 Galbiati,
16 *Pontine*
17 'Note on
and the
Tamaro,

Book IV

1: SICILY: 'THE WATER'S EDGE'

1 German Collection. Schellenberg to German Foreign Office, June 24, 1943
2 Italian Collection. Military Intelligence report, July 9, 1943
3 Simoni, *op cit* p 358
4 German Collection. War Office Archives. Rintelen report, July 19, 1943
5 Extracts from the diary of an Italian Staff Officer at the Ministry of War quoted by Tamaro, *op cit* I p 186
6 Alfieri, *op cit* pp 298–9
7 Simoni, *op cit* pp 359–60
8 German Collection. Rome telegram, July 13, 1943
9 Italian Collection. Duce-Kesselring-Ambrosio meeting July 13, 1943
10 Tamaro, *op cit* I p 190
11 Fuehrer Directives, 1942–5 p 83
12 Italian Collection. Duce-Kesselring-Ambrosio meeting July 15, 1943. This is the last document in the series
13 German Collection. Mackensen telegram, July 15, 1943
14 Tamaro, *op cit* I p 186
15 German Collection. Report by Jodl July 15, 1943, and summarized in the War Diary of the German General Staff
16 Fuehrer Conferences on Naval Affairs 1943, *op cit* pp 59–62
17 Alfieri, *op cit* pp 300–1
18 Simoni, *op cit* pp 365–6
19 Rommel, *op cit* p 430

2: THE ROMAN SCENE

1 German Collection. Rome telegram, June 1, 1943
2 Galbiati, *op cit* pp 192 ff
3 Bottai, *op cit* pp 269–70
4 *Ibid* pp 272–4
5 German Collection. Ribbentrop to Mackensen, July 15, 1943
6 Galbiati, *op cit* pp 214 ff
7 Bottai, *op cit* p 276
8 *Ibid* pp 281 ff
9 Farinacci deposition in Cersosimo, *op cit* p 5
10 Bottai, *op cit* p 282
11 *Ibid* p 287
12 Mussolini *Memoirs, op cit* p 49
13 Hagen, *op cit* p 391
14 German Collection. Dollmann to Mackensen, July 16 and 17, 1943

15 Italian Collection. Ciano to the Duce, July 17, 1943
16 Bastianini, *op cit* p 115
17 German Collection. German Legation to the Vatican to Berlin, April 14, 1943
18 *Ibid* Berne telegram, May 15, 1943
19 Printed in Tamaro, *op cit* I, pp 70 ff
20 Bastianini, *op cit* p 117
21 Simoni, *op cit* pp 362–3
22 German Collection. Dollmann to Mackensen, July 17, 1943
23 Bonomi, *op cit* pp 17 ff
24 Bonomi, *op cit* p 22
25 *Ibid* p 23
26 German Collection. German War Office Archives. Abwehr telegram, July 14, 1943
27 Cerica. Article in *Tempo,* July 19, 1956

3: Feltre

1 Alfieri, *op cit* pp 318–9
2 Italian Collection. Ambrosio diary
3 German Collection. War Diary of the German General Staff, July 19, 1943
4 Alfieri, *op cit* p 305
5 *Ibid* pp 306 ff
6 Rintelen, *op cit* p 212
7 Alfieri, *op cit* p 316
8 Mussolini, *Memoirs, op cit* pp 50–1
9 *Pontine Notes, op cit*
10 Italian Collection. Tarvisio file. Minute dated July 20. 'Summary of first conversations, Excellency Ambrosio-Marshal Keitel (in the train).' Extracts are quoted by Rossi, *Come arrivammo al armistizio* pp 335 ff
11 Alfieri, *op cit* p 309
12 *Ibid* p 313
13 *Ibid* p 315. See also Rintelen, *op cit* p 214
14 *Pontine Notes, op cit*
15 Rintelen, *op cit* p 214
16 *Pontine Notes, op cit*
17 Fuehrer Conferences on Naval Affairs 1943. P 81
18 Italian Collection. Tarvisio file 'Summary of second conversations. Excellency Ambrosio-Marshal Keitel (in the train)', dated July 20, 1943
19 Rintelen, *op cit* p 215
20 Mussolini, *Memoirs, op cit* p 51
21 *Pontine Notes, op cit*
22 Bastianini, *op cit* p 121
23 German Collection. Rommel Diary, July 20 and 21
24 Bastianini, *op cit* pp 122–3

4: 'FIVE MINUTES TO TWELVE'

1 Italian Collection. Feltre documents
2 Castellano, *op cit* pp 56–7. See also Vailati, *Badoglio Racconta*, p 363
3 Rintelen, *op cit* p 215
4 German Collection. Rintelen telegram, July 21, 1943
5 *Ibid* Rome telegram, July 24, 1943
6 *Ibid* Himmler to Bormann, July 19, 1943
7 *Ibid* Mackensen telegram, July 22, 1943
8 Goerdeler to Kluge. Between July 20 and 24, 1943. Wheeler-Bennett, *The Nemesis of Power* p 572
9 German Collection. War Office Archives. War Diary of German General Staff, July 25, 1943
10 *Ibid*
11 Interview in *Il Corriere della Sera* March 11, 1955. Ambrosio was precise in his statements. It is possible, however, that this date is not correct
12 Nino Bolla, *Il Segreto di Due Re* pp 74–5
13 Italian Collection. Ambrosio's list of appointments
14 Anfuso, *op cit* p 282
15 Mussolini, *Memoirs, op cit* p 54
16 *Ibid* p 53. Grandi has published in successive interviews varying versions of this meeting. See Indro Montanelli *Il Corriere della Sera* February 9, 1955; Giovanni Cavallotti *Oggi* June 4, 1959. The above account is largely based on the latter
17 Pellicano, *op cit* Article II
18 Bottai, *op cit* pp 290–1
19 Alfieri *L'Ultima Seduta del Gran Consiglio* reprinted from the magazine 'Epoca' of May 24, 1952, p 5
20 Puntoni, *op cit* p 141
21 Cersosimo, *op cit* pp 6–7. Ciano's deposition before his trial at Verona
22 Bottai, *op cit* p 291
23 Canevari, *La Fine del Maresciallo Cavallero,* p 28
24 Bottai, *op cit* p 291
25 Anfuso, *op cit* p 283
26 Cersosimo, *op cit* p 7
27 Cucco, *op cit* pp 97–8
28 Mussolini, *Memoirs, op cit* p 54
29 German Collection. Mackensen to Ribbentrop, July 24, 1943
30 *Ibid* Second telegram, July 24, 1943
31 *Ibid* Rome telegram (office of Military Attaché) July 24, 1943
32 Senise, *op cit* pp 197–9
33 Roatta, *Otto Milioni di Baionette,* p 262 note
34 Italian Collection. Meeting of Italian Chiefs of Staff, July 22, 1943. 6 p.m.

35 Italian Collection. Meeting of Italian Chiefs of Staff, July 22, 1943. 6 p.m.
36 Castellano, *op cit* p 62

5: The Meeting of the Grand Council

1 Mussolini, *Memoirs, op cit* p 55
2 *Ibid* pp 58–9
3 Bottai, *op cit* p 302
4 *Ibid,* pp 307–9
5 Mussolini, *Memoirs, op cit* p 80
6 Grandi, *op cit* p 49
7 Federzoni, *Memorie,* Article V, published in *L'Indipendente* (as from May 30, 1946)
8 Bottai, *op cit* pp 311–12
9 Mussolini, *Memoirs, op cit* p 63
10 Alfieri, *op cit* p 336
11 Letter from Bastianini to Mussolini, November 9, 1943, quoted in Cersosimo, *op cit* pp 180 ff
12 Bottai, *op cit* p 313
13 Galbiati, *op cit* p 232
14 Alfieri, *op cit* pp 339–40, and the offprint of his article '*L'Ultima Seduta del Gran Consiglio*'
15 Bottai, *op cit* pp 316–17
16 Alfieri, *op cit* p 340
17 Mussolini, *Memoirs, op cit* p 64

6: The Coup d'État

1 Text in the Italian Collection
2 *Ibid* Mussolini to Farinacci, October 13, 1925
3 Spampanato, *Contro Memoriale* I, p 232
4 Galbiati, *op cit* p 234
5 Pellicano, *op cit* Article 3
6 Mussolini, *Memoirs,* p 83
7 Spampanato, *op cit* I, p 232
8 Farinacci, *Diario, op cit,* July 25, 1943
9 *Pontine Notes, op cit*
10 *Ibid*
11 Mussolini, *Memoirs, op cit* p 88
12 Bastianini, *op cit* p 131 and the text of his letter in Cersosimo, *op cit* pp 181–2
13 Galbiati, *op cit* p 235
14 Host Venturi's report in Dolfin, *Con Mussolini nella Tragedia,* pp 125 ff
15 Galbiati, *op cit* pp 214 ff
16 *Pontine Notes, op cit*
17 'Note on the conversation which took place between the Duce and the Japanese Ambassador' (July 25, 1943) quoted in Tamaro, *op cit* I, p 72

18 German Collection. Mackensen telegram, July 28, 1943
19 *Ibid* Mackensen telegram July 31, 1943. 'For the Foreign Minister personally'
20 *Ibid*
21 Mussolini, *Memoirs, op cit* p 80
22 *Pontine Notes, op cit*
23 Galbiati, *op cit* p 239
24 *Ibid* p 241
25 *Pontine Notes, op cit*
26 Cucco, *op cit* pp 102 ff. This is confirmed in Graziani's book, *op cit* p 324
27 Grandi. Montanelli interview, *op cit*
28 *Ibid*
29 Ambrosio in an interview in *Il Corriere delle Sera,* March 11, 1955
30 Puntoni, *op cit* p 142
31 Cerica has described his participation in the events of July 25 in three articles published in *Tempo* (July 19, July 26, August 2, 1956). See also his speech in the Italian Senate, July 25, 1958
32 *Ibid*
33 Puntoni, *op cit* p 143
34 Mussolini, *Memoirs, op cit* p 80
35 Article in the newspaper *Meridiano d'Italia,* April 6, 1947
36 Puntoni, *op cit* p 145
37 *Pontine Notes, op cit*
38 Spampanato, *op cit* I, pp 230 ff. See also Senise, *op cit* p 206
39 Galbiati, *op cit* p 243
40 *Ibid* p 244
41 Dolfin, *op cit* p 128
42 Galbiati, *op cit* p 248 note, and a map in Appendix H
43 Roatta, *op cit* pp 262–3
44 Galbiati, *op cit* p 250
45 Jo di Benigno, *op cit* p 83
46 For the text see Tamaro, *op cit* I, p 47
47 Italian Collection. Intercepts of telephone conversations

NOTES TO APPENDIX

1 German Collection. Ribbentrop to Rahn, September 12, 1943
2 Italian Collection. Memorandum by Ambassador Rosso. 'The Withdrawal by the Germans of Political Archives' September 15, 1943
3 German Collection. Rahn to Ribbentrop, September 14, 1943
4 *Ibid* Rahn to Ribbentrop, September 17, 1943
5 *Ibid* German Foreign Office minute, September 23, 1943
6 *Ibid* German Foreign Office minute, September 28, 1943
7 *Ibid* Steengracht, October 1, 1943

8 *Ibid* Note from Private Office of the German Foreign Minister, October 2, 1943
9 *Ibid* Ribbentrop telegram, October 6, 1943 (signed Hilger)
10 *Ibid* Rome telegram (Moellhausen), October 11, 1943
11 *Ibid* Rahn telegram, October 23, 1943
12 *Ibid* Hencke memoranda for Ribbentrop: October 18, October 21, November 20, 1943
13 *Ibid* Foreign Office minute, March 21, 1944

INDEX

NOTE: In this index all references to institutions (Army, High Command, Ministry, etc.) are to those of Italy, unless otherwise stated.

ANCHOR BOOKS

EUROPEAN HISTORY

ADAMS, HENRY Mont-Saint-Michel and Chartres, A166
BAGEHOT, WALTER Bagehot's Historical Essays, ed. St. John-Stevas, A451
BARK, WILLIAM CARROLL Origins of the Medieval World, A190
BARZUN, JACQUES Darwin, Marx, Wagner, A127
BURKE, EDMUND Edmund Burke: Selected Writings and Speeches, ed. Stanlis, A334
BUTTERFIELD, HERBERT, & OTHERS A Short History of Science, A180
CASTIGLIONE, BALDESAR The Book of the Courtier, trans. Singleton, A186
CROMBIE, A. C. Medieval and Early Modern Science, 2 vols.
Vol. I—V–XIII Centuries, A167a
Vol. II—XIII–XVII Centuries, A167b
DE STAEL, MADAME Madame de Staël on Politics, Literature and National Character, trans. & ed. Berger, A429
FORSTER, E. M. Alexandria: A History and a Guide, A231
FRIED, ALBERT, & SANDER, RONALD, eds. Socialist Thought: A Documentary History, A384
GALILEO Discoveries and Opinions of Galileo, trans. Drake, A94
GREVILLE, CHARLES CAVENDISH FULKE The Great World: Portraits and Scenes from Greville's Memoirs, ed. Kronenberger, A409
HARRISON, G. B., ed. Elizabethan Journals, Vols. 1 & 2, A458a; A458b
HALEVY, ELY The Age of Tyranny, trans. Webb, A463
HOLT, ELIZABETH G. A Documentary History of Art
Vol. I—The Middle Ages and Renaissance, A114a
Vol. II—Michelangelo and the Mannerists, A114b
——, ed. From the Classicists to the Impressionists: A Documentary History of Art and Architecture in the 19th Century, A114c
HOOVER, CALVIN B. The Economy, Liberty and the State, A241
HUIZINGA, J. The Waning of the Middle Ages, A42
KENDALL, PAUL MURRAY Richard III, A455
—— The Yorkist Age, A466
LEWIS, W. H. The Splendid Century, A122
—— The Sunset of the Splendid Century: The Life and Times of Louis Auguste de Bourbon, Duc du Maine, 1670–1736, A355
LUKACS, JOHN A History of the Cold War, A322

MARX, KARL, & ENGELS, FRIEDRICH Basic Writings on Politics and Philosophy, A185
MEYERHOFF, HANS, ed. The Philosophy of History in Our Time, A164
MILL, JOHN STUART John Stuart Mill: Essays on Politics and Culture, ed. Himmelfarb, A373
MUELLER, WILLIAM A. Church and State in Luther and Calvin, A454
NAMIER, LEWIS 1848: The Revolution of the Intellectuals, A385
NEALE, J. E. Queen Elizabeth I, A105
NEVINS, ALLEN The Gateway to History, A314
OSTROGORSKI, M. Democracy and the Organization of Political Parties—Vol. I: England, ed. Lipset, A388a
PIRENNE, HENRI A History of Europe
Vol. I—From the End of the Roman World in the West to the Beginnings of the Western States, A156a
Vol. II—From the Thirteenth Century to the Renaissance and Reformation, A156b
—— Medieval Cities, A82
SERGE, VICTOR The Case of Comrade Tulayev, A349
SHATTUCK, ROGER The Banquet Years, A238
STERN, FRITZ The Politics of Cultural Despair—A Study in the Rise of Germanic Ideology, A436
SYPHER, WYLIE Four Stages of Renaissance Style, A45
TOCQUEVILLE, ALEXIS DE The Old Regime and the French Revolution, A60
TREVELYAN, G. M. History of England
Vol. I—From the Earliest Times to the Reformation, A22a
Vol. II—The Tudors and the Stuart Era, A22b
Vol. III—From Utrecht to Modern Times, A22c
TROTSKY, LEON The Russian Revolution, A170
VICO, GIAMBATTISTA The New Science of Giambattista Vico, trans. Bergin & Fisch, A254
WADDELL, HELEN The Wandering Scholars, A63
WANDRUSZKA, ADAM The House of Habsburg, trans. Epstein, A453
WEDGWOOD, C. V. The Thirty Years War, A249
WILLEY, BASIL The Seventeenth Century Background, A19
WILSON, EDMUND To the Finland Station, A6

DATE DUE

A